John Willis

Theatre World

1994-1995 SEASON

VOLUME 51

APPLAUSE

NEW YORK • LONDON
THEATRE BOOK PUBLISHERS
211 WEST 71ST STREET • NEW YORK NY • 10023

LIBRARY OF CONGRESS CATALOG CARD NO. 73-82953
ISBN 1-55783-250-1 (cloth)
ISBN 1-55783-251-X (paper)

Patricia Elliott

This volume is dedicated to our treasured friend, Patricia Elliott, not only in recognition of her honored appearances on stage and television, but also of her efforts to perpetuate Theatre World Awards and the publication of this historical record of each theatre season.

John Willis

Patricia Elliot is a
1973 Theatre World Award Winner for
A Little Night Music

Sunset Boulevard
photograph ©Joan Marcus

CONTENTS

EDITOR: JOHN WILLIS
ASSISTANT EDITOR: TOM LYNCH

Assistants: Stine Elbirk Cabrera, Herbert Hayward, Jr., Barry Monush, Christopher Morelock, Eric Ort,
John Sala, John Stachniewicz
Staff Photographers: Gerry Goodstein, Michael Riordan, Michael Viade, Van Williams
Production: Emily Franzosa, Steve Ledezma, Ruth McKee, Rachel Reiss,
Paul Sugarman, Nicholas Thorn

BROADWAY PRODUCTIONS

(JUNE 1, 1994 – MAY 31, 1995)

GRAY'S ANATOMY

By Spalding Gray; Director, Renee Shafransky; General Manager, Steven C. Callahan; Production Manager, Jeff Hamlin; Presented by Lincoln Center Theater (Andre Bishop, Artistic Director; Bernard Green, Executive Producer); Press, Merle Debuskey, Susan Chicoine; Opened in the Vivian Beaumont Theater on Sunday, June 5, 1994*

CAST

Spalding Gray

A theatrical monologue exploring traditional and alternative medicine. A return engagement of last season's performance.

* Closed June 27, 1994 after limited engagement of 8 performances.

Nigel Dickson Photo

6

DIANA RIGG: NO TURN UNSTONED

Presented by the Actors' Fund of America; At the Booth Theatre on Monday, June 20, 1994 for one night only.

The actress performs her compilation of theatre reviews.

Right: Diana Rigg

IAN McKELLEN:
A KNIGHT OUT AT THE LYCEUM

Devised/Directed by Ian McKellen; Contributors, Armistead Maupin, Edward Morgan, Peter Shaffer, Tennessee Williams; Set, Norbert U. Kolb; Sound, Cynthia J. Hawkins; Lighting, Richard Winkler; General Managers, Richard Martini, Joann Swanson; Stage Manager, Patrick Horrigan; Presented by The Cultral Festival of Gay Games IV; Press, Peter Cromarty; Previewed from Tuesday, June 21; Opened in the Lyceum Theatre on Wednesday, June 22, 1994*

CAST

Ian McKellen

A mixture of stand-up, classical acting, and gay activism in two acts. Presented as part of the Gay Games celebration in New York City.

*Closed June 25 after limited engagement

Right: Ian McKellen

7

Kelly McGillis

HEDDA GABLER

By Henrik Ibsen; Translation, Frank McGuinness; Director, Sarah Pia Anderson; Set, David Jenkins; Costumes, Martin Pakledinaz; Lighting, Marc B. Weiss; Music, Dan Moses Schreier; Sound, Douglas J. Cuomo; General Manager, Ellen Richard; Stage Manager, Jay Adler; Presented by Roundabout Theatre Company (Todd Haimes, Artistic Director; Gene Feist, Founding Director); Press, Chris Boneau/Adrian Bryan-Brown, Susanne Tighe; Previewed from Wednesday, June 8; Opened in the Criterion Center Stage Right on Sunday, July 10, 1994*

CAST

Miss Julie Tesman	Patricia Conolly
Berte	Bette Henritze
Jorgen Tesman	Jeffrey DeMunn
Hedda Gabler	Kelly McGillis
Thea Elvsted	Laura Linney
Judge Brack	Keith David
Eilert Lovborg	Jim Abele +1

UNDERSTUDIES: April Black (Julie/Berte), Sarah Long (Hedda/Thea), Michael S. Ouimet(Jorgen), Robert Jason Jackson (Judge)

An 1890 drama in four acts, performed with one intermission. The action takes place at the home of Jorgen Tesman and his wife, Hedda, in the years just after World War II.

Variety tallied 2 mixed and 6 negative reviews. *Times:* (Richards) "...verges dangerously on camp." (Canby) "Nearly everything about the revival is half-baked..." *Post:* (Barnes) "McGillis' performance is glittering and imperious." *News:* (Kissel) "Laura Linney does well..." *Newsday:* (Jacobson) "...this is the kind of concept production for which the director must bear responsibility..." *Variety:* (Gerard) "...dated soap opera..."

*Closed August 7, 1994 after 33 performances and 37 previews.

+1. Michael O'Keefe during previews.

Carol Rosegg/Martha Stewart Photos

Right: Keith David
Below: Kelly McGillis, Laura Linney

PHILADELPHIA, HERE I COME!

By Brian Friel; Director, Joe Dowling; Set, John Lee Beatty; Costumes, Catherine Zuber; Lighting, Christopher Akerlind; Sound, Philip Campanella; General Manager, Ellen Richard; Stage Manager, Lori M. Doyle; Presented by Roundabout Theatre Company (Todd Haimes, Artistic Director; Gene Feist, Founding Director); Press, Chris Boneau/Adrian Bryan-Brown/Susanne Tighe; Previewed from Wednesday, August 17; Opened in the Criterion Center Stage Right on Thursday, September 8, 1994*

CAST

Madge	Pauline Flanagan
Gareth O'Donnell (in public)	Jim True
Gareth O'Donnell (in private)	Robert Sean Leonard +1
S.B. O'Donnell	Milo O'Shea +2
Kate Doogan	Miriam Healy-Louie
Senator Doogan	Peter McRobbie
Master Boyle	Jarlath Conroy
Lizzy Sweeney	Aideen O'Kelly
Con Sweeney	James Murtaugh
Ben Burton	Robert Stattel
Ned	Joel James Forsythe
Tom	Timothy Reynolds
Joe	Gregory Grene
Canon Mick O'Byrne	Leo Leyden

UNDERSTUDIES: Robin Howard (Madge/Lizzy), Sean Dougherty (Public Gareth/Tom/Joe), Jay Snyder (Private Gareth/Ned), Robert Stattel (S.B./Canon), Ciannait Walker (Kate), Philip LeStrange (Sen. Doogan/Boyle/Con/Ben)

A new production of a 1964 play in three acts. The action takes place in the small village of Ballybeg in County Donegal, Ireland, early 1960s. For original 1966 Broadway production see *Theatre World Vol. 22.*

Variety tallied 9 favorable, 5 mixed, and 2 negative reviews. *Times:* (Richards) "In the vast category of dramas that explore the rifts between fathers and sons, Brian Friel's *Philadelphia, Here I Come!* is surely the most lyrical." (Canby) "It would be difficult to imagine a finer Public Gar than Jim True..." *Post:* (Burke) "...worth listening to again and again." *News:* (Kissel) "Too little of this bleakness is apparent in the production..." *Newsday:* (Stuart) "...sanguine and smartassed...also incredibly sad..." *Variety:* (Evans) "...close to magic, what with the casting of Jim True...and Robert Sean Leonard...Neither of these charming, garrulous performers hits a false note in their emotional pas de deux..."

*Closed October 22, 1994 after 52 performances and 25 previews.

+Succeeded by: 1. Jay Snyder 2. Robert Stattel

Carol Rosegg Photos

Top: Milo O'Shea, Robert Sean Leonard, Jim True
Right: Robert Sean Leonard, Jim True

Milo O'Shea, Pauline Flanagan, Robert Sean Leonard, Jim True

Top: Jim True, Robert Sean Leonard

SHOW BOAT

Music, Jerome Kern; Lyrics/Book, Oscar Hammerstein II; Based on the novel by Edna Ferber; Director, Harold Prince; Choreography, Susan Stroman; Orchestrations, (original) Robert Russell Bennett, (new) William David Brohn; Musical Supervisor, Jeffrey Huard; Design, Eugene Lee; Costumes, Florence Klotz; Lighting, Richard Pilbrow; Sound, Martin Levan; Dance Music Arrangements, David Krane; Mr. Prince's Assistant, Ruth Mitchell; Cast Recording, Livent Music; General Manager, Frank P. Scardino; Company Manager, Jim Brandeberry; Stage Managers, Randall Buck, Betsy Nicholson; Presented by Livent (U.S.); Press, Mary Bryant/Wayne Wolfe; Previewed from Thursday, Sept.22; Opened in the Gershwin Theatre on Sunday, October 2, 1994*

CAST

Steve	Doug LaBrecque
Queenie	Gretha Boston
Pete	David Bryant
Parthy	Elaine Stritch
Windy	Ralph Williams
Cap'n Andy	John McMartin
Ellie	Dorothy Stanley
Frank	Joel Blum
Julie	Lonette McKee
Gaylord Ravenal	Mark Jacoby
Vallon	Jack Dabdoub
Magnolia	Rebecca Luker
Joe	Michel Bell
Dealer/Jake	Bob Walton
Balcony Soloist	Lorna Hampson
Jeb	David Earl Hart
Backwoodsman/Jim	Michael O'Carroll
Young Kim	Larissa Auble
Ethel	Danielle Greaves
Landlady	Lorraine Foreman
Mother Superior/Old Lady(on the Levee)	Sheila Smith
Charlie/Radio Announcer	Michael Scott
Lottie	Louise-Marie Mennier
Dottie	Karen Curlee
Drunk	David Bryant
Fan (on the Levee)	Kim Lindsay
Kim	Tammy Anderson

ENSEMBLE: Van Abrahams, Timothy Albrecht, Derin Altay, Kevin Bagby, Hal Beasley, Timothy Robert Blevens, David Bryant, Joseph Cassidy, Roosevelt Andre Credit, Karen Curlee, Jack Dabdoub, Debbie de Coudreaux, Steve Elmore, Lorraine Foreman, Jose Garcia, Ron Gibbs, Steve Girardi, Danielle Greaves, Jeff Hairston, Lorna Hampson, Linda Hardwick, Pamela Harley, David Earl Hart, Richard L. Hobson, Edwin Hodge, Michael LaFleche, Karen Lifshey, Kim Lindsay, Jesse Means II, Louise-Marie Mennier, Kiri-Lyn Muir, Panchali Null, Mike O'Carroll, Amy Jo Phillips, Catherine Pollard, Jimmy Rivers, Michael Scott, Jill Slyter, Bob Walton, Laurie Walton, Cheryl Warfield, Jo Ann Hawkins White, Dathan B. Williams, Gay Willis, Lionel Woods, Darlene B. Young SWINGS: Dennis Daniels, David Dannehl, Tari Kelly, Ritchie McCall, Kimberley Michaels, Louise St. Cyr
CHILDREN: Larissa Auble, Kimberly Jean Brown, Joran Corneal, Edwin Hodge, Imani Parks

STANDBYS/UNDERSTUDIES: Sheila Smith (Parthy), Ralph Williams (Cap'n Andy), Andre Solomon-Glover (Joe), Mike O'Carroll (Cap'n Andy), Lorraine Foreman (Parthy/Mother Superior/Old Lady), Kim Lindsay, Gay Willis (Magnolia), Doug LaBrecque, Joseph Cassidy (Ravenal), Derin Altay, Debbie de Coudreaux (Julie), Pamela Harley, Jo Ann Hawkins White (Queenie), Richard L. Hobson, Jose Garcia (Joe), Michael Scott (Steve/Backwoods/Vallon/Jim), David Earl Hart (Steve/Windy/Pete/Drunk), Bob Walton, Steve Girardi, Ronn Gibbs (Frank), Karen Curlee, Tari Kelly (Ellie), Kiri-Lyn Muir, Karen Lifshey (Kim), Kimberly Jean Brown (young Kim), David Dannehl (Windy/Pete/Backwoods/Vallon/Jim/Jake/Jeb/Dealer/Charlie/Drunk), Dennis Daniels (Jake/Jeb/Dealer/Charlie), Kimberley Michaels, Louise St. Cyr (Ethel), Panchali Null (Landlady/Mother Superior/Old Lady), Laurie Walton, Tari Kelly (Lottie/Dottie)

Top Left:John McMartin   Top Right: Elaine Stritch
Bottom Left: Lonette McKee Bottom Right: Michel Bell

MUSICAL NUMBERS: Overture, Cottton Blossom, Cap'n Andy's Bally-hoo, Where's the Mate for Me?, Make Believe, Ol' Man River, Can't Help Lovin' Dat Man, Till Good Luck Comes My Way, Mis'ry's Comin' Aroun', I Have the Room Above Her, Life Upon the Wicked Stage, Queenie's Ballyhoo, You Are Love, Wedding Celebration, Why Do I Love You?, Dandies on Parade, Alma Redemption Mater, Bill, Goodbye My Lady Love, After the Ball, Dance Away the Night, Kim's Charleston, Finale

A new production of the 1927 musical in two acts. The action takes place along the Mississippi River and in Chicago, 1887–1927. This production uses material from previous revivals and film adaptations in addition to the 1927 original.

Variety tallied 19 favorable and 1 mixed reviews. *Times:* (Richards) "…gloriously bold reexamination of the indestructible classic…amounts to a major reappraisal of the work…" (Margo Jefferson) "…it retains our interest both because of and despite the changes each generation of artists or hacks brings to it." *Post:* (Barnes) "The score comes across as great and sweeping as ever, while Harold Prince's modern, high-tech staging treats the musical precisely like the opera it very nearly is." *News:* (Kissel) "To have so overwhelming a production of this rich, complex show seems especially important now…" *Newsday:* (Winer) "…big, strapping dances actually seem to bubble up from the stage, as cakewalks turn to can-cans and white people steal the Charleston from the blacks." *Variety:* (Gerard) "…an artistry rarely equaled and a totally modern sensitivity…"

*Closed Jan. 5, 1997 after 946 performances and 12 previews. Winner of "Tony" for Best Musical Revival.

Catherine Ashmore, Michael Cooper Photos

Top: Lonette McKee, Rebecca Luker, Michel Bell, Gretha Boston
Right: Gretha Boston, Michel Bell

WONDERFUL TOWN

Music, Leonard Bernstein; Lyrics, Betty Comden and Adolph Green; Book, Joseph Fields and Jerome Chodorov based on their play *My Sister Eileen;* Director, Richard Sabellico; Conductor, Eric Stern; Orchestrations, Don Walker; Choreography, Tina Paul; Sets, Michael Anania; Costumes, Gail Baldoni; Lighting, Jeff Davis; Sound, Abe Jacob; Presented by New York City Opera; Press, Susan Woelzl/Barry Ambrose; Opened in the New York State Theatre on Tuesday, November 8, 1994*

CAST

Tour Guide/Chef/Police	William Ledbetter
Appopolous	Larry Block
Lonigan	Don Yule
Helen	Meghan Strange
Wreck	Timothy Warmen
Violet	Amanda Green
Speedy Valenti	Carlos Lopez
Eileen Sherwood	Crista Moore
Ruth Sherwood	Kay McClelland
Fletcher/Rexford/Escort	Gary Jackson
Drunks	Mason Roberts, Louis Perry
Eskimo Pie Man/Cadet	Mason Roberts
Robert Baker	Richard Muenz
Associate Editors	John Lankston, William Ledbetter
Mr. Mallory/Police	Louis Perry
Danny/Police	Jeffrey Weber
Party Guest	Marilyn Armstrong
Trent/Waiter	Daniel Shigo
Mrs. Wade	Susan Browning
Frank Lippencott	Don Stephenson
Delivery Boy/Cadet	Larry Sousa
Chick Clark	Stephen Berger
Shore Patrolman	Ron Hilley
Brazilian Ambassador/Police	John Lankston
Flower Sellers	Paula Hotstetter, Melissa Maravell
Customer	Beth Pensiero
Children	Zoe Startz Barton, Simon Behr, Dov Lebowitz-Nowak, Sebastian Perez, Jacqueline Rosenfield, Rachel Rosenfield

STANDBYS: Dorothy Kiara (Ruth), Michele McBride (Eileen), Patrick Boll (Robert), Richard Bell (Appopolous/Chick)

MUSICAL NUMBERS: Overture, Christopher Street, Ohio, One Hundred Easy Ways, What a Waste, A Little Bit in Love, Pass the Football, Conversation Piece, A Quiet Girl, Conga, Entr'acte, My Darlin' Eileen, Swing, It's Love, Let It Come Down Ballet, Wrong Note Rag, Finale

A new production of the 1953 musical in two acts. The action takes place in and around Greenwich Village, NYC, 1939. For original Broadway production with Rosalind Russell see *Theatre World Vol. 9.*

Times: (Edward Rothstein) "Songs like "Ohio" with its plaintive melody, "A Little Bit in Love" with its charming sweetness, and the rambunctious and musically witty "Wrong Note Rag" have more life than anything that took place on stage..." (Jefferson) "What a grand score this one is...The huge New York State Theater was designed for opera and ballet, not musical comedy...I'm talking about a theater where some people sitting in the sixth row center were using opera glasses." *Post:* (Barnes) "No one would nowadays risk putting *My Sister Eileen* on Broadway. It would look and sound dated and creaky. And that is precisely how the book looks and sounds." *News:* (Kissel) "I'm so happy to see it I can overlook even those blemishes that mar its irresistible charm." *Newsday:* (Stuart) "...we waste far too much energy worrying about whether they're still relevant."

*Closed November 20, 1994 after limited run of 14 performances.

Carol Rosegg Photos

Top: Kay McClelland, Crista Moore
Left: Stephen Berger, Kay McClelland, Crista Moore, Don Stephenson, Richard Muenz

THE GLASS MENAGERIE

By Tennessee Williams; Director, Frank Galati; Set, Loy Arcenas; Costumes, Noel Taylor; Lighting, Mimi Jordan Sherin; Sound, Richard R. Dunning; Projections, John Boesche; Music, Miriam Sturm; General Manager, Ellen Richard; Stage Managers, Jay Adler, Charles Kindl; Presented by Roundabout Theatre Company (Todd Haimes, Artistic Director; Gene Feist, Founding Director); Press, Chris Boneau/Adrian Bryan-Brown/ Susanne Tighe, Cindy Valk; Previewed from Saturday, October 29; Opened in the Criterion Center Stage Right on Wednesday, November 15, 1994*

CAST

Tom ....Zeljko Ivanek
Amanda..Julie Harris
Laura ....Calista Flockhart
Jim ....Kevin Kilner

UNDERSTUDIES: Martha Randall (Amanda), Laurel Holloman (Laura), Brett Rickaby (Tom/Jim), Jordan Matter (Jim)

A new production of a 1944 drama in two acts. For original 1945 Broadway production see *Theatre World Vol. 1.*

Variety tallied 11 favorable, 4 mixed, and 2 negative reviews. *Times:* (Richards) "Ms. Flockhart has...eyes that glisten with expectation and tears...Mr. Kilner, the real discovery of this production...so resonant is William's writing..." (Canby) "...allows the audience to rediscover the beauty of the Williams dialogue..." *Post:* (Barnes) "...Julie Harris as Amanda Wingfield—a role to which her entire career now seems to have been hitherto directed." *News:* (Kissel) "In his languid manner of speaking, his supple movements and, most importantly, in the irony that often sparkles in his eyes, Ivanek suggests Williams without stooping to outright caricature." *Newsday:* (Stuart) "...a production that reinvigorates an American landmark and redoubles the play's mythic hold on our hearts." *Variety:* (Gerard) "...It leaves an audience member with something like the shivering senses of astonishment and pity..."

*Closed January 1, 1995 after 57 performances and 19 previews.

Carol Rosegg Photos

Zeljko Ivanek, Julie Harris
Top: Zeljko Ivanek, Julie Harris
Left: Calista Flockhart, Kevin Kilner

SUNSET BLVD.

Music, Andrew Lloyd Webber; Lyrics/Book, Don Black and Christopher Hampton; Based on the 1950 Billy Wilder film; Director, Trevor Nunn; Musical Staging, Bob Avian; Orchestrations, David Cullen, Lloyd Webber; Musical Supervision, David Caddick; Musical Director, Paul Bogaev; Design, John Napier; Costumes, Anthony Powell; Lighting, Andrew Bridge; Sound, Martin Levan; Cast Recording, Polydor; Production Supervisor, Peter Lawrence; Technical, Peter Feller, Arthur Siccardi; General Manager, Nina Lannan; Company Manager, Abbie M. Strassler; Stage Managers, Peter Lawrence, John Brigleb, Jim Woolley, Lynda J. Fox; Presented by The Really Useful Company; Press, Chris Boneau/Adrian Bryan-Brown/John Barlow; Previewed from Tuesday, November 1; Opened in the Minskoff Theatre on Thursday, November 17, 1994*

CAST

Norma Desmond	Glenn Close +1
Joe Gillis	Alan Campbell
Max von Mayerling	George Hearn
Betty Schaefer	Alice Ripley
Cecil B. DeMille	Alan Oppenheimer
Artie Green	Vincent Tumeo
Harem Girl/Beautician	Sandra Allen
Young Writer/Salesman/DeMilles's Asst.	Bryan Batt
Heather/2nd Masseuse	Susan Dawn Carson
Cliff/Salesman/Young Guard	Matthew Dickens
Jean/Beautician/Hedy Lamarr	Colleen Dunn
Morino/Salesman/Hog Eye	Steven Stein-Grainer
Lisa/Doctor	Kim Huber
1st Financeman/Film Actor/Salesman	Rich Herbert
Katherine/Psychiatrist	Alicia Irving
Harem Girl/Beautician	Lada Boder
Mary/1st Masseuse	Lauren Kennedy
Sheldrake/Police Chief	Sal Mistretta
John/Salesman/Victor Mature	Mark Morales
Myron/Manfred	Rick Podell
Financeman/Salesman/Party Guest	Tom Alan Robbins
Jonesy/Sammy/Salesman	David Eric
Choreographer/Salesman	Rick Sparks
Joanna/Astrologer	Wendy Walter

STANDBYS/UNDERSTUDIES: Karen Mason (Norma), Susan Dawn Carson (Norma), Bryan Batt, Matthew Dickens (Joe), Kim Huber, Lauren Kennedy (Betty), Steven Stein-Grainger(DeMille), David Eric (DeMille/Sheldrake), Matthew Dickens, Darrin Baker, Harvey Evans (Writer/Salesman/Asst./Cliff/Morino/Hog Eye/Financeman/Film Actor/Police/John/Sammy/Jonesy/Choreographer), Darrin Baker (Artie), Rosemary Loar, Darlene Wilson (Harem Girls, Beauticians/Lisa/Doctor/Heather/Masseuses/Hedy/Joanna/Astrologer/Katherine/Psychiatrist/Mary)

MUSICAL NUMBERS: Overture, Prologue, Let's Have Lunch, Surrender, With One Look, Salome, The Greatest Star of All, Every Movie's a Circus, Girl Meets Boy, New Ways to Dream, The Lady's Paying, The Perfect Year, This Time Next Year, Sunset Boulevard, As If We Never Said Goodbye, Eternal Youth Is Worth a Little Suffering, Too Much in Love to Care, Finale

A musical in two acts. The action takes place in Los Angeles, 1949–50.

Variety tallied 5 favorable, 14 mixed, and 3 negative reviews. *Times:* (Richards) "...allows Glenn Close to give one of those legendary performances people will be talking about years from now. Full of rich and swelling melodies..." *Post:* (Barnes) "It's qualities are sometimes strange but always real...It is nothing to be compared to Lloyd Webber's finest score, *Aspects of Love*." *News:* (Kissel) "The score may be static, but the way the set moves up and down is thrilling." *Newsday:* (Winer) "Close is the major reason to see Trevor Nunn's production..." *Variety* : (Gerard) "Close is as much the draw as Andrew Lloyd Webber...a memorable display of the shattered hauteur of a fabled star whom time and technology have long since passed by."

*Still playing May 31, 1995. Winner of "Best Musical" Tony Award and Best Actress in a Musical (Glenn Close).

Succeeded by: 1. Karen Mason; during vacation/illness, Betty Buckley

Joan Marcus, Craig Schwartz Photos

Top: Glenn Close
Right: George Hearn

Glenn Close

Alice Ripley, Alan Campbell

The Company

Alan Campbell

Glenn Close in *Sunset Blvd.*

THE SHADOW BOX

By Michael Cristofer; Director, Jack Hofsis; Set, David Jenkins; Costumes, Carrie Robbins; Lighting, Richard Nelson; Sound, Aural Fixation; Fights, B.H. Barry; Choreography, Nora Kasarda; Company Manager, Gordon G. Forbes; Stage Managers, William Hare, Thom Widmann; Presented by Circle in the Sqaure (Theodore Mann & Josephine R. Abady, Co-Artistic Directors; Robert Bennett, Managing Director); Press, Jeffrey Richards/Kevin Rehac, Bruce Roberts; Previewed from Friday, November 4; Opened in the Circle in the Square Uptown Theatre on Sunday, November 20, 1994*

CAST

The Interviewer ....Ron Frazier

COTTAGE ONE
Joe ....Frankie R. Faison
Steve ....Sean Nelson
Maggie..Mary Alice

COTTAGE TWO
Brian..Jamey Sheridan
Mark..Raphael Sbarge
Beverly ....Mercedes Ruehl

COTTAGE THREE
Agnes ....Marlo Thomas
Felicity ....Estelle Parsons

UNDERSTUDIES: Charles Dumas (Interviewer/Joe), Yvette Hawkins (Maggie), Grant Albrecht (Brian/Mark), Carol Locatell (Beverly/Agnes), Peggy Cosgrave (Felicity), Deji Olasimbo (Steve)

A new production of a 1977 Pulitzer Prize-winning drama in two acts. The action takes place on the grounds of a hospital. The genesis of this production was a staged reading of the play in Tuscon, Arizona, to protest the supression of the play by a Flowing Wells, AZ, high school. For original 1977 Broadway production see *Theatre World Vol. 33.*

Variety tallied 4 favorable, 8 mixed, and 2 negative reviews. *Times:* (Brantley) "The decimating effects of AIDS, and the political movements that were born in response to it, have engendered a new, more aggressive openness in dealing with death and illness..." *Post:* (Barnes) "...tautly staged and passionately acted, the production does proud by Cristofer's contrapuntal musings..." *News:* (Kissel) "...Jamey Sheridan plays... with no self-pity and Raphael Sbarge plays his lover with great understatement...Mercedes Ruehl gives such a wild, exuberant performance... Faison is beautiful...Mary Alice is touching...Estelle Parsons brings great dignity..." *Newsday:* (Stuart) "After many dark months and financial obstacles, the theater has reopened with one of those glittering all-star ensembles that used to leaven bad movies..." *Variety:* (Gerard) "...a very good, unexpectedly moving production..."

*Closed January 1, 1995 after 49 performances and 19 previews.

Martha Swope Photos

Mercedes Ruehl, Jamey Sheridan, Raphael Sbarge
Top Left: Sean Nelson, Mary Alice, Frankie R. Faison
Top Right: Marlo Thomas, Estelle Parsons

THE FLYING KARAMAZOV BROTHERS DO THE IMPOSSIBLE!

Musical Director, Doug Wieselman; General Managers, Timothy Childs, Sally Campbell Morse; Company Manager, Abby Evans; Stage Manager, Shannon Rhodes; Presented by The Imagination Company (Natasha & Boris Childs, Presidents), Herb Goldsmith Productions (Vladimir Goldsmith, President) and Jujamcyn Theatres (Fyodor Landesman, President); Press, Chris Boneau/Adrian Bryan-Brown/Bob Fennell, Jamie Morris; Previewed from Tuesday, November 15; Opened in the Helen Hayes Theatre on Sunday, November 20, 1994*

CAST

Dmitri Karamazov ....Paul Magid
Ivan Karamazov ....Howard Jay Patterson
Rakitin Karamazov ....Michael Preston
Smerdyakov Karamazov...Sam Williams
with The Kamikaze Ground Crew Orchestra

The Flying Karamazov Brothers in a brand new two-act show (with just a few old favorite bits).

Variety tallied 6 favorable and 3 mixed reviews. *Times:* (Stephen Holden) "…they convey the cheerfully anarchic attitude of unreconstructed hippies." (Canby) "…Don't send anyone to see this without explaining what and who the Flying Karamazovs is and are." *Post* :(Barnes) "…juggling must be the most unlikely art from since the ice show." *News:* (Michael Musto) "…a charmingly anarchic evening…there are questionable elements…" *Newsday:* (Stuart) "…you may be mystified by the bizarre arsenal of offerings hauled into the theater by many audience members." *Variety:* (Evans) "…return to Broadway for the fourth time, bringing along their comfortable blend of juggling, pun-filled comedy, hip improv and easy camaraderie."

*Closed January 1, 1995 after 50 performances and 7 previews.

T.L. Boston Photos

Right: Michael Preston
Below: The Flying Karamazov Brothers

GYPSY OF THE YEAR

Director, Michael Lichtefeld; Stage Managers, Kim Vernace; J. Courtney Plooard, Michael Passaro; Associate Producer, Michael Graziano; Presented by Tom Viola and Maria Di Dia; Press, Chris Boneau/Adrian Bryan-Brown, Andy Shearer; Presented in the St. James Theatre on Tuesday, November 29, 1994.

CAST INCLUDES

Jonathan Hadary (host)
Vanessa Redgrave, Eileen Atkins, Karen Mason, Davis Gaines, Brooke Shields, Dick Latessa, Victor Garber, Jane Connell, Carleton Carpenter, Donna Murphy, Carole King, Vanessa Williams, and the casts of *Carousel, Guys and Dolls* (A Guys & Dolls Goodbye), *Les Miserables* (The Book Report), *Cats, Phantom of the Opera , Grease, Nunsense 2, Damn Yankees* (Who Needs a Star?), *Beauty and the Beast, Crazy For You* (Daisy, Ego Trip), *Show Boat, Passion* (Give Me That Sondheim Style), *Tommy, Kiss of the Spider Woman, Blood Brothers,* and *Miss Saigon.*

GYPSY OF THE YEAR GYPSIES: Barbara Angeline, Robert Bianca, Andy Blankenbuehler, Linda Bowen, Myra Browning, Michael-Demby Cain, Byron Easley, Gregory Garrison, Trina Simon

The sixth annual competition for Broadway Cares/Equity Fights AIDS raised $804, 492.

T.L. Boston Photo

Left: Brooke Shields
Top: (Center) Dick Latessa, Victor Garber, and *Damn Yankees* cast

Walter Willison, Martin Van Treuren, Joan Barber,
Michael X. Martin, Erin Stoddard

Walter Charles, Jeff Keller

(center) Michael Mandell, Walter Charles and ensemble

Sean Thomas Morrissey, Elizabeth Albano, Cynthia Thole, David
Gallagher, Joy Hermalyn, Nick Corley, Matthew Mezzacappa

A CHRISTMAS CAROL

Music, Alan Menken; Lyrics, Lynn Ahrens; Book, Mike Ockrent, Lynn Ahrens; Based on the story by Charles Dickens; Director, Mike Ockrent; Choreography, Susan Stroman; Orchestrations, Michael Starobin; Musical Director, Paul Gemignani; Sets, Tony Walton; Costumes, William Ivey Long; Lighting, Jules Fisher, Peggy Eisenhauer; Sound, Tony Meola; Projections, Wendall K. Harrington; Flying by Foy; Dance Arrangements, Glen Kelly; Cast Recording, Columbia; Production Supervisor, Gene O'Donovan; Company Manager, Steven H. David; Stage Managers, Steven Zweigbaum, Clifford Schwartz; Producers, Dodger Productions, Tim Hawkins; Presented by Nickelodeon Family Classics and Madison Square Garden; Press, Chris Boneau/Adrian Bryan-Brown, Patty Onagan, Jamie Morris, Craig Karpel; Previewed from Wenesday, November 23; Opened in the Paramount Theatre on Thursday, December 1, 1994*

CAST

Scrooge ....Walter Charles
Bob Cratchit..Nick Corley
Ghost of Christmas Past ....Ken Jennings
Ghost of Jacob Marley ....Jeff Keller
Mr. Smythe ....Joseph Kolinski
Ghost of Christmas Present ....Michael Mandell
Fred ....Robert Westenberg
Scrooge's Mother/Blind Hag ....Andrea Frierson Toney
Mrs. Cratchit..Joy Hermalyn
Scrooge's Father..Michael X. Martin
Young Scrooge ....Michael Christopher Moore
Grave Digger ....Bill Nolte
Mrs. Mops ....Darcy Pulliam
Emily ....Emily Skinner
Mrs. Fezziwig..Mary Stout
Fezziwig..Gerry Vichi
Ghost of Christmas Future ....Theara J. Ward
Jonathan ....Jason Fuchs
Judge ....Michael H. Ingram
Jack Smythe ....Andy Jobe
Grace Smythe ....Lindsay Jobe
Scrooge at 12 ....Ramzi Khalaf
Old Joe/Mr. Kent..Ken McMullen
Tiny Tim..Matthew Mezzacappa
Charity Man..Robert Ousley
Young Marley..Christopher Sieber
Sally..Natalie Toro
Charity Man..Walter Willison
Charity Man..Martin Van Treben
Fan at 6 ....Mary Elizabeth Albano
Young Boy.......................Matthew F. Byrne, Justin Bartholemew Kamen
Fan at 10 ....Jacy De Filippo, Olivia Oguma
Boy ....Christopher Mark Petrizzo, P.J. Smith
Ensemble................Joan Barber, Renee Bergeron, Christophe Caballero, Betsy Chang, Candy Cook, Madeleine Doherty, Mark Dovey, Donna Dunmire, Melissa Haizlip, Don Johanson, James Judy, Eric H. Kaufman, John-Charles Kelly, David Lowenstein, Seth Malkin, Donna Lee Marshall, Carol Lee Meadows, Sean Thomas Morrissey, Karen Murphy, Tom Pardoe, Gail Pennington, Angela Piccinni, Josef Reiter, Pamela Remler, Sam Reni, Eric Riley, Rommy Sandhu, Erin Stoddard, Tracy Terstriep, David Gallagher, Arlene Pierret

DANCE CAPTAINS: Mark S. Hoebee, Cynthia Thole; SWINGS: Leslie Bell, Michael Hayward-Jones, Matthew J. Vargo, Billy Vitelli, Whitney Webster CHORAL GROUPS: Blessed Sacrament Chorus of Staten Island, PS 26 Chorus, Righteousness Unlimited, William F. Halloran Vocal Ensemble-School 22

MUSICAL NUMBERS: The Years Are Passing By, Jolly Fat and Rich, Nothing to Do With Me, Street Song, Link By Link, Lights of Long Ago, God Bless Us Everyone, A Place Called Home, Mr. Fezziwig's Annual Christmas Ball, Abundance and Charity, Christmas Together, Dancing on Your Grave, Yesterday Tomorrow and Today, Final Medley

A musical performed without intermission. The action takes place in London, 1880.

Walter Charles, Emily Skinner, Michael Christopher Moore

Times: (Richards) "...snow falls in the hall as well as onstage, which so thrilled an incredulous 8-year-old boy seated near me that he got up and danced in the aisle...a succession of ballads, waltzes and anthems..." (Canby) "The star of the production is Mr. Walton...the entire show looks to be a giant antique Christmas card whose illustrations keep changing." *Post:* (Barnes) "...curiously hearty in an extraordinarily heartless fashion." *News:* (Musto) "...$13 million spectacle that serves up some 90 actors, 50 computerized effects, 30 ghosts, oodles of snow and a set that stretches practically all the way around the arena." *Newsday:* (Winer) "The 5,100-seat hall is indeed overwhelming...extended the vast playing area halfway up the walls so we feel surrounded—no, actually embraced—by the stores and houses of late (slightly updated Dickens) Victorian London." *Variety:* (Gerard) "...it is done fluidly and—an Ockrent/Stroman trademark—with considerable humor...Menken and lyricist Lynn Ahrens have written several lovely tunes..."

*Closed January 1, 1995 after seasonal run of 71 performances and 14 previews.

Joan Marcus Photos

LAMB CHOP ON BROADWAY

Music/Musical Director/Orchestrations, Stormy Sacks; Lyrics, Rob Battan; Book, Saul Turteltaub; Additional Music, Norman Martin, Lan O'Kun, Cliff Jones; Director/Choreographer, Kevin Carlisle; Assitant Director, Randy Doney; Set, Jack McAdam, Richard D. Bluhm; Lighting/Production Supervisor, Fred Allen, Steven Shelley; Sound, Peter Fitzgerald; Production Coordinator, Robert Kernen; Stage Manager, Thom Schilling; Producers, Jim Golden, Shari Lewis; Presented by James M. Nederlander and James L. Nederlander; Press, Richard Gersh/Dana Kahn; Opened in the Richard Rodgers Theatre on Tuesday, December 6, 1994*

CAST

Shari Lewis

Kathy Jo Boss	Jeff Drew	Guy Woodson
(Big Lamb Chop)	(Big Hush Puppy)	(Big Charlie Horse)

A musical entertainment in two acts.

*Closed Dec. 11, 1994 after limited run of 8 performances.

Lamb Chop, Shari Lewis

David Moscow, Florence Stanley, Alan Rosenberg in *What's Wrong With This Picture?*

WHAT'S WRONG WITH THIS PICTURE?

By Donald Margulies; Director, Joe Mantello; Set, Derek McLane; Costumes, Ann Roth; Lighting, Brian MacDevitt; Sound, Aural Fixation; Wigs, Paul Huntley; Music, Mel Marvin; General Management, Richard Frankel Productions/Marc Routh; Stage Managers, Michael Ritchie, Barnaby Harris; Associate Producer, Ruth Kalkstein; Presented by David Stone, The Booking Office, Albert Nocciolino, Betsy Dollinger in association with Ted Snowdon; Press, Chris Boneau/Adrian Bryan-Brown, Bob Fennell, Jackie Green, David Wood, Susanne Tighe; Previewed from Tuesday, November 15; Opened in the Brooks Atkinson Theatre on Thursday, December 8, 1994*

CAST

Artie ....David Moscow
Bella ....Florence Stanley
Mort ....Alan Rosenberg
Sid ....Jerry Stiller
Ceil..Marcell Rosenblatt
Shirley ....Faith Prince

STANDBYS: Emily Zacharias (Shirley/Ceil), Paul Harman (Mort), Stan Lachow (Sid), Rose Arrick (Bella), Brad Stoll (Artie)

A comedy in two acts. The action takes place in a middle-class apartment in Brooklyn, N.Y., some years ago. Earlier versions of this play were performed at Manahttan Theatre Club and Jewish Repertory Theatre.

Variety tallied 3 mixed and 8 negative reviews. *Times:* (Richards) "The director, Joe Mantello...seems more comfortable with the serious implications of the script than with its quips and comic quibbles. But it's the comedy the audience is eager for. Mr. Moscow couldn't be more earnest... the performance likable. Mr. Stiller brings great zest..." (Canby) "...there's a peculiar moment when Mort persuades his son to model one of Shirley's dresses, only to become turned on by the sight...at that moment the members of the Brooks Atkinson audience with whom I saw the play began to disengage..." *Post:* (Barnes) "...three exceptional performances: a radiant Faith Prince...brilliantly stylized Florence Stanley... eccentrically adorable Jerry Stiller..." *News:* (Kissel) "...the play has been mugged. Uptown, it is performed so heavy handedly that almost all its virtues have been obliterated." *Newsday:* (Winer) "...the play's a mystery...Margulies does dig deeper, ultimately, than we begin to expect..." *Variety:* (Gerard) "...a throwback to the '50s Brooklyn days of whine and *tsuris*...Prince goes even farther: She's totally adorable..."

*Closed December 18, 1994 after 12 performances and 27 previews.

Joan Marcus Photos

Top Left: Faith Prince, Alan Rosenberg
Top Right: Jerry Stiller, David Moscow
Left: David Moscow, Faith Prince, Alan Rosenberg,
(front) Marcell Rosenblatt, Jerry Stiller, Florence Stanley

Jaston Williams
Top: Jaston Williams, Joe Sears

A TUNA CHRISTMAS

By Jaston Williams, Joe Sears, and Ed Howard; Director, Mr. Howard; Set, Loren Sherman; Costumes, Linda Fisher; Lighting, Judy Rasmuson; Sound, Ken Huncovsky; General Management, Marvin A. Krauss Associates; Company Manager, Carla McQueen; Stage Manager, Peter A. Still; Presented by Charles H. Duggan and Drew Dennett; Press, Pete Sanders/ Ian Rand, Glenna Freedman; Previewed from Thursday, December 8; Opened in the Booth Theatre on Thursday, December 15, 1994*

CAST ·

JOE SEARS plays	JASTON WILLIAMS plays
Thurston Wheelis	Arles Struvie
Elmer Watkins	Didi Snavely
Bertha Bumiller	Petey Fisk
Leonard Childers	Jody Bumiller
R.R. Snavely	Charlene Bumiller
Pearl Burras	Stanley Bumiller
Sheriff Givens	Vera Carp
Ike Thompson	Dixie Deberry
Inita Goodwin	Farley Burkhalter
Phoebe Burkhalter	Helen Budd
Joe Bob Lipsey	Garland Poteet

UNDERSTUDIES: Greg Currie (for Mr. Williams), Tim Mateer (for Mr. Sears)

A comedy in two acts. The action takes place in Tuna, third smallest town in Texas, on Christmas Eve. Mr. Sears and Mr. Williams performed these roles in *Greater Tuna* at the Circle in the Square Downtown in 1982 (see *Theatre World Vol. 39*).

Variety tallied 9 favorable and 1 mixed review. *Times:* (Richards) "The show, really just a series of interconnected sketches, is a hoot. The cast... is two hoots." (Canby) "...a little bit of this goes a long way..." *Post:* (Barnes) "a weird but wildly funny play..." *News:* (Kissel) "...lampooning small-town Southerners seems less imaginative than it did 11 years ago." *Newsday:* (Winer) "Sears and Williams are completely convincing as the sweet—if obliviously vicious—men and women of the town..." *Variety:* (Gerard) "...don't be surprised if some of these folks stay with you longer than you'd have suspected."

*Closed December 31, 1994 after seasonal engagement of 20 performances and 8 previews.

T.L. Boston Photos

COMEDY TONIGHT

Director, Alexander Cohen; Musical Staging, Albert Stephenson; Sets, Ray Klausen; Costumes, Alvin Colt; Lighting, Richard Nelson; Sound, Bruce D. Cameron; Musical Director, Peter Howard; Ms. Louden's Special Material, Bruce Vilanch; General Management, Marvin A. Krauss; Company Manager, Ken Silverman; Stage Manager, Bob Borod; Associate Producer, Hildy Parks; Presented by Alexander H. Cohen and Max Cooper; Press, Merle Debuskey/Susan Chicoine; Previewed from Wednesday, December 14; Opened in the Lunt-Fontanne Theatre on Sunday, December 18, 1994*

CAST

Joy Behar	Michael Davis
Dorothy Loudon	Mort Sahl

A revue performed without intermission.

Variety tallied 5 mixed and 3 negative reviews. *Times:* (Stephen Holden) "...a variety program with no direction and no center." (Canby) "...like a band of strolling players stranded in a small town, doing their shticks in return for bus tickets home." *Post:* (Barnes) "...not so much a revue as a nightclub convention..." *News:* (Kissel) "Seventy years ago, an evening like this might have been billed as vaudeville." *Newsday:* (Stuart) "...Loudon is the Beluga caviar of musical comedy..." *Variety:* (Gerard) "The ushers at the Lunt-Fontanne seemed to take a perverse delight in telling patrons the show was on its deathbed."

*Closed December 25, 1994 after 8 performances and 6 previews. The pre-Broadway tryout featured a new song, "Three," by John Kander and Fred Ebb.

T. Charles Erickson Photos

Left: Dorothy Loudon
Bottom Left: Dorothy Loudon, Mort Sahl,
(front) Michael Davis, Joy Behar
Bottom Right: Mort Sahl

A CHRISTMAS CAROL

By Charles Dickens; Adapted/Staged by Patrick Stewart; Lighting, Fred Allen; General Management, Timothy Childs, Sally Campbell Morse; Company Manager, Mitzi Harder; Executive Producer, Kate Elliott; Presented by Terri and Timothy Childs; Press, Chris Boneau/Adrian Bryan-Brown, Bob Fennell; Previewed from Tuesday, December 20; Opened in the Richard Rodgers Theatre on Thursday, December 22, 1994*

CAST

Patrick Stewart

A solo version of Dicken's Christmas tale performed with one intermission. Previously performed on Broadway in 1991 and 1992.

Variety tallied 6 favorable and 1 mixed review. *Times:* (Ben Brantley) "...supremely entertaining, supremely intelligent..." *Post:* (Barnes) "...I found myself longing to re-read all the novels." *News:* (Kissel) "I hope Stewart provides this Christmas bounty for many years to come." *Variety:* (Gerard) "Think of the world of good it would do for all those Trekkies to get beamed up to the truly amazing world Dickens conjured 150 years ago ..."

*Closed January 8 after 19 performances and 2 previews.

Jim Farber Photos

JESUS CHRIST SUPERSTAR

Music, Andrew Lloyd Webber; Lyrics, Tim Rice; Director/Choreographer, Tony Christopher; Musical Director, Craig Barna; Sets, Bill Stabile; Lighting, Rick Belzer; Costumes, David Paulin; Sound, Jonathan Deans; Stage Manager, Joe Cappelli; Special Effects, Gregg Stephens; General Management, Niko Associates; Presented by Landmark Entertainment Group, Magic Promotions & Theatricals and Tap Productions; Press, Judy Jacksina; Opened in the Paramount Theatre on Tuesday, January 17, 1995*

CAST

Jesus of Nazareth	Ted Neeley
Judas Iscariot	Carl Anderson +1
Mary Magdalene	Syreeta Wright
Caiphas	David Bedella
Annas	Danny Zolli
First Priest	Mark Slama
Second Priest	Michael Guarnera
Third Priest	Gary Bankston
Simon	Lawrence Clayton +2
Pontius Pilate	Dennis DeYoung
Tormentors	Carol Bentley, Shannon Falank, Kristen Young
Peter	Mike Eldred
King Herod	Douglass Fraser
Maid by the Fire	Karen Byers
Soldier by the Fire	Mark C. Reis
Old Man by the Fire	Pressley Sutherland
Soul Sisters	Karen Byers, J. Kathleen Lamb, Hillary Turk
Ensemble	Gary Bankston, Carol Bentley, Kevin Bernard, Karen Byers, Phil Dominguez, Mike Eldred, Shannon Falank, Robert H. Fowler, Michael Guarnera, Vanessa A. Jones, Eileen Kaden, J. Kathleen Lamb, Mark C. Reis, Mark Slama, Pressley Sutherland, Hillary Turk, Kristen Young

UNDERSTUDIES/STANDBYS: Jeffrey Watkins (Jesus/Judas/Caiphas), Danny Zolli (Jesus/Judas), Lawrence Clayton (Judas/Pilate), Vanessa A. Jones, Eileen Kaden, Hillary Turk (Mary), Pressley Sutherland (Pilate/Peter/Herod/Priests), Gary Bankston (Peter/Simon/Annas), Robert H. Fowler (Simon), Michael Guarnera (Annas), Mark Slama (Caiphas/Man), Jeffrey Watkins (Caiaphas), Kevin Bernard (Herod), Hans Kriefall (Priests/Soldier/Man), Michelle Dejean, Cindi Parise (Maid)

MUSICAL NUMBERS: Overture, Heaven on Their Minds, What's the Buzz, Strange Thing Mystifying, Everything's Alright, This Jesus Must Die, Hosanna, Simon Zealotes, Poor Jerusalem, Pilate's Dream, The Temple, I Don't Know How to Love Him, Damned for All Time, Last Supper, Gethsemane, The Arrest, Peter's Denial, Pilate and Christ, King Herod's Song, Could We Start Again Please, Judas' Death, Trial Before Pilate, Superstar, The Crucifixion, John 19:41

A new production of the 1971 musical in two acts. The action traces the last seven days of Jesus of Nazareth. For original Broadway production see *Theatre World Vol. 28.*

Times: (Holden) "…a raggedly glitzy bus-and-truck production…If nothing else…is decently sung." *Post:* (Barnes) "…part of an anniversary tour that started in Baltimore in 1991…a sorry spectacle." *News:* (Jim Farber) "…a kind of badness that really must be seen to be believed." *Newsday:* (Winer) "Somewhere in there, however, remains one of the theatre's best pop operas…"

*Closed January 29, 1995 after limited run of 16 performances.

+Succeeded by: 1. Lawrence Clayton (during illness) 2. Robert H. Fowler

Richard Feldman Photos

Top: Carl Anderson, Syreeta Wright, Ted Neeley
Center: Ted Neeley
Left: Dennis DeYoung, Ted Neeley

Brian Bedford, Remak Ramsay
Bottom Left and Right: Brian Bedford, Suzanne Bertish

THE MOLIERE COMEDIES

By Molière; Translation, Richard Wilbur; Director, Michael Langham; Sets, Douglas Stein; Costumes, Ann Hould-Ward; Lighting, Richard Nelson; Sound, Douglas J. Cuomo, One Dream; Hairstylist, David H. Lawrence; General Manager, Ellen Richard; Stage Managers, Lori M. Doyle, Jana Llynn; Presented by Roundabout Theatre Company (Todd Haimes, Artistic Director; Gene Feist, Founding Director); Press, Chris Boneau/Adrian Bryan-Brown, Susanne Tighe; Previewed from Wednesday, January 11; Opened in the Criterion Center Stage Right on Thursday, February 2, 1995*

CASTS

THE SCHOOL FOR HUSBANDS

Sganarelle	Brian Bedford
Ariste	Remak Ramsay
Isabelle	Patricia Dunnock
Leonor	Cheryl Gaysunas
Lisette	Suzanne Bertish
Valere	Malcolm Gets
Ergaste	David Aaron Baker
Magistrate	Reg Rogers
Notary	Denis Holmes
Attendant	Jeff Stafford

THE IMAGINARY CUCKOLD

Gorgibus	Remak Ramsay
Celie	Cheryl Gaysunas
Celie's Maid	Patricia Dunnock
Sganarelle	Brian Bedford
His Wife	Suzanne Bertish
Lelie	David Aaron Baker
Gros-Réne	Reg Rogers
Servant	Jeff Stafford
Mme. Sganarelle's Brother	Malcolm Gets
Villebrequin	Denis Holmes

UNDERSTUDIES: Reg Rogers (Sganarelle), Denis Holmes (Ariste/Gorgibus), Elizabeth Rainer (Isabelle/Lenor/Celie/Maid), April Black (Lisette/Mme.Sganarelle), Daniel Travis (Valere/Notary/Attendant/Servant), Nick Sullivan (Ergaste/Magistrate/Gros-Réne/Brother/Villebrequin), Jeff Stafford (Lelie)

Two comedies set in the seventeenth century. *School For Husbands* takes place in Paris. *Imaginary Cuckold* takes place in a small French town.

Variety tallied 14 favorable and 4 mixed reviews. *Times:* (Canby) "The funniest, wisest, most engaging new show in town is more than 300 years old…" *Post:* (Barnes) "…both Bedfordian faces are pure Molière—vibrant, funny and credible." *News:* (Kissel) "The cavortings could not be more fresh or delicious." *Newsday:* (Winer) "How much poorer New York would be without Brian Bedford…" *Variety:* (Gerard) "These plays are a delight, particularly in Richard Wilbur's typically ticklish translations…"

*Closed March 26, 1995 after 56 performances and 26 previews.

Carol Rosegg Photos

Nathan Lane, Randy Becker in *Love! Valour! Compassion!*

Mario Cantone, Anthony Heald, Justin Kirk, Stephen Bogardus, John Benjamin Hickey, John Glover
Top: John Glover, Randy Becker, Justin Kirk, Anthony Heald, John Benjamin Hickey, (front) Nathan Lane, Stephen Bogardus

LOVE! VALOUR! COMPASSION!

By Terrence McNally; Director, Joe Mantello; Sets, Loy Arcenas; Costumes, Jess Goldstein; Lighting, Brian MacDevitt; Sound, John Kilgore; Choreography, John Carrafa; General Manager, Victoria Bailey; Company Manager, Denise Cooper; Stage Managers, William Joseph Barnes, Ira Mont; Presented by Manhattan Theatre Club (Lynne Meadow, Artistic Director; Barry Grove, Managing Director) by special arrangement with Jujamcyn Theatres; Press, Kevin P. McAnarney/Helene Davis, Amy Lefkowitz; Previewed from Friday, January 20; Opened in the Walter Kerr Theatre on Tuesday, February 14, 1995*

CAST

Gregory Mitchell	Stephen Bogardus
Arthur Pape	John Benjamin Hickey +1
Perry Sellars	Anthony Heald +2
John Jeckyll/James Jeckyll	John Glover
Buzz Hauser	Nathan Lane +3
Bobby Brahams	Justin Kirk
Ramon Fornos	Randy Becker +4

UNDERSTUDIES: Steven Skybell (Perry/Buzz/Arthur), Gregory Mitchell (John/James), Kirk Jackson (Perry), David Norona (Bobby/Ramon)

A drama in three acts. The action takes place at a remote country house in Duchess County, New York, over the Memorial Day, 4th of July, and Labor Day weekends. This production featured a new version of "Shine On Harvest Moon" by Barbara Cook.

Variety tallied 12 favorable and 1 negative review. *Times:* (Canby) "…written, directed and acted with such theatrical skill and emotional range that it's as broadly entertaining as it is moving." *Post:* (Kissel) "This is a gold-plated, cast-iron hit if ever I saw one—charming, funny, touching and exquisitely well-acted…This is not just the funniest play to hit Broadway in many a season, it is also one of the most sincere and touching." *News:* (Kissel) "…an elegy for an innocence, a giddiness now lost and irreplaceable. The play is mostly hilarious, but the laughter is never unalloyed…I am amused by how much tongue-wagging the abundant nudity has caused…" *Newsday:* (Winer) "McNally has written the deepest, wittiest, most satisfying play of his impressive career—indeed one of the major plays of our time." *Variety:* (Gerard) "…flows with heartfelt writing and becomes quite moving…It's also very, very funny, thanks in no small measure to Lane…The ensemble is altogether winning…The sense of loss it summons is heartbreaking."

*Closed September 17, 1995 after 249 performances and 28 previews. Earlier in the season it played 72 performances and 24 previews Off-Broadway at Manhattan Theatre Club. Winner of the 1995 "Tony" for Best Play and New York Drama Critics Circle "Best American Play".

+Succeeded by: 1. Richard Bekins 2. T.Scott Cunningham 3. Mario Cantone 4. David Norona (during illness)

Martha Swope Photos

Nathan Lane, John Glover
Bottom Left: John Benjamin Hickey, Anthony Heald
Bottom Right: Stephen Bogardus, Justin Kirk

33

CALL ME MADAM

Music/Lyrics, Irving Berlin; Book, Howard Lindsay and Russel Crouse; Adaptation, Bill Russell and Charles Repole; Director, Charles Repole; Musical Director, Rob Fisher; Orchestration, Don Walker; Set, John Lee Beatty; Lighting, Richard Pilbrow, Dawn Chiang; Sound, Scott Lehrer; Choreography, Kathleen Marshall; Cast Recording, DRG; Stage Manager, Clifford Schwartz; Presented by City Center Encores (Walter Bobbie, Artistic Director); Press, Philip Rinaldi/Barbara Carroll; Opened in City Center on Thursday, February 16, 1995*

CAST

Mrs. Sally Adams	Tyne Daly
Mr. Gibson	John Leslie Wolfe
Congressman Wilkins	Christopher Durang
Kenneth Gibson	Lewis Cleale
Senator Brockbank	MacIntyre Dixon
Senator Gallagher	Ken Page
Cosmo Constantine	Walter Charles
Pemberton Maxwell	Peter Bartlett
Sebastian Sebastian	Simon Jones
Princess Maria	Melissa Errico
Grand Duchess Sophie	Jane Connell
Grand Duke Otto	Gordon Connell
Singing Ensemble	Jamie Baer, John Clonts, Colleen Fitzpatrick, Michael Hayward-Jones, Dale Hensley, David Masenheimer, Beth McVey, Lori Brown Mirabel, Rebecca Spencer, Christianne Tisdale, Brent Weber, John Leslie Wolfe
Dancers	Michael Berresse, Angelo Fraboni, Amy Heggins, JoAnn M. Hunter, Mary Ann Lamb, Darren Lee

and The Coffee Club Orchestra

MUSICAL NUMBERS: Overture, Mrs. Sally Adams, The Hostess with the Mostes' on the Ball, Washington Square Dance, Lichtenburg, Can You Use Any Money Today?, Marrying for Love, Ocarina, It's a Lovely Day, The Best Thing For You, Entr'acte, Something to Dance About, Once Upon a Time Today, They Like Ike, You're Just in Love, Finale

A concert adaptation of the 1950 musical. For original Broadway production with Ethel Merman see *Theatre World Vol. 7.*

*Closed February 18, 1995 after limited run of 4 performances.

Gerry Goodstein Photos

Right: Lewis Cleale, Melissa Errico
Below: Tyne Daly, Walter Charles

UNCLE VANYA

By Anton Chekhov; Translation, Jean-Claude van Itallie; Director, Braham Murray; Set, Loren Sherman; Costumes, Mimi Maxmen; Lighting, Tharron Musser; Sound, John Kilgore; Music, Stanley Silverman; Hairstylist, Paul Huntley; Company Manager, Gordon G. Forbes; Stage Managers, Wm. Hare, Cheryl Zoldowski; Presented by Circle in the Square (Theodore Mann, Josephine R. Abady, Co-Artistic Directors; Robert Bennett, Managing Director); Press, Jeffrey Richards/Kevin Rehac, Mimi Scott; Previewed from Friday February 3; Opened in the Circle in the Square Uptown on Thursday, February 23, 1995*

CAST

Maryina (Nanny)..Bette Henritze
Mikhail Lvovich Astrov ....James Fox
Ivan Petrovich Voinitsky (Vanya) ....Tom Courtenay
Alexander Vladimirovich Serebryakov.........................Werner Klemperer
Ilya Ilyich Telyegin...Gerry Bamman
Sofya Alexandrovna (Sonya) ....Kate Skinner
Yelena Andreyevna ....Amanda Donohoe
Maria Vasilyevna Voinitskaya...........................Elizabeth Franz
Worker...Richard Council

UNDERSTUDIES: Angela Thornton (Nanny/Maria), Richard Council (Astrov/Serebryakov), Paul Hebron (Vanya/Telyegin/Worker), Catherine Dent (Sonya/Yelena)

A four-act play (1899) performed with one intermission and one pause. The action takes place in and around the family estate.

Variety tallied 5 mixed and 4 negative reviews. *Times:* (Canby) "Anger and petulance have replaced Chekhov's evocation of longing and resignation." *Post:* (Barnes) "This is the least poetic *Vanya* I can recall, but one of the most bitterly realistic." *News* (Kissel) "It moves smoothly and amusingly, if not touchingly." *Newsday:* (Winer) "This is Chekhov without the ache—more efficient than moving..." *Variety:* (Gerard) "... closer to the conclusion of Rumpelstiltskin than to what is arguably Chekhov's bleakest comedy."

*Closed March 19, 1995 after 29 performances and 23 previews.

Gerry Goodstein Photos

Right: Amanda Donohoe, Kate Skinner
Top: James Fox, Tom Courtenay

DeLee Lively, Michael Park

SMOKEY JOE'S CAFE

Music/Lyrics, Jerry Leiber and Mike Stoller; Director, Jerry Zaks; Musical Staging, Joey McKneely; Orchestrations, Steve Margoshes; Conductor/Arranger, Louis St. Louis; Music Coordinator, John Miller; Sets, Heidi Landesman; Costumes, William Ivey Long; Lighting, Timothy Hunter; Sound, Tony Meola; Hair/Make-up, Randy Houston Mercer; Production Supervisor, Steven Beckler; Production Manager, Peter Fulbright; Original Concept, Stephen Helper, Jack Viertel; Cast Recording, Atlantic; General Management, Richard Frankel; Company Manager, Laura Green; Stage Managers, Kenneth Hanson, Maximo Torres; Presented by Richard Frankel, Thomas Viertel, Steven Baruch, Jujamcyn Theatres/Jack Viertel, Rick Steiner, Frederic H. Mayerson and Center Theatre Group/Ahmanson/Gordon Davidson; Press, Chris Boneau/Adrian Bryan-Brown, Jackie Green, Patty Onagan, Meredith Moore, Ari Cohn, Scott Walton; Previewed from Wednesday, February 8; Opened in the Virginia Theatre on Thursday, March 2, 1995*

CAST

Ken Ard	Adrian Bailey	Brenda Braxton
Victor Trent Cook	B.J. Crosby	Pattie Darcy Jones
DeLee Lively	Frederick B. Owens	Michael Park

STANDBYS: Bobby Daye, April Nixon, Kevyn Morrow, Monica Page

MUSICAL NUMBERS: Neighborhood, Young Blood, Falling, Ruby Baby, Dance with Me, Keep on Rollin', Searchin', Kansas City, Trouble, Love Me/Don't, Fools Fall in Love, Poison Ivy, Don Juan, Shoppin' for Clothes, I Keep Forgettin', On Broadway, D.W. Washburn, Saved, That is Rock & Roll, Yakety Yak, Charlie Brown, Stay a While, Pearl's a Singer, Teach Me How to Shimmy, You're the Boss, Smokey Joe's Cafe, Loving You, Treat Me Nice, Hound Dog, Little Egypt, I'm a Woman, There Goes My baby, Love Potion #9, Some Cats Know, Jailhouse Rock, Fools Fall in Love, Spanish Harlem, I Who Have Nothing, Stand By Me, Finale

A musical revue in two acts.

Variety tallied 9 favorable and 6 mixed reviews. *Times:* (Brantley) "...a strangely homogenized tribute to one of popular music's most protean songwriting teams...big, crowd-pleasing voices." *Post:* (Barnes) "...niftily staged by Jerry Zaks, with sleek, sharp and seamless choreography by newcomer Joey McNeely...sensationally well performed..." *News* (Kissel) "Theater music presupposes characters and story. These songs presuppose you want to clap your hands and dance." *Newsday:* (Winer) "...the authors of "On Broadway" have indeed made it there."

*Still playing May 31, 1995.

Joan Marcus Photos

Adrian Bailey, Ken Ard, Victor Trent Cook, Frederick B. Owens

Brenda Braxton, B.J. Crosby, DeLee Lively, Pattie Darcy Jones

Cherry Jones in *The Heiress*

Philip Bosco, Jon Tenney, Cherry Jones
Top: Frances Sternhagen, Cherry Jones

THE HEIRESS

By Ruth and Augustus Goetz; Director, Gerald Gutierrez; Sets, John Lee Beatty; Costumes, Jane Greenwood; Lighting, Beverly Emmons; Music, Robert Waldman; Sound, Aural Fixation; General Manager, Steven C. Callahan; Production Manager, Jeff Hamlin; Company Manager, Edward J. Nelson; Stage Managers, Michael Brunner, Christopher Wigle; Presented by Lincoln Center Theater (Andre Bishop, Bernard Gersten, Directors); Press, Merle Debuskey/Susan Chicoine, Wylie Strout; Previewed from Thursday, February 9; Opened in the Cort Theatre on Thursday, March 9, 1995*

CAST

Maria	Kate Finneran
Dr. Austin Sloper	Philip Bosco +1
Lavinia Penniman	Frances Sternhagen
Catherine Sloper	Cherry Jones
Elizabeth Almond	Patricia Conolly
Arthur Townsend	Karl Kenzler
Marian Almond	Michelle O'Neill
Morris Townsend	Jon Tenney +2
Mrs. Montgomery	Lizbeth Mackay

UNDERSTUDIES: Jenn Thompson (Maria/Marian), William Cain (Dr. Sloper), Amelia White (Lavinia/Elizabeth/Mrs. Montgomery), Michelle O'Neill (Catherine), Richard Thompson (Arthur/Morris)

A new production of a 1947 drama in two acts. The action takes place in Dr. Sloper's Washington Square home, New York City, 1850. For original Broadway production see *Theatre World Vol. IV.*

Variety tallied 10 favorable and 3 mixed reviews. *Times:* (Canby) "If you would like to see a first-rate production of the kind of comparatively small, well-made play that Broadway once trafficked in, you won't want to miss it." (Jefferson) "...concentrates more on the story of an unloving parent and his unwanted child." *Post:* (Barnes) "...Jones, radiant in hope, tragic in despair, chilling in conviction, resonates with passions that seem all the more vibrant for being supressed..." *News:* (Kissel) "If self-denial is quite foreign to the contemporary American mood, so is the concept of the well-made play. The combination of the two makes *The Heiress* as exotic a spectacle as New York has seen in years..." *Newsday:* (Winer) "...a delightfully old-fashioned and engrossing surprise." *Variety:* (Gerard) "...unexpected emotional vitality...the exceptional cast never falters..."

*Closed December 31, 1995 after 340 performances and 31 previews. Winner of "Tony" award for Best Play Revival and Best Actress in a Play (Cherry Jones).

+Succeeded by: 1. Donald Moffat 2. Richard Thompson (during illness), Michael Cumpsty

Philip Bosco
Bottom Left: Jon Tenney
Bottom Right: Cherry Jones, Philip Bosco

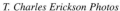
T. Charles Erickson Photos

TRANSLATIONS

By Brian Friel; Director, Howard Davies; Set, Ashley Martin-Davis; Lighting, Chris Parry; Costumes, Joan Bergin; Sound, T. Richard Fitzgerald; Production Supervisors, Fred Gallo Jr., John Woolf; Company Manager, Kathleen Lowe; Stage Managers, Susie Cordon, Allison Sommers; Presented by Noel Pearson in association with Joseph Harris; Press. Shirley Herz/Sam Rudy; Previewed from Tuesday, March 7; Opened in the Plymouth Theatre on Sunday, March 19, 1995*

CAST

Manus	Rob Campbell
Sarah	Amelia Campbell
Jimmy Jack	Donal Donnelly
Maire	Dana Delany
Doalty	David Herlihy
Bridget	Miriam Healy-Louie
Hugh	Brian Dennehy
Owen	Rufus Sewell
Captain Lancey	Geoffrey Wade
Lieutenant Yolland	Michael Cumpsty
Soldier	Hugh O'Gorman

STANDBYS/UNDERSTUDIES: Kerry O'Malley (Sarah/Bridget), Mari Nelson (Maire), Malachy McCourt (Hugh/Jimmy), Brian Mallon (Manus/Owen), Hugh O'Gorman (Lancey/Doalty/Yolland)

A new production of a 1980 Irish play in three acts (performed with one intermission). The action takes place in Baile Beag/Ballybeg, County Donegal, Ireland in 1833. For 1981 Off-Broadway production see *Theatre World Vol. 37.*

Variety tallied 6 favorable, 5 mixed, and 1 negative notice. *Times:* (Canby) "...a big, meditative, far more interesting play than you're likely to realize from the flat, mostly uninspired production..." (Jefferson) "...nothing in this production works very well..." *Post:* (Barnes) "It stays with you long past the curtain fall, offering queries for the heart, sustenance for the mind." *News:* (Kissel) "The strongest performance is that of the English actor Rufus Sewell..." *Newsday:* (Winer) "...enormously rich and moving testimony to the profound importance of language on the very essence of identity..." *Variety:* (Gerard) "Stars or no stars, it's going to be a tough sell on Broadway."

*Closed April 9, 1995 after 25 performances and 15 previews.

Tom Lawlor Photos

Top: Geoffrey Wade, Rufus Sewell
Left: Dana Delany, Donal Donnelly, Brian Dennehy

Matthew Broderick in *How To Succeed…*
Joan Marcus Photo

The Company
Top: Lillias White & male cast

HOW TO SUCCEED IN BUSINESS WITHOUT REALLY TRYING!

Music/Lyrics, Frank Loesser; Book, Abe Burrows, Jack Weinstock and Willie Gilbert; Based on the book by Shepard Mead; Director, Des McAnuff; Choreography, Wayne Cilento; Musical Director/Vocal Arrangements, Ted Sperling; Orchestrations, Danny Troob, David Siegel, Robert Ginzler; Sets, John Arnone; Costumes, Susan Hilferty; Lighting, Howell Binkley; Video, Batwin + Robin; Sound, Steve Canyon Kennedy; Hairstylist, David H. Lawrence; Cast Recording, RCA Victor; Company Manager, Marcia Goldberg; Stage Managers, Frank Hartenstein, Diane DiVita; Presented by Dodger Productions, Kardana Productions, John F. Kennedy Center for the Performing Arts; and the Nederlander Organization; Press, Chris Boneau/Adrian Bryan-Brown, John Barlow, Susanne Tighe; Previewed from Thursday, March 9; Opened in the Richard Rodgers Theatre on Thursday, March 23, 1995*

CAST

Voice of the Narrator	Walter Cronkite
J. Pierpont Finch	Matthew Broderick +1
Milt Gatch	Tom Flynn
Jenkins	Jay Aubrey Jones
Davis	William Ryall
Bert Bratt	Jonathan Freeman
Tackaberry	Martin Moran
J.B. Biggley	Ronn Carroll
Rosemary Pilkington	Megan Mullally +2
Smitty	Victoria Clark
Bud Frump	Jeff Blumenkrantz +3
Miss Krumholtz	Kristi Lynes
Office Boy/Ovington/TV Announcer	Randl Ask
Security Guard	Kevin Bogue
Henchmen	Jack Hayes, Jerome Vivona
Miss Jones	Lillias White +4
Twimble	Gerry Vichi
Hedy La Rue	Luba Mason
Toynbee	Tom Flynn
Scrubwomen	Rebecca Holt, Carla Renata Williams
Dance Soloist	Nancy Lemenager
Wickets and Wickettes	Kevin Bogue, Maria Calabrese, Jack Hayes, Nancy Lemenager, Kristi Lynes, Aiko Nakasone, Jerome Vivona, Carla Renata Williams
Wally Womper	Gerry Vichi
Ensemble	Randl Ask, Kevin Bogue, Maria Calabrese, Tom Flynn, Jack Hayes, Rebecca Holt, Jay Aubrey Jones, Nancy Lemenager, Martin Moran, Aiko Nakasone, William Ryall, Jerome Vivona, Carla Renata Williams

UNDERSTUDIES: Martin Moran (Finch), Randl Ask (Finch/Frump), Jay Aubrey Jones (Twimble/Womper), Tom Flynn (Bratt), Carla Renata Williams (Smitty/Miss Jones), Pamela Gold, Rebecca Holt (Hedy), Kristi Lynes (Rosemary), William Ryall (Biggley) SWINGS: Jeffry Denman, Tom Flagg, Pamela Gold

MUSICAL NUMBERS: Overture, How to Succeed, Happy to Keep His Dinner Warm, Coffee Break, The Company Way, A Secretary Is Not a Toy, Been a Long Day, Grand Old Ivy, Paris Original, Rosemary, Entr'acte, Love from a Heart of Gold, I Believe in You, Pirate Dance, Brotherhood of Man, Finale

A new production of the 1961 musical in two acts. The action takes place at the World Wide Wicket Company in NYC, 1961. For original Broadway production with Robert Morse and Rudy Vallee see *Theatre World Vol. 18.*

Top: Ronn Carroll, Luba Mason

Variety tallied 13 favorable, 5 mixed, and 3 negative notices. *Times:* (Canby) "...as fast, funny and glitzy as it ever was...Mr. Broderick sings. He dances...he gives a supremely legitimate performance that also happens to be priceless." *Post:* (Barnes) "...as gloriously tuneful and extravagantly witty as ever...the main modernization is simply in presentation." *News:* (Kissel) "...entertaining largely because of the brilliance of Loesser's score...the material is so witty, so compelling." *Newsday:* (Winer) "It's hard to imagine a more affectionate, more caring, more unrelentingly inventive revival...with the blithely terrific Matthew Broderick..." *Variety:* (Gerard) "...should be making people happy for a long time...*How to Succeed* is as good as it gets..."

*Closed July 14, 1996 after 548 performances and 16 previews. Winner of "Tony" award for Best Actor in a Musical (Matthew Broderick).

+Succeeded by: 1. Martin Moran (during vacation), John Stamos, Matthew Broderick 2. Kristi Lynes, Sarah Jessica Parker 3. Brooks Ashmanskas 4.Tina Fabrique

Joan Marcus Photos

DEFENDING THE CAVEMAN

By Rob Becker; Music, R.B. & Michael Barrow; Company Manager, Todd Grove; Stage Manager, Jason Lindhorst; Presented by Contemporary Productions; Press, Merle Frimark and Marc Thibodeau/Erin Dunn, Colleen Brown; Previewed from Wednesday, March 1; Opened in the Helen Hayes Theatre on Sunday, March 26, 1995*

CAST

Rob Becker

A one-man comedy performed without intermission.

Left & Below: Rob Becker

Billy Crudup, Jennifer Dundas in *Arcadia*

Robert Sean Leonard

Blair Brown

Victor Garber

Billy Crudup

ARCADIA

By Tom Stoppard; Director, Trevor Nunn; Sets/Costumes, Mark Thompson; Lighting, Paul Pyant; Sound, Charles Bugbee III; Music, Jeremy Sams; Production Manager, Jeff Hamlin; General Manager, Steven C. Callahan; Company Manager, Edward J. Nelson; Stage Managers, Alan Hall, Ruth E. Rinklin; Presented by Lincoln Center Theater (Andre Bishop, Bernard Gersten, Directors); Press, Merle Debuskey/Susan Chicoine, Wylie Strout; Previewed from Thursday, March 2; Opened in the Vivian Beaumont Theater on Thursday, March 30, 1995*

CAST

Thomasina Coverly	Jennifer Dundas
Septimus Hodge	Billy Crudup
Jellaby	Richard Clarke
Ezra Chater	Paul Giamatti
Richard Noakes	Peter Maloney
Lady Croom	Lisa Banes
Captain Brice, RN	David Mantis
Hannah Jarvis	Blair Brown
Chloe Coverly	Haviland Morris
Bernard Nightingale	Victor Garber
Valentine Coverly	Robert Sean Leonard
Gus Coverly/Augustus Coverly	John Griffin

UNDERSTUDIES: Mary Bacon (Thomasina/Chloe), Don Reilly (Septimus/Valentine), Anderson Matthews (Jellaby/Ezra/Noakes/Brice), Gloria Biegler (Lady Croom/Hannah), Terrence Caza (Nightingale/Brice), Josh Broomberg (Gus/Augustus)

A play in two acts. The action takes place in a large Derbyshire country house, 1809, and the present. Winner of the New York Drama Critics' Circle Best Play of 1995.

Variety tallied 12 favorable and 7 mixed reviews. *Times:* (Canby) "...Tom Stoppard's richest, most ravishing comedy to date, a play of wit, intellect, language, brio and, new for him, emotion. It's like a dream of levitation: you're instantly aloft, soaring, banking, doing loop-the-loops and then, when you think you're about to plummet to earth, swooping to a gentle touchdown of not easily described sweetness and sorrow." (Jefferson) "The night I saw it, large portions of the audience stood and cheered, but others left looking wan and defeated." *Post:* (Barnes) "...the best Broadway play for many, many a season. It is a work shot through with fun, passion and, yes, genius." *News:* (Kissel) "...I don't think one can praise *Arcadia* enough...Blair Brown makes Hannah vital and sexy...Jennifer Dundas is enthralling...Billy Crudup and Robert Sean Leonard exude great power...Victor Garber is absolutely delicious..." *Newsday:* (Winer) "...a high-flying ride without a stick of mechanized scenery a great aching thrill of a play." *Variety:* (Gerard) "The hunger for meaning and discovery palpable in every line of the play ultimately links both halves...look to Leonard's Valentine. With conviction and easy grace, he makes the play's heaviest lines weightless..."

*Closed August 27, 1995 after 173 performances and 31 previews. Winner of New York Drama Critics Circle Best Play

Joan Marcus Photos

Top: Blair Brown, Victor Garber
Center: David Manis, Billy Crudup, Lisa Banes
Right: Robert Sean Leonard, Blair Brown

Andrea Martin in *Out Of This World*

HAVING OUR SAY

Written/Directed by Emily Mann; Adapted from the autobiography by Sarah L. Delany and A. Elizabeth Delany; Set, Thomas Lynch; Costumes, Judy Dearing; Lighting, Allen Lee Hughes; Projections, Wendall K. Harrington, Sage Marie Carter; Music, Baikida Carroll; General Manager, Robert Cole; Company Manager, Lisa M. Poyer; Stage Managers, Martin Gold, Ed De Shae; Produced in association with Dreyfuss/James Productions; Presented by Camille O. Cosby, Judith Rutherford James; Press, Chris Boneau/Adrian Byran-Brown/Andy Shearer, Meredith Moore; Previewed from Thursday, March 16; Opened in the Booth Theatre on Thursday, April 6, 1995*

CAST

Miss Sadie Delany ....Gloria Foster
Dr. Bessie Delany..Mary Alice

STANDBYS: Frances Foster (Sadie), Novella Nelson (Bessie)

A drama in three acts. The setting is the Delany home in Mt. Vernon, NY, February 1993. The actual Delany sisters attended the production on May 13, 1995.

Variety tallied 13 favorable and 3 mixed reviews. *Times:* (Canby) "...contains dozens of characters, represents six generations and embraces nearly 200 years of black American life...The Booth stage is alive. When the actresses get going, the performance takes on the excitement of a revival meeting." (Jefferson) "...cozy domestic drama..." *Post:* (Barnes) "...it is a window on a world now lost, full of love, a little pain and a wondrous deal of hope." *News:* (Kissel) "Gloria Foster gives Sadie tremendous dignity and inner strength. Mary Alice is absolutely captivating..." *Newsday:* (Winer) "...faithful, if overly didactic and sprawling, adaptation of the published oral history...how lovely to hear about America's real history from witnesses who are such good company..." *Variety:* (Gerard) "Add performances of uncommon power by two of our most accomplished actresses, Gloria Foster and Mary Alice, and a subject that embraces the century, and you have the elements of a memorable evening of playgoing."

*Closed December 31, 1995 after 308 performances and 24 previews.

T. Charles Erickson Photos

OUT OF THIS WORLD

Music/Lyrics, Cole Porter; Book, Dwight Taylor and Reginald Lawrence; Adaptation, David Ives; Musical Director, Rob Fisher; Director, Mark Brokaw; Orchestration, Robert Russell Bennett; Set, John Lee Beatty; Lighting, Marc B. Weiss; Sound, Scott Lehrer; Choreography, John Carrafa; Cast Recording, DRG; Stage Manager, Michael F. Ritchie; Presented by City Center Encores (Walter Bobbie, Artistic Director); Press, Philip Rinaldi/Barbara Carroll; Opened in City Center on Thursday, March 30, 1995*

CAST

Mercury...Peter Scolari
Jupiter...Ken Page
Helen...Marin Mazzie
Art O'Malley...Gregg Edelman
Juno...Andrea Martin
Chloe...La Chanze
Niki Skolianos ....Ernie Sabella
Ensemble ....Rachel Coloff, Andrea Green, Marc Heller, Dale Hensley, David Masenheimer, Chris Monteleone, Christine Noll, Francis Ruivivar, John Scherer, Margaret Shafer, Dawn Spare, Elizabeth Walsh and The Coffee Club Orchestra

MUSICAL NUMBERS: Overture, Prologue, I Jupiter I Rex, Use Your Imagination, Juno's Ride, I Got Beauty, Maiden Fair, Where Oh Where?, They Couldn't Compare to You, From This Moment On (cut during out-of-town previews in 1950), What Do You Think About Men, Dance of the Long Night, You Don't Remind Me, I Sleep Easier Now, I Am Loved, Entr'acte, Climb Up the Mountain, Dance of the Dawn, No Lover for Me, Cherry Pies Ought to Be You, Hark to the Song of the Night, Nobody's Chasing Me, Finale

A concert version of the 1950 musical. For original Broadway production with Charlotte Greenwood see *Theatre World Vol. 7.*

*Closed April 1, 1995 after limited run of 4 performances.

Gerry Goodstein Photos

Mary Alice, Gloria Foster

Mary Alice, Gloria Foster

GENTLEMEN PREFER BLONDES

Music, Jule Styne; Lyrics, Leo Robin; Book, Anita Loos and Joseph Fields based on Loos' novel; Director, Charles Repole; Choreography, Michael Lichtefeld; Orchestrations, Douglas Besterman; Musical Director, Andrew Wilder; Musical Supervision/Vocal Arrangements, Michael O'Flaherty; Sets/Costumes, Eduardo Sicangco; Lighting, Kirk Bookman; Sound, T. Richard Fitzgerald; Dance Music, G. Harrell; General Management, Niko Associates; Managing Director, Fred Walker; Company Manager, Erich Hamner; Stage Managers, Donna Cooper Hilton, Kathy J. Faul; Executive Producer, Manny Kladitis; Presented by National Actors Theatre (Tony Randall, Founder/Artistic Director) in association with Goodspeed Opera House (Michael P. Price, Executive Producer); Press, Gary and John Springer; Previewed from Tuesday, March 28; Opened in the Lyceum Theatre on Monday, April 10, 1995*

CAST

Dorothy Shaw	Karen Prunzik
Lorelei Lee	KT Sullivan
Gus Esmond	Allen Fitzpatrick
Lady Phyllis Beekman	Carol Swarbrick
Sir Francis Beekman	David Ponting
Mrs. Ella Spofford	Susan Rush
Henry Spofford	George Dvorsky
Josephus Gage	Jamie Ross
Steward/Mr. Esmond Sr.	Dick Decareau
Frank/Robert Lemanteur	Craig Waletzko
George	Ken Nagy
Mime	Joe Bowerman
Louie Lemanteur	John Hoshko
Tango Couples	Paula Grider, Joe Bowerman, Lisa Hanna, Ken Nagy, Richard Costa, Lorinda Santos
Park Casino Trio	Angela Bond, John Hoshko, Craig Waletzko
Ensemble	Angela Bond, Joe Bowerman, Richard Costa, Paula Grider, Lisa Hanna, Bryan S. Haynes, John Hoshko, Ken Nagy, Wendy Roberts, Lorinda Santos, Craig Waletzko

UNDERSTUDIES: Angela Bond (Lorelei/Mrs. Spofford/Lady Beekman), Lisa Hanna (Dorothy), John Hoshko (Gus/Sr. Esmond/Steward), Dick Decareau (Josepheus/Francis), Craig Waletzko (Henry), Ken Nagy (Mime) SWINGS: Melissa Bell, Marty McDonough

MUSICAL NUMBERS: Overture, It's High Time, Bye Bye Baby, A Little Girl from Little Rock, I'm Atingle I'm Aglow, I Love What I'm Doing, Just a Kiss Apart, It's Delightful Down in Chile, Sunshine Montage, Entr'acte, Mamie is Mimi, Diamonds Are a Girl's Best Friend, A Ride on a Rainbow, Gentlemen Prefer Blondes, Homesick, You Say You Care, Keeping Cool with Coolidge, Finale

A revised version of the 1949 musical in two acts. The action takes place in New York City, Paris, and the Ile de France. For original Broadway production starring Carol Channing see *Theatre World Vol. 6*. For 1974 revision, *Lorelei*, see *Theatre World Vol. 30*. This version rearranges the musical program and uses dialogue written for the 1953 film version.

Variety tallied 2 mixed and 12 negative reviews. *Times:* (Canby) "...it's desperate, skinny and exhausted, down to its last few pennies." (Jefferson) "What can you say about a show that dies, right there on the stage in front of you?" *Post* (Barnes) "it does have a great score, among Styne's best..." *News:* (Kissel) "No one could imagine it was a show of any interest at all from the lackluster revival..." *Newsday:* (Winer) "We're missing the special excitement of Broadway...an altogether provincial staging..." *Variety:* (Gerard) "...an example of talent that can appear ample outside the theatre district but which withers in the Broadway spotlight."

*Closed April 30, 1995 after 24 performances and 16 previews.

Diane Sobolewski Photos

KT Sullivan, Karen Prunzik in *Gentlemen Prefer Blondes*

EASTER BONNET COMPETITION: BACK TO BASICS

Director, Charles Repole; Choreography, Kathleen Marshall; Musical Supervision, David Friedman, Seth Rudetsky; Assistant Director, Scott T. Stevens; Associate Choreographer, Drew Geraci; Stage Managers, James Harker, John M. Atherlay, Kim Vernace; Presented by Michael Graziano, John V. Fahey, Carol Ingram, Kevin Duncan; Producing Director, Tom Viola; Producing Consultant, Maria Di Dia; Press, Chris Boneau/Adrian Bryan-Brown, Miguel Tuason; Presented in the Palace Theatre on Monday, April 10 and Tuesday, April 11, 1995.

CAST INCLUDES

Matthew Broderick and Sarah Jessica Parker, Zoe Caldwell and Robert Whitehead, Joe Mantello and Jon Robin Baitz, Marlo Thomas and Davis Gaines, Debra Monk and Cherry Jones, Rebecca Luker and Gregory Jbara, Alix Korey, Lizbeth MacKay, Glenn Close, Victor Garber, Whoopi Goldberg, Anne Runolfsson, Billy Porter, Howard McGillin, Nancy LaMott, Maria Conchita Alonso, Helen Reddy, and cast members from *Miss Saigon, Kiss of the Spider Woman, How To Succeed..., An Inspector Calls, Crazy For You, That's Life, Grease, Beauty and the Beast, Language of Their Own, Les Ballets Trockadero, Cats, Love Valour Compassion, Hello Dolly, Fiddler on the Roof, Angels in America, Rainbow & Stars, Gentlemen Prefer Blondes, Tommy, Les Miserables, Sunset Boulevard, Damn Yankees, Smokey Joe's Café, Three Tall Women,* and *Show Boat*

BONNET DANCERS: Tim Albrecht, Joyce Chittick, Greg Garrison, Alisa Klein, Shannon Lewis, Brian Paul Mendoza, Elizabeth Mills, Malinda Shaffer, Lorna Shane, Steven Sofia, Alton White, Daniel Wright

BONNET CHORUS: Kevin Berdini, Andrea Burns, Paul Castree, Neil Cohen, Margo Grib, Elliot Levine, Rita Lilly, Rob Lorey, Anna McNeely, Hugo Munday, Beverly Myers, Kristen Nordeval, Wilbur Pauley, John Schenkweiler, Eilene Tepper, Molly Wasswemann

The ninth annual Easter fundraiser for Broadway Cares/Equity Fights AIDS raised $1,112,639.

A MONTH IN THE COUNTRY

By Ivan Turgenev; Translation, Richard Freeborn; Director, Scott Ellis; Set, Santo Loquasto; Costumes, Jane Greenwood; Lighting, Brian Nason; Sound, Tony Meola; General Manager, Ellen Richard; Stage Managers, Jay Adler, Charles Kindl; Presented by Roundabout Theatre Company (Todd Haimes, Artistic Director; Gene Feist, Founding Director); Press, Chris Boneau/Adrian Bryan-Brown, Susanne Tighe; Previewed from Tuesday, April 4; Opened in the Criterion Center Stage Right on Tuesday, April 25, 1995*

CAST

Schaaf..Rocco Sisto
Anna Semenovna..Helen Stenborg
Lizaveta Bogdanovna ....Gail Grate
Natalya Petrovna ....Helen Mirren
Mikhailo Aleksandrovich Rakitin ....Ron Rifkin
Kolya...Benjamin N. Ungar
Aleksei Nikolaevich Belyaev ....Alessandro Nivola
Matvei ....Dan Moran
Ignaty Ilich Shpigelsky...F. Murray Abraham
Verochka ....Kathryn Erbe
Arkady Sergeich Islaev ....Byron Jennings
Katya..Patricia T.A. Ageheim
Afanasy Ivanovich Bolshintsov............................John Christopher Jones

STANDBYS/UNDERSTUDIES: Suzanna Hay (Natalya), Julian Gamble (Mikhailo/Ignaty/Arkady), Dan Moran (Schaaf/Afanasy), Jennifer Garner (Verochka/Katya), Paul F. Dano (Kolya), Patricia Baxter (Anna), Ezio Cutarelli (Aleksei/Matvei)

A new production of a Russian drama in five acts with one intermission. The action takes place in Russia, 1840s. Written in 1850, the play was first staged in Russia in 1872.

Variety tallied 8 favorable, 5 mixed, and 1 negative notice. *Times:* (Jefferson) "There are so many shades and textures to this play, as, one by one, the characters acknowledge then renounce their hearts' desires." *Variety:* (Gerard) "almost always entertaining but never involving."

*Closed June 10, 1995 after 53 performances and 24 previews.

Carol Rosegg Photos

Ron Rifkin, Rocco Sisto, Helen Stenborg, Gail Grate, Dan Moran, Helen Mirren
Top: Alessandro Nivola, Helen Mirren

INDISCRETIONS
(LES PARENTS TERRIBLES)

By Jean Cocteau; Translation, Jeremy Sams; Director, Sean Mathias; Sets/Costumes, Stephen Brimson Lewis; Lighting, Mark Henderson; Sound, Jonathan F. Suffolk; Music, Jason Carr; General Management, Marvin A. Krauss; Stage Managers, Arthur Gaffin, David J. O'Brien; Presented by The Shubert Organization, Capital Cities/ABC, Roger Berlind, Scott Rubin, and The Royal National Theatre; Press, Alma Viator/Michael S. Borowski, William Schelble; Previewed from Monday, April 3; Opened in the Ethel Barrymore Theatre on Thursday, April 27, 1995*

CAST

George..Roger Rees
Leonie (Leo)..Eileen Atkins +1
Yvonne ....Kathleen Turner +2
Michael ....Jude Law +3
Madeleine ....Cynthia Nixon

STANDBYS: Leslie Hendrix (Yvonne), Sandra Shipley (Leo), Lewis Arlt (George), Jim Stanek (Michael), Carrie Preston (Madeleine)

The American premiere of a 1938 French play in three acts. The action takes place in Paris during the 1940s. The 1938 production was shut down for "immorality."

Variety tallied 15 favorable, 2 mixed, and 4 negative notices. *Times:* (Canby) "A bewitching experience...alternately hilarious and ferocious..." (Jefferson) "...brittle, brutal play...visually opulent, psychologically disorienting set...the director, Sean Mathias, throws bold strokes our way. Michael stands up in Madeleine's bathtub, stark naked and ravishing; Michael and his mother roll around on her bed, kissing passionately..." *Post* (Barnes) "All wonderfully perfect, perfectly wonderful, and to be missed at your peril." *Newsday:* (Winer) "Fabulous, trashy, gorgeous, monstrous, stylish, unbelievably happy and deeply entertaining." *Variety:* (Gerard) "...veers giddily from one extreme to another: A constant disorientation is a big part of its thrill...irrepressible Law...Rees and Atkins are nothing short of spellbinding..."

*Closed November 4, 1995 after 220 performances and 28 previews.

+Succeeded by: 1. Sandra Shipley, Dana Ivey 2. Leslie Hendrix (during illness) 3. Jim Stanek (during vacation)

Joan Marcus Photos

Jude Law, Cynthia Nixon, Eileen Atkins, Roger Rees
Top: Kathleen Turner, Jude Law

Kathleen Turner

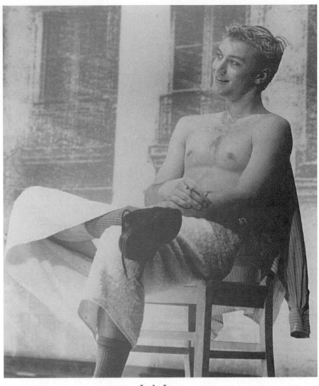

Jude Law

Roger Rees

Eileen Atkins

(top to bottom) Kathleen Turner, Jude Law, Eileen Atkins, Cynthia Nixon, Roger Rees in *Indiscretions*

THE ROSE TATTOO

By Tennessee Williams; Director, Robert Falls; Set, Santo Loquasto; Costumes, Catherine Zuber; Lighting, Kenneth Posner; Sound, John Kilgore; Dialects, K.C. Ligon; Stage Managers, Peggy Peterson, Wm. Hare; Presented by Circle in the Square (Theodore Mann, Josephine R. Abady, Co-Artistic Directors; Robert Bennett, Managing Director); Press, Jeffrey Richards/Kevin Rehac; Previewed from Friday, April 21; Opened in the Circle in the Square Uptown on Sunday, April 30, 1995*

CAST

Salvatore	Anthony Manganiello
Vivi	Jackie Angelescu
Assunda	Antonia Rey
Rosa Delle Rose	Cara Buono
Serafina Delle Rose	Mercedes Ruehl
Estelle Hohengarten	Deborah Jolly
The Strega	Irma St. Paule
Giuseppina	Carol Locatelle
Peppina	Suzanne Grodner
Violetta	Fiddle Viracola
Mariella	Elaine Bromka
Father De Leo	Dominic Chianese
A Doctor/Salesman	Philip LeStrange
Miss Yorke	Ellen Tobie
Flora	Catherine Campbell
Bessie	Kay Walbye
Jack Hunter	Dylan Chalfy
Alvaro Mangiacavallo	Anthony LaPaglia

UNDERSTUDIES: Teddy Alvaro (Salvatore/Vivi), Elaine Bromka (Miss Yorke/Bessie/Flora), Kevin Geer (Alvaro/Doc/Salesman), Suzanne Grodner (Serafina), Philip LeStrange (Fr. DeLeo), Carol Locatell (Assunta), Diane Martella (Strega/Peppina/Giuseppina), Elizabeth Rouse (Rosa/Estelle/Violetta/Mariella), Sam Trammell (Jack)

A new production of a 1951 drama in three acts. The action takes place in a village along the Gulf Coast between New Orleans and Mobile. For original Broadway production with Maureen Stapleton and Eli Wallach, see *Theatre World Vol. 7*.

Variety tallied 9 favorable and 8 mixed reviews, *Times:* (Brantley) "I can't think of a better way for New York audiences to celebrate the rites of spring." (Jefferson) "...Anthony LaPaglia enters, playing the goofy, lusty truck driver...sly but open-hearted, jaunty but awkward too, awakens Ms. Ruehl's subtler instincts, and the two of them have some fine scenes together." *Post:* (Barnes) "Mercedes Ruehl is dazzling..." *News:* (Kissel) "...Anthony LaPaglia is marvelous..." *Variety:* (Gerard) "...more infuriating than inspiring. Ruehl's sheer exuberance...could mask any production's shortcomings..."

*Closed July 2, 1995 after 73 performances and 10 previews.

Gerry Goodstein Photos

Mercedes Ruehl
Bottom Left: Mercedes Ruehl, Anthony LaPaglia
Bottom Right: Cara Buono, Dylan Chalfy

ON THE WATERFRONT

By Budd Schulberg with Stan Silverman; Director, Adrian Hall (succeeding Gordon Edelstein); Sets, Eugene Lee; Costumes, Ann Hould-Ward; Lighting, Peter Kaczorowski; Music, David Amram; Sound, Dan Moses Schreier; Hairstylist, David H. Lawrence; Stunts/Fights, Michael Giansanti; Production Supervisor, Maureen F. Gibson; General Manager, Charlotte W. Wilcox; Company Manager, Mitchell Weiss; Stage Managers, Franklin Keysar, David Hyslop, Debora F. Porazzi; Presented by Mitchell Maxwell, Dan Markley, Victoria Maxwell, Pines/Goldberg, Michael Skipper, Harvey J. Klaris, David Young, Dina Wein-Reis, James L. Simon, Palmer Video, Workin' Man Films, in association with Fred H. Krones, Hugh Hayes, Alan J. Schuster; Press, Peter Cromarty/Sara Chaiken; Previewed from Tuesday, April 18; Opened in the Brooks Atkinson Theatre on Monday, May 1, 1995*

CAST

Terry Malloy	Ron Eldard
Joey Doyle	Barry McEvoy
Mutt/J.P. Morgan	Jarlath Conroy
Bartender	Robertson Carricart
Barney	Jerry Grayson +1
Truck	Michael Mulheren
Charley Malloy	James Gandolfini +2
Little Frankie	Desmond Devenish
Moose/Interrogator	Skipp Sudduth
Runty Nolan	Lance Davis
Luke	Afemo Omilami
Ron	Leon Addison Brown
Pop Doyle	Brad Sullivan
Police	Richard Pruitt
Mrs. Collins	Alison Sheehy
Tommy	David Warshofsky
Father Barry	David Morse
Edie Doyle	Penelope Ann Miller
Johnny Friendly	Kevin Conway
Mac	Wayne Grace
Skins/Glover	Steve Ryan
Father Vincent	George N. Martin
Jimmy Conroy	Charlie Hofheimer
Bailiff	Leon Addison Brown
Longshoremen/Townspersons/Mobsters	Leon Addison Brown, Robertson Carricart, Lynn Eldredge, Kevin Hagen, Peter Linari, Richard Pruitt

UNDERSTUDIES: Skipp Sudduth (Fr. Barry/Charlie), Jarlath Conroy (Fr. Vincent/Pop), Jerry Grayson (Friendly), Barry McEvoy (Terry), Robertson Carricart (Barney/Morgan/Mutt/Runty), Richard Pruitt (Moose/Truck/Mac/Interrogator), Leon Addison Brown (Luke/Tommy/Glover), Alison Sheehy (Edie), Desmond Devenish (Jimmy/Joey), David Hyslop (Police/Bartender)

A drama in two acts. The action takes place on the New Jersey-New York waterfront. The material was previously done in a 1954 film with Marlon Brando.

Variety tallied 4 negative and 5 mixed reviews. *Times:* (Jefferson) "The show went through two directors, and that makes it hard to tell who did or didn't do what to whom. But as the night wore on and the actors wore themselves out trying to keep their words and actions from being swallowed up by a black hole of a set, you started to feel that they had been as abused and exploited as the dockworkers they were playing." *Variety:* (Gerard) "...opens on Broadway after the rockiest tryout in recent memory. There was a last-minute change of director and actors in two important roles, along with escalating preview costs that lifted the tab to some $2.6 million as the script went through numerous changes. As if that weren't enough, at the final preview, actor Jerry Grayson suffered an on-stage heart attack..."

*Closed May 7, 1995 after 8 performances and 16 previews.

+Succeeded by: 1. Robertson Carricart 2. Michael Harney

Carol Rosegg Photos

Top: Ron Eldard, Penelope Ann Miller
Center: Ron Eldard
Right: David Morse, Ron Eldard

HAMLET

By William Shakespeare; Director, Jonathan Kent; Set, Peter J. Davison; Costumes, James Acheson; Lighting, Mark Henderson; Music, Jonathan Dove; Sound, John A. Leonard; Fights, William Hobbs; Production Supervisor, Aurora Productions; General Management, David Strong Warner; Company Manager, Steven H. David; Stage Managers, Anne Keefe, Frank Lombardi; Presented by Dodger Productions, Roger Berlind, Endemol Theatre Productions, Jujamcyn Theatres, Kardana Productions, Scott Rudin and The Almeida Theatre Company; Press, Chris Boneau/Adrian Bryan-Brown/Bob Fennell; Previewed from Friday, April 14; Opened in the Belasco Theatre on Tuesday, May 2, 1995*

CAST

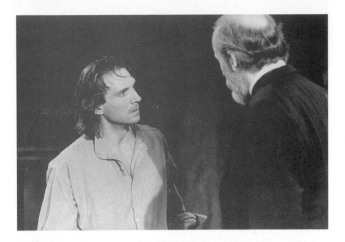

Francisco/Lucianus	Gilly Gilchrist
Barnardo	Colin Marc
Horation	Patterson Joseph
Marcellus/Captain	Terry McGinity
Ghost/Player King/Gravedigger	Terence Rigby
Hamlet	Ralph Fiennes
Laertes	Damian Lewis
Claudius	James Laurenson
Gertrude	Francesca Annis
Polonius	Peter Eyre
Ophelia	Tara FitzGerald
Reynaldo	David Melville
Rosencrantz	James Wallace
Guildenstern	Nicholas Rowe
Prologue/Gentlemen	Peter Helmer
Player Queen	Caroline Harris
Fortinbras	Rupert Penry-Jones
Priest	Gordon Langford-Rowe
Osric	Nicholas Palliser
Members of the Court	Melissa Chalsma, Denis Holmes, James Langton, Thomas Schall, Spence White

UNDERSTUDIES: Thomas Schall (Francisco), Peter Helmer (Barnardo/Rosencrantz), Colin Mace (Horatio), Denis Holmes (Marcellus/Priest), Terry McGinity (Ghost/Player King/Gravedigger), Rupert Penry-Jones (Hamlet), James Wallace (Laertes), Gilly Gilchrist (Claudius), Caroline Harris (Gertrude), Gordon Langford-Rowe (Polonius), Melissa Chalsma (Ophelia/Player Queen), Spence White (Reynaldo/Gentlemen), Nicholas Palliser (Guildenstern), James Langton (Prologue), David Melville (Lucianus/Fortinbras/Osric), Thomas Schall (Captain)

A new production of Shakespeare's drama performed in two acts. The action takes place in and near Elsinore Castle in Denmark.

Variety tallied 14 favorable, 7 mixed, and 1 negative review. *Times:* (Jefferson) "Mr. Fiennes is incredibly alive and complex...The words roll out and cushion us with their richness..." *Variety:* (Gerard) "...in the beautiful, tormented, Gertrude of Francesca Annis, almost a fresh vision of the play...This *Hamlet* literally wears his angst on his sleeve. His clothes get progressively grungier, his hair more unkempt..."

*Closed July 22, 1995 after 91 performances and 19 previews. Winner of Tony Award for Best Actor in a Play (Ralph Fiennes).

Ivan Kyncl Photos

Top: Ralph Fiennes, Peter Eyre
Center: Ralph Fiennes
Right: Tara FitzGerald, Peter Eyre

MY THING OF LOVE

By Alexandra Gersten; Director, Michael Maggio; Set, John Lee Beatty; Costumes, Erin Quigley; Lighting, Howell Binkley; Music, Rob Milburn and Michael Bodeen; Sound, Peter Fitzgerald; General Manager, Barbara Darwall; Company Manager, Judith Drasner; Stage Managers, Jane E. Neufeld, Terrence J. Witter; Presented by Barry and Fran Weissler, Jujamcyn Theatres in association with Pace Theatrical Group; Press, Pete Sanders/Michael Hartman; Previewed from Friday, April 21; Opened in the Martin Beck Theatre on Wednesday, May 3, 1995*

CAST

Elly	Laurie Metcalf
Jack	Tom Irwin
Kelly	Sheila Kelley succeeded by Jane Fleiss
Garn	Mark Blum
Kate (voice)	Erin Rice
Chris (voice)	Rebecca I. Rice

STANDBYS: Jim Abele (Jack/Garn), Jane Fleiss (Elly/Kelly)

A play in two acts. The action takes place in a modest house in an American suburb.

Variety tallied 1 favorable, 2 mixed, and 10 negative reviews. *Times:* (Jefferson) "It is a bumpy, depressing little ride." *Variety:* (Gerard) "...a devastating X-ray of a marriage ripped apart by sexual betrayal, put over by a ferocious performance from Laurie Metcalf..."

*Closed May 14, 1995 after 13 performances and 12 previews.

Carol Rosegg Photos

Tom Irwin, Laurie Metcalf in *My Thing of Love*

PAL JOEY

Music, Richard Rodgers; Lyrics, Lorenz Hart; Book, John O'Hara; Adaptation, Terrence McNally; Musical Director, Rob Fisher; Director, Lonny Price; Orchestration, Hans Spialek; Choreography, Joey McKneely; Set, John Lee Beatty; Lighting, Richard Pilbrow, Dawn Chiang; Sound, Scott Lehrer; Cast Recording, DRG; Stage Manager, Perry Cline; Presented by City Center Encores (Walter Bobbie, Artistic Director); Press, Philip Rinaldi/Barbara Carroll; Opened in City Center on Thursday, May 4, 1995*

CAST

Joey Evans	Peter Gallagher
Mike Spears	Ron Orbach
Gladys Bumps	Vicki Lewis
The Kid	Lori Werner
Terry	Mary Ann Lamb
Tilda	Dana Moore
Valerie	Mamie Duncan-Gibbs
Diane	Nora Brennan
Janet	Lynn Sterling
Linda English	Daisy Prince
Vera Simpson	Patti LuPone
Vera's Escorts	John Anthony, Christopher Sieber
Ernest (the Tailor)/Victor	John Deyle
Stage Manager/Hotel Manager	Jeff Brooks
Louis (the Tenor)	Arthur Rubin
Melba Snyder	Bebe Neuwirth
Ludlow Lowell	Ned Eisenberg
Deputy Commissioner O'Brien	Richard Council

and The Coffee Club Orchestra

MUSICAL NUMBERS: Overture, A Great Big Town, You Mustn't Kick It Around, I Could Write a Book, That Terrific Rainbow, What Is a Man, Happy Hunting Horn, Bewitched, Pal Joey (What Do I Care for a Dame?), Ballet, Entr'acte, Flower Garden of My Heart, Zip, Plant You Now Dig You Later, Den of Iniquity, Do It the Hard Way, Take Him, Finale

A staged concert of the 1940 musical.

Peter Gallagher, Patti LuPone in *Pal Joey*

Gerry Goodstein Photos

BROADWAY PRODUCTIONS FROM PAST SEASONS
THAT PLAYED THROUGH THIS SEASON

BEAUTY AND THE BEAST

Music, Alan Menken; Lyrics, Howard Ashman, Tim Rice; Book, Linda Woolverton; Director, Robert Jess Roth; Orchestrations, Danny Troob; Musical Supervision/Vocal Arrangements, David Friedman; Musical Director/Incidental Arrangements, Michael Kosarin; Choreography, Matt West; Sets, Stan Meyer; Costumes, Ann Hould-Ward; Lighting, Natasha Katz; Sound, T. Richard Fitzgerald; Hairstylist, David H. Lawrence; Illusions, Jim Steinmeyer, John Gaughan; Prosthetics, John Dods; Fights, Rick Sordelet; Cast Recording, Walt Disney Records; General Manager, Dodger Productions; Production Supervisor, Jeremiah J. Harris; Company Manager, Kim Sellon; Stage Managers, James Harker, John M. Atherlay, Pat Sosnow, Kim Vernace; Presented by Walt Disney Productions; Press, Chris Boneau/Adrian Bryan-Brown, Patty Onagan, Brian Moore, Michael Tuason; Previewed from Wednesday, March 9, 1994; Opened in the Palace Theatre on Monday, April 18, 1994*

CAST

Enchantress	Wendy Oliver
Young Prince	Harrison Beal
Beast	Terrence Mann +1
Belle	Susan Egan +2
Lefou	Kenny Raskin +
Gaston	Burke Moses +3
Three Silly Girls	Sarah Solie Shannon, Paige Price, Linda Talbott
Maurice	Tom Bosley +4
Cogsworth	Heath Lamberts
Lumiere	Gary Beach +5
Babette	Stacey Logan
Mrs. Potts	Beth Fowler +6
Chip	Brian Press
Madame de la Grande Bouche	Eleanor Glockner
Monsieur D'Arque	Gordon Stanley
Townspeople / Enchanted Objects	John Barber, Roxanne Barlow, Harrison Beal, Michael-Demby Cain, Kate Dowe, David Elder, Merwin Foard, Gregory Garrison, Jack Hayes, Kim Huber, Elmore James, Rob Lorey, Patrick Loy, Barbara Marineau, Joanne McHugh, Anna McNeely, Bill Nabel, Ms. Oliver, Vince Pesce, Ms. Price, Ms. Shannon, Mr. Stanley, Ms. Talcott, Wysandria Woolsey
Prologue Narrator	David Ogden Stiers

STANDBYS/UNDERSTUDIES: Chuck Wagner (Beast/Gaston), Kate Dowe, Alisa Klein (Enchantress/Silly Girls), Gregory Garrison, Dan Mojica (Young Prince), David Elder (Beast), Kim Huber, Paige Price (Belle), Harrison Beal, Vince Pesce (Lefou), Merwin Ford (Gaston), Bill Nabel, Gordon Stanley (Cogsworth/Lumiere), Joanne McHugh, Sarah Solie Sannon (Babette), Barbara Marineau, Anna McNeely (Mrs. Potts/Wardrobe), Linda Talcott (Chip), Rob Lorey (D'Arque) SWINGS: Ms. Klein, Mr. Mojica, Ms. Dowe, Mr. Garrison, Mr. Lorey

MUSICAL NUMBERS: Overture, Prologue (Enchantress), Belle, No Matter What, Me, Home, Gaston, How Long Must This Go On?, Be Our Guest, If I Can't Love Her, Entr'acte/Wolf Chase, Something There, Human Again, Maison des Lunes, Beauty and the Beast, Mob Song, The Battle, Transformation, Finale

A musical in two acts. An expanded, live action version of the 1992 animated film musical with additional songs. Winner of 1994 "Tony" for Best Costume Design.

*Still playing May 31, 1995.

+Succeeded by: 1. Jeff McCarthy 2. Sarah Uriarte 3. Marc Kudish 4. MacIntyre Dixon, Tom Bosley, Kurt Knudson 4. Lee Roy Reams 5. Cass Morgan

Terrence Mann, Susan Egan
Top: Sarah Uriarte, Jeff McCarthy

Joan Marcus/Marc Bryan-Brown/Walt Disney Theatrical Photos

BLOOD BROTHERS

Music/Lyrics/Book, Willy Russell; Directors, Bill Kenwright and Bob Tomson; Arrangements, Del Newman; Production Musical Director, Rod Edwards; Musical Director, Rick Fox; Musical Coordinator, Mort Silver; Sets/Costumes, Andy Walmsley; Lighting, Joe Atkins; Sound, Paul Astbury; Casting, Pat McCorkle; General Manager, Stuart Thompson; Company Manager, Bruce Klinger; Stage Managers, Mary Porter Hall, John Lucas; Associate Producer, Jon Miller; Presented by Mr. Kenwright; Press, Philip Rinaldi/Kathy Haberthur; Previewed from Wednesday, April 14, 1993; Opened in the Music Box Theatre on Sunday, April 25, 1993*

CAST

Mrs. Johnstone	Petula Clark +1
Narrator	Adrian Zmed +2
Mrs. Lyons	Regina O'Malley
Mr. Lyons	Ivar Brogger
Mickey	David Cassidy +3
Eddie	Shaun Cassidy +4
Sammy	John Schiappa
Linda	Shauna Hicks
Perkins	Sam Samuelson
Donna Marie/Miss Jones	Kerry Butler
Policeman/Teacher/Teddy Boy	Robin Haynes
Brenda	Karyn Quackenbush
Ensemble	Kerry Butler, Philip Lehl, John Schiappa, Douglas Weston, Nick Cokas, Robin d'Arcy James, Karen Quackenbush, Timothy Gulan, Gregory Watt

UNDERSTUDIES: Regina O'Malley (Mrs. Johnstone/Mrs. Lyons), Philip Lehl (Mickey/Eddie), John Schiappa, Nick Cokas (Sammy/Narrator), Sam Samuelson (Eddie), Anne Torsiglieri (Linda), Robin Haynes (Sammy/Mr. Lyons), Kerry Butler (Donna/Linda), Brian d'Arcy James (Eddie), Susan Tilson (Mrs. Johnstone/Mrs. Lyons), Karyn Quackenbush (Mrs. Lyons/Linda) SWINGS: John Soroka, Susan Tilson

MUSICAL NUMBERS: Marilyn Monroe, My Child, Easy Terms, Shoes Upon the Table, Kids Game, Prelude, Long Sunday Afternoon/My Friend, Bright New Day, That Guy, I'm Not Saying a Word, Take a Letter Miss Jones, Light Romance, Madman, Tell Me It's Not True

A musical in two acts. The action takes place in and around Liverpool. The show originally premiered in London's West End in January, 1983 and was revived there in 1988.

*Closed April 30, 1995 after 839 performances and 13 previews.

+Succeeded by: 1. Carole King, Helen Reddy 2. Domenick Allen 3. Philip Lehl 4. Ric Ryder 5. Jodi Jinks

Joan Marcus Photos

Petula Clark, David Cassidy
Bottom Left: Carole King
Bottom Right: Helen Reddy, Philip Lehl

CATS

Music, Andrew Lloyd Webber; Based on *Old Possum's Book Of Practical Cats* by T.S. Eliot; Orchestrations, David Cullen, Lloyd Webber; Prod. Musical Director, David Caddick; Musical Director, Edward G. Robinson; Sound, Martin Levan; Lighting, David Hersey; Design, John Napier; Choreography/Associate Director, Gillian Lynne; Director, Trevor Nunn; Original Cast Recording, Polydor/Really Useful Records; Casting, Johnson-Liff Associates; Company Manager, James G. Mennen; Stage Managers, Peggy Peterson, Tom Taylor, Suzanne Viverito; Executive Producers, R. Tyler Gatchell, Jr., Peter Neufeld; Presented by Cameron Mackintosh, The Really Useful Co., David Geffen, and The Shubert Organization; Press, Fred Nathan/Michael Borowski; Opened in the Winter Garden Theatre on Thursday, October 7, 1982*

CAST

Alonzo	Hans Kriefall
Bustopher/Asparagus/Growltiger	Joel Briel +1
Bombalurina	Marlene Danielle
Cassandra	Sara Henry +2
Coricopat	David E. Lidell+3
Demeter	Mercedes Perez
Grizabella	Liz Callaway
Jellylorum/Griddlebone	Nina Hennessey
Jennanydots	Carol Dilley
Mistoffelees	Lindsay Chambers
Mungojerrie	Roger Kachel
Munkustrap	Keith Bernardo
Old Deuteronomy	Ken Prymus
Plato/Macivity/Rumpus Cat	Jim T. Ruttman
Pouncival	Jacob Brent
Rum Tum Tiger	David Hibbard
Rumpleteazer	Jennifer Cody
Sillabub	Bethany Samuelsohn
Skimbleshanks	Eric Scott Kincaid
Tantomile	Jill Nicklaus
Tumblebrutus	Levansky Smith
Victoria	Nadine Isenegger
Cat Chorus	John Briel, Jay Aubrey Jones, Susan Powers, Heidi Stallings

STANDBYS/UNDERSTUDIES: Marty Benn, Joe Briel, Dawn Marie Church, Colleen Dunn, Angelo H. Fraboni, Douglas Graham, James Hadley, Amy N. Heggins, Devanand N. Janki, Jay Aubrey Jones, B.K. Kennelly, Cholsu Kim, David E. Liddell, Joe Locarro, Jack Magredey, Lisa Mayer, Rusty Mowery, Mercedes Perez, Susan Powers, Jim Raposa, Naomi Reddin, Mark Santoro, Sarah Solie Shannon, Heidi Stallings, Lynn Sterling, Sally Ann Swarm, Owen Taylor, Suzanne Viverito, Leigh Webster, Darlene Wilson, Randy Wojcik, Lily-Lee Wong

MUSICAL NUMBERS: Jellicle Songs for Jellicle Cats, Naming of Cats, Invitation to the Jellicle Ball, Old Gumbie Cat, Rum Tum Tugger, Grizabella the Glamour Cat, Bustopher Jones, Mungojerrie and Rumpleteazer, Old Deuteronomy, Aweful Battle of the Pekes and Pollicles, Jellicle Ball, Memory, Moments of Happiness, Gus the Theatre Cat, Growltiger's Last Stand, Skimbleshanks, Macavity, Mr. Mistoffolees, Journey to the Heavyside Layer, Addressing of Cats

A musical in two acts with 20 scenes.

*Still playing May 31, 1995. Winner of 1983 "Tonys" for Best Musical, Score, Book, Direction, Costumes, Lighting, and Featured Actress in a Musical (Betty Buckley as Grizabella). For original 1982 production see *Theatre World Vol. 39.*

+Succeeded by: 1. Richard Poole 2.Sara Henry, Ida Ida Gilliams 3. James Hadley 4. Philip Michael Baskerville 5. Jeanine Meyers, Kristi Sperling

Martha Swope Photos

Right and Top: Liz Callaway

Pia Zadora, Darren Kelly
Below: James Brennan and showgirls

CRAZY FOR YOU

Music, George Gershwin; Lyrics, Ira Gershwin, Gus Kahn, Desmond Carter; Book, Ken Ludwig; Conception, Mr. Ludwig and Mike Ockrent, inspired by material by Guy Bolton and John McGowan; Director, Mr. Ockrent; Choreography, Susan Stroman; Orchestrations, William D. Brohn, Sid Ramin; Musical Director, Paul Gemignani; Musical Consultant, Tommy Krasker; Dance/Incidental Arrangements, Peter Howard; Sets, Robin Wagner; Costumes, William Ivey Long; Lighting, Paul Gallo; Sound, Otts Munderloh; Casting, Julie Hughes, Barry Moss; Cast Recording, Broadway Angel; Fights, B.H. Barry; Hairstylist, Angela Gari; General Manager, Gatchell & Neufeld; Prod. Manager, Peter Fulbright; Company Manager, Richard Biederman; Stage Manager,John Bonanni; Associate Producers, Richard Godwin, Valerie Gordon; Presented by Roger Horchow and Elizabeth Williams; Press, Bill Evans/Jim Randolph, Susan L. Schulman, Erin Dunn; Previewed from Friday, January 31, 1992; Opened in the Shubert Theatre on Wednesday, February 19, 1992*

CAST

Tess	Beth Leavel +1
Patsy	Jill Matson +2
Bobby Child	James Brennan
Bela Zanger	John Jellsion +3
SheilaJudine	Hawkins Richard
Mitzi	Wendy Waring
Susie	Ida Gilliams +4
Louise	Jean Marie
Betsy	Angel L. Schworer +5
Margie	Kimberly Hester
Vera	Shannon Lewis
Elaine	Paula Legett Chase +6
Irene Roth	Kay McClelland +7
Mother	Jane Connell +8
Perkins/Custus	James Young
Moose	Gary Douglas
Mingo	Branch Woodman
Sam	Michael Duran +9
Junior	John M. Wiltberger
Custus	James Young
Pete	Fred Anderson +10
Jimmy	Michael Kubala
Billy	Ray Roderick
Wyatt	Sean Martin Hingston +11
Harry	Joel Goodness
Polly Baker	Karen Ziemba
Everett Baker	Carleton Carpenter +12
Lank Hawkins	John Hillner +13
Eugene	Stephen Temperley
Patricia	Colleen Smith Wallnau

UNDERSTUDIES: James Young (Bobby/Lank/Bela/Everett), Jill Matson (Polly), Wendy Waring (Irene), Michael Duran (Everett), Colleen Smith Wallnau (Mother), John M. Wiltberger (Eugene), Angie L. Schworer (Pastsy), Ida Gilliams (Tess), Angelique Ilo (Patricia)

MUSICAL NUMBERS: Original sources follow in parentheses: K-ra-azy for You (*Treasure Girl*, 1928), I Can't Be Bothered Now (Film: *A Damsel in Distress*, 1937), Bidin' My Time (*Girl Crazy*, 1930), Things Are Looking Up (*A Damsel in Distress*), Could You Use Me (*Girl Crazy*), Shall We Dance (Film: *Shall We Dance*, 1937), Someone to Watch Over Me (*Oh Kay*, 1926), Slap That Bass (*Shall We Dance*), Embraceable You (*Girl Crazy*), Tonight's the Night (previously unused), I Got Rhythm (*Girl Crazy*), The Real American Folk Song is a Rag (*Ladies First*, 1918), What Causes That? (*Treasure Girl*), Naughty Baby (previously unused), Stiff Upper Lip (*A Damsel in Distress*), They Can't Take That Away From Me (*Shall We Dance*), But Not for Me (*Girl Crazy*), Nice Work If You Can Get It (*A Damsel in Distress*), Finale

A musical comedy, inspired by *Girl Grazy* (1930), in two acts with seventeen scenes. The action takes place in New York City and Deadrock, Nevada, in the 1930's.

*Closed January 7, 1996 after 1,622 performances and 21 previews. Winner of 1992 "Tonys" for Best Musical, Best Choreography and Best Costumes.

+Succeeded by: 1. Bruce Adler 2. Sandy Edgerton 3. Roger Horchow, Carleton Carpenter, John Jellsion, Al Checco, John Jellison STANDBY: Karen Culp

Joan Marcus Photos

DAMN YANKEES

Music and Lyrics, Richard Adler and Jerry Ross; Book, George Abbott and Douglas Wallop; Based on Wallop's novel *The Year the Yankees Lost the Pennant*; Director/Book Revision, Jack O'Brien; Orchestrations, Douglas Besterman; Musical Supervision/Vocal Arrangements, James Raitt; Musical Coordinator, William Meade; Choreography, Rob Marshall; Sets, Douglas W. Schmidt; Costumes, David C. Woolard; Lighting, David F. Segal; Sound, Jonathan Deans; Special Effects, Gregory Meech; Hair/Makeup, J. Roy Helland; Dance Arrangements, Tom Fay, David Krane; Cast Recording, Mercury; Production Supervisor, Alan Hall; General Manager, Charlotte W. Wilcox; Company Manager, Robb Lady; Stage Managers, Douglas Pagliotti, Cosmo P. Hanson; Presented by Mitchell Maxwell, PolyGram Diversified Entertainment, Dan Markley, Kevin McCollum, Victoria Maxwell, Fred H. Krones, Andrea Nasher, The Frankel-Viertel-Baruch Group, Paula Heil Fisher, Julie Ross in association with Jon B. Platt, Alan J. Schuster, Peter Breger; Press, Peter Cromarty/Michael Hartman; Previewed from Monday, February 14, 1994; Opened in the Marquis Theatre on Thursday, March 3, 1994*

CAST

Meg Boyd	Linda Stephens
Joe Boyd	Dennis Kelly
Applegate	Victor Garber +1
Sister	Susan Mansur
Joe Hardy	Jarrod Emick +2
Rocky	Scott Wise +3
Smokey	Jeff Blumenkrantz +4
Sohovik/Narrator Voice	Gregory Jbara +5
Mickey	John Ganun +6
Vernon	Joey Pizzi
Del	Scott Robertson +7
Ozzie	Michael Winther +8
Bubba	Cory English +9
Henry	Bruce Anthony Davis
Bomber	Michael Berresse +10
Van Buren	Dick Latessa
Gloria Thorpe	Vicki Lewis +11
Betty	Paula Leggett Chase +12
Donna	Nancy Ticotin +13
Kitty	Cynthia Onrubia +14
Lulu	Meg Bussert +15
Photographer/Rita	Amy Ryder +16
Welch	Terrence P. Currier
Lola	Bebe Neuwirth +17

UNDERSTUDIES/STANDBYS: Patrick Quinn (Applegate), Valerie Wright, Nancy Ticotin (Lola), Michael Berresse, John Ganun, David Elder, Christopher Monteleone (Hardy), Scott Robertson, Allen Fitzpatrick (Boyd/Van Buren/Welch), Paula Leggett Chase, Meg Bussert (Meg), Amy Ryder, Roxie Lucas, Karen Babcock (Sister), Robyn Peterman, Linda Gabler, Malinda Shaffer (Gloria)

MUSICAL NUMBERS: Overture, Six Months Out of Every Year, Goodbye Old Girl, Blooper Ballet, Heart, Shoeless Joe from Hannibal Mo., A Little Brains a Little Talent, A Man Doesn't Know, What Ever Lola Wants (Lola Gets), Entr'acte, Who's Got the Pain, The Game, Near to You, Those Were the Good Old Days, Two Lost Souls, Finale

A revision of the 1955 musical comedy in two acts. For original Broadway production with Gwen Verdon, Ray Walston, Stephen Douglass and Jean Stapleton, see *Theatre World Vol. 11*. Winner of 1994 "Tony" for Featured Actor in a Musical (Jarrod Emick).

*Closed August 6, 1995 after 510 performances and 35 previews. The show was on hiatus from January 1, 1995 to February 28, 1995 when performances resumed. Official re-opening with Jerry Lewis was Sunday, March 12, 1995.

+Succeeded by: 1. Jerry Lewis 2. Jason Workman, Jarrod Emick, Eric Kunze 3. Rod McCune 4. Mark Chmiel 5. Louis D. Giovannetti 6. Trot Britton Johnson, Christopher Monteleone 7. Allen Fitzpatrick 8. John Bolton, Michael Winther 9. Bill Brassera 10. Robb Edward Morris, David Elder 11.Liz Larsen 12. Peggy Ayn Maas 13. Malinda Shaffer 14. Karen Babcock 15. Roxie Lucas 16. Meg Bussert 17. Nancy Tictin, Charlotte d'Amboise

Jerry Lewis

Charlotte d'Amboise

Jason Workman, Victor Garber

Carol Rosegg/Martha Swope Photos

63

GREASE

Music/Lyrics/Book by Jim Jacobs and Warren Casey; Director/Choreography, Jeff Calhoun; Orchestrations, Steve Margoshes; Musical Director/Vocal and Dance Arrangements, John McDaniel; Musical Coordinator, John Monaco; Sets, John Arnone; Costumes, Willa Kim; Lighting, Howell Binkley; Hairstylist, Patrik D. Moreton; Sound, Tom Morse; Associate Choreographer, Jerry Mitchell; Cast Recordings, RCA; General Manager, Charlotte W. Wilcox; Casting, Stuart Howard, Amy Schecter; Company Manager, Barbara Darwall; Stage Managers, Craig Jacobs, David Hyslop; Presented in associated with PACE Theatrical Group, TV Asahi; The Tommy Tune Production presented by Barry & Fran Weissler, Jujamcyn Theatres; Press, Pete Sanders/Ian Rand, Bruce Laurienzo, Meredith Oritt; Previewed from Saturday, April 23, 1994; Opened in the Eugene O'Neill Theatre on Wednesday, May 11, 1994*

CAST

Vince Fontaine..Brian Bradley +1
Miss Lynch...Marcia Lewis +2
Patty Simcox ....Michelle Blakely +3
Eugene Florczyk ....Paul Castree
Jan ....Heather Stokes
Marty ....Megan Mullally +4
Betty Rizzo ....Rosie O' Donnell +5
Doody...Sam Harris +6
Roger ....Hunter Foster
Kenickie ....Jason Opsahl
Sonny Latierri...Carlos Lopez +7
Frenchy ....Jessica Stone +8
Sandy Dumbrowski...Susan Wood +9
Danny Zuko ....Ricky Paull Goldin +10
Straight A's ....Clay Adkins, Brad Aspel, Paul
Castree, Denis Jones, Denny Tarver
Dream Mooners ....Brad Aspel, Katy Grenfell
Heartbeats...Katy Grenfell, Janice Lorraine Holt,
Lorna Shane
Cha-Cha Degregorio ....Sandra Purpuro +11
Teen Angel ....Billy Porter +12
Ensemble ....Clay Adkins, Brad Aspel, Melisssa Bell,
Gregory Cunneen, Jeff Edgerton, Katy Grenfell,
Janice Lorraine Holt, Denis Jones, Allison Metcalf,
Connie Ogden, Lorna Shane, Denny Tarver

UNDERSTUDIES: Paul Castree (Roger), Patti D'Beck (Miss Lynch), Allison Metcalf (Miss Lynch/Marty), Melissa Bell (Patty/Jan), Jeff Edgerton, Brian-Paul Mendoza (Eugene), Katy Grenfell (Jan), Lorna Shane (Marty/Rizzo/Cha-Cha), Sandra Purpuro (Rizzo), Clay Adkins (Doody/Angel), Patrick Boyd (Roger), H. Hylan Scott II (Kenickie/Danny/Vince), Denis Jones, Brian Loeffler, Brad Aspel (Sonny), Janice Lorraine Holt (Frenchy/Angel, Carrie Ellen Austin (Frenchy), Michelle Blakely (Sandy), Gregory Cunneen, Hunter Foster (Kenicke/Danny), Scott Moon, Jason Opsahl (Vince), Jeanna Schweppe (Cha-Cha/Sandy)

A new production of the 1972 musical in two acts with thirteen scenes. The action takes place in and around Rydell High, 1950s. For original Broadway production see *Theatre World Vol. 29.*

*Still running May 31, 1996.

+Succeeded by: 1. Micky Dolenz, Brian Bradley, "Cousin" Brucie Morrow 2. Mimi Hines, JoAnne Worley 3.Christine Toy, Carrie Ellen Austin 4. Sherie Rene Scott, Leah Hocking 5. Maureen McCormick, Brooke Shields, Joley Fisher, Tia Riebling 6. Ray Walker 7. Brad Kane, Nick Cavarra 8. Monica Lee Gradischek 9. Susan Moniz 10. Adrian Zmed, Ricky Paull Goldin, Jon Secada 11. Jennifer Cody 12. Mary Bond Davis, Charles Gray, Jennifer Holliday, Charles Gray

Carol Rosegg, Stan Schnier/Carmen Schiavone Photos

Top: Brooke Shields
Right: Carlos Lopez, Jason Opsahl, Monica Lee Gradischek, Ray Walker, Jon Secada, Leah Hocking, Hunter Foster, Heather Stokes, Tia Riebling

AN INSPECTOR CALLS

By J.B. Priestley; Director, Stephen Daldry; Design, Ian MacNeil; Lighting, Rick Fisher; Music, Stephen Warbeck; Sound, T. Richard Fitzgerald; Special Effects, Gregory Meeh; Fights, B.H. Barry; Production Supervisor, Jeremiah J. Harris; Casting, Julie Hughes, Barry Moss; Company Manager, Victoria Stevenson; Stage Managers, Sally Jacobs, Judith Binus; Presented by Noel Pearson, The Shubert Organization, Capital Cities/ABC, Joseph Harris and The Royal National Theatre; Press, Alma Viator/Bill Cannon, William Schelbe; Previewed from Thursday, April 14, 1994; Opened in the Royale Theatre on Wednesday, April 27, 1994*

CAST

Arthur Birling ....Philip Bosco +1
Gerald Croft ....Aden Gillett +2
Sheila Birling ....Jane Adams +3
Sybil Birling ....Rosemary Harris +4
Edna ....Jan Owens
Eric Birling ....Marcus D'Amico +5
Inspector Goole..Kenneth Cranham +6
Boy..Christopher Marquette +7

STANDBYS: George Morfogen (Arthur), John Lantz (Goole), Jeffrey Donovan (Gerald), Catherine Wolf (Sybil/Edna), Kali Rocha (Sheila), Mark Elliot (Boy)

A new production of a 1945 thriller performed without intermission. The action takes place in Brumley, an industrial city in the Yorkshire, spring 1912. For original 1947 Broadway production see *Theatre World Vol. 4.* Winner of 1994 "Tony's" for Best Revival of a Play, Featured Actress in a Play (Jane Adams), Best Direction of a Play, Best Scenic Design and Best Lighting Design.

*Closed May 28, 1995 after 454 performances and 14 previews.

+Succeeded by: 1. Roy Cooper 2. Maxwell Caulfield 3. Susannah Hoffmann 4. Sian Phillips 5. Harry Carnahan 6. Nicholas Woodeson 7. Frank John Galasso

Joan Marcus Photos

Sian Phillips, Maxwell Caulfield in *An Inspector Calls*

JACKIE MASON: POLITICALLY INCORRECT

Written/Created by Jackie Mason; Production Design/Lighting, Neil Peter Jampolis; Sound, Bruce Cameron; Company Manager, Beth Riedmann; Stage Manager, Don Myers; Presented by Jyll Rosenfeld; Press, Robert M. Zarem; Previewed from Monday, March 21, 1994; Opened in the Golden Theatre on Tuesday, April 5, 1994*

CAST

Jackie Mason

An evening of political comedy. Prior Mason Broadway engagements were *The World According to Me* (1986–88) and *Brand New* (1990–91).

*Closed June 4, 1995 after 347 performances and 13 previews.

Left: Jackie Mason

KISS OF THE SPIDER WOMAN

Music, John Kander; Lyrics, Fred Ebb; Book, Terrence McNally; Based on the novel by Manuel Puig; Director, Harold Prince; Orchestrations, Michael Gibson; Musical Director, Jeffrey Huard; Dance Music, David Krane; Choreography, Vincent Paterson; Additional Choreography, Rob Marshall; Sets/Projections, Jerome Sirlin; Costumes, Florence Klotz; Lighting, Howell Bikley; Sound, Martin Levan; Mr. Prince's Assistant, Ruth Mitchell; Cast Recordings (Chita Rivera) RCA, (Vanessa Williams) Mercury; Casting, Johnson-Liff & Zerman; Company Manager, Alan R. Markinson; Stage Managers, Bonnie Panson, Michael Pule; Presented by Livent (U.S.); Press,Mary Bryant; Previewed from Monday, April 19, 1993; Opened in the Broadhurst Theatre on Monday, May 3, 1993*

CAST

Molina...Howard McGillin
Warden..Herndon Lackey
Valentin ....Brian Mitchell
Esteban ....Philip Hernandez
Marcos ....Michael McCormick
Spider Woman/Aurora.............................Vanessa Williams +1
Aurora's Men/Prisoners ....Gregory Mitchell, Robert Montano, Dan O'Grady, Raymond Rodriguez, Andre E. Carthen, David Marques, Troy Myers
Prisoner...Darius de Haas +2
Molina's Mother ....Merle Louise +3
Marta ....Kirsti Carnahan
Escaping Prisoner...Colton Green +4
Tortured Prisoner...Raymond Rodriguez
Religious Fanatic/Prisoner ....John Norman Thomas +5
Amnesty Int'l Obserber/Prisoner Emilio.........................Bob Stillman +6
Prisoner Fuentes...Gary Schwartz +7
Gabriel/Prisoner ....Jerry Christakos
Window Dresser at Montoya's/Prisoner.....................Robert Montano +8

STANDBYS/UNDERSTUDIES: Nancy Hess (Spider Woman/Aurora/Marta), Bob Stillman (Molina), Barbara Andres (Mother), Philip Hernandez (Valentin), Vincent D'Elia (Esteban), John Norman Thomas (Marcos), Michael McCormick (Warden), Dan O'Grady (Gabriel) SWINGS: Mark Bove, Colton Green, David Marques

MUSICAL NUMBERS: Prologue, Her Name Is Aurora, Over the Wall, Blubloods, Dressing Them Up/I Draw the Line, Dear One, Where You Are, Marta, Come, I Do Miracles, Gabriel's Letter/My First Woman, Morphine Tango, You Could Never Shame Me, A Visit, She's a Woman, Gimme Love, Russian Movie/Good Times, The Day After That, Mama It's Me, Anything for Him, Kiss of the Spider Woman, Only in the Movies

A musical in two acts with nineteen scenes and prologue. The action takes place in a prison in Latin America, sometime in the recent past.

*Closed July 2, 1995 after 906 performances and 16 previews. Winner of 1993 "Tony" Awards for Best Musical, Leading Actor in a Musical (Brent Carver), Leading Actress in a Musical (Chita Rivera), Featured Actor in a Musical (Anthony Crivello), Book of a Musical, Costume Design, and Best Score (tie). Winner of New York Drama Critics Circle for Best Musical.

+Succeeded by:1. Maria Conchita Alonso 2. John Aller 3. Mimi Turque 4. Troy Myers 5. Robert DuSold 6.Jeff Bannon 7. Vincent D'Elia 8. John Aller

Catherine Ashmore Photos

Top: Vanessa Williams
Left: Brian Mitchell, Howard McGillin

Craig Schulman
Below: Catherine Hickland

LES MISERABLES

By Alain Boublil and Claude-Michel Schonberg; Based on the novel by Victor Hugo; Music, Mr. Schonberg; Lyrics, Herbert Kretzmer; Original French Text, Mr. Boublil and Jean-Marc Natel; Additional Material, James Fenton; Direction/Adaptation, Trevor Nunn and John Caird; Orchestral Score, John Cameron; Musical Supervisor, Robert Billig; Musical Director, Tom Helm; Design, John Napier; Lighting, David Hersey; Costumes, Andreane Neofitou; Casting, Johnson-Liff & Zerman; Original Cast Recording, Geffen; General Manager, Alan Wasser; Company Manager, Robert Nolan; Stage Managers, Marybeth Abel, Mary Fran Loftus, Brent Peterson; Executive Producer, Martin McCallum; Presented by Cameron Mackintosh; Press, Marc Thibodeau/Merle Frimark; Previewed from Saturday, February 28; Opened in the Broadway Theatre on Thursday, March 12, 1987* and moved to the Imperial Theatre on October 16, 1990.

CAST

PROLOGUE: Craig Schulman(Jean Valjean), Robert Cuccioli +1 (Javert), Dave Clemmons, Joel Robertson, Michael X. Martin, Ken Krugman, Matt McClanahan, Drew Eshelman, Ron Bohmer, Michael Berry, Craig Rubano (Chain Gang), Bryan Landrine (Farmer), Mr. Krugman (Labourer), Lucille DeCristofaro (Innkeeper's Wife), Gary Lynch (Innkeeper), Nicholas F. Saverine (Bishop), Tom Donoghue, Paul Avedidian (Constables)

MONTREUIL-SUR-MER 1823: Susan Gilmour +2 (Fantine), Mr. Robertson (Foreman), Mr. Landrine, Mr. McClanahan (Workers), Jean Fitzgibbons, Nicola Boyer, Connie Kunkle, Dianne Della Piazza (Women Workers), Jessie Janet Richards (Factory Girl), Mr. Berry, Mr. Clemmons, Mr. McClanahan (Sailors), Ms. DeCristofaro, Ms. Doherty, Ms. Kunkle, Jodie Langel, Ms. Richards, Sarah Uriarte, Jennifer Lee Andrews, Jessica-Snow Wilson (Whores), Ms. Fitzgibbons (Old Woman), Ms. Boyer (Crone), Mr. Saverine (Pimp/Fauchelevent), Mr. Martin (Bamatabois)

MONTFERMEIL 1823: Lacey Chabert, Jessica Scholl, Savannah Wise (Young Cosette/Young Eponine), Diana Rogers(Mme. Thenardier), Drew Eshelman (Thenardier), Mr. Landrine (Drinker), Mr. Krugman, Ms. Snow-Wilson (Young Couple), Mr. Lynch (Drunk), Paul Avedisian, Ms. Doherty (Diners), Mr. Saverine, Mr. Martin, Mr. Clemmons, Ms. Fitzgibbons, Ms. Richards, Ms. DeCristofaro (Drinkers), Mr. Berry (Young Man), Ms. Kunkle, Ms. Langel(Young Girls), Ms. Boyer, Mr. McClanahan (Old Couple), Mr. Robertson, Mr. Donohue (Travelers)

PARIS 1832: Sean Russell, Brandon Espinoza (Gavroche), Ms. DeCristofaro (Beggar Woman), Ms. Richards (Young Prostitute), Mr. Lynch (Pimp), Sarah Uriarte +4 (Eponine), Mr. Krugman (Montparnasse), Mr. Donoghue (Babet), Mr. Clemmons (Brujon), Mr. Saverine (Claquesous), Ron Bohmer (Enjolras), Craig Rubano (Marius), Jennifer Lee Andrews (Cosette), Mr. Robertson (Combeferre), Mr. Berry (Feuilly), Mr. Landrine (Courfeyrac), Mr. McClanahan (Joly), Mr. Martin (Grantaire), Mr. Avedisian (Lesgles), Mr. Lynch (Jean Prouvaire)

UNDERSTUDIES: Joel Robertson, Bryan Landrine, Nicholas F. Saverine, Dave Clemmons (Valjean), Gary Lynch, Michael X. Martin (Javert), Paul Avedisian, Joseph Kolinski, Wayne Scherzer (Bishop), Jean Fitzgibbons, Kerrianne Spellman (Fantine), Ken Krugman, Mr. Saverine (Thenardier), Ms. Fitzgibbons, Nicola Boyer (Mme. Thenardier), Jessica Snow-Wilson, Jodie Langel (Eponine/Cosette), Tom Donoghue, Matt McClanahan (Marius), Mr. Avedisian, Michael Berry (Enjolras), Lacey Chabert (Gavroche) SWINGS: Christa Justus, Joseph Kolinski, Wayne Scherzer, Kerrianne Spellman

MUSICAL NUMBERS: Prologue, Soliloquy, At the End of the Day, I Dreamed a Dream, Lovely Ladies, Who Am I?, Come to Me, Castle on a Cloud, Master of the House, Thenardier Waltz, Look Down, Stars, Red and Black, Do You Hear the People Sing?, In My Life, A Heart Full of Love, One Day More, On My Own, A Little Fall of Rain, Drink with Me to Days Gone By, Bring Him Home, Dog Eats Dog, Soliloquy, Turning, Empty Chairs at Empty Tables, Wedding Chorale, Beggars at the Feast, Finale

A dramatic musical in two acts with four scenes and prologue.

*Still playing May 31, 1995. Winner of 1987 "Tonys" for Best Musical, Best Score, Best Book, Best Featured Actor and Actress in a Musical (Michael Maguire, Frances Ruffelle), Direction of a Musical, Scenic Design and Lighting.

+ Succeeded by: 1. Merwin Ford 2. Paige O'Hara 3. Gina Ferrall 4. Jessica Snow-Wilson, Shanice

Joan Marcus Photos

MISS SAIGON

Music, Claude-Michel Schonberg; Lyrics, Richard Maltby, Jr., Alain Boublil; Adapted from Boublil's French lyrics; Book, Mr. Boublil, Mr. Schonberg; Additional Material, Mr. Maltby, Jr.; Director, Nicholas Hytner; Musical Staging, Bob Avian; Orchestrations, William D. Brohn; Musical Supervisors, David Caddick, Robert Billig; Associate Director, Mitchell Lemsky; Design, John Napier; Lighting, David Hersey; Costumes, Andreane Neofitou, Suzy Benzinger; Sound, Andrew Bruce; Conductor, Edward G. Robinson; Stage Managers, Tom Capps, Sherry Cohen, Beerly Jenkins; Cast Recording (London), Geffen; Presented by Cameron Mackintosh; Press, Marc Thibodeau/Merle Frimark-Erin Dunn; Previewed from Saturday, March 23, 1991; Opened in the Broadway Theatre on Thursday, April 11, 1991*

CAST

SAIGON – 1975

The Engineer..Alan Muraoka +1
Kim ....Rona Figueroa , Emy Basic
Gigi...Imelda De Los Reyes
Mimi...Zoie Lam
Yvette..Chloe Stewart
Yvonne...Mirla Criste
Bar Girls ....Margaret Ann Gates, Ai Goeku, Emily
                                        Hsu, Elizabeth Paw, Roxanne Taga
Chris...Eric Kunze +2
John...Keith Byron Kirk +3
Marines...................................Donnell Aarone, Erik Bates, Robert Bartley,
                              C.C. Brown, Jay Douglas, Leonard Joseph,
                              Norman Kauahi, Howard Kaye, Kevin Neil
                              McCready, Matthew Pedersen, Jeff Reid,
                              Robert Weber, Welly Yang
Barmen..........................Zar Acayan, Alan Ariano, Eric Chang, Ming Lee
Vietnamese Customers..........Tito Abeleda, Francis J. Cruz, Darrell Autor,
                              JimHarrison, Juan P. Pineda, Ray Santos
Army Nurse...Heidi Meyer
Thuy ....Yancey Arias
Embassy Workers, Vendors, etc ....Company

HO CHI MINH CITY (FORMERLY SAIGON) – APRIL 1978

Ellen ....Tami Tappan +4
Tam..Melanie Carabuena, Justin Lee Wong
Guards ....Mr. Cruz, Mr. Pineda
Dragon Acrobats...............................Mr. Autor, Mr. Harrison, Mr. Weber
Asst. Commissar..Mr. Yang
Soldiers ....Mr. Abeleda, Mr. Acayan, Mr. Ariano,
                                        Mr. Kauahi,Mr. Santos
Citizens, Refugees ....Company

USA – SEPTEMBER 1978

Conference Delegates ....Company

BANGKOK – OCTOBER 1978

Hustlers ....Mr. Acayan, Mr. Harrison, Mr.
                                        Kauahi, Mr. Santos, Mr. Yang
Moulin Rouge Owner ....Mr. Cruz
Inhabitants, Bar Girls, Vendors, Tourists....................................Company

SAIGON – APRIL 1975

Shultz ....Howard Kaye
Doc ....Erik Bates
Reeves ....C.C. Brown
Gibbons ....Kevin Neal McCready
Troy ....Leonard Joseph
Nolen...Donnell Aarone
Huston ....Matthew Pederson
Frye ....Jay Douglas
Marines, Vietnamese...Company

BANGKOK – OCTOBER 1978

Inhabitants, Moulin Rouge Customers ....Company

Raul Aranas

UNDERSTUDIES: Norman Kauahi, Ming Lee, Ray Santos (Engineer), Imelda de los Reyes, Elizabeth Paw, Chloe Stewart, Roxanne Taga (Kim), Erik Bates, Robert Bartley, Jay Douglas (Chris), Donnell Aarone, C.C. Brown, Leonard Joseph (John), Heidi Meyer (Ellen), Zar Acayan, Jim Harrison, Marc Oka, Juan P. Pineda, Welly Yang (Thuy) SWINGS: Eric Chan, Sylvia Dohi, Frank J. Maio, Marc Oka, Fay Rusli, Jeff Siebert

MUSICAL NUMBERS: The Heat is on in Saigon, Movie in My Mind, The Transaction, Why God Why?, Sun and Moon, The Telephone, The Cere-mony, Last Night of the World, Morning of the Dragon, I Still Believe, Back in Town, You Will Not Touch Him, If You Want to Die in Bed, I'd Give My Life for You, Bui-Doi, What a Waste, Please, Guilt Inside Your Head, Room 317, Now That I've Seen Her, Confrontation, The American Dream, Little God of My Heart

A musical in two acts. The action takes place in Saigon, Bangkok, and the USA between 1975–79.

*Still playing May 31, 1995. Winner of 1991 "Tonys" for Leading Actor in a Musical (Jonathan Pryce), Leading Actress in a Musical (Lea Salonga) and Featured Actor in a Musical (Hinton Battle).

+ Succeeded by: 1. Raul Aranas 2. Peter Lockyer, Jay Douglas (during vacation) 3. Norm Lewis 4. Misty Cotton

Joan Marcus Photos

THE PHANTOM OF THE OPERA

Music, Andrew Lloyd Webber; Lyrics, Charles Hart; Additional Lyrics, Richard Stilgoe; Book, Mr. Stilgoe, Mr. Lloyd Webber; Director, Harold Prince; Musical Staging/Choreography, Gillian Lynne; Orchestrations, David Cullen, Mr. Lloyd Webber; Based on the novel by Gaston Leroux; Design, Maria Bjornson; Lighting, Andrew Bridge; Sound, Martin Levan; Musical Direction/Supervision, David Caddick; Conductor, Jack Gaughan; Cast Recording (London), Polygram/Polydor; Casting, Johnson-Liff & Zerman; General Manager, Alan Wasser; Company Manager, Michael Gill; Stage Managers, Steve McCorkle, Bethe Ward, Richard Hester, Barbara-Mae Phillips; Presented by Cameron Mackintosh and The Really Useful Theatre Co.; Press, Merle Frimark, Marc Thibodeau; Previewed from Saturday, January 9, 1988; Opened in the Majestic Theatre on Tuesday, January 26, 1988*

CAST

The Phantom of the Opera	Davis Gaines
Christine Daae	Tracy Shayne
	Laurie Gayle Stephenson (alternate)
Raoul, Vicomte de Chagny	Ciaran Sheehan +1
Carlotta Giudicelli	Elena Jeanne Batman
Monsieur Andre	Jeff Keller
Monsieur Firmin	George Lee Andrews
Madame Giry	Leila Martin
Ubaldo Piangi	Frederic Heringes
Meg Giry	Tener Brown
M. Rever	Thomas James O'Leary
Auctioneer	Richard Warren Pugh
Porter/Marksman	Gary Lindemann
M. Lefevre	Kenneth Waller
Joseph Buquet	Philip Steele
Don Attilio/Passarino	Peter Atherton
Slave Master/Solo Dancer	Thomas Terry
Flunky/Stagehand	Jack Hayes
Policeman	Thomas Sandri
Page	Patrice Pickering
Porter/Fireman	Maurizio Corbino
Spanish Lady	Marci DeGonge-Manfredi
Wardrobe Mistress/Confidante	Mary Leigh Stahl
Princess	Raissa Katona
Madame Firmin	Melody Johnson
Innkeeper's Wife	Teresa Eldh
Ballet Chorus of the *Opera Populaire*	Harriet M. Clark,

Alina Hernandez, Cherylyn Jones, Lori MacPherson, Tania Philip, Kate Solmssen, Christine Spizzo

UNDERSTUDIES: Jeff Keller (Phantom), Raissa Katona, Laurie Gayle Stephenson (Christine), Gary Lindemann, James Romick (Raoul), Peter Atherton, Paul Laureano (Firmin), Richard Warren Pugh (Firmin/Piangi), George Lee Andrews, James Thomas O'Leary,Mr. Romick (Andre), Marcy DeGonge-Manfredi, Teresa Eldh, Melody Johnson (Carlotta), Patrice Pickering, Mary Leigh Stahl (Giry), Maurizio Corbino (Piangi), Cherilyn Jones, Kate Solmssen, Lori MacPherson (Meg), Thomas Terry (Master) Paul B. Sadler, Jr. (Dancer)

MUSICAL NUMBERS: Think of Me, Angel of Music, Little Lotte/The Mirror, Phantom of the Opera, Music of the Night, I Remember/Stranger Than You Dreamt It, Magical Lasso, Notes/Prima Donna, Poor Fool He Makes Me Laugh, Why Have You Brought Me Here?/Raoul I've Been There, All I Ask of You, Masquerade/Why So Silent?, Twisted Every Way, Wishing You Were Somehow Here Again, Wandering Child/Bravo Bravo, Point of No Return, Down Once More/Track Down This Murderer, Finale

A musical in two acts with nineteen scenes and a prologue. The action takes place in and around the Paris Opera house, 1881–1911.

*Still playing May 31, 1995. Winner of 1988 "Tonys" for Best Musical, Leading Actor in a Musical (Michael Crawford), Featured Actress in a Musical (Judy Kaye), Direction of a Musical, Scenic Design and Lighting. The title role has been played by Michael Crawford, Timothy Nolen, Cris Groendaal, Steve Barton, Jeff Keller, Kevin Gray, Marc Jacoby, and Marcus Lovett and Davis Gaines.

+Succeeded by: 1. Brad Little

Joan Marcus/Clive Barda Photos

Brad Little, Tracy Shayne

Top: Davis Gaines

THE WHO'S TOMMY

Music/Lyrics, Pete Townshend; Book, Mr. Townshend, Des McAnuff; Director, Mr. McAnuff; Additional Music/Lyrics, John Entwistle, Keith Moon; Choreography, Wayne Cilento; Orchestrations, Steve Margoshes; Musical Supervision/Direction, Joseph Church; Musical Coordinator, John Miller; Sets, John Arnone; Costumes, David C. Woolard; Lighting, Chris Parry; Projections, Wendall K. Harrington; Sound, Steve Canyon Kennedy; Video, Batwin + Robin Productions; Hairstylist, David H. Lawrence; Special Effects, Gregory Meeh; Flying by Foy; Fights, Steve Rankin; Cast Recording, RCA; Company Manager, Sandy Carlson; Stage Managers, Karen Armstrong, Dan Hild; Executive Producers, David, Strong, Warner, Inc., Scott Zieger/Gary Gunas; Associate Producer, John F. Kennedy Center for the Performing Arts; Presented by Pace Theatrical Group and Dodger Productions with Kardana Productions; Press, Chris Boneau/Adrian Bryan-Brown/Susanne Tighe; Previewed from Monday, March 29, 1993; Opened in the St. James Theatre on Thursday, April 22, 1993*

CAST

Mrs. Walker ....Laura Dean +1
Captain Walker ....Jonathan Dokuchitz +2
Uncle Ernie ....Paul Kandel
Minister/Mr. Simpson ....Bill Buell
Minister's Wife ....Jeanine Morick
Nurse ....Lisa Leguillou
Officer #1/Hawker ....Michael McElroy +3
Officer #2 ....Timothy Warmen +4
Allied Soldier #1/1st Pinball Lad ....Donnie Kehr +5
Allied Soldier #2..Michael Arnold +6
Lover/Harmonica Player......................................Lee Morgan
Tommy, Age 4 ....Emily Hart +7, Kimberly Hannon +7
(alternating performances)
Tommy ....Michael Cerveris +8
Judge/Kevin's Father/News Vendor/DJ ....Tom Flynn +9
Tommy, Age 10..Buddy Smith +10
Cousin Kevin ....Anthony Barrile
Kevin's Mother..Maria Calabrese +11
Local Lads/Security Guards.................Adrian Bailey, Paul Dobie, Aaron Ellis, Matthew Farnsworth, Clarke Thorell, Matt Zarley, Kevin Cahoon, Jim Newman, Alton White
Local Lasses ....Angela Garrison, Lacey Hornkohl, Pam Klinger, Lisa Leguillou, Sara Miles, April Nixon, Jolie Jenkins
The Gypsy ....Cheryl Freeman
2nd Pinball Lad..Clarke Thorell
Specialist..Steven Cates
Specialist's Assistant..Angela Garrison
Sally Simpson..Sherie Scott +12
Mrs. Simpson ....Pam Klinger

UNDERSTUDIES: Peter Ermides, Matt Zarley (Tommy/Cousin Kevin), Angela Garrison, Pam Klinger (Mrs. Walker), Todd Hunter, Jim Newman, Tom Rocco (Walker), Bill Buell, Tom Rocco (Ernie), April Nixon (Gypsy), Aaron Ellis, Peter Ermides (Kevin) SWINGS: Victoria Lecta Cave, Joyce Chittick, Steve Dahlem, Peter Ermides, Doug Friedman, Todd Hunter

MUSICAL NUMBERS: Overture, Captain Walker, It's a Boy, We've Won, Twenty-One, Amazing Journey, Sparks, Christmas, See Me Feel Me, Do You Think It's Alright, Fiddle About, Cousin Kevin, Sensation, Eyesight to the Blind, Acid Queen, Pinball Wizard, Underture (Entr'act), There's a Doctor, Go to the Mirror, Listening to You, Tommy Can You Hear Me, I Believe My Own Eyes (new song), Smash the Mirror, I'm Free, Miracle Cure, Tommy's Holiday Camp, Sally Simpson, Welcome, We're Not Going to Take It, Finale

A musical in two acts with twenty-two scenes. The action takes place mostly in London between 1941–63. *Tommy* originated as a 1969 rock opera album.

*Closed June 17, 1995 after 899 performances and 28 previews. Winner of 1993 "Tonys" for Direction of a Musical, Scenic Design, Lighting Design, Choreography, and Best Score (tie).

+Succeeded by: 1. Jessica Molaskey, Christy Tarr 2. J. Mark McVey 3. Adrian Bailey, Alton White 4. Matthew Farnsworth, Jim Newman 5. Matt Zarley 6. Aaron Ellis 7. Nicole Zeidman, Crysta Macalush, (alternates) Kelly Mady, Caitlin Newman, Rachel Ben Levenson 8. Peter Ermides 9. Tom Rocco 10. Travis Jordan Greisler, Michael Zeidman 11. Sara Miles, Jolie Jenkins 12. Lacey Hornkohl

Marcus/Bryan-Brown Photos

Top: Ensemble
Below: Michael Cerveris

OFF-BROADWAY PRODUCTIONS FROM PAST SEASONS
THAT PLAYED THROUGH THIS SEASON

ALL IN THE TIMING

By David Ives; Director, Jason McConnell Buzas; Sets, Bruce Goodrich; Costumes, Sharon Lynch; Lighting, Deborah Constantine; Sound, Jim van Bergen; Music, Bruce Coughlin; General Manager, Maria Di Dia; Company Manager, Bob Reilly; Stage Managers, Christine Catti, Bill McComb; Presented by Estragon Productions and Primary Stage Company (Casey Childs, Artistic Director); Press, Tony Origlio/Stephen Murray, Michael Cullen, William McLaughlin; Opened at the John Houseman Theatre on Thursday, February 17, 1994*

CAST

Michael Countryman +1		Wendy Lawless +2
Ted Neustadt +3	Nancy Opel +4	Robert Stanton +5

PROGRAM: Sure Thing, Words Words Words, The Universal Language, Philip Glass Buys a Loaf of Bread, The Philadelphia, Variations on the Death of Trotsky

Six one-act comedies.

*Closed May 20, 1995 after 526 performance at the Houseman. The production originated at Primary Stages on November 24, 1993 where it played 80 performances.

+Succeeded by :1. Philip Hoffman, Stuart Zagnit 2. Kathy Morath 3. Danny Burstein 4. Jan Neuberger 5. Jason Graae, Ray Wills

Carol Rosegg, Andrew Leynes Photos

Nancy Opel, Robert Stanton
Bottom Left: Michael Countryman, Robert Stanton, Nancy Opel
Bottom Right: Michael Countryman, Nancy Opel, Ted Neustadt

THE FANTASTICKS

Music, Harvey Schmidt; Lyrics/Book, Tom Jones; Director, Word Baker; Original Musical Director/Arrangements, Julian Stein; Design, Ed Wittstein; Musical Director, Dorothy Martin; Stage Managers, Kim Moore, James Cook, Steven Michael Daly, Christopher Scott; Presented by Lore Noto; Associate Producers, Sheldon Baron, Dorothy Olim, Jules Field, Cast Recording, MGM/Polydor; Opened in the Sullivan Street Playhouse on Tuesday, May 3, 1960*

CAST

The Boy	Josh Miller
The Girl	Lisa Mayer
The Girl's Father	William Tost
The Boy's Father	Gordon G. Jones
Narrator/El Gallo	Robert Vincent Smith
Mute	Paul Blankenship
Old Actor	Bryan Hull
Man Who Dies	Joel Bernstein

UNDERSTUDIES: Paul Blankenship (Boy), Jill Colgan (Girl), William Tost, Gordon G. Jones (Both Fathers)

MUSICAL NUMBERS: Overture, Try to Remember, Much More, Metaphor, Never Say No, It Depends on What You Pay, Soon It's Gonna Rain, Abduction Ballet, Happy Ending, This Plumb is Too Ripe, I Can See It, Plant a Radish, Round and Round, They Were You, Finale

A musical in two acts suggested by *Les Romanesques* by Edmond Rostand.

*Still playing May 31, 1995. The world's longest running musical celebrated its 35th anniversary during the season.

Chuck Pulin Photo

Lisa Mayer, Josh Miller
Top: (Back) Dorothy Martin, Paul Blankenship, Robert Vincent Smith, Hank Whitmire, (middle) William Tost, Josh Miller, Lisa Mayer, Gordon G. Jone, (front) Bryan Hull, Joel Bernstein

PERFECT CRIME

By Warren Manzi; Director, Jeffrey Hyatt; Set, Jay Stone; Costumes, Nancy Bush; Lighting, Jeff Fontaine; Sound, David Lawson; Stage Manager, Joseph Millett; Presented by The Actors Collective in association with the Methuen Company; Press, Michelle Vinvents, Paul Lewis, Jeffrey Clarke; Opened in the Courtyard Playhouse on April 18, 1987* and later transferred to the Second Stage, 47th St. Playhouse, Intar, Harold Clurman Theatre, Theatre Four, and currently The Duffy Theatre.

CAST

Margaret Thorne Brent	Catherine Russell
Inspector James Ascher	Gene Terinoni
W. Harrison Brent	David Butler
Lionel McAuley	J. A. Nelson
David Breuer	Dean Gardner

UNDERSTUDIES: Lauren Lovett (Females), J. R. Robinson (Males)

A mystery in two acts. The action takes place in Windsor Locks, Connecticut.

*Still playing May 31, 1995.

Right: David Butler in *Perfect Crime*

STOMP

Created/Directed by Luke Cresswell and Steve McNicholas; Lighting, Mr. McNicholas, Neil Tiplady; Production Manager, Pete Donno; General Management, Richard Frankel/Marc Routh; Presented by Columbia Artists Management, Harriet Newman Leve, James D. Stren, Morton Wolkowitz, Schuster/Maxwell, Galin/Sandler, and Markley/Manocherian; Press, Chris Boneau/Adrian Bryan-Brown, Jackie Green, Bob Fennell; Previewed from Friday, February 18, 1994; Opened in the Orpheum Theatre on Sunday, February 27, 1994*

CAST

Luke Cresswell	Nick Dwyer	Sarah Eddy	Theseus Gerard
Fraser Morrison	David Olrod	Carl Smith	Fiona Wilkes

SWINGS: Everett Bradley, Allison Easter

An evening of percussive performance art. The ensemble uses everything but conventional percussion to make rhythm and dance.

*Still playing May 31, 1995.

Stuart Morris, Steve McNicholas Photos

Left: Fraser Morrison, Theseus Gerard, Luke Cresswell, Carl Smith in *Stomp*

THREE TALL WOMEN

By Edward Albee; Director, Lawrence Sacharow; Set, James Noone; Costumes, Muriel Stockdale; Lighting, Phil Monat; General Management, Brent Peek; Company Manager, Roy Gabay; Stage Managers, R. Wade Jackson, John Henbest; Presented by Elizabeth I. McCann, Jeffrey Ash, Daryl Roth in association with Leavitt/Fox Mages, and the Vineyard Theatre; Press, Shirley Herz/Sam Rudy, Miller Wright, Wayne Wolfe; Opened in the Promenade Theatre on Tuesday, April 5, 1994*

CAST

A ....Myra Carter +1
Lucille Patton (alternate)
B ....Marian Seldes +2
C...Jordan Baker +3
The Boy ....Michael Rhodes +4

UNDERSTUDIES: Melissa Bowen (C), Lucille Paton (A), Kathleen Butler (B), John Henbest (Boy)

A drama in two acts. Winner of the 1994 Pulitzer Prize and the New York Drama Critics Circle Best Play.

*Closed August 26, 1995 after 582 performances. The production originated January 27, 1994 at the Vineyard Theatre where it played 47 performances before moving to the Promenade.

+Succeeded by: 1. Lucille Patton, Marian Seldes 2. Joan Van Ark 3. Christine Rounder 4. John Henbest (during vacation)

Carol Rosegg Photos

Left: Joan Van Ark
Below: Marian Seldes, Myra Carter, Jordan Baker

TONY N' TINA'S WEDDING

By Artificial Intelligence; Conception, Nancy Cassaro (Artistic Director); Director, Larry Pellegrini; Supervisory Director, Julie Cesari; Musical Director, Lynn Portas; Choreography, Hal Simons; Design/Decor, Randall Thropp; Costumes/Hairstyles/Makeup, Juan DeArmas; General Manager, Leonard A. Mulhern; Company Manager, James Hannah; Stage Managers, Bernadette McGay, W. Bart Ebbink; Presented by Joseph Corcoran & Daniel Cocoran; Press, David Rothenberg/Terence Womble; Opened in the Washington Square Church & Carmelita's on Saturday, February 6, 1988*

CAST

Valentia Lynne Nunzio, the bride ....Justine Rossi
Anthony Angelo Nunzio, the groom ....Tony Meola
Connie Mocogni, maid of honor ....Susan Laurenzi
Barry Wheeler, best man ....Timothy Monagan
Donna Marsala, bridesmaid ....Susan Campanero
Dominick Fabrizzi, usher ....Joseph Barbara
Marina Gulino, bridesmaid ....Cheryl Giuliano
Johnny Nunzio, usher/brother of the groom.....................Nick Gambella
Josephine Vitale, mother of the bride ....Victoria Barone
Joseph Vitale, brother of the bride..................................Richard Falzone
Luigi Domenico, great uncle of the bride ....Stan Winston
Rose Domenico, aunt of the bride......................................Cayte Thorpe
Sister Albert Maria, cousin of the bride ....Fran Gennuso
Anthony Angelo Nunzio, Sr., father of the groom ....Dan Grimaldi
Madeline Monroe, Mr. Nunzio's girlfriend...........................Karen Cellini
Grandma Nunzio, grandmother to the groom.....................Elaine Unnold
Michael Just, Tina's ex-boyfriend ....Anthony T. Lauria
Father Mark, parish priest ....Gary Schneider
Vinnie Black, caterer...Tom Karlya
Loretta Black, wife of the caterer ....Victoria Constan
Mick Black, brother of the caterer ....Robert R. Oliver
Nikki Black, daughter of the caterer ....Jodi Grant
Mikie Black, son of the caterer..John Walter
Pat Black, sister of the caterer ....Maria Gentile
Rick Demarco, the video man ....Kerry Logan
Sal Antonucci, the photographer...Tony Patellis

An environmental theatre production. The action takes place at a wedding and reception.

*Still playing May 31, 1995 after moving to St. John's Church and Vinnie Black's Coliseum.

Blanche Mackey Photo

Below: Justine Rossi, Tony Meola in *Tony N' Tina's Wedding*

Blue Man Group in *Tubes*

TUBES

Created and Written by Matt Goldman, Phil Stanton, Chris Wink; Director, Marlene Swartz; Artistic Coordinator; Caryl Glaab; Sets, Kevin Joseph Roach; Lighting, Brian Aldous; Costumes, Lydia Tanji, Patricia Murphy; Sound, Raymond Schilke; Computer Graphics, Kurisu-Chan; Stage Manager, Kevin Cunningham; Press, David Rothenberg; Opened at the Astor Place Theatre on Thursday, November 7, 1991*

CAST

Blue Man Group (Matt Goldman, Phil Stanton, Chris Wink)

An evening with the performance group, performed without intermission.

*Still playing May 31, 1995.

Martha Swope Photo

PRODUCTIONS FROM PAST SEASONS
THAT CLOSED DURING THIS SEASON

PRODUCTION	OPENED	CLOSED	PERFORMANCES
All in the Timing	11/24/93	5/20/95	526 Houseman 80 Primary Stages
Angels in America: Millennium Approaches	5/4/93	12/4/94	367 & 21 previews
Angels in America: Perestroika	11/23/93	12/4/94	216 & 26 previews
Blood Brothers	4/25/93	4/30/95	839 & 13 previews
Broken Glass	4/24/94	6/26/94	73 & 15 previews
Carousel	3/24/94	1/17/95	322 & 46 previews
Forever Plaid	5/4/90	6/12/94	1,811 performances
Guys and Dolls	4/14/92	1/8/95	1,143 & 33 previews
An Inspector Calls	4/27/94	5/28/95	454 and 14 previews
Laughter on the 23rd Floor	11/22/93	8/27/94	320 & 24 previews
Medea	4/7/94	6/26/94	82 & 9 previews
Nunsense	12/3/85	10/16/94	3,672 performances
Passion	5/9/94	1/7/95	280 & 52 previews
Sally Marr and Her Escorts	5/5/94	6/19/94	50 & 27 previews
She Loves Me	6/10/93	6/19/94	Atkinson294 & 11 pre Criterion 61 & 31 pre
The Sisters Rosensweig	3/18/93	7/16/94	Bdwy 556 & 18 pre OffBdwy 142 & 29 pr
Twilight: Los Angeles 1992	4/17/94	6/19/94	72 & 7 previews

Anna Deavere Smith in
Twilight: Los Angeles, 1992

Rosemary Harris in *An Inspector Calls*

Michael Hayden in *Carousel*

Brad Kane, Louis Zorich in *She Loves Me*

David Marshall Grant, Marcia Gay Harden in
Angels in America

OFF-BROADWAY PRODUCTIONS
(June 1, 1994–May 31, 1995)

(St. Mark's Studio) Thursday, June 2–25, 1994 (9 performances and 4 previews) Faux-Real Theatre Co. presents:
HTEBCAM; Director/Adaptation, Mark Greenfield; Set, Michael Casselli; Costumes, Kristy Irish; Lighting, Sarah Sidman; Music, Atchade Assongba; Stage Manager, Christopher Nelson; Press, Jim Baldassare CAST: Steven Weber (Macduff Jr./Fleance), Bryan Webster (Htebcam), Christine Tracy (2nd Witch), Rookie Tiwari (3rd Witch), Eric Dean Scott (Macduff), Michelle R. Oplinger, Jill Kramer (Apparations), Elizabeth Napier (1st Witch), John Nagle (Malcolm), Nicholas Mortimer (Banquo), Wanda McDaniel (Lady Macduff), Jerry Jaffe (Duncan), Glenn Healey (Murderer/Porter), Shawna Gladhill (Lady Htebcam), Sergi Bosch (Ross), Daria Balling (Messenger/Old Man), Keith Ayers (Siward), Joel Arandia (Doctor)
A reworking of Shakepeare's *Macbeth* with the text performed in reverse.

(Watermark Theatre at the Ohio) Thursday, June 2–19, 1994 (13 performances and 4 previews) Watermark Theatre presents:
WAITING AT THE WATER'S EDGE by Lucinda Coxon; Director, Nela Wagman; Music, David Rothenberg; Set, Sarah Lambert; Costumes, Cynthia Dumont; Lighting, Joe Saint; Stage Manager, Bernadette McGay; Press, Shirley Herz/Sam Rudy, Wayne Wolfe CAST: Isabel Keating (Vi), Patricia Scanlon (Su), Simon Brooking (Will), Sharon Laughlin (Therese), Craig Ugoretz (David)
A drama in two acts. The action takes place in England and America, 1920s.

(Theatre Off Park) Friday, June 3–18 transferred to Judith Anderson Theatre June 21–25, 1994 (13 performances and 3 previews)
JUDY AT THE STONEWALL INN by Thomas O'Neil; Director, Kenneth Elliott; Set, Harry Lines; Costumes, Patrick M. Chevillot; Lighting, Vivien Leone; Stage Manager, Brian Winkowski; Press, Fred Nathan/Michael Borowski CAST: Teddy Coluca (Carmen), Mark Krassenbaum (Brendan), Bryce Jenson (Jimmy), M.W. Reid (Jackson), Wade Wilkinson (Hugh), Richard Cuneo (Winston), Drue Penella (Michael), Hur Rangel (Jesus), Jackie Sanders (Judy)
A two-act drama about Judy Garland's influence on the Stonewall riots. The action takes place in NYC on June 27, 1969; the day of Judy's funeral and the first riot.

(Marymount Manhattan Theatre) Friday, June 3–11, 1994 (4 performances) American Chamber Opera Co. presents:
LOVE AND MARRIAGE; Conductor, Douglas Anderson
HELLO OUT THERE by Jack Beeson; Adapted from play by William Saroyan; Director, Jennifer Vermont Davis; Music Director, Jorge Martin CAST: Lisa Pierce, Michael Willson, Mark Victor Smith
TROUBLE IN TAHITI by Leonard Bernstein; Director, Diane Schenker; Music Director, Howard Meltzer CAST: Sharon Babbitt, Allan Roberts, Cynthia Madison, C. Anson Hedges, John Uehlein
A double-main of chamber operas.

(Cucaracha Theatre) Friday, June 3–25, 1994 (15 performances) Cucaracha Theatre presents:
APOCRYPHA; Director, Travis Preston; Dramaturgy, Royston Coppenger; Score, David Van Tieghem; Set, Christine Jones; Costumes, Mary Myers; Lighting, Brian Aldous; Press, Mary McBride CAST: Sung Yun Cho, Pamela Gray, Kirk Jackson, Reese Madigan, Chuck Montgomery, Mollie O'Mara, John Gould Rubin, Francine Zerfas
A work-in-progress unmasking and redefining myths and preoccupations.

Bryan Webster, Nicholas Mortimer in *Htebcam*

Simon Brooking, Isabel Keating in *Waiting at the Water's Edge*

(center)Jackie Sanders, Teddy Coluca, Bryce Jensen, Richard Cuneo, Mark Krassenbaum, Hur Rangel, M.W. Reid, Drue Pennella in *Judy at the Stonewall Inn*

(CSC Theatre) Friday, June 3, 1994 one ticket, inc. presents:
BOX OFFICE OF THE DAMNED; Music/Lyrics/Book/Musical Direction by Michael James Ogborn; Director/Choreographer, Barry McNabb; Set/Costumes, Loyce L. Arthur; Lighting, Delano Lopez; Stage Manager, Rich Borutta; Press, Carol Van Keuren CAST: Marcy McGuiggan (Marcy—Box Office Manager), Larry Hansen (Larry—Asst. Box Office Manager), Kristin Chenoweth(Kristy—New Girl), Jessica Hendy (Jessica—Clerk), Mark Agnes (Mark—House Manager), James Anderson (James—Clerk)
MUSICAL NUMBERS: A Season You'll Never Forget, Please Hold, Festival Fever, Mrs. Levittown's Complaints, Go Away Mrs. Levittown, Just Say No, Vive La Matinee, I'm in the Show, We See It All, Our Exchange Policy, Remember Me, New Non-Union Usher Polka, Finale Act One, Ladies Please!, One Ticket, Stranger, Daddy Long Legs, 8:00 Auto Pilot, Incantation to the T.M.I., Curtain Speech, Subscribe, Late, Clerk 2 Clerk, General Public Burn-Out, Finale Act Two
A two-act musical comedy set in and around a theatre box office.

(Perry St. Theatre) Saturday, June 4–June 26, 1994 (20 performances and 4 previews) Glocca Morra Productions present:
SIMPLY COLE PORTER; Conceived and Performed by Deborah Ausemus and J. Kent Barnhart; Director, Francis J. Cullinan; Set, Ron Kadri; Costumes, Baker S. Smith; Lighting, Brenda Veltre; Press, Chris Boneau/Adrian Bryan-Brown, Hillary Harrow, Jamie Morris
An intimate two-act musical revue.

(Theatre at St. Peter's) Monday June 6–13 (2 limited performances) The Broadway Dozen presents:
QUILT—A Musical Celebration; Music/Musical Director, Michael Stockler; Additional Music, Robert Lindner; Lyrics, Jim Morgan; Book, Mr. Morgan, Merle Hubbard, John Schak; Director, John Margulis; Press, Jeffrey Richards/Kevin Rehac CAST: Jeff Binder, Angela Bullock, Jeff Hayenga, Sara Krieger, Kimberly Mahon, Ron Palillo, Nancy Ringham, Linda Stephens, Ty Taylor, Russ Thzcker, Lillias White, Matt Zarley, Kurt Ziskie
MUSICAL NUMBERS: Something Beautiful, Karen's Songs: 9am–12 noon–3:30pm–10pm, At a Distance, Todd's Song, Hot Sex, Living with the Little Things, In the Absence of Angels, Could You Do Me a Favor, Robert Knows, I Believe in You, Victim of AIDS, Autobiography, One Voice
A two-act musical based on stories that inspired panels of the NAMES Project AIDS Quilt.

(Paradise Theater) Wednesday, June 8–July 1, 1994 (12 performances and 3 previews) Paradise Theater Co. presents:
THE AMAZING ADVENTURES OF TENSE GUY; Music/Lyrics/Book by Alan Ball; Director, Matthew Lenz; Set/Lighting, John Lasiter; Costumes, Vicki March; Musical Director, Carol McCann; Choregography, Thom Fogarty, Jim Hoskins, Fights, Byron Jennings; Stage Manager, Karen Usher; Press, Peter Cromarty/Michael Hartman CAST: Marc Ashmore, Enid Graham, Carol Halstead, Mark Hirschfield, David Levine, Phil Lombardo, Camryn Manheim, Connie Rotunda, Kyle Shannon, Andrew Watts
Alarm Dog Rep in a two-act comedy with music. The action takes place in New York City and the Planet America Corporation.

(Naked Angels) Wednesday, June 8–26, 1994 (16 performances) Naked Angels (Artistic Director, Toni Kotitc) presents:
ESCAPE FROM HAPPINESS by George F. Walker; Director, Joe Brancato; Set, Nancy Deren; Lighting, Eric Thoben; Costumes, MaryAnn D. Smith; Sound, Roger Raines; Stage Manager, Peggy R. Samuels CAST: Matt McGrath (Junior), Catherine Kellner (Gail), Marsha Mason (Nora), Betsy Aidem (Dian Black), Tom Bloom (Mike Dixon), Edmond Genest (Tom), Melinda Mullins (Elizabeth), Jodie Markell (Mary Ann), Michael Mastrototaro (Stevie Moore), Rolly Moore (Paul Austin)
A play in three acts. The action takes place in the kitchen of an old house in the east end of a large city.

(One Dream Theatre) Wednesday, June 8–26, 1994 (15 performances) Blue Heron Theatre Co. presents:
DOUBLE BILL by David Henry Hwang; Director, William A. Finlay; Score, Richard E. Cornell
AS THE CROW FLIES CAST: Ryohei Hoshi, Jean Mura, Gloria Sauve
THE SOUND OF A VOICE CAST: Marshall Factora, Shanah Luhmann

William Gibson

Leighton Edmundson

Marcy McGuigan, Kristy Chenoweth in *Box Office of the Damned*

J. Kent Barnhart, Deborah Ausemus in *Simply Cole Porter*

Andrew Watts in *Amazing Adventures of Tense Guy*

(Harold Clurman Theatre) Friday, June 10–19, 1994 (10 performances) AMAS Musical Theatre (Artistic Director, Rosetta LeNoire) presents: **LEGACY;** Music/Lyrics, Holly B. Francis and Arden Altino; Lighting, Kurt S. Nelson; Set/Costumes, The Company; Director, James L. Moody; Musical Director, Ms. Francis; Choreography, Felicia Kennerly ; Stage Manager, Christinea Davis CAST: Leonardo Arias, Natalie Bridges, Sanya Brown, Sonia Calderon, Sofie Camacho, Frederick Cheng, Natasha Creightney, Carrie Gaffney, Rick Gonzalez, Kandace Gray-Kollins, Selina Hernandez, Salisha Jackson, Cara Jedell, Thalia Kalamaras, Cory Kaufman, Alexandra Lucas, Jason Marin, Dashielle McKee, Dennis Moore, Lawrence A. Neals, Justine Peacock, Amelia Ramirez, Dafina Roberts, Janna Schiavo, Adjowah Scott, Miriam Silverman, Lola St. Vil, Juliana Souza, Tomisha Taylor, Priscilla Urena, Noelia Warnette, Isa Vasquez, Andrea White Jakeina Wingate MUSICAL NUMBERS: Conditions of the World, Star Spangled Banner, Once Upon a Time, Paycheck Away from the Streets, We've Got Something Goin' On, Good Morning Heat Ache, Isn't That the Way, Running, Walk Him Up, Let's Learn to Be Friends, If We're Suppose to Be in Love, Never E-Nuff Time, But This Is

A two-act musical developed by the AMAS/Eubie Blake Youth Theatre.

(Pier 25) Saturday, June 18–July 17, 1994 (26 performances) En Garde Arts presents:
STONEWALL, NIGHT VARIATIONS; Written/Directed by Tina Landau; Music, Ricky Ian Gordaon; Film, Jennie Livingston; Sets, James Schuette; Costumes, Elizabeth Fried; Lighting, Brian Aldous; Sound, John Gromada, Chriss Todd; Stage Manager, Stacey-Jo Marine CAST: Keith Abramson, Bill Buddendorf, John Burns, Patricia A. Chilsen, Katie Firth, Molly Lahr, Nicole Levy, Gail Thomas (Angels), Otis B. Banks, Dan Casto (Bar Boys/Supremes), Tiffani K. Barbour (Angel/Isley Brother), Aydin Bengisu (Rudolpho Genovese), Yvonne Brechbuhler, Helena Webb (Superstars), Drae Campbell, Eliza Gagnon, Carys Wayne (Dykes), Michael Casselli, Brian O'Donnell, Neil Potter (Cops), Veronica Cruz (Superstar/ Isley Brother), Daniel (Angel/Dancer), Andrea Darriau (Andy Warhol), Paolo De Paola (Michelangelo Genovese), Ford Evanson (David Von Ronk), Ramsey Faragallah (Cop/Seymour Pine), Clare Giarratana (Bianca Maria De Gallo), Jennifer Gordon (Sunflower), Ruth Hackett (Billie), Tyrone Mitchell Henderson (Wanda N. Price), Jon Holden (Hustler/Jim Fourrat), Roberta Kastelic (Hippie), Bruce Katzman (Eliot Shomberg), Amy Lowenthal (Plainclothes Cop), Joseph Mahan (Barker), Jim Mahady (Angel Leader), Michael Malone (Francis Sinclair), Theresa McCarthy (Trish Phillips), Rita Menu (Josie), Barney O'Hanlon (Howie Raskin), Janice O'Rourke (Lisa), Bo Offenbaker (Drag Queen), Stephen Peters (Bar Boy), Brian Quirk, Beau Van Donkelaar (Hustlers), Alison Russo (Dyke/Ginny Apuzzo/Isley Brother), Michael St. Clair (Queen of Queens/Supreme), Nick Sakai (Tony the Bartender), Camilia Sanes (Geneva), Sharon Scruggs (Angie Romano), Raymond Shelton (Beat Cop), Steven Skybell (Matt Branfield), Joseph Small (Barfly), Stephen Speights (Keith-cop), Daryl Terry (Ed Murphy/Mermaid), Will Warren (Splits), Stefanie Zadravec (Ultra-Violet)
MUSICAL NUMBERS: Bring Me Your Tired, Secret Love, Little One, Adolescent's Song, City of Ships I & II, Vigil Strange, Prayer, Anthem

A remembrance of the events surrounding the Stonewall riots, 25 years prior. The performance takes place outdoors on a Hudson River pier.

(Irish Arts Center) Saturday, June 18–Aug. 28, 1995 Donald Kelly, Diane Krausz, and Jeremy Steinberg present:
SANCTIFYING GRACE by Lou Di Maggio and Colin Quinn; Director, Robert Moresco; Set, David Raphel; Lighting, Mauricio Saavedra Pefaur; Costumes, Susanne Coghlin; Stage Manager, John Brophy; Press, Glenn Schwartz CAST: Colin Quinn

A monologue set in Brooklyn during the 1970s.

(John Houseman Studio) Wednesday, June 22–July 17, 1994 (24 performances) Epoch Theatre presents:
SEARCH AND DESTROY by Howard Korder; Director, Joe Reynolds and **NEW YORICK, NEW YORICK** by Joe Reynolds and David Davalos, also with *Smoke* by Laurence Klavan, *If Men Played Cards Like Women Do* by George S. Kaufman, and *Bed and Breakfast* by Richard Dresser
Sets, Shawn Lewis; Lighting, Ellen Bone; Press, Howard and Barbara Atlee CASTS INCLUDE: Anthony DiMaria, James Donato, Jeani Finnerty, Sean Fri, Phillip Hinch, Elissa Piszel, Pamela Jean Shaffer, Dan Sturges, Kip Veasey, J. Paul Boehmer, Cassandra Brooks, Ed Baker

Repertory by the Epoch Theatre. *SEARCH AND DESTROY* is a drama. *NEW YORICK* is six one acts, including 15 minute versions of *Death of a Salesman, Hamlet,* and a combination of the two.

Colin Quinn in *Sanctifying Grace*

Peter Morris in *Truth about Ruth*

(Village Theatre) Thursday, June 23–July 17, 1994 (17 performances) Village Theatre Co. presents:
DELIRIUM by Daniel O'Brien; Director, Paull Moss; Set, Daniel Jagendorf; Lighting, Donald Brill   CAST: Jill Chamberlain, Larry Reinhardt-Meyer, Andrew Douglas Roth

(Henry St. Settlement) Thursday, June 23–July 17, 1994 (13 performances and 3 previews) New Federal Theatre (Producing Director, Woodie King, Jr.) presents:
THE SPRIT MOVES; Written/Performed by Trazana Beverley; Director, A. Dean Irby; Set/Lighting, Jeff Richardson; Musical Director, Charles Lovell; Press, Max Eisen/Kathryn Kinsella
One woman's spiritual journey in two acts.

(Town Hall) Friday, June 24, 1994 (1 performance only) Ballroom Communications, VG Productions and the International Drag Festival present:
CHARLES BUSCH'S DRESSING UP!; Director, Kenneth Elliot; Musical Director, Dick Gallagher, Press, Tony Origlio CAST: Charles Busch, Charles Pierce, Milton Berle, Randy Allen, Ira Siff, Louise DuArt, Imperial Court of New York
An evening of drag entertainment.

(45th St. Theatre) Saturday, June 25–July 1994 Michael & Barbara Ross present:
MY PLAYGROUND by I.C. Howe; Director, Peter Joseph Triolo; Set, Bill Dunckley; Lighting, Alan Sporing; Costumes, Phyllis Begley; Sound, Kenny Sheehan; Press Maya/Penny Landau   CAST: T. Gregory Belle, Cameron Hixon, Jim McNicholas, Mick Preston
A drama involving an upperclass woman returning to the playground of her youth.

(Actors' Playhouse) Tusday, June 28–July 1994 Postage Stamp Xtravaganzas in association with Turnip Festival Co. presents:
THE TRUTH ABOUT RUTH: The Musical Memoirs of a Bearded Lady; Music, Brad Ellis; Lyrics/Book, Peter Morris; Director/Musical Staging, Phillip George; Musical Director, Pete Blue; Sets, B.T. Whitehill; Costumes, Randy Carfagno, Gene Lauze; Lighting, Mark Vogeley; Stage Manager, Julie Charette; Press, Tony Origlio/William McLaughlin CAST: Peter Morris succeeded by Toni DiBuono (Ruth Fields), David Lowenstein (All Men in Her Life)
MUSICAL NUMBERS: The Truth About Ruth, Hit That High Note, Home Sweet Home, Sermonette, Hello Hello, Love Nest, You're Unique, Bang, Dear Ruth/Ruth's Hit Parade, This Is the Place to Be, Face the Fact, Ballad of Mrs. Bluebird, Fabo Soap Jingle, Let Me Possess You, Low, If I Were Beautiful, Finale
A musical comedy in two acts. Previously a one-act cabaret show at the Duplex under the title *The Remarkable Ruth Fields*.

(Lookinglass Theatre) Thursday, June 30–July 17, 1994 (12 performances) The Looking Glass Theatre presents:
HAMLET by William Shakespeare; Director, Shela Xoregos; Set, Nicholas Schlee; Musical Director, Gene Abrams; Sound, Kenn Dovel; Fights, Ian Marshall; Stage Manager, Jeanne Jaconson CAST: Rufus Collins (Hamlet), Cathrine Hesselbach (Ophelia), Olivia Negron (Queen), Daniel Nalbach (Polonius), Michael Simpson (Laertes), William Beckwith (Claudius), Peter Johnson (Ghost), James Colby, Kevin Elden, Maria Galante, Jim Ivey, Stephen Largay, James Riggs

(Atlantic Theatre) Wednesday, July 6–16, 1994 (10 performances) Roundabout Theatre Conservatory Ensemble Co. presents:
THE KENTUCKY CIRCLE by Robert Schenkkan; Director, Paul Leishman; Music, Jim Buck; Costumes, Kristy Irish; Stage Manager, Donna Stiles CAST: Taro Alexander, Kathleen Bloom, Beth Carr, William Christopher, Tim Deak, Ana DelCastillo, Christian Gerard, Sabrina S. Gordon, Abby Imber, Rick Larson, Bill Lettich, Charles May, Patrick McCaffrey, John McDermott, Amy Muzilla, Susan Pasquantonio, Osvaldo Plascencia, Alfred Preisser, Paul Schulz, Bart Shattuck, Rochelle Stempel, Jean Streit, Peter Vouras, Bethlyn Weidler, Ken Weitzman
A new production of the Pulitzer Prize-winning drama.

Trazana Beverly in *The Spirit Moves*

Milton Berle in *Charles Busch's Dressing Up*

Randy Allen, Charles Busch, Louise DuArt, Ira Siff in *Charles Busch's Dressing Up*

Carol Rosegg

(Actor's Attic) Wednesday, July 6–17, 1994 (10 performances) Silent Echo Productions in association with the Hotel Macklowe Artists Guild presents:
PERSONAL AFFAIRS by Judd Lear Silverman; Director, Charles Maryan; Lighting, William M. Kradlak; Set, Laura Lambert; Costumes, Lana Fritz; Press, Michael Cullen
CASTS: *SETTLING ACCOUNTS* with Marla Manning (Anne), James Breckenridge (Dennis)
CORRECT ADDRESS with Sean Hagerty (Adam), James Breckenridge (Jeff)
 Two one-acts about two couples; one straight, one gay.

(John Jay Theatre) Thursday, July 7–9, 1994 (4 performances)
SHLEMEIL THE FIRST with Music/Orchestrations by Hankus Netsky; Lyrics, Arnold Weinstein; Based on a play by Isaac Bashevis Singer; Conceived/Adapted by Robert Brustein; Director/Choreographer, David Gordon; Musical Director, Zalmen Mlotek; Set, Robert Israel; Costumes, Catherine Zuber; Lighting, Robert Isreal; Sound, Christopher Walker; Press, Ellen Zeisler/Grant Lindsey CAST: Larry Block (Schlemiel), Charles Levin (Gronam Ox), Rosalie Gerut, Marilyn Sokol, Remo Airaldi, Tryna Rytza, Benjamin Evett, Scott Cunningham, Vontress Mitchell
 A musical comedy set in the village of Chelm. Presented as part of Lincoln Center's Serious Fun festival.

(Theatre Row Theatre) Saturday, July 9–30, 1994 (11 performances and 5 previews) Art & Work Ensemble (Derek Todd, Artistic Director) presents:
THE MANCHURIAN CANDIDATE by John Lahr; Based on the novel by Richard Condon; Director, Perry Liu; Set, Miguel Lopez-Castillo; Lighting, Steven Rust; Costumes, Brenda Renfroe; Composer/Sound, Adam Wolfensohn; Slides, Kipling Berger, Jorger Vasconcelos; Stage Manager, Melanie S. Armer; Press, Joanne Comerford CAST: David Frank (Ben Marco), Lawrence Kopp (Raymond Shaw), Ann Guilford-Grey (Eleanor Iselin), Richard Bourg (Sen. Iselin), Alicia Genetski (Eugenie Cheyney), Jeremy Johnson (Sen. Jordan), Tricia Kiley (Jocie Jordan), Jesse Newman (Corp. Melvin/Secretary's Aid), Steve Capone (Pvt. Mavole/Ivan), Gregory St. John (Holborn Gaines), R.J. Chesney (O'Neill), Jayne Ross (Gina Malvole/Secretary of Defense), Laura Gillis (Doctor/First Lady), Juan Rivero (Doctor/Floor Manager), Toshiro Yamamoto (Reporter/Doctor), Rob Corddry (Butler/Billy Fasolino), Alden Crews (Gen.Jorgenson/President), Demethress Gordon (Ellen/Cheerleader)
 A thriller set in a post-Cold War future. The original 1959 novel was previously adapted as a 1962 film.

(Nat Horne Theatre) Wednesday, July 13–Aug. 6, 1994 (16 performances) Love Creek Productions (Le Wilhelm, Executive Artistic Director) presents:
THE TIDE IS HIGH by B. Scharolais; Director, George Cron; Set, Viola Bradford; Lighting, Richard Kent Green; Stage Manager, Bart Tangredi; Press, Francine L. Trevens CAST: Sharon Fallon (Sharon), Cecelia Frontero (Toni), Addie O' Donnell (Beth), Tracy Newirth (Ronnie), Joanie Schumacher (Myra), Kirsten Walsh (Ona), Michael Duvert (Intruder)
 A thriller performed without intermission.

Marla Manning, James Breckenridge in *Personal Affairs*

**Richard Bourg, Lawrence Kopp, Ann Guilford-Grey
in *The Manchurian Candidate***

(Lamb's Theatre) Tuesday, July 12–Sept. 30, 1994 Elohim Unlimited in association with Jesse L. DeVore, Jr. presents:
FAITH JOURNEY; Music, George Broderick; Lyrics, Mr. Broderick, Clarence Cuthbertson; Book, Mr. Cuthbertson; Director, Chuck Patterson; Visual, Elizabeth Bello; Costumes, Nancy Brous; Choreography, Barry Carrington; Stage Manager, Kimberly K. Harding; Press, David Rothenberg CAST: Craig Anthony Grant (Paul), Loreal Steiner (Lucille), Claude Jay (Amos), Janet Weeden (Ruby), Hanry C. Rawls (JP), Clarencia Shade (Sister Bell), Robert L. Evans (Brother), Claudette Evans (Traci), Jeff Benish (Police/Jason)
MUSICAL NUMBERS: Somebody's Knocking, I Made a Vow, Justice is Knocking, Over My Head, Best of Both Worlds, Should I Wait, Decide, Don't Take Your Love, One Day, We Got a Movement, By Any Means Necessary, To Be Loved For Who I Am, Help Me Find a Way, I Wanna Be Ready, I Got to Go/I Just Wanna Be Loved, Ain't Gonna Let Nobody Turn Me 'Round, Woke Up This Morning, There's a War in Mississippi, We Shall Overcome, My Country Tis of Thee, Freedom/Walk Together, I Find a Friend in You, I Miss You, Finale
 A musical in two acts based on the life of Martin Luther King, Jr.

**Left: Joanie Schumacher, Tracy Newirth,
Sharon Fallon in *The Tide Is High***

(John Jay Theatre) Wednesday, July 13–16, 1994 (4 performances)
THE NOTEBOOKS OF LEONARDO DA VINCI; Adapted/Directed by Mary Zimmerman; Sets, Scott Bradley; Costumes, Allison Reeds; Lighting, T.J. Gerckens; Sound, Michael Bodeen; Music, Miriam Sturm, Mr. Bodeen; Stage Manager, Kimberly Osgood; Press, Ellen Zeisler/Grant Lindsey CAST: Krzstof Donohue, Laura Eason, Mariann Mayberry, Krzysztof Pieczynski, Paul Oakley Stoval, Marc Vann, Tracy Walsh, Meredith Zinner

A performance culled from 5000 pages of notes by Leonardo da Vinci, 1475–1519. Presented as part of Lincoln Center's Serious Fun festival.

(Wings Theatre) Thursday, July 14–Aug. 20, 1994 (23 performances) Wings Theatre Co. (Jeffery Corrick, Artistic Director; Michael Hillyer, Associate Director) presents:
THE MAGIC FORMULA by Sidney Morris; Director, John Wall; Costumes, Mark D. Sorensen; Set, John Wall, Leon Munier; Lighting, Philip Widmer; Stage Manager, William Doyle; Press, Robert Ganshaw CAST: Michael Dunn Litchfield (David Winters), Mark Robert Gordon (Rubin Buber), Roy Aaron (Dr. Max Buber)

A drama in two acts. The action takes place in Los Angeles, 1949.

(Vineyard Theatre) Tuesday, July 17–Aug. 6, 1994 (15 performances and 3 previews) National Asian American Theatre Co. presents:
OUR TOWN by Thornton Wilder; Director, Mia Katigbak; Set, Mylene Santos; Lighting, Ellen E. Bone; Costumes, Ronna Rothenberger; Stage Manager, Victoria Epstein; Press, Shirley Herz/Wayne Wolfe, Jennifer Talansky, Wentworth Miller CAST: Konrad Aderer (Howie Newsome), Kawie Manuel Atwood (Mrs. Soames), J.B. Barricklo (Joe Crowell/Man in Audience/Baseball Player), Gusti Bogard (Mrs. Webb), Isaac Ho (Baseball Player/Dead Man), Carol A. Honda (Mrs. Gibbs), David Kimo Ige (George Gibbs), Yumi Iwama (Emily Webb), Noriko Kashiwakura (Woman in Audience/Dead Woman), Glenn Kubota (Dr. Gibbs), Ron Nakahara (Mr. Webb), Jorge Ortoll (Prof. Willard/Joe Stoddard), Ralph Pena (Simon Stimson), James Saito (Stage Manager/Sam Craig), Luis A. Salvador (Wally Webb/Si Cromwell), Michelle V. Salvador (Rebecca Gibbs), Stanford Yukinaga (Constable Warren)

An Asian-American production of the 1938 drama in two acts.

(28th St. Theatre) Tuesday, July 26–Aug. 6, 1994 (11 performances) Katy Bolger and Constance McCord present:
WAITING FOR GODOT by Samuel Beckett; Director, Constance McCord; Lighting, Steven L. Shelley; Set, Mark Bloom; Costumes, Michael Piatowski; Stage Manager, K.A. Smith; Press, Howard and Barbara Atlee CAST: Mitch Tebo (Estragon), Sheriden Thomas (Vladimir), McCaffrey Calhoun (Lucky), Donavon Dietz (Pozzo), Carter Spurrier (Boy)

A drama in two acts. The action takes place on a country road.

Mariann Mayberry, Paul Oakley Stovall, Meredith Zinner, Christopher Piecynski in *Notebooks of Leonardo Da Vinci*

Jo Harvey Allen, Barry Tubb in *Chippy*

(John Jay Theatre) Wednesday, July 27–30, 1994 (4 performances)
CHIPPY by Jo Harvey Allen and Terry Allen; Music, Jo Harvey Allen, Terry Allen, Butch Hancock, Joe Ely; Additional Music, Wayne Hancock, Jo Carol Pierce; Director, Evan Yionoulis; Set, Terry Allen, Donald Eastman; Costumes, Veronica Worts; Lighting, Ken Posner; Sound, Darron L. West, Paul Vincent Longo; Stage Manager, Erica Schwartz CAST: Jo Harvey Allen (Chippy), Terry Allen (Ghost), Joe Ely (Tuck), Butch Hancock (Buddy), Wayne Hancock (Mr. Jukebox), Robert Earl Keen (Charles Travis), Jill Parker-Jones (Ruth), Jo Carol Pierce (Doris), Barry Tubb (Roy)

A musical in two acts. The action takes place in West Texas, 1930s–60s.

(Synchronicity Space) Wednesday Aug. 3–7, 1994 (5 performances) American Casino Productions presents:
THE SLOPE by Angelo Parra; Director, Pat Weber Sones; Set, Mark Symczak; Lighting, David Alan Comstock CAST: Julia Levo, Glenn Fitzgerald

A drama involving an anti-lesbian attack in Brooklyn.

(Eighty Eight's) Sunday, Aug. 7–Sept. 25, 1994 (7 performances) Eighty Eight's presents:
LITTLE WHITE LIES!; Director/Arrangements, David Berk; Musical Director, Dick Gallagher CAST: Harvey Evans, Rosemary McNamara, Sam Stoneburner, Margaret Wright

The Walter Donaldson songbook.

(front) Harvey Evans, Rosemary McNamara, Sam Stoneburner, Margaret Wright in *Little White Lies*

Morten Gunnar Larsen, Vernel Bagneris in *Jelly Roll!*

Rosemary Almonte, Lydia Montes, (rear) Wanda Arraiga, Carmen Gutierrez, Yetta Gottesman in *Real Women Have Curves*

Julie Halston

(47th St. Theatre) Wednesday, Aug. 10, 1994–March 30, 1995 transferred to Kaufman Theatre April 1–July 3, 1995 Michael and Barbara Ross with Susan Melman present:
JELLY ROLL!; Music/Lyrics, Jelly Roll Morton; Book, Vernel Bagneris; Choreography, Pepsi Bethel; Lighting, John McKernon; Set, Mike Fish; Sound, One Dream, Darren Clark; Stage Manager, Michael Chudinski; Press, Shirley Herz/Miller Wright CAST: Vernel Bagneris succeeded during vacation by Marion J. Caffey (Jelly), Morten Gunnar Larsen succeeded by Butch Thompson during vacation (Accompanist)
A musical biography performed without intermission. A previous version was seen at Michael's Pub for nearly a year.

(Prospect Park) Thursday, Aug. 25–Sept. 4, 1994 (10 performances) Kings County Shakespeare Co. presents:
THE TEMPEST by William Shakespeare; Director, Deborah Wright Houston; Movement, Liz Shipman; Music, Peter Griggs; Set, Kim Hensen; Lighting, Athomas Goldberg; Costumes, Renee Elizabeth Wright; Stage Manager, Paul Marquis; Press, Jonathan Slaff CAST: Mark Schulte (Prospero), Gary Morabito (Antonio), Jeffrey Eugene Williams (Ferdinand), Matthew Hutton (Gonzalo), Mark McGriff (Francisco), Bill Cohen (Stephano), Randy Aromando (Caliban), Gerald A. Small (Valet), Kathryn Gay Wilson (Alonsa), Karen Eterovich (Sebastian), Maria Hansen (Miranda), Renee Bucciarelli (Adrian), Vicki Hirsch (Trincula), Amy Schwartzman (Ariel), Lisa-Erin Allen, Jack Benton, Mallory Catlett, Cheryl Clark, David Ethan, Chris Ferris, Patrick Leader (Ensemble)
This version sets the action in the 1830s.

(Looking Glass Theatre) Thursday, Aug. 25–Sept. 11, 1994 (12 performances) The Looking Glass Theatre presents:
THE WICKLOW PLAYS by J.M. Synge; Costumes, Elizabeth Rice; Lighting, David Brody
IN THE SHADOW OF THE GLEN Director, John Regis
THE TINKER'S WEDDING Director, David Brody
CASTS: Anne Marie Brennan, Robert Michael Kane, John Keating, Lynda Kennedy, Emmett McConnell, Judy Ramaker, Marla Stollar
Two Irish one-acts.

(Gramercy Arts Theatre) Saturday, Aug. 27–Dec. 29, 1994 (14 performances and 7 previews) Repertorio Espanol presents:
REAL WOMEN HAVE CURVES by Josefina Lopez; Director, Susana Tubert; Set/Costumes, Robert Weber Federico; Press, Susan L. Schulman CAST: Wanda Arriaga, Carmen Gutierez, Yetta Gottesman, Gina Maria Paoli, Lydia Montes, Rosemary Almonte, Vanessa Aspillaga, Sofia Oviedo
A comedy about five women.

(Westside Theatre/Upstairs) Tuesday, Aug. 30–Oct. 30, 1994 (57 performances and 15 previews) Scottie Held & Ann Baker present:
FIRST NIGHT by Jack Neary; Director, Tony Giordano; Set/Lighting, Neil Peter Jampolis; Costumes, David Murin; Sound, Raymond D. Schilke; Stage Manager, Tom Aberger; Press, Peter Cromarty/Michael Hartman CAST: Daniel McDonald (Danny), Lannyl Stephens (Meredith)
A two-act comedy set in a Boston video store on New Year's Eve.

(Primary Stages) Thursday, Sept. 1–Oct. 2, 1994 Primary Stages presents:
LAUGHING MATTERS; Written/Performed by Nick Ulett; Director, Nick Podell; Set/Lighting, Bruce Goodrich
A one-man monologue.

(Synchronicity Space) Thursday, Sept. 1–18, 1994 (14 performances) The 11th Hour Theatre Collective presents:
COLD SWEAT by Neal Bell; Direction/Design, Gail Noppe-Brandon; Lighting, Jeff Segal CAST: Susan Peters (Alice), Harry Danner, Joseph Edwards, Max Frescoln, Thom Goff, Douglas Hall, Jeanne Horn, Lara Koritzke, Betty McKinley, Ron Trenouth
A drama involving a Doctor becoming preoccupied with death.

(Eighty-Eights) Friday, Sept. 2, 1994–Jan. 25, 1995 (Alternating Schedule)
JULIE HALSTON: THE HONEYMOON IS OVER
A comic monologue.

Amy Brentano, David Bishins in *The Nest*

Allan Arinao

Anthony M. Brown, Helen Harrelson in *Mother and Child*

(Theatre for the New City) Wednesday, Sept. 7–Oct. 2, 1994 (20 performances) Tectonic Theater Project presents:
THE NEST by Franz Xaver Kroetz; Translation, Roger Downey; Director, Moises Kaufman; Sets, Marsha Ginsberg; Costumes David Zinn; Lighting, Kevin Adams; Sound, Vanessa Weinberg; Puppets, Basil Twist; Press, Keith Sherman/Jim Byk CAST: David Bishins (Kurt), Amy Brentano (Martha)

A drama set, in this version, in suburban America.

(Hudson Guild Theatre) Thursday, Sept. 8–18, 1994 Rogue Repertory Co. presents:
THE COMEDY OF ERRORS by William Shakespeare; Director, Erica Gould; Set, Doug Huszti; Costumes, Kaye Voyce; Lighting, David Lander CAST INCLUDES: Rainard Rachele (Aegeon), Erik Jensen (Dromio of Syracuse), David Haugen (Dromio of Ephesus), T.J. Glenn (Luce), Keith Grumet (Antipholus of Syracuse), David Ledingham (Antipholus of Ephesus), Ariane Brandt (Luciana), Jonathan Miller (Dr. Pinch), Cady McClain (Adriana)

(Primary Stages) Sunday, Sept. 11–Oct. 3, 1994 (8 performances)
FINAL CURTAIN; Written/Performed by Arlene Sterne; Director, Russell Treyz; Press, Tony Origlio/Stephen Murray

Moments from the lives of three great stage actresses-Sarah Bernhardt, Ellen Terry, and Eleonora Duse.

(McGinn/Cazale Theatre) Monday, Sept. 12–Oct. 1, 1994 (11 performances and 10 previews) American Theatre Ensemble presents:
MOTHER AND CHILD; Written/Directed by Matthew Lombardo; Set/Costumes, Alvin Colt; Lighting, Peter L. Smith; Stage Manager, Kimberly Russell; Press, Shirley Herz/Miller Wright CAST: Helen Harrelson (Mother), Anthony M. Brown (Child)

A drama performed without intermission. The action takes place in a New York hospital room, Christmas Eve.

(Cucaracha Theatre) Wednesday, Sept. 14–Oct. 1, 1994 (12 performances) Cucaracha presents:
UNCLE VANYA; Adapted by Howard Barker; Director, Kirk Jackson; Music, John Hoge; Lighting, Brian Aldous; Costumes, Mary Myers; Sets, Russell Parkman CAST: Andrew Borba, Joey Golden, Dale Goodson, Pamela Gray, Lori Johnson, Marie Kalish, Vivian Lanko, Chuck Montgomery, John Gould Rubin

(Currican Theatre) Thursday, Sept. 15–25, 1994 (10 performances) Marten Sameth and Associates present:
THE CARETAKER by Harold Pinter; Director, Jeffrey Guyton; Lighting, David Casteneda; Set, Zaniz Jakulowski; Music/Sound, David Schommer, Michael Paris; Stage Manager, Amie C. Hennessey; Press, Howard and Barbara Atlee CAST: Gerard J. Schneider (Mick), Jim Kramer (Aston), Marten Sameth (Davies)

A drama in three acts performed with one intermission. The action takes place in West London.

(Charles Ludlam Theatre) Thursday, Sept. 15–Dec. 18, 1994 (70 performances and 12 previews) The Ridiculous Theatrical Company (Everett Quinton, Artistic Director; Adele Bove, Managing Director) presents:
A MIDSUMMER NIGHT'S DREAM by William Shakespeare; Director, Everett Quinton; Set, T. Greenfield; Costumes, Ramona Ponce; Lighting, Richard Currie; Sound, Mark Bennett; Wigs/Makeup, Zsamira Ronquillo; Choreography, Barbara Allen; Stage Manager, Lars Umlaut; Press, Philip Rinaldi/Tony Stavick CAST: Everett Quinton (Nick Bottom/Egeus/Pyramis), Beth Dodye Bass (Titania), John Cassaras (Demetrius), Eureka (Oberon), Michael Goldfried (Philostrate/Robin Starveling), Lisa Herbold (Peter Quince), Noelle Kalom (Hippolyta), Wilfredo Medina (Lysander), Grant Neale (Robin Goodfellow), Mel Nieves (Snug/Lion/Titania's Fairy), Lenys Sama (Francis Flute/Thisbe), Tim Sozen (Thesus/Moth), Jimmy Szczepanek (Helena), Michael Van Meter (Tom Snout/Wall/Titania's Fairy), Christine Weiss (Hermia)

The Ridiculous Company meets Shakespeare for the first time. Performed with one intermission.

Left: Marten Sameth in *The Caretaker*

85

(Perry St. Theatre) Friday, Sept. 16–Oct. 9, 1994 (16 performances and 2 previews) The Barrow Group (Seth Barrish, Artistic Director) presents: **GHOST IN THE MACHINE** by David Gilman; Director/Music, Seth Barrish; Set, Michael McGarty; Costumes, Markas Henry; Lighting, Howard Werner; Sound, One Dream; Stage Manager, Christine Lemme; Press, Shirley Herz/Wayne Wolfe, Stephen Barry CAST: Reade Kelly (Wes), Lee Brock (Nancy), Stephen Singer (Matt), Susan Floyd (Kim), Herbert Rubens (Harper), Ken Leung (Minh Schumann)

A psychological thriller performed without intermission. The action takes place in a Cambridge, Mass. home and Harvard University.

(28th St. Theater) Wednesday, Sept. 21–Oct. 9, 1994 (12 performances and 4 previews) Katy Bolger presents: **BROKEN ENGLISH** by Geraldine Sherman; Director, Stephen Hollis; Set, James Wolk; Lighting, Christine Methot; Costumes, Paula Scofield; Sound, Lewis Flinn; Stage Manager, Lori Lundquist; Press, Chris Boneau/Adrian Bryan-Brown, Bob Fennell CAST: Fleur Phillips (Ruth), Ahvi Spindell (Karl), Mary Testa (Trude), Maxine Taylor-Morris (Miss Singer)

A drama in two acts. The action takes place in London, 1956.

(Nat Horne Theatre) Wednesday, Sept. 21–25, 1994 (5 performances) Love Creek Productions (Le Wilhelm, Artistic Director) presents: **DOWN DARK, DECEPTIVE STREETS** by Glenn Alterman; Director, Jeffrey J. Albright CAST: Michael Cannis, Donna Davidge, Paul Kawecki, Bob Manus, Taryn Quinn, Scott Sparks, Bart Tangredi, Trey Webster

Four short plays: *Goin' Round on Rock Solid Ground, Once in a Blue Moon, The Danger of Strangers,* and *Like Family*.

(Greenwich St. Theatre) Thursday, Sept. 22–Oct. 16, 1994 (13 performances and 3 previews) Chain Lightning Theatre (Todd Pieper, Artistic Director; Claire Higgins, Producer) presents: **CRAIG'S WIFE** by George Kelly; Director, Kricker James; Set, Teresa Stroh; Lighting, Jeff Croiter; Costumes, Devin Quigley; Stage Manager, Brian D. White; Press, Jim Baldassare CAST: Carol Emshoff (Miss Austen), Blainie Logan (Mrs. Harold), Cheryl Horne (Mazie), Ginger Grace (Mrs. Craig), Brandee Graff (Ethel Landreth), Tad Jones (Walter Craig), Cam Kornman (Mrs. Frazier), Monty Bonnell (Billy Birkmire), Sandford Stokes (Joseph Catelle), Jeff Woods (Harry), Max Faugno (Tailor's Boy/Expressman/Delivery Boy)

A three-act drama performed with one intermission. This play won the 1926 Pulitzer Prize.

(Intar Theatre) Thursday, Sept. 22–Oct. 9, 1994 (13 performances and 3 previews) C. George Scala, F and M Productions, and The Field Company present: **A FIELD IN HEAT** by Ricky Spears; Director, Michael Piatkowski; Lighting, Trad A. Burns; Sets, Ted Simpson; Costumes, Brenda Renfroe; Stage Manager, John J. Harmon; Press, Shirley Herz/Sam Rudy CAST: Christina Burz (Annie Golden), Ray Pirkle (Donnie Golden), Todd Lewis (Bill Barnes), Jill Jackson (Martha), Jennifer Petsche (Aggie), Steve Sherling (Joe Evans), Justin Malone (Bobbie Joe)

A drama in two acts. The action takes place in a small farmhouse somewhere in the dust bowl of America, 1954.

Ken Leung in *Ghost in the Machine*

Mary Testa, Fleur Phillips, Ahvi Spindell in *Broken English*

(Pelican Studio) Thursday, Sept. 22–Oct. 8, 1994 (9 performances and 2 previews) New Perspectives Theatre Co. (Melody Brooks, Artistic Director) presents: **POST MORTEM** by Jennifer Christman; Director, Kathleen M. Powers; Lighting, Jennifer Tanzer; Press, Jim Baldassare CAST: Maureen Brooks, Dina Comolli, Carolyn Dilley, Dawn Greenidge, Chris Tolliver, Nancy Ward, Janice Williams

A drama set at a baby shower.

(Blue Angel) Tuesday, Sept. 27, 1994– Mark Dunn & Danielle Chappard present: **LES INCROYABLES;** Co-Directed by Les Incroyables and Jean Marie Riviere; Set, Daniel Ettinger; Lighting/Stage Manager, Laurent Legal; Costumes, Michel Prosper; Dance Captain/Additional Choreography, Jean Laurent Martinez; Press, David Rothenberg/Manuel Igrejas, Hugh Hayes CAST: Les Incroyables (Michel Prosper, Gilles Jean, Daniel Rohou), Ivan Arino, Tony Burrer, Lee Cherry, Carolyn Doherty, Jamie Gustis, Marianne Hettinger, Irene Kent, Adriana Nogueira, Katia Rios, Rebecca Sherman

New edition of a Parisian musical revue which played at Kaptain Banana last season.

Left: Christina Burz in *Field in Heat*

(Fools Company Space) Wednesday, Sept. 28–Oct. 15, 1994 (12 performances and 2 previews) Working Lights Unlimited presents:
THE BLINDFOLD by Jose Lopez Rubio; Translation, Marion Peter Holt; Director, Sara Louise Lazarus; Sets, Ariel Goldberger; Costumes, Cathy Small; Lighting, Matthew J. Williams; Stage Manager, Jennifer Creighton; Press, Jonathan Slaff CAST: D. Candis Paule (Carmen), Ellen Berman (Emilia), Rica Martens (Aunt Carolina), Richard-Charles Hoh (Uncle Gerard), Steve Parris (Buyer), Constance Stellas (Beatriz), Harry Danner (Villalba), Cary Barker (Henrietta), Russell Stevens (Quintana), Louise Gallanda (Matilde)

A comedy in three acts. The action takes place in Madrid, 1954.

(Currican Theatre) Thursday, Sept. 29–Oct. 16, 1994 (16 performances) Igloo, The Theatrical Group presents:
THE KILLER INSIDE ME by Jim Thompson; Adapted/Directed by Christopher Peditto; Set, Sarah Lambert; Lighting, David Sullivan; Costumes, Family Jewels Vintage Clothing; Music, Marc Ribot; Fights, Rick Sordelet; Stage Manager, Brion Lopez; Press, Chris Parsons CAST: Christopher Peditto (Lou Ford), Fia Porter (Waitress/Helene/Nurse), Maria Bello (Joyce Lakeland), James Kissane succeeded by Glenn Wilson (Joe Rothman), Donna Jean Fogel (Amy Stanton), Sean P. Reilly (Bum), John Henry Cox (Chester Conway), Christopher Centrella (Elmer Conway), Shane Stevens (Johnnie Pappas), Jeff Stafford (Jeff Plummer), Scott Thomson (Bob Maples), Phillip Baltazar (Howard Hendricks), William Rothlein (Dr. Ford), Martin Rudy (Billy Boy Walker)

A dark drama set in a small Texas town.

(29th St. Rep Theatre) Thursday, Sept. 29–Dec. 4, 1994 (36 performances and 6 previews) The 29th St. Repertory Theater and Darren Lee Cole present:
KILLER JOE by Tracy Letts; Director, Wilson Milam; Set, Richard Meyer; Costumes, Liz Elkins; Lighting, Jeremy Kumin; Fights, David Brimmer; Stage Manager, Brad Rohrer; Press, Shirley Herz/Miller Wright CAST: Thomas Wehrle (Chris Smith), Linda June Larson (Sharla Smith), Leo Farley (Ansel Smith), Danna Lyons (Dottie Smith), David Mogentale (Killer Joe Cooper)

A satiric drama in two acts. The setting is a trailer home on the outskirts of Dallas.

(Playhouse on Vandam) Sunday, Oct. 2, 1994–still playing May 31, 1995 Dana Matthow presents:
GRANDMA SYLVIA'S FUNERAL; Conceived by Glenn Wein and Amy Lord Blumsack; Created by Wein, Blumsack and the original company; Director, Mr. Wein; Design, Leon Munier; Lighting, David J. Lander; Costumes, Peter Janis; Choreography, Joanna Rush; Stage Manager, Margaret Bodriguian; Press, John and Gary Springer, Sharon Rothe CAST: Paul Eagle (Dave Schildner), David Ellzey , Bill Kraus (Rabbi Michael Wolfe), Holgie Forrester (Elsie Duey), Ron Gilbert (Jerry Grossman), Karen Ginsburg (Dori Grossman), Sheri Goldner (Marlena Weiss Grossman), Sondra Gorney (Helen Krantz), Brooke Johnson (Ava Gerard), Marc Kamhi (Mark Grossman), Morgan Lavere (Vlad Helsenrott), Simone Lazer (Dr. Rachel Rosenbaum), Janice Mautner (Melinda Franklin), Brocton Pierce (Dr. Byron Franklin), David Eric Rosenberg (SkyBoy/Stuart Grossman), Joanna Rush (Natalie Chasen), Tom Darpi (Fredo Iannuzzi), Stanley Allan Sherman (Harvey Grossman), Helen Siff (Helga Helsenrott), Justine Slater (Risa Iannuzzi), Glenn Wein (Gary Grossman), Barry Weinberger (Todd Grossman)

A theatrical funeral in two acts. The action takes place at the Helsenrott Jewish Mortuary and includes a "mitzvah meal."

Christopher Peditto, Maria Bello in *The Killer Inside Me*

Grandma Sylvia's Funeral

(227 Waverly Place) Tuesday, Oct. 4–29, 1994 (15 performances and 5 previews) LASO Productions/Karen Hauser presents:
BANNER by Kathleen Clark; Director, Alison Summers; Set, George Xenos; Lighting, Chris Dallos; Costumes, Andy Wallach; Sound, Kurt Kellenberger; Press, Chris Boneau/Adrian Bryan-Brown/Meredith Westgate-Moore CAST: Lois Robbins (Banner Lee Winston), Michael Piontek (Price Winston), Steven Barkhimer (Matthew Joley), Schuyler Grant (Tess Tipton), Maduka Steady (G.W. Jackson), James Doerr (Doc Forbes)

A drama in two acts. The setting is a small town in the Tennessee Smokey Mountains, 1939.

Left: Lois Robbins, Michael Piontek in *Banner*

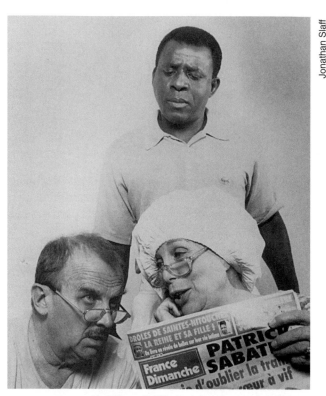

Fred Burrell, Elizabeth Perry,
(top) Adboulaye N'Gom in *A Modest Proposal*

Craig Green, Richard Grunn, Natalie Ross in *Madwoman of Chaillot*

(Public/LuEsther Hall) Tuesday, Oct. 4–29, 1994 (22 performances and 10 previews) Young Playwrights Inc. (Sheri M. Goldhirsch, Artistic Director; Brett W. Reynolds, Managing Director) presents:
THE 1994 YOUNG PLAYWRIGHTS FESTIVAL; Sets, Allen Moyer; Costumes, Karen Perry; Lighting, Pat Dignan; Sound, Raymond D. Schilke; Stage Managers, Elise-Ann Konstantin, Rick Steiger; Press, Serio Coyne/Alan Cohen, Kris Moran
THE BASEMENT AT THE BOTTOM AT THE END OF THE WORLD by Nadine Graham; Director, Gloria Muzio CAST: Amber Kain (Daneen), Mark Rosenthal (Paul)
THE MOST MASSIVE WOMAN WINS by Madeleine George; Director, Phyllis S.K. Look CAST: Candace Taylor (Sabine), Amy Ryder (Carly), Elaina Davis (Rennie), Suzanne Costallos (Cel)
THE LOVE OF BULLETS by Jerome D. Hairston; Director, Brett W. Reynolds CAST: Sandra Daley (Sydney), Harold Perrineau (Darius), Curtis McClarin (Mattie), Candace Taylor (Evan), Victor Mack (Dick Banks)
The 13th year of the Festival founded by Stephen Sondheim in 1981. All scripts are from writers 18 or younger.

(Ubu Rep Theater) Tuesday, Oct. 4–24, 1994 (15 performances and 3 previews) Ubu Repertory presents:
A MODEST PROPOSAL by Tilly; Translation, Richard Miller; Director, Saundra McClain; Set, Watoku Ueno; Lighting, Greg MacPherson; Costumes, Carol Ann Pelletier; Stage Manager, Teresa Conway; Press, Jonathan Slaff CAST: Elizabeth Perry (Aimee), Fred Burrell (Raymond), Melissa Chalsma (Cristelle), Elizabeth Hess (Marie-Jo), Abdoulaye N'Gom (Modeste)
A comedy set in Brittany.

(Cucaracha Theatre) Wednesday, Oct. 5–22, 1994 (12 performances) Cucaracha presents:
STAIRWAY TO HEAVEN by Jennifer Houlton and Caroline Seymour; Director, Sara Driver; Lighting, Fern Gnesin; Sets, Penelope Wish CAST: Caroline Seymour, Jennifer Houlton, Suzanne Fletcher, Robert Adanto

(The Hamlet of Bank St. Theatre) Wednesday, Oct. 5–23, 1994 (15 performances) Euro-Plays presents:
GEORGE BERNARD AND STELLA by Jesse Torn; Director, Fred Horton; Press, Howard and Barbara Atlee CAST: Dennis Bowman (Shaw), Eileen Kenney (Stella), Maude Boylan (Charlotte), Barry Holmes, J. Stephen Hall, Irish McGettricks, Dick Henley, Jimmy Lee, Debbie Horton
A drama about the love triangle between George Bernard Shaw, the actress Stella (Mrs. Patrick) Campbell, and Shaw's wife Charlotte Payne-Townshend.

(Clark Studio) Saturday, Oct. 8–16, 1994 (10 performances) Cressid Productions presents:
THE WINTER'S TALE by William Shakespeare; Director, Deloss Brown; Music, Raphael Crystal; Press, Maya/Penny Landau CAST: William Christian (Polixenes), James Glossman, Joseph Holmgren, Jeremy Johnson, Miranda Kent, Becky Killy, Susan Knott, Michael Laurence, Christopher Marquette, Evan Miller, Paul Murphy, Phil Powers, James Riggs, Leigh Rose, Mary Lou Shriber, Gregory Sobeck, Cynthia Sopheia, Cornelia Whitcomb, Peter Ashton Wise

(Metropolitan Playhouse) Sunday, Oct. 8–30, 1994 (14 performances) Parsifal's Productions Inc. presents:
THE MADWOMAN OF CHAILLOT by Jean Giraudoux; Translation, Maurice Valency; Director, Rebecca Taylor; Musical Director, Mark Goodman; Choreography, Lindsey Hanahan; Music, Michael Paris; Costumes, Larry Callahan; Puppets, Richard Grunn; Set, Edward Pierce; Lighting, Tim Stephenson; Masks, Nat Thomas CAST: Kate Anthony (Irma), Christopher Baez (Shoelace Peddler), Susan Barrett (Street Performer), Steve Boles (President), Elizabeth Bove (Constance), Jack Frankel (Baron/Adolphe), Gary Glor (Waiter/Press Agents), Craig Green (Ragpicker/Bongos), Richard Grunn (Police/Sergeant), Amy N. Hawkes (Paulette), Cynthia Hewett (Broker), James-Howard Laurence (Josephine/Dr. Jardin), William Prael (Little Man/Doorman/Sewerman), Danielle LaViscount (Therese), Natalie Ross (Countess), Robert Ruffin (Prospector), Henry Sidel (Deaf Mute), Sharron Amy Swartz (Flower Girl), Mary Wadkins (Gabrielle), Robert Wilson (Pierre)
A satire on modern society.

Alice Haining, Melinda Eades, Carlin Glynn, Kerrianne Spellman in *The Cover of Life*

Patricia Scanlon, Sean Runnett, (rear) Jordan Lage in *Blaming Mom*

(American Place Theatre) Tuesday, Oct. 11–Nov. 20, 1994 (29 performances and 19 previews) T. Harding Jones Entertainment, Frederick B. Vogel, Herb Goldsmith Productions, Angels of the Arts, and Snapshot Theatrical Productions present:
THE COVER OF LIFE by R.T. Robinson; Director, Peter Masterson; Set, Amy Shock; Costumes, Lindsay W. Davis; Lighting, Marc B. Weiss; Sound, Jeremy Grody; Music, Randy Courts; Stage Manager, Marjorie Horne; Press, Richard Kornberg/Bill Schelble, Thomas Naro, Don Summa CAST: Sara Botsford succeeded by Leslie Hendrix (Kate Miller), Alice Haining (Tood), Melinda Eades (Weetsie), Carlin Glynn (Aunt Ola), Kerrianne Spellman (Sybil), Cynthia Darlow (Addie Mae), David Schiliro (Tommy)
A drama in two acts. The action takes place in New York City and Sterlington, Louisiana, 1943.

(LaMAMA) Thursday, Oct. 13–23, 1994 (11 performances) LaMAMA ETC presents:
IS THAT ALL THERE IS?; Director, Kfir Yefel; Choreography, Amir Hosseinpou; Design, Duncan MacAskill; Costumes, Paul Edwards; Lighting, Rita Ann Kogler; Press, Judy Jacksina CAST: Liliane Montevecchi, Amir Hosseinpour, Sarah Toner, Floyd G. Hendricks
A theatre/dance piece based on the life of Russian aristocrat, Lou Salome.

(Watermark Theatre) Thursday, Oct. 13–30, 1994 (13 performances and 3 previews) The Watermark Theatre (Nela Wagman, Artistic Director) presents:
BLAMING MOM and **SOUPY AND ADENA** by David Edelstein; Director, Nela Wagman; Set, Sarah Lambert; Lighting, Joe Saint; Press, Shirley Herz/Sam Rudy, Stephen Barry CASTS: Sean Runnett (Willie), Patricia Scanlon (Lucy), Tucker Smith, Marie Dame, Kristen Lee Kelly (Adena), Jordan Lage (Soupy)
Two one-act comedies.

(Irish Arts Center) Friday, October 14, 1994–Feb.26, 1995 Irish Arts Center presents:
PUBLIC ENEMY by Kenneth Branagh; Director, Nye Heron; Set, David Raphel; Lighting, Susan Roth; Costumes, Mimi Maxmen; Music/Sound, Nico Kean; Stage Manager, John Brophy; Press, Marianne, Don Kelly CAST: George Coe (Thompson), Paul Ronan (Tommy Black), Brian D'Arcy James (Davey Boyd), Tony Coleman (Geordie Pearson), Bernadette Quigley (Kitty Rogers), Patti Allison (Ma), Neal Jones (Robert Black), James Beecher (Kevin O'Donnell)
A crime drama in two acts. The action takes place in Belfast, mid-eighties.

(Folksbiene Playhouse) Saturday, Oct. 15, 1994–Jan. 29, 1995 (40 performances) Folksbiene Playhouse (Tova Ronni, Artistic Director; Morris Adler, President) presents:
MIRELE EFROS by Jacob Gordin; Translation, Pearl Krupit; Director, Bryna Wasserman Turetsky; Costumes, Tzili Charney; Lighting, Betsy Finston; Set, Michael McGarty; Stage Manager, Judith Scher; Press, Max Eisen/Kathryn Kinsella CAST: Shifra Lerer (Makhle), Norman Kruger (Shalmen), Felix Fibich (Nukemste), Mina Bern (Khane-Dvoyre), Zypora Spaisman (Mirele Efros), Richard Carlow (Yosele), Mark Ethan Toporek (Doyne), Raquel Yossiffon (Sheyndele), David J. Waletzky (Shloymele)
An 1898 Yiddish drama in two acts.

(Lamb's Theatre) Sunday, Oct. 16–17, 1994 (2 limited performances) Musicals in Concert and BT McNicholl present:
MUSIC IN THE AIR; Music, Jerome Kern; Lyrics/Book, Oscar Hammerstein II; Director, James Hammerstein; Musical Director, James Stenborg; Stage Manager, Maureen F. Gibson; Press, Rob Hargraves CAST INCLUDES: Lynne Wintersteller, Jason Workman, John Fiedler, Emily Loesser, Keith Jurosko, Dennis Kelly
A concert version of the 1932 musical.

Left: Bernadette Quigley, Paul Ronan in *Public Enemy*

89

(Carnegie Hall/Weill Hall) Wednesday, Oct. 19–23, 1994 (6 performances) Carnegie Hall presents:
VERY WARM FOR MAY with Music by Jerome Kern; Lyrics/Book, Oscar Hammerstein; Director/Conductor, John McGlinn; Orchestrations, Robert Russell Bennett; Press, Mari Beth Bittan CAST: Gregory Jbara (Kenny), Robert Nichols (Will Graham/Eddie Schlessinger), Brent Barrett (Johnny Graham), Donna Lynne Champlin (May Graham), Marguerite Shannon (Liz Spofford), Karl duHoffman (Sonny Spofford), James Ludwig (Raymond Sibley), Damon Kirschenmann (Lowell Pennyfeather), Jon Lovitz (Ogdon Quiler), Elizabeth Futral (Carroll), John Hancock (Charles), Jeanne Lehman (Winnie Spofford), Cory Fay (Alvin), Jennifer Casey Cabot (Miss Wasserman), Lucy Schaufer (Miss Hyde), Marc Heller (Mr. Pratt), Edward Albert (Mr. McGee), Beverly Thiele (Alice), Dulce Reyes (Sylvia), Jeffrey Lentz (Stanley)
MUSICAL NUMBERS: Overture, In Other Words Seventeen, Me and the Roll and You, Ogdon's Characterization, Quartette, All the Things You Are, May Tells All, Heaven In My Arms, Rhumba, That Lucky Fellow, L'Histoire De Madame De La Tour, That Lucky Lady, The Strange Case of Adam Standish Ballet, Dance Da-Da, Rehearsal Sequence, Schottische Scena, All in Fun, Waltz Speciality, In the Heart of the Dark, High Up in Harlem, Harlem Boogie-Woogie, Finale
A concert version of a 1939 musical in two acts.

(Primary Stages) Wednesday, Oct. 19–Nov. 27, 1994 (40 performances) transferred to Westside Theatre Dec. 8, 1994–Mar. 5, 1995 Primary Stages Company (Casey Childs, Artistic Director), in association with the Herrick Theatre Foundation on transfer, presents:
YOU SHOULD BE SO LUCKY by Charles Busch; Director, Kenneth Elliott; Set, B.T. Whitehill; Lighting, Michael Lincoln; Costumes, Suzy Benzinger; Sound, Aural Fixation; Song, Dick Gallagher; Stage Manager, John Frederick Sullivan; Press, Tony Origlio/Stephen Murray CAST: Stephen Pearlman (Mr. Rosenberg), Charles Busch (Christopher), Nell Campbell (Polly), Matthew Arkin (Walter), Julie Halston (Lenore), Jennifer Kato (Wanda Wang)
A comedy in two acts. The setting is a small Greenwich Village apartment.

(Sanford Meisner Theatre) Thursday, Oct. 20–Nov. 6, 1994 (9 performances and 3 previews) The Promethean Theatre Co. (Dan Roentsch, Artistic Director) presents:
MARY STUART by Friedrich Schiller; Translation, Charles E. Passage; Director/Set/Lighting, Dan Roentsch; Costumes, Maggie Kulick; Press, Shirley Herz/David Lotz CAST: Katrina Ferguson (Mary Stuart), Deborah Mathieu (Queen Elizabeth), Stephen Byers, Hugh Cole, Steve Crow, Alan Dolderer, Michael Feigin, Michael Keyloun, Christopher Knott, Jack Lewis, Ann Marie Morelli
A drama about the 30 year religious and royal battle between Mary Stuart and Elizabeth Tudor.

Nell Campbell, Jennifer Kato, Matthew Arkin, Charles Busch, Julie Halston in *You Should Be So Lucky*

Clea Rivera, Diego Taborda in *The Crossroads*

(Tribeca Performing Arts Center) Thursday, Oct. 20–Nov. 13, 1994 (13 performances and 3 previews) Ensemble International Theatre and Tribeca Performing Arts Center present:
THE CROSSROADS by Juan Tovar; Translation, Joe Martin, Iona Weissberg; Based on the writings of Juan Rulfo; Director, Susana Tubert; Press, Shirley Herz/Sam Rudy CAST: Diego Taborda, Roberto Rodriguez, George Bass, Doris Difarnecio, Axel Cintron, Mary Magdalena Hernandez, Camilla Sanes, Clea Rivera, Miguel Parga, Elissa Olin
A dramatic rendering of Juan Rulfo's stories.

(Douglas Fairbanks Theater) Friday, Oct. 21, 1994–Feb. 26, 1995 Twice Blessed Company presents:
NUNSENSE 2: THE SEQUEL; Music/Lyrics/Book/Direction by Dan Goggin; Choreography, Felton Smith; Orchestrations, Michael Rice, David Nyberg; Musical Director, Mr. Rice; Set, Barry Axtell; Lighting, Paul Miller; Sound, Jim van Bergen; Stage Manager, Paul J. Botchis; Press, Pete Sanders/Ian Rand, Glenna Freedman CAST: Nancy E. Carroll (Sister Mary Regina), Semina De Laurentis (Sister Mary Amnesia), Carolyn Droscoski (Sister Robert Anne), Elizabeth Dargan Doyle (Sister Mary Leo), Terri White (Sister Mary Hubert), Teri Gibson (Alternate)
MUSICAL NUMBERS: Overture, Jubilatedo, Nunsense the Magic Word, Winning Is Just the Beginning, Prima Ballerina, Biggest Still Ain't the Best, I've Got Pizazz, The Country Nun, Look Ma I Made It, Padre Polka, The Classic Queens, A Hat and Cane Song, Angeline, We're the Nuns to Come to, What Would Elvis Do?, Yes We Can, I Am Here to Stay, What a Catastrophe, No One Cared Like You, Gloria in Excelsis Deo, There's Only One Way to End Your Prayers, Finale
A musical in two acts. The action takes place at Mt. Saint Helen's School Auditorium six weeks after the action of the 1985 musical *Nunsense*.

(clockwise from Top L) Terri White, Nancy E. Carroll, Carolyn Droscoski, Semina DeLaurentis, Susan Emerson in *Nunsense 2*

90

(Curran Theatre) Friday, Oct. 21–Nov. 6, 1994 (16 performances) Currican Theatre Co. (Andrew Miller, Artistic Director) presents:
THE BORDERLINE by Jim Grimsley; Director, Dean Gray; Set, Rob Odorisio; Lighting, Jack Mehler; Costumes, Jonathan Green; Sound, Michael Keck; Press, Howard and Barbara Atlee CAST: Lawrence Lau (Gordon Hammond), Elizabeth Lewis Corley (Helen Hammond), David Van Pelt (Jake), Eleanor Rollins (Sarah McCord)

A drama set in the rural south.

(Theatre Four) Monday, Oct. 27–Dec. 18, 1994 (37 performances and 3 previews) The Irish Repertory Theatre presents:
MOTHER OF ALL THE BEHANS; Adapted by Peter Sheridan; from book by Brian Behan; Additional Material, Rosaleen Linehan; Set/Costumes, Chisato Yoshimi; Lighting, Tony Wakefield; Stage Manager, Kathe Mull; Press, Chris Boneau/Adrian Bryan-Brown/Susanne Tighe, Meredith Moore, David Wood CAST: Rosaleen Linehan (Kathleen Behan)

A one-woman play on the life of a Dublin mother.

(Minetta Lane Theatre) Tuesday, Oct. 25–Dec. 4, 1994 (30 performances and 18 previews) Thomas Viertel, Steven Baruch, Richard Frankel, Jack Viertel, Dasha Epstein, Margery Klain, Leavitt/Fox/Mages, and Daryl Roth present:
DAS BARBECU; Music, Scott Warrender; Lyrics/Book, Jim Luigs; Director, Christopher Ashley; Musical Staging, Stephen Terrell; Orchestrations, Bruce Coughlin; Musical Director, Jeff Halpern; Music Supervision/Dance Arrangements, Michael Kosarin; Sets/Costumes, Eduardo Sicangco; Lighting, Frances Aronson; Sound, T. Richard Fitzgerald; CAST Recording, Varese Sarabande; Press, Chris Boneau/Adrian Bryan-Brown/Andy Shearer, Bob Fennell, Jackie Green CAST: Carolee Carmello (Gutrune/Freia/et al.), Julie Johnson (Narrator/Fricka/Erda/et al.), Sally Mayes (Brunnhilde/et al.), Jerry McGarity (Siegfried/Alberich/et al.), J.K. Simmons (Wotan/Hagen/et al.)
MUSICAL NUMBERS: A Ring of Gold in Texas, What I Had in Mind, Hog-Tie Your Man, Makin' Guacamole, Rodeo Romeo, County Fair, Public Enemy Number 1, A Little House for Me, River of Fire, If Not Fer You, Slide a Little Close, Barbecue for Two, After the Gold Is Gone, Wanderin' Man, Turn the Tide, Closing

A musical comedy in two acts inspired by Wagner's *Ring* cycle. The action takes place in Texas.

(One Dream Theatre) Thursday, Oct. 27–Nov. 13, 1994 (11 performances and 3 previews) Zena Group presents:
FAITH'S BODY by Gilbert Girion; Director, Tom McDermott, Jr.; Set, Deborah R. Rosen; Lights, Russell H. Chiampa; Sound, Darron West; Music, Paul Ruest; Press, Chris Boneau/Adrian Bryan-Brown/Bob Fennell CAST: Jeremy Gold, Laura John, Josh Liveright, Maggie Low, Chris Marobella, Johanna Pfaelzer

A drama set in Southern California.

Rosaleen Linehan in *Mother of All the Behans*

Sally Mayes, Carolee Carmello, Julie Johnson in *Das Barbecu*

(Creative Place Theatre) Thursday, Oct. 27–30, 1994 (4 performances) January Stevens presents:
PORTER PEACE by Edward Musto; Based on stories by Adam Stuart, Andre Dubus, Richard Rothstein, and Christopher Leitch; Director, Duane Fletcher; Lighting, William Kradlak II; Costumes, Amy Swobeda; Set, Jude Damski
ARMISTICE CAST: Anita Logan (Vera), Dana Watkins (Mark)
SEPARATE FLIGHTS CAST: Elizabeth Gee (Beth), Daniel Weiss (Robert), Elizabeth Soychak (Peggy), James Breckenridge (Lee)
O.D. FEELIN CAST: Allison Furman (Angel/Orchid), Adam J. Brooks (Cash/Duke), Charles Derbyshire (J.B./Mr. Bigg)
Three one-act plays.

(Westbeth Music Hall) Thursday, Oct. 27–Nov. 20, 1994 (15 performances and 1 preview) Kindred Productions in association with The Triumvirate presents:
HAMLET by William Shakespeare; Director, Scott Noflet Carr; Lighting, Jennifer L. Karger; Costumes, Beowulf Boritt; Fights, Ian Rose; Stage Manager, Lisa I. Blanco; Press, Tony Origlio/Michael Cullen CAST: Tony Cormier (Claudius), Jean Richards (Gertrude), Lawrence Preston (Hamlet), Robert Francis Perillo (Polonius), Harry Bouvy (Laertes/4th Player), Kathryn Newbrough (Ophelia), Benjamin Chelsea (Horatio), Heather Margaret Murphy (Rosencrantz/Lady of the Court), Mark Schaller (Guildenstern/Soldier/Thief), Tom Reuel (Osric), J. Mark Danly (Marcellus/Captain/Priest), Jonathan Smit (Player King/Gravedigger/Soldier/Thief), Laurie Wickens (Player Queen/Voltemand), Jennifer Gordon (3rd Player/2nd Gravedigger/Reynaldo/Messenger), James McClure (Fortinbras/Ghost/Courtier)

This production sets the action in Berlin's 1930s cabaret society.

Lawrence Preston, Kathryn Newbrough in *Hamlet*

91

Milo O'Shea, Kitty Sullivan in *Alive Alive Oh!*

(front) Harriet D. Foy, (Clockwise from Top L) Jan Maxwell,
Cass Morgan, Kathleen Mahony-Bennett, Julie Prosser in *Inside Out*

Joshua Taylor, Paul Ellis, Ellen Orenstein,
Georgia M. Corbo in *You Can't Win*

(Henry St. Settlement) Thursday, Oct. 27–Nov. 20, 1994 (16 performances)
New Federal Theatre (Woodie King Jr., Producing Director) presents:
BESSIE SPEAKS by China Clark; Director, Dwight R.B. Cook; Musical
Director/Arrangements, Grenoldo Frazier; Choreography, Louis Johnson;
Costumes, Judy Dearing; Set, Chris Cumberbatch; Lighting, Ric Rogers;
Stage Manager, Yvette Coit; Press, Max Eisen/Kathryn Kinsella CAST:
Debbi Blackwell-Cook (Bessie Smith), Troy Blackwell-Cook (Spirit),
Grenoldo Frazier (A Conductor)
MUSICAL NUMBERS: Gimme a Pigfoot, Haunted House Blues, I've
Got What It Takes, Amazing Grace, Alexander's Ragtime Band, There'll
Be a Hot Time in the Old Town Tonight, Smooth Tounged Negro, Down
Hearted Blues, Body and Soul, Taint Nobody's Bizness If I Do, I Ain't
Goin' to Play Second Fiddle, Back Water Blues, Devil's Gonna Git You,
Nobody Knows You When You're Down and Out, St. Louis Blues, Wasted
Life Blues, It Makes My Love Come Down, After You've Gone, Back
Mountain Blues, On Revival Day
A two-act musical biography of jazz great Bessie Smith. The action
takes place in the early 1900s.

(Theatre Four) Friday Oct. 28–Dec. 18, 1994 (35 performances and 4
previews) The Irish Repertory Theatre presents:
ALIVE, ALIVE OH; Written/Conceived by Milo O'Shea and Kitty
Sullivan; Lighting, Gregory Cohen; Set, David Raphel; Sound, Richard
Clausen; Stage Manager, Pamela Edington; Press, Chris Boneau/Adrian
Bryan-Brown/Susanne Tighe, Meredith Moore, David Wood CAST:
Milo O'Shea, Kitty Sullivan, Michael Lavine
Irish songs, poetry, Vaudevilles, drama, and pantomime.

(Cherry Lane Theatre) Friday, Oct. 28, 1994–Jan. 1, 1995 (74 perfor-
mances) Marc Routh, Richard Frankel, Randy Kelly, Carol Ostrow, and
George Tunick present:
INSIDE OUT; Music, Adryan Russ; Lyrics, Ms. Russ, Doug Haverty;
Book, Mr. Haverty; Director, Henry Fonte; Choreography, Gary Slavin;
Orchestrations, Ned Ginsburg; Musical Director/Vocal Arrangements, E.
Suzan Ott; Set, Rob Odorisio; Costumes, Gail Brassard; Lighting, Douglas
O'Flaherty; Stage Manager, Craig Palanker; Press, Chris Boneau/Adrian
Bryan-Brown/Andy Shearer, David Wood, Patty Onagan CAST: Ann
Crumb (Dena), Harriett D. Foy (Grace), Kathleen Mahony-Bennett
(Molly), Jan Maxwell (Liz), Cass Morgan (Chlo), Julie Prosser (Sage)
MUSICAL NUMBERS: Inside Out, Thin, Let It Go, I Can See You Here,
If You Really Loved Me, Yo Chlo, Behind Dena's Back, No One Inside,
Grace's Nightmare, All I Do Is Sing, Never Enough, I Don't Say Anything,
Passing of a Friend, Things Look Different, Do It at Home, Reaching Up
A musical comedy in two acts. The action follows six women who meet
weekly for group therapy. An earlier version, titled *Roleplay,* ran at the Vil-
lage Theatre in 1992.

(Soho Rep) Monday, Oct. 31–Nov. 27, 1994 (18 performances and 1
preview) Soho Rep presents:
SWOOP by Mac Wellman; Director, Julian Webber; Set/Lighting, Kyle
Chepulis; Costumes, James Sauli; Music, David van Tieghem; Sound, John
Kilgore; Stage Manager, Christine Lemme; Press, Martin Blank CAST:
Zivia Flomenhaft, Lauren Hamilton, John Leslie Harding, John Nesci
Vampires circle over Manhattan at the end of the twentieth century.

(Playhouse 125) Tuesday, Nov. 1–26, 1994 (16 performances and 5 pre-
views) Irondale Ensemble Project presents:
YOU CAN'T WIN; Written/Conceived by Jim Niesen, Joshua Taylor, and
the Irondale Ensemble; Adapted from the book by Jack Black; Director, Mr.
Niesen; Set, Kennon Rothchild; Lighting/Costumes, Hilarie Blumenthal;
Press, Peter Cromarty/Sara Chaiken CAST: Paul Ellis (Jack Black), Robin
Kurtz (Julie)
The adventures of a hobo and petty criminal turned librarian.

(Judith Anderson Theatre) Tuesday, Nov. 1–27, 1994 (21 performances
and 7 previews) Women's Project & Productions (Julia Miles, Artistic Di-
rector) presents:
WHY WE HAVE A BODY by Claire Chafee; Director, Evan Yionoulis;
Set, Peter B. Harrison; Lighting, Donald Holder; Costumes, Teresa Snider-
Stein; Sound, Janet Kalas; Stage Manager, Renee Lutz; Press, Shirley
Herz/Miller Wright CAST: Nancy Hower (Mary), Jayne Atkinson (Lili),
Trish Hawkins (Eleanor), Deborah Hedwall (Renee)
A comedy about four women.

Peter Giles, Juliet Kerr, Sean Hagerty in *Genesis*

**Adina Porter, Brenda Bakke, Dina Spybey,
Bernadette Penotti, Seth Gilliam, Kelly Wolf in** *Girl Gone*

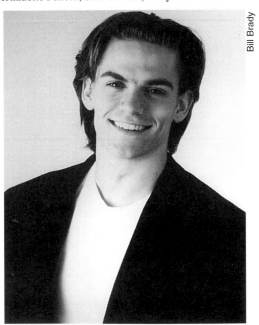

(Creative Voices Theatre) Wednesday, Nov. 2–Dec. 3, 1994 (11 performances and 5 previews) Creative Voices Theatre Co. (Kathy Towson, Managing Producer) presents:
TELL VERONICA by Tony Jerris; Director, Jeffrey J. Albright; Lighting/Sound, Kathy Towson; Set, Mr. Jerris; Press, Kevin P. McAnarney CAST: CaSandra Brooks (Babs), Lee Steinhardt (June), Lisa O'Brien (April), Wende O'Reilly (May-Louise), Jeff Paul (Brad), Joanie Schumacher (Veronica)

A new two-act comedy about t.v. talk shows.

(Neighborhood Playhouse) Thursday, Nov. 3–20, 1994 (14 performances) Deep River Productions in association with the Neighborhood Playhouse School of the Theatre presents:
GENESIS: The Mary Shelly Play by Mary Humphrey Baldridge; Director, Kathleen Patricia Cullen; Set, Harold G. Baldridge; Costumes, Astrid Brucker; Lighting, William M. Kradlak II; Sound, Dan Mendeloff; Stage Manager, David Semonin; Press, Tony Origlio/Michael Cullen CAST: Peter Giles (Lord Byron), Cameron Miller (Claire Godwin), Jay Gordon (Dr. Polidori), Juliet Kerr (Mary Godwin Shelley), Sean Hagerty (Percy Bysshe Shelley)

A drama in two acts. The action takes place at Lake Geneva, summer 1816.

(Samuel Beckett Theater) Thursday, Nov. 3–13, 1994 (10 performances) Africa Arts Theater Company:
TOWER OF BURDEN by Onukaba Adinoyi Ojo; Director, Adusah Boakye; Set, Christopher Nelson; Costumes, Blythe Colombo; Lighting, Zdenick Kriz; Sound/Stage Manager, Kevin G. Ewing, III; Press, Jonathan Slaff CAST: Arthur French (Okino), Richarda Abrams (Oiza), Messeret (Inya), Tamika Lamison (Hawker), William Francis Smith (Leader), Ahmat Jallo (Anate)

An African comedy about a man who upsets the order of things.

(Manhattan Class Company) Sunday, Nov. 6–Dec. 18, 1994 (26 performances and 7 previews) Manhattan Class Co. presents:
GIRL GONE by Jacquelyn Reingold; Director, Brian Mertes; Music, Delfeayo Marsalis; Choreography, Mark Dendy; Sets, Christine Jones; Lighting, Scott Zielinski; Costumes, Karen Perry; Sound, John Gromada; Stage Manager, James Marr; Press, Peter Cromarty/Michael Hartman CAST: Kelly Wolf (Tish), Brenda Bakke (Jean), Adina Porter (Carla/Dancer #1), Dina Spybey (Baby June/Dancer #2), Bernadette Penotti (Roxanne/Dancer #3), David Thornton (Danny), Seth Gilliam (Sam), Jack Gwaltney (Bobby)

A suspense drama performed without intermission. The action centers around a topless club.

(Eighty-Eight's) Monday, Nov. 7–Dec. 11, 1994 (5 limited performances) Eighty-Eight's presents:
I WON'T DANCE; Musical Director, Christopher Denny; Press, Jeffrey Richards/Kevin Rehac, Bruce Roberts CAST: Jon Marshall Sharp, Sandy Brown, Dana Stackpole, Natascia Diaz, Happy McPartlin

The noted dancer sings (and dances) in a musical entertainment. An earlier version of the show was performed in June 1994 at Steve McGraw's.

(Sanford Meisner Theater) Tuesday, Nov. 8–19, 1994 (12 performances) Psi/Clone Entertainment presents:
THIRTY YEARS FROM THIRTY by Mike O'Malley; Director, John Znidarsic; Press, Chris Boneau/Adrian Bryan-Brown/Jamie Morris CAST: Jim Barry, Jack Carey., Victoria Labalme, Richard Munroe, Mike O'Malley, Jackie Phelan, Maria Sucharetza

A play about post-college adults' struggles.

(Workhouse Theatre) Wednesday, Nov. 9, 1995–
PROSTHETICS AND THE TWENTY-FIVE THOUSAND DOLLAR PYRAMID by Adam Rapp; Director, Peter Flynn; Press, Jeffrey Richards/Kevin Rehac CAST: Anthony Rapp, Lauren Howard, Tim Devlin, Brendan Burke, Michael Camacho

A comedy about an All-American jock…who is gay.

Left: Jon Marshall Sharp in *I Won't Dance*

(N.Y. Film Academy) Wednesday, Nov. 9–17, 1994 (9 performances) Trust Theatre Co. presents:
BODIES, REST, AND MOTION by Roger Hedden; Director, Marcus Olson; Set, Todd Dyer; Lighting, Brian Decker; Sound, Hector Millia; Costumes, Valerie Gatchell; Stage Manager, Pam Warwick; Press, John and Gary Springer CAST: David Lawton (Nick), Emilie Ward (Carol), Joann Passantino (Beth), Anthony Michael Ruivivar (Sid), E.J. Morrison (Man/Mr. August/Newlywed), Sarah Bradley (Elizabeth), Jennie Ventriss (Mrs. Dotson/Newlywed)

A drama in two acts. The action takes place in Enfield, Connecticut.

(Currican Theatre) Thursday, Nov. 10–27, 1994 (14 performances) Little Molasses Theatre Co. presents:
CASH COW by Sander Hicks; Director, Lee Gundersheimer; Design, Aaron Cantor; Press, Howard and Barbara Atlee CAST: Frank Bartell, Thomas Coate, Sander Hicks, Jennie Maguire, David Rainey, Ann Zupa

A drama set in a twenty-four hour copy shop.

(Intar Theatre) Friday, Nov. 11–Dec. 4, 1994 (20 performances and 6 previews) Willow Cabin Theatre Compnay presents:
ANATOMY OF SOUND by Norman Corwin; Adapted/Directed by Edward Berkeley; Sets, Miguel Lopez-Castillo; Costumes, Dede Pochos, Tasha Lawrence; Lighting, Matthew McCarthy; Choreography, Nora Kasarda; Press, Jim Baldassare CAST: John Billeci, Fiona Davis, Kenneth Favre, Ken Forman, Laurence Gleason, Tasha Lawrence, Richard Long, Dede Pochos, Linda Powell, Maria Radman
PROGRAM: *Anatomy of Sound, The Undecided Molecule, Daybreak, El Capitan and the Corporal, Untitles, 14 August*

Six fully-staged radio plays from the 1940s.

(Musical Theatre Works/Linhart Theatre) Sunday, Nov. 13–27, 1994 (10 performances) Musical Theatre Works (Anthony J. Stimac, Executive Director) presents:
THE NEW YORKERS; Music/Lyrics, Cole Porter; Book, Herbert Fields; Based on a story by Peter Arno and E. Ray Goetz; Director, Anthony J. Stimac; Choreography, Lois Englund; Musical Director, Milton Granger; Arrangements, Milton Granger, Louis St. Louis; Lighting, Richard Latta; Press, Jeffrey Richards/Kevin Rehac CAST: Wynn Harmon (Hillary Trask), Jeanne Jones (Lola McGee), Sean McDermott (Al Spanish), Les Marsden (Jimmy Deegan), William Metzo (Feet McGeehan/Dr. Cortland Jenks), Tara O'Brien (Mrs. DePeyster), Patti Perkins (Mrs. Gloria Wentworth), Jack Savage (Feliz/Plague/Mildew), Robin Skye (Mona Low), Lannyl Stephens (Alice Wentworth), Clif Thorn (James Livingston), Raymond Thorne (Dr. Windham Wentworth), Lisa Arturo, Randy Donaldson, Mindy Franzese, Christopher Harrod, Emily Hsu, Timothy Kasper, Michelle Kittrell, Jeff Williams
MUSICAL NUMBERS: Just One of Those Things, Go Into Your Dance, Where Have You Been?, Say It with Gin, I Happen to Like New York, I'm Getting Myself Ready for You, Love for Sale, Most Gentlemen Don't Like Love, Rap-a-Tap on Wood, Ev'rybodee Who's Anybodee, But He Never Said He Loved Me, You're Too Far Away, Sing Sing for Sing Sing, The Extra Gal, When Love Comes Your Way, Let's Fly Away, Take Me Back to Manhattan, It Only Happens in Dreams

A 1930 musical comedy in two acts. The action takes place in New York City, 1930.

Joann Passantino   **Anthony Michael Ruivivar**
in *Bodies, Rest, and Motion*

Carol Rosegg

Willow Cabin Theatre Co. in *Anatomy of Sound*

(Sylvia & Danny Kaye Playhouse) Sunday, Nov. 13, 1994 (1 performance only) Jeffrey Finn Productions in association with Varese Sarabande Theatricals presents:
UNSUNG MUSICALS; Director/Choreography, Niki Harris; Musical Director, Tom Fay; Orchestrations, Larry Moore; Projections, Ian Hill, Wendall K. Harrington; Press, Viator/Michael Borowski CAST INCLUDES: Christine Baranski, Laurie Beechman, Liz Callaway, Jason Graae, Harry Groener, Timothy Jerome, Liz Larsen, Mary McCatty, Crista Moore, Michelle Nicastro, Lynnette Perry, Sal Viviano, Lee Wilkof, Lynne Winsterseller

A celebration of unrecorded Broadway musicals including *Welcome to the Club, Smile, Drat! The Cat!, The First, La Strada, Sherry!, The Vamp, One Two Three Four Five, We Take the Town, The Bone Room, How Do You Do I Love You, Foxy,* and *A Broadway Musical.*

(Holy Trinity) Thursday, Nov. 17–Dec. 11, 1994 (14 performances and 2 previews) Triangle Theatre Co.(Anne Chapin, Charles R. Johnson, Co-Artistic Directors) presents:
GUNPLAY by Frank Higgins; Director, Charles R. Johnson; Sets, William Moser; Costumes, Carol Brys; Lighting, Nancy Collings; Press, Susan Chicoine CAST: Chris Hietkko, Charlotte Maier, Joanna Rhinehart, Scott Whitehurst

A play about society's fascination with guns.

Left: Chris Hietikko, Joanna Rhinehart in *Gunplay*

Carol Rosegg

(Union Square Theatre) Wednesday, Nov. 16, 1994–Mar. 19, 1995 (129 performances and 6 previews) Lewis Allen, Robert Fox Ltd., Julian Schlossberg with Mitchell Maxwell and Alan J. Schuster present:
VITA & VIRGINIA; adapted by Eileen Atkins from the correspondence between Vita Sackville-West and Virginia Woolf; Director, Zoe Caldwell; Sets, Ben Edwards; Costumes, Jane Greenwood; Lighting, Rui Rita; Music/Sound, John Gromada; Stage Manager, Dianne Trulock; Press, Bill Evans/Jim Randolph CAST: Vanessa Redgrave (Vita Sackville-West), Eileen Atkins (Virginia Woolf)

A drama in two acts.

(Samuel Beckett Theatre) Thursday, Nov. 17–Dec. 11, 1994 (9 performances and 7 previews) Lark Theatre Company presents:
COMMEDIA TONITE!; Conceived by John Clinton Eisner and Erin B. Mee; Music/Lyrics/Musical Director, Frank Schiro; Based on *The Three Cuckolds* translated from the Italian by Leon Katz and *Revue Sketches* by Howard Dietz, George S. Kaufman, Dick Poston, and Billy K. Wells; Director/Choreography, Erin B. Mee; Sets, Larry Gruber; Lighting, Ed McCarthy; Costumes, Carol Brys; Commedia dell'Arte Consultant, Mace Perlman; Magic Consultant/Stage Manager, Dale Soules; Press, Chris Boneau/Adrian Bryan-Brown/Patty Onagan, Meredith Westgate-Moore CAST: Olga Bagnasco, Josie Chavez, Michael Cone, Peter Daniel, Stephen Gleason, John C. Havens, Ilyana Kadushin, Shaun Powell, Jeremy Shamos, Kim Alan Winslow

A musical comedy combining the Italian play *The Three Cuckolds* with revue sketches *The Still Alarm, On the American Plan, Stocks,* and others.

(Theatre Ten Ten) Thursday, Nov. 17–Dec. 10, 1994 (14 performances and 1 preview) Ten Ten Players present:
ARMS AND THE MAN by George Bernard Shaw; Director, David S. Macy; Set, Mike Allen; Lighting, Anthony Brian Sciarra; Costumes, Edmund Felix; Arrangements, John Canary; Stage Manager, Joe Pinter CAST: John Canary (Nicola), Katherine Harber (Catherine Petkoff), Max Jacobs (Major Petkoff), John Loprieno (Sergius Saranoff), Lynn Marie Macy (Louka), Katherine Puma (Raina Petkoff), Mark Muszynski (Russian Soldier), Rob Rogerson (Capt. Bluntschli)

A centennial production.

Left & Top: Vanessa Redgrave, Eileen Atkins in *Vita & Virginia*

(Samuel Beckett Theatre) Tuesday, Nov. 22–Dec. 7, 1994 (6 performances) Roundtable presents:
DANCING AT LUGHNASA by Brian Friel; Director, Deb Guston; Set, Myrna E. Durante; Lighting, Charlie Spickler; Dances, Theresa Cornish; Stage Manager, Suzanna Cramer; Press, Howard and Barbara Atlee CAST: Michael Walczak (Michael), Patricia Davey (Chris), Jane Jakimetz (Maggie), Caroline Palmer (Agnes), Anita Marton (Rose), Gayle Kelly Landers (Kate), Howard Atlee (Jack), William Maul (Gerry)

A drama in two acts. The action takes place in Ballybeg, County Donegal, Ireland, in August 1936.

(Perry St. Theatre) Wednesday, Nov. 23, 1994–Feb. 11, 1995 Eric Clapton, PW Productions and Paul Stuart Graham present:
THE TRUMAN CAPOTE TALK SHOW by Bob Kingdom; Director, Kevin Knight
in repertory with
DYLAN THOMAS: RETURN JOURNEY; Devised by Bob Kingdom from the writings of Dylan Thomas; Director, Anthony Hopkins
Design, Kevin Knight, Andrew Leigh; Stage Manager, Rupert Tebb; Press, Judy Jacksina CASTS: Bob Kingdom

One man theatrical portraits of two writers.

(Westbeth Theatre Center) Tuesday, Nov. 29–Dec. 17, 1994 (15 performances) returned Jan. 18–Mar. 26, 1995 (41 performances and 9 previews) Bank Street Productions in association with Westbeth Theatre Center (Arnold Engleman, Producing Director) presents:
BODY SHOP; Music/Lyrics/Book by Walter Marks; Director, Sue Lawless; Choreography, Tony Stevens; Music Director/Orchestrations, Deborah Hurwitz; Set, Tim Goodmanson; Costumes, Franne Lee; Lighting, Don Coleman; Sound, Scott Stauffer; Stage Manager, Laura Josepher; Press, (1st run)Shirley Herz/David Lotz, (return) Jim Baldassare CAST: Tiffany Cooper succeeded by Paesan Wilson (Keisha), Justin DiCostanzo (Esmeralda), Donna Drake (Leanne), Susan Flynn (Tiffany Silver), Beth Glover (Samantha), Christopher Scott succeeded by Russell Goldberg(Franklin Francesa/Others), Jodi Stevens (Doris), Marine Jahan (Angeline)
MUSICAL NUMBERS: Desire, Maybe It's Not Too Late, You're a Natural, Suffer, Esmeralda (1st run), Angeline(return)You Like Me, My Turn, Class Act, Doris' Nightmare, A Matter of Time, Mr. Maybe, The Woman in Me, Find a Way, Virtual Sexuality, Finale

A musical in two acts. The action takes place in a small-town strip club.

(Actors' Playhouse) Tuesday, Nov. 29– Elliot Martin and Ron Shapiro in association with Robert R. Blume present:
ME AND JEZEBEL by Elizabeth Fuller; Director, Mark S. Graham; Set/Lighting, Gordon Link; Stage Manager, Katie Rader; Press, Jeffrey Richards/Kevin Rehac CAST: Elizabeth Fuller (Herself), Louise DuArt (Bette Davis)

A comedy in two acts. The action takes place in Westport, CT, spring 1985. Based on the true experiences of the author, the play was performed earlier in the season at the Blaroom with Randy Allen as Bette Davis. Mr Allen fell ill during the rehearsal period for this version.

Bob Kingdon in *Truman Capote Talk Show*

Carol Rosegg

(clockwise from L) Jodi Stevens, Justine DiConstanzo, Susan Flynn, Beth Glover, Tiffany Cooper, Donna Drake in *Body Shop*

(Greenwich St. Theatre) Wednesday, Nov. 30–Dec. 18, 1994 (11 performances and 4 previews) Chain Lightning Theatre (Claire Higgins, Producer; Todd Pieper, Artistic Director) presents:
SHORT PLAY FESTIVAL; Lighting, Scott Clyve; Stage Manager, Jason Brouillard; Press, Jim Baldassare
SHELTER by Sanford Stokes; Director, Todd Pieper CAST: Kricker James (Flash), Max Faugno (Jinx), Leslie Colucci (Baby Cakes)
LIVE WITNESS by Jim Neu; Director, Joel Goldes CAST: Cheryl Horne, Jerry Mettner
OLDER PEOPLE by John Ford Noonan; Director, Marvin Starkman CAST: Mark Barkan, Tina Bruno, Les Goldman, Cam Kornman, Frank O'Brian, Sandi Skoknick

(Judson Church) Wednesday, Nov. 30, 1994–Jan. 1, 1995 (23 performances and 6 previews) Working Theatre, Downtown Art Co. and Judson Church present:
HEROES AND SAINTS by Cherrie Moraga; Director, Albert Takazauckas; Set, Ann Paterson; Lighting, Kurt Landisman; Costumes, Deborah Nadoolman; Press, David Rothenberg CAST: Isaiah Cazares, Doris DiFarnecio, Matt Edwards, Elsie Hilario, Adriana Inchausregui, Mario Mendoza, Claudia Rocofort, Jualkyris Santiago, Marta Vidal

A drama about Chicano farm workers.

Carol Rosegg

Louise DuArt, Elizabeth Fuller in *Me and Jezebel*

(30th St. Theatre) Wednesday, Nov. 30–Dec. 17, 1994 (11 performances and 4 previews) Outlaw Entertainment by special arrangement with the Miranda Theatre Co. presents:
SHADES OF GREY by Kirk Aanes; Director, Nick Gregory; Set, Leonel Valle; Lighting, Jeff Croiter; Stage Manager, David Smith; Press, Peter Cromarty/Michael Hartman CAST: Jan Leslie Harding (Lois), Stewart Clarke (Tom), Brian Tarantina (Ringo)

A comedy performed without intermission. The action takes place in the SoHo artists section of New York City.

(St. Bart's Playhouse) Thursday, Dec. 1–11, 1994 (7 performances) Ireneusz and George Gordon present:
THE JEWELER'S SHOP by Karol Wojtyla (Pope John Paul II); Director, Eric Wykurz; Press, Peter Cromarty/Michael Hartman CAST: Ed Hardesty, Mona Kruski, Kerry Casserly, Robert K. Casserly, Christina Fuller, Rachelle Fleming, Jerry Rago, John Sacco

A drama in three acts. Pope John Paul II wrote, acted and directed in his native Poland during WWII.

(Main St. Theatre) Thursday, Dec. 1–19, 1994 (16 performances) Main St. Theatre & Dance Alliance presents:
JUST ANOTHER LOUSY MUSICAL by Worth Howe, Nancy Howe and John W. Calder, III; Director, Worth Howe; Choreography, Diana Baffa-Brill; Musical Director/Arrangements, Bob McDowell; Costumes, Cathy Kross; Lighting, Michael Gottlieb CAST: Natalie Kaye Arazi, Tom Dusenbury, Richard P. Gang, Joe Heffernan, Dane Knell, Emily Lester, Alicia Litwin, David B. McDonald, Robb McKindles, Julia Simpson, Jordan Trumbo

(Pulse Ensemble Theatre) Thursday, Dec. 1–19, 1994 (14 performances and 1 preview) Pulse Ensemble (Alexa Kelly, Artistic Director) presents:
OH WHAT A LOVELY WAR by Joan Littlewood, Theatre Workshop and Charles Clinton; Director, Alexa Kelly; Musical Director, Marc di Minno; Costumes, Fran Cole; Set, Keven Lock; Lighting, Jeffrey S. Koger; Sound, Mitchell Simchowitz; Choreography, Barry McNabb; Stage Manager, Dana Ortiz; Press, Susan L. Schulman CAST: Simon Boughey, Katherine Brecka, Dan Browning, Ezio Catarelli, Sandra Loftman Drakes, Mark Eis, Kate Fitzgerald, Patrick Hillan, Schecter Lee, Brian O'Sullivan, Richard Penn, Paula Roth, Penelope Smith, Jay Veduccio

A new production of the 1963 British musical satire. The original NYC production opened at the Broadhurst in September, 1964.

(CSC Theatre) Thursday, Dec. 1–23, 1994 (19 performances and 5 previews) Falstaff presents:
MACBETH by William Shakespeare; Director, Jack Stehlin; Set, Mark Symczak; Costumes, Jennifer Difiglia; Lighting, Adam Silverman; Movement, Daniel Banks; Video, Damond Gallagher; Stage Manager, Catherine Norberg; Press, Tony Origlio/Stephen Murray CAST: Patrice Johnson (Weird Sister/Gentlewoman), Stacy Rukeyser (Lady Macduff/Weird Sister), Luisa Sermol (Scottish Doctor/Weird Sister), Jeff Guyton (Caitness/Fleance), William Meisle (Duncan/Porter/Old man/Siward), Neal Huff (Malcolm/Murderer/Son to Macduff), Mark Feurstein (Doanlbain/Seyton), Troy Ruptash (Lennox), John Fitzgibbon (Rosse), Jack Stehlin (Macbeth), Matt Servitto (Banquo), Alyssa Bresnahan (Lady Macbeth/Young Siward), Sebastian Roche (Macduff/Murderer)

Performed with one intermission.

Stewart Clarke, Jan Leslie Harding in *Shades of Grey*

Jack Stehlin, Alyssa Bresnahan in *Macbeth*

(Harold Clurman Theater) Friday, Dec. 2–11, 1994 (13 performances) Heritage Productions present:
DAMES AT SEA; Music, Jim Wise; Lyrics/Book, George Haimsohn, Robin Miller; Director, Bob Bogdanoff; Choreography, Mark Santoro; Musical Director, Ed Goldschneider; Set/Lighting, James Hunter; Costumes, Bridget Bartlett; Sound, B.C. Keller; Stage Manager, David Winitsky CAST: Sally Ann Swarm (Mona Kent), Stephen Belida (Hennesey/Captain), Connie SaLoutos (Joan), Kristin Chenoweth (Ruby), Tom Stuart (Dick), Stephen Hope (Lucky)
MUSICAL NUMBERS: Wall Street, It's You, Broadway Baby, That Mister of Mine, Choo-Choo Honeymoon, Sailor of My Dreams, Singapore Sue, Good Times are Here to Stay, Dames at Sea, The Beguine, Raining in My Heart, There's Something about You, Echo Waltz, Star Tar, Let's Have a Simple Wedding

A musical comedy in two acts.

Tom Stuart in *Dames at Sea*

(Soho Rep) Friday, Dec. 2–17, 1994 (11 performances) abode Theatre Co. presents:
THE EIGHT: Reindeer Monologues by Jeff Goode CAST INCLUDES: James McCauley, Erin Quinn Purcell, Vin Knight
  A black comedy about Santa's reindeer.

(Theatre Row Theatre) Thursday, Dec. 8–18, 1994 Riverside Opera Ensemble presents:
WHERE OR WHEN...; Music, Richard Rodgers; Lyrics, Lorenz Hart; Conception/Direction, Stephen Pickover; Musical Director/Arrangements, Nathan Matthews; Choreography, Robin Reseen; Set, Michael Fagin; Costumes, Clifford Capone; Lighting, Richard Coumbs; Stage Manager, Robert V. Thurber; Press, Maryellen Kernaghan CAST: Hunter Bell, Betsi Morrison, Jay Poindexter, Michael Ricciardone, Dawn Spare, Sonja Stuart
  A musical revue in two acts.

(Intar Theatre) Thursday, Dec. 8–18, 1994 (8 performances and 2 previews) PASSAJJ Productions presents:
ONCE/TWICE; Music/Lyrics, Adaptation by Paul Dick; Director, Thomas Gruenwald; Musical Director, Jonathan Smith; Set/Lighting, Jack Mehler; Costumes, Crystal Thompson; Choreography, Brian Barrentine; Stage Manager, Elizabeth Reeves; Press, Tony Origlio/Tim Flaherty, Stephen Murray
ONCE; Based on the play *A Sunny Morning* by Serafin and Joaquin Alvarez Quintero CAST: Richard Ianni (Don Gonzalo), Ellen Martin (Dona Laura), Michelle Colwill (Petra), Brian Barrentine (Juanito), Lawrence Asher (Park Attendant)
  MUSICAL NUMBERS: Changing Seasons, A Sunny Morning, When You Grow Old: Senile Old Lady-Crabby Old Man, Thirty Years Ago, In a Villa in Valencia, His Dream, Once, Finale
TWICE; Based on the play *The Boor* by Anton Chekhov CAST: Richard Ianni (Grigori Smirnov), Ellen Martin (Elena Popov), Lawrence Asher (Luka), Brian Barrentine (Alexi), Michelle Colwill (Olga)
  MUSICAL NUMBERS: Woe, My My the Master Is Dead, Faithful Forever, A Year of Mourning in Two Minutes, Go, If the Answer Is No, Madrigal for a Misogynist, Show Me a Man, What a Woman, Faithful Forever, Changing Seasons
  Two one-act musicals.

(Judith Anderson Theatre) Friday, Dec. 9–18, 1994 (9 performances) The Other Theatre presents:
THREE BY BECKETT; Sets, Jun Maeda; Lighting, Katy Orrick, Beverly Emmons; Sound, John Gromada; Costumes, Mary Brecht; Press, Shirley Herz/David Lotz
THAT TIME (1974); Director, Joseph Chaikin CAST: Ron Faber
PLAY (1963); Director, Mary Forcade CAST: Wendy vanden Heuvel, Henry Steele, Rosemary Quinn
NOT I (1972); Director, Luly Santangelo CAST: Wendy vanden Heuvel
  Three rarely seen Samuel Beckett one-acts.

Kamron Hinatsu

Brooke Smith, John Cameron Mitchell in *Little Monsters*

(Cucaracha Theater) Saturday, Dec. 10–29, 1994 (13 performances) Seraphim Theater Company presents:
LITTLE MONSTERS by Alan Bowne; Director, David Saint; Set, Brad Stokes; Lighting, Ken Posner; Costumes, Laura Cunningham; Sound, Michael Tkach; Fights, Rick Sordelet; Stage Manager, John Harmon; Press, Viator/Michael Borowski CAST: John Cameron Mitchell (Kip), Gil Bellows (3-Yard), Brooke Smith (Gooey), Yusef Bulos (Maurice)
  A drama in two acts. The action takes place in a New York apartment.

(Metropolitan Playhouse) Saturday, Dec. 10–31, 1994 (16 performances) Parsifal's Productions presents:
THE BUTTERFINGERS ANGEL by William Gibson; Director, Mary Ethel Schmidt; Musical Direction, Patrick Barnes; Choreography, Teri Seier; Dances, Diana Walker; Fights, Robert Ruffin; Costumes, Donna Lettman; Set, Martin Kooi; Lighting, Brian Orter; Stage Manager, Suzanne Rose; Press, Richard Grunn CAST: Patrick Barnes, David Marantz, Jack Serra (Lout/King), Dennis Carrig (Joseph), Kristin Stewart Chase (Sheep), Page Clements (Tree), William Driscoll (Angel), Craig Green (Man in Grey), John Kooi (Donkey), Stephen LaViscount (Cow), Chris McGinn, Sharron Amy Swartz (A Woman), Leah McSweeney (Girl), Terri Towns (Mary)
  A re-telling of the Nativity story.

Gerry Goodstein

Ron Faber in *That Time*

98

(Harold Clurman Theater) Thursday, Dec. 15, 1994–Mar. 12, 1995 The Christabelle Co. presents:
ANDREW MY DEAREST ONE by Mary Mitchell; Director, Tanya Kane-Parry; Set, Salvatore Tagliarino, Eddie Krumins; Sound, David Ferdinand/One Dream; Lighting, Jeffery S. Koger; Stage Manager, Valerie Lau-Kee; Press, Wesley Stahler CAST: Jason Tyler White, Rafael Petlock (Andrew-alternating), Brenda Smiley (Nancy Sue)

An unusual love story in two acts. The action takes place in Manhattan.

(Charles Ludlam Theater) Wednesday, Dec. 28, 1994–April 22, 1995 (83 Performances and 17 previews) The Ridiculous Theatrical Co. presents:
CARMEN; Adapted/Directed by Everett Quinton; Sets, Tom Greenfield; Sound, Mark Bennett; Lighting, Richard Currie; Costumes, Mr. Quinton, Cory Lippiello,Toni Nanette Thompson; Choreography, Barbara Allen; Stage Manager, Amy Deaton Smith; Press, Philip Rinaldi/Tony Stavick CAST: Larry McLeon (Rita/Beverly Howard/Odalee/Mercedes), Michael Van Meter (Anita/Carolina Garrison/Odaloo/Frasquita), Jimmy Szczepanek (Chita/Dottie Olinski/Odalaa/Manuela), Julia Dares (Capt. Zoriega/Torre Adore), Lenys Sama (Don Johnson), Cheryl Reeves (Micaela), Everett Quinton (Carmen), Eureka (Warden Harper), Beth Dodye Bass (Lily Pastia)

A comic Carmen.

(John Houseman Theatre) Sunday, Jan. 1–Feb. 18, 1996 (330 performances) John Houseman Theatre Co. (Eric Krebs, Artistic Director) presents:
TOO JEWISH?; Written/Performed by Avi Hoffman; Musical Director, Ben Schaechter; Press, David Rothenberg
MUSICAL NUMBERS: Overture, *Afn Pripetshik*, *Afn Veg Shteyt a Boym*, *Odenameya*, Yiddish Medley, Not on the Top, Cardova the Bronx Casanova, I'm a Litvak She's a Galitz, *Oom-glick* Blues, *Heym Afn Range*, #4 *Humentash* Lane, Quiet Evening, I Can't Wait Till You Arrive, Faith in Whom

A musical comedy revue from the Yiddish theatre.

(28th St. Theater) Wednesday, Jan. 4–28, 1995 (18 performances and 6 previews) Tidewater Productions in association with Jerry Scher presents:
L.A. by Angus Fraser; Director, William Piserchio; Set, Curtis Phillips; Lighting, Juliet Hampel; Sound, David H. Barash; Stage Manager, Brian D. White; Press, Jim Baldassare CAST: David James O'Brien (Bobby), Michael Ouimet (Frank), Glory (Theresa V. Ferraro (Glory)

A black comedy set in L.A., six months after the 1992 riots.

Rafael Petlock, Brenda Smiley in *Andrew My Dearest One*

Lenys Sama, Everett Quinton in *Carmen*

Kathleen Larson, Steve Allen in *The Mikado*

(Looking Glass Theatre) Thursday, Jan. 5–Mar. 12, 1995 (24 performances) Looking Glass Theatre (Justine Lambert, Artistic Director) presents:
THE PLAYBOY OF THE WESTERN WORLD by J.M. Synge; Director, David Brody; Stage Manager, Frances Smyth PRESS: John Regis (Christy Mahon), Judy Ramakers (Widow Quinn), Phoebe Jonas (Pegeen Mike), John Keating, Emmett McConnell, Lorraine Maguire

(Symphony Space) Thursday, Jan. 5–15, 1995 (10 performances) New York Gilbert & Sullivan Players present
THE MIKADO or The Town of Titipu; Music, Sir Arthur Sullivan; Libretto, W.S. Gilbert; Directors, Albert Bergeret, Bill Fabris; Music Director, Mr. Bergeret; Lighting, Keith Kalohelani; Set, Albere; Costumes, Gail J. Wofford, Kayko Nakamura; Press, Francine L. Trevens CAST: Steve Allen (Mikado of Japan), Marc Heller (Nanki-Poo), Stephen O'Brien (Ko-Ko), Philip Reilly (Pooh-Bah), Cedric Cannon (Pish-Tush), Belinda Bronaugh, Lynne Vardaman (Yum-Yum), Katie Geissinger, Carrie Wilshusen (Pitti-Sing), Karen Dixon, Monika Kendall (Peep-Bo), Kathleen Larson, Joy Hermanlyn (Katisha), Shannon Carson, Karen Cholhan, Joanne Cuccia, Charlotte Detrick, Katie Neuser, Margaretha Ohse, Jenny Ryan, Luisa Sauter (Schoolgirls); Jeff Bannon, Christopher Carey, Shawn Churchman, Michael Collins, Gary Dimon, Alan Hill, Travis Messinger, Sal Midolo (Noblemen), Mark Edmonds, Victoria Devany, Laura Palladino, Paul Sigrist (Coolies/Matrons), David Benetello, Charles Bergeret, Genevieve Bergeret, Rebecca Stein Morhaim (Children)

The 1885 operetta in two acts. The setting is a Japanese garden.

(Samuel Beckett Theatre) Friday, Jan. 6–15, 1995 (7 performances and 2 previews) AST Co./New Day Rep presents:
THE REHEARSAL or Love's Punishment by Jean Anouilh; Director, John Daines; Set, Paul Wonsek; Lighting, Philip D. Widmer; Costumes, Lee J. Austin; Stage Manager, Randy Lawson; Press, Jeffrey Richards/Kevin Rehac CAST: Peter Johnson (M. Damiens), David Denson (Valet), Amy Danis (Countess), Shannon Daley (Maid), George Millenbach (Count), Fiona Hutchison (Hortensia), Robert Ierardi (Hero), Jerry Della Salla (Villebosse), Sarah Graham Hayes (Lucille)

A comedy in two acts. The action takes place in France at a rehearsal of *The Double Inconstancy*, 1950.

(Intar Theatre) Wednesday, Jan. 11–29, 1995 (14 performances and 4 previews) Intar Hispanic American Arts Center (Max Ferrz, Artistic Director; David Minton, Managing Director) presents:
HEART OF THE EARTH: A POPOL VUH STORY; Music, Glen Valez; Book, Cherrie Moraga; Conception/Direction/Masks/Puppets by Ralph Lee; Choreography, Sigfrido Aguilar; Set, Donald Eastman; Costumes, Caryn Neman; Lighting, Katy Orrick, Ken Allaire; Press, Shirley Herz/Miller Wright CAST: Caroline Stephanie Clay (Tecolote/Rat/Wooden Man), Curtiss Cook (Cucumatz/Patriarchal Pus), Doris Difarnecio (Daykeeper/Ixmucane/Bat), William Ha'o (Ixpiyacoc/Blood Sausage), Joe Herrera (Hunapu I and II), Adriana Inchaustegui (Ixquic/Blood Woman/Conejo), David Norona (Vucub/Ixbalanque)

A drama performed without intermission. The action is based on ancient Mayan myths.

(Synchronicity Space) Thursday, Jan. 12–29, 1995 (14 performances) The Jewish Theater of New York presents:
ONE HUNDRED GATES by Tuvia Tenenbom; Director, Howard Rosen CAST: Reiko Aylesworth, Alexander Barnett, Suzanne Friedline, Alice Greenberg, Eric Kuttner, Jenny Mandel, John Marino, Charles Roden, Michael Suvorov

A drama set in Jerusalem.

(Soho Rep) Thursday, Jan. 12–Feb. 12, 1995 (24 performances) Soho Rep presents:
THE HOUSE OF YES by Wendy MacLeod; Director, Julian Webber; Set, Sarah Lambert; Costumes, James Sauli; Lighting, Joe Saint; Music, David van Tieghem; Sound, John Kilgore; Press, Holly Becker CAST: Chris Eigeman (Marty), Neal Huff (Anthony), Allison Janney (Mrs. Pascal), Jodie Markell (Jodie-O), Kim Soden (Lesley)

A comedy about incest and murder.

(Miranda Theatre) Wednesday, Jan. 18–Feb. 11, 1995 (14 performances and 6 previews) Miranda Theatre Co. (Valentina Fratti, Artistic Director; Cathy Trinant Buxton, Executive Director) presents:
KIDNAPPED by Sean O'Connor; Director, Jude Schanzer; Set, Eric Lowell Renschler; Lighting, Scott Griffin; Costumes, Patrick Bevilacqua, Rodney Munoz; Fights, B.H. Barry; Music, George Bonds; Stage Manager, Jason Brouillard; Press, Peter Cromarty/Michael Hartman CAST: Sally Frontman (Marylee), Raymond Haigler (Tyrone), Earle Hugens (Happy Man/Young Man/Tyrone Jr.), Ibi Janko (Nurse MacNamara/Betty Ann Pomeroy/Madonna), Tim McCracken (Dr. Barden/Scoutmaster/Daniel Boone), Clark Middleton (Joe), Andre Sogliuzzo (Barney/Jed), Jo Twiss (Nurse Connelly/Mrs. McKensie/Betsy Ross), George Bonds (Singer)

A dark comedy in two acts. The action travels through time with descendants of Daniel Boone and Betsy Ross.

George Millenbach, Fiona Hutchison in *The Rehearsal*

Heart of the Earth

(Primary Stages) Wednesday, Jan. 18–Feb. 19, 1995 (13 performances and 21 previews) Primary Stages (Casey Childs, Artistic Director) presents:
I SENT A LETTER TO MY LOVE; Music, Melissa Manchester; Lyrics, Jeffrey Sweet, Ms. Manchester; Book, Mr. Sweet; Based on the novel by Bernice Rubens; Director, Pat Birch; Musical Director, Aaron Hagan; Arrangements, Ms. Manchester, Mr. Hagan; Set, James Noone; Lighting, Kirk Bookman; Costumes, Rodney Munoz; Sound, Jim Van Bergen; Stage Manager, Colleen Marie Davis; Press, Tony Origlio/Stephen Murray CAST: Lynne Winterstellar (Amy), Robert Westenberg (Stan), John Hickok (Jimmy), Bethe B. Austin (Gwen), Meagen Fay (Miss Morgan)
MUSICAL NUMBERS: Prologue, Across the Lake, God Never Closes a Door, What I Am, Lady Seeks Gentleman, Grass Between My Toes, Your Prince, Very Truly Yours, Rosy Red, Pants Angela, Perfect Timing, Chance of You, I Never Knew, Someone in a Chair, The Day I Meet My Friend, Last Night, Change in the Air

A musical in two acts. The action takes place in a small town in Ohio, 1954.

Left: Robert Westenberg, Lynne Wintersteller, Bethe B. Austin in *I Sent a Letter to My Love*

(One Dream Theatre) Thursday, Jan. 19–Feb. 12, 1995 (19 performances) One Dream (Laine Valentino and David Ferdinand, Artistic Directors) presents:
LIVING IN PIECES; Written/Performed by Julie Flanders; Director, Stephen Jobes; Lighting, Christien Methot; Costumes, Markas Henry; Movement, Todd Williams; Press, David Rothenberg
A darkly comic monologue.

(American Place Theatre) Wednesday, Jan. 25–Mar. 26, 1995 American Place Theatre presents:
BEAUTY'S DAUGHTER; Written/Performed by Dael Orlandersmith; Director, Peter Askin; Set, Joel Reynolds; Lighting, Jane Reisman; Sound, Bruce Ellman; Press, Jonathan Slaff
The poet/performer creates a variety of characters.

(Judith Anderson Theatre) Thursday, Jan. 26–Feb. 4, 1995 (9 performances) Fertile Ground presents:
NIAGARA FALLS AND SO DO I; Written/Performed by Gary Schiro; Director, Robert Burns; Lighting, Roma Flowers; Press, David Rothenberg
A monologue about returning home.

(St. Clement's) Friday, Jan. 27–April 8, 1995 (44 performances and 30 previews) Theatre for a New Audience (Jeffrey Horowitz, Artistic/Producing Director; Michael Solomon, General Manager) presents:
HENRY VI by William Shakespeare; Director, Barry Kyle; Sets, Derek McLane; Costumes, Constance Hoffman; Lighting, Donald Holder; Music, Michael Ward; Fights, J. Allen Suddeth; Movement, Daniel Banks; Stage Manager, James Latus; Press, Merle Debuskey/Susan Chicoine, Wylie Strout CAST: Philip Goodwin (Henry VI), John Campoin (York), Robert Stattel (Humphrey/Old Clifford/Father), Jack Wetherall (Warwick), Ellen Barber (Countess/Eleanor Cobham/Lady Grey), Nicole Callender (Joan/Asnath/Lady Bona), Geoffrey P. Cantor (Somerset/Smith/Lord Rivers/Son), George Demas (Alencon/Basset/Talbot's Army/Guard/Sheriff), Curzon Dobell (Suffolk/James Cromer/Clarenece), Arthur French (Duke of Bedford/Salisbury/Iden), Pamela Gray (Margaret/Porter), Gaby Gulielmetti (Young Henry/Prince of Wales), Mark Hammer (Beaufort/Winchester/Lord Saye/Northumberland), David Patrick Kelly (Talbot/Jack Cade/Simpcox, John Montgomery), Frank Lowe (Mortimer/Exeter), Mark Niebuhr (2nd Messenger/Burgandy/Simpcox's Wife/Stafford/Edward), Tom Oppenheim (Reignier/Bolingbroke/Oxford), Heath Patellis (John Talbot/Earl of Rutland), Michael Rudko (Dauphin/Hume/Butcher/Lewis of France), Trellis Stepter (Richard Crookback/3rd Messenger.Margery Jourdain/1st Murderer), Jamie C. Ward (Gargrave/Vernon/Captain/Servant/Messenger/Soldier/Officer of Ireland/Montague), John Wojda (Bastard of Orleans/John Stanley/2nd Murderer/Walter Whitmore/Hastings/Young Clifford), Sean Grissom, Jules Cohen (Music performers)
Shakespeare's trilogy distilled into *The Contention (Part I)* and *The Civil War (Part II).*

Lisa M. Bostnar, Ronda Music, Paula Ewin, Jennifer Gordon in *Dancing at Lughnasa*

Curzon Dobell, Pamela Gray, Philip Goodwin in *Henry VI*

June Havoc, Shirl Bernheim in *Old Lady's Guide to Survival*

(Lamb's Theatre) Saturday, Jan. 28–Mar. 5, 1995 (22 performances and 20 previews) Daniel Mayer Selznick presents:
THE OLD LADY'S GUIDE TO SURVIVAL by Mayo Simon; Director, Alan Mandell; Set, Douglas W. Schmidt; Costumes, Marianna Elliott; Lighting, Dennis Parichy; Sound, Jim Capenos; Stage Manager, Susan Slagle; Press, Keith Sherman/Jim Byk, Stuart Ginsberg CAST: June Havoc (Netty), Shirl Bernheim (Shprintzy)
A drama in two acts. The action takes place in San Diego, California.

(Theatre Row Theatre) Tuesday, Jan. 31–Feb. 18, 1995 (15 performances) The Playful Repertory Co. presents:
THE GREEN TURTLE by Patrick Gabridge; Director, Michael MacKenzie Wills; Set, Eric Lowell Renschler; Lighting, Traci Klainer-McDonnell; Press, Richard Kornberg/Tom Naro CAST: Cheryl Ann Allen, Dean Bradshaw, Teddy Coluca, Dana Grant, Jill Leslie, Tim Miller, Alex Roe, Jayne Ross, JoAnn Wahl
A drama set in an old diner.

(Sanford Meisner Theatre) Thursday, Feb. 2–19, 1995 (12 performances) Perkasie Productions presents:
DANCING AT LUGHNASA by Brian Friel; Director, Steven Keim; Costumes, Blythe Columbo; Stage Manager, Fran Feil CAST: Alan Walker (Michael), Ronda Music (Chris), Paula Ewin (Maggie), Lisa M. Bostnar (Agnes), Jennifer Gordon (Rose), Mary Aufman (Kate), John Szura (Jack), Stephen Kaiser (Gerry)
A drama in two acts. The action takes place in Ballybeg, County Donegal, Ireland in 1936.

(Ohio Theater) Thursday, Feb. 2–20, 1995 (29 performances) Watermark Theater presents:
WORDFIRE FESTIVAL '95; Press, Shirley Herz/Stephen Barry
MY LEFT BREAST: Written/Performed by Susan Miller; Director, Nela Wagman
JUST BENEATH MY SKIN; Written/Performed by Patricia Scanlon
ONE MORMON SHOW; Written/Performed by Emmett Foster
LATER THAT NIGHT PERFORMERS: Tom Burnett, Kevin Draine, Tim Moeagan, David Simpatico, Toni Schlesinger, Brad Zimmerman
 Solo spoken word performances.

(Metropolitan Playhouse) Thursday, Feb. 2–4, 1995 (4 performances) Parsifal's Productions presents:
THE MORALITY OF DEATH by Robert Ruffin; Director, Rebecca Taylor CAST: Patrick Barnes, David Carson, Michelle deFranco, Sandra Drakes, John Fritz, Gary Glor, Craig Green, Amy N. Hawkes, Cynthia Hewett, Kirk Oberholtzer
 A twisted morality play.

(Musical Theatre Works) Friday, Feb. 3–12, 1995 (10 performances) Musical Theatre Works (Anthony J. Stimac, Artistic Director) presents:
OEDIPUS-PRIVATE EYE; Music, Matthew Sklar; Lyrics/Book/Direction, Chad Beguelin; Musical Director, Fred Lassen; Choreography, Patricia Wilcox; Press, Jeffrey Richards/Kevin Rehac CAST: George Merrick (Oedipus), Andrew Driscoll, Nicola Egan, Terence Goodman, Jan Maxwell, Lynette Perry, Gwen Stewart, Bellamy Young
 A musical transporting the ancient Greek tragedy to the 1940s.

(Synchronicity Space) Friday, Feb. 3–19, 1995 (13 performances) Synchronicity Theatre Group presents:
PORTRAIT OF A WOMAN by Michael Vinaver; Director, Peter Sylvester; Set, Mark Symczak; Lighting, David Alan Comstock CAST: Chris Burmester, Julianne Carpenter, Nora Colpman, Bill Dante, Max Miller, Bruce Mohat, John Moraitis, Terry O'Brien, Peter Palazzo, Cate Smit, Wayne Tetrick
 A drama, based on actual events, set in Paris during the early 1950s.

(Florence Mission) Friday, Feb. 3–26, 1995 (18 performances) Florence Mission Project in association with the McNight Foundation presents:
THE BEEKEEPER'S DAUGHTER; Written/Directed by Karen Malpede; Set, Maxine Willi Kleine; Costumes, Sally Ann Parsons; Lighting, Tony Giovanetti CAST: George Bartenieff, Lee Nagrin, Christen Clifford, Brendan Corbalis, Carolyn Goelzer
 A drama set on a Greek island.

(Theatre Off Park) Friday, Feb. 3–11, 1995 (6 performances and 3 previews) SDD Productions in conjunction with Betty and Harold Levitt, and Kathleen Ruen present:
MOST MEN ARE; Music/Lyrics/Book/Musical Direction by Stephen Dolginoff; Director, Daniel Simmons; Arrangements, Michael Patrick Walker, James Conant; Lighting, Jeffrey Zeidman; Graphics, Linda Thomas; Stage Manager, Melinda Berk; Press, Shirley Herz/Sam Rudy, Stephen Barry CAST: James Heatherly (Scott), Joel Carlton (Russ), Terrance Flynn (Larry), Mark Peters (Jack)
MUSICAL NUMBERS: Overture, You Won't Die Alone, Not That Strong, Scott, He Can Still Hear You, What If, Daddy'd Playboy Magazines, Something Bound to Begin, The Perfect Place on Christopher Street, I Couldn't Care Less, Never Disappointed Him, Potential, Steal My Thunder, We Could Rent a Movie, Away, When I Come Home at Night, Gotta Get Outta Here, Most Men Are, Better Not to Know, My Body, Urban Legend, Maybe Some Weekend
 A musical performed without intermission. The action takes place in New York City and concerns three important men in one young man's life—father, brother, and lover.

(Hamlet of Bank Street) Saturday, Feb. 4–26, 1995 (13 performances and 3 previews) Carry Me Ackee Productions and Westbeth Artists Residents Council presents:
ACTS OF FAITH; Written/Directed by Stephen Mantin; Press, Mayre Ferrer CAST: Jack Marks (Sidney Salaman), Sheila Evans (Cynthia Johnson)

Emmett Foster, Patricia Scanlon, Susan Miller in *Wordfire Festival*

(top to bottom) Mark Peters, James Heatherly, Joel Carter in *Most Men Are*

102

Joan Marcus

Robert Prosky, Ken Howard, John Cunningham in *Camping with Henry and Tom*

(Lucille Lortel Theatre) Tuesday, Feb. 7–May 7, 1995 (88 performances) Daryl Roth, Wind Dancer Theatre, Randall L. Wreghitt in association with Lucille Lortel present:
CAMPING WITH HENRY & TOM by Mark St. Germain; Director, Paul Lazarus; Set, James Leonard Joy; Costumes, Ann Hould-Ward; Lighting, Phil Monat; Sound, Otts Munderloh; Stage Manager, Renee Lutz; Press, Philip Rinaldi/James Morrison CAST: John Cunningham (Henry Ford), Ken Howard (Warren G. Harding), Robert Prosky (Thomas Alva Edison), John Prosky (Col. Edmund Starling)
A fact-suggested comedy in two acts. The action takes place in the woods outside Licking Creek, MD on July 24, 1921.

(American Place Theatre) Wednesday, Feb. 8–March 26, 1995 (24 performances and 11 previews) American Place Theatre (Wynn Handman, Artistic Director; Susannah Halston, Executive Director) presents:
SPOONBREAD AND STRAWBERRY WINE by Norma Jean Darden and Carole Darden; Director, Josh Broder; Set, Kennon Rothchild; Lighting, Christopher Boll; Songs, Jou Jou Papailler; Stage Manager, Sue Jane Stoker; Press, Jonathan Slaff CAST: Norma Jean Darden, Jou Jou Papailler
An evening of food, songs and family discoveries.

Jonathan Slaff

**Jou Jou Papailler, Norma Jean Darden
in** *Spoonbread and Strawberry Wine*

(St. Peter's) Thursday, Feb .9–26, 1995 (12 performances) Barry Cole and Barry McNabb in association with the York Theatre Co. present:
LOVE FOR BETTER & VERSE; Concieved/Written/Performed by Barbara Feldon; Director, Barry McNabb; Set, James Morgan; Lighting, Mary Jo Dondlinger; Music, Ed Linderman; Sound, Eric Tallorico, Jim van Bergen; Stage Manager, Alan Bluestone; Press, Keith Sherman/Jim Byk, Stuart Ginsberg
Compilation of poetry, prose, and song.

(West Bank Downstairs) Thursday, Feb. 9–March 19, 1995 (30 performances) West Bank presents:
KING MACKEREL & THE BLUES ARE RUNNING by Bland Simpson and Jim Wann; Additional Material, Jerry Leath Mills, Cass Morgan, John Dos Passos; Director, John L. Haber; Design, Fred Buchholz; Lighting, Joe Kentner; Sound, Hank Meiman; Stage Manager, Kevin Brannick; Press, Chris Boneau/Adrian Bryan-Brown/Jim Campbell CAST:Don Dixon, Bland Simpson, Jim Wann (The Coastal Cohorts)
MUSICAL NUMBERS: King Mackrel & the Blues are Running, Corncake Inlet Inn, Food Chain, Timeless, Ain't that Something?, Rushing the Season, Joyride, Whose Idea Was This?, Down By the Edge of the Sea, Georgia Rose, Kitty hawk and Jockey's Ridge, Sand Mountain Song, Sound Side, Shag Baby, Maco Light, Ethiope's Ear, To Catch a King, Home on the River, A Mighty Storm, I'm the Breeze, Beautiful Day
Songs and stories of the Carolina coast in two acts.

Keith Sherman

Barbara Feldon in *Love for Better & Verse*

103

(Westside Theatre/Downstairs) Friday, Feb. 10–July 1, 1995 (145 performances and 19 previews) Jeffrey Richards, Richard Gross, Jamie deRoy present:
THE COMPLEAT WORKS OF WLLM SHKSPR ABRIDGED by Adam Long, Daniel Singer, and Jess Winfield; Director, Mr. Winfield; Set, Edward Gianfrancesco; Lighting, Phil Monat; Costumes, Sa Winfield; Sound, Jim van Bergen; Press, Jeffrey Richards/Kevin Rehac CAST: Christopher Duva, Peter Jacobson, Jon Patrick Walker

A comic deconstruction of the Shakesperian Canon in 105 minutes.

Christopher Duva, Jon Patrick Walker, Peter Jacobson
in Compleat Works of Wllm Shkspr (Abridged)

(Judith Anderson Theatre) Friday, Feb. 10–Mar. 5, 1995 (19 performances and 4 previews) Willow Cabin Theatre Co. (Edward Berkleley, Artistic Director) presents:
TWELFTH NIGHT by William Shakespeare; Director, Edward Berkeley; Set/Costumes, Anne C. Patterson; Lighting, Matthew McCarthy; Stage Manager, Cynthia Tuohy; Press, Jim Baldassare CAST: John Billeci (Antonio/Capt.), John Bolger (Orsinio/2nd Officer), David Cheaney (Sebastian/Valentine/1st Officer), Kenneth Favre (Andrew Aguecheek), Ken Forman (Toby Belch), Anthony Gelsomino (Fabian), Laurence Gleason (Malvolio), Angela Nevard (Maria/Priest), Linda Powell (Olivia/Curio), Christine Radman (Feste), Maria Radman (Viola)

Performed in two acts. The action takes place in Illyria, the world of the unknown.

(Ubu Repertory Theatre) Tuesday, Feb. 14–26, 1995 (13 performances and 1 preview) Ubu Repertory (Francoise Kourlisky, Artistic Director) presents:
THE TROPICAL BREEZE HOTEL by Maryse Conde; Translation, Barbara Brewster Lewis, Catherine Temerson; Director, Shauneille Perry; Set, Watoku Ueno; Lighting, Greg MacPherson; Costumes, Carol Ann Pelletier; Sound, Julia Pena; Stage Manager, Teresa Conway; Press, Jonathan Slaff CAST: Jane White (Emma), Patrick Rameau (Ishmael)

A drama set in Paris.

Patrick Rameau, Jane White in *Tropical Breeze Hotel*

(Kaufman Theatre) Tuesday, Feb. 14–Mar. 12, 1995 (16 previews and 16 performances) Martin R. Kaufman presents:
CIRCUS LIFE by Murray Schisgal; Director, Larry Arrick; Set, Edward Gianfrancesco; Costumes, Mimi Maxmen; Lighting, Robert Jared; Sound, Darren Clark; Stage Manager, Andrea Testani; Press, David Rothenberg CAST: Mike Burstyn (Nick Schwab), Keith Langsdale (Howard Corey), Tresha Rodriguez ("Bobbie" Bluestone)

A comedy in two acts. The action takes place at the law firm of Corey and Schwab.

(Miranda Theatre) Wednesday, Feb. 15–Mar. 11, 1995 (15 performances and 4 previews) Miranda Theatre Co. presents:
REGRETS ONLY/KNOWING THE QUESTIONS; Written and Performed by Jamie Berger; Director, Roberta D'Alois; Press, Peter Cromarty

Two monologues.

(Kraine Theater) Wednesday, Feb. 15–Mar. 3, 1995 (15 performances) Peccadillo Theater Company presents:
TINY CLOSETS by William Inge; Director, Dan Wackerman; Sets/Lighting, Katherine Spencer; Costumes, Susan Soetaert; Press, Cris Parker
THE TINY CLOSET CAST: Howard Atlee (Mr. Newbold), leigh armor (Mrs. Crosby), Cam Kornman (Mrs. Hergesheimer)
THE BOY IN THE BASEMENT CAST: Constance Kane (Mrs. Scranton), Robert Buckley (Spencer Scranton), Howard Atlee (Mr. Scranton), Jeremy Klavens (Joker Evans), leigh armor (corpse)
A MURDER CAST: Cam Kornman (Landlady), Dale Carman (Man), Jim Sweeney (Houseman)

Three "repression era" one-acts.

(Currican Theatre) Tuesday, Feb. 16–Mar. 5, 1995 (16 performances) Deborah Pickul Osborne presents:
LUCIA MAD by Don Nigro; Director, Kevin Osborne; Press, Howard and Barbara Atlee CAST: Julie Jirousek (Lucia), James Rutledge (Beckett), Jay Devlin (JamesJoyce), Maybeth Ryan (Nora), Stephen Ahern (McGreevy/Jung), Ron Piretti (Pimp/Napoleon)

A dark comedy that takes place when James Joyce was finishing *Finnegan's Wake* in Paris.

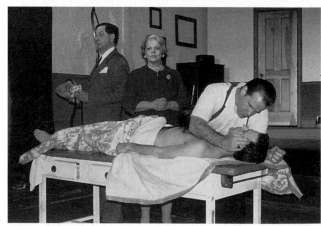

Howard Atlee, Constance Kane, Robert Buckley,
Jeremy Klavens in *Tiny Closets*

(Cucaracha Theatre) Thursday, Feb. 23–Mar. 18, 1995 (15 performances) Cucaracha presents:
BUDD; Written/Directed by Richard Caliban; Music, John Hoge; Lighting, Brian Aldous; Set, Kyle Chepulis; Costumes, Mary Myers; Sound, John Huntington; Stage Manager, Alexia Prichard CAST: Adrienne Shelly, Mollie O'Mara, Joey L. Golden, Chuck Montgomery, Stephen Brantley, Alicia Miller

A NYC performance artist moves to the suburbs.

(Blue Angel) Friday, Feb. 24–Nov. 26, 1995 William Repicci & Michael Minichiello in association with Ken Jillson & Robert Massimi present:
SWINGTIME CANTEEN; Book, Linda Thorsen Bond, William Repicci and Charles Busch; Director, Kenneth Elliott; Special Material, Dick Gallagher; Choreography, Barry McNabb; Set, B.T. Whitehill; Costumes, Robert Mackintosh; Lighting, Michael Lincoln; Orchestrations, Bob McDowell; Musical Director, Lawrence Yurman; Stage Manager, J. Andrew Burgreen; Press, David Rothenberg/David Lotz, David Gersten CAST: Alison Fraser succeeded by Charles Busch(Marian Ames), Debra Barsha (Topeka Abotelli), Emily Loesser (Katie Gammersflugel), Marcy McGuigan (Jo Sterling), Jackie Sanders (Lilly McBain), (from Sept.) Maxine Andrews

A musical, utilizing 1940s standards, performed without intermission.

(Variety Arts Theatre) Friday, Feb. 24, 1995–Feb. 25, 1996 Julian Schlossberg and Jean Doumanian present:
DEATH DEFYING ACTS; Director, Michael Blakemore; Sets, Robin Wagner; Costumes, Jane Greenwood; Lighting, Peter Kaczowski; Sound, Jan Nebozenko; Production Supervisor, Steven Zweigbaum; Press, Chris Boneau/Adrian Bryan Brown/Jackie Green, Andy Shearer
AN INTERVIEW by David Mamet CAST: Paul Guilfoyle (Attorney), Gerry Becker (Attendant)
HOTLINE by Elaine May CAST: Gerry Becker (Ken), Paul Guilfoyle (Dr. Russell), Paul O'Brien (Marty), Linda Lavin (Dorothy), Aasif Mandvi (Delivery Boy)
CENTRAL PARK WEST by Woody Allen CAST: Debra Monk (Phyllis), Linda Lavin (Carol), Gerry Becker (Howard), Paul Guilfoyle (Sam), Tari T. Signor (Juliet)
SUCCEEDING CAST: Valerie Harper (for Lavin), Kelly Bishop (for Monk)
Three one-act comedies.

Marcy McGuigan, Debra Barsha, Alison Fraser, Emily Loesser, Jackie Sanders in *Swingtime Canteen*

Below: Paul Guilfoyle, Linda Lavin, Gerry Becker, Debra Monk in *Death Defying Acts*

Joan Marcus

(Greenwich St. Theatre) Thursday, Mar. 2–26, 1995 (16 performances) Chain Lightning Theatre presents:
EDWARD II by Christopher Marlowe; Director, Todd Pieper; Lighting, Scott Clyve; Costumes, Arturo Lopez; Stage Manager, Brian White CAST: Josh Adler (Leicester/Rice Howell), Brina Bishop (Margaret), Monty Bonnell (Pembroke/Trussel), Frank Nelson Bradley (Beaumont/Sir John), Betty Burdick (Lancaster), Ben Chelsea (Levune/Metrevis), Glen Cruz (Baldock), Max Faugno (Edward III), Brian James Grace (Herald/Abbot), Joel Goldes (Edward II), Joseph Holgrem (Gaveston), Cheryl Horne (Queen Isabella), Kelly Huck (Warwick), Kricker James (Old Spencer/Old Mortimer), Lynn Laurence (Lightborn), Michael McFadden (James/Gurney), Jerry Mettner (Canterbury), Roderick O'Grady (Mortimer, Jr.), Andrew Rothkin (Young Spencer), Lyle Walford (Edmund/Earl)
History of medieval England re-set in the 1930s.

(224 Waverly Place) Thursday, Mar. 2–Apr. 16, 1995 (28 performances) AXIS Theatre Co. presents:
DOWN THERE by Randy Sharp and Michael Gump; Press, Bruce Lynn CAST INCLUDES: Michael Gump, Paul Dawson
A Grand Guignol play based on a 1960s torture murder in Indianapolis.

(Primary Stages) Friday, Mar. 3–Apr. 9, 1995 (41 performances) Primary Stages presents:
DON JUAN IN CHICAGO by David Ives; Director, Robert Stanton; Set, Bob Phillips; Costumes, Jennifer von Mayrhauser; Lighting, Deborah Constantine; Music/Sound, David van Tieghem; Fights, B.H. Barry; Stage Manager, Christine Catti; Press, Tony Origlio CAST: Simon Brooking (Don Juan), Larry Block (Leporello), Peter Bartlett (Mephistopheles), J. Smith-Cameron (Dona Elvira), Nancy Opel (Sandy), Mark Setlock (Mike), T. Scott Cunningham (Todd), Dina Spybey (Zoey)
A comic retelling of the Don Juan myth in three acts.

(Kraine Theatre) Wednesday, Mar. 8–May 14, 1995 (50 performances) Cooper Square Players present:
SEDUCED by Sam Shepard; Director, Frank Licato; Lighting, Donalee Katz; Costumes, Beth Suhocki; Set, Jon Moss, Tara Solomon; Choreography, Alicia Harding; Stage Managers, Adrian Wattenmaker, Jordon Polon; Press, Howard and Barbara Atlee CAST: Paul D'Amato (Henry Malcolm Hackemore), Nick Sandow (Raul), Maryann Towne (Luna), Alicia Harding (Miami)
A drama about eccentric billionaire Howard Hughes.

(Manhattan Class Company) Wednesday, Mar. 8–Apr. 1, 1995 (19 performances and 4 previews) Manhattan Class Co. presents:
CLASS 1–ACTS; Sets, Rob Odorisio; Lighting, Darrel Maloney; Costumes, Judy Jerald Sackheim; Sound, Stuart Allyn; Stage Managers, Elizabeth Timperman, Jenny Peek, Erica Blum, Liz Reddick; Press, Peter Cromarty/Hugh Hayes
THE ROCKS HAVE EARS; Written/Performed by Tom Burnett
IT'S ALMOST LIKE A FAVOR THAT I DO by Patrick Breen; Director, Brian Mertes CAST: Neal Huff (Eddie), Cara Buono (Jan)
HARD HATS by Rafael Lima; Director, Max Mayer CAST: James Colby (Smitty), Dan Moran (Becker)
SWEET TALK by Peter Lefcourt; Director, Stephen Willems CAST: Linda Marie Larson (Ginny), Julie Boyd (Delilah), Keith Reddin (John)
Seventh annual one-act festival.

Daisy Taylor

(top to bottom) Cheryl Horne, Joel Holmgren, Joel Goldes in *Edward II*

Roya

Keith Reddin, Linda Marie Larson, Julie Boyd in *Class 1–Acts*

(Alice's Fourth Floor) Wednesday, Mar. 8–25, 1995 (12 performances and 4 previews) AGBU-Arts presents:
THANTOS by Ron Simonian; Director, Sidonie Garrett; Stage Manager, John L. Kerst; Press, Tony Origlio/Stephen Murray CAST: Richard Augustine (Ted), Phil Fiorini (Sam), R.D. Mangels (Larry), Tess Brubeck (Mary), Matthew Rapport (Security)
A dark comedy in two acts. The action takes place in a hotel room.

(William Redfield Theatre) Thursday, Mar. 9–26, 1995 (13 performances and 3 previews) re-opened at Theatre Off Park Rattlestick Productions presents:
2 BOYS IN A BED ON A COLD WINTER'S NIGHT by James Edwin Parker; Director, Thomas Caruso; Set/Costumes, William F. Moser; Lighting, Ed McCarthy; Stage Manager, Eric Sirois; Press, Shirley Herz/Miller Wright CAST: Paul Rice succeeded by Robert Gomes (Daryl), Michael Curry (Peter)
A drama performed without intermission. The action takes place in NYC during winter.

Michael Curry, Robert Gomes
in 2 Boys in a Bed on a Cold Winter's Night

Robert DiScalfani

(Theatre Row Theatre) Thursday, Mar. 9–19, 1995 (11 performances and 1 preview)
THE OCCUPATION by Evelyn Rothstein; Director, Lisa Juliano; Music, Charles Nix; Press, Maya/Penny Landau CAST: Judy Dodd, Martha Gilpin, Larry Petersen, Mark Schaller, Les Shenkel, Jeff Skowron
A drama about a German military doctor occupying a Jewish family's Russian home.

(John Houseman Studio) Friday, Mar. 10–26, 1995 (10 performances) Untitles Theatre Co. #61 presents:
BRIMSTONE AND TREACLE by Dennis Potter; Director, Edward Einhorn; Press, Howard and Barbara Atlee CAST: Marcus Powell (Mr. Bates), Susanne Wasson (Mrs. Bates), Jason Katz (Martin), Elizabeth Yager (Pattie)
A play about a satanic young man who visits a British family.

(Perry St. Theatre) Friday, Mar. 10–Apr. 2, 1995 (16 performances and 3 previews) The Barrow Group presents:
TRUST by Steven Dietz; Director, Larry Green; Set, Michael McGarty; Costumes, Markas Henry; Lighting, Russell Champa; Sound, One Dream; Stage Manager, Shelli Aderman; Press, Shirley Herz/Wayne Wolfe CAST: Elizabeth Rice (Becca), Ilene Kristen (Leah), Lee Brock (Gretchen), Amy Hargreaves (Holly), Holter Graham (Cody), Seth Barrish (Roy)
A drama in two acts. The action takes place in an American city.

(Judith Anderson Theatre) Friday, Mar. 10–Apr. 9, 1995 (26 performances and 5 previews) Maxemmus Theatre presents:
INCOMMUNICADO by Tom Dulack; Director, Richard Corley; Sets, Christine Jones; Lighting, Rand Ryan; Costumes, Patricia Sarnataro; Sound, Donna Riley; Music, David Van Tieghem; Press, Denise Robert CAST: Tom Aldredge (Ezra Pound), Darryl Theirse (MP), Scott Whitehurst (Till), Brian Dykstra (Forbes), Baxter Harris (Muller)
A drama about American poet, Ezra Pound, in prison for treason, Italy, 1945.

(Metropolitan Playhouse) Saturday, Mar. 11–Apr. 2, 1995 (15 performances) Parsifal's Productions presents:
DARK SUN by Lisette Lecat Ross; Director, Mark Hirschfield; Lighting, Brian Orter; Costumes, Diana Walker; Set, William Marshall; Sound, Mark Hirschfield; Stage Manager, Doreen Chila; Press, David Zarko CAST: Craig Green (Sipho/Black Police), Vincent Masterpaul (White Police), Mary Ethel Schmidt (Lydia), Daniel Whitner (Simon)
A drama in two acts. The action takes place in Soweto, South Africa, 1988.

(28th St. Theatre) Saturday, Mar. 11–Apr. 2, 1995 (14 performances and 2 previews) Playwrights' Preview Productions presents:
KOKORO (TRUE HEART) by Velina Hasu-Houston; Director, Tina Chen; Set, Jeff Cowie, Eiko Yamaguchi; Lighting, Robert Lott; Costumes, Eiko Yamaguchi; Sound, Gian David Bianciardi; Stage Manager, Si Siorek; Press, Francine L. Trevens CAST: Ako, Elaina Davis, Ryohei Hoshi, Dorothy Kiara, Shanah Luhmann, Midori Nakamura
A drama which mixes Japanese Kabuki and contemporary staging.

Holter Graham in *Trust*

Carol Rosegg

Tom Aldredge in *Incommunicado*

Jonathan Slaff

(Russian Tea Room) Sunday, Mar. 12–transferred to Eighty-Eights on April 12, 1995 for alternating schedule
THE MILLENIUM APPROACHES: AND I'M NOT READY; Written and Performed by Julie Halston
A comic monologue.

(Ubu Rep Theater) Tuesday, Mar. 14–24, 1995 (14 performances) Ubu Repertory presents:
ANOTHER STORY by Julius Amedee Laou; Translation, Richard Miller; Director, Francoise Kourilsky; Set, Watoku Ueno; Lighting, Greg MacPherson; Music, Genji Ito; Costumes, Carol Ann Pelletier; Stage Manager, Teresa Conway; Press, Jonathan Slaff CAST: ERila L. Heard (Sawa), Robert Morgan (Abraham Ben Israel), La Tonya Borsay (Adelaide Beaulieu), Andrea Smith (Mory Haidara), Duane McLaughlin
The history of the Caribbean through music and drama.

Left: Erika L. Heard in *Another Story*

(Soho Rep) Tuesday, Mar. 14–Apr. 16, 1995 (16 performances each)
The Basic Theatre presents:
TITUS ANDRONICUS and **MEASURE FOR MEASURE** by William Shakespeare; Directors, Lester Shane (Titus), Jared Hammond (Measure); Sets, Mark Symczak; Lighting, Jeff Segal; Costumes, Desiree Petitjean, Michael Moore, Patty Burke; Music/Sound, Dean Myers; Press, Tony Origlio/Michael Cullen   CASTS: Eric Brandenburg, Judith Lightfoot Clarke, Robert Corddry, Tony Cormier, Ezio Cutarelli, Robert Devaney, Kevin Dwyer, Mark Eis, Robert English, Jason Green, Dean Harrison, Greg Hubbard, Bill Laney, Christopher Marino, Tony Meindl, Tinne Metcalf, Jonathan Miller, Philip Munson, Kathryn Newbrough, Deborah Ostrowsky, Greg Petroff, John Prave, Beckett Royce, Marilyn Salinger, Greig Sargeant, Tristan Smith, Jason Stevens, Douglas Stewart, Ross Tatum, Chris Tolliver, Stewart Walker
Performed in repertory.

(29th St. Repertoire) Tuesday, Mar. 14–Apr. 9, 1995 (28 performances)
Altered Stages presents:
I KILLED MY BROTHER; Written/Performed by Nelson Jewell; Press, Ron Koch
An autobiographical monologue.

(One Dream Theatre) Thursday, Mar. 16–26, 1995 (8 performances and 4 previews) Flock Theater Company presents:
A LIE OF THE MIND by Sam Shepard; Director, April Shawhan; Set, Steven Capone; Lighting, Jeff Nellis; Music, Tom Shaner; Stage Manager, Rebecca Cammisa; Press, Shirley Herz/Stephen Barry   CAST: David Phillips (Jake), Sam Trammell (Frankie), Jeannie Zusy (Beth), Kyle McMurray (Mike), Suzanne Sheperd (LOrraine), Irene Glezos (Sally), Paul Geier (Baylor), Rosemary McNamara (Meg)
A drama in three acts.

(Eighty-Eights) Monday, Mar. 20–May 1, 1995 (7 Monday performances)
LITTLE BY LITTLE with Music by Brad Ross; Lyrics, Ellen Greenfield, Hal Hackady; Book, Ms. Greenfield, Annette Jolles; Director, Ms. Jolles; Press, Merle Frimark & Marc Thibodeau/Erin Dunn   CAST: Michael Gruber, Tia Speros, Sarah Uriarte
A musical about the lives and loves of three friends.

Kirk Acevedo in *Robert Zucco*

**Tracy Newirth, Britton Herring,
Faye Jackson in *Found in the Garden***

(Harold Clurman Theatre) Tuesday, Mar. 21–Apr. 15, 1995 (18 performances) Love Creek Productions presents:
FOUND IN THE GARDEN: FRAGMENTS OF SHRAPNEL by Le Wilhelm; Director, Philip Galbraith; Set, Viola Bradford; Lighting, Richard Kent Green; Sound, Hanry Marsden Davis; Stage Managers, Louise Bylicki, Winni Troha; Press, Annie Chadwick   CAST: Claire Cousineau (Helen Ann), Jed Dickson (J.E.), Cynthia Granville (Martha/Louise), Richard Kent Green (Sam), Britton Herring (Wayne), Ron Hirt (Ez), Faye Jackson (Deanna), Jackie Jenkins (Olean), Michelle Matzeder (Leslie), Tracy Newirth (Mattie) (Paradise Falls Girl), Katherine Parks (Freda), Jeff Paul (David), Devin Quigley (Terry), Laura Shapanus (Mary Ann), Trey Webster (Jimmy Wade/Hub), Joseph Will (Jimmy Clines/Jimmy Jack), Kate Zahorsky (Clara Sue)
A drama in three acts. The setting is small town America during the 1950s.

(Next Stage Co.) Wednesday, Mar. 22–26, 1995 (5 performances) Next Stage Company presents:
UTTERLY WILDE!!!; Created from the Words and Writings of Oscar Wilde by Marc H. Glick; Music/Lyrics, John Franceschina; Director, Drew Scott Harris; Musical Director/Arrangements, George Kramer; Lighting, David Castaneda; Press, Judy Jacksina   CAST: Marc H. Glick (Oscar Wilde)
MUSICAL NUMBERS: Deja Vu, Two Loves, I Want to Make Magic, Wasted Days, Dearest of All Boys, Romantic Experience, Joshua, To My Wife, I'll Never Give Up on Bosie, Ballad of Reading Gaol
A musical biography. The action takes place at Paris' Hotel D'Alsace, 1899.

(Cucaracha Theater) Friday, Mar. 24–Apr. 21, 1995 Cucaracha presents:
ROBERTO ZUCCO by Bernard-Marie Koltes; Translation, Royston Coppinger; Director, Travis Preston CAST INCLUDES: Kirk Acevedo (Roberto), Marylouise Burke

(West Bank Downstairs) Friday, Mar. 24–Apr. 8, 1995 (8 performances) Denise Cooper and Susan Wilber present:
THE SECRET OF LIFE by David Simpatico; Director, Roger Mrazek; Costumes, Shelley Norton; Lighting, David Comstock; Set, Kermit Cole; Press, Judy Jacksina   CAST: Jane Young, Donna Villella, Bob Yarnall, Anne Lilly, Susan Kurowski, William Flatley
Six characters face an emotional crisis.

Michael Lamont

Michael Lamont

Dan Butler   **Greg Louganis**

in *The Only Thing Worse You Could Have Told Me…*

Joan Marcus

Ed Begley Jr., Shelton Dane, Felicity Huffman in *The Cryptogram*

(Actors' Playhouse) Sunday, Mar. 26–Sept. 16, 1995 (175 performances and 9 previews) Scott Allyn presents:
THE ONLY THING WORSE YOU COULD HAVE TOLD ME…by Dan Butler; Director, Randy Brenner; Set, James Noone; Costumes, Parker Poolc; Lighting, Ken Billington; Sound, Jim Van Bergen; Stage Manager, M.A. Howard; Press, Peter Cromarty/Hugh Hayes CAST: Dan Butler succeeded by Greg Louganis
A whirlwind tour of the gay American landscape performed without intermission.

(Lamb's Theatre) Tuesday, Mar. 28–Apr. 16, 1995 (36 performances) Arthur Cantor presents:
ST. MARK'S GOSPEL; Lighting, Lloyd Sobel; Design Associate, Bruce Goodrich; Stage Manager, Jim Ring; Production Associate, Marc Firek; Press, Mr. Cantor CAST: Alec McCowen
Repeat engagement of solo rendition of the gospel.

(Battery Park City) Tuesday, Mar .28–June 4, 1995 AT&T presents:
ALEGRIA; Written/Directed by Franco Dragone; Costumes, Dominique; Set, Michael Crete; Choreography, Debra Brown; Music, Rene Dupere; Lighting, Luc Lafortune; Press, Marc Thibodeau CAST: Cirque Du Soleil
Cirque du Soleil's eighth production in ten years.

(Westside Theatre/Upstairs) Tuesday, Mar. 28–June 4, 1995 (62 performances and 18 previews) Frederick Zollo, Nicolas Paleologos, Gregory Mosher and Jujamcyn Theatres in association with Herb Albert and Margo Lion present:
THE CRYPTOGRAM; Written/Directed by David Mamet; Set, John Lee Beatty; Costumes, Harriet Voyt; Lighting, Dennis Parichy; Stage Manager, Carol Dawes; Press, Bill Evans/Tom D'Ambrosio CAST: Shelton Dane (John), Ed Begley, Jr. (Del), Felicity Huffman (Donny)
A drama performed without intermission. The action takes place in Donny's living room, 1959.

Carol Rosegg

Paxton Whitehead, Carole Shelley in *London Suite*

(Union Square Theatre) Tuesday, Mar. 28–Sept. 3, 1995 (169 performances and 15 previews) Emanuel Azenberg and Leonard Soloway present:
LONDON SUITE by Neil Simon; Director, Daniel Sullivan; Sets, John Lee Beatty; Costumes, Jane Greenwood; Lighting, Ken Billington; Sound, Tom Clark; Wigs/Hair, Paul Huntley; Stage Manager, John Vivian; Press, Bill Evans/Terry Lilly CAST: Carole Shelley succeeded by Harriet Harris (Mrs. Semple/Diana/Mrs. Sitgood), Paxton Whitehead succeeded by Paul Hecht (Billy/Sidney/Dr. McMerlin), Kate Burton succeeded by Monique Fowler (Lauren/Grace/Annie), Jeffrey Jones succeeded by Munson Hicks (Brian/Mark), Brooks Ashmanskas (Bellman)

Four one act plays that take place in an old but very fashionable hotel in London, much like the Connaught Hotel. Program: *Settling Accounts, Going Home, Diana & Sidney, The Man on the Floor.*

Carol Rosegg

Kate Burton, Paxton Whitehead, Jeffrey Jones, Brooks Ashmanskas in *London Suite*

(Intar Theatre) Wednesday, Mar. 29–May 7, 1995 (25 performances and 11 previews) Intar Hispanic American Arts Center presents:
A ROYAL AFFAIR by Luis Santeiro; Director, Max Ferra; Set, Loren Sherman; Lighting, Phil Monat; Costumes, Donna Zakowska; Sound, Bruce Ellman; Press, Shirley Herz/Miller Wright CAST: Tobi Brydon (Edna), Andriana Inchaustegui (Marie Antoinette), Gary Perez (Rene), Martiza Rivera (Hilda), Ed Trucco (Count Fersen), Marta Vidal (Luz)

A comedy about an illegal alien who dreams of working for royalty.

(William Redfield Theatre) Wednesday, Mar. 29–Apr. 23, 1995 (16 performances and 7 previews)
MEMORIES OF AN UNKNOWN CELEBRITY; Written/Performed by Michael Mindlin; Director, Phyllis Newman; Press, Tony Origlio/Michael Cullen

A monologue about show business.

(Ubu Rep Theatre) Friday, Mar. 31–Apr. 9, 1995 (10 performances) Libra Ensemble presents:
THE CAGE by Mario Fratti; Director, Robert Kalfin; Set, Alexander Solodukho; Lighting, Robert Williams; Costumes, Gail Cooper; Fights, B.H. Barry; Stage Manager, Alida Gunn; Press, Richard Biles CAST: Mark Heismann (Christano), Nicholas Keene, David Hirsh (Delivery Boys), Carol Harris (Mother), Karen Ann Welch (Nella), Jud Meyers (Sergio), John Monteleone (Pietro), Caroline Strong (Chiara)

A drama in two acts. The action takes place in an Italian industrial city, 1970s.

(30th St. Theatre) Wednesday, Apr. 5–10, 1995 Creative Voices presents:
GIN AND BITTERS by Susan Cinoman; Director, Alison Sommers; Press, Kathy Towson CAST: John Augustine, Geneva Carr, Chris Hury, Kay Walbye

A Philadelphia-set comedy about a gay writer and an actress.

Mark Heimann, Caroline Strong, Carol Harris in *The Cage*

(Minetta Lane Theatre) Wednesday, Apr. 5–Oct. 1, 1995 (199 performances and 7 previews) Bill Kenwright presents:
TRAVELS WITH MY AUNT by Graham Greene; Adaptor/Director, Giles Havergal; Set/Costumes, Stewart Laing; Lighting, Gerry Jenkinson; Stage Manager, Jane Grey; Press, Philip Rinaldi/Barbara Carroll, Kathy Haberthur, James LL Morrison CAST: Jim Dale succeeded by Larry Linville (Henry Pulling/Augusta Bertram), Brian Murray (Henry Pulling/Richard Pulling/Vicar/Miss Keene/Tooley/Italian Girl/Frau General Schmidt/O'Toole/Yolanda), Martin Rayner (Henry Pulling/Taxi Driver/Wordsworth/Det. Sgt. Sparrow/Hatty/Mr. Visconti/Col. Hakim, Miss Paterson/Spanish Gentleman), Tom Beckett (Henry Pulling/Girl in Jodphurs/Wolf/Hotel Receptionist/Bodyguard)

A comedy in two acts. All roles are performed by the four-man cast.

(HERE) Friday, Apr. 7–22, 1995 (10 performances) HERE presents:
PHAEDRA; Written/Directed by Matthew Maguire CAST: Andy Paris, Nicole Alifante, Socorro Santiago, George Bartenieff, Ray Xifo, Verna Hampton

A modern spin on the Greek classic.

(28th St. Theatre) Friday, Apr. 7–30, 1995 (18 performances and 5 previews) Willow Cabin Theatre Company presents:
GOOSE AND TOMTOM by David Rabe; Director, Adam Oliensis; Set, Miguel Lopez-Castillo; Lighting, Matthew McCarthy; Costumes, Tasha Lawrence; Press, Jim Baldassare CAST: Laurence Gleason (Tomtom), Joe Pacheco (Goose), Tasha Lawrence (Lorraine), Angela Nevard (Lulu), John Billeci (Bingo), Ken Forman (Man 1), Joseph Adams (Man 2), Bjarni Thorsson (Man 3)

A drama in two acts. Performed as a workshop at the Mitzi Newhouse in 1986 with Madonna, Sean Penn, and Harvey Keitel.

Brian Murray, Jim Dale, Tom Beckett, Martin Rayner in *Travels with My Aunt*

(Carnegie Hall) Saturday, Apr. 8, 1995 (1 performance only) Peter Bogyo presents:
ANYONE CAN WHISTLE with Music/Lyrics by Stephen Sondheim; Book, Arthur Laurents; Staging, Herbert Ross; Musical Director, Paul Gemignani; Orchestrations, (original) Don Walker, Jonathan Tunick; Set, Heidi Landesman; Costumes, Theoni V. Aldredge; Lighting, Jules Fisher; Sound, Otts Munderloh; Choreographic Associate, Robert LaFosse; CAST Recording, Columbia; Press, Elizabeth Eynon, Steve Asher CAST: Angela Lansbury (Hostess), Chip Zien (Treasurer Cooley), Ken Page (Chief Magruder), Walter Bobbie (Comptroller Schub), Madeline Kahn (Cora Hoover Hooper), Sterling Clark, Harvey Evans, Evan Pappas, Eric Riley, Tony Stevens (The Boys), Maureen Moore (Mrs. Schroeder), Bernadette Peters (Fay Apple), Scott Bakula (J. Bowden Hapgood), Nick Wyman (Dr. Detmold), Harolyn Blackwell (Soprano), Sterling Clark (Western Union Boy), Sandra Brown, Stacy Caddell, Lisa Lockwood, Robert LaFosse, Jon Marshall Sharp (Ballet), Joan Barber, Mary Bentley-LaMar, Gerry Burkhardt, Susan Cella, Nick Corley, Madeleine Doherty, Colleen Fitzpatrick, Joy Franz, Philip Hoffman, Michael Ingram, Betsy Joslyn, Joseph Kolinski, David Lowenstein, Seth Malkin, Donna Lee Marshall, Michael X. Martin, Marin Mazzie, Maureen Moore, Karen Murphy, Bill Nolte, Robert Ousley, Darcy Pulliam, Sam Reni, Nancy Ringham, Francis Ruivivar, Martin Van Treuren, Whitney Webster, Walter Willison, John Leslie Wolfe
MUSICAL NUMBERS: Overture, Me and My Town, I'm Like the Bluebird, Miracle Song, There Won't Be Trumpets, The Interrogation, Prelude, Hooray for Hapgood, Come Play with Me, Anyone Can Whistle, A Parade in Town, Everybody Says Don't, I've Got You to Lean On, See What It Gets You, Cookie Chase, There's Always a Woman, With So Little To Be Sure Of, Finale

An AIDS benefit concert of the 1964 musical for Gay Men's Health Crisis.

**Left: Scott Bakula, Bernadette Peters
Above: (left) Angela Lansbury, (right) Madeline Kahn
in *Anyone Can Whistle***

(Playhouse 91) Saturday, Apr. 8–23, 1995 (10 performances and 5 previews) The Eclectic Theatre Co. in association with Gary Perlman presents: **THE FALL GUY** by Tsuka Kohei based on his play *Kamata Koshinkyoku;* Adaptation, Gary Perlman; Director, Mako; Set, Yoichi Aoki; Costumes, Eiko Yamaguchi; Lighting, Betsy Finston; Sound, Raymond Schilke; Music, Yukio Tsuji; Stage Manager, Sue Jane Stoker; Press, Pete Sanders, Michael Hartman   CAST: Stephen Lee (Wakadanna), Roger Ma (Shinji), Kaipo Schwab (Makoto), Arthur Acuna (Takashi), Gordon Synn (Tachibana Taro), Ryohei Hoshi (Tachibana Jiro), Frank Kamai (Tachibana Saburo), Mimosa (Konatsu), Keenan Shimizu (Director), Evan Lai (Asst. Director), Andrew Pang (Ginshiro), Keone Young (Yasu), Yukio Tsuji (Musician)

A three-act Japanese drama performed with one intermission. The action takes place in a Kyoto movie studio.

(Naked Angels) Monday, Apr. 10–29, 1995 (16 performances) Naked Angels presents: **FUNKY CRAZY BOOGALOO BOY;** Written/Directed by Ned Eisenberg; Set, Franne Lee; Costumes, Daniele Hollywood; Lighting, Eric Thoben; Sound, Roger Raines; Fights, Rick Sordelet; Stage Manager, Janice Jackson   CAST: Sharon Bart, Mark Feurstein, Ronald Guttman, Jean Claude LaMarre, Eric LaRay Harvey, Shawn Randall, Eleanor Reissa, Vanessa Ruane, Albert S., Anjua Warfield

(Perry St. Theatre) Thursday, Apr. 13–May, 1995 The Glocca Morra Company presents: **MORTICIANS IN LOVE** by Christi Stewart-Brown; Director, Jennifer Mendenhall; Set, Michael McGarty; Lighting, Russell H. Champa; Costumes, Susan Anderson; Sound, One Dream; Stage Manager, Bethany Ford; Press, Shirley Herz/Wayne Wolfe   CAST: Bernadette Flagler (Lydia Drury), Carol Monda (Limer), Eric Nolan (Charlie), Warren Keith (St. John Homebody), Gabriela May Ladd (Monika)

A black comedy in two acts. The action takes place in the back room of the Eternal Acres funeral home.

(28th St. Theatre) Thursday, Apr. 13–30, 1995 (15 performances) Africa Arts Theatre Company presents: **THE SWAMP DWELLERS** by Wole Soyinka; Director, Patricia Floyd; Design, Delano Lopez; Costumes, Kenneth J. Wyrtch; Lighting, Zdenek Kriz; Stage Manager, Nanci Mere; Press, Jonathan Slaff   CAST: Arthur French, Geany Masai, Daniel Whitner, Todd Anthony-Jackson, Christopher Kirk Allen, Rochelle Henderson, James Abe

A drama blending Yoruban folk drama with European dramatic form.

Andrew Pang, Mimosa, Keone Young in *The Fall Guy*

Arthur French, Todd Anthony Jackson, James Abe, Christopher Kirk Allen in *The Swamp Dwellers*

(Sanford Meisner Theatre) Thursday, Apr. 13–23, 1995 (12 performances) Case Goodmen Productions presents: **FRANKIE & JOHNNY IN THE CLAIR DE LUNE** by Terrence McNally; Director, M.R. Goodley; Set, Bill Wood; Lighting, Robert Campbell; Costumes, Darlene C. Ritz; Sound, Dominic Cuskern; Stage Manager, Jennifer Baker; Press, Mary Ruth Goodley   CAST: Karen Case Cook (Frankie), Joseph J. Menino (Johnny), Dominic Cuskern (Marlon)

A drama in two acts.

(Ohio Theatre) Friday, Apr. 14–29, 1995 (10 performances and 4 previews) The Rorschach Group presents: **XXX LOVE ACT** by Cintra Wilson; Director, Troy Hollar; Set/Costumes, Joe Egan; Lighting, Jeff Croiter; Sound, Raymond Schilke; Press, Pete Sanders/Michael Hartman   CAST: Lynn Cohen, Jennifer Esposito, Adam Nelson, Courtney Rackley, Daniel Reinish, Nadine Stevnovitch, Shea Whigham

A drama loosely based on Jim and Artie Mitchell, two brothers who built a pornography empire in San Francisco.

Left: *XXX Love Act*

(Douglas Fairbanks Theater) Friday, Apr. 14, 1995–Mar. 24, 1996 (342 performances and 31 previews) Michael Leavitt, Fox Theatricals, Leonard Soloway, Peter Breger, Jerry Frankel, Dennis J. Grimaldi and Steven M. Levy present:
PARTY by David Dillon; Set, James Noone; Costumes, Gail Cooper-Hecht; Lighting, Ken Billington; Sound, Tom Clark; Stage Manager, Bruce Greenwood; Press, Bill Evans/Jim Randolf, Terry M. Lilly, Tom D'Ambrosio CAST: David Pevsner succeeded by Marc Wolf (Kevin), Ted Bales succeeded by Craig Dawson (Ray), Larry Alexander succeeded by Tom Humphreys (Philip), Kellum Lewis succeeded by Tony Meindl (Brian), Tom Stuart succeeded by Achilles Tsakirdis (Peter), Jay Corcoran (James), Vince Gatton succeeded by Jason Mauro (Andy)

A New York-set two-act comedy involving a truth-or-dare game in which everyone ends up naked.

(McGinn/Cazale Theatre) Sunday, Apr. 16–17, 1995 (2 performances) Fourth Annual Cabaret Series presents:
DEJA REVUE; Assembled by Gordon Connell; Director, Estelle Parsons; Staging/Choreography, Bick Goss; Costumes, Santo Loquasto CAST: Jeanne Arnold, Gordon Connell, Ronny Graham, Carol Morley, Estelle Parsons, Rex Robbins, Stan Keen, William Roy

A return to the heyday of cabaret.

(Promenade Theatre) Sunday, Apr. 16–June 25, 1995 (14 performances and 7 previews) Julian Schlossberg and Ben Sprecher present a Nichols & May Production:
WORD OF MOUTH; Written/Performed by James Lecesne; Director, Eve Ensler; Set, Bradley Wester; Lighting, Brian Aldous; Sound, Ray Schilke; Stage Manager, Bern Gautier; Press, Bill Evans/Terry Lilly

One man creates ten characters. Performed without intermission.

(Dont Tell Mama) Tuesday, Apr. 18–May 28, 1996 (5 performances)
SWIRL; Created/Directed by Terry Walsh; Press, Judy Jacksina CAST: Mimi Bessette, Brenda Braye, Meghan Duffy, Judith Marie Walton

The story of the making of a girl group.

(John Houseman Studio) Tuesday, Apr. 18–June 4, 1995 The New Group presents:
ECSTACY by Mike Leigh; Director, Scott Elliott; Set, Kevin Price, Zaniz; Costumes, Eric Becker; Lighting, Benjamin Pearcy; Sound, Raymond D. Schilke; Music, Tom Kochan CAST: John Wojda (Roy), Caroline Seymour (Jean), Marian Quinn (Dawn), Zaniz Jakubowski (Val), Jared Harris, Tim Smallwood (Len), Patrick Fitzgerald (Mick)

A drama in two acts. The action takes place in a Northwest London bed-sit, winter, 1979.

Above: Vince Gatton, Tom Stuart, Kellum Lewis in *Party*

Below: James Lecesne in *Word of Mouth*

(Theatre Row Theatre) Tuesday, Apr. 18–23, 1995 (7 performances)
The Big Face presents:
HOLY GHOSTS by Romulus Linney; Director, John Zibel; Lighting, Ken Allaire; Lighting/Sound/Stage Manager, Patrick Davila   CAST: Mark Bennington (Howard Rudd), Bruce Coulter (Coleman Shedman), David John Dean (Rogers Canfield), Richard Derry (Musician), Crew Hoakes (Virgil Tides), Ted Kenneally (Billy Boggs), Cam Kornman (Mrs. Wall), Kirsten Lambertsen (Nancy Shedman), Wendell Laurent (Obediah Buckhorn, Jr.), Elizabeth Logun (Bonnie Bridge), William Preston (Obediah Buckhorn, Sr.), Brandt Reiter (Orin Hart), Roswell Smith (Cancer Man), Sharon Talbot (Lorena Cosburg), Lincoln Watson (Carl Specter), Trina Wilson (Muriel Boggs)
A drama in two acts. The setting is the rural south.

(Theatre Off Park) Wednesday, Apr. 19–May 6, 1995 (14 performances and 5 previews) Nightlight Productions presents:
THE SECRET SITS IN THE MIDDLE by Lisa-Maria Radano; Director, Deena Levy; Set, Andy Warfel; Lighting, Chris Dallos; Sound, Matthew Agrell; Stage Manager, Jenny Dewar; Press, Peter Cromarty/Bill Klemm CAST: Andrea Maulella (Angela), Marnie Pomerantz (Tina), Kate Shein (Person), Brian Vincent (Sonny), John Di Benedetto (Mr. Runey)
A two-act drama set in Brooklyn.

(30th St. Theatre) Thursday, Apr. 20–May 7, 1995 (15 performances and 1 preview) Blue Heron Theatre presents:
CHIKAMATSU'S FOREST by Edward Sakamoto; Director, Tom Prewitt; Set/Costumes, Christopher Thomas; Lighting, Glen Fasman; Choreography, Lu Yu, Yung Yung Tsuai; Music, Peter Gingerich; Stage Manager, Charles Michael Edmonds; Press, Ardelle Striker   CAST: Phillip Baltazar (Noritoshi), Willy Corpus (Niko/Fujo), Ron Domingo (Yasai/Yaki), Paul Jung (Stranger/Jobei), Shanah Luhmann (Asako), Ben Wang (Ino), Lu Yu (Chikamatsu)
A drama using elements of Japanese Kabuki and Bunraku (puppet) theatre.

(Playhouse 125) Thursday, Apr. 20–May 14, 1995 (16 performances) The Theatre Beneath the Sand presents:
THE CONQUEST OF THE SOUTH POLE by Manfred Karge; Translation, Ralf E. Remshardt, Caron Cadle, Calvin MacLean; Director, Nigel Maister; Set, Scott A. Perich; Lighting, Clay Brown; Costumes, Nan Young; Fights, Edward F. Vassallo; Stage Manager, Rachel E. Boschen; Press, Jonathan Slaff   CAST: Christopher Mako (Benno Slupianek), Dominic Compertore (Buscher), William McCall (Braukmann), Edward F. Vassallo (Erwin Seiffert), Linnea Pyne (Luise), Sergio Cacciotti (Frankieboy), Peggy Jo Brenneman (Rosi), Kevin Connell (Rudi)
A German drama performed without intermission.

(Eighty-Eights) Thursday, Apr. 20–May 6, 1995 (9 performances)
AN OFF BROADWAY CABARET; Musical Director, Shelly Markham CAST: Bonnie Franklin, Michael Hawkins, Byron Nease, Teri Ralston

William Preston in *Holy Ghosts*

Lisa Maizlish

Paul Jung, Lu Yu, Shanah Luhmann in *Chikamatsu's Forest*

(A Theater) Thursday, Apr. 20–May 7, 1995 (13 performances and 4 previews) Circuit Rider Theater Co. presents:
YOUNG HITLER Written/Performed by Marshall Davis; Director, Keith Fadelici; Set, Tamar Cohn; Costumes, Anne Lommel; Lighting, Jennifer Tanzer; Sound, Casey Warren; Press, Richard Kornberg/Don Summa
The action takes place in a Bavarian prison, 1924.

(White St. Theater) Friday, Apr. 21–May 27, 1995 (21 performances and 2 previews) Irondale Ensemble Project presents:
GHOST SONATA by August Strindberg; Translation, Harry G. Carlson; Director, Johan Petri; Set, Ken Rothchild; Costumes/Lighting, Hilarie Blumenthal; Music/Sound, Kato Hideki; Press, Tony Origlio/Stephen Murray   CAST: Terry Greiss (Hummel), Joshua Taylor (Arkenholz), Robin Kurtz (Adele), Georgina Corbo (Amalia), Michael-David Gordon (Johansson), Paul Ellis (Bengtsson), Jim Niesen (Colonel), Vicky Gilmore (Dark Lady/Cook), D. Zhoninsky (Baron)

(Performing Garage) Saturday, Apr. 22–June 4, 1995 The Wooster Group presents:
THE HAIRY APE by Eugene O'Neill; Director, Elizabeth LeCompte; Set, Jim Clayburgh; Lighting, Jennifer Tipton; Music, John Lurie; Press, Alexandra Paxton   CAST: Willem Dafoe, Peyton Smith, Kate Valk, Roy Faudree, Paul Lazar, Scott Renderer, Dave Shelley
A comedy of ancient and modern life in eight scenes.

Jonathan Slaff

Edward Vassallo, William McCall in *Conquest of the South Pole*

(Gramercy Arts Theatre) Sunday, Apr. 23–June 23, 1995 (6 performances and 11 previews) Repertorio Espanol presents:
LIFE IS A DREAM by Pedro Calderon de la Barca; Director, Rene Buch; Set/Costumes, Robert Weber Federico; Press, Susan L. Schulman CAST INCLUDES: Maria Jose Alvarez (Rosaura), Ricardo Barber (Clarin), Quique Arce (Segismundo), Rene Sanchez
    A 1636 Spanish drama.

(Harold Clurman Theatre) Wednesday, Apr. 26–May 13, 1995 (16 performances) Love Creek Productions present:
PIRANDELLO 3 by Luigi Pirandello; Director, Le Wilhelm; Set, Viola Bradford; Lighting, Richard Kent Green; Press, Colin Campbell CAST: Annie Chadwick, Henry Marsden Davis, Alan Denny, Roslyne Hahn, David Pincus, Scott Sparks, Bart Tangredi
    Three one-acts: *The Man with the Flower in His Mouth, The License,* and *I'm Dreaming.*

(Ridiculous Theatre) Wednesday, Apr. 26–May 21, 1995 (19 performances and 5 previews) Luli Inc. presents:
NELLIE-A-GO-GO!; Director, Mark Owen; Lighting, David Alan Comstock; Costumes, Thomasine Dolan; Wigs, Chris Starling; Stage Manager, Jonathan Nye; Press, Philip Rinaldi/Tony Stavick CAST: Nora Burns, Mike Jefferson, Tony Markham, Terrence Michael, Maggie Moore, Julie Wheeler (The Nellie Olesons)
    Gay sketch comedy.

(Sanford Meisner Theatre) Wednesday, Apr. 26–30, 1995 (7 performances) INCOACT presents:
LONELY TOO LONG; Written/Directed by Chuck Blasius; Set, Steven Marcus; Sound, Audible Difference; Press, Chris Boneau/Adrian Bryan-Brown/Bob Fennell CAST: John Alban Coughlan (John), Sarah Zinsser (The Women), Rob Gomes(The Men)
    A comedy about finding love.

Rob Gomes, Sarah Zinsser, John Alban Coughlan in *Lonely Too Long*

(Redfield Theater) Thursday, Apr. 27–May 13, 1995 (12 performances) The Working Playground presents:
BABY LUV by Joan Ratner; Director, Tony Phelan CAST: Muriel Gould, Amy Rosenfeld, Elayne Wilks
and **MOTIVATION FOR THE MEAT OF LIFE;** Written/Directed by Kaethe Fine CAST: Calude Wampler, Tim Williams
Sets, Johnny Poux; Lighting, Michael Gottlieb; Press, Laura Segal
    Two version of contemporary urban life.

(Synchronicity Space) Thursday, Apr. 27–May 14, 1995 (14 performances) Synchronicity Space presents:
JACOB'S BLANKET by Geoffrey Hassman; Director, James Knopf; Set, Jordan Jacobs; Lighting, David Alan Comstock; Stage Manager, Paul Miller; Press, John Amato CAST: Gary Dennis, Lanie Lewis, Peter-Michael Marino, Janice Messitte, Jane Ross, Alexandria Sage, Alixx Schottland, Len Stanger
    A "comic tragedy" involving an upper middle class Jewish family in Long Island.

(Soho Rep) Thursday, Apr. 27–May 28, 1995 SoHo Rep presents:
SKIN by Naomi Iizuka; Director, John Edward McGrath; Set, Paul Clay; Video, Myra Paci CAST: Adam Stein (Jones), Karenjune Sanchez (Mary)
    A drama performed without intermission.

(HERE) Thursday, Apr. 27–May 14, 1995 (19 performances and 7 previews) Music-Theatre Group and HOME for Contemporary Theatre and Art present:
EXTRAORDINARY MEASURES; Written/Directed by Eve Ensler; Composer, William Harper; Set, Bradley Wester; Lighting, Michael Chybowski; Costumes, Donna Zakowska; Sound, Richard Jansen; Stage Manager, Lori Lundquist; Press, Shirley Herz/Sam Rudy CAST: James Lecesne, Jeannine Otis, Serafina Martino, Christine Sperry
    A music-theatre work inspired by the life of teacher/director Paul Walker.

(Irish Arts Center) Thursday, Apr. 27–June 30, 1995 (51 performances and 14 previews) The Irish Arts Center presents:
THE DONAHUE SISTERS by Geraldine Aron; Director, Nye Heron; Sets, David Raphel; Lighting, Mauricio Saavedra Pefaur; Costumes, Mimi Maxmen; Sound/Music, Nico Kean; Stage Manager, Kurt Wagemann CAST: Alma Cuervo (Rosie), Terry Donnelly (Annie), Carolyn McCormick succeeded by Olivia Tracey (Dunya)
and **BAR AND GER** CAST: John Keating (Bar), Aedin Moloney (Ger)
    Two Irish plays.

(Samuel Beckett Theatre) Friday, Apr. 28–May 14, 1995 Gilgamesh Theatre Group presents:
THE GEOGRAPHY OF LUCK by Marlene Meyer; Director, Guy Giarrizzo; Press, Jeffrey Richards/Kevin Rehac, Richard Guido CAST: Michael Patterson (Dixie), Charles Dumas (Dutchy), Jan Munroe, Herbert Rubens, Elizabeth M. Schofield, Brian Shnipper, Lainie R. Siegel, Suzanne Von Eck
    A drama set in Las Vegas.

Terry Donnelly, Carolyn McCormick,
Alma Cuervo in *Donahue Sisters*

(Theatre Row Theatre) Friday, Apr. 28–May 14, 1995 (13 performances and 2 previews) Salamander Repertory presents:
RICHARD III by William Shakespeare; Director, Albert Asermely; Costumes, Neville Bean; Press, Jonathan Slaff CAST: Joel Leffert (Richard), Nancy Nichols (Queen Elizabeth), Warren Kelly (Buckingham), John FitzGibbon (Clarence), Rik Walter (Tyrell), Kate Anthony, Jonathan Bell, Michael Briney, John Mark Campbell, Paul Connor, Liam Craig, Robert Devaney, Gordon Gray, Francis E. Hodgins, Kathleen Huber, Randall Rapstine, Joan Shepard, James Tosney, John H. Walker

The action is set in the fifteenth century.

(Kampo Cultral Center) Tuesday, May 2–27, 1995 (27 performances) Women's Project & Productions presents:
THE LAST GIRL SINGER by Deborah Grace Winer; Director, Charles Maryan; Set, Atkin Pace; Lighting, John Gleason; Costumes, Lana Fritz; Sound, Darren Clark; Musical Director, John Wallowitch; Incidental Music, Barbara Carroll; Stage Manager, Christopher Nilne; Press, Shirley Herz/Miller Wright CAST: Kelly Bishop (Ila Farrell), Bill Tatum (Kip Winston), Charlotte Maier (Dorothy Hohenemser)

A comedy about a movie star trying to become a cabaret singer.

(Theatre Four) Tuesday, May 2, 1995–Apr. 28, 1996 Nancy Richards, Judith Resnick, Evangeline Morphos in association with Carol Ostrow and Manhattan Theatre Club present:
AFTER-PLAY by Anne Meara; Director, David Saint; Set, James Youmans; Costumes, Jane Greenwood; Lighting, Don Holder; Sound, John Gromada; Stage Manager, Pamela Singer; Press, Richard Kornberg/Thomas Naro, Don Summa CAST: Lance Reddick (Raziel), Merwin Goldsmith (Marty Guteman), Anne Meara (Terry Guteman), Larry Keith succeeded by Jerry Stiller (Phil Shredman), Barbara Barrie succeeded by Rita Moreno, Jane Powell (Renee Shredman), Rochelle Oliver (Emily Paine), John C. Vennema (Matthew Paine)

A comedy performed without intermission. The action takes place in Manhattan. Originated earlier in the season at Manhattan Theatre Club.

Right: Kate Anthony, Joel Leffert in *Richard III*
Below: Anne Meara, Barbara Barrie in *After-Play*

Jonathan Slaff

Joan Marcus

(Ensemble Studio Theatre) Wednesday, May 3–June 11, 1995 (12 performances each series) Ensemble Studio Theatre presents:
MARATHON '95 Artistic Director, Curt Dempster; Sets, Kert Lundell, Mike Allen; Lighting, Greg MacPherson; Costumes, Lourdes Garcia, Austin Sanderson; Sound, Jeff Taylor; Press, Jim Baldassare
SERIES A: *The Wreck on the Five-Twenty-Five* by Thorton Wilder; Director, Richard Lichte CAST: Deborah Hedwall, James Murtaugh, Melinda Hamilton
The Ryan Interview, or How It Was Around Here by Arthur Miller; Director, Curt Dempster CAST: Mason Adams, Julie Lauren
A Dead Man's Apartment by Edward Allan Baker; Director, Ron Stetson CAST: Ilene Kristen, David McConeghey, Bill Cwikowski, Alexandra Lee
Flyboy by Yvonne Adrian; Director, Maggie Mancinelli CAST: Polly Adams, Adam Fox, Salty Loeb, Ellen Mareneck, Richard Mover, Dan Ziskie
SERIES B: *Credo* by Craig Lucas; Director, Kirsten Sanderson CAST: Marcia Jean Kurtz
Sonny DeRee's Life Flashes Before His Eyes by Bill Bozzone; Director, Keith Reddin CAST: Joseph Siravo, Holter Grahame, Suzanne Shepard
Water and Wine by Stuart Spencer; Director, Nicholas Martin CAST: Frank Biancamano, Chris Ceraso, Justin Theroux, Ed Setrakian
Rain by Garry Williams; Director, Jamie Richards CAST: Kristin Griffith, Richmond Hoxie, Carrie Luft, Heather Robinson, Nicholas Joy
SERIES C: *No One Will Be Immune* by David Mamet; Director, Curt Dempster CAST: Robert Joy, David Rasche
Freud's House by Laurence Klavan; Director, Charles Karchmer CAST: Scott Sherman, Ann Talman
Dearborn Heights by Cassandra Medley; Director, Irving Vincent CAST: Cecelia Antoinette, Linda Powell
   Eighteenth annual spring festival of one act plays.

Julie Lauren, Mason Adams in *Marathon '95*

(American Place Theatre) Wednesday, May 3–June 4, 1995 (19 performances and 11 previews) American Place Theatre presents:
COMING THROUGH Adapted/Directed by Wynn Handman; Set, Vladimir Shpitalnik; Lighting, Rui Rita; Costumes, Kim Wilcox; Stage Manager, Sue Jane Stoker; Press, Jonathan Slaff CAST: David Kener (Manny Steen), Shawn McNesby (Mary Cox), Thomas Pennacchini (Salvatore Crosetti), Mara Stephens (Regina Sass Tepper), David Warren (John Suren Babaian)
   A drama adapted from recorded interviews of the Ellis Island Oral History Project.

Ilene Kristen, David McConeghey in *Marathon '95*

(The Supper Club) Wednesday, May 3–13, 1995 (12 performances) Jujamcyn Theatres presents:
THE DECLINE OF THE (MIDDLE) WEST Lyrics, Fran Landesman; Book, Arnold Weinstein; Director, Susan H. Schulman; Musical Director, Michael Rafter CAST: Robert Michael Baker, Anita Gillette, Paul Harman, Betsy Joslyn, Michelle Pawk
   A musical set around the Crystal Palace nightclub in St. Louis, 1950s and early 1960s.

(Merchant's House Museum) Wednesday, May 3–20, 1995 (12 performances) The Other Theatre presents:
A DOLL'S HOUSE by Henrik Ibsen; Translation, Eva Le Gallienne; Director, Carol Fox Prescott; Set, Betsy McDonald; Lighting, Benjamin Pearcy; Costumes, Kasia Maimone; Sound, Dave Meschter; Choreography, Luly Santangelo; Stage Manager, Miriam Auerbach; Press, Sue Latham CAST: Wendy vanden Heuvel (Nora), Robert Emmet (Torvald), Marlene Schmidt (Helene), Rosemary Quinn (Kristine), Stephen Ringold (Krogstad), Kim Moore (Dr. Rank)
   Performed in three acts.

(Watermark Theater) Thursday, May 4, 1995– Edward Vilga presents:
ACTS OF DESIRE by Neena Beber; Director, Nela Wagman; Set, Sarah Lambert; Costumes, Kitty Leech; Lighting, Joe Saint; Press, Judy Jacksina CAST: Robert Bella, Lauren Hamilton, Jake-Ann Jones, Richard Long
   Four one-act plays.

(Phoenix Gallery) Thursday, May 4–14, 1995 (6 performances)
RUSH HOUR by Stan Vogel; Director, Nora Colpman CAST: Mike Bailey, Nicole Bouras, Iris Dorbian, Carmel Forte, Steven Marvisch, Bonnie Perlman, Caroline Roman, Jami Simon, Stewart Steinberg, Mark Stone
   An urban fantasy.

**(center) Wynn Handman,
(clockwise from far right) Mara Stephens, Thomas Pennacchini, Shawn McNesby, David Kener, David Warren of *Coming Through***

(Cherry Lane Theatre) Tuesday, May 9–July 1, 1995 Stewart F. Lane presents:
FORTUNE'S FOOLS by Frederick Stroppel; Director, John Rando; Set/Projections, Loren Sherman; Costumes, David Murin; Lighting, Phil Monat; Sound, Jim van Bergen; Stage Manager, Christopher De Camillis; Press, Keith Sherman/Jim Byk, Stuart Ginsberg CAST: Tuc Watkins (Jay Morrison), Danton Stone (Chuck Galluccio), Dorrie Joiner (Gail Hildebrandt), Marissa Chibas (Bonnie Sparks)

A comedy in two acts.

(Colony Theater) Wednesday, May 10–21, 1995 (12 performances) The Epoch Theatre presents:
THE END OF THE DAY by Jon Robin Baitz; Director, Alexander Steele CAST: J. Paul Boehmer, CaSandra Brooks, David Cheaney, Hilary Gilford, Phillip Hinch, Dan Sturges

(Triad) Wednesday, May 10–July 15, 1995 (71 performances and 8 previews) Channel Zero Productions in association with Martin & McCall Productions present:
LOOSE LIPS: A Dangerous Revue by Kurt Andersen, Lisa Birnbach and Jamie Malanowski; Director, Martin Charnin; Set, Ken Foy; Lighting, Ken Billington; Music, Keith Levenson; Costumes, Joan Vass; Stage Manager, Nancy Wernick; Press, Peter Cromarty/Philip Thurston CAST: James Biberi, Scott Bryant, Sara Pratter, Keith Primi, Ingrid Rockefeller, Luke Toma GUESTS: Harry Shearer

The National Transcript Players in a revue of outrageous utterances.

(Linhart Theatre) Wednesday, May 10–21, 1995 (13 performances) Musical Theatre Works presents:
THE RINK with Music by John Kander; Lyrics, Fred Ebb; Book, Terrence McNally; Director, Jay Berkow; Musical Director, Kevin Wallace; Choreography, Joey McKneely CAST: Lisa Accardi, Michael Cone, Billy Hartung, Julie Johnson, John MacInnis, Christopher Monteleone; Matthew Orlando, Lorraine Serabian, Dan Sklar

A new production of the 1984 musical set at a decaying roller rink.

Luke Toma, Ingrid R. Rockefeller, Sara Pratter, James Biberi, Scott Bryant, Keith Primi in *Loose Lips*

Dion Graham, Clarence Felder, Matthew Lewis in *2*

Tuc Watkins, Marissa Chibas in *Fortune's Fools*

(Naked Angels) Wednesday, May 10–27, 1995 (16 performances) Naked Angels presents:
SATURDAY, MOURNING CARTOONS by Patrick Breen; Directors, Jace Alexander, Tina Ball, Jo Bonney, Toni Kotite, Fisher Stevens; Set, George Xenos; Costumes, Martha Bromelmeier; Lighting, John-Paul Szczepanski; Sound, Roger Raines; Stage Manager, Darlene Zimbardi CAST: Patrick Breen, Peter Dinklage,, Paul S. Eckstein, Ned Eisenberg, Preston Foerder, Neal Huff, Michelle Hurd, Jodie Markell, Rica Martens, Michael Mastro, Geoffrey Nauffts, Adina Porter, Tim Ransom, Billy Strong, Tom Toner, Bradley White
PROGRAM: *Flood, St. Stans, Wounded Personage, Midnight,* and *Morning Rain*

Four short plays and a talkie.

(Primary Stages) Wednesday, May 10–June 11, 1995 (34 performances) Primary Stages presents:
2: GOERING AT NUREMBERG by Romulus Linney; Director, Thomas Bullard; Set, E. David Cosier; Lighting, Jeffrey S. Koger; Costumes, Teresa Snider-Stein; Sound, Darron L. West, Casey L. Warren; Fights, Jake Turner; Stage Manager, Christine Lemme; Press, Tony Origlio/Stephen Murray CAST: Matthew Lewis (Counsel), Dion Graham (Sergeant), Kevin Cutts (Captain), Craig Wroe (Commandant), Clarence Felder (Hermann Goering), Peter Ashton Wise (Psychiatrist), Laurie Kennedy (Goering's Wife), Alexandra Cohen-Spiegler (Goering's Daughter)

A drama in two acts. The action takes place at the Palace of Justice, Nuremberg, Germany.

(St. Bart's Playhouse) Thursday, May 11–20, 1995 (8 performances) St. Bart's Players present:
NEW FACES OF 1952; Songs/Sketches by Ronnie Graham, Peter DeVries, Arthur Siegel & June Carroll, Alan Melville, Sheldon M. Harnick, Luther Davis & John Cleveland, Melvin Brooks, Murray Grand & Elisse Boyd, Paul E. Lynde and Michael M. Brown; Director, Christopher Catt; Musical Director, Steven Silverstein; Choreography, Stacey Brown Einhorn; Press, Maryellen Conroy CAST: Eric B. Bettelheim, Barbara Blomberg, Melissa Broder Brown, Tracey Cassidy, Corissa Ginsberg, Michael Guy, Mike Irizarry, Joe Kassner, Hope Landry, Alice Muir, Jane Southall, Martin Wallace

A new production of the best known "New Faces" revue.

(Theater for the New City) Thursday, May 11–June 4, 1995 (16 performances) Theater for the New City presents:
THE CAUSE by Yolanda Rodriguez; Director, Crystal Field; Lighting, Donald L. Brooks; Set, Mark Marcante; Stage Manager, Ian Gordon; Press, Jonathan Slaff CAST: Joel Arandia, Israel Cruz, Juan De Larosa, Joseph C. Davies, Sol Echeverria, Pietro Gonzales, Bob Grimm, Jerry Jaffe, Carlos Linares, Mark Marcante, Raul Martinez, Craig Meade, Tessa Martina Morales, Ana Veronica Munoz, Jessy Ortiz, Primy Rivera, Krystal Trinidad, Rookie Tiwari, Michael Vazquez, Venus Velaquez
A three-act drama based on the Puerto Rican independence movement.

(One Dream) Friday, May 12-June 4, 1995 (18 performances) Zena Group presents:
VERTIGO PARK by Mark O'Donnell; Director, Matt Ames; Set, Deborah R. Rosen; Costumes, Lois J. Eastlund; Lighting, Russell H. Champa; Sound, Kurt Kellenberger; Press, Chris Boneau/Adrian Bryan-Brown/ Bob Fennell CAST: Christopher Marobella (Van Walker), Margaret Howard (Carlotta), Josh Liveright (Cliff), Jeremy Gold, Joseph Goscinski, Linda Ames Key, Lisa McNulty, Belinda Morgan, Shaun Powell, Jay Rosenbloom, Andrew VanDusen
A comic saga of decades of (imaginary) American history.

(Ubu Rep Theatre) Friday, May 12–28, 1995 (15 performances) M.A.R.S. Theatre Co. in association with Irish Repertory presents:
MEASURE FOR MEASURE by William Shakespeare; Adaptation, Connor Smith; Director, Kathe Mull CAST: India Cooper, Helen Coxe, Andrew Crawford, Fiona Davis, Sally Goodwin, Gretchen Koerner, Carol London, Ellen McLaughlin, Honor Moor, Jeannie Naughton, Terri O'Neal, Tony Reilly, Paul Soule, Kip Veasy
A reverse-gender adaptation.

Anna Munoz, Krystal Trinidad, Venus in *The Cause*

Ezra Knight, Kate Forbes in *Othello*

Terumi Mattews, Dina Spybey in *Dates and Nuts*

(Tribeca Performing Arts Center) Monday, May 15–25, 1995 (3 Doll and 6 Othello performances) The Acting Company presents:
A DOLL HOUSE by Henrik Ibsen; Translation, Gerry Bamman and Irene B. Berman; Director, Zelda Fichandler; Sets, Douglas Stein; Costumes, Marjorie Slaiman; Lighting, Dennis Parichy; Sound, Susan R. White; Press, Jeffrey Richards/Kevin Rehac, Michelle Lambert CAST: Kate Forbes (Nora), Mark Lewis (Torvald), Kathleen Christal (Kristine Linde), Anthony Ward (Nils), Derek Meader (Dr. Rank), Shona Tucker (Nurse), Stevie Ray Dallimore (Henrik), Eimly and Ted Kaplan, Ada and Gabriel Meyers (Helmer Chldren)
in repertory with
OTHELLO by William Shakespeare; Director, Penny Metropulos; Sets, Michael Vaughn Sims; Costumes, James Scott; Sound/Music, Deena Kaye CAST: Kevin Orton (Roderigo), Allen Gilmore (Iago), Derek Meader (Brabantio), Ezra Knight (Othello), Anthony Ward (Cassio), Kate Forbes (Desdemona), Frank Deal (Duke), Mark Lewis (Lodovico), Andy Paterson (Gratiano/Clown), Gregory Lamont Allen (Solino), Stevie Ray Dallimore (Montano), Shona Tucker (Emilia), Kathleen Christal (Bianca)

(Theater Off Park) Tuesday, May 16–June 11, 1995 (22 performances and 7 previews) Weissberger Theater Group presents:
DATES AND NUTS by Gary Lennon; Director, Donald Douglass; Set, Kalina Ivanov; Lighting, Joe Saint; Costumes, Christopher Del Coro; Sound, Darren Clark; Stage Manager, Cheryl Zoldowski; Press, Gary and John Springer CAST: Dina Spybey (Mary), Terumi Matthews (Eve), Mark Nassar (Al), Thomas Michael Allen (Donald)
A comedy performed without intermission. The action takes place in New York City.

(Kraine Theatre) Wednesday, May 17–June 4, 1995 (15 performances) Peccadillo Theatre Co. presents:
THE SILVER CORD by Sidney Howard; Director, Dan Wackerman; Set/ Lighting, Katherine Spencer; Costumes, Susan Soetaert; Press, Howard and Barbara Atlee CAST: Christine Mosere (Hester), William Steel (David), Cris Parker (Christina), Jeff Woods (Robert), Dale Carman (Mrs. Phelps)
A three-act 1926 drama performed with one intermission. The action takes place in Mrs. Phelps home during winter.

James Ludwig

Carolee Carmello, James Ludwig

in *jon & jen*

(Lambs Little Theatre) Tuesday, May 16–Sept. 1995 Lamb's Theatre Co. and Carolyn Rossi Copeland present:
jon & jen with Music by Andrew Lippa; Lyrics, Tom Greenwald; Book, Mr Lippa and Mr. Greenwald; Director, Gabriel Barre; Orchestrations, Jason Robert Brown; Musical Director, Joel Fram; Set, Charles E. McCarry; Costumes, D. Polly Kendrick; Lighting, Stuart Duke; Stage Manager, Mary Ellen Allison; Press, Kevin P. McAnarney CAST: Carolee Carmello succeeded by Michele Pawk (Jen), James Ludwig (John)
MUSICAL NUMBERS: Welcome to the World, Christmas, Think Big, Dear God, Hold Down the Fort, Timeline, Out of My Sight, Run and Hide, Old Clothes, Little League, Just Like You, Bye Room, What Can I Do?, Smile of Your Dreams, Graduation, The Road Ends Here, That Was My Way, Every Goodbye Is Hello
A musical drama in two acts. The action takes place in America and Canada, 1952–72.

(Grove St. Playhouse) Thursday, May 18–July 24, 1995 The Glines presents:
LADY-LIKE by Laura Shamas; Director, Vivian Sorenson; Set/Lighting, David Jensen; Costumes, Yvonne De Moravia; Sound, Mark Sterling; Choreography, Janet Bogardus; Stage Manager, Courtney Halliday; Press, Shirley Herz/Wayne Wolfe CAST: Angel McKinney (Sarah Ponsonby), Laura Jane Salvato (Lady Eleanor Butler), Jenny Bass (Mary Carryll)
A two-act drama based on the lives of three women who fled Ireland for Wales, 1778–1831.

Right: Laura Jane Salvato, Angela McKinney in *Lady-Like*

(Theater for the New City) Thursday, May 18–June 11, 1995 (14 performances and 2 previews) Theater for the New City presents:
THE HEART IS A LONELY HUNTER by Carson McCullers; Adapted/Directed by David Willinger; Set, Clark Fidelia; Lighting, Zdenek Kriz; Costumes, Tanya Serdiuk; Music, Richard Roque; Press, Jonathan Slaff CAST: Jonathan Cook (Biff Brannon), Tony Greenleaf (John Singer), Ralph Navarro (Spiros), Caesar Paul Del Trecco (Parker/Kelly/Simms/Others), Bryan Schany (Harry/Spareribs/Others), Mari Prentice (Whore/Alice Brannon/Others), Brian Whelehan Husband/Sheriff/Others), Tony Rowe (Storekeeper/Weird Man/Others), Shane Blodgett (Jake Blount), Lea Antolini (Mick Kelly), Dennis R. Jones (Dr.Benedict/Mady Copeland/Others), Kolawole Ogundiran (Willie Copeland/Lunatic/Others), Aixa Kendrick (Portia Copeland)

A drama in two acts. The action takes place in a small city in the South, late 1930s.

(Synchronicity Space) Friday, May 19–June 4, 1995 (13 performances) Synchronicity Theatre Group presents:
THE GOOD WOMAN OF SETZUAN by Bertolt Brecht; Director, Cap Pryor; Set, Mark Symczak; Lighting, David Alan Comstock; Music, Stefan Wolpe; Musical Director, John Dresher CAST: Jody Barrett, Michael Birch, Rachel Bones, Chris Burmester, Bill Dante, John Dresher, Jeff Kronson, Michael Lewis, Cappy Lyons, Bruce Mohat, John Moratis, Bricken Sparacino, Barbara J. Spence, Samme Johnston Spolan

(Puerto Rican Traveling Theatre) Wednesday, May 24–July 2, 1995 (42 performances) The Puerto Rican Traveling Theatre presents:
SIMPSON STREET (LA CALLE SIMPSON) by Eduardo Gallardo; Translation, Toni Diaz, Miriam Colon; Director, Alba Oms; Set, Carl Baldasso; Lighting, Peter Greenbaum; Stage Manager, Fernando Quinn; Press, Max Eisen/Louisa Benton CAST: Anamaria Correa (Angela), Martha De La Cruz (Elva Cruz), Selenis Leyva (Sonia Sanchez), Iraida Polanco (Rosa Sanchez), Carmen Rosario (Lucy), Douglas Santiago (Miguel Rodriguez)

A drama in two acts. The action takes place in the South Bronx, NYC. Performances alternate English and Spanish.

(Duo Theatre) Friday, May 26–June 18, 1995 Duo Theatre presents:
CHEZ GARBO with Music by Michelangelo Alasa' and David Welch; Lyrics/Book/Direction, Mr. Alasa'; Stage Manager, Paul Wontorek CAST: Lynne Charnay (Greta Garbo), Tony Louden (Joe Herrera), Michelle Powers (Young Garbo), Reet Roos Varnik (Linda Weinstar) MUSICAL NUMBERS: Never, I See Myself, I Have Always Collected, Just Let Me Love You, Where Does One Turn To, An Artist Til the End, As I Do, Roses, In a Perfect World, How You've Changed, Dreamers, It's Not Like We Have Forever

A musical set in Garbo's East Side living room.

Jonathan Slaff

Tony Greenleaf, Ralph Navarro in *The Heart Is a Lonely Hunter*

Jonathan Slaff

Dennis R. Jones, Aixa Kendrick in *The Heart Is a Lonely Hunter*

Marilyn Chris in *The Lobster Reef*

(Greenwich St. Theatre) Tuesday, May 30–June 4, 1995 (7 performances)
THE KATHY AND MO SHOW: PARALLEL LIVES by Kathy Najimy and Mo Gaffney; Director, Alan Wynroth; Press, Gary and John Springer CAST: Getchie Argetsinger, Jeanie Kanaley

Two new actresses fill in for the creators in a comedy revue.

(Theatre Row Theatre) Wednesday, May 31–June 17, 1995 (15 performances and 6 previews) HAI Theatre Festival presents:
THE LOBSTER REEF by Eda LeShan; Director, Max Daniels; Set, Miguel Lopez-Castillo; Lighting, Doug Cox; Costumes, Gay Howard; Sound, Brian Hallas; Stage Manager, Frank Laurents; Press, David Rothenberg/David E. Gersten CAST: Marilyn Chris (Ellen)

A one-woman play about fighting cancer.

(William Redfield Theatre) Wednesday, May 31–June 4, 1995 (7 performances) Shotgun Productions presents:
THE CHOICE by Claire Luckham; Director, Linda S. Nelson; Set, Matthew P. Katz; Lighting, Alexandra De Collibus; Costumes, Elissa T. Iberti; Stage Manager, Genia Jo Domico; Press, Mimi Scott CAST: Judith Barcroft (Writer), Bruce G. Bradley (Consultant), Paul McGrane (Ray), Alison Larkin (Sal), Leslie Rohland (Midwife), Jeffrey Poritz (Brother)

A drama set in London.

OFF BROADWAY COMPANY SERIES

AMERICAN JEWISH THEATRE

Twenty-first Season

Artistic Director, Stanley Brechner; Managing Director, Ruth Ann Nightengale; Development, Norman Golden; Press, Jeffrey Richards/ Kevin Rehac, Bruce Roberts, Mimi Scott

Saturday, Nov. 5–Dec. 4, 1994 (29 performances)
HEY BUDDY by Bryan Goluboff; Director, George Ferencz; Set, James Wolk; Costumes, Sally J. Lesser; Lighting, Ernie Barbarash; Music, Sam Mastandrea; Sound, Bruce Ellman; Stage Manager, Kelly Varley CAST: Anthony Grasso (Sal), Justin McCarthy (Eric), David Vadim (Terry), Mark Auerbach (Danny)
A drama performed without intermission. The action takes place in Valley Stream, NY, 1983.

Saturday, Jan. 7–Feb. 5, 1995 (32 performances)
HAVE YOU SPOKEN TO ANY JEWS LATELY? by Bruce Jay Friedman; Director, Michael Rudman; Set, James Wolk; Costumes, Jennifer Di Figlia; Lighting, Deborah Constantine; Sound, Bruce Ellman; Stage Manager, Alexander D Carney CAST: Penny Balfour (Margaret/ Cabaret Artist), Brennan Brown (Tom/Local), Gene Canfield (Lee/Super), Richard M. Davidson (Sid/Bar Patron), Judith Granite (Mrs. Goldman), Christina Haag (Flannery), Larry Pine (Jack), Stephen Singer (Danny)
A hallucination in two acts. The action takes place somewhere in the Northeast during the off season, near future.

Saturday, Mar. 4–Apr. 2, 1995 (32 performances)
MIAMI STORIES; Sets/Lighting, Paul Wonsek; Costumes, Gail Brassard; Sound, Bruce Ellman; Stage Manager, Alexander D Carney
A WEN by Saul Bellow; Director, Charles Karchmer CAST: Barbara Spiegel (Marcella Menelik), Richard M. Davidson (Solomon Ithimar)
THE MAGIC BARREL by Laurence Klavan and Martin Blank; Adapted from Bernard Malamud story; Director, Stanley Brechner CAST: Bernie Passeltiner (Pinye Salzman), Jonathan Brody (Leo Finkle), Dana Smith (Lily H)
IF WALLS COULD TALK by Laurence Klavan; Director, Charles Karchmer CAST: Dana Smith (Arlene), Jonathan Brody (Gilbert), Bernie Passeltiner (Gaggy), Michael Marcus (Uncle Jack), Marvin Chatinover (Gus), Richard M. Davidson (Uncle Ike), Barbara Spiegel (Madge), Judith Granite (Aunt/Woman in Puce)
Three one-act plays set in Miami.

Saturday, Apr. 22–May 28, 1995 (41 performances)
SHABBATAI; Music/Lyrics/Book by Michael Shubert and Michael Edwin; Director, Stanley Brechner; Musical Director, Wendell Smith; Choreography, Joe Locarro; Set, Paul Wonsek; Lighting, David I. Taylor; Costumes, Gail Baldoni; Sound, Fox and Perla; Stage Manager. Alexander D Carney CAST: Rex Hays (Nehemiah), Romain Fruge (Shabbatai), Sam Scalamoni (High Rebbe), Steve Liebman (Middle Rebbe), Darrell Carey (Low Rebbe), Henry James Smith (Young Shabbatai/Boy), Maggi-Med Reed (Sarah), Ken Jennings (Nathan of Gaza)
MUSICAL NUMBERS: Tikkun, Bad Boy, A Good man, Messiah?, Not Another False Messiah, Why Shabbatai, Life Sucks When You're Jewish, People Would Rather Listen to Lies, Redemption Through Sin, Bad Love, Lets Talk Turkey, The Place No One Ever Goes, Good Old Ways, Olam Haba' ah, Confession, It's All How You Look at Things, The Apostasy, Finale
A musical in two acts. The action takes place in the Ottoman Empie, 1639–76.

Carol Rosegg, Gerry Goodstein, Brian Stanton Photos

Larry Pine, Penny Balfour, (rear) Richard M. Davidson, Brennan Brown in *Have You Spoken To Any Jews Lately?*
Top: Mark Auerbach, Anthony Grasso in *Hey Buddy*

Neil Patrick Harris in *Luck, Pluck & Virtue*

Giancarlo Esposito, Anthony Rapp in *Trafficking in Broken Hearts*

ATLANTIC THEATER COMPANY

Artistic Director, Neil Pepe; Managing Director, Joshua Lerner; General Manager, David Topchik; Production Manager, Matthew Silver; Sound, One Dream; Press, Chris Boneau/Adrian Bryan-Brown, Andy Shearer

Thursday, Dec. 8, 1994–Jan. 7, 1995 (29 performances)
TRAFFICKING IN BROKEN HEARTS by Edwin Sanchez; Director, Anna D. Shapiro; Set/Lighting, Kevin Rigdon; Costumes, Laura Cunningham; Music, Max Shapiro; Fights, Rick Sordelet CAST: Giancarlo Esposito (Papo), Neil Pepe (Brian), Anthony Rapp (Bobby)
A drama performed without intermission. The action takes place in New York City.

Tuesday, Jan. 24–Feb. 25, 1995 (34 performances)
MISSING PERSONS by Craig Lucas; Director, Michael Mayer; Set, David Gallo, Lauren Helpern; Lighting, Howard Werner; Costumes, Laura Cunningham; Music, Jill Jaffe CAST: Mary Beth Peil (Addie), Todd Weeks (Hat), John Cameron Mitchell (Steve), Mary McCann (Joan), Camryn Manheim (Gemma), Jordan Lage (Tucker)
A play in two acts. The action takes place in Swarthmore, PA at Thanksgiving, 1994.

Saturday, Mar. 18–Apr. 9, 1995 (26 performances)
LUCK, PLUCK & VIRTUE; Written/Directed by James Lapine; Based on the novel *A Cool Million* by Nathaniel West; Music, Allen Shawn; Lyrics, Ellen Fitzhugh; Sets, Derek McLane; Costumes, Laura Cunningham, Martin Pakledinaz; Lighting, Don Holder; Fights, B.H. Barry; Stage Manager, Kelley Kirkpatrick CAST: Neil Patrick Harris (Lester Price), Adriannie Krstansky (Show Girl), Chris Bauer (Kaplan), Steven Goldstein (Hoffman), Marge Redmond (Mother), MacIntyre Dixon (Nathan Whipple), Elaina Davis (Betty Ferris), Siobhan Fallon (Vendor), Geoffrey Owens (Wellington), Stephen Lee Anderson (Rev. Shaye)
A comedy performed without intermission.

Gerry Goodstein Photos

John Cameron Mitchell, Mary Beth Peil in *Missing Persons*

123

BROOKLYN ACADEMY OF MUSIC

President/Executice Producer, Harvey Lichtenstein; Executive Vice-President, Karen Brooks Hopkins; Producing Director, Joseph V. Melillo; Press, William Murray/Heidi Feldman, Ellen Zeisler/Suzanne Ford

Tuesday, Oct. 4–9, 1994 re-opened Dec. 6–10, 1994 (14 performances)
AS YOU LIKE IT by William Shakespeare; Director, Declan Donnellan; Design, Nick Ormerod; Music, Paddy Cunneen; Lighting, Judith Greenwood; Stage Manager, Marcus Bray CAST: Scott Handy (Orlando de Boys), Jonathan Chesterman (Oliver de Boys), Sean Francis (Jaques de Boys/Le Beau), Richard Cant (Adam/Audrey), Steve Watts (Dennis/Martext), David Hobbs (Duke Frederick/Banished Duke), Simon Coates (Celia), Adrian Lester (Rosalind), Peter Needham (Touchstone), Paul Kissaun (Charles/Corin), Michael Gardiner (Jaques), Rhashan Stone (Amiens/William), Gavin Abbott (Silvius), Wayne Cater (Phebe)
The "Cheek by Jowl" company in an all-male version of Shakespeare's comedy.

Wednesday, Nov. 2–6, 1994 (4 performances)
GAUDEAMUS by Sergei Kaledin; Adapted/Directed by Lev Dodin; Sets, Alexei Porai-Koshits; Stage Manager, Olga Dazidenko CAST: Oleg Dmitriev, Sergei Kargin, Jurii Kordonsky, Natalia Kromina, Igor Koniaev, Igor Nikolaev, Tatiana, Andrei Rostovsky, Vladimir Seleznev, Artem Tsypin, Dmitrii Vitov, Igor Cherenvich, Oleg Gaianov, Alexander Koshkarev, Sergei Kuryshev, Julia Moreva, Maria Nikiforova, Irina Tychinina, Arkadii Sharogradsky
19 improvisations after the story *Construction Battalion* performed by the Maly Drama Theatre of St. Petersburg and the Academy of Theatre Arts of St. Petersburg.

Saturday, Mar. 11–Apr. 9, 1995 (26 performances)
THE MAN WHO; Adapted/Directed by Peter Brooks; Based on the book *The Man Who Mistook His Wife for a Hat* by Oliver Sacks; Collaborator, Marie-Helene Estienne; Music, Mahmoud Tabrizi-Zadeh; Lighting/Stage Manager, Philippe Vialatte CAST: David Bennent, Sotigui Kouyate, Bruce Myers, Yoshi Oida
A drama performed without intermission.

Wednesday, Apr. 26–30, 1995 (5 performances)
THE MOUNTAIN GIANTS by Luigi Pirandello; Director, Giorgio Strehler; Set, Ezio Frigerio CAST: Piccolo Teatro di Milano featuring Andrea Jonasson, Franco Graziosi
An unfinished 1936 drama.

Wednesday, May 17–25, 1995 (6 performances)
GORODISH; Written/Directed by Hillel Mittelpunkt; Music, Ori Vidislavski; Sets, Eitan Levy; Costumes, Michael Laor; Lighting, Benzion Munitz CAST: Igal Naor (Gorodish), Avi Kushnir (Epstein), Yonathan Cherchi (Moshe Dayan), Dov Navon (Friedman), Elisheva Michaeli (Golda Meir), Noa Arad-Brenner (Dalia)
and **FLEISCHER** by Igal Even-Or; Director, Amit Gazit CAST INCLUDES: Joseph Carmon (Arye), Zaharirah Charifai (Berta)
Two drama performed in repertory by Cameri Theatre of Tel Aviv.

Wednesday, May 31–June 3, 1995 (4 performances)
THE WINTER'S TALE by William Shakespeare; Director, Ingmar Bergman; Sets/Costumes, Lennart Mork; Choreography, Donya Feuer; Music, Carl Jonas Love Almquist CAST: Bibi Andersson (Paulina), Irene Lindh (Songe), Pierre Wilkner (Almquist/Dion), Borje Ahlstedt (Leontes), Pernilla August (Hermoine), Anna Bjork (Mamillus), Kristina Tornqvist (Perdita), Krister Henriksson (Polyxenes), Jakob Eklund (Florizel), Gosta Pruzelius (Camillo), Ingvar Kjellson (Antigonus), Jan Blomberg (Cleomenes), Monica Nielsen (Emilia/Dorcas), Anna von Rosen Sundelius (Amalia/Mopsa), Oscar Ljung (Archidamus/Warden), Tord Peterson (Old Shepard), Per Mattsson (Clown), John Zacharias (Judge), Reine Brynolfsson (Autolycus), Gerd Hagman (Gerontes), Jan Nyman (Mariner), Ingvar Kjellson (Old Courtier), Kristina Adolphson (Time), Members of Royal Dramatic Theatre of Sweden
Performed in two acts.

Cheek by Jowl, Bengt Wanselius Photos

Bibi Andersson in *The Winter's Tale*

Peter Needham in *As You Like It*

124

Andrew Polk, Barbara Gulan in *The Truth-Teller*

Fritz Weaver, Jonathan Hogan in *The Professional*

CIRCLE REPERTORY COMPANY

Twenty-sixth Season

Artistic Director, Tanya Berezin; Executive Director, Milan Stitt; Managing Director, Meredith Freeman; Lab Artistic Director, Michael Warren Powell; Literary Manager, Lynn M. Thomson; Development Director, Eileen Jear; Press, Tom D'Ambrosio, Jeffrey Richards/Kevin Rehac, Richard Guido

Wednesday, Nov. 2–Dec. 11, 1994 (31 performances and 16 previews)
3 POSTCARDS; Book, Craig Lucas; Music/Lyrics, Craig Carnelia; Director/Musical Staging, Tee Scatuorchio; Musical Director, Steve Freeman; Set, Derek McLane; Costumes, Toni-Leslie James, Lighting, Tom Sturge CAST: Steve Freeman (Bill), David Pittu (Walter), Johanna Day (Big Jane), Amy Kowallis (Little Jane), Amanda Naughton (K.C.)
MUSICAL NUMBERS: Opening, She Was K.C., What the Song Should Say, See How the Sun Shines, I've Been Watching You, 3 Postcards, The Picture in the Hall, A Minute, I'm Standing in This Room
  A new revision of a 1987 musical performed without intermission. The setting is a New York restaurant.

Thursday, Jan. 26–Feb. 26, 1995 (24 performances and 15 previews)
THE TRUTH-TELLER by Joyce Carol Oates; Director, Gloria Muzio; Set, Stephan Olson; Lighting, Peter Kaczorowski; Costumes, Ellen McCartney; Sound, Janet Kalas; Stage Manager, Denise Yaney CAST: Lynn Hawley (Hedda Culligan), Andrew Polk (Saul Schwartz), John Seitz (Tiny Culligan), Kathleen Widdoes (Nora Culligan), Barbara Gulan (Maggie Culligan), Craig Bockhorn (Biff Culligan), Richard Seff (Nelly Rockefeller)
  A comedy in two acts. The action takes place in an affluent suburb of Buffalo, NY.

Friday, Apr. 28–June 4, 1995 (30 performances and 15 previews)
THE PROFESSIONAL by Dusan Kovacevic; Adapted/Translated by Bob Djurdjevic; Director, Peter Craze; Set, Edward T. Gianfrancesco; Costumes, Mary Myers; Lighting, Brian Aldous; Sound, Chuck London; Stage Manager, Denise Yaney CAST: Fritz Weaver (Luke), Jonathan Hogan (Teya), Jan Maxwell (Martha), Lachlan Macleay succeeded by James Coyle (Lunatic), Ward Asquith (Gravedigger)
  A drama performed without intermission.

Gerry Goodstein Photos

Amanda Naughton, Amy Kowallis, Johanna Day, David Pittu in *3 Postcards*

125

CLASSIC STAGE COMPANY (CSC)

Twenty-eighth Season

Artistic Director, David Esbjornson; Managing Director, Patricia Taylor; Production Manager, Matthew Maraffi; Press, Denise Roberts

Tuesday, Oct. 11–Nov. 13, 1994 (35 performances)
THE SCARLET LETTER by Phyllis Nagy; Adapted from novel by Nathaniel Hawthorne; Director, Lisa Peterson; Set, Neil Patel; Costumes, Michael Krass; Lighting, Kenneth Posner; Music/Sound, Mark Bennett; Stage Manager, Carol Dawes CAST: Cynthia Nixon (Hester Prynne), Dan Daily (Master Brackett), Erin Cressida Wilson (Pearl), Bill Cwikowski (Gov. Bellingham), Sheila Tousey (Mistress Hibbins), Stephen Caffrey (Arthur Dimmesdale), Jon DeVries (Roger Chillingworth)
　A drama in two acts. The action takes place in Boston, 300 years ago.

Wednesday, Nov. 16–27, 1994 (14 performances)
THE DREAM EXPRESS Written/Directed by Len Jenkin; Musical Director, John Kilgore CAST: Deirdre O'Connell, Steve Mellor
　The original outlaw lounge act.

Tuesday, Jan. 31–Mar. 5, 1995 (35 performances)
IPHIGENIA AND OTHER DAUGHTERS by Ellen McLaughlin; Director, David Esbjornson; Set, Narelle Sissons; Costumes, Susan Hilferty; Lighting, Christopher Akerlind; Music/Sound, Gina Leishman; Stage Manager, Crystal Huntington CASTS: *Iphigenia in Aulis:* Susan Heimbinder (Iphigenia), Kathleen Chalfant (Clytemnestra) *Electra:* Sheila Tousey (Electra), Kathleen Chalfant (Clytemnestra), Deborah Hedwall (Chrysothemis), Seth Gilliam (Orestes) *Iphigenia in Tauris:* Susam Heimbinder (Iphigenia), Seth Gilliam (Orestes), Jasmine Curry, Carley Dubicki, Cari Kosins, Karen Sackman, Jill Vinci
　A trilogy performed without intermission.

Tuesday, Apr. 18–May 21, 1995 (31 performances)
AMPHITRYON by Eric Overmyer; Director, Brian Kulick; Set/Costumes, Mark Wendland; Lighting, Kevin Adams; Stage Manager, Lisa Iacucci CAST: Peter Francis James (Jupiter), Arthur Hanket (Mercury), Gina Torres (Alcmena), Katherine Leask (Goddess of Night/Charis), David Edward Jones (Mr. Dawn/Capt./Colonel), Ken Cheeseman (Sosia),
　A comedy in two acts.

T. Charles Erickson Photos

Peter Francis James, Gina Torres in *Amphitryon*
Bottom: Seth Gilliam, Sheila Tousey in
Iphigenia and Other Daughters

126

JEWISH REPERTORY THEATRE

Twenty-first Season

Artistic Director, Ran Avni; Managing Director, Steven M. Levy; Company Manager, James Grosso; Press, Shirley Herz/Wayne Wolfe, Sam Rudy, Miller Wright

(All Productions at Playhouse 91) Saturday, June 4–Sept. 16 transferred to Theatre East before closing April 30, 1995 (292 performances)
THAT'S LIFE! with Music by Rick Cummins, Dick Gallagher, Ben Schaechter, Carolyn Sloan; Lyrics, Adele Ahronheim, Susan DiLallo, Dan Kael, Stacey Luftig, June Siegel, Glenn Slater, Carolyn Sloan, Cheryl Stern, Greer Woodward; Conceived/Directed/Choreographed by Helen Butleroff; Musical Director, Christopher McGovern; Orchestrations, Sande Campbell, Mr. McGovern; Set, Fred Kolo; Costumes, Gail Cooper-Hecht; Lighting, Betsy Finston; Sound, Robert Campbell; Stage Manager, D.C. Rosenberg CAST: David Beach, Lisa Rochelle, Stephen Berger succeeded by Robert Michael Baker, Cheryl Stern, Steve Sterner
MUSICAL NUMBERS: More Than 5700 Years, It's Hard to Be a Patriarch Today, Endangered Species, It's Beyond Me, Tap My Potential, Power Babies, Rhinoplasty, Ina Schoolyard in Brooklyn, My Calling, Funny How Things Happen, A Share of Paradise, Mama I Want to Sit Downstairs, Gorgeous Kay, We Could All Be Jewish If We Tried a Little Harder, Observant in My Way, I Can Pass, Geshrunken Meshuggenah Rag, Jews in Groups, Bei Mir Bist du Rap, Fathers and Sons, Consciousness Karma, Finale
A musical revue in two acts.

Saturday, Oct. 29–Nov. 20, 1994 (24 performances)
THE GIFT HORSE by Michael Hardstark; Director, Robert Kalfin; Set/Lighting, James Tilton; Costumes, Gail Cooper-Hecht; Sound, Steve Shapiro; Stage Manager, Alan M. Fox CAST: Brian Rose (Saul Louderman), Ed Kershen (Phil Louderman), Lex Monson (Willy Slacks), J.J. Reap (Herman Dorfknocker), Sue Brady (Marilyn Krantz), Ronnie Farer (Estelle Louderman), Bernie Passeltiner (Isaac Cantor), Eric Kushnick (Ralph Louderman), Jon Avner (Abe the Babe Riess)
A comedy in two acts. The action takes place in West Hollywood, 1959.

Saturday, Jan. 7–29, 1995 (24 performances)
LIVING PROOF by Gordon Rayfield; Director, Allen Coulter; Set, Michael Bottari, Ronald Case; Costumes, Joan Fedyszyn; Lighting, Betsy Finston; Sound, Donna Riley; Stage Manager, Kristin Newhouse CAST: Michael D. Gallagher (Ryan), Amy Hargreaves (Tiffany), Lee Brock (Claire), Lee Sheperd (Andrew), Rebecca Waxman (Dylan), Jeffrey Spolan (Henry)
A comedy in two acts. The action takes place in Broadlawn, NJ, a wealthy suburb.

Saturday, Mar. 11–Apr. 2, 1995 (24 performances)
AWAKE AND SING! by Clifford Odets; Director, Larry Arrick; Set, Ursula Belden; Costumes, Gail Cooper-Hecht; Lighting, Betsy Finston; Sound, Darren Clark; Stage Manager, Alan Fox CAST: Stephen Mailer (Ralph Berger), David Rosenbaum (Myron Berger), Amanda Peet (Hennie Berger), Salem Ludwig (Jacob Berger), Tovah Feldshuh (Bessie Berger), Tim Zay (Schlosser), Stephen Lang (Moe Axelrod), Avery Schreiber (Uncle Morty), Jeff Casper (Sam Feinschreiber)
A new production of the 1935 drama in three acts. The setting is the Bronx, mid-1930s.

Top: Stephen Lang, Tovah Feldshuh in *Awake and Sing!*
Below: David Beach, Stephen Berger,
Steve Sterner, Cheryl Stern in *That's Life!*

Saturday, May 6–28, 1995 (24 performances)
ANGEL LEVINE with Music/Lyrics/Book by Phyllis K. Robinson; Based on story by Bernard Malamud; Director, Peter Bennett; Musical Director/Arrangements, Phillip Namanworth; Choreography, Hope Clarke; Set, Harry Feiner; Costumes, Tzili Charney; Lighting, Spencer Mosse; Sound, Darren Clark; Stage Manager, Dwight R.B. Cook CAST: Michael Ingram (Finkel), Jordan Leeds (Dr. Morton Scharf), Marilyn Sokol (Fanny), Andre De Shields (Alexander Levine), Pauline Frommer (Muriel), Curtiss I' Cook (Night Singer), Charles E. Wallace (Archibald Taylor), Tina Fabrique (Bella), Vanessa A. Jones, Reggie Phoenix, Julie Pasqual (Ensemble)
MUSICAL NUMBERS: Finkel's Lament, The Name Is Levine, Come Spring, Black Is the Color of Night, It's a Gift, Only Believe, Can It Happen, Nobody Believes in Me, You Can't Sing the Blues When You Tango, Something to Live For, I'm Only Human, Hand Song, Come to the Wild Side, God Made the Grass Be Green, Making a Living, Checkered Suit Fancy Tie Two-Tone Leather Spats, Levine's Turn, Finale
A musical in two acts. The action takes place in New York City, 1948.

Gerry Goodstein/Carol Rosegg-Martha Swope Photos

LINCOLN CENTER THEATER

Tenth Season

Artistic Director, Andre Bishop; Executive Producer, Bernard Gersten; General Manager, Steven C. Callahan; Production Manager, Jeff Hamlin; Development Director, Hattie K. Jutagir; Press, Merle Debuskey/Susan Chicoine, Wylie Strout, Owen Levy

(Off-Bdwy productions at Mitzi E. Newhouse Theater) Friday, Nov. 11, 1994–Mar. 26, 1995 (129 performances and 27 previews)
HAPGOOD by Tom Stoppard; Director, Jack O'Brien; Sets, Bob Crowley; Costumes, Ann Roth; Lighting, Beverly Emmons; Projections, Wendall K. Harrington; Sound, Scott Lehrer; Music, Bob James; Stage Manager, Jeff Lee CAST: Stockard Channing (Hapgood), Clifton Davis succeeded by David Wolos-Fonteno (Wates), David Lansbury (Ridley), Graeme Malcolm (Radio Voices), Boris McGiver (Russian/Intern/Radio Voices), Brian F. O'Byrne (Merryweather), Yaniv Segal (Joe), Josef Sommer (Blair), David Strathairn (Kerner), Michael Winther (Maggs)
An espionage drama in two acts. The action takes place in London, 1989.

Right: David Lansbury, Stockard Channing in *Hapgood*
Below: Stockard Channing, David Strathairn, David Lansbury, Josef Sommer in *Hapgood*

Thursday, May 11–Aug. 6, 1995 (70 performances and 31 previews)
TWELVE DREAMS; Written/Directed by James Lapine; Sets, Adrianne Iobel; Costumes, Martin Pakledinaz; Lighting, Peter Kaczorowski; Sound, Dan Moses Schreier; Music, Allen Shawn; Dance Staging, Lar Lubovitch; Stage Manager, Beverley Randolph   CAST: Harry Groener (Charles Hatrick), Mischa Barton (Emma Hatrick), Kathleen Chalfant (Jenny), Jan Rubes (Professor), Matthew Ross (Sanford Putnam), Donna Murphy (Dorothy Trowbridge), Meg Howrey (Miss Banton), Brittany Boyd (Rindy)

A new production of a 1981 drama in two acts. The action takes place in a New England university town, December, 1936.

For other Lincoln Center Theater productions: *Arcadia*, *The Heiress*, see BROADWAY CALENDAR.

Ken Howard, Joan Marcus Photos

Top: Meg Howrey, Mischa Barton,
Brittany Boyd in *Twelve Dreams*
Right: Donna Murphy, Harry Groener in *Twelve Dreams*

(clockwise from Left) **Frank Whaley, Peter Frechette, Nick Phelps, Jonathan Marc Sherman, Robert Sean Leonard** in *The Great Unwashed*

MALAPARTE THEATRE COMPANY

Third Season

Artistic Director, Ethan Hawke; Producing Director, Jason Blum; Managing Director, Troy Hollar; Set Designer, Alexander Dodge; Lighting Designer, Jeff Croiter; Production Stage Manager, Elizabeth Timperman

(All plays at Theatre Row Theatre) Friday, Oct. 7–23, 1994 (15 performances)
VEINS AND THUMBTACKS by Jonathan Marc Sherman; Director, Ethan Hawke; Costumes, Therese Bruck; Sound, Raymond Schilke CAST: Frank Whaley (Jimmy Bonaparte), Lynn Cohen (Grandmother), Jenny Robertson (Annie), Matthew Weiss (Chapel Owner), Nicole Burdette (Nurse), Jose Zuniga (Arturo Constantini), Calliope Thorne (Tralice), Jenny Matthews (Wendy Bonaparte)
A drama performed without intermission. The setting is New Jersey.

Frank Whaley, Lynn Cohen in *Veins and Thumbtacks*

Friday, Nov. 4–12, 1994 (8 performances)
HESH by Matthew Weiss; Director, Frank Pugliese; Assistant Director, James Waterston; Costumes, Therese Bruck, Mimi O'Donnell, Laura Yates; Sound, Raymond Schilke CAST: Ned Eisenberg (Hesh), Ethan Hawke (Sammy), Nadia Dajani (Bianca), Frank Whaley (Jacob), Missy Yager (Gwen)
A drama in two acts. The action takes place in Rye, NY and NYC, 1974–91.

Friday, Nov. 18–Dec. 4, 1994 (15 performances)
THE GREAT UNWASHED by Nicole Burdette; Director, Max Mayer; Costumes, Arden, Jana C. Kelley; Sound, Michael Clark CAST: Peter Frechette (Bud), Jenny Robertson (Bridgit "Jesse" James), Nick Phelps (Hood), Robert Sean Leonard (Fr. Michael Casey), Frank Whaley (Tom Casey), Ethan Hawke (Beau Casey), Martha Plimpton (Katie), Jonathan Marc Sherman (Eddie), Lynn Cohen (Mrs. Casey)
A drama in two acts.

Malaparte readings and musical evenings were held in New York City and at Vassar.

Anna Thompson Photos

Frank Whaley, Ethan Hawke, Robert Sean Leonard
in a Malaparte Coffeehouse

130

Nathan Lane, Stephen Spinella in Manhattan Theatre Club's *Love! Valour! Compassion!*

MANHATTAN THEATRE CLUB

Twenty-third Season

Artistic Director, Lynne Meadow; Managing Director, Barry Grove; General Manager, Victoria Bailey; Associate Artistic Director, Michael Bush; Play Development, Kate Loewald; Development Director, Mark Hough; Press, Helene Davis, Amy Lefkowitz, Barbara Carroll

(Stage I) Tuesday, Oct. 11, 1994–Jan. 1, 1995 (72 performances and 24 previews) transferred to Broadway Jan. 20, 1995
LOVE! VALOUR! COMPASSION! by Terrence McNally; Director, Joe Mantello; Sets, Loy Arcenas; Costumes, Jess Goldstein; Lighting, Brian MacDevitt; Sound, John Kilgore; Choreography, John Carrafa; Stage Manager, William Joseph Barnes CAST: Stephen Bogardus (Gregory Mitchell), John Benjamin Hickey (Arthur Pape), Stephen Spinella (Perry Sellars), John Glover (John Jeckyll), Nathan Lane (Buzz Hauser), Justin Kirk (Bobby Brahms), Randy Becker (Ramon Fornos), John Glover (James Jeckyll)
A drama in three acts. The action takes place in a remote house in Duchess County, New York on Memorial Day weekend, 4th of July weekend, and Labor Day weekend.

(Stage II) Tuesday, Oct. 25–Dec. 18, 1994 (41 performances and 23 previews)
DURANG DURANG by Christopher Durang; Director, Walter Bobbie; Set, Derek McLane; Costumes, David C. Woolard; Lighting, Brian Nason; Sound, Tony Meola; Stage Manager, Perry Cline
MRS. SORKEN CAST: Patricia Elliott (Mrs. Sorkin)
FOR WHOM THE SOUTHERN BELLE TOLLS CAST: Lizbeth Mackay (Amanda), Keith Reddin (Lawrence), David Aaron Baker (Tom), Patricia Randell (Ginny)
A STYE OF THE EYE CAST: Marcus Giamatti (Jake), Becky Ann Baker (Ma), Patricia Elliott (Dr. Martina), Keith Reddin (Agnes/Beth), Lizbeth Mackay (Meg), David Aaron Baker (Wesley), Patricia Randell
NINA IN THE MORNING CAST: David Aaron Baker (Narrator), Patricia Randell (Maid), Patricia Elliott (Nina), Keith Reddin (James/Robert/LaLa), Marcus Giamatti (Foote)
WANDA VISIT CAST: Marcus Giamatti (Jim), Lizbeth Mackay (Marsha), Becky Ann Baker (Wanda), David Aaron Baker (Waiter)
BUSINESS LUNCH AT THE RUSSIAN TEA ROOM CAST: Keith Reddin (Chris), Patricia Elliott (Margaret), Marcus Giamatti (Waiter), Patricia Randell (Melissa Stearn)
One-act comedies.

(Stage II) Tuesday, Jan. 10–Mar. 5, 1995 (59 performances and 24 previews) transferred to Theatre Four on May 2, 1995.
AFTER-PLAY by Anne Meara; Director, David Saint; Set, James Youmans; Costumes, Jane Greenwood; Lighting, Don Holder; Sound, John Gromada; Stage Manager, Lisa Iacucci CAST: Merwin Goldsmith (Marty Guteman), Rue McClanahan (Terry Guteman), Larry Keith (Phil Shredman), Barbara Barrie (Renee Shredman), Lance Reddick (Raziel), Rochelle Oliver (Emily Paine), John C. Vennema (Matthew Paine)
A comedy in two acts. The aetting is a Manhattan restaurant.

(Stage I) Tuesday, Jan. 31–Apr. 9, 1995 (56 performances and 24 previews)
HOLIDAY HEART by Cheryl L. West; Director, Tazewell Thompson; Set, Riccardo Hernandez; Costumes, Tom Broecker; Lighting, Jack Mehler; Sound, James Wildman; Fights, Brad Waller; Stage Manager, James Fitzsimmons CAST: Afi McClendon (Niki Dean), Keith Randolph Smith (Holiday Heart), Maggie Rush (Wanda Dean), Ron Cephas Jones (Silas Jericho), Alimi Nallard (Ricky/Mark)
A drama in two acts. The action takes place in South Chicago.

Top: Penny Fuller, Buck Henry in *Three Viewings*

(Stage II) Tuesday, Mar. 14–Apr. 30, 1995 (32 performances and 24 previews)
THREE VIEWINGS by Jeffrey Hatcher; Director, Mary B. Robinson; Set, James Noone; Costumes, Michael Krass; Lighting, Pat Dignan; Sound, Bruce Ellman; Stage Manager, Tom Aberger
TELL TALE CAST: Buck Henry (Emil)
THE THIEF OF TEARS CAST: Margaret Whitton (Mac)
THIRTEEN THINGS ABOUT ED CARPOLOTTI CAST: Penny Fuller (Virginia)
Three monologues set in a midwestern funeral parlor.

(American Place Theatre) Wednesday, Mar. 29–May 28, 1995 (39 performances and 32 previews)
NIGHT AND HER STARS by Richard Greenberg; Director, David Warren; Set, Derek McLane; Costumes, Walker Hicklin; Lighting, Peter Kaczorowski; Projections, Wendall K. Harrington; Music/Sound, Michael Roth; Stage Manager, Ruth Kreshka CAST: Patrick Breen (Herb Stempel), Keith Charles (Mark Van Doren), Peter Frechette (Dan Enright), Ileen Getz (Toby Stempel), Jordan Lage (Al Freedman), David Andrew MacDonald (Jack Barry), Reese Madigan (Warren Corso), Linda Pierce (Doris), John Slattery (Charles Van Doren)
A drama in two acts. The action concerns the TV quiz show scandals of the 1950s.

(Stage I) Tuesday, May 2–Sept. 23, 1995 (167 performances) transferred to John Houseman Theatre on Sept.29, 1995
SYLVIA by A.R. Gurney; Director, John Tillinger; Set, John Lee Beatty; Costumes, Jane Greenwood; Lighting, Ken Billington; Sound, Aural Fixation; Stage Manager, Roy Harriss CAST: Sarah Jessica Parker (Sylvia), Charles Kimbrough succeeded by John Cunningham (Greg), Blythe Danner succeeded by Mariette Hartley (Kate), Derek Smith (Tom/Phyllis/Leslie)
A two-act comedy about loving your dog. The setting is New York City.

(Stage II) Thursday, May 18–July 2, 1995 (56 performances)
THE RADICAL MYSTIQUE; Written/Directed by Arthur Laurents; Set, Thomas Lynch; Costumes, Theoni V. Aldredge; Lighting, Kenneth Posner; Sound, Bruce Ellman; Stage Manager, Sandra Lea Carlson CAST: Mary Beth Fisher (Josie Gruenwald), Sharon Washington (Janice Catlett), Oren J. Sofer (Father Gruenwald), Kevin J. O'Rourke (Tad Gruenwald), Jake Weber (Merriwell)
A drama in two acts. The action takes place in Greenwich Village at the end of the sixties.

Joan Marcus, Martha Swope Photos

Lance Reddick, Rue McClanahan, Merwin Goldsmith in *After-Play*

Charles Kimbrough, Sarah Jessica Parker in *Sylvia*

Peter Frechette, John Slattery in *Night and Her Stars*

Maggie Rush, Afi McClendon, Keith Randolph Smith in *Holiday Heart*

Oren J. Sofer, Sharon Washington, Kevin O'Rourke,
Mary Beth Fisher in *Radical Mystique*

Marcus Giamatti, Lizbeth Mackey,
Becky Ann Baker in *Durang Durang*

MINT THEATRE COMPANY

Third Season

Executive Artistic Director, Kelly Morgan; Producing Artistic Director, Jonathan Bank; Financial Director, Andrew Chipok; Company Manager, Rachel Hoyer; Press, David Rothenberg, Fran Burch

Thursday, July 21–31, 1994 (8 performances)
IRVING BERLIN RAGTIME REVUE; Director, Robert Dahdah; Choreography, Craig Meade; Music Director, Mark Victor Smith; Set/Lighting, Donald L. Brooks; Costumes, James Bidgood; Stage Manager, S.D. Wagner CAST: Judy Ayres (Justine Johnstone/Marion Davies), Del Matthew Bigtree (Irving Berlin), John Cloutman (George M. Cohan/Ted Snyder), Donna Marie Conti (Mary Garden/Fanny Brice/Irene Castle), Carla Hall (Gaby Deslys/Baroness Rosen), Alvin Le-Bass (Bert Williams), Rebecca Thomas (Valeska Suratt), Jerry Williams (Frank Tinney/Richard Whiting/Vernon Castle)
  A musical revue in two acts.

Thursday, Sept. 8–Oct. 2, 1994 (16 performances)
PEANUTS AND CRACKER JACK by Jerry Slaff; Director, William Strempek; Set, Christopher H. Jones; Lighting, Craig Caccamise; Sound, Carmen Borgia; Stage Manager, Cristine Ann Richmond CAST: J. Bryan McMillen (Dave Webster), Richard Willis (Whitey Lamonica), Craig Mason (Announcers)
  A comedy in two acts. The action takes place in the NY Yankees locker room and dugout, early 1970s.

Friday, Oct. 7–30, 1994 (15 performances)
LADY WINDERMERE'S FAN by Oscar Wilde; Director, James B. Nicola CAST: Jennifer Rohn, Barbara Reierson, Terico Bretas, Barbara Becker, Peter Husovsky, Craig Dean Mason, James Conant, Julie Mer

Wednesday, Jan. 11–Apr. 9, 1995 (59 performances and 18 previews)
UNCLE BOB by Austin Pendleton; Director, Kelly Morgan; Set, Jeffrey Pajer; Lighting, Craig Caccamise; Sound, Carmen Borgia; Costumes, Paula Godsey CAST: George Morfogen (Bob), Adam Sumner Stein (Josh)
  A drama performed without intermission.

Thursday, Apr. 20–May 14, 1995 (17 performances)
QUALITY STREET by J.M. Barrie; Director, Jonathan Bank; Set, Curtis Phillips; Lighting, Mark T. Simpson; Costumes, Paula Godsey; Sound, Francys Olivia Burch CAST: Lisa M. Bostnar (Phoebe Throssel), Barbara Becker (Susan Throssel), Deborah Thomas (Mary Willoughby), Jennifer Blaine (Fanny Willoughby), Ayelet Kaznelson (Henrietta Turnbull), Karen Oster (Patty), Jada Roberts (Charlotte Parratt), K. Elson (Harriet), Jennifer Kennedy (Isabella), Shauna Lewis (Beveridge), Shakiea Lewis (Elizabeth), Tim Goldrick (Valentine Brown), David Richard (Sergeant), Nick Dantos (Ensign Blades), Felix Solis (Lt. Spicer), Jarius Steed (Arthur Wellesly Tomson), Jonathan Rosa (William Smith), William Adams (George Williams)
  A 1901 four-act play performed with one intermission.

Bob Newey Photos

Top: George Morfogen, Adam Stein in *Uncle Bob*
Center: Tim Goldrick, Lisa M. Bostnar in *Quality Street*
Right: J. Bryan McMillen, Richard Willis
in *Peanuts and Cracker Jack*

Paul Calderon, James Colby, Nelson Vasquez in New York Shakespeare Festival's *Blade to the Heat*

Lisa Gay Hamilton, Malcolm Gets, Joel De La Fuente, Nance Williamson in *Two Gentlemen of Verona*

NEW YORK SHAKESPEARE FESTIVAL

Fortieth Season

Producer, George C. Wolfe; Managing Director, Jason Steven Cohen; Associate Producers, Rosemarie Tichler, Kevin Kline; General Manager, Sally Campbell Morse; Press, Carol Fineman, Terence Womble, Eugenie Hero

(Delacorte/Central Park) Thursday, June 23–July 24, 1994 (28 performances)
THE MERRY WIVES OF WINDSOR by William Shakespeare; Director, Daniel Sullivan; Set, John Lee Beatty; Costumes, Ann Hould-Ward; Lighting, Allen Lee Hughes; Sound, Tom Morse; Music, Stanley Silverman; Stage Manager, Jess Lynn CAST: Millie Chow (Anne Page), Brian Coats (John), John Ellison Conlee (John), Enrico Colantoni (Nym), Kevin Dewey (Simple), David Alan Grier (Master Frank Ford), George Hall (Justice Shallow), Walker Jones (Abraham Slender), Andrea Martin (Mistress Quickly), Reggie Montgomery (Hugh Evans), Brian Murray (Falstaff), Chris O'Neill (Bardolph), Kevin Orton (John Rugby), Miguel Perez (George Page), Alec Phoenix (Fenton), Tonya Pinkins (Mistress Ford), Bray Poor (Pistol), Steve Ryan (Host), Rocco Sisto (Dr. Caius), Pedro James Vasquez (Robin), Margaret Whitton (Mistress Page), C.J. Wilson (Robert), Candace Marie Bennett, Jennifer Carroll, Shelton Dane, Jesse Ontiveros, Nick Sullivan, Collette Wilson (Ensemble)
The comedy performed in two acts is the 25th production of the NYSF Shakespeare Marathon.

(Delacorte/Central Park) Thursday, Aug. 4–Sept. 4, 1994 (22 performances)
TWO GENTLEMEN OF VERONA by William Shakespeare; Director, Adrian Hall; Set, Eugene Lee; Costumes, Catherine Zuber; Lighting, Ken Billington; Sound, Tom Morse; Music, Richard Cumming; Stage Manager, Lisa Buxbaum CAST: Joel De La Fuente (Valentine), Robert Dorfman (Speed), Herb Foster (Sir Eglamour), Peter J. Gerety (Launce), Malcolm Gets (Proteus), Lisa Gay Hamilton (Silvia), Thomas Ikeda (Panthino), Marc Damon Johnson (2nd Outlaw), Camryn Manheim (Lucetta), Daniel Mastrogiorgio (3rd Outlaw), Jerry Mayer (Antonio), Brett Rickaby (Outlaw), Jack Ryland (Duke of Milan), Steven Skybell (Thurio), Nance Williamson (Julia), Brian Coats, John Ellison Conlee, Tracey Copeland, Christopher Duva, Jeff Stafford, Kristi Wedemeyer (Ensemble)
The comedy performed in two acts is the 26th production of the NYSF Shakespeare Marathon.

(Public/Anspacher) Tuesday, Oct. 18–Dec. 4, 1994 (38 performances and 18 previews)
BLADE TO THE HEAT by Oliver Mayer; Director, George C. Wolfe; Set, Riccardo Hernandez; Costumes, Paul Tazewell; Lighting, Paul Gallo; Sound, Dan Moses Schreier; Fights, Michael Olajide, Jr.; Stage Manager, Gwendolyn M. Gilliam CAST: Carlton Wilborn (Garnet), Chuck Patterson (Three-finger Jack), Jaime Tirelli (Alacran), Paul Calderon (Mantequilla Decima), Kamar De Los Reyes (Pedro Quinn), James Colby (Reporter/Announcer/Referee), Maricela Ochoa (Sarita Malacara), Nelson Vasquez (Wilfred Vinal)
A drama in two acts. The action is set in 1959.

(Public/Shiva) Tuesday, Oct. 18–Dec. 31, 1994 (45 performances)
SOME PEOPLE; Written/Performed by Danny Hoch; Director, Jo Bonney; Lighting, David Castaneda; Stage Manager, Sarah Sidman
One-man show creating 11 New York characters.

(Public/Shiva) Thursday, Oct. 27–Dec. 31, 1994 (34 performances and 3 previews)
THE DIVA IS DISMISSED by Jenifer Lewis and Charles Randolph-Wright; Director, Mr. Randolph-Wright; Musical Director, Michael Skloff; Lighting, David Castaneda CAST: Jenifer Lewis
One-woman musical memoir. Performed in repertory with Some People.

Top: David Drake, B.D. Wong in *A Language of Their Own*

(Public/Newman) Tuesday, Nov. 1–Dec. 18, 1994 (40 performances and 16 previews)
SIMPATICO; Written/Directed by Sam Shepard; Set, Loy Arcenas; Costumes, Elsa Ward; Lighting, Anne Militello; Sound, Tom Morse; Music, Patrick O'Hearn; Stage Manager, Ruth Kreshka CAST: Ed Harris (Carter), Fred Ward (Vinnie), Marcia Gay Harden (Cecilia), James Gammon (Simms), Welker White (Kelly), Beverly D'Angelo (Rosie)
A drama in three acts. The action takes place in Cucamonga, San Dimas, Lexington and Midway, Kentucky.

(Public/Martinson) Tuesday, Dec. 6, 1994–Jan. 15, 1995 (32 performances and 16 previews)
THE PETRIFIED PRINCE with Music/Lyrics by Michael John LaChiusa; Book, Edward Gallardo; Based on screenplay by Ingmar Bergman; Director, Harold Prince; Musical Staging, Rob Marshall; Orchestrations, Jonathan Tunick; Musical Director, Jason Robert Brown; Sets, James Youmans; Costumes, Judith Dolan; Lighting, Howell Binkley; Sound, Jim Bay; Stage Manager, Bonnie Metzgar CAST: Loni Ackerman (Roberta), Gabriel Barre (Franz), Geoffrey Blaisdell (Gen. Montesquieu), Robert Blumenfeld (Judge Schied), Alan Braunstein (Napoleon), Candy Buckley (Queen Katarina), Ralph Byers (Pope Pius VII), Marilyn Cooper (Mama Chiaramonte), Alexander Gaberman (Prince Samson), Timothy Jerome (Cardinal Pointy), Mal Z. Lawrence (King Maximillian/Abbe Sebastian/Fernando/Gypsy King), George Merritt (Gen. Petschul), Judith Moore (Nursemaid), Daisy Prince (Elise), Jane White (Madame Paulina), Mindy Cooper, Wendy Edmead, Nicholas Garr, Amy N. Heggins, Darren Lee, David Masenheimer, Dana Moore, Troy Myers, Casey Nicholaw, Cynthia Sophiea, Mark Anthony Taylor, Sally Ann Tumas (Ensemble)
MUSICAL NUMBERS: Move, There Are Happy Endings, His Family Tree, The Easy Life, Abbe's Appearance, Samson's Thoughts, Pointy's Lament, A Woman in Search of Happiness, Napoleon's Nightmare, Dormez-Vous, One Little taste, Never Can Tell, Look Closer Love, Stay, Without Me, Animal Song, Samson's Epiphany, Fernando's Suicide, Addio Bambino, What the Prince Is Saying, I Would Like to Say, Finale
A musical in two acts. The action takes place in Slavonia, 1807.

(Public/LuEsther) Tuesday, Dec. 13, 1994–Jan. 8, 1995 (13 performances and 25 previews)
HIM by Christopher Walken; Director, Jim Simpson; Set/Lighting, Kyle Chepulis; Costumes, Franne Lee; Musical Director/Sound, Mike Nolan; Choreography, John Carrafa; Stage Manager, Kristen Harris CAST: Christopher Walken (Him), Rob Campbell (Bro), Larry Block (Doc/Borden/Taxman/Stylagi), Barton Heyman (Joe/Mel), Peter Appel (Al/Disappointed Fan/Stylagi), Ellen McElduff (Nurse/Dolores/Journalist)

A play about "the king" performed without intermission.

(Public/Anspacher) Tuesday, Jan. 17–Feb. 26, 1995 (48 performances)
THE MERCHANT OF VENICE by William Shakespeare; Director, Barry Edelstein; Sets, John Arnone; Costumes, Catherine Zuber; Lighting, Mimi Jordan Sherin; Sound, darren Clark; Music, Michael Torke; Stage Manager, William H. Lang CAST: Peter Jay Fernandez (Gratiano), Jay Goede (Bassanio), Gail Grate (Nerissa), Earle Hyman (Tubal/Duke of Venice), Robert Jason Jackson (Prince of Morocco), Byron Jennings (Antonio), Walker Jones (Old Gobbo/Prince of Arragon/Stephano), Nina Landey (Jessica), Ron Leibman (Shylock), Paul Mullins (Salerio), Tom Nelis (Lancelot), Billy Porter (Solanio), Peter Rini (Balthazar), Laila Robins (Portia), Willis Sparks (Lorenzo), Cornel Womack (Leonardo)

Performed with one intermission. This is production #27 in the NYSF Shakespeare Marathon.

(Public/Martinson) Tuesday, Feb. 7–Mar. 12, 1995 (25 performances and 15 previews)
SILENCE, CUNNING, EXILE by Stuart Greenman; Director, Mark Wing-Davey; Set, Derek McLane; Costumes, Catherine Zuber; Lighting, Christopher Akerlind; Sound, John Gromada; Fights, Nels Hennum; Stage Manager, Thom Widmann CAST: Elizabeth Marvel (Suzie), Denis O'Hare (Donald), Margaret Whitton (Beryl), Tim Hopper (Frank), Fiona Davis (Nicole), Adina Porter (Kiki), Matte Osian (Transient/Boyfriend/Inert Man), Rocco Sisto (Isaac), Michael Lynch (Transvestite), Jerry Mayer (Prostitute), Timothy Wheeler (Acquaintance/Party Man)

A two-act drama based on the life of photographer Diane Arbus.

Anna Maria Horsford, Terry Alexander, Andre De Shields in *Dancing on Moonlight*

Rob Campbell, Christopher Walken in *Him*

Ed Harris, Marcia Gay Harden in *Simpatico*

Rocco Sisto, David Alan Grier, Reggie Montgomery, Tonya Pinkins in *The Merry Wives of Windsor*

(Public/Anspacher) Tuesday, Apr. 4–30, 1995 (32 performances)
DANCING ON MOONLIGHT by Keith Glover; Director, Marion McClinton; Set, Riccardo Hernandez; Costumes, Karen Perry; Lighting, Paul Gallo; Sound, Dan Moses Schreier; Music, Max Roach; Choreography, Donald Byrd; Fights, David Leong; Stage Manager, Jana Llynn CAST: Adina Porter (Anansi), Kevin Jackson (Apollotis), Terry Alexander (Dady Jerry), Anna Maria Horsford (Neptune), Badja Djola (Eclipse), Andre De Shields (Sorry Charlie), Kim Yancey (La Ronda), Ray Anthony Thomas (Robber Lee)

A drama in two acts with prologue. The action takes place in Harlem, 1935–60.

(Public/Shiva) Tuesday, Apr. 4–May 28, 1995 (46 performances and 18 previews)
A LANGUAGE OF THEIR OWN by Chay Yew; Director, Keng-Sen Ong; Set, Myung Hee Cho; Costumes, Michael Krass; Lighting, Scott Zielinski; Music, Liang-Xing Tang; Fights, J. Steven White; Stage Manager, Buzz Cohen CAST: B.D. Wong (Ming), Francis Jue (Oscar), David Drake (Robert), Alec Mapa (Daniel)

A drama in two acts.

(Public/Martinson) Tuesday, Apr. 11–May 21, 1995 (15 performances and 33 previews)
DOG OPERA by Constance Congdon; Director, Gerald Gutierrez; Set, John Lee Beatty; Costumes, Toni-Leslie James; Lighting, Brian McDevitt; Sound, Otts Munderloh; Stage Manager, Marjorie Horne CAST: Albert Macklin (Peter Szczepanek), Kristine Nielsen (Madeline Newell), Kevin Dewey (Jackie), Rick Holmes (Steven/Chris/David/Tim/Hank), Sloane Shelton (Bernice/Ruby/Dale Williamson/Doris/Maureen), Eduardo Andino (Joe's Lover/Street Man/Stavros/Paul/Arapahoe), Richard Russell Ramos (Charlie Szczepanek/Brad/Sunny)

A comedy in two acts.

Michael Daniel, Martha Swope Photos

John Christopher Jones, Marisa Tomei in *Slavs!*

Studio production of *Rent*

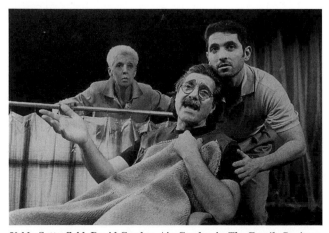

Valda Setterfield, David Gordon, Ain Gordon in *The Family Business*

NEW YORK THEATRE WORKSHOP

Artistic Director, James C. Nicola; Managing Director, Nancy Kassak Diekmann; Associate Artistic Director, Christopher Grabowski; General Manager, Esther Cohen; Press, Richard Kornberg/Bill Schelble, Barbara Carroll, Sandra Manley, Tom Naro, Don Summa

Friday, June 10–July 9, 1994 (30 performances)
101 HUMILIATING STORIES; Written/Performed by Lisa Kron; Director, John Robert Hoffman; Set, Amy Shock; Costumes, Jose Gutierrez, Chip White; Stage Manager, Janet M. Clark
A comic monologue.

Thursday, Sept. 8–Oct. 22, 1994 (45 performances)
THE SECRETARIES; Written/Performed by The Five Lesbian Brothers; Set, James Schuette; Costumes, Susan Young; Lighting, Nancy Schertler; Sound, Darron L. West; Fights, J. Allen Suddeth; Stage Manager, Janet M. Clark CAST: Maureen Angelos (Dawn Midnight/Buzz Benikee), Babs Davy (Ashley Elizabeth Frantangelo), Dominique Dibbell (Patty Johnson), Peg Healey (Susan Curtis), Lisa Kron (Peaches Martin)
A comedy performed without intermission.

Saturday, Oct. 29–Nov. 6, 1994 (7 performances)
RENT with Music/Lyrics/Book by Jonathan Larson; Director, Michael Greif; Musical Director, Tim Weil; Set/Costumes, Angela Wendt; Lighting, Blake Burba; Sound, S.R. White; Original Concept/Additional Lyrics, Billy Aronson; Stage Manager, Kristen Harris CAST: Anthony Rapp (Mark Cohen), Tony Hoylen (Roger Davis), Pat Briggs (Tom Collins), Mark Setlock (Angel Dumott Schunard), Sarah Knowlton (Maureen Johnson), Shelley Dickinson (Joanne Jefferson), Daphne Rubin-Vega (Mimi Marquez), Michael Potts (Benjamin Coffin III), Erin Hill (Blockbuster Rep.), Deirdre Boddie-Henderson, Gilles Chiasson, Sheila Kay Davis, John Lathan, Jesse Sinclair Lenat
MUSICAL NUMBERS: Message #1, Rent, Cool/Fool, Today for You/Business, Female to Female, He Says, Right Brain, Light My Candle, Christmas Bells, Message #2, Another Day, Sante Fe, I'll Cover You, Will I?, Over It, Over the Moon, La Vie Boheme, I Should Tell You, Message #3, Seasons of Love, Out Tonight, Message #4, Without You, Message #5, Contact, Goodbye Love, Real Estate, Open Road, Message #6, Finale
A studio production of a two-act rock musical based on *La Boheme*. The action takes place in the East Village.

Friday, Nov. 25, 1994–Jan. 29, 1995 (64 performances and 18 previews)
SLAVS! Thinking About the Longstanding Problems of Virtue and Happiness by Tony Kushner; Director, Lisa Peterson; Set, Neil Patel; Costumes, Gabriel Berry; Lighting, Christopher Akerlind; Sound, Darron L. West; Stage Manager, Christopher DeCamillis CAST: Barbara Eda-Young (First Babushka/Mrs. Shastlivyi), Mary Shultz (2nd Babushka/Bonfila Bezhukhovna Bonch-Bruevich), Ben Hammer (Vassily Vorovilich Smukov), Gerald Hiken (Serge Esmereldovich Upgobkin/Big Babushka), Joseph Wiseman (Aleksii Antedilluvianovich Prelapsarianov), David Chandler (Yegor Tremens Rodent), John Christopher Jones (Ippolite Ippopolitovitch Popolitpov), Marisa Tomei (Katherina Serafima Gleb), Mischa Barton (Vodya Domik)
A play about the fall of the Soviet Union performed without intermission. The action takes place in Moscow, Siberia, and elsewhere, 1985–92.

Tuesday, Mar. 14–Apr. 16, 1995 (14 performances and 21 previews)
THE FAMILY BUSINESS; Written/Directed/Choreographed by Ain Gordon and David Gordon; Set/Costumes, Anita Stewart; Lighting, Stan Pressner; Sound, David Meschter; Stage Manager, Ed Fitzgerald CAST: Valda Setterfield, Ain Gordon, David Gordon

Friday, May 12–June 18, 1995 (35 performances and 11 previews)
PRISONER OF LOVE by Jean Genet; Translation, Barbara Bray; Adaptation, JoAnne Akalaitis; Ruth Maleczech, Chiori Miyagawa; Music, Philip Glass; Director, JoAnne Akalaitis; Set/Costumes, Amy Shock; Lighting, Frances Aronson; Stage Manager, Mireya Hepner CAST: Ruth Maleczech
A drama performed without intermission.

Joan Marcus Photos

Top: Mirla Criste, Zar Acayan, Lydia Gaston in *Rita's Resources*
Below: Tina Chen, John Lee in *Arthur & Leila*

PAN ASIAN REPERTORY

Eighteenth Season

Artistic/Producing Director, Tisa Chang; Artistic Associate, Ron Nakahara; General Manager, Russell Murphy; Press, Denise Robert

(All productions at St. Clement's) Tuesday, Oct. 4–22, 1994 (21 performances)
ARTHUR & LEILA by Cherylene Lee; Director, Ron Nakahara; Set, Robert Klingelhoefer; Lighting, William Simmons; Costumes, Eiko Yamaguchi; Sound, Ty Sanders; Stage Manager, Patt Giblin CAST: Tina Chen (Leila), Jon Lee (Arthur)
A drama set in Los Angeles.

Tuesday, Nov. 1–19, 1994 (21 performances)
YELLOW FEVER by R. A. Shiomi; Director, Andrew Tsao; Sets, Robert Klingelhoeffer; Lighting, Richard Schaefer; Costumes, Eiko Yamaguchi; Stage Manager, Lisa Ledwich CAST: Robert Baumgardner, David Beyda, Carol A. Honda, Eleanora Kihlberg, Glenn Kubota, Gay Reed, James Saito, Michael Twaine
A detective play.

Tuesday, Apr. 25–May 13, 1995 (21 performances)
RITA'S RESOURCES by Jeannie Barroga; Director, Kati Kuroda; Set, Dunsi Dai; Costumes, Hugh Hanson; Lighting, Richard Schaefer; Sound, Gayle Jeffery; Stage Manager, Lisa Ledwich CAST: Luna Borromeo (Rita), Mirla Criste (Arlette), Lydia Gaston (Marnie), Marshall Factora (Joe), Zar Acayan (Bob), Cortez Nance Jr. (Freddie), Gay Reed (Dee Jay/Voices)
A comedy in two acts. The action takes place in a mixed neighborhood, 1974.

Carol Rosegg Photos

139

PEARL THEATRE COMPANY

Eleventh Season

Artistic Director, Shepard Sobel; Managing Director, Parris Relkin; Development Director, Lawrence Swann; Artistic Associate, Joanne Camp; Set Designer, Robert Joel Schwartz; Fight Director, Rick Sordelet; Press, Chris Boneau/Adrian Bryan-Brown, Bob Fennell

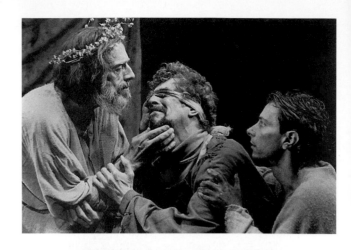

(All productions at Theatre 80) Thursday, Sept. 8–Oct. 22, 1994 (33 performances and 12 previews)
KING LEAR by William Shakespeare; Director, Shepard Sobel; Lighting, Stephen Petrilli; Costumes, Deborah Rooney; Sound, Donna Riley; Stage Manager, Jana Llynn CAST: Thomas Schall (Kent), Chris O'Neill (Gloucester), Brian Evaret Chandler (Edmund), Robert Hock (Lear), Joanne Camp (Goneril), Rachel Botchan (Cordelia), Robin Leslie Brown (Regan), Ray Virta (Albany/Martin), Kurt Ziskie (Cornwall/Doctor), Bradford Cover (Burgandy/Knight), Greg Steinbruner (France/Oswald/Herald), Arnie Burton (Edgar), Jennifer Thomas (Fool), Michael Jason Klein (Curan), John Wellmann (Old Man/Jacques/Soldier), William Wurch (George/Soldier)
Performed with one intermission.

Friday, Oct .28–Dec. 10, 1994 (35 performances and 10 previews)
THE BEAUX STRATAGEM by George Farquhar; Director, Mary Lou Rosato; Lighting, Stephen Petrilli; Costumes, Leslie Yarmo; Sound, Sheafe Walker CAST: Michael James Reed (Aimwell), Michael Butler (Archer), Robin Leslie Brown (Dorinda), Joanne Camp (Mrs. Sullen), Robert Hock (Boniface), Bradford Cover (Scrub), Arnie Burton (Foigard), Derek Meader (Gibbet/Bellair), Jennifer Thomas (Cherry/Old Woman), Anna Minot (Lady Bountiful), Kurt Ziskie (Mr. Sullen), William Wurch (Hounslow), Rachel Botchan (Gipsy), Greg Steinbruner (Sir Charles), John E. Sauer (Bagshot)
A 1706 Restoration comedy.

Friday, Dec.16, 1994–Jan. 28, 1995 (34 performances and 10 previews)
THE VENETIAN TWINS by Carlo Goldoni; Translation, Michael Feingold; Director, John Rando; Lighting, Stephen Petrilli; Costumes, Deborah Rooney; Sound, Casey L. Warren; Stage Manager, Lynn Bogarde CAST: Rachel Botchan (Rosaura), Robin Leslie Brown (Columbina), John Wylie (Professor/Tiburzio), Greg Steinbruner (Brighella), Arnie Burton (Zanetto/Tonio), Clement Fowler (Pancrazio), Jennifer Thomas (Beatrice), Michael James Reed (Florindo), Kevin Black (Lelio), Bradford Cover (Porter/Constable)
A 1748 comedy in two acts. The action takes place in Verona, 1746.

Friday, Feb. 3–Mar. 12, 1995 (29 performances and 10 previews)
OEDIPUS AT COLONUS by Sophocles; Translation, Theodore Howard Banks; Lighting, Philip D. Widmer; Costumes, Deborah Rooney; Sound, Donna Riley; Stage Manager, Amanda W. Sloan CAST: Robert Hock (Oedipus), Jennifer Thomas (Antigone), Lou Cilla (Citzen), Rachel Botchan (Ismene), Bernard K. Addison (Theseus), Robert Blackburn (Creon), Bradford Cover (Polyneices), John E. Sauer (Guard), Chet Carlin (Messenger), Fred Burrell, Mr. Carlin, Mr. Ciulla (Chorus)
Performed without intermission.

Friday, Mar. 24–May 7, 1995 (41 performances and 10 previews)
MRS. WARREN'S PROFESSION by Bernard Shaw; Director, Alex Dmitriev; Costumes, Deborah Rooney; Lighting, Philip D. Widmer; Sound, Casey L. Warren; Stage Manager, Colleen Marie Davis CAST: Chelsea Altman (Vivie), John Braden (Crofts), Bradford Cover (Frank), Robert Hock (Reverand), Woody Sempliner (Praed), Margo Skinner (Mrs. Warren)

Carol Rosegg, Tom Bloom Photos

**Top: Robert Hock, Chris O'Neill, Arnie Burton in *King Lear*
Center: Arnie Burton, Rachel Botchan in *Venetian Twins*
Right: Bradford Cover, Chelsea Altman in *Mrs. Warren's Profession***

PLAYWRIGHTS HORIZONS

Twenty-fourth Season

Artistic Director, Don Scardino; Managing Director, Leslie Marcus; General Manager, Lynn Landis; Associate Artistic Director, Tim Sanford; Production Manager, Jack O'Connor; Press, Philip Rinaldi/James Morrison, Barbara Carroll, Kathy Haberthur

Friday, Sept. 16, 1994–Jan.1, 1995 (103 performances and 21 previews)
A CHEEVER EVENING by A.R. Gurney; Based on stories by John Cheever; Director, Don Scardino; Set, John Lee Beatty; Costumes, Jennifer von Mayrhauser; Lighting, Kenneth Posner; Sound, Aural Fixation; Stage Manager, Lloyd Davis, Jr. CAST: John Cunningham, Jack Gilpin, Julie Hagerty, Mary Beth Peil, Robert Stanton, Jennifer Van Dyck
Performed in two acts. The action takes place in Manhattan's east side, northern suburbs, and the New England coast.

(Studio) Wednesday, Oct. 5–16, 1994 (17 performances)
BABY ANGER; Written/Directed by Peter Hedges; Lighting, Annie Padien; Costumes, Therese Bruck; Sound, Michael Clark CAST: Patrick Breen, Shelton Dane, Travis DeLingua, Moira Driscoll, Barbara Garrick, Stephanie Gatschet, Paul Giamatti, Judith Moreland, Damian Young
A dark comedy about parenthood.

Friday, Feb. 10–Mar. 26, 1995 (25 performances and 28 previews)
JACK'S HOLIDAY with Music/Lyrics by Randy Courts; Book/Lyrics, Mark St. Germain; Director, Susan H. Schulman; Musical Staging, Michael Lichtefeld; Orchestrations, Douglas Besterman; Musical Director/Vocal Arangements, Steve Tyler; Sets, Jerome Sirlin; Costumes, Catherine Zuber; Lighting, Robert Wierzel; Sound, Dan Moses Schreier; Stage Manager, Perry Cline CAST: Judy Blazer (Mary Healey), Nicolas Coster (Max), Allen Fitzpatrick (Jack), Herb Foster (Spencer/Rev. Parkhurst/Sgt. Deehan), Alix Korey (Shakespeare/Elizabeth/Mrs. Parkhurst/Molly), Mark Lotito (Clubber Williams/John), Michael X. Martin (Rev. Billis/Dr. Rourke/Samuel/Edward), Michael Mulheren (Humpty Jackson), Greg Naughton (Will Bolger), Dennis Parlato (Inspector Thomas Byrnes), Anne Runolfsson (Sarah/Suzy/Edith), Henry Stram (Snatchem Leese), Lauren Ward (Jennie/Servant/Daisy), Lou Williford (Gallus Mag)
MUSICAL NUMBERS: Changing Faces, City of Dreams, Letters #1-4, Tricks of the Trade, Never Time to Dance, The Line, What I Almost Said, The Hands of God, You Never Know Who's Behind You, What Land Is This?, Stage Blood, If You Will Dream of Me, Don't Think About It, All You Want Is Always, Pandarus' Song, Finale
Jack the Ripper visits 1891 New York City in a two-act musical drama.

Top: Jack Gilpin, Julie Hagerty in *A Cheever Evening*
Right: Judith Hawking, Nancy Giles in *Police Boys*
Below: Judy Blazer, Allen Fitzpatrick in *Jack's Holiday*

Saturday, Apr. 15–May 26, 1995 (13 performances and 34 previews)
POLICE BOYS by Marion McClinton; Director, Donald Douglass; Sets, Riccardo Hernandez; Costumes, Judy Dearing; Lighting, Jan Kroeze; Music/Sound, Don DiNicola; Fights, David Leong; Stage Manager, Andrea J. Testani CAST: Larry Gilliard Jr. (Signifying Monkey), Richard Brooks (Commanche), Akili Prince (Royal Boy), Judith Hawking (Teddy/Meredith Fellows), Lelnad Gantt (Benjamin Santiago Bowie), Chuck Cooper (Capt. Jabali Abdul LaRouche), Nancy Giles (Sgt. Ruth "Babe Ruth" Milano), Russell Andrews (Superboy Beauchamp)
A drama in two acts. The action takes place in a police station in a future you can touch with your hand.

(Studio) Wednesday, May 17–28, 1995 (15 performances)
SOMEWHERE IN THE PACIFIC by Neal Bell; Director, Mark Brokaw; Set, Riccardo Hernandez; Lighting, Anne Padien; Costumes, Therese Bruck; Sound, Michael Clark; Stage Manager, Michael Ritchie CAST: Ross Bickell (Capt. Albers), Ari Fliakos (Interrogator/Soldier), Michael Gaston (Chotlowski), Leo Marks (Billy DuPre), Silas Weir Mitchell (McGuiness), Peter Rini (DeLucca), Ross Salinger (Interrogator/Soldier), Charlie Schiff (Duane), Adam Trese (Hobie)
A drama performed without intermission. The action is set in hostile Japanese waters, July 1945.

T. Charles Erickson, Joan Marcus Photos

141

PUERTO RICAN TRAVELING THEATRE

Artistic Director, Miriam Colon Valle; Managing Director, Geoff Shlaes; Lighting Designer, Peter Greenbaum; Press, Max Eisen/Louisa Benton

(Parks Tour) Thursday, July 28–Aug. 28, 1994 (29 performances)
THE FICKLE FINGER OF LADY DEATH by Eduardo Rodriguez-Solis; Translation, Carlos Morton; Dirctor, Jorge Huerta; Set/Costumes, Monica Raya; Musical Director, Sergio Garcia-Marruz; Stage Manager, Fernando Quinn CAST: Ivonne Caro, Tony Chiroldes Carbia, Miriam Cruz, Oscar De La Fe Colon, Jorge Oliver, Sandra Rodriguez
  A musical fable.

Wednesday, Apr. 5–May 14, 1995 (42 performances)
YEPETO by Roberto Cossa; Translation, Jack Agueros; Director, Rafael Acevedo; Set, Eric Lowell Renschler; Stage Manager, Robin C. Gillette CAST: Priscilla Garita (Cecilia), Bruno Irizarry (Roberto), Nelson Roberto Landrieu (Professor)
  A drama performed without intermission.

Wednesday, May 24–July 2, 1995 (42 performances)
SIMPSON STREET by Eduardo Gallardo; Translation, Toni Diaz, Miriam Colon; Director, Alba Oms; Set, Carl Baldasso; Stage Manager, Fernando Quinn CAST: Anamaria Correa (Angela), Martha De La Cruz (Elva Cruz), Selenis Leyva (Sonia Sanchez), Iraida Polanco (Rosa Sanchez), Carmen Rosario (Lucy), Douglas Santiago (Miguel Rodriguez)
  A drama in two acts. The action takes place in the South Bronx, NYC.

Priscilla Garita, Bruno Irizarry in *Yepeto*

Tony Chiroldes, Yvonne Caro in *Fickle Finger of Lady Death*

Douglas Santiago, Carmen Rosario in *Simpson Street*

SECOND STAGE THEATRE

Sixteenth Season

Artistic Director, Carole Rothman; Producing Director, Suzanne Schwartz Davidson; Associate Producer, Carol Fishman; Marketing Director, Harold Marmon; Literary Manager/Dramaturg, Erin Sanders; Production Manager, George Lentino; Press, Richard Kornberg/Bill Schelble, Don Summa, Thomas Naro

Thursday, June 9–July 30, 1994 (34 performances and 18 previews)
THE FAMILY OF MANN by Theresa Rebeck; Director, Pamela Belin; Set, Derek McLane; Lighting, Natasha Katz; Costumes, Lindsay W. Davis; Music/Sound, Jeremy Dyman Grody; Stage Manager, James Fitzsimmons CAST: David Garrison (Ed/Dave), Richard Cox (Bill), Julie White (Belinda/Sissy), Lisa Gay Hamilton (Clara), Robert Duncan McNeill (Ren/Buddy), Anne Lange (Sally/Ginny), Reed Birney (Steve/Uncle Willy)

A dark comedy in two acts. The action takes place in Los Angeles.

(Lucille Lortel) Tuesday, Sept. 27, 1994–Jan. 1, 1995 (83 performances and 33 previews)
UNCOMMON WOMEN & OTHERS by Wendy Wasserstein; Director, Carole Rothman; Set, Heidi Landesman; Costumes, Jennifer von Mayrhauser; Lighting, Richard Nelson; Sound, Janet Kalas; Stage Manager, Roy Harris CAST: Stephanie Roth (Kate Quinn), Mary McCann (Samantha Stewart), Julie Dretzin (Holly Kaplan), Haviland Morris (Muffet DiNicola), Jessica Lundy succeeded by Annabelle Gurwitch (Rita Altabel), Rosemary Murphy (Mrs. Plumm), Robin Morse (Susie Friend), Danielle Ferland (Carter), Joan Buddenhagen (Leilah), Forrest Sawyer (Man's Voice)

A new production of a 1977 drama. The action takes place at a women's college and a restaurant, 1972–78.

Tuesday, Nov. 22, 1994–Jan. 15, 1995 (44 performances and 20 previews)
ZOOMAN AND THE SIGN by Charles Fuller; Director, Seret Scott; Set, Marjorie Bradley Kellogg; Costumes, Karen Perry; Lighting, Michael Gilliam; Sound, Janet Kalas; Stage Manager, Elise-Ann Konstantin CAST: Larry Gilliard Jr. (Zooman), Oni Faida Lampley (Rachel Tate), Tony Todd (Reuben Tate), Stephen M. Henderson (Emmett Tate), Alex Bess (Victor Tate), Willie Stiggers Jr. (Russell Adams), Ed Wheeler (Donald Jackson), Saundra McClain (Ash Boswell), Kim Bey (Grace Georges)

A drama set in Philadelphia, summer 1981.

Wednesday, Feb. 22–Apr. 15, 1995 (20 performances and 28 previews)
RUSH LIMBAUGH IN NIGHT SCHOOL; Written/Directed/Performed by Charlie Varon; Developed with David Ford; Director, Martin Higgins; Lighting, Donald Holder; Set, Sherri Adller; Stage Manager, Elaine Bayless

A "mockumentary" in two acts. The action takes place in New York City, 1996.

Tuesday, May 9–July 1, 1995 (13 performances and 40 previews)
CRUMBS FROM THE TABLE OF JOY by Lynn Nottage; Director, Joe Morton; Set, Myung Hee Cho; Lighting, Donald Holder; Costumes, Karen Perry; Sound, Mark Bennett; Stage Manager, Delicia Turner CAST: Kisha Howard (Ernestine Crump), Nicole Leach (Ermina Crump), Daryl Edwards (Godfrey Crump), Ella Joyce (Lily Ann Green), Stephenie Roth (Gerte Schulte)

A drama in two acts. The action takes place in Brroklyn, 1950. *Susan Cook Photos*

Top: Reed Birney, Robert Duncan McNeil, Julie White, Anne Lange, Richard Cox in *Family of Mann*

Center: Joan Buddenhagen, Robin Morse, Mary McCann, Julie Dretzin in *Uncommon Women and Others*

Right: Tony Todd, Oni Faida Lampley in *Zooman and the Sign*

SIGNATURE THEATRE COMPANY

Fourth Season

Founding Artistic Director, James Houghton; Managing Director, Thomas C. Proehl; Associate Director, Elliot Fox; Lighting Designer, Jeffrey S. Koger; Press, Philip Rinaldi/James Morrison

Friday, Sept. 23–Oct. 23, 1994 (24 performances)
TALKING PICTURES by Horton Foote; Director, Carol Goodheart; Sets, Colin D. Young; Costumes, Teresa Snider-Stein, Jonathan Green; Stage Manager, Bethany Ford CAST: Samantha Reynolds (Katie Bell Jackson), Sarah Paulson (Vesta Jackson), Hallie Foote (Myra Tolliver), Frank Girardeau (Mr. Jackson), Alice McLane (Mrs. Jackson), Seth Jones (Willis), Isaiah G. Cazares (Estaquio Trevino), Eddie Kaye Thomas (Pete), Susan Wands (Gladys), Ed Hodson (Ashenback), Kenneth Cavett (Gerard Anderson)
A drama set in Harrison, Texas, 1929.

Friday, Nov. 4–Dec. 4, 1994 (24 performances)
NIGHT SEASONS; Written/Directed by Horton Foote; Sets, E. David Cosier; Costumes, Barbara A. Bell, Teresa Snider-Stein; Music, Donald Pippin; Stage Manager, Mary Ellen Allison CAST: Jean Stapleton (Josie Weems), Hallie Foote (Laura Lee Weems), Devon Abner (Lawrence), George Bamford (Mercer Hadley), Jo Ann Cunningham (Rosa), Frank Girardeau (Skeeter Weems), Michael Hadge (Thurman Weems), Howard Hensel (Barsoty), James Pritchett (Weems), Barbara Caren Sims (Dolly), Elizabeth Stearns (Delia), Beatrice Winde (Doris), Ted Zurkowski (Chestnut)
A drama set in Harrison, Texas, 1923–63.

Friday, Jan. 27–Feb. 26, 1995 (24 performances)
THE YOUNG MAN FROM ATLANTA by Horton Foote; Director, Peter Masterson; Sets, E. David Cosier; Costumes, Teresa Snider-Stein, Jonathan Green; Stage Manager, Dean Gray CAST: Ralph Waite (Will Kidder), Devon Abner (Tom Jackson), Christina Burz (Miss Lacey), Seth Jones (Ted Cleveland Jr.), Carlin Glynn (Lily Dale), James Pritchett (Pete Davenport), Frances Foster (Clara), Michael Lewis (Carson), Beatrice Winde (Etta Doris)
A drama set in Houston, Texas, 1950. Winner of the 1995 Pulitzer Prize.

Friday, Mar. 10–Apr. 9, 1995 (24 performances)
LAURA DENNIS by Horton Foote; Director, James Houghton; Sets, E. David Cosier; Costumes, Jonathan Green; Stage Manager, Bethany Ford CAST: Missy Yager (Laura Dennis), Peter Sarsgaard (Harvey Griswold), Becky Ann Baker (Lena Abernathy), Hallie Foote (Velma Dennis), Victoria Fischer (Pud Murphy), Stacey Moseley (Annie Laurie Davis), Pamela Lewis (Mrs. Murphy), Barbara Caren Sims (Fay Griswold), Horton Foote Jr. (Andrew Griswold), Andrew Finney (Seymour Mann), Janet Ward (Ethel Dennis), Eric Williams (Stewart Wilson), Michael Hadge (Edward Dennis)
A drama performed without intermission. The setting is Harrison, Texas, 1938.

Susan Johann Photos

Top: Carlin Glynn, Ralph Waite in *The Young Man from Atlanta*
Right: Hallie Foote, Eddie Kaye Thomas in *Talking Pictures*

VINEYARD THEATRE

Fourteenth Season

Artistic Director, Douglas Aibel; Executive Director, Barbara Zinn Krieger; Managing Director, Jon Nakagawa; Press, Shirley Herz / Sam Rudy

Thursday, Dec. 8, 1994–Jan. 8, 1995 (20 performances and 12 previews)
AMERICA DREAMING by Chiori Miyagawa; Music, Tan Dun; Director, Michael Mayer; Choreography, Doug Carone; Music Director, Bruce Gremo; Set, Riccardo Hernandez; Costumes, Michael Krass; Lighting, Michael Chybowski; Stage Manager, Crystal Huntington CAST: Liana Pai (Yuki), Billy Crudup (Robert), Beth Dixon, Joel De La Fuente, Ann Harada, Virginia Wing, Michael Lewis, P.J. Brown, Aleta Hayes, Si-Zheng Chen
A music-theatre piece produced with Music-Theatre Group.

Monday, Dec. 26–31, 1994 (12 afternoon performances)
APPELEMANDO'S DREAMS with Music by James Kurtz; Libretto, Barbara Zinn Krieger; Writer, Patricia Polacco; Director/Choreographer, Lisa Brailoff; Set, Wendy Ponte; Costumes, David Brooks; Lighting, A.C. Hickox; Stage Manager, Patt Giblin CAST: Suzanne Grodner (Mayor's Wife), Mark Peters (Mayor), April Armstrong (Mother), Clif Thorn (Teacher), Siri Howard (Petra), Jackie Angelescu (Dorma), Joey Hannon (Appelemando)
A one-act opera set in the middle of nowhere.

Thursday, Feb. 9–Mar. 21, 1995 (23 performances and 19 previews)
RAISED IN CAPTIVITY by Nicky Silver; Director, David Warren; Set, James Youmans; Costumes, Teresa Snider-Stein; Lighting, Donald Holder; Music/Sound, John Gromada; Stage Manager, Christopher De Camillis CAST: Peter Frechette (Sebastian Bliss), Patricia Clarkson (Bernadette Dixon), Brian Kerwin (Kip Dixon), Leslie Ayvazian (Hillary MacMahon/Miranda Bliss), Anthony Rapp (Dylan Taylor Sinclair/Roger)
A dark comedy in two acts: *Bread and Water* and *Forty Dollars and a New Suit*.

Friday, Apr. 21–May 21, 1995 (15 performances and 17 previews)
PHAEDRA by Elizabeth Egloff; Director, Evan Yionoulis; Set, James Youmans; Costumes, Constance Hoffman; Lighting, Donald Holder; Sound, Donna Riley; Music, Thomas Cabaniss; Stage Manager, Elizabeth M. Berther CAST: Randy Danson (Phaedra), David Chandler (Narrator), Mark Rosenthal (Hippolytus), Sam Tsoutsouvas (Theseus), Susan Blommaert (Nurse), Mark Smaltz (Boss), Fanni Green (Secretary), David Greenspan (Messenger)
A drama performed without intermission

Carol Rosegg, Susan Johann Photos

Patricia Clarkson, Peter Frechette in *Raised in Captivity*

Anthony Rapp, Peter Frechette in *Raised in Captivity*

Jackie Angelescu, Joey Hannon, Siri Howard in *Appelemando's Dreams*

Liana Pai, Billy Crudup in *America Dreaming*

WPA THEATRE
(Workshop of the Players Art)

Eighteenth Season

Artistic Director, Kyle Renick; Managing Director, Lori Sherman; Business Manager, Mark Merriman; Sound Design, Aural Fixation/Guy Sherman; Press, Jeffrey Richards/Kevin Rehac, Richard Guido

Thursday, Oct. 6–Nov .6, 1994 (21 performances and 11 previews)
UNEXPECTED TENDERNESS by Israel Horovitz; Director, Steve Zuckerman; Set, Edward Gianfrancesco; Lighting, Richard Winkler; Costumes, Mimi Maxmen; Stage Manager, Mark Cole CAST: Jonathan Marc Sherman (Roddy Stern), Steve Ryan (Elder Roddy Stern), Caitlin Clarke (Molly Stern), Steve Ryan (Archie Stern), Karen Goberman (Sylvie Stern), Scotty Bloch (Haddie Stern), Sol Frieder (Jacob Stern), Paul O'Brien (Willie)
A drama in two acts. The action takes place in a small New England town, early 1950s.

Tuesday, Jan. 3–Feb. 5, 1995 (16 performances and 19 previews)
THE SUGAR BEAN SISTERS by Nathan Sanders; Director, Evan Yionoulis; Set, David Gallo; Lighting, Jack Mehler; Costumes, Mary Myers; Stage Manager, Gail Eve Malatesta CAST: Annie Golden (Videllia Sparks), Beth Dixon (Willie Mae Nettles), Margo Martindale (Faye Clementine Nettles), David Lee Smith (Bishop Crumley), Sheila Harper Linnette (Reptile Woman)
A comedy in two acts. The action takes place in Sugar Bean, Florida.

Jonathan Marc Sherman, Caitlin Clarke in *Unexpected Tenderness*

Thursday, Mar. 16–Apr. 16, 1995 (20 performances and 13 previews)
WATBANALAND by Doug Wright; Director, Christopher Ashley; Set, Rob Odorisio; Lighting, Doug Holder; Costumes, Anne C. Patterson; Stage Manager, Kate Broderick CAST: Lisa Emery (Flo), Emily Skinner (Marilyn), David Chandler (Park), Ken Garito (Dash), Susan Greenhill (Penelope Wax), Dion Graham (Yobo Munde)
A drama with 25 short scenes. The action takes place in NYC, Watbanaland and Springfield.

Thursday, May 25–July 2, 1995 (21 performances and 19 previews)
HUNDREDS OF HATS with Lyrics by Howard Ashman; Music, Alan Menken, Jonathan Sheffer, Marvin Hamlisch; Conception/Direction, Michael Mayer; Choreography, John Ruocco; Musical Director, Helen Gregory; Orchestrations, Steven Bishop; Set, Mark Beard; Lighting, Jack Mehler; Stage Manager, Kay Foster CAST: John Ellison Conlee, Bob Kirsh, Philip Lehl, Amanda Naughton, Nancy Opel
MUSICAL NUMBERS: Hero, In Our Hands, 30 Miles from the Banks of the Ohio, Firestorm Consuming Indianapolis, Rhode Island Tango, Belle, Skid Row, Song for a Hunter College Graduate, Thank God for the Volunteer Fire Brigade, Cheese Nips, A Little Dental Music, Aria for a Cow, Hundreds of Hats, Growing Boy, Les Poissons, Maria's Song, Suddenly Seymour, Since You Came to This Town, Day in the Life of a Fat Kid in Philly, Part of Your World, Somewhere That's Green, Disneyland, Your Day Begins Tonight, A Magician's Work, Babkak Omar Aladdin Kassim, Daughter of Prospero, Kiss the Girl, How Quick They Forget, Poor Unfortunate Souls, We'll Have Tomorrow, Proud of Your Boy, High Adventure, Sheridan Square, Daughter of God
A two-act musical revue focusing of the lyrics of Howard Ashman including many songs cut from plays and films.

Gerry Goodstein, Carol Rosegg Photos

**Center: Annie Golden, Margo Martindale in *Sugar Bean Sisters*
Left: Philip Lehl, John Ellison Conlee, Amanda Naughton, Bob Kirsh, Nancy Opel in *Hundreds of Hats***

YORK THEATRE COMPANY

Twenty-sixth Season

Producing Director, Janet Hayes Walker; Managing Director, Joseph V. De Michele; One World Arts Foundation: Executive Director, W. Scott McLucas; Artistic Director, George Rondo; Press, Keith Sherman/Jim Byk, Stuart Ginsberg

(All shows at St. Peter's) Tuesday, Sept. 20–Oct. 23, 1994 (30 performances and 5 previews)
DOWN BY THE OCEAN by P.J. Barry; Set, James Morgan; Costumes, Elizabeth Besom; Lighting, Stan Pressner; Sound, Jim van Bergen; Stage Manager, Cathleen Wolfe   CAST: Dennis parlato (Dan Bailey), Sam Groom (David Emerson (Sam Groom), Ross Bickell (Peter Carmody), Melina Kanakaredes (Isabelle), John Newton (Wally Monahan), Pamela Burrell (Lil Donavan Carmody)
   A drama in three acts. The action takes place in Jericho, Rhode Island, 1946–60.

Tuesday, Dec. 13, 1994–Jan. 22, 1995 (34 performances and 8 previews)
A DOLL'S LIFE with Music by Larry Grossman; Lyrics/Book, Betty Comden and Adolph Green; Director, Robert Brink; Musical Director, David Kirshenbaum; Set, James Morgan; Costumes, Patricia Adshead; Lighting, Mary Jo Dondlinger; Sound, Jim van Bergen; Stage Manager, Alan Bluestone   CAST: Paul Blankenship (Hamsun/Karl/Guest/Jailer/Ambassador/Power Patron), Tom Galantich (Johan Blecker), Catherine Anne Gale (Respectable Woman/Guest/Cannery Girl/Jacquel Le Beau), Jill Geddes (Nora Helmer), Tamara Hayden (Lady of the Evening/Singer/Secretary/Camilla Forrester), Jeff Herbst (Otto Bernick), Seth Jones (Torvald Helmer), Michael Klashman (Pimp/Gustafson/Call Boy/Loki/Kloster), Eileen Mc Namara (Waitress/Selma/Berta), Howard Pinhasik (Conductor/Dr. Berg/Peterson/Muller/Zetterling), Paul Schoeffler (Eric Didrickson), Robin Skye (Astrid Klemnacht), Jennifer Laura Thompson (Lady of the Evening/Jailed Woman/Helga/Bridgit)
MUSICAL NUMBERS: What Now?, A Woman Alone, Letter to the Children, Arrival in Christiania, New Year's Eve, Stay With Me Nora, Arrival, Loki and Baldur, You Interest Me, Departure, Letter from Klemnacht, Learn to Be Lonely, Rats and Mice and Fish, Jailer Jailer, Rare Wines, You Puzzle Me, No More Mornings, There She Is, Power, At Last, Can't You Hear I'm Making Love To You
   A revised version of a 1982 two-act musical featuring new songs. The action takes place in Norway, 1879–1883.

Tuesday, Apr. 11–30, 1995 (21 performances)
CLOTHES FOR A SUMMER HOTEL by Tennessee Williams; Director, Tony Giordano; Music, Michael Valenti; Lighting, Mary Jo Dondlinger; Sound, Jim van Bergen; Stage Manager, Robert D. Uttrich   CAST: Robert Duncan (Edouard/Intern), Diane Kagan (Zelda Fitzgerald), Robert LuPone (Scott Fitzgerald), Terrence Markovich (Gerald Murphy), Maeve McGuire (Sara Murphy), Conrad Osborn (Dr. Zeller), Shwaneen Rowe (Hadley Hemingway), Doug Stender (Ernest Hemingway)
   A drama in two acts. The action takes place in an asylum in No. Carolina.

Saturday, May 6–21, 1995 (12 performances–4 perf. each)
MUSICALS IN MUFTI; Concert versions of musicals
ONWARD VICTORIA with Music by Keith Herrmann; Lyrics/Book, Charlotte Anker, Irene Rosenberg; Director, Adele Aronheim; Musical Director, David Kirshenbaum
MATI HARI with Music by Edward Thomas; Lyrics/Book/Direction, Martin Charnin
GOLDEN BOY with Music by Charles Strouse; Lyrics, Lee Adams, Strouse; Book, Leslie Lee; Director, Jeffrey B. Moss

Monday, May 8–20, 1995 (14 performances)
SACRIFICE TO EROS by Fredeick Timm; Director, Lisa Juliano; Presented by Libra Productions in association with York Theatre Co.; Press, Penny M. Landau   CAST: Steven Ditmyer (Jesse), Larry Petersen (Tom), Diane Ciesla (Edna), John Marino, Michael Gilpin, Judith Lightfoot Clarke
   A drama in two acts. The action takes place in rural Wisconsin, 1934.

Carol Rosegg Photos

Melina Kanakaredes, Sam Groom in *Down by the Ocean*

Jill Geddes, Jeff Herbst in *A Doll's Life*

PROFESSIONAL REGIONAL COMPANIES

ACTORS THEATRE OF LOUISVILLE

Louisville, Kentucky
Thirty-first Season

Producing Director, Jon Jory; Executive Director, Alexander Speer; Associate Director, Marilee Hebert-Slater; Set Desingers, Paul Owen, Virginia Dancy, Elmon Webb, Neil Patel; Costume Designers, Hollis Jenkins-Evans, Myra Colley-Lee, Marcia Dixcy, Gabriel Berry, Laura Patterson, Lewis D. Rampino, James Schuette, Maria E. Marrero, Nanzi J. Adzima, Delmar L. Rinehart Jr.; Lighting Designers, T.J. Gerckens, Mimi Jordan Sherin, Michitomo Shiohara, Karl E. Haas, Brian Scott, Mimi Jordan Sherin; Public Relations Director; James Seacat; Public Relation Associates, Margaret Costello, Jennifer McMaster, Joseph W. Hans

PRODUCTIONS & CASTS

DANCING AT LUGHNASA by Brian Friel; Director, Jon Jory CAST: Tom Nelis (Michael), Karen Grassle (Kate), Sarah Burke (Maggie), Pamela Stewart (Agnes), Edith Meeks (Rose), Connan Morrissey (Chris), Lou Sumral (Gerry), Bob Burrus (Jack)

SOMEONE WHO'LL WATCH OVER ME by Frank McGuiness; Director, Rob Bundy CAST: William McNulty (Edward), A. Bernard Cummings (Adam), V Craig Heidenreich (Michael)

I HATE HAMLET by Paul Rudnick; Director, Frazier W. Marsh CAST: Peggity Price (Felicia), David Andrew Macdonald (Deirdre), Adale O'Brien (Lillian), V Criag Heidenreich (Barrymore), William McNulty (Gary)

William McNulty, Ellen Lauren in *Adding Machine*

Faran Tahir, Vilma Silva in *Beast on the Moon*

A CHRISTMAS CAROL by Charles Dickens; Adaptation, Jon Jory and Marcia Dixcy; Director, Frazier W. Marsh CAST: Fred Major (Scrooge), Vaughn McBride, V Craig Heidenreich, Ann Hodapp, Raphael Nash, Sarah Burke, Adale O'Brien, Mark Sawyer-Dailey, David Andrew Macdonald, Bob Burrus, Brent J. Bauer, Stephanie Jaggers, Dustin Longstreth, S. Kyle Parker, Lou Sumrall, Linda Larkin, Pip Tulou, Jennifer Morris, Leah Price, James A. Harris, Ken Barnett, Lisa Kringel, Larry Barnett, Eric Shepard

THE GIFT OF THE MAGI by O. Henry; Adaptation/Music/Lyrics by Peter Ekstrom; Director, Jennifer Hubbard; Music Director, Scott Kasbaum CAST: Jessica Hendy (Della), Timothy Thomas (Jim)

THE ADDING MACHINE by Elmer L. Rice; Director, Anne Bogart CAST: William McNulty (Mr. Zero), Kristine Nielsen (Mrs. Zero), Ellen Lauren (Daisy Diana Dorothea Devore/Mrs Three), Fred Major (Boss), Denise Gientke, Jamison Newlander, Glory Kissel, David McMahon, Bob Burrus, Jennifer Hubbard, V Criag Heidenreich, Sarah Burke, Mark Sawyer-Dailey, Adale O'Brien, Andrew Weems, Eric Munro Johnson, Evan Prizant, Mitch Melder, Jan Harlin

SMALL LIVES/BIG DREAMS; Adapted from Chekov; Conceived/Directed by Anne Bogart CAST: J. Ed Araiza, Will Bond, Kelly Maurer, Barney O'Hanlon, Karenjune Sanchez

THE MEDIUM; Inspired by the life and predictions of Marshall McLuhan; Conceived/Directed by Anne Bogart CAST: J. Ed Araiza, Will Bond, Ellen Lauren, Kelly Maurer, Stephen Webber

CORPSE! by Gerald Moon; Director, Carl Schurr CAST: V Craig Heidenreich (Evelyn Farrant/Rupert Farrant), Adale O'Brien (Mrs. McGee), Fred Major (Major Powell), Mark Sawyer-Dailey (Hawkins)

BETWEEN THE LINES by Regina Taylor; Director, Shirley Jo Finney CAST: Ellen Bethea (Nina), Dee Pelletier (Becca), Lizan Mitchell (Mother/Angela Davis), Jacinto Taras Riddick (Jonathan/George Jackson), Gordon Joseph Weiss (Rufus), Ashley Savage (Mercedes), Denise Gientke (Pam/Nancy/Nadine), Andre Pyle (Supervisor/Marcus), Jamison Newlander, Leah Price

CLOUD TECTONICS by Jose Rivera; Director, Tina Landau CAST: Camilia Sanes (Celestina del Sol), Robert Montano (Anibal de la Luna), Javi Mulero (Nelson de la Luna)

MIDDLE-AGED WHITE GUYS by Jane Martin; Director, Jon Jory CAST: Karenjune Sanchez (R.V.), John Griesemer (Roy), Bob Burrus (Clem), Karen Grassle (Mona), Leo Burmester (Moon), Larry Larson (King), Anne Pitoniak (Mrs. Mannering)

BEAST ON THE MOON by Richard Kalinoski; Director, Laszlo Marton CAST: Ray Fry (Gentleman), Faran Tahir (Aram Tomasian), Vilma Silva (Seta Tamasian), Dustin Longstreth (Vincent)

BELOW THE BELT by Richard Dresser; Director, Gloria Muzio CAST: William McNulty (Hanrahan), V Craig Heidenreich (Dobbit), Fred Major (Merkin)

TRUDY BLUE by Marsha Norman; Director, George de la Pena CAST: Joanne Camp (Ginger), Leo Burmester (Don), Karenjune Sanchez (Maria /Admirer), Karen Grassle (Sue), Ann Bean (Connie/Sales/Waitress), Anne Pitoniak (Annie), Larry Larson (Swami Voice/Sales/Publisher), Tony Coleman (James), Jennifer Carpenter (Beth), Larry Barnett (Charlie), James McDaniel (Waiter)

A SEMINAR FOR RESPONSIBLE LIVING by Jane Anderson; Director, Lisa Peterson CAST: Kenneth L. Marks (Bob Dooley), Susan Knight (Helen/Arden)

JULY 7, 1994 by Donald Margulies; Director, Lisa Peterson CAST: Susan Knight (Kate), Kenneth L. Marks (Mark), Miriam Cruz (Senora Soto), Myra Taylor (Ms. Pike), Edward Hyland (Caridi), Sandra Daley (Paula)

Carmilia Sanes, Javi Mulero, Robert Montano in *Cloud Tectonics*

Anne Pitoniak in *Middle-Aged White Guys*

HELEN AT RISK by Dana Yeaton; Director, Frazier W. Marsh CAST: Adale O'Brien (Helen), V Craig Heidenreich (Ronnie Guyette), William McNulty

YOUR OBITUARY IS A DANCE by Bernard Cummings; Director, Lorna Littleway CAST: Jacinto Taras Riddick (Tommy), Marcella Lowery (Nella)

HEAD ON by Elizabeth Dewberry; Director, Shirley Jo Finney CAST: Adale O'Brien (Anne), Dee Pelletier (Therapist)

FROM THE MISSISSIPPI DELTA by Dr. Endesha Ida Mae Holland; Director, Tazewell Thompson CAST: Tonia Rowe (One), Lisa Renee Pitts (Two), Crystal Laws Green (Three)

THE STRANGE CASE OF DR. JEKYLL AND MR. HYDE by David Edgar based on story by Robert Louis Stevenson; Director, Jon Jory CAST: William McNulty (Utterson), T. Ryder Smith (Enfield), Jennifer Carpenter (Lucy), Ryan Haeseley (Charles), Mark Zeisler (Henry Jekyll), Jennifer Hubbard (Katherine), Libby Christopherson (Annie Loder), David Valcin (Mr. Hyde), Ed Hyland (Poole), Fred Major Dr. Lanyon), Anita Vassdal, Mark Sawyer-Dailey

FOREVER PLAID by Stuart Ross; Director/Choreographer, Karma Camp; Musical Director, Scott Kasbaum CAST: Jamison Stern (Francis), Sean Frank Sullivan (Sparky), Christopher Eaton Bailey (Jinx), Matt McClanahan (Smudge)

Richard Trigg Photos

ALLENBURY PLAYHOUSE

Boiling Springs, Pennsylvania

Producer, John J. Heinze; Artistic Director, Production Stage Manager, Richard J. Frost; Production Coordinator, Cate Van Wickler; Set Desinger, Robert Klingelhoefer; Lighting, Richard J. Frost; Costumes, Lourdes Garcia; Musical Director, Robert Felstein; Choreography, Kathleen Conry, David Wanstreet; Public Relations, Bob Crawford

PRODUCTIONS & CASTS

NUNSENSE II: The Second Coming…;Music/Lyrics/Book by Dan Goggin; Director, Michael Haney   CAST: Lorraine Serabian (Mary Regina), Debbie Lee Jones (Mary Hubert), Kathleen Conry (Robert Anne), Helen Hedman (Mary Paul), Fern-Marie Aames (Mary Leo)

OKLAHOMA! with Music by Richard Rodgers; Lyrics/Book, Oscar Hammerstein; Director, Richard J. Frost CAST: Debbie Lee Jones (Aunt Eller), Thomas Ladd (Curly), Jennifer Westfeldt (Laurey), Bill Eissler (Skidmore), Maurice Villalobos (Fred), Allen Jeffrey Rein (Slim), David Wanstreet (Will Parker), Christopher Hartmann (Jud), Melissa Blake (Ado Annie), Les Marsden (Gertie), Fern-Marie Aames (Ellen), Andrea Andresakis (Fay/Dream Laurey), Eric Kaufman (Joe/Dream Curly), Meghan Shanaphy (Kate), Monique Cash (Virginia), Tina Guice (Sylvie), Nick Cosco (Carnes), Adrian Martinez (Cord), Jennifer Chaiken (Arminia), Bill Blacksmith (Mike), Rusty Ross (Tom), Sean Kieron Deming (Chet), Jennifer Miller (Pigtails)

MEET ME IN ST. LOUIS with Music/Lyrics by Hugh Martin and Ralph Blane; Book, Sally Benson; Director, Michael Haney CAST: Debbie Lee Jones (Katie), Joel Carlton (Lon), Amy Warner (Mrs. Smith), Traci Fatula (Tootie), Melissa Blake (Esther), David Coxwell (Grandpa), Jennifer Westfeldt (Rose), Mary Jo Maxton (Agnes), Nick Cosco (Mr. Smith), Christopher Hartmann (Warren), Thomas Ladd (John Truitt), Christopher Budden (Douglas), Monique LaVielle Cash (Lucille), Allen Jeffrey Rein (Clinton), Andrea Andresakis (Ida), Meghan Shanaphy (Eve), Maurice Villalobos, Fern-Marie Adams, Jennifer Chaiken, Melissa R. Frey, Tina Guice, Bill Blacksmith, Adrian Martinez, Rust Ross

I HATE HAMLET by Paul Rudnick; Director, Michael Haney CAST: Jennifer Chaiken (Felicia), Scott DeFreitas (Andrew), Fern-Marie Aames (Deirdre), Amy Warner (Lillian), David Coxwell (John Barrymore), Les Marsden (Lefkowitz)

DEATHTRAP by Ira Levin; Director, Michael Haney CAST: David Coxwell (Sidney), Amy Warner (Myra), Christopher Hartmann (Clifford), Catherine Blaine (Helga), Les Marsden (Porter)

SHIRLEY VALENTINE by Willy Russell; Director, Michael Haney CAST: Amy Warner (Shirley)

Thomas Ladd, Chris Hartman in *Oklahoma*

Scott DeFreitas, David Coxwell, Fern-Marie Aames in *I Hate Hamlet*

MARK TWAIN'S ADAM & EVE DIARIES; Adapted/Directed by Michael Haney CAST: Mr. Haney (Adam), Amy Warner (Eve)

LOST IN YONKERS by Neil Simon; Director, Michael Haney CAST: David Malkoff (Jay), Peter L. Wilson (Arty), David Coxwell (Eddie), Amy Warner (Bella), Jayne Heller (Grandma), Tony Freeman (Louie), Catherine Blaine (Gert)

RIGHT BED, WRONG HUSBAND by Neil and Catherine Schaffner; Director, Robert J. Frost CAST: Jason Mitchell (Ted), David Coxwell (Martin), Tony Freeman (Claude), Morgan Sills (Hubert), Michelle Portch (Ruth), Amy Warner (Evelyn), Mary Rausch (Myra)

FOREVER PLAID by Stuart Ross; Director, Michael Haney; Musical Director, Ed Goldschneider; Choreography, Dan Brunson CAST: Bob Bucci (Frankie), Dan Brunson (Sparky), Steven Michael Daley (Jinx), Dan Guller (Smudge)

THE SECRET GARDEN with Music by Lucy Simon; Lyrics/Book, Marsha Norman; Director, Michael Haney; Musical Director, Ed Goldschneider CAST: Jennifer Marshall (Lily), Jennifer Murray (Mary), Matthew Picheny (Fakir), Bernadette Drayton (Ayah), Kim Saltarelli (Rose), Steven Michael Daley (Lennox), Brian J. Gill (Wright), Morgan Sills (Shaw), Ed Hammond (Holmes), Jessica L. Kell (Claire), Andrea Andresakis (Alice), Jason Mitchell (Shelley), Carrie J. Ranck (Indian), Michelle Portch (Cholera Bearer), Martha Baker (Dreamer), Kim Moore (Archibald), Dan Brunson (Neville), Amy Warner (Mrs. Medlock), Melissa Blake (Martha), Bob Bucci (Dickon), Nick Cosco (Ben), Brian Massey (Colin), Claudia Alick (Headmistress)

Bookwalter Photos

Amy Warner, Jayne Heller in *Lost in Yonkers*

AMERICAN CONSERVATORY THEATRE

San Francisco, California
Twenty-ninth Season

Artistic Director, Carey Perloff; Administrative Director, Thomas W. Flynn; Associate Producer, James Haire

PRODUCTIONS & CASTS

ANGELS IN AMERICA: MILLENNIUM APPROACHES and **PERESTROIKA;** by Tony Kushner; Director, Mark Wing-Davey; Sets, Kate Edmunds; Costumes, Catherine Zuber; Lighting, Christopher Akerlind CASTS: Cristine McMurdo-Wallis (Aleksii/Hannah/Doctor/Ethel Rosenberg/Asiatica/Rabbi), Lise Bruneau (Angel/Mormon/Nurse/Ella/So. Bronx Woman), Gregory Wallace (Belize/Lies/Oceania), Julia Gibson (Harper/Africani/Heller), Steven Culp (Joseph/Mormon/Europa), Garret Dillahunt (Prior/Man in Park), Peter Zapp (Roy Cohn/Antartica), Ben Shenkman (Louis/Australia)

HOME by David Storey; Director, Carey Perloff; Set. Dawn Swiderski; Costumes, Callie Floor; Lighting, Peter Maradudin CAST: William Paterson (Harry), Raye Birk (Jack), Joy Carlin (Kathleen), Ruth Kobart (Marjorie), Tom Lenoci (Alfred)

ROSENCRANTZ AND GUILDENSTERN ARE DEAD by Tom Stoppard; Director, Richard Seyd; Set, Kate Edmunds; Costumes, D.F. Draper; Lighting, Peter Maradudin CAST: Dan Hiatt (Guildenstern), Ray Porter (Rosencrantz), Jarion Monroe (Player), Jack Halton, Christopher Paul Hart, Tony Stovall, Peter James Meyers (Tragedians), Boris Undorf (Alfred), Ken Grantham (Claudius), Wanda McCaddon (Gertrude), George Ward (Polonius), Jamison Jones (Hamlet), Elisabeth Imboden (Ophelia), Tom Lenoci (Ambassador/Soldier), Michael Fitzpatrick (Horatio)

THE PLAY'S THE THING by Ferenc Molnar; Adaptation, P.G. Wodehouse; Director, Benny Sato Ambush CAST: Ken Grantham (Mansky), Ken Ruta (Turai), Don Burroughs (Albert), Joe Bellan (Dwornitschek), Stephen Markle (Almady), Kimberly King (Ilona), Dan Hiatt (Mell), Michael Fitzpatrick, Gabriel Sebastian (Lackeys)

OTHELLO by William Shakespeare; Director, Richard Seyd; Sets, Kate Edmunds; Costumes, Shigeru Yaji; Lighting, Peter Maradudin CAST: Dan Hiatt (Roderigo), Tony Amendola (Iago), Ken Grantham (Brabantio), Steven Anthony Jones (Othello), Remi Sandri (Cassio), Tom Blair (Duke), Mark Booher (Lodovico), Tom Lenoci (Gratiano), Maura Vincent (Desdemona), Michael Fitzpatrick (Montano), Domenique Lozano (Emilia), Bren McElroy (Bianca), Darren Bridgett

HECUBA by Euripides; Translation, Timberlake Wertenbaker; Director, Carey Perloff; Set, Kate Edmunds; Costumes, Donna Zakowska; Lighting, Peter Maradudin CAST: Olympia Dukakis (Hecuba), Darren Bridgett (Polydorus), Viola Davis (Chorus Leader), Elisabeth Imboden (Polyxena), Ken Ruta (Odysseus), Gerald Hiken (Talthibios), Remi Barclay Bosseau (Servent), James Carpenter (Agamemnon), Stephen Markle (Polymestor), Dylan Hackett, Eli Marienthal, James Milber, Ari Rosenman (Sons), Bob Brown, Catherine Rose Crowther, Deborah Dietrich, Irina Mikhailova, Janet Kutulas, Julie Graffagna, Michele Simon, Shira Cion, Tatiana Sarbinska

Tom Chargin, Ken Friedman Photos

Top: Garret Dillahunt, Lise Bruneau in *Angels in America*

Center: Maura Vincent, Tony Amendola, Steven Anthony Jones in *Othello*

Right: Olympia Dukakis, Remi Barclay Bouseau, Shirley Roecca, Ken Ruta in *Hecuba*

ARENA STAGE

Washington, D.C.
Forty-fourth Season

Artistic Director, Douglas C. Wager; Executive Director, Stephen Richard; Founding Director, Zelda Fichandler; Executive Director Emeritus, Thomas C. Fichandler; Production Manager, Dennis A. Blackledge; Communications Dircetor, Regan M. Byrne; Communications Intern, Amanda C. Fazzone

PRODUCTIONS & CASTS

A PERFECT GANESH by Terrence McNally; Director, Laurence Maslon; Costumes, Marina Draghici; Lighting, Nancy Schertler CAST: Jeffery V. Thompson (Ganesha), Andrew Weems (Man), Halo Wines (Margaret), Tana Hicken (Katherine)

THE ODYSSEY by Derek Walcott; Music, Galt MacDermot; Director, Douglas C. Wager; Music Director, Michael Keck; Choreography, Carol La Chapelle; Movement/Fights, David S. Leong; Sets, Thomas Lynch; Costumes, Paul Tazewell; Lighting, Allen Lee Hughes CAST: Wendell Wright (Blind Billy), Casey Biggs (Odysseus), Cordelia Gonzalez (Penelope), Teagle F. Bougere (Telemachus), Marilyn Coleman (Eurycleia), Gary Sloan (Antinous), Ralph Cosham (Eumaeus), Henry Strozier (Menelaus), T J Edwards (Eurylochus), Kristina Nielsen (Nausicaa), Yvonne Racz (Anemone), Crystal Simone Wright (Chloe), Richard Bauer (Cyclops), Stephenie Pope (Circe), Helen Carey (Anticlea), M. E. Hart (Achilles), Michael W. Howell (Thersites), Ernest Robert Mercer (Wrestler), Cornell Womack (Leodes), Dominic Dickerson, Kieron Anthony Pickett Lee (Boy)

MISALLIANCE by George Bernard Shaw; Director, Kyle Donnelly; Sets, Loy Arenas; Costumes, Paul Tazewell; Lighting, Michael Philippi CAST: David Marks (Johnny), JD Cullum (Bentley), Ellen Karas (Hypatia), Halo Wines (Mrs. Tarleton), Henry Strozier (Summerhays), Richard Bauer (John), Hank Stratton (Joey), Pamela Nyberg (Lina), T J Edwards (Gunner)

Crystal Simone Wright, Casey Biggs, Yvonne Racz in *The Odyssey*

Mary Beth Peil, Gary Sloan in *Month in the Country*

LONG DAY'S JOURNEY INTO NIGHT by Eugene O'Neill; Director, Douglas C. Wager; Set, Ming Cho Lee; Costumes, Paul Tazewell; Lighting, Scott Zielinski CAST: Richard Kneeland (James), Tana Hicken (Mary), Caset Biggs (James Jr.), Rainn Wilson (Edmund), Holly Twyford (Cathleen)

HEDDA GABLER by Henrik Ibsen; Translation, Christopher Hampton; Director/Designer, Liviu Ciulei; Costumes, Marina Draghici; Lighting, Allen Lee Hughes CAST: Halo Wines (Miss Tesman), June Hansen (Berte), Richard Howard (George), Pamela Nyberg (Hedda), Lily Knight (Mrs. Elvsted), Francois Giroday (Eilert)

I AM A MAN by OyamO; Director, Donald Douglas; Music, Olu Dara; Sets, Riccardo Hernandez; Costumes, Paul Tazewell; Lighting, Allen Lee Hughes CAST: Olu Dara (Bluesman), Wendell Wright (Jones), Jeffery V. Thompson (Rev. Moore), Henry Strozier (Mayor), David Marks (Solicitor), Ellis Foster (Councilman), Franchelle Stewart Dorn (Alice Mae), Ralph Cosham (Rev. Weatherford), Stephanie Pope (Miss Secretary), Teagle F. Bougere (Swahili), D'Monroe (Cinnamon), Michael W. Howell (Willins), Lee Sellars (Joshua)

WHAT THE BUTLER SAW by Joe Orton; Director, Frank Dowling; Set, Frank Hallinan Flood; Costumes, Paul Tazewell; Lighting, Christopher V. Lewton CAST: Andrew Weems (Dr. Prentice), Sevanne Martin (Geraldine), Helen Carey (Mrs. Prentice), Gabriel Macht (Nicholas), Milo O'Shea (Dr. Rance), Edward Gero (Sgt. Match)

A MONTH IN THE COUNTRY by Brian Friel; Based on Turgenev; Director, Kyle Donnelly; Sets, Linda Buchanan; Costumes, Lindsay W. Davis; Lighting, Rita Pietraszek CAST: Richard Bauer (Schaaf), Tana Hicken (Lizaveta), Halo Wines (Anna), Mary Beth Peil (Natalya), Melissa Flaim (Katya), Gary Sloan (Michel), Joseph Fuqua (Aleksey), Ralph Cosham (Matvey), Henry Strozier (Ignaty), Kristina Nielson (Vera), Wendell Wright (Arkady), Jeffery V. Thompson (Afanasy)

Joan Marcus Photos

ARIZONA THEATRE COMPANY

Tucson and Phoenix, Arizona
Twenty-eighth Season

Artistic Director, David Ira Goldstein; Managing Director, Robert Alpaugh; Public Relations Director, Marion Owsnitzki

PRODUCTIONS & CASTS

NOISES OFF by Michael Frayn; Director, David Ira Goldstein; Set, Jeff Thomson; Costumes, David Kay Mickelsen; Lighting, Don Darnutzer CAST: Lynne Griffin (Dotty), Don Sparks (Lloyd), Benjamin Livingston (Garry), Diane Stilwell (Brooke), Kelly Going (Poppy), Peter Silbert (Frederick), Suzanne Bouchard (Belinda), Bob Sorenson (Tim), Apollo Dukakis (Selsdon)

BLUES IN THE NIGHT; Conceived/Directed by Sheldon Epps; Musical Director, Ronald P. Metcalf; Set/Lighting, Douglas D. Smith; Costumes, Marianna Elliott CAST: Roz Ryan (Lady from Road), Alisa Gyse-Dickens (Woman of the World), Vanita Harbour (Girl with Date), Dennis C. Rowland (Man in Saloon)

THE OLD MATADOR by Milcha Sanchez-Scott; Director, Peter C. Brosius; Set, Greg Lucas; Lighting, Michael Gilliam; Costumes, Tina Cantu Navarro CAST: Valente Rodriguez (Cookie), Ismael East Carlo (Enrique), Ivonne Coll (Margarita), Erica Ortega (Jesse), Christopher Aponte (Paco), Michele Mais (Evelina), Laurence Ballard (Fr. Steven), Fred Sugerman (Angel), Miguel Rodriguez (Guitar), Step Raptis (Percussion), Ricardo Esquival, Miguel Ortega (Kids)

DANCING AT LUGHNASA by Brian Friel; Director, Matthew Wiener; Choreography, Jim Corti; Set, R. Michael Miller; Costumes, Rose Pederson; Lighting, Rick Paulsen CAST: Lawrence Hecht (Michael), Michele Marsh (Kate), Deborah Van Valkenburgh (Maggie), Michele Farr (Agnes), Corliss Preston (Rose), Jessica Knoblauch (Chris), Charles Shaw Robinson (Gerry), Charles Lanyer (Jack)

DRACULA by Steven Dietz; Adapted from novel by Bram Stoker; Director, David Ira Goldstein; Sets, Bill Forrester; Costumes, David Kay Mickelsen; Lighting, Don Darnutzer CAST: David Pichette (Renfield), Britt Sady (Mina), Suzanne Bouchard (Lucy), David Ellenstein (Harker), Benjamin Livingston (Seward), Patrick Page (Dracula), Peter Silbert (Van Helsing), Adam Burke, Jamie Lynn Hines, Aubdon O. Morales, Renee Serino

THE CONVICTS RETURN; Written/Performed by Geoff Hoyle; Developed by Tony Taccone, Mr. Hoyle; Director, Mr. Taccone; Set, Bill Forrester; Lighting, Tracy Odishaw

Tim Fuller Photos

Top: Apollo Dukakis, Don Sparks, Bob Sorenson in *Noises Off*

Center: Deborah Van Valkenburgh, Jessica Knoblauch, Michele Marsh, Michele Farr, Corliss Preston in *Dancing at Lughnasa*

Right: David Ellenstein, Patrick Page in *Dracula*

153

CALDWELL THEATRE COMPANY

Boca Raton, Florida
Nineteenth Season

Artistic/Managing Director, Michael Hall; Associate Artistic Director, Tina Paul; Sets, Frank Bennett(Design Director), Tim Bennett; Costume Desingers, Patricia Bowes, Penny Koleos Williams; Lighting Designer, Thomas Salzman; Company Manager, Patricia Burdett; Publicity Manager, Paul Perone

PRODUCTIONS & CASTS

COWGIRLS; Music/Lyrics/Concept by Mary Murfitt; Book, Betsy Howie; Director, Eleanor Reissa; Musical Director, Mary Ehlinger CAST: Mary Ehlinger, Brook Ann Hedick, Betsy Howie, Audrey Lavine, Mary Murfitt, Claudia Schneider

BUT NOT FOR ME by Christopher Cooper, Michael Hall, Dana P. Rowe and Avery Sommers; Director, Michael Hall; Musical Director, Dana P. Rowe CAST: Avery Sommers, Dana P. Rowe

THE HASTY HEART by John Patrick; Director, Joe Warik CAST: John Archie, W. Paul Bodie, David Cass, Jon Brent Curry, David DeBesse, Sean Patrick Fagan, John Goulet, Leslie Scarlett Mason, Tony Meindl

THE PRICE by Arthur Miller; Director, Michael Hall CAST: Philip Clark, Pat Nesbit, Kip Niven, Allen Swift

COMPANY with Music/Lyrics, Stephen Sondheim; Book, George Furth; Director/Choreographer, Tina Paul; Musical Director, Kevin Wallace CAST: Carole Caselle, Kim Cozort, Jessica Frankel, Maribeth Graham, Peter Gunther, Wayne LaGette, Rita Rehn, Robert Riley, Connie Saloutos, Wayne Steadman, Meghan Strange, Barry J. Tarallo, Barbara Tirrell, Court Whishman

CRIMES OF THE HEART by Beth Henley; Director, Michael Hall CAST: Viki Boyle, Kim Cozort, Scott Hudson, Kenneth Kay, Pat Nesbit, Toby Poser

DAMES AT SEA with Music by Jim Wise; Lyrics/Book, George Haimsohn and Robin Miller; Director/Choreographer, Tina Paul; Musical Director, David Truskinoff CAST: Carl J. Danielsen, Barbara Folts, Mark Manley, Joel Newsome, Rita Rehn, Melodie Wolford

SHOLEM ALECHEM; Adapted/Edited by Nehemiah Persoff

Paul Perone photos

Mary Ehlinger, Brook Ann Hedick, Mary Murfitt in *Cowgirls*

Avery Sommers in *But Not for Me*

John Goulet, David DeBesse in *Hasty Heart*

(clockwise from bottom center) Peter Gunther, Maibeth Graham, Barry J. Tarallo, Rita Rehn, Court Whisman, Meghan Strange, Wayne LeGette in *Company*

154

CENTER STAGE

Baltimore, Maryland

Artistic Director, Irene Lewis; Managing Director, Peter W. Culman; Artistic Administrator, Del W. Risberg; Production Manager, Kathryn Davies; Stage Managers, Julianne Franz, Michael B. Paul; Communications Director, Linda Anne Geeson

PRODUCTIONS & CASTS

THE CHERRY ORCHARD by Anton Chekhov; Translation, Elisaveta Lavrova; Director, Irene Lewis; Set, Tony Straiges; Costumes, Jess Goldstein; Lighting, Mimi Jordan Sherin   CAST: Stephen Markle (Lopakhin), Lynn Hawley (Dunyasha), Ken Cheeseman (Yepikhodov), Carrie Preston (Anya), Lois Smith (Ranyevskaya), Colette Kilroy (Varya), James J. Lawless (Gayev), Janni Brenn (Charlotta), George Bartenieff (Simeonov-Pishchik), Tucker McCrady (Yasha), George Hall (Firs), Reg Rogers (Petya), Eeggor Fainbereft (Passeby), Matthew Ramsey (Stationmaster), Liam Hughes (Postmaster), Alex David Balchowicz, Ted R. Frankenhauser, Dann Garrett, Kurt Herring, Brad Reiss, Thomas Rinaldi

TWO TRAINS RUNNING by August Wilson; Director, Marion Isaac McClinton; Set, Neil Patel; Costumes, Paul Tazewell; Lighting, Allen Lee Hughes CAST: Clayton LeBouef (Wolf), Anthony Chisholm (Memphis), Rosalyn Coleman (Risa), John Henry Redwood (Holloway), Willis Burks (Hambone), Keith Glover (Sterling), Damien Leake (West)

SLAVS! by Tony Kushner; Director, Lisa Peterson; Set, Michael Yeargan; Costumes, Gabriel Berry; Lighting, Robert Wierzel CAST: Caitlin O'Connell (1st Babushka/Dr. Bonch-Bruevich), Ludmila Bokievsky (2nd Babushka/Mrs. Domik), James J. Lawless (Vassily/Big Babushka), James Greene (Serge), Ronny Graham (Aleksii), Lee Wilkof (Poppy), Christopher McCann (Yegor), Katie MacNichol (Kat), Meredith Friend, Maren E. Rosenberg

HAPPY END with Music by Kurt Weill; Lyrics/Book, Bertolt Brecht; Adaptation, Michael Feingold; Director, Irene Lewis; Musical Director, Mark Bennett; Choreography, Willie Rosario; Sets, Christopher Barreca; Costumes, Catherine Zuber; Lighting, James F. Ingalls CAST: Joe Pichette (Professor), Kevin McClarnon (Baby Face), Ed Dixon (Mommy), Tony Marinyo (Governor), Clayton LeBouef (Reverand), William Parry (Bill), William Foeller (Cop), Sharon Scruggs (Fly), Beata Fido (Miriam), Pamela Isaacs (Holiday), Jennifer Smith (Sister Mary), Pebble Kranz (Sister Jane), Ken Jennings (Brother Jackson), Mary Stout (Stone), Michael Bennett (Brother Ben), Ted R. Frankenhauser, dan garrett, Thomas Rinaldi

CITIZEN RENO by Reno; Director, Tina Landau; Design, Heather Carson CAST: Reno, Tom Nelis, Toona Platonica Amora Maybe-a

HANNAH SENESH; Written/Directed by David Schechter; Music, Steven Lutvak; Set, David M. Barber; Costumes, David Burdick; Lighting, Mark McCullough CAST: Lori Wilner (Hannah), Dan Garrett (Nazi)

BIG BUTT GIRLS, HARD-HEADED WOMEN; Director, Idris Ackamoor; Set, David M. Barber; Lighting, Mark L. McCullough

THE SHOW-OFF by George Kelly; Director, Irene Lewis; Set, Hugh Landwehr; Costumes, Paul Tazewell; Lighting, Pat Collins CAST: Anne Torsiglieri (Clara), Pamela Payton-Wright (Mrs. Fisher), Bo Foxworth (Joe), Katie MacNichol (Amy), Steve Irish (Frank), Jefferson Mays (Aubrey), James J. Lawless (Mr. Fisher), Kevin McClarnon (Mr. Gill), T J Edwards (Mr Rogers)

Richard Anderson Photos

**Top: Stephen Markle, Lois Smith James J. Lawless in *Cherry Orchard*
Center: Clayton LeBouef, Keith Glover in *Two Trains Running*
Right: Anne Torsilieri in *The Show-Off***

CENTER THEATRE GROUP
Ahmanson/Doolittle Theatres

Los Angeles, California
Twenty-eighth Season

Artistic Director/Producer, Gordon Davidson; Managing Director, Charles Dillingham; General Manager, Douglas C. Baker; Press Director, Tony Sherwood; Press Assistant, Nicole Gorak

PRODUCTIONS & CASTS

RACING DEMON by David Hare; Director, Richard Eyre; Design, Bob Crowley; Lighting, Mark Henderson; Music, George Fenton CAST: Oliver Ford Davies (Rev. Espy), Richard Pasco (Rev. Allen), Adam Kotz (Rev. Ferris), Adrian Scarborough (Rev. "Streaky" Bacon), Michael Bryant (Rev. Henderson), Nicholas Day (Rev. Heffernan), Saskia Wickham (Frances Parnell), Joy Richardson (Stella Marr), Barbara Leigh-Hunt (Heather Espy), Alastair Gailbraith (Ewan Gilmour), Paul Moriarty (Tommy Adair), Robert Tunstall, Roger Swaine, Doyne Byrd, Judith Coke, Julie Hewlett, Tacye Nichols

SMOKEY JOE'S CAFE: The Songs of Leiber and Stoller; Music/ Lyrics by Jerry Leiber and Mike Stoller; Director, Jerry Zaks; Choreography, Joey McKneely; Sets, Heidi Landesman; Costumes, William Ivey Long; Lighting, Timothy Hunter; Conductor, Louis St. Louis CAST: Ken Ard, Adrian Bailey, Brenda Braxton, Victor Trent Cook, B. J. Crosby, Pattie Darcy Jones, DeLee Lively, Frederick B. Owens, Robert Torti, Bobby Daye, Cee-Cee Harshaw, Kevyn Morrow, Monica Pege

MISS SAIGON; See Broadway section for creative credits; Director, Nicholas Hytner; Musical Director, Kevin Stites CAST: Kevin Gray (Engineer), Jennifer Paz (Kim), Peter Lockyer (Chris), Keith Byron Kirk (John), Allen D. Hong (Thuy), Tami Tappan (Ellen), Melanie Mariko Tojio ("Kim" alternate), Missy Aguilar, Susan Ancheta, Philip Michael Baskerville, Randy Bettis, Miguel Braganza II, Frankie Braxton, Carter Alden Chang, Kevin Chinn, Melinda Chua, Leo Daignault, Dexter Echiverri, Ariel Felix, Johnny Fernandez, John-Michael Flate, Joseph Anthony Foronda, Steve Geary, Marie Gulmatico, General MacArthur Hambrick, Moon Hi Hanson, Donny Honda, david Jennings, Bridget Bernell Johnston, Owen Johnston II, Paul Martinez, Pat McRoberts, Henry Menendez, Charles Munn, Sandy Shimoda Nagel, Paul Nakauchi, Jenni Padua, Stephanie Park, Jeff Pierce, Donna Pompei, Michael Raimondi, Ray Rochelle, Ariel A. Rodriguez, John-Paul Stewart, Jade K. Stice, Larry Sullivan Jr., Charles West

THE WOMAN WARRIOR; Adaptation by Deborah Rogin; Based on novels *The Woman Warrior* and *China Men* by Maxine Hong Kingston; Director, Sharon Ott; Choreography, Daniel Pelzig; Set, Ming Cho Lee; Costumes, Susan Hilfery; Lighting, Peter Maradudin CAST: Michael Paul Chan, Francois Chau, Tsai Chin (Brave Orchid), John Cho, Janis Chow, David Furumoto, Alsion Gleason, Charles Hu, Yunjin Kim, Dian Kobayashi, Emily Kuroda, Brian Kwan, Dana Lee, Page Leong, Kim Miyori (Fa Mu Lan), Wood Moy, Soon-Tech Oh (Father), Liana Pai (Daughter), Luo Yong Wang (Father's Youth), Donna Mae Wong, Man Wong, Jenny Woo, Peide Yao, Tricia Dong, Alberto Isaac, Sharon Omi

LAUGHTER ON THE 23RD FLOOR by Neil Simon; Director, Jerry Zaks; Set, Tony Walton; Costumes, William Ivey Long; Lighting, Tharron Musser CAST: Howard Hesseman (Max), Lewis J. Stadlen (Milt), Matthew Arkin (Lucas), Alan Blumenfeld (Ira), Michael Countryman (Val), Anthony Cummings (Kenny), Alsion Martin (Carol), Michelle Schumacher (Helen), J.K. Simmons (Brian), Jason Brill, Laurie Graff, Daniel Hagen, John Plumpis

Jay Thompson, John Haynes, Carol Rosegg Photos

Top: Janis Chow, Donna Mae Wong, Jenny Woo, Emily Kuroda (on bed) in *Woman Warrior*

Center: Oliver Ford Davies in *Racing Demon*

Right: Alan Blumenfeld, Matthew Arkin, Anthony Cummings, Michael Countryman, J.K. Simmons, Howard Hesseman in *Laughter on the 23rd Floor*

Brenda Braxton, B.J. Crosby, DeLee Lively, Pattie Darcie Jones in the Ahmanson's *Smokey Joe's Cafe*

Peter Kelly Gaudreault, Jane Lind in the Mark Taper's *Black Elk Speaks*

CENTER THEATRE GROUP
Mark Taper Forum

Los Angeles, California
Twenty-eighth Season

Artistic Director, Gordon Davidson; Managing Director, Charles Dillingham; Producing Director, Robert Egan; General Manager, Karen S. Wood; Associate Producing Director, Corey Madden; Press Director, Nancy Hereford

PRODUCTIONS & CASTS

FLOATING ISLANDS: Part I—The Family Business: The Modern Ladies of Guanabacoa and In the Eye of the Hurricane; Part II—After the Revolution: Fabiola and Broken Eggs; by Eduardo Machado; Director, Oskar Eustis; Sets, Eugene Lee; Costumes, Marianna Elliott; Lighting, Paulie Jenkins CAST: Victor Argo (Arturo/Oscar/Alfredo), Marissa Chibas (Manuela/Rosa/Clara/Mimi), Miriam Colon (Maria Josefa/Manuela), Alma Cuervo (Manuela/Sonia), Kamala Dawson (Lizette), Josie de Guzman (Dolores/Sonia), Wanda De Jesus (Adelita/Miliciana/Miriam), Rosana De Soto (Cusa), Shawn Elliott (Mario/Osvaldo), Gloria Mann (Sara), William Marquez (Antonio), Tim Perez (Miguel/Fernando), Jaime Sanchez (Ernesto/Alfredo), Joe Urla (Oscar Hernandez/Osvaldo/Miliciano/Oscar), Yul Vazquez (Hugo/Pedro/Adam Rifkin)

BLACK ELK SPEAKS; Adapted by Christopher Sergel from book by John G. Neihardt; Director, Donovan Marley; Set, Bill Curley; Costumes, Andrew V. Yelusich; Lighting, Don Darnutzer CAST: John Belindo (Kiowa Chief/Gen. Crook), Stuart Bird (Lt. Ortiz/Shakopee/William Bent/Dancer), Jack Burning (Elder/Black Kettle/Arapaho Chief), Janice Conway (Taino), Luke Dubray (Spirit Guide/Dancer), James Apaumut Fall (Taino/Navajo/Wowinapa/John Finerty), Peter Kelly Gaudreault (Gen. Carleton/Lt. Cramer/Crazy Horse/Gen. Custer), Jane Lind (Lucy/Yellow Woman/Eagle Spirit), Kenneth Little Hawk (Priest/Cheyenne Chief/Crazy Horse father), Kenneth Martines (Andrew Jackson/Little Crow)/Taylor), David Medina (Hoksila), Miguel Najera (Manuelito/Col. Chivington/Gen. Sherman), Gracie Red Shirt-Tyon (Show Dancer), Andrew Roa (Corporal/Major Wyncoop/Red Cloud), Maria Antoinette Rogers (Grandmother/Crazy Horse Mother), Ned Romero (Black Elk), Adam Sanchez (Clown Spirit/Galbraith/Col. Carrington), Larry Swalley (Medecine Bottle/Lakota Chief/Dancer), Stephan Ray Swimmer (Dancer), Kateri Walker (Taino/Cross-Over Spirit/Dancer), Seth Bissonette, Bernard Cottonwood, Dane LeBeau, Dennis Yerry

Audra McDonald, Zoe Caldwell in *Master Class*

Left: Tim Perez, Miriam Colon, Jaime Sanchez, Shawn Elliott in *Floating Islands*

Below: Joe Urla, Yul Vazquez in *Floating Islands*

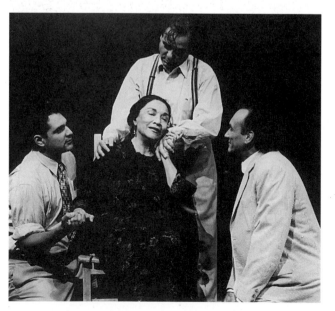

THREE HOTELS by Jon Robin Baitz; Director, Joe Mantello; Set, Loy Arcenas; Costumes, Jess Goldstein; Lighting, Brian MacDevitt CAST: Richard Dreyfuss (Kenneth), Christine Lahti (Barbara), Evan Acosta (Attendant)

MASTER CLASS by Terrence McNally; Director, Leonard Foglia; Set, Michael McGarty; Costumes, Jane Greenwood; Lighting, Brian MacDevitt CAST: John Achorn (Stagehand), Zoe Caldwell (Maria Callas), Karen Kay Cody (Sophie), David Loud (Manny), Audra McDonald (Sharon), Jay Hunter Morris (Tony)

THE YELLOW BOAT by David Saar; Director, Peter C. Brosius; Choreography, Carol Guidry; Set, Victoria Petrovich; Costumes, Lydia Tanji; Lighting, R. Stephen Hoyes CAST: Joshua Fardon, Leslie Ishii, Kenneth Martines, Anne O'Sullivan, Kevin Sifuentes, Torri Whitehead-Winn

HYSTERIA by Terry Johnson; Director, Phyllida Lloyd; Set/Costumes, Mark Thompson; Lighting, Chris Parry CAST: Anna Gunn (Jessica), Richard Libertini (Salvador Dali), David Margulies (Sigmund Freud), Kenneth Mars (Abraham Yahunda), Jack Axelrod, Fiona Hale, BobbyRuth Mann, Liann Pattison, Marra Racz, Katherine Talent

Jay Thompson Photos

Top Left: Christine Lahti in *Three Hotels*
Top Right: Richard Dreyfuss in *Three Hotels*
Right: Kenneth Mars, David Margulies in *Hysteria*

159

CINCINNATI PLAYHOUSE IN THE PARK

Cincinnati, Ohio
Thirty-fifth Season

Producing Artistic Director, Edward Stern; Executive Director, Buzz Ward; Production Manager, Shawn Nolan; Stage Managers, Bruce E. Coyle, Jenifer Morrow, Susann Pollock; Public Relations Director, Peter Robinson; Public Relations Assistant, John P. Bruggen

PRODUCTIONS & CASTS

A MIDSUMMER NIGHT'S DREAM by William Shakespeare; Director, Martin L. Platt; Choreography, Dennis Poole; Sets, Russell Parkman; Costumes, Susan Tsu; Lighting, Robert Wierzel CAST: Greg Thornton (Theseus/Oberon), Leslie Hendrix (Hippolyta/Titania), Spike McClure (Philostrate/Puck), David McKinney, Aaron Ishmael-Memphis Mingo (Indian Boys), Donald Christopher (Egeus), Shelley Delaney (Hermia), Scott Whitehurst (Lysander), Craig Wroe (Demetrius), Jackie Farrington (Helena), Charles Antalosky (Quince), Ray Dooley (Bottom), Russ Jolly (Flute), David Hemsley Caldwell (Snout), John Milligan (Starveling), David B. Heuvelman (Snug), Gary Anaple , John Timothy Baldwin, Richard Kelly, Lavinia Magliocco Howes, Kathryne Gardette, Wendi Rohan, Victor D. Dickerson, Lynne Manijeh Mostaghim, Lynette Ferguson

KELLY & DU by Jane Martin; Director, Madeleine Pabis; Set, Robert Barnett; Costumes, Jeanette de Jong; Lighting, John R. Lasiter CAST: Beverly May (Du), Alan Mixon (Walter), Jane Fleiss (Keeley), Brian Dykstra (Cole), Claire Cundiff (Guard), Robert J. Brown, Alastar Brown (Orderlies)

INSPECTING CAROL by Daniel Sullivan and the Seattle Rep Theatre Company; Director, Edward Stern; Sets, James Leonard Joy; Costumes, Dorothy L. Marshall; Lighting, Peter E. Sargent CAST: Pamela Wiggins (M.J. McMann), Russ Jolly (Wellacre), Glynis Bell (Zorah), Chris Van Strander (Beatty), Darrie Lawrence (Dorothy), Thomas Ligon (Carlton), Anderson Matthews (Hewlitt), Dale E. Turner (Parsons), Jack Cirillo (Emery), Brett Pearsons (Frances), Tony Hoty (Vauxhall), Liz Comstock (Betty)

BEEHIVE by Larry Gallagher; Director/Choreographer, Pamela Hunt; Musical Director, Darren R. Cohen; Set, Jim Morgan; Costumes, John Carver Sullivan; Lighting, Mary Jo Dondlinger CAST: Adinah Alexander, Angela Lockett, Virginia McMath, Gayle Samuels, Cathy Trien, Kathy Wade

Right: (rear) Paul DeBoy, Matthew Rauch, Katherine Heasley in *Brothers Karamazov*

Below: Elain Graham, Crystal Laws Green, Irma P. Hall in *Jar the Floor*

A CHRISTMAS CAROL; Adaptation by Howard Dallin; Director, Michael Haney; Sets, John Leonard Joy; Costumes, David Murrin; Lighting, Kirk Bookman CAST: Alan Mixon (Scrooge), Torben Brooks, Patrick Frederic, Craig Wroe, Steven Dennis, Gregory Procaccino, Shelley Delaney, Andrew Chaney, Annie Gill, Herbert Mark Parker, Dale Hodges, R. Ward Duffy, Mary Proctor, Kristen Schwarz, Sara G. Fischer, Ben Sands, Christopher Bissonnette, Regina Pugh, Petra Van Nuis, Benjamin Endress, Christina Seymour, Jake Sieving, Brandon West, Jason White, Emily Bissonnette, Monique L. Cash, Julie Hasl Miller

JAR THE FLOOR by Cheryl L. West; Director, Clinton Turner Davis; Set, Robert Barnett; Costumes, Myrna Colley-lee; Lighting, Phillip Monat CAST: Irma P. Hall (MaDear), Elain Graham (MayDee), Crystal Laws Green (Lola), Tamika Lamison (Vennie), Drew Richardson (Raisa)

THE CARETAKER by harold Pinter; Director, Charles Towers; Set, Ursula Belden; Costumes, Lisa Molyneux; Lighting, James Sale CAST: Jason Antoon (Mick), Jack Willis (Aston), David A. Penhale (Davies)

THE BROTHERS KARAMAZOV; Adapted by Anthony Clarvoe from novel by Dostoyevsky; Director, Brian Kulick; Set/Costumes, Mark Wendland; Lighting, Max De Volder CAST: Robert Elliott (Fydor/Judge/Devill), Michael Chaban (Dmitri), Michael Ornstein (Ivan), Matthew Rauch (Alyosha), Ed Shea (Smerdyakov/Plotkinov), Joneal Joplin (Zosima/Mussyalovich/D.A.), Paul DeBoy (Rakitin/Plastunov), Susan Ericksen (Katya), Katherine Heasley (Grushenka), Brooks Almy (Samsonov/Fenya)

HOMETOWN HEROES by Ed Graczyk; Director, Edward Stern; Set, Paul R. Short; Costumes, Hollis Jenkins-Evans; Lighting, Jackie Manassee CAST: Ralph Waite (Willie), M. Emmet Walsh (Joe)

DRACULA by Hamilton Deane and John L. Balderston; Director, Stephen Hollis; Set, David Crank; Costumes, Elizabeth Covey; Lighting, Kirk Bookman CAST: Christine Dye (Miss Wells), Chris Hietikko (Harker), Donald Christopher (Seward), James Doerr (Van Helsing), Keith McDermott (Renfield), Duffy Hudson (Butterworth), Nancy Bell (Lucy), Ray Dooley (Dracula)

BANJO DANCING; Written/Collected by Stephen Wade with Milton Kramer; Director/Set/Lighting, Mr. Kramer CAST: Stephen Wade

Sandy Underwood Photos

Top: Ralph Waite, M. Emmet Walsh in
Cincinnati Playhouse's *Hometown Heroes*

Center: Andrew Dunn, Council Cargle,
Wm. Boswell, Tony Lucas in *Carpool*

Bottom: Tony Lucas, Benita Charles, Wm. Banks,
Natalie Chillis, Jeffry Chastang in *Kate's Sister*

DETROIT REPERTORY THEATRE

**Detroit, Michigan
Thirty-seventh Season**

Artistic/Managing Director, Bruce E. Millan; Production Manager, Richard Smith; Set Design, Richard Smith, Mr. Millan; Lighting Design, Kenneth Hewitt, Jr.; Costume Design, B.J. Essan; Publicity Manager, Dee Andrus

PRODUCTIONS & CASTS

CARPOOL by Laura Hembee; Director, Barbara Busby CAST: Andrew Dunn (Arthur), Tony Lucas (Carl), Harold Hogan (Gene), Council Cargle (Raymond), William Boswell (Willard), Mark Bishop (Passenger)

KATE'S SISTER by Maisha Baton; Director, Charlotte Nelson CAST: Bill Banks (Sgt. Lucas), Benita Charles (Kate), Jeffry Chastang (Thomas), Natalie A. Chillis (Janie), Tony Lucas (Papa)

THE CHANCELLOR'S TALE by Paul Mohrbacher; Director, Andrew Dunn CAST: J. Center (Joseph), Rick Hudson (Frank), Charlotte J. Nelson (Ellen), Dennis T. Kleinsmith (Peter)

LATER LIFE by A.R. Gurney; Director, Bruce Millan CAST: Council Cargle (Austin), Dorry Peltyn (Ruth), Barbara Busby (Women), Thomas Emmott (Men)

Bruce Millan Photos

161

GEORGE STREET PLAYHOUSE

New Brunswick, New Jersey

Producing Artistic Director, Gregory S. Hurst; Managing Director, Diane Claussen; Associate Artistic Director, Wendy Liscow; Marketing and Public Relations Director, Rick Engler; Production Manager, Edson Womble; Development Director, Ann M. Poskocil; Press Manager, Stacey Colosa

PRODUCTIONS & CASTS

KEELEY AND DU by Jane Martin; Director, Wendy Liscow; Set, Deborah Jasien; Costumes, Hilary Rosenfeld; Lighting, Donald Holder CAST: Amanda Carlin (Keely), Mary Fogarty (Du), Robert Hogan (Walter), John Leonard Thompson (Cole)

RELATIVITY by Mark Stein; Director, Gregory S. Hurst; Set, Deborah Jasien; Costumes, Barbara Forbes; Lighting, Donald Holder, John Lasiter CAST: Michael Rupert (Neil), Kit Flanagan (Audrey), Doris Belak (Vera), Laura Sametz (Susan), David S. Howard (Kirby)

MR. RICKEY CALLS A MEETING by Ed Schmidt; Director, Sheldon Epps; Set, Marjorie Bradley Kellogg; Costumes, Toni Leslie James; Lighting, David S. Segal CAST: Ray Ford (Young Clancy Hope), Tom Brennan (Branch Rickey), Sterling Macer, Jr. (Jackie Robinson), Isiah Whitlock (Joe Louis), Willie C. Carpenter (Paul Robeson), Allie Woods, Jr. ("Bojangles" Robinson), Lawrence James (Clancy Hope at 64)

A RAISIN IN THE SUN by Lorraine Hansberry; Director, Seret Scott; Set, Atkin Pace; Costumes, Karen Perry; Lighting, Brian Nason CAST: Brenda Pressley (Ruth Younger), Joey Allen (Travis Younger), Scott Lawrence (Walter Lee Younger), Ayo Haynes (Beneatha Younger), Sheila Gibbs (Lena Younger), Maduka Steady (Joseph Asagai), Tyrone Mitchell Henderson (George Murchison), Eddie Lee Murphy III (Bobo), Charles Geyer (Karl Lindner), Georgeric Davis, Busairi Savage (Moving Men)

OPAL with Music/Lyrics/Book by Robert Nassif Lindsey; Director/Choreographer, Lynne Taylor-Corbett; Set, Micheal R. Smith; Costumes, Ann Hould-Ward; Lighting, Tom Sturge; Musical Director, James Stenborg; Orchestrations, Douglas Besterman CAST: Mana Allen (Girl That Has No Seeing), Jackie Angelescu (Opal), Christopher Chew (Man Who Wears Gray Neckties), Erin Hill (Thought Girl With The Far-Away Look In Her Eyes), Julie Johnson (Mamma), Marni Nixon (Sadie McKibben), Hal Davis, Deb G. Girdler, Judy Malloy, Ed Sala (Narrators)

OFF-KEY with Music by Richard Adler; Lyrics, Bill C. Davis, Mr. Adler; Book, Mr. Davis; Director/Choreographer, Marcia Milgrom Dodge; Set, Narelle Sissons; Costumes, Gail Brassard; Lighting, Christopher Akerlind; Musical Director, Darren R. Cohen CAST: Christopher Sieber (Austin Quinn), Lannyl Stephens (Donna), Paul Binotto (Ronald), Mana Allen (Ruth), Amanda Naughton (Lauren), Michael Greenwood (Charles), Christy Baron (Diane), Derek Gentry (Lionel), Reathel Bean (Mr. Lester), Robert Vargas (Alex), Marcell Rosenblatt (Mrs. Liebowitz), Frank Raiter (Mr. Garfinkle), M. Eliot Beisner (Officer Pitts)

OF MICE AND MEN by John Steinbeck; Director, Susan Kerner; Set, R. Michael Miller; Costumes, Deirdre Sturges Burke; Lighting, Tom Sturge CAST: Conan McCarty (George), Bill Christ (Lennie), David S. Howard (Candy), Michael Barry Greer (Boss), Guy Chandler Roberts (Curley), Clover Devaney (Curley's Wife), Peter Bretz (Slim), Lou Sumrall (Carlson), Christopher Haas (Whit), Stephen M. Henderson (Crooks)

Miguel Pagliere Photos

Top: Paul Binotto, Mana Allen, Christopher Sieber in *Off-Key*
Center: Marni Nixon, Jackie Angelescu in *Opal*
Right: Ayo Haynes, Brenda Pressley, Sheila Gibbs in *Raisin in the Sun*

GOODMAN THEATRE

Chicago, Illinois

Artistic Director, Robert Falls; Executive Director, Roche Schulfer; Press Directors, Cindy Bandle, Mario LaCorte, David A. Ham

PRODUCTIONS & CASTS

A LITTLE NIGHT MUSIC with Music/Lyrics by Stephen Sondheim; Book, Hugh Wheeler; Director, Michael Maggio; Set, John Lee Beatty; Costumes, Virgil C. Johnson; Lighting, Michael S. Philippi; Choreography, Danny Herman; Musical Director, Bradley Vieth CAST: Jessica Boevers (Fredrika), Rich Brunner (Lindquist), Kelly Cronin (Mrs. Nordstrom), Sheila Savage (Mrs. Anderssen), Stephen Branch (Erlanson), Anne Kanengeiser (Mrs. Segstrom), Paula Scrofano (Desiree), John Herrera (Carl-Magnus), Andy Taylor (Henrik), Kimberly Karen Johnson (Anne), Mark Zimmerman (Fredrik), Hollis Resnik (Charlotte), Christopher Vasquez (Frid), Rengin Altay (Petra), Ann Stevenson Whitney (Madame Armfeldt), Jamie Pachino (Malla), Lisa Menninger (Osa), Tracy Hultgren (Bertrand)

THE MERCHANT OF VENICE by William Shakespeare; Director, Peter Sellars; Costumes, Dunya Ramicova; Lighting, James F. Ingalls CAST: Geno Silva (Antonio), Joe Quintero (Salerio), Richard Coca (Solanio), John Ortiz (Brassanio), Rene Rivera (Lorenzo), Carlos Sanz (Gratiano), Lori Tan Chinn (Nerissa), Midori Nakamura (Balthaser), Dorcas M. Johnson (Stephano), Paul Butler (Shylock), Tyrone Beasley (Prince of Morocco/Jailer), Philip Seymour Hoffman (Launcelot), Del Close (Old Gobbo/Duke of Venice), David Anzuelo (Leonardo), Portia Johnson (Jessica), Anjul Nigam (Prince of Arragon), Ernest Perry Jnr. (Tubal)

A CHRISTMAS CAROL by Charles Dickens; Adaptation, Tom Creamer; Director, Chuck Smith; Set, Joseph Nieminski; Lighting, Robert Christen CAST: Tom Mula (Scrooge), Paul Amandes, Jeff Parker, Greg Vinkler, Christopher Vasquez, John Reeger, Mary Ernster, Mark L. Montgomery, Phillip Doyle, Marites Cumba, Dwain A. Perry, James Sie, Bradley Mott, E. Faye Butler, Marci Kipnis, Jaye Tyrone Stewart, Aisha deHaas, Alyson Horn, Gregory K. Hirte, Kareth M. Schaffer, Robert Artee Pittman, Rengin Altay, Cheryl Hamada, Paul Slade Smith, William Schwartz, Jordan Loperena

SEVEN GUITARS by August Wilson; Director, Walter Dallas; Set, Scott Bradley; Costumes, Constanza Romero; Lighting, Christopher Akerlind CAST: Michele Shay (Louise), Ruben Santiago-Hudson (Canewell), Tommy Hollis (Red), Viola Davis (Vera), Albert Hall (Hedley), Jerome Preston Bates (Floyd), Rosalyn Coleman (Ruby)

**Jenny Bacon, Jane C. Cho,
Christopher Donahue in *Journey to the West***

Calista Flockhart, Bruce Norris in *Three Sisters*

THREE SISTERS by Anton Chekhov; Translation, Richard Nelson; Director, Robert Falls; Set/Costumes, Santo Loquasto; Lighting, James F. Ingalls CAST: Bruce Norris (Baron Nikolai Tuzenbach), Calista Flockhart (Irina), Jenny Bacon (Masha), Susan Bruce (Olga), Zak Orth (Andrei Prozorov), Ellen Karas (Natasha), B.J. Jones (Fyodor Kulygin), Ned Schmidtke (Alexander Vershinin), Marc Vann (Vassily Solyony), Howard Witt (Ivan Chebutykin), Christopher Walz (Fedotik), Christopher Eudy (Rode), Dennis Kennedy (Ferapont), Etel Billig (Anfisa), Heidi Mokrycki (Maid), Patrick Billingsley, Chris Farrell, Patricia Gallagher, Marci Kipnis, Roderick Peeples

JOURNEY INTO THE WEST; Adapted/Directed by Mary Zimmerman; Set, Scott Bradley; Costumes, Allison Reeds; Lighting, T.J. Gerckens; Music, William Schwarz, Miriam Sturm, Michael Bodeen CAST: Jance C. Cho (Buddah), Christopher Donahue (Jade Emperor/T'ang Emperor), Jenny Bacon (Kuan Yin), Douglas Hara (Monkey), Marc Vann (Woodsman), Lisa Tejero (Subodhi), Tim Rhoze (Dragon King), David Kersnar (Yama), Maulik Pancholy (Moksa), Bruce Norris (Tripitaka T'ang), Manao DeMuth (Green Orchid), Steve Pickering (Pig), Paul Oakley Stovall (Sha Monk), Tracy Walsh (Fisherman Chang)

ANOTHER MIDSUMMER NIGHT with Music by Jeffrey Lunden; Lyrics/Book, Arthur Perlman; Director, Michael Maggio; Set, Linda Buchanan; Costumes, Catherine Zuber; Lighting, Robert Christen; Choreography, Danny Herman; Musical Director, Bradley Vieth; Orchestrations, Bruce Coughlin CAST: Michael Rupert (Larry), Mary Ernster (Actress/Titania), Nick Wyman (Director/Oberon), Jim Walton (Dan), Kathleen Rowe McAllen (Heather), Jessica Molaskey (Helen), Hollis Resnik (Nicki), David Coronado (Pete), Ora Jones (Fran), Robert D. Mammana (Reporter), Jim Corti (Puck), Jennifer Rosin (Cobweb), Lisa Menninger (Peaseblossom)

SIN by Wendy MacLeod; Director, David Petrarca; Set, Scott Bradley; Costumes, Allison Reeds; Lighting, Robert Christen CAST: Amy Morton (Avery), Tim Rhoze (Man-Lust), David Pasquesi (Michael-Sloth), Steve Carell (Date-Greed), Karen Vaccaro (Helen-Gluttony), Kyle Colerider-Krugh (Fred-Envy), Steve Pickering (Jason-Wrath), Jeffrey Hutchinson (Gerald-Pride)

GERTRUDE STEIN: EACH ONE AS SHE MAY; Adapted/Directed by Frank Galati; Music, Reginald Robinson, Miriam Sturm; Set, Mary Griswold; Costumes, Birgit Rattenborg Wise; Lighting, Robert Christen CAST: Cheryl Lynn Bruce, Rick Worthy (Narrators), Jacqueline Williams (Melanctha), Johnny Lee Davenport (Dr. Campbell)

VIVISECTIONS FROM THE BLOWN MIND by Alonzo D. Lamont, Jr.; Director, Chuck Smith; Set. James Dardenne; Costumes, Michael Alan Stein; Lighting, Todd Hensley CAST: Michelle Elise Duffy (Angelique), Darryl Alan Reed (Castro), Daniel J. Bryant (Dusty), Cedric Young (Goliath)

Eric Y. Exit, Liz Lauren Photos

GOODSPEED OPERA HOUSE

East Haddam, Connecticut
Thirty-first Season

Executive Director, Michael P. Price; Associate Producer, Sue Frost; Casting Director, Warren Pincus; Publc Relations Director, Jennifer Wislocki; Press, Max Eisen/Kathryn Kinsella

(1994 PRODUCTIONS)

KISS ME, KATE with Music/Lyrics by Cole Porter; Book, Bella and Sam Spewack; Director, Ted Pappas; Musical Director, Michael O'Flaherty; Choreography, Liza Gennaro; Set, James Noone; Costumes, Michael Krass; Lighting, Kirk Bookman CAST: Steve Barton (Fred/Petruchio), Marilyn Caskey (Lilli/Katharine), David Ponting (Harry/Baptista), Leah Hocking (Lois/Bianca), Michael E. Gold (Ralph), Laura Kenyon (Hattie), Peter Gregus (Johnny), Kevin Bogue (Paul), Michael Gruber (Bill/Lucentio), James Allen Baker (Cab), Mark Lotito, Kevin McClarnon (Gunmen), Kenneth Garner (Harrison), Bob Freschi (Gremio), Michael Cone (Hortensio), Paul A. Brown, Pamela Gold, Kimberly Herosian, Nadine Isenegger, Nancy St. Alban, Elizabeth Steers

SHENANDOAH with Music by Gary Geld; Lyrics, Peter Udell; Book, James Lee Barrett, Mr. Udell, Mr. Rose; Director/Choreographer, J. Randall Hugill; Musical Director, Michael O'Flaherty; Set, James Morgan; Costumes, John Carver Sullivan; Lighting, Mary Jo Dondlinger CAST: Walter Charles (Charlie), Marc Kudish (Jacob), Michael Park (James), James Ludwig (Nathan), Bill Whitefield (John), Stephanie Douglas (Jenny), James Van Der Beek (Henry), P.J. Smith (Robert), Allison Clifford (Anne), James H. Wiggins III (Gabriel), Russell Leib(Rev. Boyd/Tinkham), Richard Roland (Sam), Jon Vandertholen (Johnson/Engineer), Alex Sharp (Lieutenant), Luke Lynch (Carol), Scott M. Beck (Corporal), Michael Sharon, Mr. Lynch, Mr. Sharp (Marauders), Gary Slavin, Bill Fennelly (Soldiers), Margaret Shafer, Colleen Stanton

GENTLEMEN PREFER BLONDES with Music by Jule Styne; Lyrics, Leo Robin; Book, Joseph Fields and Anita Loos; Director, Charles Repole; Musical Director, Andrew Wilder; Choreography, Michael Lichtefeld; Sets/Costumes, Eduardo Sicangco; Lighting, Kirk Bookman; Orchestrations, Douglas Besterman CAST: Karen Prunczik (Dorothy), KT Sullivan (Lorelei), Allen Fitzpatrick (Gus), Carol Swarbrick (Lady Beekman), David Ponting (Francis Beekman), Susan Rush (Ella Spofford), George Dvorsky (Spofford), Jamie Ross (Josephus), Dick Decareau (Steward/Esmond Sr.), Craig Waletzko (Frank/Robert), Ken Nagy (George), Joe Bowerman (Mime), John Hoshko (Louie), Paula Grider, Lisa Hanna, Richard Costa, Lorinda Santos, Angela Bond, Bryan S. Haynes, Wendy Roberts

(clockwise from upper left) **Terry Burrell, Lewis Cleale, Alvaleta Guess, Michael McGrath, Valerie Wright, Kathy Fitzgerald, Gregg Burge** in *Swinging on a Star*
Bottom: **P.J. Smith, Michael Park, Walter Charles** in *Shenandoah*

GOODSPEED-AT-CHESTER/NORMA TERRIS

CAPTAINS COURAGEOUS with Music by Frederick Freyer; Lyrics/Book, Patrick Cook; Director, David Warren; Musical Director, Bob Goldstone; Choreography, John Carrafa; Set, James Youmans; Costumes, Teresa Snider-Stein; Lighting, Don Holder CAST: Mark Ankeny (Murphy), Buddy Crutchfield (Tom/Elliot), Terrance Flynn (Hermans/Attendant), Jonathan Hadley (Simon), Walter Hudson (Simon), Kevin Jeffers (Peters), Larry Keith (Troop), Ramzi Khalaf (Harvey), George Kmeck (Walters), Michael Christopher Moore (Evans), Colin Munro (Dan), Charles Pistone (Manuel), Vernon Spencer (Doc), Richard Thomsen (Ollie), Roy Alan Wilson (Cheyne/Harris), Christopher Yates (Stephens)

SWINGING ON A STAR; Lyrics by Johnny Burke; Music, Mr. Burke, Erroll Garner, Robert Haggart, Arthur Johnston, James Monaco, Harold Spina, Jimmy Van Heusen; Conceived/Written/Directed by Michael Leeds; Choreography, Kathleen Marshall; Musical Director/Orchestrations, Barry Levitt; Costumes, Judy Dearing; Lighting, Richard Nelson CAST: Gregg Burge, Terry Burrell, Lewis Cleale, Kathy Fitzgerald, Alvaleta Guess, Michael McGrath, Valerie Wright

STARCROSSED: The Trial of Galileo; Music, Jeanine Tesori; Lyrics, Book, Keith Levenson and Alexa Junge; Director, Martin Charnin; Musical Director, Michael O'Flaherty; Choreography, Daniel Pelzig; Set, Kenneth Foy; Costumes, Gail Brassard; Lighting, Ken Billington CAST: Tom Treadwell (Inquisitor/Astrologer), Ed Dixon (Galileo), Neal Mayer (Ponti), Cordell Stahl (Barberini), Elizabeth Richmond (Mara), Kevin Berdini (Doge), Phillip Officer (Simon Faber), Ellyn Arons (Princess), Catherine Ruivivar, Jennifer Neuland (Soloists), Tim Bohle, Jane Brockman, Barbara Pflaumer, David Alan Quart

Diane Sobolewski Photos

Buddy Crutchfield in Goodspeed's *Captains Courageous*

KT Sullivan, Allen Fitzpatrick in
Goodspeed's *Gentlemen Prefer Blondes*

Timothy Altmeyer, Jeffries Thaiss,
Lorca Simons in *Midsummer Night's Dream*

GREAT LAKES THEATRE FESTIVAL

Cleveland, Ohio

Artistic Director, Gerald Freedman; Managing Director, Anne B. DesRosiers; Associate Artistic Director, John Ezell; Associate Directors, Bill Rudman, Victoria Bussert; Production Manager, Anthony M. Forman; Communications Director, Zandra Wolfgram

PRODUCTIONS & CASTS

SHAKESPEARE FOR MY FATHER; Conceived/Written/Performed by Lynn Redgrave; Director, John Clark; Lighting, Thomas R. Skeleton

A MIDSUMMER NIGHT'S DREAM by William Shakespeare; Director, Gerald Freedman; Set, John Ezell; Costumes, James Scott; Lighting, Mary Jo Dondlinger CAST INCLUDES: Michael Early (Oberon/Theseus), Monica Bell (Titania/Hippolyta), John Buck Jr. (Egeus), Lorca Simons (Helena), Anne M. Hasenzahl (Hermia), Timothy Altmeyer (Lysander), Jeffries Thaiss (Demetrius), Marc Damon Johnson (Puck)

A CHRISTMAS CAROL by Charles Dickens; Adaptation, Gerald Freedman; Director, Rob Ruggiero; Sets, John Ezell, Gene Emerson Freidman; Costumes, James Scott; Lighting, Mary Jo Dondlinger CAST INCLUDES: William Leach (Scrooge), Michael Krawic, John Buck Jr., Maryann Nagel, Charles Tuthill, Kevin McCarty, Sheila Heyman, Don Mayo, Helene Weinberg

SCHOOL FOR WIVES by Molière; Director, Victoria Bussert; Set, Tony Fanning; Costumes, James Scott; Lighting, Norman Coates CAST: John Woodson (Arnolf), Jennifer Roszell (Agnes), Paul Boehmer (Horatio), John Tillotson (Chrisaldo), Steve Routman (Alain), Sheila Heyman (Georgette), Bill Busch (Enrico), John Buck Jr. (Oronte)

THE BAKKHAI by Euripides; Translation, Robert Bagg; Director, Gerald Freedman; Set, John Ezell; Costumes/Masks, Barbara Kessler; Lighting, Mary Jo Dondlinger CAST: Alyssa Bresnahan, Kermit Brown, John Buck Jr., Sheridan Crist, Marlowe Daniels, Tom Evert, Steve Irish, Edwina King, Mary Kukich, Tanny McDonald, Kelly Parsley, Amy Tarachow, Mark Tomasic, Charles Tuthill, Jeremy Webb, Suana Weingarten de Evert

Roger Mastroianni, Sarah Turner Photos

Neil Maffin, Joe Quintero in *Clean*

Below: Julie Dretzin, Richard Topol,
Gordon MacDonald in *A Dybbuk*

Right: Richard Thomas in *Richard III*

HARTFORD STAGE

Hartford, Connecticut
Thirty-first Season

Artistic Director, Mark Lamos; Managing Director, Stephen J. Albert; Associate Director, Bartlett Sher; Production Manager, Candice Chirgotis; Public Relations Director, Herb Emanuelson

PRODUCTIONS & CASTS

RICHARD III by William Shakespeare; Director, Mark Lamos; Set, Christine Jones; Costumes, Constance Hoffman; Lighting, Darrel Maloney CAST: Richard Thomas (Richard III), John Bolger, Orlagh Cassidy, John Cayer, Helmar Augustus Cooper, Joan Copeland, Leland Gantt, Spruce Henry, John Michael Higgins, Peter Francis James, Nafe Katter, Daniel Oreskes, Alec Phoenix, Anne Pitoniak, Gordana Rashovich, Peter Von Berg, Deron Bayer, Dick Boland, Thomas S. Czerkawski, Robert Dolan, Joshua Donoghue, Eric Stephen Evenson, Bill Mullen, Hayden Reed Sakow, Colin Stevenson, David Watson, Ed Wierzbicki

SUDDENLY LAST SUMMER and **THE POET** by Tennessee Williams; Director, JoAnne Akalaitis; Sets, Marina Draghici; Costumes, David C. Woolard; Lighting, Jennifer Tipton CAST: Lisa Arrindell Anderson, Marylouise Burke, Mark Deakins, Anita Gillette, Dawn Akemi Saito, Myra Lucretia Taylor, Todd Weeks

SPUNK; Three Tales by Zora Neale Hurston; Adapted by George C. Wolfe; Music, Chic Street Man; Director, Reggie Montgomery; Sets, Edward Burbridge; Costumes, Karen Perry; Lighting, Donald Holder CAST: Chad L. Coleman, Tina Fabrique, LaChanze, John Lathan, Keb' Mo', Raymond Anthony Thomas

A DYBBUK by S. Ansky; Adaptation, Tony Kushner; Translation, Joachim Neugroschel; Director, mark lamos; Set, John Conklin; Costumes, Jess Goldstein; Lighting, Pat Collins CAST: Yusef Bulos, Eddie Crodad, Julie Dretzin, Mark Feurstein, Nancy Franklin, Sam Gray, Michael Hayden, David Little, Robert LuPone, Gordon MacDonald, Herman Petras, Judith Roberts, Elizabeth Sastre, Michael Stuhlbarg, Richard Topol, Daniel Zelman, David Alan Basche, Thomas S. Czerkawski, Eric Stephen Evenson, Mellini S. Kantayya, Peter Papadopoulos, Alison Russo, Caleb Sekeres, H.A. Shemonsky, Lisa Terezakis

CLEAN by Edwin Sanchez; Director, Graciela Daniele; Costumes, Eduardo Sicango; Lighting, David F. Segal CAST: Joe Quintero (Gustavito), Paula Pizzi (Mercy), Mateo Gomez (Kiko), Neil Maffin (Father), Nelson Vasquez (Junior), A. Bernard Cummings (Norry)

T. Charles Erickson Photos

HUNTINGTON THEATRE COMPANY

Boston, Massachusetts
Thirteenth Season

Producing Director, Peter Altman; Managing Director, Michael Maso; Marketing/Public Relations Director, Rosemary C. Clinton; Press Representative, Martin Blanco

PRODUCTIONS & CASTS

THE WOMAN WARRIOR: A Girlhood among Ghosts; Adaptation by Deborah Rogin; Based on the novels *The Woman Warrior* and *China Men* by Maxine Hong Kingston; Director, Sharon Ott; Set, Ming Cho Lee; Costumes, Susan Hilferty; Lighting, Peter Maradudin; Music, John Jang CAST: Kim Miyori (Fa Mu Lan), David Furumoto (Ancient/Baron/Druggist/Grandfather), Dian Kobayashi (Ancient/Psychiatrist/Ah Po), Soon-Teck Oh (Fathers), Lisa Lu (Mother/Brave Orchid), Michael Edo Keane (Husband/Delivery), Lydia Look (Daughter), Miko Lee (Sister), Donna Mae Wong (Young Sister), Jonathan Cho (Brother), Brian Kwan (Younger Brother/Railroad Owner), Janis Chow (Silent Girl/Wife), Mel Duane Gionson (Woodrow/Doctor/Kau Goong), David Johann (Worldster/Dai Bak), Emily Kuroda (Mother's Youth/Teacher), Lisa Tejero (Railroad Owner/Aunt), Wang Luoyong(Father's Youth), Wood Moy (Ah Goong), Charles Hu, Man Wong, Janis Chow

PTERODACTYLS by Nicky Silver; Director, Mark Brokaw; Set, Allen Moyer; Costumes, Susan E. Mickey; Lighting, Pat Dignan CAST: Christopher Collet (Todd Duncan), Nile Lanning (Emma Duncan), Allan Heinberg (Tommy McKorckle), Marian Mercer (Grace Duncan), Dennis Creaghan (Arthur Duncan)

AS YOU LIKE IT by William Shakespeare; Director, Edward Gilbert; Set, Marjorie Bradley Kellogg; Costumes, Mariann Verheyen; Lighting, Dennis Parichy CAST: Aloysius Gigl (Orlando), Joel Friedman (Adam), Arthur Pearson (Oliver), R. Scott Olmstead (Dennis/1st Lord), Michael Glumicich (Charles/2nd Lord), Emilie Talbot (Celia), Monica Bell (Rosalind), Les Marsden (Touchstone), Ron Siebert (Le Beau), Craig Spidle (Duke Frederick/Martext), Clarence Felder (Duke Senior), Kurt Ziskie (Amiens), Jim Loutzenhiser (1st Lord/William), Edmund Wyson (2nd Lord/Jacques), Ronald H. Siebert (Corin), Gregory Simmons(Silvius), Munson Hicks (Jaques), Julie Oda (Audrey), Regin Altay (Phoebe), Janelle Dempsey, Jasmine Hillard, Joe Hedreick, Matthew Krouner (Pages/Hymen)

Above: Christopher Collet, Nile Lanning,
Allan Heinberg in *Pterodactyls*
Below: Esther Rolle, Hassan El-Amin in *Raisin in the Sun*

THE GUARDSMAN by Ferenc Molnar; Translation, Frank Marcus; Director, Jacques Cartier; Set, James Leonard Joy; Costumes, Lindsay W. Davis; Lighting, Roger Meeker CAST: Timothy Landfield (Nandor), Kandis Chappell (Ilona), Edwin C. Owens (Bela), Tammy Grimes (Mother), Patricia Tamagini (Maid), Ralph Buckley (Creditor), Tamara Daniel (Usherette), Timothy O'Neil (Porter)

A RAISIN IN THE SUN by Lorraine Hansberry; Director, Kenny Leon; Set, Marjorie Bradley Kellogg; Costumes, Susan E. Mickey; Lighting, Ann G. Wrightson CAST: Marguerite Hannah (Ruth), Kemal Hassan Collins, Jean-Pierre R. Jacquet (Travis), Hassan El-Amin (Walter Lee), B.W. Gonzalez (Beneatha), Esther Rolle (Lena), Adrian Roberts (Joseph), Geoffrey D. Williams (George), Joseph Culliton (Karl), Donald (Bobo), Ricardo Engerman, Lonnie Farmer (Moving Men)

Richard Feldman Photos

167

ILLINOIS THEATRE CENTER

Park Forest, Illinois
Nineteenth Season

Artistic Director, Steve S. Billig; Managing Director, Etel Billig; Set Designer, Wayne Adams

PRODUCTIONS & CASTS

THE DARK AT THE TOP OF THE STAIRS by William Inge; Director, Steve S. Billig; Costumes, Mary Ellen O'Meara; Lighting, Jonathan Roark CAST: Gary Houston, Adrienne Rieck, Judy McLaughlin, Phil Hollingsworth, Nina Garza, Nicole Steen, Brandon McShaffrey, David Weiss Lipshutz, Matthew Davis

LETTICE AND LOVAGE by Peter Shaffer; Director, Steve S. Billig; Lighting, Jonathan Roark; Costumes, Pat Decker CAST: Don McGrew, Alexandra Murdoch

THE GIFTS OF THE MAGI with Music by Randy Courts; Lyrics, Mr. Courts and Mark St. Germain; Book, Mark St. Germain; Based on stories by O. Henry; Director, Steve S. Billig; Musical Director, Jonathan Roark; Costumes, Mary Ellen O'Meara; Lighting, Archway Designs CAST: Peter Reynlds, Laura Reisch, Benjamin D. Dooley, Bernard Rice, Pamela Turlow, Steve S. Billig

GUILTY CONSCIENCE by Richard Levinson and William Link; Director, Wayne Adams; Lighting, Jonathan Roark; Costumes, Pat Decker CAST: Tony Carsella, Shelley Crosby, Pamela Turlow, Robert Alan Smith

THE VOICE OF THE PRAIRIE by John Olive; Director, Steve S. Billig; Costumes, Mary Ellen O'Meara; Lighting, Jonathan Roark CAST: Gary Houston, Connie McGrail, Benjamin D. Dooley

THE GOD OF ISAAC by James Sherman; Director, Steve S. Billig; Costumes, Mary Ellen O'Meara; Lighting, Jonathan Roark CAST: Marc Moritz, Beth Kathan, Franette Liebow, Rebecca Borter, Howard Hahn, Wayne Adams

SOME ENCHANTED EVENING with Music by Richard Rodgers; Lyrics, Oscar Hammerstein; Director, Steve S. Billig; Musical Direction, Jonathan Roark; Choreography, Brandon McShaffrey; Costumes, Pat Decker; Lighting, Archway Design CAST: Marc Moritz, Shelley Crosby, James Braunstein, Pat Fitch, Sara E. Baur

Todd Panagopoulous Photos

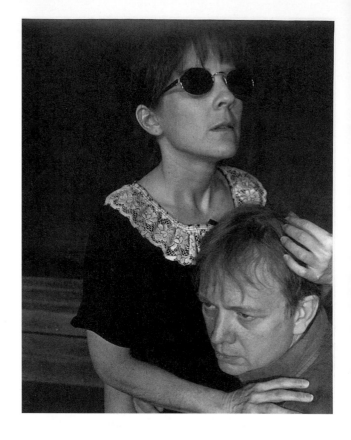

Above: Connie McGrail, Gary Houston in *Voice of the Prairie*
Below Left: Pam Turlow, Steve Billig,
Bernard Rice in *Gift of the Magi*

Below: Howard Hahn, Marc Moritz in *God of Isaac*

JUPITER THEATRE

Jupiter, Florida

Executive Producer, Richard C. Akins; Artistic Director, Avery Schreiber; Producer, Brian M. Cronin; Associate Producer, Norb Joerder; General Manager, Paulette Winn; Costume Designer, Vickie K. Bast; Public Relations Director, Pamela Smith

PRODUCTIONS & CASTS

THE MUSIC MAN with Music/Lyrics/Book by Meredith Wilson; Director, Richard C. Akins; Choreography, Norb Joerder; Musical Director, Douglass G. Lutz; Set, Mark Beaumont; Lighting, Ginny Adams CAST: Gregory Harrison (Harold Hill), Ann Kittredge (Marian), Harvey Phillips (Mayor), Lourelene Snedeker (Eulalie), Penny Larsen (Mrs. Paroo), Tim Fauvell (Marcellus), Catrina Honadle (Ethel), Ed Romanoff (Charlie), Eric J. Keiper (Jacey), Jordan Seth Peck (Ewart), Jeff Morrall (Oliver), Rick Losco (Olin), Kay Ostrenko (Mrs. Squires), Leigh Bennett (Maud), Geraldine O'Mahoney (Alma), Kevin Krum (Tommy), Tara Tobin (Zaneeta), Cherie Bebout (Amaryllis), Mike Bebout, Dawn Agnese, Katie Angell, Bryan T. Donovan, Lisa Hookailo, Michael Lundy, Mickey Mchale, Nick Swafford, Alsion Barberio, Amy Bebout, Christopher Graf, Dominick Nesci, Carrie Specksgoor, Heather Young, Philip Young

THE MOST HAPPY FELLA with Music/Lyrics/Book by Frank Loesser; Director/Choreographer, Norb Joerder; Musical Director, Douglass G. Lutz; Sets, Jeff Modereger; Lighting, Ginny Adams CAST: David Holliday (Tony), Rebecca Spencer (Amy/Rosabella), Ed Romanoff (Joe), Lourelene Snedeker (Marie), Brian Quinn (Herman), Renee Dobson (Cleo), Eric J. Keiper (Doc), Wayne Steadman (Cashier), James Coelho (Pasquale), Larry French (Giuseppe), Kevin C. Bogan (Ciccio), Kenn Christopher (Al), Jayme McDaniel (Jake), Bryan T. Donovan (Clem), Michael Lundy (Max), Jordan Seth Peck (Priest), Susan Brady Keiper, Melinda Parrish, Robyn Soliani, Dawn Agnese, Katie Angell, Kevin Krum, Mickey Mchale

I DO! I DO! with Music by Harvey Schmidt; Lyrics/Book, Tom Jones; Director/Choreographer, Norb Joerder; Musical G. Lutz; Set, Mark Beaumont; Lighting, Ginny Adams CAST: Lee Meriwether (Agnes), Tom Urich (Michael)

THE ODD COUPLE by Neil Simon; Director, Thomas Somerville; Set, Mark Beaumont; Lighting, Ginny Adams CAST: Irv West (Speed), Kris Johnson (Murray), Elias Eliadis (Roy), Jordan Seth Peck (Vinnie), Richard Akins, Jack Cole (Oscar), William Christopher (Felix), Carole Healey (Gwendolyn), Barbara Altz (Cecily)

THE SECRET GARDEN with Music by Lucy Simon; Lyrics/Book, Marsha Norman; Director/Choreographer, Andrew Glant-Linden, Musical Director, Lllisa Collins; Lighting, William Hepner CAST: Stephanie Roberts (Mary), Frank Mastrone (Archibald), Ryan Hopkins (Colin), David Elledge (Neville), Sheila Allen (Mrs. Medlock), Ellen Zachos (Martha), Jack Evans (Dickon), Harvey Phillips (Ben), Leigh Bennett (Mrs. Winthrop/Claire), Jeff Morrall (Albert), Katie Angell (Rose), Susan Brady Keiper (Lily), Bryan T. Donovan (Lt. Wright), Steven Garrett (Lt. Shaw), Wayne Steadman (Holmes), Kendra Munger (Alice), Kay Ostrenko (Ayah), Greg Skura (Fakir), Kristen Anderson (Jane), Katie Grant (Agatha), Ronnie Karam (Edmond), Edward Kemper (William), Nathanael Fisher (Timothy), Rodney Perkins (Jamison), Michelle Gerard (Catherine)

A WONDERFUL LIFE with Music/Lyrics by David Nehls; Adaptation/Book, Michael Tilford; Based on the 1946 film; Director/Choreographer, Norb Joerder; Musical Director, Lisa Collins; Set, Mark Beaumont; Lighting, Robert D. Clark CAST: Louis Seeger Crume (Joseph/Peter Bailey), Tim Fauvell (Clarence), John Tessier (Young George/Paperboy/Pete), Elliot Taubenslag (Gower/Chairman), Elias Eliadis (Uncle Billy), Harvey Phillips (Potter), Reed Armstrong (George Bailey), Nathanael Fisher (Clerk), Rodney Perkins (Ernie), Steven Garrett (Bert), Geraldine O'Mahoney (Tillie), Edward Kemper (Harry), Kay Daphne (Mrs. Bailey), Kay Ostrenko (Violet), Brent Sexton (Sam Wainwright), Mary Illes (Sam), Allison Barberio (Young Mary/Janey), Sheila Allen (Ma Hatch), Michelle Gerard (Miss Jones), Ronnie Karem (Smith), Greg Skura (Carter), Katherine Speaker (Zuzu)

Russ Thacker in *Will Rogers Follies*

THE WILL ROGERS FOLLIES with Music by Cy Coleman; Lyrics, Betty Comden and Adolph Green; Book, Peter Stone; Director/Choreographer, Norb Joerder; Musical Director, Liisa Collins; Lighting, Robert D. Clark CAST: Russ Thacker (Will Rogers), Kimberly Wells (Ziegfeld's Favorite), Greg Skura (Wiley), Rudy Tronto (Clem), Michele Aster, Cynthia Green, Gina Lamparella, Heather Morris, Kathleen O'Rawe, Jennifer Sagan (Will's Sisters/Betty's Sisters), Marylee Graffeo (Betty), Curtis Fonger, John Tessier (Will Jr.), Elizabeth Sekora, Andrea Willson (Mary), Denton Clark, Ryan Hopkins (James), Patrick Collins, Murphy Hopkins (Freddy), Rodney Perkins (Stage Manager), Gary Steven Martin (Roper/Wrangler), Robert Abdoo, Michael Martino, Ashton Byrum (Wranglers), Ms. Morris, Kay Ostrenko, Ms. Aster, Kathy Dacey, Cynthia Green, Louisa Kendrick, Ms. lamparella, Ms. O'Rawe, Ms. Sagan, Charisse R. Singleton (New Ziegfeld Girls), Richard C. Akins (Ziegfeld's Voice), Kristine Anderson, Nathanael Fisher, Michelle Gerard, Katie Grant, Ronnie Karam, Edward Kemper, Kendra Munger

CABARET with Music by John Kander; Lyrics, Fred Ebb; Book, Joe Masteroff; Director/Choreographer, Norb Joerder; Musical Director, Lisa Collins; Set, Mark Beaumont; Lighting, Ginny Adams CAST: Norb Joerder (M.C.), Christopher Carl (Clifford), Jimmy W. Evans (Ernst), Greg Skura, Edward Kemper (Officials), Susan Willis (Fraulein Schneider), Harvey Phillips (Schultz), Connie Saloutos (Sally Bowles), Heather Morris, Kay Ostrenko (Two Ladies), Lisa Guignard, Cynthia Green, Karen L. Shoecraft, Kristen Anderson, Katie Grant, Ronnie Karam (Bobby), Nathaniel Fisher (Victor/Gorilla), Lisa Guignard, Gary Steven Martin, Marc Carmen, Fred Murdock, Kristen Anderson, Nathanael Fisher, Michelle Gerard, Katie Grant, Kendra Munger

Greg Allikas Photos

LA JOLLA PLAYHOUSE

San Diego, California

Artistic Director, Des McAnuff; Managing Director, Terrence Dwyer; Associate Artistic Director, Robert Blacker; Production Manager, Mark Maltby; Communications Director, Joshua Ellis

PRODUCTIONS & CASTS

HARVEY by Mary Chase; Director, Douglas Hughes; Set, Hugh Landwehr; Costumes, Linda Fisher; Lighting, Greg Sullivan CAST: Marianne Owen (Myrtle May), Peggy Pope (Veta), Jeff Weiss (Elwood P. Dowd), Angela Reed (Miss Johnson), Avril Gentles (Ethel), Katie Forgette (Nurse Ruth), Tom Spiller (Duane), Christopher Evan Welch (Dr. Sanderson), Rick Tutor (Dr. Chumley), Peggy O'Connell (Betty), Glenn Mazen (Judge) Kevin C. Loomis (Lofgren)

THE TRIUMPH OF LOVE by Pierre Carlet De Chambain De Marivaux; Translation, James Magruder; Director, Lisa Peterson; Set, Marina Draghici; Costumes, Jack Taggart; Lighting, Tim Becker CAST: Angie Phillips (Leonide), Laurie Williams (Corine), Paul Giamatti (Harlequin), Silas Weir Mitchell (Dimas), David Hunt (Agis), Beth Dixon (Leontine), Tony Amendola (Hermocrate)

THERESE RAQUIN by Neal Bell; Based on novel by Emile Zola; Director, Michael Greif; Set, Marina Draghici; Costumes, Mark Wendland; Lighting, Kenneth Posner CAST: Beth Dixon (Madame Raquin), Paul Giamatti (Camille), Angie Phillips (Therese), Tony Amendola (Michaud), Silas Weir Mitchell (Olivier), Laurie Williams (Suzanne), Kent Davis (Grivet), David Hunt (Laurent)

THE GOOD PERSON OF SETZUAN by Bertolt Brecht; Adaptation, Tony Kushner; Music/Lyrics, David Hidalgo and Louie Perez; Director, Lisa Peterson; Musical Director, Doug Wieselman; Set, Robert Brill; Costumes, Candice Donnelly; Lighting, James F. Ingalls CAST: Gedde Watanabe (Wang/Nephew), Charlayne Woodard (Shen Te/Shui Ta), Francine Torres (Mrs. Shin/Boy), Diane Rodriguez (Wife/Mrs. Yang), Isiah Whitlock Jr. (Husband/Police/Old Man/Priest), David Wiater (Unemployed/Prostitute), Matthew Henerson (Lin To/Waiter), Ching Valdes-Aran (Mi Tzu/Old Woman), Lou Diamond Phillips (Brother/Yang Sun), Alison Tatlock (Sister-in-Law), Chris De Oni (Grandfather/Shu Fu), Maria Striar (Niece)

MUMP & SMOOT IN "FERNO"; Written/Created/Performed by Michael Kennard and John Turner; Director, Karen Hines; Set, Campbell Manning; Lighting, Michel Charbonneau

HOW TO SUCCEED IN BUSINESS WITHOUT REALLY TRYING with Music/Lyrics by Frank Loesser; Book, Abe Burrows, Jack Weinstock, Willie Gilbert; Director, Des McAnuff; Choreography, Wayne Cilento; Musical Director, Ted Sperling; Orchestrations, Danny Troob CAST: Walter Cronkite (Narrator), Matthew Broderick (J. Pierrepont Finch), Robert Mandan (Biggley), Megan Mullally (Rosemary), Jonathan Freeman (Bratt), Dawnn Lewis (Smitty), Jeff Blumenkrantz (Bud), Lillias White (Miss Jones), Ernie Sabella (Twimble/Womper), Tom Flynn (Gatch/Toynbee), Kristi Lynes (Miss Krumholtz), Luba Mason (Hedy), Jay Aubrey Jones (Jenkins), Martin Moran (Tackaberry), William Ryall (Davis), Randl Ask (Office Boy/Ovington/Announcer), Rebecca Holt, Carla Renata Williams (Scrubwomen), Nancy Lemenager (Dance Solo), Kevin Bogue (Guard), Jack Hayes, Jerome Vivona, Maria Calabrese, Jack Hayes, Aiko Nakasone

Ken Howard Photos

Top: Charlayne Woodard, Lou Diamond Phillips in
Good Person of Setzuan

Center: Angie Phillips in *Therese Raquin*

Right: Lillias White, Matthew Broderick in *How to Succeed…*

LONG WHARF THEATRE

New Haven, Connecticut
Thirtieth Season

Artistic Director, Arvin Brown; Executive Director, M. Edgar Rosenblum; Literary Consultant, John Tillinger; Artistic Administrator, Janice Muirhead; General Manager, John Conte; Press and Marketing Director, Robert Wildman; Press Representative, Jeff Fickes

PRODUCTIONS & CASTS

PADDYWACK by Daniel Magee; Director, John Tillinger; Set, James Youmans; Costumes, Candice Donnelly; Lighting, Ken Billington CAST: Patricia Kilgarriff, Sarah Long, James Nesbitt, Alexandro Nivola, Michael O'Kagan, Denis O'Hare

SATURDAY, SUNDAY, MONDAY by Eduardo de Filippo; Translation, Thomas Simpson; Director, Arvin Brown; Set, Marjorie Bradley Kellogg; Costumes, David Murin; Lighting, Dennis Parichy   CAST: James Andreassi, Donald Berman, Geoffrey P. Cantor, Dominic Chianese, Janis Dardaris, Marin Hinkle, Lauren Klein, Michelle Kronin, Richard Merrell, Jan Miner, Peter Rini, Frank Savino, Stephanie Silverman, George A. Sperdakos, Saul Stein, Richard Venture

ARSENIC AND OLD LACE by Joseph Kesselring; Director, John Tillinger; Set, James Noone; Costumes, David Murin; Lighting, Ken Billington CAST: Paul Benedict, John Deyle, Tim Donoghue, Joyce Ebert, John Elsen, Jack Gilpin, Blaise Lamphier, Daniel Southern, Richard Spore, Doug Stender, Jill Tasker, Jan Triska, Joanne Woodward

Patricia Kilgarriff, James Nesbitt in *Paddywack*

**Joyce Ebert, Jack Gilpin, Joanne Woodward,
Richard Spore in** *Arsenic and Old Lace*

CEREMONIES IN DARK OLD MEN by Lonne Elder III; Director, L. Kenneth Richardson; Set, Donald Eastman; Costumes, Mary Mease Warren; LIghting, Frances Aronson CAST: Helgar Augustus Cooper, O.L. Duke, Curtis McClarin, Sharon Washington, Dondre T. Whitfield, Samuel E. Wright

BANJO DANCING; Written/Performed by Stephen Wade; Director, Milton Kramer

THE ENTERTAINER by John Osborne; Director, Arvin Brown; Set, Hugh Landwehr; Costumes, Jess Goldstein; Lighting, Mark Stanley CAST: Patricia Dunnock, Joyce Ebert, George Ede, Frank Lowe, Joseph Maher, Jud Meyers, Stephen Turner

STAGE II

TRAVELS WITH MY AUNT by Graham Greene; Adapted/Directed by Giles Havergal; Set/Costumes, Stewart Laing; Lighting, Mimi Jordan Sherin CAST: Tom Beckett, Jim Dale, Brian Murray, Martin Rayner

A SWELL PARTY by John Kane and David Kernan; Music/Lyrics, Cole Porter; Director, Virginia Davis Irwin; Musical Director, Don Rickenback; Lighting, M. Linda Knox CAST: Amy James, John Knox-Johnston, Patty O'Connor, Don Rickenback

SOME PEOPLE; Written/Performed by Danny Hoch; Director, Jo Bonney; Lighting, Sarah Sidman

IN THE HEART OF AMERICA by Naomi Wallace; Director, Tony Kushner CAST: Firdous Bamji, Lanny Flaherty, Irene Glezos, Wai Ching Ho, David Van Pelt

RULER OF MY DESTINY by Jocelyn Meinhardt; Director, Pamela Berlin CAST: Angela Marie Bettis, Malachy Cleary, Diana Henry, Charlie Hofheimer, Carrie Luft, Jenny Maguire, Priscilla Shanks

T. Charles Erickson Photos

Martin Rayner, Jim Dale, Brian Murray in *Travels with My Aunt*

**Dondre T. Whitfield, Samuel E. Wright,
Curtis McClarin in Ceremonies in** *Dark Old Men*

LOOKINGGLASS THEATRE COMPANY

Chicago, Illinois

Artistic Director, Philip R. Smith; Managing Director, David Catlin; Producing Director, Kate Churchill; Public Relations Director, Stephanie Howard

PRODUCTIONS & CASTS

(Goodman Theatre) **UP AGAINST IT**; Based on an unproduced screenplay by Joe Orton; Adapted and Directed by Bruce Norris; Set, Michael Lapthorn; Costumes, Allison Reeds; Lighting, Shannon McKinney CAST: Lance Baker (Ian McTurk), Christine Dunford (Constance Boon), Hannah Fowlie (Prime Minister), Raymond Fox (Jack Ramsay), Joy Gregory (Patricia Drumgoole), Douglas Hara (Christopher Low), Stephanie Howard (Mrs. O'Scullion), David Kersnar (Ramsay's Father/Fr. Brody), Rick Sims (Fatman/Musician), Joey Slotnick (The Mayor O'Scullion/Prison Guard), Philip R. Smith (Bernard Coates), Heidi Stillman (Rowena Torrence)

HERE AFTER; Conceived/Directed by Royd Climenhaga; Set, Michael Lapthorn; Lighting, Kenneth Moore; Costumes, Heather Ann Priest CAST: Thomas J. Cox, Christine Dunford, Raymond Fox, Nadine George, Morgan McCabe, Michael Rohd, Sophia Skiles, Andrew White, Meredith Zinner

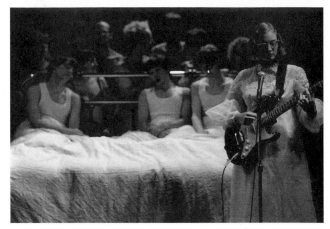

Joy Gregory and *Up Against It* cast

**Lookingglass Theatre Company: (top) David Catlin, Larry DiStasi,
(center) Douglas Hara, Thomas J. Cox, Joy Gregory, Mary Zimmerman, David Schwimmer, Phillip R. Smith, Andrew White,
(bottom) Christine Dunford, Heidi Stillman, David Kersnar, John Musial, Laura Eason, Temple Williams III**

MCCARTER THEATRE

Princeton, New Jersey

Artistic Director, Emily Mann; Managing Director, Jeffrey Woodward; Special Programming, W.W. Lockwood, Jr.; Associate Director/Staff Producer, Loretta Greco; General Manager, Kathleen Kund Nolan; Marketing Press, David Mayhew, Daniel Y. Bauer

PRODUCTIONS & CASTS

THE MATCHMAKER by Thornton Wilder; Director, Emily Mann; Set, Tony Straiges; Costumes, Jennifer von Mayrhauser; Lighting, Peter Kaczorowski CAST: Jerome Kilty (Horace), Richard Thompson (Ambrose), Laurence O'Dwyer (Joe), Barbara Lester (Gertrude), Kenneth L. Marks (Cornelius), Vivienne Benesch (Ermengarde), Elizabeth Franz (Dolly Levi), Danny Gerard (Barnaby), Alyson Reed (Irene), Hynden Walch (Minnie), Edwin C. Owens, Jamison Selby, Marylouise Burke, Barbara Lester

ROUGH CROSSING by Tom Stoppard; Songs, Andre Previn, Mr. Stoppard; Director, Michael Maggio; Set, John Lee Beatty; Costumes, Tom Broecker; Lighting, Kenneth Posner; Musical Director, David Bishop CAST: Mark Nelson (Dvornichek), John Christopher Jones (Turai), Douglas Weston (Adam), Lewis J. Stadlen (Gal), Randy Graff (Natasha), Munson Hicks (Ivor), Grace Jordan, Tamlyn Brooke Shusterman, Christine Siracusa (Chorus Ladies)

A CHRISTMAS CAROL by Charles Dickens; Adaptation, David Thompson; Director, Loretta Greco; Set, Michael Anania; Costumes, Lindsay W. Davis; Lighting, Peter Kaczorowski CAST: Robin Chadwick (Scrooge), Anthony Fusco (Crachit), David Moynihan (Marley), Douglas Weston, Erika L. Heard, Evalyn Baron, Karen Tsen Lee, Polly Pen, Karen Garvey, John Hickok, Richard Thompson, Edwin C. Owens, Susan Owen, Kim Brockington, Cate Woodruff, Jorge V. Ledesma, Penny Cornwall, Regin Forman, Seth Herzog, Pam Fabri Pisani, Barry Tropp

HAVING OUR SAY: The Delany Sisters First 100 Years; Written/Directed by Emily Mann; Adapted from the book by Sarah L. Delany and A. Elizabeth Delany with Amy Hill Hearth; Set, Thomas Lynch; Costumes, Judy Dearing; Lighting, Allen Lee Hughes CAST: Gloria Foster (Sadie), Mary Alice (Bessie)

MIRANDOLINA by Carlo Goldoni; Adaptation/Direction/Translation by Stephen Wadsworth; Set, Thomas Lynch; Costumes, Martin Pakledinaz; Lighting, Christopher Akerlind CAST: Robin Chadwick (Marchese), Sebastian Roche (Count), Derek Smith (Fabrizio), John Michael Higgins (Cavaliere), Mary Lou Rosato (Mirandolina), Laurence O'Dwyer (Servant), Elizabeth Van Dyke (Ortensia), Wendy Kaplan (Desianza), Sewell Whitney, Reid Armbruster, Maggie Laccy, Rhonda King

WONDERFUL TENNESSEE by Brian Friel; Director, Douglas Hughes; Set, Anita Stewart; Costumes, Catherine Zuber; Lighting, Michael Chybowski CAST: Denis O'Hare (Terry), Mia Dillon (Berna), Paul Blankenship (George), Colleen Quinn (Trish), Henry Stram (Frank), Kathryn Meisle (Angela)

T. Charles Erickson Photos

Top: John Christopher Jones, Mark Nelson in *Rough Crossing*

Center: Mary Alice, Gloria Foster in *Having Our Say*

Right: Hynden Walch, Danny Gerard, Kenneth L. Marks in *The Matchmaker*

MEADOW BROOK THEATRE

Rochester, Michigan
Twenty-ninth Season

Artistic Director, Geoffrey Sherman; Managing Director, Gregg Bloomfield; Cultral Affairs Director, Stuart Hyke; Set Designer, Peter W. Hicks; Lighting, Reid G. Johnson; Costumes, Barbara Jenks; Public Relations Director, Michael C. Vigilant

PRODUCTIONS & CASTS

NOISES OFF by Michael Frayn; Director, Donald Ewer CAST: Jenny Turner (Dotty/Mrs. Clackett), Randell Haynes (Lloyd, Guy Paul (Garry/Roger), Shirleyann Kaladjian (Brooke/Vicki), Suzi Regan (Poppy), Richard A. Schrot (Frederick/Philip/Sheikh), Sherry Skinker (Belinda/Flavia), Alexander Webb (Tim), Donald Ewer (Selsdon/Burgler)

TO KILL A MOCKINGBIRD by Harper Lee; Adaptation by Christopher Sergel; Director, Randal Myler CAST: Maureen McDevitt (Jean), Mike Kopera (Jem), Maggie Keenan-Bolger (Scout), Thomas D. Mahard (Walter/Gilmer), Michael Kevin (Atticus), Angela Bullock (Calpurnia), Laurie V. Logan (Mrs. Dubose), Andrew Keenan-Bolger (Dill), David Duchene (Radley/Boo), Roy K. Dennison (Judge), James Anthony (Heck), Roderick Aird (Bob), James Sephers III (Rev. Sykes), Dale Dickey (Mayella), Ray Anthony Thomas (Tom), Donna Lewis, Lynch R. Travis, Roxanne Wellington, Gregory A. Wilson

A CHRISTMAS CAROL by Charles Dickens; Adapted/Directed by Charles Nolte CAST: Booth Colman (Scrooge), James Anthony, Mary Benson, Paul Hopper, Adrianne Kriewall, Thomas D. Mahard, Maureen McDevitt, Richard A. Schrot, John Siebert, Thomas M. Suda, Peter Gregory Thomson, Roxanne Wellington, Gregory A. Wilson

BENEFACTORS by Michael Frayn; Director, Jay Broad; Lighting, David F. Segal CAST: Kevin Jackson (David), Judith Moreland (Jane), Samuel Maupin (Colin), Claire Beckman (Sheila)

I HATE HAMLET by Paul Rudnick; Director, Howard J. Millman; Set/Lighting, Dale F. Jordan; Costumes, Dana Harnish Tinsley CAST: Tessie Hogan (Felicia), Craig Mathers (Andrew), Jessica Walling (Deidre), Taina Elg (Lillian), Alan Coates (Barrymore), David Breitbarth (Lefkowitz)

THE GLASS MENAGERIE by Tennessee Williams; Director, Bob Bundy; Lighting, Dennis Parichy CAST: Daniel Pardo (Tom), Peggy Cowles (Amanda), Amy Lammert (Laura), J. Paul Boehmer (Jim)

SHE LOVES ME with Music by Jerry Bock; Lyrics, Sheldon Harnick; Book, Joe Masteroff; Director, Robert Spencer; Musical Director, John Lehr Opfar; Choreography, Mary Jane Houdina CAST: Eric Brooks (Ladislav), Billy Miller (Arpad), Lora Jeanne Martens (Ilona), Joseph Gram (Kodaly), Scott Mikita (Georg), Wil Love (Maraczek), Lisa Rochelle (Amalia), Brian Svhulz (Keller), Paul Hopper (Waiter), Scott Peerbolte (Busboy), Shirley Benyas, Thomas Cooch, Michael Denham Smith, Amy Dolan-Malaney, Shirleyann Kaladjian, Karen Sheridan, Lynne Sherwood

Rick Smith Photos

Top: Donald Ewer, Alexander Webb, Shirleyann Kaladjian in *Noises Off*

Center: Amy Lammert, J. Paul Boehmer in *The Glass Menagerie*

Left: Lora Jeanne Martens, Joseph Gram in *She Loves Me*

174

NEW JERSEY SHAKESPEARE FESTIVAL

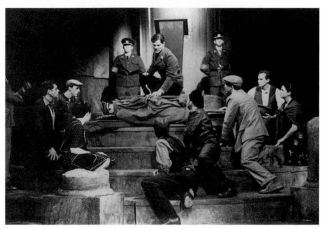

Drew University, Madison, New Jersey

Artistic Director, Bonnie J. Monte; Managing Director, Michael Stotts; Marketing Director, Mark Rossier

PRODUCTIONS(1995)

LOVE'S LABOUR'S LOST by William Shakespeare; Director, Daniel Fish; Set, James Kronzer; Costumes, Kaye Voyce; Lighting, Peter West CAST: Simon Billig (Ferdinand), Mark Niebhur (Berowne), Gregory Jackson (Longaville), Berton Schaeffer (Dumaine), Craig Wallace (Boyet), Greg Derelian (Marcade), John Tillotson (Armado), Ken Kliban (Holofernes), John Wellman (Nathaniel), Liam Craig (Dull), Bradford Cover (Costard), Holly Imper (Moth), Vivienne Benesch (Princess), Jenna Stern (Rosaline), Amanda Ronconi (Katherine), Kate Hampton (Maria), Mia Barron (Jaquenetta)

THE HOMECOMING by Harold Pinter; Director, Bonnie J. Monte; Set, Shelley Barclay; Costumes, Hugh Hanson; Lighting, Bruce Auerbach CAST: Frederick Neumann (Max), Paul Mullins (Lenny), Robert Hock (Sam), Tom Delling (Joey), Patrick Stretch (Teddy), Laila Robins (Ruth)

JULIUS CAESAR by William Shakespeare; Adaptation, Orson Welles; Director, Dennis Delany; Set, Rob Odorisio; Costumes, Mary Peterson; Lighting, Christopher Gorzelnik   CAST: Joseph Barbarino (Flavius), Alexis Brentani (Portia), Matthew Boston (Casca), Robin Chadwick (Caesar), Steven Dennis (Cinna), Greg Derelian (Marullus), Danielle Duvall (Soothsayer), Holly Imper (Lucius), Tomas O'Cenneally, David Patton (Servants), Robert Krakovski (Cassius), Robert LuPone (Brutus), David Andrew Macdonald (Antony), William Mierzejewski (Cobbler), Berton Schaeffer (Mettulus), Craig Wallace (Decius), Alsion Weller (Calpurna)

THE COUNTRY WIFE by William Wycherley; Director, Robert Kalfin; Set, Andrew Hall; Costumes, Austin K. Sanderson; Lighting, Scott Zielenski CAST: Peter Bradbury (Horner), Kevin Henderson (Harcourt), Greg Derelian (Dorilant), Howard Samuelsohn (Pinchwife), Paul Mullins (Sparkish), Larry Swansen (Fidget), Allison Daugherty (Mrs. Pinchwife), Elizabeth Van Dyke (Alithea), Sue Brady (Lady Fidget), Danielle Duvall (Dainty), June Ballinger (Mrs. Squeamish), Sylvia Gassell (Old Lady Squeamish), Tomas O'Cenneally (Quack), Allison Weller (Lucy), Dan Dudden (Clasp), Jack Moran (Boy), Amy Hutchins, Nurit Monicelli, Jay Tomasko, Lara Walters

ARTISTS AND ADMIRERS by Alexander Ostrvsky; Adapted/Directed by Bonnie J. Monte; Set, Rob Odorisio; Costumes, Hwa Park; Lighting, Michael Giannitti CAST: Judith Anna Roberts (Domna), Herman Petras (Narokov), Roy Cockrum (Prince), james Michael Reilly (Bakin), Amanda Ronconi (Negina), Kate Hampton (Nina), Edmond Genest (Velikatov), Bruce Turk (Melusov), Tom Brennan (Tragedian), W. David Wilkins (Migaev), David Mandel (Vasya), Kathy Mattingly (Matryona), Joe Mihalchick (Waiter), William Mierzejewski (Conductor), Kristin Kwasniewski, Tracey Donvito (Ballerinas)

MACBETH by William Shakespeare; Director, Ulla Neuerburg; Set, Gail Rothschild; Costumes, Audrey Fisher; Lighting, Gary L. Marlin CAST: Bruce Turk (Weird Sister/Malcolm), David Mandel (Weird Sister/Donalbain), Doug Webster (Weird Sister/Caitness/Captain), Patrick Morris (Macbeth), Rebecca Ortese (Lady Macbeth), Dan Berkey (Duncan/Macduff), Renee Buchiarelli (Lady Macduff/Porter), Dennis Green (Banquo), Ty Jones (Fleance/Ross), Norman Field (Angus), James Christopher Tracy (Lennox)

Gerry Goodstein Photos

Top: Patrick Stretch, Paul Mullins, Laila Robins in
The Homecoming

Center: (center) David Andrew Macdonald and *Julius Caesar* **cast**

Left: Peter Bradbury, Sue Brady in *The Country Wife*

OLD GLOBE THEATRE

San Diego, California
Sixtieth Season

Artistic Director, Jack O' Brien; Executive Producer, Craig Noel; Managing Director, Thomas Hall; Public Relations Director, Charlene Baldridge; Public Relations Associate, David Tucker

PRODUCTIONS & CASTS

TWELFTH NIGHT by William Shakespeare; Director, Laird Williamson; Set, Ralph Funicello; Costumes, Andrew V. Yelusich; Lighting, Chris Parry CAST: Marcia Cross (Viola), Jefrey Alan Chandler (Feste), Jonathan McMurtry (Captain/Priest), Rob Devaney, Maurice Mendoza, Leonard Stewart (Sailors/Officers), John Hutton (Orsinio), Brian Taylor (Valentine), Mark Hill (Curio), Michael Medico (Medico), William Anton (Toby Belch), Katherine McGrath (Maria), Steve Jones (Fabian), Dan Shor (Aguecheek), Jacqueline Antaramian (Olivia), Tracey Atkins, Anna Cody, Elisa Llamido (Handmaidens), James Jaboro (Zoltan), Don Sparks (Malvolio), Steven Flynn (Sebastian), Leonard Stewart (Antonio), Rhys Laval Green, Calixto Hernandez (Guards/Servants)

LATER LIFE by A. R. Gurney; Director, Nicholas Martin; Set, Allen Moyer; Costumes, David C. Woolard; Lighting, Michael Gilliam CAST: Frank Converse (Austin), Jennifer Harmon (Ruth), Linda Atkinson (Women), Richard Easton (Men)

OLEANNA by David Mamet; Director, Jack O'Brien; Set, Robert Brill; Costumes, David C. Woolard; Lighting, Ashley York Kennedy CAST: Kathleen Dennehy (Carol), William Anton (John)

MADAME MAO'S MEMORIES by Henry Ong; Director, Seret Scott; Set/Costumes, Andrew V. Yelusich; Lighting, Michael Gilliam CAST: Kim Miyori (Madame Mao), Mauricio Mendoza (1st Guard), David Natale (2nd Guard)

SOMEONE WHO'LL WATCH OVER ME by Frank McGuinness; Director, Sheldon Epps; Set, Greg Lucas; Costumes, Dione Lebhar; Lighting, Michael Gilliam CAST: Terry Alexander (Adam), Richard Easton (Michael), Cotter Smith (Edward)

HOME by David Storey; Director, Craig Noel; Set, Greg Lucas; Costumes, David C. Woolard; Lighting, Kent Dorsey CAST: Donald Burton (Jack), Anne Gee Byrd (Marjorie), Katherine McGrath (Kathleen), Jonathan McMurtry (Harry), Leo Stewart (Alfred)

WONDERFUL TENNESSEE by Brian Friel; Director, Craig Noel; Set, Greg Lucas; Costumes, Andrew V. Yelusich; Lighting, Kent Dorsey CAST: George Deloy (Terry), Robin Pearson Rose (Berna), Thomas S. Oleniacz (George), Deborah Taylor (Trish), Tim Donoghue (Frank), Deborah May (Angela)

THE WAY OF THE WORLD by William Congreve; Adaptation, Dakin Matthews; Director, Jack O'Brien; Set, Ralph Funicello; Costumes, Lewis Brown; Lighting, Kent Dorsey CAST: Marc Wong, Dhyana Burtnett (Ghosts), Mark Harelik (Fainall), Byron Jennings (Mirabel), James R. Winker (Witwoud), Charley Lang (Petulant), Tom Ramirez (Witwoud), Henry J. Jordan (Waitwell), Mary Louise Wilson (Lady Wishfort), Carolyn McCormick (Mrs. Millamant), Lillian Garrett-Groag (Mrs. Marwood), Jennifer Schelter (Mrs. Fainall), Monique Fowler (Foible), Eve Holbrook (Mincing), Anna Cody (Peg/Betty), Michael Brandt, David Natale, Patrick Munoz (Servants)

MUCH ADO ABOUT NOTHING by William Shakespeare; Director, Jack O'Brien; Set, William Bloodgood; Costumes, Lewis Brown; Lighting, David F. Segal CAST: Keene Curtis (Leonato), William Anton (Don Pedro), Richard Easton (Benedick), Jonathan Walker (Claudio), Maurice Mendoza (Balthazar), Don Sparks (Don John), Leo Stewart (Conrade), Marc Wong (Borachio), Nike Douglas (Hero), Katherine McGrath (Beatrice), Henry J. Jordan (Antonio), Anna Cody (Margaret), Elisa Llamido (Ursula), Dakin Matthews (Dogberry), Jonathan McMurtry (Verges), David Natale (Sexton), Michael Brandt (Friar/Messenger), Mark Hill, J.D. Black, Christopher Whenry, Fred Benedetti, George Svoboda, Tracey Atkins, Rachel French

Jonathan Walker, Richard Easton, Keene Curtis, Nike Doukas, Anna Cody, Katherine McGrath in *Much Ado About Nothing*

Michael Learned, Katherine McGrath, Erika Rolfsrud in *Dancing at Lughnasa*

FULL GALLOP by Mark Hampton and Mary Louise Wilson; Director, Nicholas Martin; Set, Allen Moyer; Costumes, Michael Krass; Lighting, David F. Segal CAST: Mary Louise Wilson (Diana Vreeland)

TIME OF MY LIFE by Alan Ayckbourn; Director, Craig Noel; Set, Greg Lucas; Costumes, Christina Haatainen; Lighting, Kent Dorsey CAST: Sada Thompson (Laura), Ramon Bieri (Gerry), Don Sparks (Glyn), Peter Krause (Adam), Lynne Griffin (Stephanie), Jennifer Stratman (Maureen), Tony Ramirez (Calvinu/Tuto/Aggi/Dinka/Bengie)

DANCING AT LUGHNASA by Brian Friel; Director, Andrew J. Traister; Set, Ralph Funicello; Costumes, Marianna Elliott; Lighting, Barth Ballard CAST: Joel Anderson (Michael), Michael Learned (Kate), Katherine McGrath (Maggie), Robin Pearson Rose (Agnes), Sally Snythe (Rose), Erika Rolfsrud (Chris), James O'Neil (Gerry), Richard Easton (Jack)

HEDDA GABLER by Henrik Ibsen; Adaptation, Christopher Hampton; Director, Sheldon Epps; Set, Ralph Funicello; Costumes, Marianna Elliott; Lighting, Ashley York Kennedy CAST: Patricia Fraser (Juliana), Trina Kaplan (Berte), John Leonard Thompson (George), CCH Pounder (Hedda), Dawn Saito (Thea), Ron Glass (Judge), John Campion (Eilert)

PUDDIN' PETE: Fable of a Marriage by Cheryl L. West; Director, Gilbert McCauley; Set, Greg Lucas; Costumes, Yslan Hicks; Lighting, Michael Gilliam CAST: Elizabeth Omilami (Puddin), Kevin E. Jones (Pete), Robert Barry Fleming (Serpent), Cara Rene (White Woman), Lisa Louise Langford (Black Woman), Jonathan Earl Peck (Black Man), Mark Hutter (White Man)

Ken Howard Photos

PAPER MILL PLAYHOUSE

Millburn, New Jersey
Sixty-fifth Season

Executive Producer, Angelo Del Rossi; Artistic Director, Robert Johanson; General Manager, Geoffrey Cohen; Public Relations Director, Meara Nigro

PRODUCTIONS & CASTS

SINGIN' IN THE RAIN with Music/Lyrics by Nacio Herb Brown and Arthur Freed; Book, Betty Comden and Adolph Green; Director, James Rocco; Choreography, Linda Goodrich, Mr. Rocco; Musical Director, Steve Tyler; Sets, Michael Anania; Costumes, Gregg Barnes; Lighting, Timothy Hunter CAST: Patti Wyss (Dora), Stewart M. Gregory (Rod/Coach), Conny Sasfai (Olga), John Howell (Baron Toulon), Sara Beth Lane (Zelda), Charles Goff (Simpson), Austin Murphy (Dexter), Randy Rogel (Cosmo), Michael Gruber (Don Lockwood), Deborah Jolly (Lina Lamont), Ryan Loftus Sciaino (Young Don), Julia Occhiogrosso (Young Cosmo), Jim Athens (Bartender/Sid), Candy Cook (Stripper), Seth Hoff (Bouncer), Machel Duncan (Showgirl), Christina Saffran (Kathy Selden), Kevin McMahon (Police/Tenor/Engineer), Daniela Panessa, Mr. Hoff (Tango Couple), Patti Wyss (Miss Dinsmore), Jeffrey J. Bateman, Theresse Friedemann, T. Scott Hoag, Julie McDonald, Ashley Mortimer, Allison K. Myers, Joel Newsome, Bran Pace, Josh Rhodes, Parisa Ross, Vincent Sandoval, Coleen Ann Sexton, Natalie Van Kleef

OLIVER with Music/Lyrics/Book by Lionel Bart; Director, Robert Johanson; Musical Director, Jim Coleman; Choreography, Daniel Stewart; Sets, Michael Anania; Costumes, Gregg Barnes; Lighting, F. Mitchell Dana CAST: David Lloyd Watson (Oliver/Strawberry Seller), Lynda DiVito (Gate Woman), Betty Winsett (Sally), David Vosburgh (Bumble), Norma Crawford (Widow), Lou Williford (Martha/Mrs. Sowerberry), Diane Pennington (Annie/Rose Seller), Keith Perry (Sowerberry/Grimwig), Karen DiConcetto (Charlotte), Kirk McDonald (Claypole), Robert Creighton (Artful Dodger), George S. Irving (Fagin), Jim Raposa (Charley), Judy Mclane (Nancy), Christopher Innvar (Sykes), Stella (Bull's Eye), Aileen Quinn (Bet), Michael Allison (Brownlow), Christina Gillespie (Mrs. Bedwin), Erin Eagan (Milkmaid), Gregory Butler (Knife-Grinder), Tony Lawson (Long Song Seller), Benjamin Bedenbaugh, Crystal-Eve, Samantha Robyn Lee, Cindy Marchionda, Mr. McDonald, Derrick McGinty, Matthew Jason Pichney, Alonzo Saunders (Fagin's Gang), Lauren Bass, Justin Bocitto, Nancy Braun, Matthew Fasano, Timothy Girrbach, C. Jay Hardy, Amanda Johnson, Jacqueline Macri, Jennifer Margulis, Allison Marks, Patrick McAndrew, Grace Ann Pisani, Jessica Waxman, J.B. Adams, Craig A. Benham, Michael Stever

FOREVER PLAID; Written/Directed/Choreographed by Stuart Ross; Musical Director, David Gursky; Set, Neil Peter Jampolis; Lighting, Jane Reisman; Costumes, Debra Stein CAST: Robert Lambert (Frankie), David Engel (Smudge), Roy Chicas (Jinx), Jonathan Brody (Sparky)

THE PRISONER OF ZENDA by Peter Manos; Based on novel by Anthony Hope; Director, Robert Johanson; Sets, Michael Anania; Costumes, Gregg Barnes; Lighting, Ken Billington CAST: Michael James Reed (Robert/Michael), Nancy Bell (Rose/Princess Flava), Jonathan Wade (Prince Rudolph/Rassendyll), Steve Boles (Burton/Johann/Jailer), Therese M. McLaughlin (Olive/Frieda), John Wylie (Col. Sapt), Robert Carin (Rupert), Teel James Glenn (Detchard), J. David Brimmer (Bersonin), Sean Dougherty, Tito Enriquez, Al Espinoza, Corinna May, Andrew Palmer

BRIGADOON with Music by Frederick Loewe; Lyrics/Book, Alan Jay Lerner; Director, David Holdgrive; Musical Director, Jim Coleman; Design, Desmond Heeley; Lighting, Mark Stanley; Choreography, Greg Ganakas CAST: Joseph Mahowald (Tommy), P.J. Benjamin (Jeff), Kenneth Kantor (Archie), Alex Sanchez (Harry), Gregory Butler (Angus), Jim Gricar (Sandy/Frank), Michael Shelle (Andrew), Lee Merrill (Fiona), Tania Philip (Jean), Leah Hocking (Meg), John Clonts (Charlie), Elizabeth Ferrell, Joan Mirabella (Maggie), Burt Edwards (Lundie), Eric H. Kaufman, Steven Ochoa (Sword Dancers), Don Rey (Stuart), George Kmeck (MacGregor), Stephen Fox (Bagpiper), Erin Dilly (Jane), Christopher Adams, James Allen Baker, Linda Bowen, Joy Hermalyn, Alexia Hess, Sylvia Hummell, Renee Lawless-Orsini, Laurie LeBlanc, Wendy Lockett, Christopher Lynn, Ashley Mortimer, Max Perlman, David Alan Quart, Dana Stackpole, Tina P. Stafford, John Summers

Nancy Bell, Jonathan Wade in *Prisoner of Zenda*

Robert Creighton, David Lloyd Watson in *Oliver!*

PETER PAN with Music by Mark Charlap, Jule Styne; Lyrics, Carolyn Leigh, Betty Comden, Adolph Green; Director, Robert Johanson; Choreography, Daniel Pelzig; Musical Director, Fred Lassen; Sets, Michael Anania; Costumes, Gregg Barnes; Lighting, F. Mitchell Dana CAST: Becky Watson (Wendy), Jeff Seelbach (John), Dana Solimando (Liza), Jeffrey Force (Michael), Jim Raposa (Nana), Elizabeth Walsh (Mrs. Darling/Peter's Mother), Christopher Innvar (Mr. Darling/Capt. Hook), Tinker Bell (Herself), Robert Johanson succeeded by Robert Creighton (Peter Pan), Robert Creighton (Slightly), Jared Gertner (Tootles), Kirk McDonald (Curly), Derrick McGinty (Nibs), Jennilee Morse, Michelle Caggiano (Twins), Debbi Fuhrman (Pug), Tommy Roeder (Whizzy), Ken Jennings (Smee), Joe Heffernan (Starkey), Seth Charles Malkin (Genghis), John Bolton (JUkes), Michael Ambrozy (Cecco), Bill E. Dietrich (Noodler), David Jordan (Rasputin), Albert Christmas (Yurk), Christopher Sieber (Napoleoni), Melody Meitrott (Cookson/Mermaid), Brad Musgrove (Crocodile), Dana Solimando (Tiger Lily), Lori Bennett (Jane), Ginger Thatcher (Neverbird), Miguel A. Aviles, Steve Bajusz, Steve Camanella, Jeff Elsass, Bryan S. Haynes, Melissa Kelly, Michael Krivak, Allegra Libonati, Christian Libonati, Michele Maly, Brad Musgrove, Taina Perez, Jacqueline Ritchie

Gerry Goodstein, Jerry Dalia Photos

PLAYMAKERS REPERTORY COMPANY

Chapel Hill, North Carolina

Producing Director, Milly S. Barranger; Associate Producing Director, David Hammond; Managing Director, Zannie Giraud Voss; Production Manager, Michael Rolleri; Sets/Costumes, Judy Adamson, Kay McKay Cole, Bobbi Owen; General Manager, David zum Brunnen; Communications Director, Patti Thorp

PRODUCTIONS: *A Streetcar Named Desire* by Tennessee Williams; Director, Michael Wilson; *2* by Romulus Linney; Director, David Hammond; *Beauty and the Beast* by Tom Huey; Conception/Direction by Michael Wilson; *The Visit* by Friedrich Durrenmatt; Translation, Maurice Valency; Director, David Hammond; *Charley's Aunt* by Brandon Thomas; Director, David Hammond; *Macbeth* by William Shakespeare; Director, David Wheeler

RESIDENT COMPANY: David Adamson, Mark Ariail, Michael Babbitt, Patricia Barnett, Jeff Betz, David M. Brooks, Thomas D. Carr, James Cartmel, Brian Christopher, Kim Ann Clay, Dede Corvinus, Peter Dillard, Julie Fishell, Matt Fleming, Heather Grayson, Michael Hunter, Paige Johnson, Fiona Jones, Michael H. King, Rob Kramer, Nancy Lane, Brent Langdon, Julie Padilla Moreno, Susanna Rinehart, Shannon Roberts, John Rosenfeld, John Stamper, Jody Strimling, Ken Strong, Christine Suhr, Alex Teller, Craig Turner, Ed Wagenseller

GUEST ARTISTS: *Actors:* Paul Benedict, Rhonda Bond, Richard Burgwin, Rafeal Clements, Nick Chinlund, Thaddeus L. Daniels, Clarence Felder, Anthony Fusco, Annalee Jefferies, Alex Loria, Matthew Lewis, Matthew Mabe, DeAnn Mears, Alan Nebelthau, Patrick Rameau, Eric Woodall *Designers:* Bill Clarke, Jeff Cowie, Laura Cunningham, Johnna Doty, John Gromada, Mark Hartman, Yvette Helin, Christine Jones, Ashley York Kennedy, Michael Lincoln, Caryn Neman, Russell Parkman, Adam Vernick, Robert Wierzel

Will Owens Photos

Top: Dede Corvinus, James Cartmel, Michael Hunter in *Beauty and the Beast*

Center: Jeff Betz, Matthew Mabe, Thomas D. Carr in *Charley's Aunt*

Below Left: Alex Loria, Anthony Fusco in *Macbeth*

Below Right: DeAnn Mears in *The Visit*

REPERTORY THEATRE OF ST. LOUIS

St. Louis, Missouri

Artistic Director, Steven Woolf; Managing Director, Mark D. Bernstein; Public Relations, Judy Andrews

PRODUCTIONS & CASTS

THE CAINE MUTINY COURT MARTIAL by Herman Wouk; Director, Steven Woolf; Set, Michael Ganio; Costumes, J. Bruce Summers; Lighting, Max De Volder CAST: R. Ward Duffy (Maryk), Jim Abele (Greenwald), Richard Esvang (Challee), Joneal Joplin (Blakely), Robert Elliott (Queeg), Paul DeBoy (Keefer), Dana Snyder (Urban), Chris Hietikko (Keith), Peter Byger (Southard), Whit Reichert (Lundeen), Steve Routman (Bird), Scott De Broux (Stenographer)

BLACK COFFEE by Agatha Christie; Director, Susan Gregg; Set, John Ezell; Costumes, James Scott; Lighting, Phillip Monat CAST: Steve Routman (Tredwell/Graham), Mana Allen (Lucia), Christiane McKenna (Caroline), Paul DeBoy (Richard), Alison Bevan (Barbara), Bill Bowers (Edward), Noble Shropshire (Carelli), Peter Byger (Claud/Japp), Joe Palmieri (Hercule Poirot), Eric Swanson (Hastings), David S. Stewart (Johnson)

INSPECTOR CAROL by Daniel Sullivan and the Seattle Repertory Resident Company; Director, Edward Stern; Set, James Leonard Joy; Costumes, Dorothy L. Marshall; Lighting, Peter E. Sargent CAST: Pamela Wiggins (M.J.), Russ Jolly (Wayne), Glynis Bell (Zorah), Chris Van Strandler (Luther), Darrie Lawrence (Dorothy), Thomas Ligon (Sidney), Anderson Matthews (Phil), Dale E. Turner (Walter), Jack Cirillo (Kevin), Brett Pearsons (Bart), Tony Hoty (Larry), Zoe Vonder Haar (Betty)

THE BROTHERS KARAMAZOV by Anthony Clarvoe; Based on novel by Dostoyevsky; Director, Brian Kulick; Set/Costumes, Mark Wendland; Lighting, Max De Volder CAST: Robert Elliott (Fyodor/Judge/Devil), Michael Chaban (Dmitri), Michael Ornstein (Ivan), Matthew Rauch (Alyosha), Ed Shea (Smerdyakov/Plotkinov), Joneal Joplin (Fr. Zosima/Mussyalovich/D.A.), Paul DeBoy (Rakitin/Plastunov), Susan Ericksen (Katya), Katherine Heasley (Grushenka), Brooks Almy (Fenya/Samsonov)

MAN AND SUPERMAN by George Bernard Shaw; Director, John Going; Set, James Wolk; Costumes, Jeffrey Struckman; Lighting, Howard Werner CAST: Ron Randell (Roebuck), Tina Marie Moulton (Parlormaid), David Harum (Octavius), Martin LaPlatney (John), Katherine Leask (Ann), Pauline Flanagan (Mrs. Whitefield), Zoe Vonder Haar (Miss Ramsden), Kathleen Mahony-Bennett (Violet), Peter Bradbury (Henry), Chris Hietkko (Hector), Richert Easley (Malone)

BORN YESTERDAY by Garson Kanin; Director, Timothy Near; Set, John Roslevich Jr.; Costumes, Dorothy L. Marshall; Lighting, Glenn M. Dunn CAST: Susie Wall (Helen), Scott Freeman (Paul), Gary Glasgow (Asst. Manager), Whit Reichert (Eddie), Tony Hoty (Harry Brock), Rebecca MacLean (Billie Dawn), J.G. Hertzler (Devery), Alan Benson (Barber), Hope Boynton (Manicurist), Richard Dix (Hedges), Dolores Sutton (Mrs. Hedges)

SHIRLEY VALENTINE by Willy Russell; Director, Alyson Reed; Set/Costumes, Arthur Ridley; Lighting, Max De Volder CAST: Brooks Almy

OFF THE ICE by Barbara Field; Director, Susan Gregg; Set/Lighting, Dale F. Jordan; Costumes, John Carver Sullivan CAST: Kim Sebastian (Beth), Alison Stair Neet (Jo), Carol Schultz (Meg), Sherry Skinker (Amy), Sybyl Walker (Eliza)

ESMERALDA with Music/Lyrics by Steven Lutvak; Book, Kathryn Placzek and David Schechter; Director, Mr. Schechter; Based on an adaptation of Victor Hugo's *Hunchback of Notre Dame* by Andrew Dallmeyer; Musical Director, Michael Horsley; Set, John Ezell; Costumes, James Scott; Lighting, Peter E. Sargent CAST: Price Waldman (Pierre), Kimberly JaJuan (Esmeralda), Steve Blanchard (Phoebus), George Merritt (Frollo), Suzanne Costallos (Clothilde), Marian Murphy (Fleur), Jennifer Jonassen (Innkeeper)

Judy Andrews Photos

Right: Joneal Joplin, Robert Elliott, Michael Ornstein, Paul DeBoy, Michael Chaban in *Brothers Karamazov*

Carol Schultz, Sherry Skinker, Sybyl Walker in *Off the Ice*

Kimberly JaJuan in *Esmeralda*

179

SAN DIEGO REPERTORY THEATRE

San Diego, California
Nineteenth Season

Producing Director, Sam Woodhouse; Artistic Director, Douglas Jacobs; General Manager, John Redman; Production Manager, Joan T. Foster; Communications Director, Mark Hiss

PRODUCTIONS & CASTS

FLYIN' WEST by Pearl Cleage; Director, Floyd Gaffney; Set, Ron Ranson; Lighting, Brenda Berry; Costumes, Judy Watson CAST: Damon J. Bryant (Wil), Sarah Davis (Minnie), Irma P. Hall (Miss Leah), Dominic Hoffman (Frank), Jackie Mari Roberts (Fannie), Sylvia M'Lafi Thompson (Sophie)

TURBO TANZI by Claire Luckham; Music, Chris Monks; Director, Douglas Jacobs; Musical Director, Pea Hicks; Fights, Christopher Villa; Set, John Redman; Costumes, Judy Watson; Lighting, John Philip Martin CAST: Spike Sorrentino (Referee), Vanessa Townsell-Crisp (Mom), Todd Blakesley (Dad), Robin Sheridan (Platinum Sue), Tyler Mane (Rebel), Laurie Williams (Turbo Tanzi)

A CHRISTMAS CAROL by Charles Dickens; Adaptation, Douglas Jacobs; Music, Steve Gunderson; Director, Will Roberson; Choreography, Javier Velasco; Set, Amy Shock; Lighting, Ashley York Kennedy; Costumes, Todd Roehrman CAST: Tom Lacy (Scrooge), Priscilla Allen, Damon Bryant, Jessica Bryant, Darla Cash, Kellie Evans-O'Connor, Melinda Gibb, Steve Gouveia, Steve Gunderson, Tim Irving, Maurice Mendoza, Alton Williams-Sellers, Jenny Selner, Myche Taylor, Chad Lee Williamson, Shana Wride

HAMLET by William Shakespeare; Director, Todd Salovey; Music, Beth Custer; Set, Amy Shock; Costumes, Mary Larson; Lighting, John Philip Martin CAST: Michael Behrens (Rosencrantz), Darla Cash (Gertrude), Linda CASTro (Player/Lucianus/Osrick), Beth Custer (Player), Shanesia Davis (Ophelia/Fortinbras), Matthew Henerson (Horatio), Dana Hooley (Player Queen/Voltemand), Douglas Jacobs (Claudius), Antonio T.J. Johnson (Barnardo/Reynaldo/Priest), Jefferson Mays (Hamlet), Catalina Maynard (Marcella/Player King), Felton Perry (Polonius/Francisco), Kevin White (Laertes/Guilderstern), Sam Woodhouse (Ghost/Gravedigger)

EL PASO BLUE; Written/Directed by Octavio Solis; Music, Michael "Hawkeye" Herman; Set, Michelle Riel; Costumes, Cheryl Lindley; Lighting, Jose Lopez CAST: Pace Ebbesen (Duane), Delia MacDougall (Sylvie), Monica Sanchez (China), Leon Singer (Jefe), Vic Trevino (Al)

GOODNIGHT DESDEMONA GOOD MORNING JULIET by Ann-Marie MacDonald; Director, Sam Woodhouse; Set, Michelle Riel; Costumes, Janice Louise Benning; Lighting, Jose Lopez CAST: Jennifer Barrick (Juliet/Student/Soldier), Ron Campbell (Romeo/Iago/Ghost), Darla Cash (Ledbelly), Shanesia Davis (Desdemona/Ramona/Mercutio), Jonathan Fried (Othello/Tybalt/Nurse/Claude Night)

Ken Jacques Photos

**Top: Irma P. Hall, Jackie Mari Roberts,
Sylvia M'Lafi Thompson in *Flyin' West***

Center: Jefferson May, Felton Perry, Sam Woodhouse in *Hamlet*

Right: Delia MacDougall, Leon Singer in *El Paso Blue*

SOUTH COAST REPERTORY

Costa Mesa, California

Producing Artistic Director, David Emmes; Artistic Director, Martin Benson; Managing Director, Paula Tomei; Marketing/Communications Director, John Mouledoux

PRODUCTIONS & CASTS

A STREETCAR NAMED DESIRE by Tennessee Williams; Director, martin Benson; Set, Michael Devine; Costumes, Walter Hicklin; Lighting, Jane Reisman CAST: Lea Charisse Woods (Neighbor), K.T. Vogt (Eunice), Jeff Meek (Stanley), Elizabeth Dennehy (Stella), Mikael Salazar (Steve), Jimmie Ray Weeks (Mitch), Vetza Trussell (Flower Seller/Matron), Kandis Chappell (Blanche), Art Koustik (Pablo), Nolan Yates (Young Collector), Don Took (Doctor)

GREEN ICEBERGS by Cecilia Fannon; Director, David Emmes; Set, Robert Brill; Costumes, Ann Bruice; Lighting, Tom Ruzika CAST: Hal Landon Jr. (Waiter), Nike Doukas (Veronica), Robert Curtis-Brown (Claude), Annie LaRussa (Beth), Jeff Allin (Justus)

A CHRISTMAS CAROL by Charles Dickens; Adaptation, Jerry Patch; Director, John-David Keller; Set, Cliff Faulkner; Costumes, Dwight Richard Odle; Lighting, Tom and Donna Ruzika CAST: Hal Landon Jr. (Scrooge), Devon Raymond, Art Koustik, Hisa Takakuwa, William Robert Jenkins Jr., Richard Soto, Ron Boussom, Terry Mowrey, R. Anders Porter, Aaron Cohen, Ryan Kegel, Sharon Omi, Marissa Mann, Kelliann Klein, Christopher Duval, John Ellington, Howard Shangraw, John-David Keller, Alma Martinez, Don Took, Richard Doyle, Danielle Noble, Megan Wall-Wolff, Sam Well, Gianennio Salucci, Ashly Paige Spector, Katy Brandes, Jamie Burkart, Matthew Cooper, Lauren Thomas, Erin Williams, Marty Glyer, Blake Oliver

THE MISANTHROPE by Molière; Translation, Richard Wilbur; Director, David Chambers; Set, Ralph Funicello; Costumes, Shigeru-Yaji; Lighting, Chris Parry CAST: John Vickery (Alceste), Richard Frank (Philinte), Mikael Salazar (Oronte), Lynnda Ferguson (Celimene), Art Koustik, Luck Hari (Eliante), Ron Boussom (Clitandre), Bill Mondy (Acaste), Don Took (Guard), Cindy Katz (Arsinoe), John Ellington (Dubois)

GHOST IN THE MACHINE by David Gilman; Director, David Emmes; Set, Gerard Howland; Costumes, Dwight Richard Odle; Lighting, Tom Ruzika CAST: Stephen Rowe (Wes), Wendy Robie (Nancy), Michael Canavan (Matt), Jane Fleiss (Kim), Hal Landon Jr. (Llewelyn), Eric Steinberg (Minh)

**Jeff Allin, Hal Landon Jr., Annie LaRussa,
Robert Curtis-Brown, Nike Doukas in *Green Icebergs*
Bottom: David Fenner, James Parks in *Pterodactyls***

BLITHE SPIRIT by Noel Coward; Director, William Ludel; Set, Cliff Faulkner; Costumes, Ann Brucie; Lighting, Doc Ballard CAST: Marnie Crossen (Edith), Mary Layne (Ruth), Nicholas Hormann (Charles), John-David Keller (Bradman), Mary Kay Wulf (Mrs. Bradman), Jean Stapleton (Madame Arcati), Nike Doukas (Elvira)

THE CHERRY ORCHARD by Anton Chekhov; Translation, Paul Schmidt; Set, Ming Cho Lee; Costumes, Walker Hicklin; Lighting, Peter Maradudin CAST: Megan Cole (Liubov), Luck Hari (Anya), Cindy Katz (Varya), Raye Birk (Leonid), John Vickery (Yermoli), John Walcutt (Petya), Richard Doyle (Boris), Fran Bennett (Carlotta), David Fenner (Semyon), Amanda Carlin (Dunyasha), Alan Mandell (Firs), Jon Matthews (Yasha), Art Koustik (Homeless Man), Christopher DuVal (Stationmaster), Daniel Cordova (Postmaster)

LATER LIFE by A.R. Gurney; Director, Mark Rucker; Set, Mark Wendland; Costumes, Dwight Richard Odle; Lighting, Lonnie Alcaraz CAST: Richard Doyle (Austtin), Melinda Peterson (Ruth), Ron Boussom (Men), Jane A. Johnston (Women)

JAR THE FLOOR by Cheryl L. West; Director, Benny Sato Ambush; Set, Emily T. Phillips; Costumes, Myrna Colley-Lee; Lighting, Paulie Jenkins CAST: Fran Bennett (MaDear), Juanita Jennings (MayDee), Ann Weldon (Lola), Jackie Mari Roberts (Vennie), Jodi Thelen (Raisa)

LA POSADA MAGICA by Octavio Solis; Music, Marcos Loya; Director, Jose Cruz Gonzalez; Set, Cliff Faulker; Costumes, Shigeru Yaji; Lighting, Lonnie Alcaraz CAST: Ruben Sierra (Horacio), Edna Alvarez (Consuelo), Christine Avila (Caridad), Teresa Velarde (Mom/Mariluz), Vic Trevino (Refugio/Buzzard), George Galvan (Papi/Josecruz), Phillip Daniel Rodriguez (Eli/Lauro/Bones), Ruth Livier (Gracie), Marcos Loya, Lorenzo Martinez

WIT by Margaret Edson; Director, Martin Benson; Set, Cliff Faulkner; Costumes, Kay Peebles; Lighting, Paulie Jenkins CAST: Megan Cole (Vivian), Richard Doyle (Harvey/Bearing), Mary Kay Wulf (Susie), Patricia Fraser (Ashford/Housekeeper), Brian Drillinger (Jason), Christopher DuVal, Kyle Jones (Technicians/Students), Stacy L. Porter (Fellow/Student)

PTERODACTYLS by Nicky Silver; Director, Tim Vasen; Set, Michael Vaughn Sims; Costumes, Todd Roehrman; Lighting, Jane Reisman CAST: James Parks (Todd), Clea Lewis (Emma), David Fenner (Tommy), Joan Stuart Morris (Grace), Don Took (Arthur)

FAITH HEALER by Brian Friel; Director, Barbara Damashek; Set, John Iacovelli; Costumes, Julie Keen; Lighting, Tom Ruzika CAST: Hal Landon Jr. (Frank), Karen Landry (Grace), Ron Boussom (Teddy)

Henri DiRocco Photos

181

STUDIO ARENA THEATRE

Buffalo, New York
Thirtieth Season

Artistic Director, Gavin Cameron-Webb; Producing Director, Raymond Bonnard; Production Manager, Charles Grammer; Marketing Director, Courtney J. Walsh; Public Relations Manager, Julie Kopfer

PRODUCTIONS & CASTS

HARVEY by Mary Chase; Director, Nagle Jackson; Set, James Kronzer; Costumes, Liz Covey; Lighting, William H. Grant III CAST: Eileen Dugan (Myrtle Mae), Adale O'Brien (Veta), John Schuck, Christopher Wynkoop(Elwood P. Dowd), Jeanne Cairns (Ethel), Yvette Thor (Ruth), Brian Howe (Duane), Tom Dunlop (Dr. Sanderson), Christopher Wynkoop, Irv Weinstein (Dr. Chumley), Jeannine Moore (Betty), Barry Boys (Judge), Laverne Clay (Lofgren)

A SHAYNA MAIDEL by Barbara Lebow; Director, Gavin Cameron-Webb; Set/Costumes, G.W. Mercier; Lighting, Rachel Budin CAST: Brenda Foley (Rose), Arn Weiner (Mordechai), Greta Lambert (Lusia), Scott Klavan (Duvid), Twyla Hafermann (Hanna), Sharon Cornell (Mama)

A CHRISTMAS CAROL by Charles Dickens; Adaptation, Amlin Gray; Director, Raymond Bonnard; Set/Lighting, Paul Wonsek; Costumes, Mary Ann Powell CAST: Robert Spencer (Scrooge), Timothy Wahrer, Eric Coates, Saul Elkin, Julian Gamble, Gerald Finnegan, Susan Coon, A. Luana Kenyatta, Hugh Kelly, Brenda Foley, Sonia Medina, Erin L. Lush, Wilson Freeman, Daniel Torres, Andrew Hermann, Jeff Brunell, Andria Chatman, Katie Principe, Jill Testman, Mia Moody, Nick Sanni, Gareth MacCubin, Carolyn Gioia, Alliah Agostini, Marc Franco, Darren Harper, Kate Loconti, April Adams

OVER THE TAVERN by Tom Dudzick; Director, Terence Lamude; Set, Russell Metheny; Lighting, John McClain; Costumes, Maureen Carr CAST: Yvon Pasquarello (Rudy), Jeanne Cairns (Sister Clarissa), Susanne Marley (Ellen), Chad Vahue (Georgie), Jamie Bennett (Eddie), Fleur Phillips (Annie), Tom Bloom (Chet), Bob de la Plante

THE SNOW BALL by A.R. Gurney; Director, Mark Brokaw; Choreography, John Carrafa; Set, Allen Moyer; Costumes, Jess Goldstein; Lighting, Kenneth Posner CAST: Dennis Creaghan (Cooper), Becky Watson (Young Kitty), Michael O'Steen (Young Jack), Jay Potter (Billy), Alex Bond (Heather), Marion McCorry (Lucy), Curt Karibalis (Fritz/Saul), Michael Saposnick (Dunn/Smithers), Connor Smith (Calvin), Cynthia Hood (Barbara), Lisa Ludwig (Ginny/Interviewer), Leslie Lyles (Liz), Colleen Gaughan (Mary), James Carruthers (Van Dam/Hall), Ross Bickell (Jack), Suzanne Dawson (Kitty)

DIAL M FOR MURDER by Frederick Knott; Director, Frederick King Keller; Set, Robert Cothran; Lighting, Joseph Appelt; Costumes, Elizabeth Haas Keller CAST: Elizabeth Roby (Margot), Michael MacCauley (Max), Jeff Woodman (Tony), Richard Wesp (Lesgate), Julian Gamble (Inspector), David Douglas (Police)

MA RAINEY'S BLACK BOTTOM by August Wilson; Director, Claude E. Purdy; Set, David Potts; Lighting, Phil Monat; Costumes, Kay Kurta Silva CAST: Rohn Thomas (Sturdyvant), Morgan Lund (Irvin), Thomas Martell Brimm (Cutler), Alex Allen Morris (Toledo), Anthony Chisholm (Slow Drag), Kim Sullivan (Levee), Theresa Merritt (Ma Rainey), Jesse Swartz (Police), Kathi A. Bentley (Dussie Mae), Victor Mack (Sylvester)

I HATE HAMLET by Paul Rudnick; Director, Gavin Cameron-Webb; Set, Dale Jordan; Lighting, Richard Devin; Costumes, Catherine Norgren CAST: Bess Brown Kregal (Felicia), William Gonta (Andrew), Brenda Foley (Deirdre), Jeanne Cairns (Lillian), Tom Spackman (Barrymore), Brad Bellamy (Lefkowitz)

K.C. Kratt Photos

Top: *Snow Ball* cast
Center: John Schuck in *Harvey*
Left: Scott Pechenik, Greta Lambert in *A Shayna Maidel*

182

TRINITY REPERTORY COMPANY

Providence, Rhode Island
Thirty-first Season

Artistic Director, Oskar Eustis; Managing Director, Patricia Egan; Public Relations, Lucinda Dohanian Welch

PRODUCTIONS & CASTS

THE WINTER'S TALE by William Shakespeare; Director, Dakin Matthews; Set, Eugene Lee; Costumes, William Lane; Lighting, Michael Giannitti CAST: Timothy Crowe (Leontes), Cynthia Strickland (Hermione), Whitney Haring-Smith (Mamillius), Allen Oliver (Antigonus), Phyllis Kay (Paulina), Brian McEleney (Camillo), Barbara Orson (Emilia), John Thompson (Cleomenes), Brienin Bryant (Dion/Dorcas), Jonathan Fried (Polixenes), Tony Estrella (Florizel), Robert J. Colonna, Fred Sullivan Jr. (Sheepherders), Candice Rose (Perdita), Jodie Rufty (Mopsa), Peter Gerety (Autolycus), Chris Turner (Time), Rachel Maloney, Kevin Fallon (Bawdy Planet)

THE WAITING ROOM by Lisa Loomer; Director, David Schweizer; Set, Michael McGarty; Costumes, William Lane; Lighting, Russell Champa CAST: June Kyoko Lu (Forgiveness), Anne Scurria (Victoria), Rose Weaver (Brenda), Janice Duclos (Wanda), William Damkoehler (Douglas), Ed Shea (Oliver), Stephen Berenson (Ken), Dan Welch (Larry), Chil Kong (Blessing), Gabriel Diamond, Robert Grady (Orderlies)

A CHRISTMAS CAROL by Charles Dickens; Adaptation, Adrian Hall and Richard Cumming; Music, Mr. Cumming; Director, Peter Gerety; Set, David Rotondo; Costumes, William Lane; Lighting, Russell Champa CAST: Timothy Crowe (Scrooge), Brian McEleney, David Kane, Frankie O'Brien, Robert J. Colonna, Allen Oliver, Jonathan Fried, Fred Sullivan Jr., Viola Davis, Phyllis Kay, Nance Williamson, Kurt Rhoads, Lisa Lane, Jared Danielian, Cedric Lilly, Candice Rose, Dolores Dermody, Jevon Coehlho, Jed Pilkington, Rosanna Campbell, Alex Newby, Fiona Gerety, Anna Henderson, Benjamin Simon, Alexandra Bolotow, Matt Fagin, Elise Fargnoli, Heather Baron, Sharah Connor-Johnson, Amy Dziobek

FROM THE MISSISSIPPI DELTA by Dr. Endesha Ida Mae Holland; Director, Kent Gash; Set, Edward E. Haynes Jr.; Costumes, William Lane; Lighting, R. Stephen Hoyes CAST: Rose Weaver (One), Brienin Bryant (Two), Barbara Meek (Three)

THE ILLUSION by Tony Kushner; Adapted from *L'Ilusion Comique* by Pierre Corneille; Director, Brian Kulick; Set, Mark Wendland; Costumes, William Lane; Lighting, Heather Carson CAST: William Damkoehler (Pridamant), Dan Welch (Amanuensis/Geronte), Anne Scurria (Alcanre), Shawn Hamilton (Calisto/Clindor/Theogenes), Shannon Holt (Melibea/Isabelle/Hippolyta), Phyllis Kay (Elicia/Lyse/Clarina), Allen Oliver (Pleribo/Adraste/Florilame), Timothy Crowe (Matamore), Jodie Rufty, Robert Casey, Gabriel Diamond, Matthew Fagin (Amanuensis)

SLAVS! by Tony Kushner; Director, Oskar Eustis; Set, Eugene Lee; Costumes, William Lane; Lighting, Christopher Akerlind CAST: Barbara Meek (1st Babushka/Mrs. Domik), Anne Scurria (2nd Babushka/B), Robert J. Colonna (Vashka/Big Babushka), Brian McEleney (Serge), Timothy Crowe (Aleksii), William Damkoehler (Poppy), Fred Sullivan Jr. (Yegor), Lisa Lane (Kat), Sarah E. Galli, Scarlett Shore (Vodya)

GOD'S HEART by Craig Lucas; Director, Norman Rene; Set, Eugene Lee; Costumes, Walker Hicklin; Lighting, Debra J. Kletter CAST: Ray Ford (Carlin), Phyllis Kay (Janet/Carol), Ed Shea (David/Customer/Reese), Harriet Harris (Eleanor), Janice Duclos (Barbara), Brienin Bryant (Angela/Whitney), Avaan Patel (Aria/Volunteer/Nurse), Rosalyn Coleman (Dr. Farkas/Cashmere/Valerie), Barbara Orson (Patty)

AVNER THE ECCENTRIC; Lighting, Jeff Norberry

Marc Morelli Photos

Top: Janice Duclos, Harriet Harris (on screen),
Phyllis Kay in *God's Heart*

Center: Anne Scurria, Lisa Lane in *Slavs!*

Left: Timothy Crowe, Cynthia Strickland,
Candice Rose, Phyllis Kay in *The Winter's Tale*

183

YALE REPERTORY THEATRE

New Haven, Connecticut

Artistic Director, Stan Wojewodski Jr.; Managing Director, Victoria Nolan; Press Director, Joyce Friedmann; Press and Marketing Associate, Frances Oliver

PRODUCTIONS & CASTS

ANTIGONE IN NEW YORK by Janusz Glowacki; Translation, Mr. Glowacki and Joan Torres; Director, Liz Diamond; Set, Daphne C. Klein; Costumes, Emily Beck; Lighting, Brian Haynsworth CAST INCLUDES: Bill Raymond, John Seitz

THE MARRIAGE OF FIGARO/FIGARO GETS A DIVORCE by Pierre Caron de Beaumarchais and Odon von Horvath; Adaptation, Eric Overmyer; Director, Stan Wojewodski Jr.; Music, Kim D. Sherman; Set, Derek McLane; Costumes, Jess Goldstein; Lighting, Stephen Strawbridge CAST INCLUDES: Carolyn McCormick, Jennie Israel, Ann Mallory, Lynn Hawley

TWELFTH NIGHT Or What You Will by William Shakespeare; Director, Mark Rucker; Set, Ritirong Jiwakanon; Costumes, Sarah Eckert; Lighting, Brian Haynsworth CAST INCLUDES: John Bland, Mercedes Herrero, Greer Goodman, Amy Malloy

SLAVS! by Tony Kushner; Director, Lisa Peterson; Set, Micahel Yeargan; Costumes, Gabriel Berry; Lighting, Robert Wierzel CAST INCLUDES: Ronny Graham, James Greene

UNCLE VANYA by Anton Chekhov; Translation, Paul Schmidt; Director, Len Jenkin; Set, Emily Beck; Costumes, Anita Yavich; Lighting, Jennifer Tipton

LE BOURGEOIS AVANT-GARDE by Charles Ludlam; Director, Liz Diamond; Set, Hyun-joo Kim; Costumes, Elizabeth Fried; Lighting, Robert Wierzel CAST INCLUDES: Sarah Knowlton, Stuart Sherman

T. Charles Erickson Photos

Top: John Bland, Mercedes Herrero, Greer Goodman, Amy Malloy in *Twelfth Night*

Right: Bill Raymond, John Seitz in *Antigone in New York*

Below Left: Ronny Graham, James Greene in *Slavs!*

Below Right: Carolyn McCormick, Jennie Israel, Amy Malloy, Lynn Hawley in *Marriage of Figaro*

NATIONAL TOURING COMPANY HIGHLIGHTS

ANGELS IN AMERICA

By Tony Kushner; Director, Michael Mayer; Production Supervisor, George C. Wolfe; Sets, David Gallo; Costumes, Michael Krass; Lighting, Brian MacDevitt; Stage Manager, Tom Guerra; Presented by Jujamcyn Theatres, Mark Taper Forum and Dodger Touring; Press, Laura Matalon; Tour opened in Chicago on September 6, 1994.

CAST

Roy Cohn/Prior II..Jonathan Hadary
Louis Ironson..Peter Birkenhead
Mr. Lies/Belize..Reg Flowers
Harper Pitt/Martin Heller ....Kate Goehring
Joe Pitt/Prior I/Eskimo...................................Philip Earl Johnson
Rabbi/Henry/Hannah Pitt/Ethel Rosenberg ....Barbara Robertson
Prior Walter/Man in Park ....Robert Stella
Emily/Ella Chapter/Angel/So. Bronx Woman....................Carolyn Swift
UNDERSTUDIES: Demitri Corbin (Belize), Timothy Hendrickson (Prior/Joe), John Herrera (Cohn/Louis), Carmen Roman (Hannah), Sarah Underwood (Harper/Angel)

Two dramas, *Millennium Approaches* and *Perestroika,* performed in repertory.

Joan Marcus Photo

Peter Birkenhead, Robert Stella in *Angels in America*

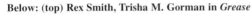

Below: (top) Rex Smith, Trisha M. Gorman in *Grease*

GREASE

For creative credits and musical numbers see Broadway Calendar

CAST

Miss Lynch ....Sally Struthers +1
Patty Simcox...Melissa Papp
Eugene Florczyk...Christopher Youngsman
Jan ....Robin Irwin
Marty ....Deirdre O'Neil
Betty Rizzo ....Angela Pupello
Doody ....Scott Beck +2
Roger ....Nick Cavarra +3
Kenickie..Douglas Crawford
Sonny Latierri...Danny Cistone
Frenchy ....Beth Lipari
Sandy Dumbrowski ....Trisha M. Gorman
Danny Zuko ....Rex Smith +4
Vince Fontaine...Davy Jones +5
Cha-Cha..Jennifer Cody +6
Teen Angel...Kevin-Anthony

A new production of the 1972 musical.

+Succeeded by: 1. Dody Goodman 2. Ric Ryder 3. Erick Buckley 4. Adrian Zmed 5. Micky Dolenz 6. Michelle Bombacie

HELLO DOLLY

Music/Lyrics, Jerry Herman; Book, Michael Stewart; Director/Choreographer, Lee Roy Reams; Associate Choreographer, Bill Bateman; Musical Director, Tim Stella; Sets, Oliver Smith; Lighting, Ken Billington; Costumes, Jonathan Bixby; Sound, Peter J. Fitzgerald; Production Supervisor, Jerry Herman; Stage Manager, Thomas P. Carr; Presented by Manny Kladitis, Magic Promotions and Theatricals, and PACE Theatrical; Press, Chris Boneau/Adrian Bryan-Brown/Dennis Crowley; Tour opened in Denver, July, 1994.

CAST

Mrs. Dolly Gallagher Levi	Carol Channing
Ernestina	Monica M. Wemitt
Ambrose Kemper	James Darrah
Horse	Sharon Moore, Michele Tibbitts
Horace Vandergelder	Jay Garner
Ermengarde	Christine DeVito
Cornelius Hackl	Michael DeVries +1
Barnaby Tucker	Cory English
Minnie Fay	Lori Ann Mahl
Irene Malloy	Florence Lacey
Mrs. Rose	Elizabeth Green
Danny	Julian Brightman
Rudolph	Steve Pudenz
Judge	Bill Bateman
Clerk	Halden Michaels

COMPANY: Joahn Bantay, Desta Barbieri, Kimberly Bellmann, Bruce Blanchard, Stephen Bourneuf, Holly Cruikshank, Simone Gee, Jason Gillman, Milica Govich, Elizabeth Green, Donald Ives, Dan LoBuono, Jim Madden, Halden Michaels, Michael Quinn, Robert Randle, Mitch Rosengarten, Mary Setrakian, Clarence M. Sheridan, Randy Slovacek, Roger Preston Smith, Ashley Stover SWINGS: Jennifer Joan Joy, Matthew A. Sipress

UNDERSTUDIES: Florence Lacey (Dolly), Julian Brightman (Barnaby), Jim Madden (Cornelius), Steve Pudenz (Vandergelder), Mary Setrakian (Irene), Christine DeVito (Minnie), Dan LoBuono (Ambrose), Michele Tibbitts (Ermengarde), Elizabeth Green (Ernestina), Halden Michaels (Judge), Roger Preston Smith (Rudolph/Clerk), Milica Govich (Mrs. Rose)

MUSICAL NUMBERS: Overture, I Put My Hand In, It Takes a Woman, Put On Your Sunday Clothes, Ribbons Down My Back, Motherhood, Dancing, Before the Parade Passes By, Elegance, Waiter's Gallop, Hello Dolly, Polka Contest, It Only Takes a Moment, So Long Dearie, Finale

A new production of the 1964 musical.

+Succeeded by: 1. Jim Walton during vacation

Joan Marcus Photos

Top: Carol Channing

Right: Jay Garner, Carol Channing

KISS OF THE SPIDER WOMAN

For creative credits and musical numbers, see Broadway—Opened Past Seasons section; Presented by Livent (U.S.); Press, Mary Bryant

PRINCIPAL CAST

Molina..Juan Chioran +1
Warden ....Mark Zimmerman
Valentin...John Dossett +2
Spider Woman/Aurora ....Chita Rivera +3
Molina's Mother ....Rita Gardner
Marta ....Juliet Lambert

A musical set in Latin America.

+Succeeded by: 1. Jeff Hyslop 2. Dorian Harewood 3. Carol Lawrence, Chita Rivera

Catherine Ashmore Photo

Top: Chita Rivera and male ensemble

Right: Jeff Hyslop

187

THE WHO'S TOMMY

For creative credits and musical numbers see Broadway—Opened Past Seasons section; Musical Director, Wendy Bobbitt; Company Manager, Alan Ross Kosher; Production Stage Manager, Randall Whitescarver; Presented by PACE Theatrical Group and DODGER Productions; Press, Laura Matalon, Ginny Ehrich, Tim Choy, Wayne McWorter; Tour opened in Dallas' Music Hall on October 12, 1993.

CAST

Mrs. Walker	Jessica Molaskey +1
Capt. Walker	Jason Workman +2
Uncle Ernie	William Youmans +3
Minister	Daniel Marcus
Minister's Wife	Bertilla Baker
Nurse	Aiko Nakasone
Officer #1	Destan Owens
Officer #2	Steve Dahlem
Allied Soldier #1	Chris Ghelfi
Allied Soldier #2	Darrian C. Ford
Lover/Harmonica Player	Alec Timmerman
Tommy, age 4	Kelly Mady, Caitlin Newman, Rachel Ben Levenson
Tommy	Steve Isaacs
Judge/Kevin's father/Vendor/D.J.	Tom Rocco
Tommy, age 10	Robert Mann Kayser +4
Cousin Kevin	Roger Bart +5
Kevin's Mother	Betsy Allen
Local Lads/Security Guards	Mr. Timmerman, Mr. Ford, Mr. Ghelfi, Anthony Galde, Clarke Thorell, Mr. Dahlem
Local Lasses	Hilary Morse, Ms. Nakasone, Valerie DePena, Carla Renata Williams, Cindi Klinger, Ms. Allen
Hawker/Specialist	Destam Owens
The Gypsy	Kennya Ramsey
1st Pinball Lad	Anthony Galde
2nd Pinball Lad	Clarke Thorell
Specialist's Assistant	Valerie DePena
Sally Simpson	Hilary Morse
Mrs. Simpson	Cindi Klinger
Mr. Simpson	Daniel Marcus
Other Ensemble	Bertilla Baker

UNDERSTUDIES: Chris Gelfi, Alec Timermann (Tommy/Kevin), Craig Lawlor (Tommy at 10), Bertilla Baker, Christy Tarr (Mrs. Walker), Steve Dahlem, Vincent D'Elia (Capt. Walker), Daniel Marcus, Tom Rocco (Ernie), Tracey Langran, Carla Renata Williams (Gypsy) SWINGS: Vincent D'Elia, Tracey Langran, Christy Tarr, Randy Wojcik

A musical based based on the 1969 concept album.

Succeeded by: 1. Christy Tarr 2. Jordan Leeds 3. Stephen Lee Anderson 4. Brett Levenson

Marcus/Bryan Brown Photos

Top: Anthony Galde, Roger Bart, Clarke Thorell

Right: Jessica Molaskey, Jason Workman

1995 THEATRE WORLD AWARD RECIPIENTS
(Outstanding New Talent)

GRETHA BOSTON
of *Show Boat*

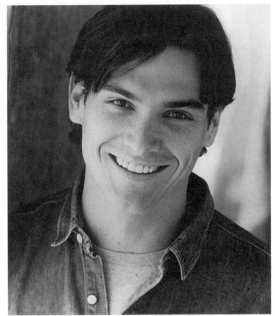

BILLY CRUDUP
of *Arcadia*

RALPH FIENNES
of *Hamlet*

BEVERLY D'ANGELO
of *Simpatico*

189

CALISTA FLOCKHART
of *The Glass Menagerie*

KEVIN KILNER
of *The Glass Menagerie*

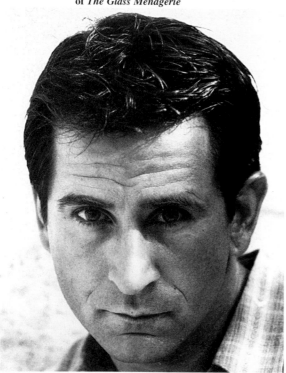

ANTHONY LAPAGLIA
of *The Rose Tattoo*

JULIE JOHNSON
of *Das Barbecu*

HELEN MIRREN
of *A Month in the Country*

JUDE LAW
of *Indiscretions*

RUFUS SEWELL
of *Translations*

VANESSA WILLIAMS
of *Kiss of the Spider Woman*

Julie Andrews

Alec Baldwin

Elizabeth McGovern

PREVIOUS THEATRE WORLD AWARD WINNERS

1944-45: Betty Comden, Richard Davis, Richard Hart, Judy Holliday, Charles Lang, Bambi Linn, John Lund, Donald Murphy, Nancy Noland, Margaret Phillips, John Raitt
1945-46: Barbara Bel Geddes, Marlon Brando, Bill Callahan, Wendell Corey, Paul Douglas, Mary James, Burt Lancaster, Patricia Marshall, Beatrice Pearson
1946-47: Keith Andes, Marion Bell, Peter Cookson, Ann Crowley, Ellen Hanley, John Jordan, George Keane, Dorothea MacFarland, James Mitchell, Patricia Neal, David Wayne
1947-48: Valerie Bettis, Edward Bryce, Whitfield Connor, Mark Dawson, June Lockhart, Estelle Loring, Peggy Maley, Ralph Meeker, Meg Mundy, Douglass Watson, James Whitmore, Patrice Wymore
1948-49: Tod Andrews, Doe Avedon, Jean Carson, Carol Channing, Richard Derr, Julie Harris, Mary McCarty, Allyn Ann McLerie, Cameron Mitchell, Gene Nelson, Byron Palmer, Bob Scheerer
1949-50: Nancy Andrews, Phil Arthur, Barbara Brady, Lydia Clarke, Priscilla Gillette, Don Hanmer, Marcia Henderson, Charlton Heston, Rick Jason, Grace Kelly, Charles Nolte, Roger Price
1950-51: Barbara Ashley, Isabel Bigley, Martin Brooks, Richard Burton, Pat Crowley, James Daley, Cloris Leachman, Russell Nype, Jack Palance, William Smithers, Maureen Stapleton, Marcia Van Dyke, Eli Wallach
1951-52: Tony Bavaar, Patricia Benoit, Peter Conlow, Virginia de Luce, Ronny Graham, Audrey Hepburn, Diana Herbert, Conrad Janis, Dick Kallman, Charles Proctor, Eric Sinclair, Kim Stanley, Marian Winters, Helen Wood
1952-53: Edie Adams, Rosemary Harris, Eileen Heckart, Peter Kelley, John Kerr, Richard Kiley, Gloria Marlowe, Penelope Munday, Paul Newman, Sheree North, Geraldine Page, John Stewart, Ray Stricklyn, Gwen Verdon
1953-54: Orson Bean, Harry Belafonte, James Dean, Joan Diener, Ben Gazzara, Carol Haney, Jonathan Lucas, Kay Medford, Scott Merrill, Elizabeth Montgomery, Leo Penn, Eva Marie Saint

1954-55: Julie Andrews, Jacqueline Brookes, Shirl Conway, Barbara Cook, David Daniels, Mary Fickett, Page Johnson, Loretta Leversee, Jack Lord, Dennis Patrick, Anthony Perkins, Christopher Plummer
1955-56: Diane Cilento, Dick Davalos, Anthony Franciosa, Andy Griffith, Laurence Harvey, David Hedison, Earle Hyman, Susan Johnson, John Michael King, Jayne Mansfield, Sara Marshall, Gaby Rodgers, Susan Strasberg, Fritz Weaver
1956-57: Peggy Cass, Sydney Chaplin, Sylvia Daneel, Bradford Dillman, Peter Donat, George Grizzard, Carol Lynley, Peter Palmer, Jason Robards, Cliff Robertson, Pippa Scott, Inga Swenson
1957-58: Anne Bancroft, Warren Berlinger, Colleen Dewhurst, Richard Easton, Tim Everett, Eddie Hodges, Joan Hovis, Carol Lawrence, Jacqueline McKeever, Wynne Miller, Robert Morse, George C. Scott
1958-59: Lou Antonio, Ina Balin, Richard Cross, Tammy Grimes, Larry Hagman, Dolores Hart, Roger Mollien, France Nuyen, Susan Oliver, Ben Piazza, Paul Roebling, William Shatner, Pat Suzuki, Rip Torn
1959-60: Warren Beatty, Eileen Brennan, Carol Burnett, Patty Duke, Jane Fonda, Anita Gillette, Elisa Loti, Donald Madden, George Maharis, John McMartin, Lauri Peters, Dick Van Dyke
1960-61: Joyce Bulifant, Dennis Cooney, Sandy Dennis, Nancy Dussault, Robert Goulet, Joan Hackett, June Harding, Ron Husmann, James MacArthur, Bruce Yarnell
1961-62: Elizabeth Ashley, Keith Baxter, Peter Fonda, Don Galloway, Sean Garrison, Barbara Harris, James Earl Jones, Janet Margolin, Karen Morrow, Robert Redford, John Stride, Brenda Vaccaro
1962-63: Alan Arkin, Stuart Damon, Melinda Dillon, Robert Drivas, Bob Gentry, Dorothy Loudon, Brandon Maggart, Julienne Marie, Liza Minnelli, Estelle Parsons, Diana Sands, Swen Swenson
1963-64: Alan Alda, Gloria Bleezarde, Imelda De Martin, Claude Giraud, Ketty Lester, Barbara Loden, Lawrence Pressman, Gilbert Price, Philip Proctor, John Tracy,

Timothy Daly

Kathleen Turner

Jason Workman

Lester, Barbara Loden, Lawrence Pressman, Gilbert Price, Philip Proctor, John Tracy, Jennifer West

1964-65: Carolyn Coates, Joyce Jillson, Linda Lavin, Luba Lisa, Michael O'Sullivan, Joanna Pettet, Beah Richards, Jaime Sanchez, Victor Spinetti, Nicolas Surovy, Robert Walker, Clarence Williams III

1965-66: Zoe Caldwell, David Carradine, John Cullum, John Davidson, Faye Dunaway, Gloria Foster, Robert Hooks, Jerry Lanning, Richard Mulligan, April Shawhan, Sandra Smith, Leslie Ann Warren

1966-67: Bonnie Bedelia, Richard Benjamin, Dustin Hoffman, Terry Kiser, Reva Rose, Robert Salvio, Sheila Smith, Connie Stevens, Pamela Tiffin, Leslie Uggams, Jon Voight, Christopher Walken

1967-68: David Birney, Pamela Burrell, Jordan Christopher, Jack Crowder (Thalmus Rasulala), Sandy Duncan, Julie Gregg, Stephen Joyce, Bernadette Peters, Alice Playten, Michael Rupert, Brenda Smiley, Russ Thacker

1968-69: Jane Alexander, David Cryer, Blythe Danner, Ed Evanko, Ken Howard, Lauren Jones, Ron Leibman, Marian Mercer, Jill O'Hara, Ron O'Neal, Al Pacino, Marlene Warfield

1969-70: Susan Browning, Donny Burks, Catherine Burns, Len Cariou, Bonnie Franklin, David Holliday, Katharine Houghton, Melba Moore, David Rounds, Lewis J. Stadlen, Kristoffer Tabori, Fredricka Weber

1970-71: Clifton Davis, Michael Douglas, Julie Garfield, Martha Henry, James Naughton, Tricia O'Neil, Kipp Osborne, Roger Rathburn, Ayn Ruymen, Jennifer Salt, Joan Van Ark, Walter Willison

1971-72: Jonelle Allen, Maureen Anderman, William Atherton, Richard Backus, Adrienne Barbeau, Cara Duff-MacCormick, Robert Foxworth, Elaine Joyce, Jess Richards, Ben Vereen, Beatrice Winde, James Woods

1972-73: D'Jamin Bartlett, Patricia Elliott, James Farentino, Brian Farrell, Victor Garber, Kelly Garrett, Mari Gorman, Laurence Guittard, Trish Hawkins, Monte Markham, John Rubinstein, Jennifer Warren, Alexander H. Cohen (Special Award)

1973-74: Mark Baker, Maureen Brennan, Ralph Carter, Thom Christopher, John Driver, Conchata Ferrell, Ernestine Jackson, Michael Moriarty, Joe Morton, Ann Reinking, Janie Sell, Mary Woronov, Sammy Cahn (Special Award)

1974-75: Peter Burnell, Zan Charisse, Lola Falana, Peter Firth, Dorian Harewood, Joel Higgins, Marcia McClain, Linda Miller, Marti Rolph, John Sheridan, Scott Stevensen, Donna Theodore, Equity Library Theatre (Special Award)

1975-76: Danny Aiello, Christine Andreas, Dixie Carter, Tovah Feldshuh, Chip Garnett, Richard Kelton, Vivian Reed, Charles Repole, Virginia Seidel, Daniel Seltzer, John V. Shea, Meryl Streep, A Chorus Line (Special Award)

1976-77: Trazana Beverley, Michael Cristofer, Joe Fields, Joanna Gleason, Cecilia Hart, John Heard, Gloria Hodes, Juliette Koka, Andrea McArdle, Ken Page, Jonathan Pryce, Chick Vennera, Eva LeGallienne (Special Award)

1977-78: Vasili Bogazianos, Nell Carter, Carlin Glynn, Christopher Goutman, William Hurt, Judy Kaye, Florence Lacy, Armelia McQueen, Gordana Rashovich, Bo Rucker, Richard Seer, Colin Stinton, Joseph Papp (Special Award)

1978-79: Philip Anglim, Lucie Arnaz, Gregory Hines, Ken Jennings, Michael Jeter, Laurie Kennedy, Susan Kingsley, Christine Lahti, Edward James Olmos, Kathleen Quinlan, Sarah Rice, Max Wright, Marshall W. Mason (Special Award)

1979-80: Maxwell Caulfield, Leslie Denniston, Boyd Gaines, Richard Gere, Harry Groener, Stephen James, Susan Kellermann, Dinah Manoff, Lonny Price, Marianne Tatum, Anne Twomey, Dianne Wiest, Mickey Rooney (Special Award)

1980-81: Brian Backer, Lisa Banes, Meg Bussert, Michael Allen Davis, Giancarlo Esposito, Daniel Gerroll, Phyllis Hyman, Cynthia Nixon, Amanda Plummer, Adam Redfield, Wanda Richert, Rex Smith, Elizabeth Taylor (Special Award)

1981-82: Karen Akers, Laurie Beechman, Danny Glover, David Alan Grier, Jennifer Holliday, Anthony Heald, Lizbeth Mackay, Peter MacNicol, Elizabeth McGovern, Ann Morrison, Michael O'Keefe, James Widdoes, Manhattan Theatre Club (Special Award)

1982-83: Karen Allen, Suzanne Bertish, Matthew Broderick, Kate Burton, Joanne Camp, Harvey Fierstein, Peter Gallagher, John Malkovich, Anne Pitoniak, James Russo, Brian Tarantina, Linda Thorson, Natalia Makarova (Special Award)

1983-84: Martine Allard, Joan Allen, Kathy Whitton Baker, Mark Capri, Laura Dean, Stephen Geoffreys, Todd Graff, Glenne Headly, J.J. Johnston, Bonnie Koloc, Calvin Levels, Robert Westenberg, Ron Moody (Special Award)

1984-85: Kevin Anderson, Richard Chaves, Patti Cohenour, Charles S. Dutton, Nancy Giles, Whoopi Goldberg, Leilani Jones, John Mahoney, Laurie Metcalf, Barry Miller, John Turturro, Amelia White, Lucille Lortel (Special Award)

1985-86: Suzy Amis, Alec Baldwin, Aled Davies, Faye Grant, Julie Hagerty, Ed Harris, Mark Jacoby, Donna Kane, Cleo Laine, Howard McGillin, Marisa Tomei, Joe Urla, Ensemble Studio Theatre (Special Award)

1986-87: Annette Bening, Timothy Daly, Lindsay Duncan, Frank Ferrante, Robert Lindsay, Amy Madigan, Michael Maguire, Demi Moore, Molly Ringwald, Frances Ruffelle, Courtney B. Vance, Colm Wilkinson, Robert DeNiro (Special Award)

1987-88: Yvonne Bryceland, Philip Casnoff, Danielle Ferland, Melissa Gilbert, Linda Hart, Linzi Hately, Brian Kerwin, Brian Mitchell, Mary Murfitt, Aidan Quinn, Eric Roberts, B.D. Wong, Special Awards: Tisa Chang, Martin E. Segal.

1988-89: Dylan Baker, Joan Cusack, Loren Dean, Peter Frechette, Sally Mayes, Sharon McNight, Jennie Moreau, Paul Provenza, Kyra Sedgwick, Howard Spiegel, Eric Stoltz, Joanne Whalley-Kilmer, Special Awards: Pauline Collins, Mikhail Baryshnikov

1989-90: Denise Burse, Erma Campbell, Rocky Carroll, Megan Gallagher, Tommy Hollis, Robert Lambert, Kathleen Rowe McAllen, Michael McKean, Crista Moore, Mary-Louise Parker, Daniel von Bargen, Jason Workman, Special Awards: Stewart Granger, Kathleen Turner

1990-91: Jane Adams, Gillian Anderson, Adam Arkin, Brenda Blethyne, Marcus Chong, Paul Hipp, LaChanze, Kenny Neal, Kevin Ramsey, Francis Ruivivar, Lea Salonga, Chandra Wilson, Special Awards: Tracey Ullman, Ellen Stewart

1991-92: Talia Balsam, Lindsay Crouse, Griffin Dunne, Larry Fishburne, Mel Harris, Jonathan Kaplan, Jessica Lange, Laura Linney, Spiro Malas, Mark Rosenthal, Helen Shaver, Al White, Special Awards: *Dancing at Lughnasa* company, *Plays for Living.*

1992-93: Brent Carver, Michael Cerveris, Marcia Gay Harden, Stephanie Lawrence, Andrea Martin, Liam Neeson, Stephen Rea, Natasha Richardson, Martin Short, Dina Spybey, Stephen Spinella, Jennifer Tilly. Special Awards: John Leguizamo, Rosetta LeNoire.

1993-94: Marcus D'Amico, Jarrod Emick, Arabella Field, Adam Gillett, Sherry Glaser, Michael Hayden, Margaret Illman, Audra Ann McDonald, Burke Moses, Anna Deavere Smith, Jere Shea, Harriet Walter.

Brooke Shields of *Grease* (Special Theatre World Award 1995)

THEATRE WORLD AWARDS

Presented in the Roundabout Theatre on Monday, May 22, 1995.

Top: Patricia Elliott, Jennifer Holliday, Cynthia Nixon, Maxwell Caulfield, Juliette Koka, Victor Garber; Fredricka Weber; John McMartin, Dorothy Loudon, B.D. Wong, Nancy Giles, Ken Howard, Dinah Manoff, Alec Baldwin

Below: Dorothy Loudon, Ralph Fiennes; Rufus Sewell, Juliette Koka; Helen Mirren, Kevin Kilner, Julie Johnson, Ralph Fiennes, Gretha Boston, Billy Crudup, Rufus Sewell

Third Row: Dorothy Loudon, B.D. Wong, Nancy Giles; Julie Johnson, Kevin Kilner; Ken Howard, Dinah Manoff, Alec Baldwin

Bottom: Victor Garber, Alec Baldwin; Anthony LaPaglia, Helen Mirren, Kevin Kilner; Jennifer Holliday, Dorothy Loudon

Photos by Michael Riordan, Michael Viade, Peter Warrick, Jack Williams, Van Williams

Top: Billy Crudup, Victor Garber; Cynthia Nixon; John McMartin, Gretha Boston, Harry Groener; Ralph Fiennes

Below: Mr. and Mrs. Len Cariou; Patricia Elliott; Anthony LaPaglia, Helen Mirren; Fredricka Weber

Third Row: Parents of Vanessa Williams accepting for her; Jude Law; Mr. and Mrs. Michael Hayden; Howard McGillin; Jennifer Holliday, Maxwell Caulfield

Botom Row: Lee Kirk, Ken Page, Ernestine Jackson; Dinah Manoff, Alec Baldwin; Ralph Fiennes; Jordan Baker, Kevin Kilner

Photos by Michael Riordan, Michael Viade, Peter Warrick, Jack Williams, Van Williams

PULITZER PRIZE PRODUCTIONS

1918–Why Marry?, 1919–no award, 1920–Beyond the Horizon, 1921–Miss Lulu Bett, 1922–Anna Christie, 1923–Icebound, 1924–Hell-Bent fer Heaven, 1925–They Knew What They Wanted, 1926–Craig's Wife, 1927–In Abraham's Bosom, 1928–Strange Interlude, 1929–Street Scene, 1930–The Green Pastures, 1931–Alison's House, 1932–Of Thee I Sing, 1933–Both Your Houses, 1934–Men in White, 1935–The Old Maid, 1936–Idiot's Delight, 1937–You Can't Take It with You, 1938–Our Town, 1939–Abe Lincoln in Illinois, 1940–The Time of Your Life, 1941–There Shall Be No Night, 1942–no award, 1943–The Skin of Our Teeth, 1944–no award, 1945–Harvey, 1946–State of the Union, 1947–no award, 1948–A Streetcar Named Desire, 1949–Death of a Salesman, 1950–South Pacific, 1951–no award, 1952–The Shrike, 1953–Picnic, 1954–The Teahouse of the August Moon, 1955–Cat on a Hot Tin Roof, 1956–The Diary of Anne Frank, 1957–Long Day's Journey into Night, 1958–Look Homeward, Angel, 1959–J.B., 1960–Fiorello!, 1961–All the Way Home, 1962–How to Succeed in Business without Really Trying, 1963–no award, 1964–no award, 1965–The Subject Was Roses, 1966–no award, 1967–A Delicate Balance, 1968–no award, 1969–The Great White Hope, 1970–No Place to Be Somebody, 1971–The Effect of Gamma Rays on Man-in-the-Moon Marigolds, 1972–no award, 1973–That Championship Season, 1974–no award, 1975–Seascape, 1976–A Chorus Line, 1977–The Shadow Box, 1978–The Gin Game, 1979–Buried Child, 1980–Talley's Folly, 1981–Crimes of the Heart, 1982–A Soldier's Play, 1983–'night, Mother, 1984–Glengarry Glen Ross, 1985–Sunday in the Park with George, 1986–no award, 1987–Fences, 1988–Driving Miss Daisy, 1989–The Heidi Chronicles, 1990–The Piano Lesson, 1991–Lost in Yonkers, 1992–The Kentucky Cycle, 1993–Angels in America: Millenium Approaches, 1994–Three Tall Women, 1995–Young Man from Atlanta

NEW YORK DRAMA CRITICS CIRCLE AWARDS

1936–Winterset, 1937–High Tor, 1938–Of Mice and Men, Shadow and Substance, 1939–The White Steed, 1940–The Time of Your Life, 1941–Watch on the Rhine, The Corn Is Green, 1942–Blithe Spirit, 1943–The Patriots, 1944–Jacobowsky and the Colonel, 1945–The Glass Menagerie, 1946–Carousel, 1947–All My Sons, No Exit, Brigadoon, 1948–A Streetcar Named Desire, The Winslow Boy, 1949–Death of a Salesman, The Madwoman of Chaillot, South Pacific, 1950–The Member of the Wedding, The Cocktail Party, The Consul, 1951–Darkness at Noon, The Lady's Not for Burning, Guys and Dolls, 1952–I Am a Camera, Venus Observed, Pal Joey, 1953–Picnic, The Love of Four Colonels, Wonderful Town, 1954–Teahouse of the August Moon, Ondine, The Golden Apple, 1955–Cat on a Hot Tin Roof, Witness for the Prosecution, The Saint of Bleecker Street, 1956–The Diary of Anne Frank, Tiger at the Gates, My Fair Lady, 1957–Long Day's Journey into Night, The Waltz of the Toreadors, The Most Happy Fella, 1958–Look Homeward Angel, Look Back in Anger, The Music Man, 1959–A Raisin in the Sun, The Visit, La Plume de Ma Tante, 1960–Toys in the Attic, Five Finger Exercise, Fiorello!, 1961–All the Way Home, A Taste of Honey, Carnival, 1962–Night of the Iguana, A Man for All Seasons, How to Succeed in Business without Really Trying, 1963–Who's Afraid of Virginia Woolf?, 1964–Luther, Hello Dolly!, 1965–The Subject Was Roses, Fiddler on the Roof, 1966–The Persecution and Assassination of Marat as Performed by the Inmates of the Asylum of Charenton under the Direction of the Marquis de Sade, Man of La Mancha, 1967–The Homecoming, Cabaret, 1968–Rosencrantz and Guildenstern Are Dead, Your Own Thing, 1969–The Great White Hope, 1776, 1970–The Effect of Gamma Rays on Man-in-the-Moon Marigolds, Borstal Boy, Company, 1971–Home, Follies, The House of Blue Leaves, 1972–That Championship Season, Two Gentlemen of Verona, 1973–The Hot l Baltimore, The Changing Room, A Little Night Music, 1974–The Contractor, Short Eyes, Candide, 1975–Equus, The Taking of Miss Janie, A Chorus Line, 1976–Travesties, Streamers, Pacific Overtures, 1977–Otherwise Engaged, American Buffalo, Annie, 1978–Da, Ain't Misbehavin', 1979–The Elephant Man, Sweeney Todd, 1980–Talley's Folley, Evita, Betrayal, 1981–Crimes of the Heart, A Lesson from Aloes, Special Citation to Lena Horne, The Pirates of Penzance, 1982–The Life and Adventures of Nicholas Nickleby, A Soldier's Play, (no musical), 1983–Brighton Beach Memoirs, Plenty, Little Shop of Horrors, 1984–The Real Thing, Glengarry Glen Ross, Sunday in the Park with George, 1985–Ma Rainey's Black Bottom, (no musical), 1986–A Lie of the Mind, Benefactors, (no musical), Special Citation to Lily Tomlin and Jane Wagner, 1987–Fences, Les Liaisons Dangereuses, Les Misérables, 1988–Joe Turner's Come and Gone, The Road to Mecca, Into the Woods, 1989–The Heidi Chronicles, Aristocrats, Largely New York (Special), (no musical), 1990–The Piano Lesson, City of Angels, Privates on Parade, 1991–Six Degrees of Separation, The Will Rogers Follies, Our Country's Good, Special Citation to Eileen Atkins, 1992–Two Trains Running, Dancing at Lughnasa, 1993–Angels in America: Millenium Approaches, Someone Who'll Watch Over Me, Kiss of the Spider Woman, 1994–Three Tall Women, Anna Deavere Smith (Special), 1995–Arcadia, Love! Valour! Compassion!, Special Award: Signature Theatre Company

AMERICAN THEATRE WING ANTOINETTE PERRY (TONY) AWARD PRODUCTIONS

1948–Mister Roberts, 1949–Death of a Salesman, Kiss Me, Kate, 1950–The Cocktail Party, South Pacific, 1951–The Rose Tattoo, Guys and Dolls, 1952–The Fourposter, The King and I, 1953–The Crucible, Wonderful Town, 1954–The Teahouse of the August Moon, Kismet, 1955–The Desperate Hours, The Pajama Game, 1956–The Diary of Anne Frank, Damn Yankees, 1957–Long Day's Journey into Night, My Fair Lady, 1958–Sunrise at Campobello, The Music Man, 1959–J.B., Redhead, 1960–The Miracle Worker, Fiorello! tied with The Sound of Music, 1961–Becket, Bye Bye Birdie, 1962–A Man for All Seasons, How to Succeed in Business without Really Trying, 1963–Who's Afraid of Virginia Woolf?, A Funny Thing Happened on the Way to the Forum, 1964–Luther, Hello Dolly!, 1965–The Subject Was Roses, Fiddler on the Roof, 1966–The Persecution and Assassination of Marat as Performed by the Inmates of the Asylum of Charenton under the Direction of the Marquis de Sade, Man of La Mancha, 1967–The Homecoming, Cabaret, 1968–Rosencrantz and Guildenstern Are Dead, Hallelujah Baby!, 1969–The Great White Hope, 1776, 1970–Borstal Boy, Applause, 1971–Sleuth, Company, 1972–Sticks and Bones, Two Gentlemen of Verona, 1973–That Championship Season, A Little Night Music, 1974–The River Niger, Raisin, 1975–Equus, The Wiz, 1976–Travesties, A Chorus Line, 1977–The Shadow Box, Annie, 1978–Da, Ain't Misbehavin', 1979–The Elephant Man, Sweeney Todd, 1980–Children of a Lesser God, Evita, Morning's at Seven, 1981–Amadeus, 42nd Street, The Pirates of Penzance, 1982–The Life and Adventures of Nicholas Nickleby, Nine, Othello, 1983–Torch Song Trilogy, Cats, On Your Toes, 1984–The Real Thing, La Cage aux Folles, 1985–Biloxi Blues, Big River, Joe Egg, 1986–I'm Not Rappaport, The Mystery of Edwin Drood, Sweet Charity, 1987–Fences, Les Misérables, All My Sons, 1988–M. Butterfly, The Phantom of the Opera, 1989–The Heidi Chronicles, Jerome Robbins' Broadway, Our Town, Anything Goes, 1990–The Grapes of Wrath, City of Angels, Gypsy, 1991–Lost in Yonkers, The Will Rogers' Follies, Fiddler on the Roof, 1992–Dancing at Lughnasa, Crazy For You, Guys & Dolls, 1993–Angels in America: Millennium Approaches, Kiss of the Spider Woman, 1994–Angels in America: Perestroika, Passion, An Inspector Calls, Carousel, 1995–Love! Valour! Compassion! (play), Sunset Boulevard (musical), Show Boat (musical revival), The Heiress (play revival)

**Above: Terrence McNally (author),
Joe Mantello (director)
of *Love! Valour! Compassion!***

**Left: Rebecca Luker, Lonette McKee
in *Show Boat***

Right: Glenn Close in *Sunset Boulevard*

**Below: Robert Sean Leonard,
Blair Brown in *Arcadia***

F. Murray
Abraham

Eileen Atkins

Howard Atlee

Becky Ann Baker

Darrin Baker

Stockard
Channing

BIOGRAPHICAL DATA ON THIS SEASON'S CASTS

ABRAHAM, F. MURRAY. Born Oct. 24, 1939 in Pittsburgh, PA. Attended U. Tex. Debut 1967 OB in *The Fantasticks* followed by *An Opening in the Trees, 14th Dictator, Young Abe Lincoln, Tonight in Living Color, Adaptation, The Survival of St. Joan, The Dog Ran Away, Fables, Richard III, Little Murders, Scuba Duba, Where Has Tommy Flowers Gone?, Miracle Play, Blessing, Sexual Perversity in Chicago, Landscape of the Body, The Master and Margarita, Biting the Apple, The Sea Gull, The Caretaker, Antigone, Uncle Vanya, The Golem, The Madwoman of Challiot, Twelfth Night, Frankie and Johnny in the Clair de Lune, A Midsummer Night's Dream, A Life in the Theatre,* Bdwy in *The Man in the Glass Booth* (1968), *6 Rms Riv Vu, Bad Habits, The Ritz, Legend, Teibele and Her Demon, Macbeth, Waiting for Godot, Angels in America, Month in the Country.*

ACAYAN, ZAR. Born Jan. 2, 1967 in Manila, PI. Attended UC/Berkeley, UCLA. Bdwy debut 1991 in *Miss Saigon,* OB in *Day Standing on Its Head, Children of Eden, Rita's Resources.*

ACKERMAN, LONI. Born Apr. 10, 1949 in New York City. Attended New School. Bdwy debut 1968 in *George M!,* followed by *No No Nanette, So Long 174th Street, The Magic Show, Evita, Cats,* OB in *Dames at Sea, Starting Here Starting Now, Roberta in Concert, Brownstone, Diamonds, Petrified Prince.*

ADAMS, MASON. Born Feb. 26, 1919 in New York City. Graduate U. Wisc. Bdwy credits include *Get Away Old Man, Public Relations, Career Angel, Violet, Shadow of My Enemy, Tall Story, Inquest, Trial of the Catonsville 9, The Sign in Sidney Brustein's Window,* OB in *Meegan's Game, Shortchanged Review, Checking Out, The Sop Touch, Paradise Lost, The Time of Your Life, Danger: Memory, The Day Room, Rose Quartet, The Ryan Interview.*

ADAMS, POLLY. Born in Nashville, TN. Graduate Stanford U., Columbia U. Bdwy debut 1976 in *Zalmen, or the Madness of God,* OB in *Ordway Ames-gay, The Free Zone, Flyboy.*

ADDISON, BERNARD K. Born Jan. 16, 1993 in Columbia, SC. Graduate USC, UNC. Debut 1995 OB in *Oedipus at Colonus.*

AKO. Born Oct. 18 in Japan. Debut 1986 in *Shogun Macbeth* followed by *Kokoro, Sleeping Beauty.*

ALDREDGE, TOM. Born Feb. 28, 1928 in Dayton, OH. Attended Daton U., Goodman Theatre. Bdwy debut 1959 in *The Nervous Set,* followed by *UTBU, Slapstick Tragedy, Everything in the Garden, Inherit, Engagement Baby, How the Other Half Loves, Sticks and Bones, Where's Charley?, Leaf People, Rex, Vieux Carre, St. Joan, Stages, On Golden Pond, The Little Foxes, Into the Woods, Two Shakespearean Actors,* OB in *The Tempest, Between Two Thieves, Henry V, The Premise, Love's Labour's Lost, Troilus and Cressida, The Butter and Egg Man, Ergo, Boys in the Band, Twelfth Night, Colette, Hamlet, The Orphan, King Lear, The Iceman Cometh, Black Angel, Getting Along Famously, Fool for Love, Neon Psalms, Richard II, The Last Yankee, Incommunicado.*

ALEXANDER, TERRY. Born Mar. 23, 1959 in Detroit, MI. Graduate Wayne State U. Bdwy debut 1971 in *No Place to Be Somebody,* OB in *Rashomon, The Glass Menagerie, Breakout, Naami Court, Streamers, Julius Caesar, Nongogo, Sus, Playboy of the West Indies, Dancing on the Moonlight.*

ALICE, MARY. Born Dec. 3, 1941 in Indianola, MS. Debut 1967 OB in *Trials of Brother Jero* followed by *The Strong Breed, Duplex, Thoughts, Miss Julie, House Party, Terraces, Heaven and Hell's Agreement, In the Deepest Part of Sleep, Cockfight, Julius Caesar, Nongogo, Second Thoughts, Spell #7, Zooman and the Sign, Glasshouse, The Ditch, Take Me Along, Departures, Marathon '80, Richard III, Watermelon Rinds,* Bdwy in *No Place to be Somebody* (1971), *Fences, Shadow Box, Having Our Say.*

ALLEN, DOMINICK. Born Oct. 5, 1958 in Glasgow, Scot. Attended Royal Scottish Academy of Music & Drama. Bdwy debut 1995 in *Blood Brothers.*

ALLEN, STEVE. Born in New York City Dec. 26, 1921. Attended Az. State Col., Drake U. Bdwy debut 1953 in *Pink Elephant* followed by OB in *Mikado* (1995).

ALLER, JOHN. Born July 5, 1957 in Cuba. Graduate Hofstra U. Debut 1985 OB in *Pacific Overtures* followed by *Encore, Miami,* Bdwy in *Rags* (1985), *Chess, Kiss of the Spiderwoman.*

ALLISON, PATTI. Born June 26, 1942 in St. Louis, MO. Graduate Webster Col., Ind. U. Bdwy debut 1978 in *Angel* followed by *Orpheus Descending,* OB in *Brimstone, Public Enemy.*

ALONSO, MARIA CONCHITA. Born June 26, 1957 in Cienfuegos, Cuba. Attended schools in Venezuela and Switzerland. Bdwy debut 1995 in *Kiss of the Spiderwoman.*

ALTAY, DERIN. Born Nov. 10, 1954 in Chicago, IL. Attended Goodman Sch., Am. Consv. Bdwy debut 1981 in *Evita* followed by *Show Boat.*

AMBROSE, JOE. Born Apr. 7, 1931 in Chicago, IL. Graduate Rutgers U., AADA, Columbia U. Debut 1986 OB in *Buried Child* followed by *Diary of a Scoundrel, The Crucible, Hotel Paradiso,* Bdwy in *An Inspector Calls* (1994).

AMERSON, TAMMY. Born Aug. 21, 1969 in Charleston, SC. Bdwy debut 1981 in *Evita* followed by *Show Boat* (1994).

ANDERSON, FRED. Born July 11, 1964 in Memphis, TN. Attended NC Sch. of Arts, Joffrey Ballet Sch. Debut 1988 OB in *Lost in the Stars,* followed by *Telltale Hearts,* Bdwy in *Crazy for You* (1992).

ANDRÉS, BARBARA. Born Feb. 11, 1939 in New York City. Graduate Catholic U. Bdwy debut 1969 in *Jimmy,* followed by *The Boy Friend, Rodgers and Hart, Rex, On Golden Pond, Doonesbury, Kiss of the Spiderwoman,* OB in *Threepenny Opera, Landscape of the Body, Harold Arlen's Cabaret, Suzanna Andler, One-Act Festival, Company, Marathon '87, Arms and the Man, A Woman Without a Name, First is Supper, Fore!*

ANDREWS, GEORGE LEE. Born Oct. 13, 1942 in Milwaukee, WI. Debut OB in *Jacques Brel Is Alive and Well...,* followed by *Starting Here Starting Now, Vamps and Rideouts, The Fantasticks,* Bdwy in *A Little Night Music* (1973), *On the 20th Century, Merlin, The Phantom of the Opera, A Little Night Music* (NYCO).

APPEL, PETER. Born Oct. 19, 1959 in New York City. Graduate Brandeis U. Debut 1987 OB in *Richard II* followed by *Henry IV Part I, Midsummer Night's Dream, Saved from Obscurity, Titus Andronicus, Taming of the Shrew, Good Times are Killing Me, Him.*

ARGETSINGER, GETCHIE. Born Oct. 29, 1947 in Youngstown, OH. Attended St. Bonaventure U, U. Grenobile. Debut 1981 OB in *Italian Straw*

Hat followed by *Kathy and Moe Show* (1995).

ARLT, LEWIS. Born Dec. 5, 1949 in Kinston, NY. Graduate Carnegie Tech. Bdwy debut 1975 in *Murder Among Friends* followed by *Piaf, Orpheus Descending, Blithe Spirit, Benefactors, The Real Thing, Indiscretions,* OB in *War and Peace, Misanthrope, Fallen Angels, Ethan Frome, The Interview, Mutual Benefit Life, Applause, House across the Street, Real Estate.*

ARNOLD, JEANNE. Born July 30 in Berkeley, CA. Graduate U. Cal. Debut 1955 OB in *Threepenny Opera* followed by *Take Five, Demi-Dozen-Medium Rare, Put It In Writing, Beggar's Opera, Marry Me! Marry Me!, Valentine's Day, Deja Revue,* Bdwy in *Happy Time, Coco.*

ASHER, LAWRENCE. Born July 30, 1948 in Cleveland, OH. Graduate Stanford, Yale. Debut 1974 OB in *The Proposition* followed by *Rise of David Levinsky, Once/Twice,* Bdwy in *Most Happy Fella* (1979).

ASQUITH, WARD. Born Mar. 21 in Philadelphia, PA. Graduate U. Pa., Columbia U. Debut 1979 OB in *After the Rise* followed by *Kind Lady, Incident at Vichy, Happy Birthday Wanda June, Another Part of the Forest, Little Foxes, Sherlock Holmes & the Hands of Othello, Macbeth, Real Inspector Hound, Uncle Vanya, Cyrano de Bergerac, What the Butler Saw, The Professional.*

ATKINS, EILEEN. Born June 16, 1934 in London, Eng. Attended Guildhall Schl. Bdwy debut 1966 in *The Killing of Sister George,* followed by *The Promise, Viva! Viva! Regina!, The Night of the Tribades, Indiscretions,* OB in *Prin, A Room of One's Own, Vita and Virginia.*

ATKINSON, JAYNE. Born Feb. 18, 1959 in Bournemouth, Engl. Graduate Northwestern U., Yale. Debut 1986 OB in *Bloody Poetry,* followed by *Terminal Bar, Return of Pinocchio, The Art of Success, The Way of the World, Appointment with a High Wire Lady, Why We Have a Body,* Bdwy in *All My Sons* (1987).

ATLEE, HOWARD. Born May 14, 1926 in Bucyrus, OH. Graduate Emerson Col. Debut 1990 OB in *Historical Productions,* followed by *The 15th Ward, The Hells of Dante, What a Royal Pain in the Farce, Rimers of Eldtrich, Dream Alliance, Vampyr Theatre, Captain!, Tiny Closets.*

AUBLE, LARISSA. Born Jan. 18, 1985 in Newark, NJ. Debut 1993 OB in *Annie Warbucks,* Bdwy in *Show Boat* (1994).

AUERBACH, MARK. Born Sept. 4, 1967 in New York City. Graduate Niagra U. Debut 1994 OB in *Hey Buddy.*

AUGUSTINE, JOHN. Born Mar. 5, 1960 in Canton, OH. Attended Baldwin-White Col. Debut in 1988 OB in *Young Playwrights Festival '88,* followed by *Insatiable/Temporary People, A Walk on Lake Erie, Marathon '91, Seven Blowjobs, Gin and Bitters, Durang Durang.*

AVNER, JON. Born June 24, 1953 in New York City. Graduate Syracuse U., St. John's U. Debut 1986 OB in *Murder on Broadway,* followed by *Radio Roast, Crimes of Passion, World of Sholem Aleichem, Penguin Blues, Rasputin, Sarah, Currents Turned Awry, Gift Horse.*

BAGNERIS, VERNEL. Born July 31, 1949 in New Orleans, LA. Graduate Xavier U. Debut 1979 OB in *One Mo' Time,* followed by *Staggerlee, Further Mo', Jelly Roll Morton: A Me-Morial, Jelly Roll Morton: Hoo Dude, Jelly Roll,* all of which he wrote.

BAILEY, ADRIAN. Born Sept. 23, in Detroit, MI. Graduate U. Detroit. Bdwy debut 1976 in *Your Arms Too Short to Box with God,* followed by *Prince of Central Park, Jelly's Last Jam, Smokey Joe's Cafe,* OB in *A Thrill a Moment, Johnny Pye.*

BAIRD, JUDY. Born June 23, 1953 in New York City. Attended Queen's College, Pace U. Bdwy debut 1994 in *An Inspector Calls.*

BAKER, BECKY ANN (formerly Gelke). Born Feb. 17, 1953 in Ft. Knox, KY. Graduate Wky. U. Bdwy debut 1978 in *The Best Little Whorehouse in Texas* followed by *A Streetcar Named Desire* (1988), OB in *Altitude Sickness, John Brown's Body, Chamber Music, To Whom It May Concern, Two Gentlemen of Verona, Bob's Guns, Buzzsaw Berkeley, Colorado Catechism, Jeremy Rudge, Laura Dennis.*

BAKER, DARRIN. Born May 7, 1965 in Toronto, Can. Attended Center for Actors. Bdwy debut 1994 in *Sunset Blvd.*

BAKER, DAVID AARON. Born Aug. 14, 1963 in Durham, NC. Graduate U. Tex., Juilliard. Bdwy debut 1993 in *White Liars/Black Comedy* followed by *Abe Lincoln in Illinois, Flowering Peach, Molière Comedies,* OB in *Richard III, 110 in the Shade* (NYCO), *Durang Durang.*

BAKER, ROBERT MICHAEL. Born Feb. 28, 1954 in Boston, MA. Attended Boston U., AADA. Debut 1984 OB in *Jessie's Land* followed by *Enter Laughing, Happily Ever After, Company, The Education of Hyman Kaplan, Yiddle with a Fiddle, Carnival, Decline of the Middle West, That's Life!* Bdwy in *Guys and Dolls* (1992).

BALL, JERRY. Born Dec. 16, 1956 in New Lexington, OH. Graduate Capitol U., NYU. Debut 1995 OB in *Buk—Life and Times of Charles Bukowski.*

BAMFORD, GEORGE. Born Nov. 6, 1944 in Dundalk, MD. Attended Frostberg State Col., AADA, Peabody Cons. Debut 1973 OB in *Anna K.* followed by *The Kid, Killer's Head, Yanks 3 Detroit 0, Sweet Bird of Youth, Quick Bright Things, Night Seasons.*

BAMMAN, GERRY. Born Sept. 18, 1941 in Independence, KS. Graduate Xavier U., NYU. Debut 1970 OB in *Alice in Wonderland* followed by *All Night Long, Richard III, Oedipus Rex, Midsummer Night's Dream, He and She, Johnny on the Spot, Museum, Henry V, Our Late Night, Sea Gull, Endgame, Road,* Bdwy in *Accidental Death of an Anarchist* (1984), *Execution of Justice, Uncle Vanya.*

BANES, LISA. Born July 9, 1955 in Chagrin Falls, OH. Graduate Julliard. Debut 1980 OB in *Elizabeth I* followed by *Call from the East, Look Back in Anger* for which she received a Theatre World Award, *My Sister in This House, Antigone, Three Sisters, Cradle Will Rock, Isn't It Romantic, Fighting International Fat, Ten By Tennessee, On the Verge, Emily,* Bdwy in *Rumors* (1988), *Arcadia.*

BARBER, ELLEN. Born in Aug. in Brooklyn, NY. Graduate Bard Col. Debut 1970 OB in *Mod Donna* followed by *Moonchildren, Apple Pie, Funeral March for a One Man Band, Starluster, Awake and Sing, Occupations, Poor Murderer, Pantagleize, Modern Ladies of Guanabacoa, Poisoner of the Wells, Souvenirs, Heaven, Shlemel the First, Knepp, Henry VI,* Bdwy in *Good Doctor* (1973), *Fame.*

BARCROFT, JUDITH. Born July 6 in Washington, D.C. Attended Northwestern U., Stephens Col. Bdwy debut 1965 in *The Mating Game* followed by *Dinner at 8, Plaza Suite, All God's Chillun Got Wings, Betrayal, Elephant Man, Shimada,* OB in *M. Amilcar, Cloud 9, For Sale, Songs of Twilight, Solitaire/Double Solitaire, Breaking the Prairie Wolf Code, Rough for Theatre II, Play, The Choice.*

BARKER, JEAN. Born Dec. 20 in Philadelphia, PA. Attended U. PA, Am. Th. Wing. Debut 1953 OB in *The Bold Soprano* followed by *Night Shift, A Month in the Country, Portrait of Jenny, About Iris Berman, Goodnight Grandpa, Victory Bonds, Cabbagehead, Oklahoma Samovar, Titus Andronicus, Flags Unfurled,* Bdwy in *The Innkeepers* (1956), *Prisoner of Second Avenue, Tchin Tchin, The Inspector General.*

BARNES, PATRICK. Born Sept. 13, 1961 in Columbus, OH. Graduate Oh. State U. Debut 1987 OB in *Blue is for Boys* followed by *Soul Survivor, Them Within Us, The American Clock, Mortality of Death.*

BARRE, GABRIEL. Born Aug. 26, 1957 in Brattleboro, VT. Graduate AADA. Debut 1977 OB in *Jabberwock* followed by *T.N.T., Bodo, The Baker's Wife, The Time of Your Life, Children of the Sun, Wicked Philanthropy, Starmites, Mistress of the Inn, Gifts of the Magi, The Tempest, Return to the Forbidden Planet, The Circle, Where's Dick?, Forever Plaid, Jacques Brel, Show Me Where the Good Times Art Marathon Dancing, El Greco, Petrified Prince Bdwy in Rags* (1986), *Starmites, Anna Karenina, Ain't Broadway Grand.*

BARRIE, BARBARA. Born May 23, 1931 in Chicago, IL. Graduate U. Tex. Bdwy debut 1955 in *The Wooden Dish* followed by *Happily Never After, Company, Selling of the President, Prisoner of Second Ave., California Suite, Torch Song Trilogy,* OB in *The Crucible, Beaux Stratagem, Taming of the Shrew, Twelfth Night, All's Well That Ends Well, Horseman, Pass By, Killdeer, Big and Little, Backer's Audition, Isn't It Romantic, Mi Vida Loca, After-Play.*

BARSHA, DEBRA. Born Mar. 19, 1959 in Syracuse, NY. Attended Eastman School of Music. NY debut OB 1991 in *Tony 'n' Tina's Wedding* followed by *Swingtime Canteen.*

BARTENIEFF, GEORGE. Born Jan. 24, 1933 in Berlin, Ger. Bdwy debut 1947 in *The Whole World Over,* followed by *Venus Is, All's Well That Ends Well, Quotations from Chairman Mao Tse-Tung, The Death of Bessie Smith, Cop-Out, Room Service, Unlikely Heroes,* OB in *Walking in Waldheim, Memorandum, The Increased Difficulty of Concentration, Trelawny of the Wells, Charley Chestnut Rides the IRT, Radio (Wisdom): Sophia Part I, Images of the Dead, Dead End Kids, The Blonde Leading the Blonde, The Dispossessed, Growing Up Gothic, Rosetti's Apologies, On the Lam, Samuel Beckett Trilogy, Quartet, Help Wanted, A Matter of Life and Death, The Heart That Eats Itself, Coney Island Kid, Cymbeline, Better People, Blue Heaven, He Saw His Reflection, Phaedra, Beekeeper's Daughter.*

BARTLETT, PETER. Born Aug. 28, 1942 in Chicago, IL. Attended Loyola U., LAMDA. Bdwy debut 1969 in *A Patriot for Me,* followed by *Gloria and Esperanza,* OB in *Boom Boom Room, I Remember the House Where I was Born, Crazy Locomotive, A Thurber Carnival, Hamlet, Buzzsaw Berkeley, Learned Ladies, Jeffrey, The Naked Truth, Don Juan in Chicago.*

BATT, BRYAN. Born Mar. 1, 1963 in New Orleans, LA. Graduate Tulane U. Debut 1987 OB in *Too Many Girls,* followed by *The Golden Apple, Jeffrey,* Bdwy in *Starlight Express* (1987), *Sunset Blvd.*

BAVAN, YOLANDE. Born June 1, 1942 in Ceylon. Attended U. Colombo. Debut 1964 OB in *Midsummer Night's Dream* followed by *Jonah, House* *of Flowers, Salvation, Tarot, Back Bog Beast Bait, Leaves of Grass, End of the War, Bald Soprano, The Leader, Stories from Sri Lanka,* Bdwy in *Heathen* (1972), *Snow White, Chronicle of a Death Foretold.*

BEASLEY, HAL. Born Dec. 19, 1957 in New York City. Graduate Brooklyn Col. Bdwy debut 1994 in *Show Boat.*

BECKER, BARBARA. Born in Brooklyn, NY. Graduate SUNY/Potsdam. Debut 1981 OB in *Cry Havoc* followed by *27 Wagons Full of Cotton, Four by Four, House of Bernarda Alba, Fat Lucy, Lady Windermere's Fan, Quality Street.*

BECKER, GERRY. Born Apr. 11, 1951 in St. Louis, MO. Graduate U. MO., St. Louis U. Bdwy debut 1993 in *Song of Jacob Zulu,* OB in *Death Defying Acts.*

BECKER, RANDY. Born June 6, 1970 in Amsterdam, NY. Graduate Brown U. Debut 1994 OB and 1995 Bdwy in *Love! Valour! Compassion!*

BECKER, ROB. Born in San Jose, CA in 1956. Bdwy debut 1995 in *Defending the Caveman.*

BECKETT, TOM. Born in Whittier, CA. Graduate Yale U. Debut 1995 OB in *Travels with My Aunt.*

BEDFORD, BRIAN. Born Feb. 16, 1935 in Morley, Engl. Attended RADA. Bdwy debut 1960 in *Five Finger Exercise* followed by *Lord Pengo, The Private Ear, The Astrakhan Coat, The Unknown Soldier and His Wife, The Seven Descents of Myrtle, Jumpers, The Cocktail Party, Hamlet, Private Lives, School for Wives, The Misanthrope, Two Shakespearean Actors, Timon of Athens, Molière Comedies,* OB in *The Knack, The Lunatic the Lover and the Poet.*

BEGLEY, ED, JR. Born Sept. 16, 1949 in Hollywood, CA. Attended Valley Col. Debut 1995 OB in *The Cryptogram.*

BERGER, STEPHEN. Born May 16, 1954 in Philadelphia, PA. Attended U. Cinn. Bway debut 1982 in *Little Me* followed by *Wonderful Town* (NYCO), OB in *Nite Club Confidential, Mowgli, Isn't It Romantic, Hello Muddah Hello Fadduh, Beau Jest, That's Life!*

BERK, DAVID. Born July 20, 1932 in New York City. Graduate Manhattan Sch. of Music. Debut 1958 OB in *Eloise* followed by *Carnival, So Long 174th St., Wonderful Town, Anyone Can Whistle, The Meehans, June Moon, Pal Joey, Time of the Cuckoo, Little White Lies.*

BERN, MINA. Born May 5, 1920 in Poland. Bdwy debut 1967 in *Let's Sing Yiddish* followed by *Light Lively and Yiddish, Sing Israel Sing, Those Were the Days,* OB in *The Special, Old Lady's Guide to Survival.*

BERNHEIM, SHIRL. Born Sept. 21, 1921 in New York City. Debut 1967 OB in *A Different World* followed by *Stage Movie, Middle of the Night, Come Back Little Sheba, One-Act Festival, EST Marathon '93, Old Lady's Guide to Survival.*

BERTISH, SUZANNE. Born Aug. 7, 1951 in London, Engl. Attended London Drama School. Bdwy debut 1981 in *Nicholas Nickleby,* followed by *Salome, Molière Comedies,* OB in *Skirmishes* for which she received a Theatre World Award, followed by *Rosemersholm, Art of Success.*

BESSETTE, MIMI. Born Jan. 15, 1956 in Midland, MI. Graduate TCU, RADA. Debut 1978 OB in *The Gifts vf the Magi,* followed by *Bugles at Dawn, On the 20th Century, Opal, Swirl,* Bdwy (1978) in *The Best Little Whorehouse in Texas.*

BICKELL, ROSS. Born Jan. 14. 1947 in Hackensack. NJ. Graduate Boston U. Debut 1971 OB in *The Sweetshop Myrium,* followed by *Privates on Parade, Down by the Ocean, Somewhere in the Pacific,* Bdwy in *A Few Good Men* (1990).

BILL, JENNIFER. Born Nov. 21, 1964 in Cleveland, OH. Graduate Northwestern U. Debut 1995 OB in *Night and Her Stars.*

BILLECI, JOHN. Born Apr. 19, 1957 in Brooklyn, NY. Graduate Loyola Marymount U. Debut 1993 OB in *3 by Wilder* followed by *As You Like It, SSS Glencairn, Twelfth Night, Goose and TomTom, Anatomy of Sound,* Bdwy (1993) in *Wilder Wilder Wilder.*

BISHOP, KELLY (formerly Carole). Born Feb. 28, 1944 in Colorado Springs, CO. Bdwy debut 1967 in *Golden Rainbow,* followed by *Promises Promises, On the Town, Rachel Lily Rosenbloom, A Chorus Line* for which she received a Theatre World Award, *Six Degrees of Separation,* OB in *Piano Bar, Changes, The Blessing, Going to New England, Six Degrees of Separation, Pterodactyls, Last Girl Singer, Death Defying Acts.*

BLACKBURN, ROBERT. Born Jan. 21, 1925 in Montgomery, AL. Attended Columbia U. Credits include *As You Like It, King Lear, Misanthrope, Volpone, Henry IV, Octoroon, Hamlet, Black Wednesday, Evening with Richard Nixon, Oedipus at Colonus.*

BLAZER, JUDITH. Born Oct. 22, 1956 in *Oh Boy!,* followed by *Roberta in Concert, A Little Night Music, Company, Babes in Arms, Hello Again, Jack's Holiday,* Bdwy in *Me and My Girl, A Change in the Heir.*

BLOCH, SCOTTY. Born Jan. 28 in New Rochelle, NY. Attended AADA. Debut 1945 OB in *Craig's Wife* followed by *Lemon Sky, Battering Ram,*

Richard III, In Celebration, An Act of Kindness, The Price, Grace, Neon Psalms, Other People's Money, Walking The Dead, EST Marathon '92, The Stand-In, Unexpected Tenderness, Bdwy in *Children of a Lesser God* (1980).

BLOCK, LARRY. Born Oct. 30, 1942, in New York City. Graduate URI. Bdwy debut 1966 in *Hail Scrawdyke,* followed by *La Turista, Wonderful Town* (NYCO), OB in *Eh?, Fingernails Blue as Flowers, Comedy of Errors, Coming Attractions, Henry IV Part 2, Feuhrer Bunker, Manhattan Love Songs, Souvenirs, The Golem, Responsible Parties, Hit Parade, Largo Desolato, The Square Root of 3, Young Playwrights Festival, Hunting Cockroaches, Two Gentlemen of Verona, Yellow Dog Contract, Temptation, Festival of 1 Acts, The Faithful Brethern of Pitt Street, Loman Family Picnic, One of the All-Time Greats, Pericles, Comedy of Errors, The Work Room, Don Juan in Chicago, Him.*

BLUM, JOEL. Born May 19, 1952 in San Francisco, CA. Attended Marin Col., NYU. Bdwy debut 1976 in *Debbie Reynolds on Broadway,* followed by *42nd Street, Stardust, Radio City Easter Show, Show Boat* (1994), OB in *And the World Goes Round.*

BLUM, MARK. Born May 14, 1950 in Newark, NJ. Graduate U. PA, U. MN. Debut 1976 OB in *The Cherry Orchard,* followed by *Green Julia, Say Goodnight Gracie, Table Settings, Key Exchange, Loving Reno, Messiah, It's Only a Play, Little Footsteps, Cave of Life, Gus & Al, Laureen's Whereabouts,* Bdwy in *Lost in Yonkers* (1991), *My Thing of Love.*

BLUMENFELD, ROBERT. Born Feb. 26, 1943 in New York City. Graduate Rutgers, Columbia U. Bdwy debut 1970 in *Othello,* OB in *Fall and Redemption of Man, Tempest, The Dybbuk, Count Dracula, Nature and Purpose of the Universe, House Music, The Keymaker, Epic Proportions, Tatterdemalion, Iolanthe, Temple, Friends in High Places, Rough Crossing, Petrified Prince.*

BLUMENKRANTZ, JEFF. Born June 3, 1965 in Long Branch, NJ. Graduate Northwestern U. Debut 1986 OB in *Pajama Game,* Bdwy (1987) in *Into the Woods,* followed by *3 Penny Opera, South Pacific, Damn Yankees, How to Succeed* (1995).

BOGARDUS, STEPHEN. Born Mar. 11, 1954 in Norfolk, VA. Princeton graduate. Bdwy debut 1980 in *West Side Story,* followed by *Les Miserables, Falsettos, Allegro in Concert, Love! Valour! Compassion!* (also OB), OB in *March of the Falsettos, Feathertop, No Way to Treat a Lady, Look on the Bright Side, Falsettoland.*

BOLERNO, DANNY. Born Nov. 1, 1962 in Los Angeles, CA. Attended East LA Col. Bdwy debut (1993) in *Joseph and the Amazing Technicolor Dreamcoat.*

BOLTON, JOHN (KEENE). Born Dec. 29, 1963 in Rochester, NY. Graduate St. John Fisher Col. Debut 1991 OB in *Cinderella,* Bdwy in *Damn Yankees* (1994).

BOND, ANGELA. Born Jan. 17, 1959 in Richmond, VA. Graduate Rolloins Col. Bdwy debut in *Gentlemen Prefer Blondes* (1995).

BORTS, JOANNE. Born June 12, 1961 in Syosset, NY. Graduate SUNY/Binghamton. Debut 1985 in *The Golden Land* followed by *On Second Ave.,* Bdwy in *Fiddler on the Roof* (1990).

BOSCO, PHILIP. Born Sept. 26, 1930 in Jersey City, NJ. Graduate Catholic U. Credits: *Auntie Mame, Rape of the Belt, Ticket of Leave Man, Donnybrook, A Man for All Seasons, Mrs. Warren's Profession,* with LCRep in *A Great Career, In the Matter of J. Robert Oppenheimer, The Miser, The Time of Your Life, Camino Real, Operation Sidewinder, Amphitryon, Enemy of the People, Playboy of the Western World, Good Woman of Setzuan, Antigone, Mary Stuart, Narrow Road to the Deep North, The Crucible, Twelfth Night, Enemies, Plough and the Stars, Merchant of Venice, A Streetcar Named Desire, Henry V, Threepenny Opera, Streamers, Stages, St. Joan, The Biko Inquest, Man and Superman, Whose Life Is It Anyway?, Major Barbara, A Month in the Country, Bacchae, Hedda Gabler, Don Juan in Hell, Inadmissable Evidence, Eminent Domain, Misalliance, Learned Ladies, Some Men Need Help, Ah Wilderness!, The Caine Mutiny Court Martial, Heartbreak House, Come Back Little Sheba, Loves of Anatol, Be Happy for Me, Master Class, You Never Can Tell, Devil's Disciple, Lend Me a Tenor, Breaking Legs, Fiorello in Concert, An Inspector Calls, The Heiress.*

BOSTON, GRETIIA. Born Apr. 18, 1959 in Crossett, AR. Attended U. Tex., U. Ill. Bdwy debut in *Show Boat* (1994) for which she received a Theatre World Award.

BOVE, ELIZABETH. Born Sept. 30 in Melbourne, Australia. Graduate U. Tex. Debut 1986 OB in *Witness for the Prosecution,* followed by *House of Bernarda Alba, Country Girl, The Maids, Round & Peakheads, The Dream Cure, House of the Dog, Shadow Box, Kiss the Blarney Stone, Moon for the Misbegotten, No Exit, Madwoman of Chaillot.*

BOVE, MARK. Born Jan. 9, 1960 in Pittsburgh, PA. Bdwy debut in *West Side Story* (1980) followed by *Woman of the Year, Chorus Line, Kiss of the*

Spider Woman.

BOVSHOW, BUZZ. Born May 14, 1956 in Hollywood, CA. Graduate UC/San Diego, U. Ind. Debut 1987 OB in *Second Avenue* followed by *J. P. Morgan Saves the Nation.*

BOYD, CAMERON. Born Sept. 6, 1984 in Carmel, NY. Bdwy debut 1992 in *Four Baboons Adoring the Sun* followed by *Abe Lincoln in Illinois,* OB in *Missing Persons.*

BOYD, JULIE. Born Jan. 2 in Kansas City, MO. Graduate U. Utah, Yale. Bdwy debut 1985 in *Noises Off,* followed by OB in *Only You, Working Acts, Hyde in Hollywood, Nowhere, A Distance from Calcutta, The Orphanage, Class-1-Acts.*

BRADLEY, BRIAN. Born Oct. 19, 1954 in Philadelphia, PA. Graduate U. Fla. Bdwy debut 1994 in *Grease.*

BRAUNSTEIN, ALAN. Born Apr. 30, 1947 in Brooklyn, NY. Debut 1962 OB in *Daddy Come Home* followed by *Rhinegold, Petrified Prince,* Bdwy in *Hair, Jesus Christ Superstar, Dude, Oliver.*

BRECKA, KATHERINE. Born Sept. 2, 1956 in Jacksonville, FL. Graduate Am. Consv. Th. Debut 1991 OB in *Measure for Measure.*

BREEN, (J.) PATRICK. Born Oct. 26, 1960 in Brooklyn, NY. NYU graduate. Debut 1982 OB in *Epiphanyu,* followed by *Little Murders, Blood Sports, Class I Acts, Baba Goya, Chelsea Walls, Naked Rights, The Substance of Fire, Saturday Morning Cartoons, A Fair Country, Night and Her Stars,* Bdwy in *Brighton Beach Memoirs* (1983).

BRENNAN, JAMES. Born Oct. 31, 1950 in Newark, NJ. Bdwy debut 1974 in *Good News,* followed by *Rodgers and Hart, So Long, 174th Street, Little Me, I Love My Wife, Singin' in the Rain, 42nd Street, Me and My Girl, Crazy for You,* OB in *Juba.*

BRENNAN, NORA. Born Dec. 1, 1953 in East Chicago, IN. Graduate Purdue U. Bdwy debut 1980 in *Camelot,* followed by *Cats, Pal Joey.*

BRIAN, MICHAEL. Born Nov. 14, 1958 in Utica, NY. Attended Boston Consv. Debut 1979 OB in *Kennedy's Children* followed by *Street Scene, Death of von Ricthofen as Witnessed from Earth, Lenny and the Heartbreakers, Gifts of the Magi, Next Please!, Love in Two Countries,* Bdwy in *Baby* (1984), *Big River, Guys and Dolls.*

BRILL, FRAN. Born Sept. 30 in PA. Attended Boston U. Bdwy debut 1969 in *Red White and Maddox,* OB in *What Every Woman Knows, Scribes, Naked, Look Back in Anger, Knuckle, Skirmishes, Baby with the Bathwater, Holding Patterns, Festival of One Acts, Taking Steps, Young Playwrights Festival, Claptrap, Hyde in Hollywood, Good Grief, Desdemona.*

BROCK, LEE. Born July 1, 1959 in Denver, CO. Graduate U. Ok. Debut 1994 OB in *Ghost in the Machine* followed by *Trust, Living Proof.*

BRODERICK, MATTHEW. Born Mar. 21, 1963 in New York City. Debut 1981 OB in *Torch Song Trilogy,* followed by *The Widow Claire, A Christmas Memory,* Bdwy 1983 in *Brighton Beach Memoirs* for which he received a Theatre World Award, followed by *Biloxi Blues, How to Succeed…*(1995).

BRODY, JONATHAN. Born June 16, 1963 in Englewood, NJ. Debut 1982 OB in *Shulamith,* followed by *The Desk Set, Eating Raoul, Theda Bara and the Frontier Rabbi, Miami Stories,* Bdwy in *Me and My Girl* (1986), *Sally Marr and Her Escorts.*

BROGGER, IVAR. Born Jan. 10 in St. Paul, MN. Graduate U. Minn. Debut 1979 OB in *In The Jungle of Cities,* followed by *Collected Works of Billy the Kid, Magic Time, Cloud 9, Richard III, Clarence, Madwoman of Chaillot, Seascapes with Sharks and Dancer, Second Man, Twelfth Night, Almost Perfect, Up 'N' Under, Progress, Juno, Madwoman of Chaillot,* Bdwy in *Macbeth* (1981), *Pygmalion* (1987), *Saint Joan, Blood Brothers.*

BROMKA, ELAINE. Born Jan. 6 in Rochester, NY. Graduate Smith Col. Debut 1975 OB in *The Dybbuk,* followed by *Naked, Museum, The Son, Inadmissible Evidence, The Double Game, Cloud 9, Light Up the Sky,* Bdwy in *Macbeth* (1982), *Rose Tattoo* (1995).

BROOKING, SIMON. Born Dec. 23, 1960 in Edinburgh, Scot. Graduate SUNY/Fredonia, U. Wash. Debut 1989 OB in *American Bagpipes,* followed by *The Mortality Project, Prelude & Liebestod, Rough Crossing, Rumor of Glory, King Lear, Waiting at the Water's Edge, Able Bodied Seaman, Don Juan in Chicago,* Bdwy in *Candida* (1993).

BROOKS, JEFF. Born Apr. 7, 1950 in Vancouver, Can. Attended Portland State U. Debut 1976 OB in *Titanic,* followed by *Fat Chances, Nature and Purpose of the Universe, Actor's Nightmare, Sister Mary Ignatius Explains It All, Marathon '84, The Foreigner, Talk Radio, Washington Heights,* Bdwy in *A History of the American Film* (1978), *Lend Me a Tenor, Gypsy, Nick & Nora, Guys & Dolls, Pal Joey.*

BROWN, ANTHONY M. Born July 14, 1962 in Springfield, VA. Graduate Fl. St. U., Juilliard. Debut 1993 OB in *Jeffrey* followed by *Mother and Child.*

BROWN, BLAIR. Born Apr. 23, 1947 in Washington, DC. Attended Pine Manor School. Debut OB in *Comedy of Errors* followed by *Threepenny Opera,* Bdwy in *Secret Rapture* (1989), *Arcadia.*

BROWN, BRANDY. Born in 1976 in Mobile, AL. Bdwy debut 1987 in *Les Miserables.*

BROWN, KIMBERLY JEAN. Born Nov. 16, 1984 in Gaithersburg, Md. Bdwy debut 1992 in *Four Baboons Adoring the Sun* followed by *Show Boat.*

BROWN, P.J. Born Nov. 5, 1956 in Staten Island, New York City. Graduate Boston Col. Debut 1990 OB in *Othello* followed by *America Dreaming,* Bdwy in *Grapes of Wrath* (1990).

BROWN, ROBIN LESLIE. Born Jan. 18, in Canandaigua, NY. Graduate LIU. Debut 1980 OB in *The Mother of Us All,* followed by *Yours Truly, Two Gentlemen of Verona, Taming of the Shrew, The Mollusc, The Contrast, Pericles, Andromache, Macbeth, Electra, She Stoops to Conquer, Berneice, Hedda Gabler, A Midsummer Night's Dream, Three Sisters, Major Barbara, The Fine Art of Finesse, Two by Schnitzler, As You Like It, Ghosts, Chekhov Very Funny, Beaux Stratagem, God of Vengeance, Good Natured Man, Twelfth Night, Little Eyolf, Ventian Twins, King Lear.*

BROWN, WILLIAM SCOTT. Born Mar. 27, 1959 in Seattle, WA. Attended UWA. Debut 1986 OB in *Juba,* Bdwy in *Phantom of the Opera* (1988).

BROWNING, DAN. Born Sept. 6, 1952 in Covington, KY. Graduate E. Ky. U., Rutgers U. Debut 1994 OB in *Oh What a Lovely War.*

BROWNING, SUSAN. Born Feb. 25, 1941 in Baldwin, NY. Graduate Penn. State. Bdwy debut 1963 in *Love and Kisses,* followed by *Company* for which she received a Theatre World Award, *Shelter, Goodtime Charley, Big River, Company in Concert, Wonderful Town* (NYCO), OB in *Jo, Dime a Dozen, Seventeen, The Boys from Syracuse, Collision Course, Whiskey, As You Like It, Removalists, Africanus Instructus, The March on Russia.*

BRYANT, DAVID. Born May 26, 1936 in Nashville, TN. Attended TN State U. Bdwy debut 1972 in *Don't Play Us Cheap,* followed by *Bubbling Brown Sugar, Amadeus, Les Miserables, Show Boat,* OB in *Up in Central Park, Elizabeth and Essex, Appear and Show Cause.*

BUCKLEY, BETTY. Born July 3, 1947 in Big Springs, TX. Graduate TCU. Bdwy debut 1969 in *1776* followed by *Pippin, Cats, Mystery of Edwin Drood* (also OB), *Song and Dance, Carrie, Carrie, Sunset Blvd.,* OB in *Ballad of Johnny Pot* (1971), *What's a Nice Country Like You, Circle of Sound, I'm Getting My Act Together, Juno's Swans.*

BUCKLEY, CANDY. Born Mar. 10 in Albuquerque, MN. Graduate TCU, U. Tex., Trinity. Debut 1994 OB in *Petrified Prince.*

BUONO, CARA. Born Mar. 1, 1971 in Bronx, New York City. Debut 1994 OB in *Spookhouse* followed by *Patience and Sarah, Once Removed, Hidden Parts, Evening Star, Class 1-Acts,* Bdwy in *Some Americans Abroad* (1990), *Rose Tattoo.*

BURK, TERENCE. Born Aug. 11, 1947 in Lebanon, IL. Graduate S. IL. U. Bdwy debut 1976 in *Equus,* OB in *Religion, The Future, Sacred and Profane Love, Crime and Punishment.*

BURNETT, ROBERT. Born Feb. 28, 1960 in Goshen, NY. Attended HB Studio. Bdwy debut 1985 in *Cats.*

BURNHAM, MARGARET. Born May 29 in Painsville, OH. Graduate Wooster Col. Debut 1988 OB in *A Midsummer Night's Dream* followed by *Reckonings, The Former Mrs. Meis, Pericles, Love's Labour's Lost, After the Ball.*

BURRELL, FRED. Born Sept. 18, 1936 in Cedar Rapids, IA. Graduate UNC, RADA. Bdwy debut 1964 in *Never Too Late,* followed by *Illya Darling, Cactus Flower, On Golden Pond,* OB in *The Memorandum, Throckmorton, Texas, Voices in the Head, Chili Queen, The Queen's Knight, In Pursuit of the Song of Hydrogen, Unchanging Love, More Fun Than Bowling, A Woman without a Name, Sorrows of Fredrick, Voice of the Prairie, Spain, Democracy and Esther, Last Sortie, Rough/Play, Life is a Dream, Taming of the Shrew, Twelfth Night, Modest Proposal, Oedipus at Colonus.*

BURRELL, PAMELA. Born Aug 4, 1945 in Tacoma, WA. Bdwy debut 1966 in *Funny Girl,* followed by *Where's Charley?, Strider, Sunday in the Park with George, Red Shoes,* OB in *Arms and the Man* for which she received a Theatre World Award, *Berkeley Square, The Boss, Biography: A Game, Strider: Story of a Horse, A Little Madness, Spinoza, After the Dancing in Jericho, Down by the Ocean.*

BURSE-MICKLEBURY, DENISE. Born Jan. 13 in Atlanta, Ga. Graduate Spellman Col., Atlanta U. Debut 1990 OB in *Ground People* for which she received a Theatre World Award, followed by *A Worm in the Heart, Robert Johnson: Trick the Devil.*

BURSTEIN, DANNY. Born June 16, 1964 in New York City. Graduate U. Cal/San Diego. Moscow Art Theatre. Debut 1991 OB in *The Rothschilds, Weird Romance, Merrily We Roll Along, All in the Timing,* Bdwy in *A Little Hotel on the Side* (1992), *The Sea Gull, Saint Joan, Three Men on a Horse, Flowering Peach.*

BURSTYN, MIKE (formerly Burstein). Born July 1, 1945 in the Bronx, NY. Bdwy debut 1968 in *The Megilla of Itzak Manger* followed by *Inquest,*

Barnum, Ain't Broadway Grand, Fiorello in Concert, OB in *Wedding in Shtetl, Prisoner of Second Avenue, The Rothschilds, Circus Life.*

BURTON, ARNIE. Born Sept. 22, 1958 in Emmett, ID. Graduate U. Az. Bdwy debut 1983 in *Amadeus,* OB in *Measure for Measure, Major Barbara, Schnitzler One Acts, Tartuffe, As You Like It, Ghosts, Othello, Moon for the Misbegotten, Twelfth Night, Little Eyolf, Mollusc, Venetian Twins, Beaux Stratagem, King Lear.*

BURTON, KATE. Born Sept. 10, 1957 in Geneva, Switz. Graduate Brown U., Yale. Bdwy debut 1982 in *Present Laughter,* followed by *Alice in Wonderland, Doonesbury, Wild Honey, Some Americans Abroad, Jake's Women,* OB in *Winners* for which she received a 1983 Theatre World Award, *Romeo and Juliet, The Accrington Pals, Playboy of the Western World, Measure for Measure, London Suite.*

BURZ, CHRISTINA D. Born Nov. 20, 1962 in Cookeville, TN. Graduate U.Cal./Berkley, Am.Consv.Th. Debut 1994 OB in *Field in Heat* followed by *Young Man from Atlanta.*

BUSCH, CHARLES. Born Aug. 23, 1954 in Hartsdale, NY. Graduate Northwestern U. Debut OB 1985 in *Vampire Lesbians of Sodom,* followed by *Times Square Angel, Psycho Beach Party, The Lady in Question, Red Scare on Sunset, Charles Busch Revue, You Should Be So Lucky,* all of which he wrote, and *Swingtime Canteen* (co-writer).

BUSSERT, MEG. Born Oct. 21, 1949 in Chicago, IL. Attended U.Ill. Bdwy debut 1980 in *The Music Man* for which she received a Theatre World Award, followed by *Brigadoon, Camelot, New Moon, The Firefly, Damn Yankees,* OB in *Lola, Professionally Speaking, Mexican Hayride, An Evening with Loesser and Sondheim.*

BUTLER, DAN. Born Dec. 2, 1954 in Huntington, IN. Attended Ind.U./Purdue, San Jose St. Bdwy debut 1982 in *The Hothouse* followed by *Biloxi Blues,* OB in *True West* (1983), *Walk the Dog Whistle, Domino, Wrestlers, Emerald City, Lisbon Traviata, Much Ado about Nothing, Early One Evening at the Rainbow Bar & Grill, Only Thing Worse You Could Have Told Me* which he wrote.

BUTTRAM. JAN. Born June 19, 1946 in Clarksville, TX. Graduate N.Tx. St.U. Debut 1974 OB in *Fashion* followed by *Startup, Camp Meeting, German Games,* Bdwy in *Best Little Whorehouse…* (1978).

BYERS, RALPH. Born Jan. 10, 1950 in Washington, DC. Graduate Wm.& Mary Col., Catholic U. Debut 1975 OB in *Hamlet* folowed by *Julius Caesar, Rebel Women, No End of Blame, Henry IV Part I, Petrified Prince,* Bdwy in *Herzl* (1976), *Goodbye Fidel, Big River, Sunday in the Park with George.*

CAHN, LARRY. Born Dec. 19, 1955 in Nassau, NY. Graduate Northwestern U. Bdwy debut 1980 in *The Music Man* followed by *Anything Goes, Guys and Dolls,* OB in *Susan B!, Jim Thorpe All American, Play to Win.*

CAIN, WILLIAM. Born May 27, 1931 in Tuscaloosa, AL. Graduate U. Wash., Catholic U. Debut 1962 OB in *Red Roses for Me,* followed by *Jericho Jim Crow, Henry V, Antigone, Relatively Speaking, I Married an Angel in Concert, Buddha, Copperhead, Forbidden City, Fortinbras,* Bdwy in *Wilson in the Promise Land* (1970), *You Can't Take It with You, Wild Honey, The Boys in Autumn, Mastergate, A Streetcar Named Desire, The Heiress.*

CALABRESE, MARIA. Born Dec. 7, 1967 in Secone, PA. Bdwy debut 1991 in *The Will Rogers Follies, My Favorite Year, How to Succeed…* (1995).

CALLAWAY, LIZ. Born Apr. 13, 1961 in Chicago, IL. Debut 1980 OB in *Godspell,* followed by *The Matinee Kids, Brownstone, No Way to Treat a Lady, Marry Me a Little, 1-2-3-4-5,* Bdwy in *Merrily We Roll Along* (1981), *Baby, The Three Musketeers, Miss Saigon, Cats, Fiorello in Concert.*

CALUD, ANNETTE Y. Born Nov. 1963 in Milwaukee, WI. Graduate IL. Col.of Optometry. Bdwy debut 1991 in *Miss Saigon.*

CAMP, JOANNE. Born Apr. 4, 1951 in Atlanta, GA. Graduate Fl.Atlantic U., Geo.Wash.U. Debut 1981 OB in *The Dry Martini,* followed by *Geniuses* for which she received a Theatre World Award, *June Moon, Painting Churches, Merchant of Venice, Lady from the Sea, The Contrast, Coastal Disturbances, The Rivals, Andromache, Electra, Uncle Vanya, She Stoops to Conquer, Hedda Gabler, The Heidi Chronicles, Importance of Being Earnest, Medea, Three Sisters, A Midsummer Night's Dream, School for Wives, Measure for Measure, Dance of Death, Two Schnitzler One-Acts, Tartuffe, Lips Together Teeth Apart, As You Like It, Moon for the Misbegotten, Phaedra, Little Eyolf, Beaux Stratagem, King Lear,* Bdwy in *The Heidi Chronicles* (1989), *Sisters Rosensweig.*

CAMPBELL, ALAN. Born Apr. 22, 1957 in Homestead, FL. Graduate U.Miami. Debut 1982 OB in *Boogie-Woogie Rumble of a Dream Deferred* followed by *Almost a Man, On Shiloh Hill,* Bdwy in *Sunset Blvd.* (1994).

CAMPBELL, AMELIA. Born Aug. 4, 1965 in Montreal, Can. Graduate Syracuse U. Debut 1988 OB in *Fun,* followed by *Member of the Wedding, Tunnel of Love, Five Women Wearing the Same Dress, Wild Dogs, Intensive Care,* Bdwy in *Our Country's Good* (1991), *A Small Family Business,*

Translations.

CAMPBELL, COLIN. Born Jan. 24, 1962 in Seattle, WA. Attended NYU. Debut 1982 OB in *Rabbit Ears* followed by *Real O'Brien, Her Hair, Norman Conquests, Titus Andronicus, Macbeth, Hamlet, Gambler, Baptists, Fashion Police, Banana Creme Pie.*

CANNIS, MICHAEL. Born May 13, 1957 in Miami, FL. Graduate UCLA. Debut 1990 OB in *Savage in Limbo* followed by *Dreamtime, Currents Turned Awry, The Party, Half & Half, Danger of Strangers, Salesmen Don't Ride Bicycles, Down Dark Deceptive Streets.*

CANTONE, MARIO. Born Dec. 9, 1959 in Boston, MA. Graduate Emerson Col. Bdwy debut 1995 in *Love! Valour! Compassion!*

CARABUENA, PHILIP LEE. Born Oct. 18, 1986 in New York City. Bdwy debut 1991 in *Miss Saigon.*

CARMELLO, CAROLEE. Born in Albany, NY. Graduate SUNY/Albany. Bdwy debut 1989 in *City of Angels* followed by *Faslettos,* OB in *I Can Get it for You Wholesale,* (1991) *Hello Again, Goose, Case of the Dead Flamingo Dancer, john & jen, Das Barbecu.*

CARNAHAN, KIRSTI. Born June 29 in Evanston, IL. Attended U.Cinn. Bdwy debut 1983 in *Baby,* followed by *The Three Musketeers, Kiss of the Spider Woman,* OB in *Hang on to the Good Times, Mortally Fine.*

CARLIN, CHET. Born Feb. 23, 1940 in Malverne, NY. Graduate Ithaca Col., Catholic U. Bdwy debut 1972 in *Evening with Richard Nelson,* OB in *Under Gaslight, Lou Gehrig Did Not Die of Cancer, Graffitti, Crystal and Fox, Golden Honeymoon, Arms and the Man, Arsenic and Old Lace, The Father, Comedy of Errors, Never the Sinner, Emperor Charles, Oedipus at Colonus.*

CARPENTER, CARLETON. Born July 10, 1926 in Bennington, VT. Attended Northwestern U. Bdwy debut 1944 in *Bright Boy* followed by *Career Angel, Three to Make Ready, Magic Touch, John Murray Anderson's Almanac, Hotel Paradiso, Box of Watercolors, Hello Dolly!, Crazy for You,* OB in *Stage Affair, Boys in the Band, Dylan, The Greatest Fairy Story Ever Told, A Good Old Fashioned Revue, Miss Stanwyck Is Still in Hiding, Rocky Road, Apollo of Bellac, Light up the Sky, Murder at Rutherford House.*

CARROLL, NANCY E. Born in Haverhill, MA. Graduate Cin.Consv. Debut 1990 OB in *Nunsense,* followed by *Balancing Act, Nunsense II.*

CARTER, MYRA. Born Oct. 27, 1930 in Chicago, IL. Attended Glasgow U. Bdwy debut 1957 in *Major Barbara* followed by *Maybe Tuesday, Present Laughter,* OB in *Trials of Oz, Abingdon Square, Three Tall Women.*

CASPER, JEFF. Born May 27, 1963 in Syracuse, NY. NYU. Graduate. Debut 1995 OB in *Awake and Sing.*

CASSERLY, KERRY. Born Oct. 26, 1953 in Minneapolis, MN. Attended U.Minn. Bdwy debut 1980 in *One Night Stand* followed by *Chorus Line, My One and Only,* OB in *Jewler's Shop.*

CASTAY, LESLIE. Born Dec. 11, 1963 in New Orleans, LA. Graduate Tulane U. Debut 1985 OB in *The Second Hurricane,* followed by *Too Many Girls, The Hunchback of Notre Dame,* Bdwy in *Threepenny Opera* (1989), *Guys and Dolls.*

CASTREE, PAUL. Born in Rockford, IL. Graduate U.IL. Debut 1992 OB in *Forever Plaid,* Bdwy in *Grease* (1994).

CAULFIELD, MAXWELL. Born Nov. 23, 1959 in Glasgow, Scot. Debut 1979 OB in *Class Enemy* for which he received a Theatre World Award, followed by *Crimes and Dreams, Entertaining Mr. Sloan, Inheritors, Paradise Lost, Salonika,* Bdwy 1995 in *Inspector Calls.*

CEBALLOS, RENE (M). Born Apr. 7, 1953 in Boston, MA. Attended San Fran.U. Bdwy debut 1977 in *A Chorus Line,* followed by *Dancin', Cats, Dangerous Games, Grand Hotel, Chronicle of a Death Foretold,* OB in *Tango Apasionado.*

CHALFANT, KATHLEEN. Born Jan. 14, 1945 in San Francisco, CA. Graduate Stanford U. Bdwy debut 1975 in *Dance with Me,* followed by *M. Butterfly, Angels in America,* OB in *Jules Feiffer's Hold Me, Killings on the Last Line, The Boor, Blood Relations, Signs of Life, Sister Mary Ignatius Explains it All, Actor's Nightmare, Faith Healer, All the Nice People, Hard Times, Investigation of the Murder in El Salvador, 3 Poets, The Crucible, The Party, Iphigenia and Other Daughters, Cowboy Pictures, Twelve Dreams.*

CHALFY, DYLAN. Born June 22, 1970 in Sarsota, FL. Debut 1994 OB in *Blood Guilty,* Bdwy 1995 in *Rose Tattoo.*

CHANDLER, DAVID. Born Feb. 3, 1950 in Danbury, CT. Graduate Oberlin Col. Bdwy debut 1980 in *The American Clock* followed by *Death of a Salesman, Lost in Yonkers,* OB in *Made in Heaven, Black Sea Follies, The Swan, Watbanaland, Phaedra, Slavs!*

CHANG, BETSY. Born Aug. 24, 1963 in Oakland, CA. Attended UC Berkeley. Bdwy debut 1988 in *42nd Street* followed by *Cats, Joseph and the Amazing Technicolor Dreamcoat, Shogun the Musical, Christmas Carol.*

CHANNING, CAROL. Born Jan. 31, 1921 in Seattle, WA. Attended Bennington Col. Bdwy debut 1941 in *No for an Answer* followed by *Let's Face*

It, Proof through the Night, Lend an Ear for which she received a Theatre World Award, *Gentlemen Prefer Blondes, Wonderful Town, The Vamp, Show Girl, Hello Dolly!* (1964/1978/1995), *Four on a Garden, Lorelei.*

CHANNING, STOCKARD. Born Feb. 13, 1944 in New York City. Attended Radcliffe Col. Debut 1970 in *Adaptation/Next*, followed by *The Lady and the Clarinet, The Golden Age, Woman in Mind, Hapgood*, Bdwy in *Two Gentlemen of Verona, They're Playing Our Song, The Rink, Joe Egg, House of Blue Leaves, Six Degrees of Separation* (also OB), *Four Baboons Adoring the Sun, Normal Heart benefit.*

CHARLES, WALTER. Born Apr. 4, 1945 in East Stroudsburg, PA. Graduate Boston U. Bdwy debut 1973 in *Grease*, followed by *1600 Pennsylvania Avenue, Knickerbocker Holiday, Sweeney Todd, Cats, La Cage aux Folles, Aspects of Love, Me and My Girl, 110 in the Shade* (NYCO), *Christmas Carol.*

CHARNAY, LYNNE. Born Apr. 1 in New York City. Attended U.Wis, Columbia, AADA. Debut 1950 OB in *Came the Dawn* followed by *Ram's Head, In a Cold Hotel, Amata, Yerma, Ballad of Winter Soldiers, Intimate Relations, Play Me Zoltan, Grand Magic, Time of Your Life, Nymph Errant, Nude with Violin, American Power Play, Salon, Three Not from the Twilight Zone, Chez Garbo*, Bdwy in *Sunday Man, Tonight in Samarkand, Juli Jake and Uncle Joe, Family Affair, Broadway, Inspector General, Grand Tour.*

CHASE, PAULA LEGGETT. Born Sept. 2, 1961 in Evansville, IN. Graduate Ind. U. Bdwy debut 1989 in *A Chorus Line* followed by *Crazy for You, Damn Yankees.*

CHATINOVER, MARTIN. Born Apr. 24, 1927 in Los Angeles, CA. Graduate Yale, NYU. OB in *Crucible, Archy and Mehitabel, Yank in Beverly Hills, Shay, God Bless You Mr. Rosewater, Man in the Glass Booth, Miami Stories.*

CHECCO, AL. Born July 21, 1922 in Pittsburgh, PA. Attended Carnegie Tech. Bdwy debut 1948 in *Lend an Ear* followed by *Leave It to Jane, Carnival in Flanders, Gazebo, Two on the Aisle, Damn Yankees, Buttrio Sq., Inspector Calls, Crazy for You.*

CHENG, KAM. Born Mar. 28, 1969 in Hong Kong. Attended Muhlenberg Col. Bdwy debut 1991 in *Miss Saigon.*

CHEN, TINA. Born Nov. 2 in Chung King, China. Graduate Brown U. Debut 1972 OB in *Maid's Tragedy* followed by *Family Devotions, Midsummer Night's Dream, Empress of China, Year of the Dragon, Tropical Tree, Madame de Sade, Arthur and Leila*, Bdwy in *King and I, Love Suicide at Schofield Barracks.*

CHENOWETH, KRISTIN D. Born July 24, 1968 in Tulsa, OK. Graduate Ok.City U. Debut 1994 OB in *The Box Office of the Damned* followed by *Dames at Sea.*

CHIANESE, DOMINIC. Born Feb. 24, 1932 in New York City. Graduate Brooklyn Col. Debut 1952 OB in *American Savoyards* followed by *Winterset, Jacques Brel is Alive, Ballad for a Firing Squad, City Scene, End of the War, Passione, Midsummer Night's Dream, Recruiting Officer, Wild Duck, Oedipus the King, Hunting Scenes, Operation, Midnight Climax, Rosario and the Gypsies, Bella Figura, House Arrest, The Return*, Bdwy in *Oliver!, Scratch, Water Engine, Richard III, Requiem for a Heavyweight, Rose Tattoo.*

CHIBAS, MARISSA. Born June 13, 1961 in New York City. Graudate SUNY/Purchase. Debut 1983 OB in *Asian Shade*, followed by *Sudden Death, Total Eclipse, Another Antigone, Fresh Horses, Fortune's Fools*, Bdwy in *Brighton Beach Memiors* (1984), *Abe Lincoln in Illinois.*

CHRIS, MARILYN. Born May 19, 1939 in New York City. Bdwy debut 1966 in *The Office*, followed by *Birthday Party, 7 Descents of Myrtle, Lenny*, OB in *Nobody Hears a Broken Drum, Fame, Juda Applause, Junebug Graduates Tonight, Man is Man, In the Jungle of Cities, Good Soldier Schweik, The Tempest, Ride a Black Horse, Screens, Kaddish, Lady from the Sea, Bread, Leaving Home, Curtains, Elephants, The Upper Depths, Man Enough, Loose Connections, Yard Sale, God of Vengeance, Lobster Reef.*

CHRISTAKOS, JERRY. Born Sept. 9, 1960 in Chicago, IL. Attended U. Az. Bdwy debut 1993 in *Kiss of the Spider Woman.*

CHRISTIAN, WILLIAM. Born Sept. 30, 1955 in Washington, DC. Graduate Catholic U., American U. OB in *She Stoops to Conquer, A Sleep of Prisoners, American Voices, Member of the Wedding, Them That's Got, Winter's Tale.*

CIESLA, DIANE. Born May 20, 1952 in Chicago, IL. Graduate Clark Col. Debut 1980 OB in *Uncle Money*, followed by *Afternoons in Vegas, The Taming of the Shrew, Much Ado about Nothing, Macbeth, Cinderella, Sacrifice to Eros.*

CIULLA, CELESTE. Born Sept. 10, 1967 in New York City. Graduate Northwestern U., Harvard. Debut 1992 OB in *Othello*, followed by *The Good Natured Man, Phaedra, Fair Fight.*

CLARKE, CAITLIN. Born May 3, 1952 in Pittsburgh, PA. Graduate Mt. Holyoke Col., Yale U. Debut 1981 OB in *No One To Blame* followed by *Lorenzaccio, Summer, Quartermaine's Terms, Thin Ice, Total Eclipse, 3*

Birds Alighting on a Field, Unexpected Tenderness, Bdwy in *Teaneck Tanzi* (1983), *Strange Interlude, Arms and the Man, Figaro.*

CLARKE, RICHARD. Born Jan. 31, 1933 in England. Graduate U. Reading. With LCRep in *St. Joan* (1968), *Tiger at the Gates, Cyrano de Bergerac*, Bdwy in *Conduct Unbecoming, The Elephant Man, Breaking the Code, The Devils Disciple M. Butterfly, Six Degrees of Separation, Two Shakespearean Actors, Arcadia*, OB in *Old Glory, Trials of Oz, Looking Glass, Trelawney of the Wells.*

CLOSE, GLENN. Born May 19, 1947 in Greenwich, CT. Graduate Wm. & Mary Col. Bdwy debut 1974 with Phoenix Co. in *Love for Love, Member of the Wedding*, and *Rules of the Game*, followed by *Rex, Crucifer of Blood, Barnum, The Real Thing, Benefactors, Death and the Maiden, Sunset Blvd.*, OB in *The Crazy Locomotive, Uncommon Women and Others, Wine Untouched, Winter Dancers, Singular Life of Albert Nobbs, Joan of Ark at the Stake, Childhood.*

COATS, WILLIAM ALAN. Born Dec. 3, 1957 in Raleigh, NC. Graduate U.Cinn. Debut 1983 OB in *Tallulah* followed by Bdwy in *Crazy for You.*

CODY, JENNIFER. Born Nov. 10, 1969 in Rochester, NY. Graduate SUNY/Fredonia. Debut 1992 OB in *Anyone Can Whistle*, Bdwy in *Cats* (1994), *Grease.*

COHEN, BILL. Born Jan. 12, 1953 in Brooklyn, NY. Yale Graduate. Debut 1984 OB in *Child's Play* followed by *Man Who Killed the Buddah, Festival of 1-Acts, Tempest.*

COHEN, LYNN. Born Aug. 10 in Kansas City, Mo. Graduate Northwestern U. Debut 1979 OB in *Don Juan Comes Back From the Wars* followed by *Getting Out, The Arbor, The Cat and the Canary, Suddenly Last Summer, Bella Figura, The Smash, Chinese Viewing Pavillion, Isn't it Romatic, Total Eclipse, Angelo's Wedding, Hamlet, Love Diatribe, A Couple with a Cat, XXX Love Acts*, Bdwy in *Orpheus Descending* (1989).

COLL, IVONNE. Born Nov. 4 in Fajardo, PR. Attended UPR, LACC. Debut 1980 OB in *Spain 1980* followed by *Animals, The Wonderful Ice Cream Suit, Cold Air, Fabiola, Concerto in Hi-Fi, Quintuplets, A Burning Beach, The Promise, Blood Wedding, La Puta Vida, Pancho Diablo*, Bdwy in *Goodbye, Fidel* (1980), *Shakespeare on Broadway: Macbeth, As You Like It, Romeo and Juliet, Chronicle of a Death Foretold.*

CONE, MICHAEL. Born Oct. 7, 1952 in Fresno, CA. Graduate U. Wash. Bdwy debut 1980 in *Brigadoon*, OB in *Bar Mitzvah Boy, The Rink, Commedia Tonite!*

CONNELL, GORDON. Born Mar. 19, 1923 in Berkley, CA. Graduate U.Cal, NYU. Bdwy debut 1961 in *Subways are for Sleeping* followed by *Hello Dolly!, Lysistrata, Human Comedy* (also OB), *Big River*, OB in *Beggars Opera, Butler Did It, With Love and Laughter, Deja Review.*

CONNELL, JANE. Born Oct. 27, 1925 in Berkeley, CA. Attended U.Cal. Bdwy debut in *New Faces of 1956* followed by *Drat! The Cat!, Mame* (1966/83), *Dear World, Lysistrata, Me and My Girl, Lend Me a Tenor, Crazy For You*, OB in *Shoestring Revue, Threepenny Opera, Pieces of Eight, Demi-Dozen, She Stoops to Conquer, Drat!, Real Inspector Hound, Rivals, Rise and Rise of Daniel Rocket, Laughing Stock, Singular Dorothy Parker, No No Nanette in Concert.*

CONOLLY, PATRICIA. Born Aug. 29, 1933 in Tabora, E. Africa. Attended U. Sydney. With APA in *You Can't Take It With You, War and Peace, School for Scandal, Wild Duck, Right You Are, We Comrades Three, Pantagleize, Exit the King, Cherry Orchard, Misanthrope, Cocktail Party, Cock-a-doodle Dandy* followed by *Stretcar Named Desire, Importance of Being Earnest, The Circle, Small Family Business, Real Inspector Hound/ 15 Minute Hamlet, Heiress*, OB in *Blithe Spirit, Woman in Mind.*

CONROY, FRANCES. Born in 1953 in Monroe, GA. Attended Dickinson Col., Juilliard, Neighborhood Playhouse. Debut 1978 OB with the Acting Co. in *Mother Courage, King Lear, The Other Half* followed by *All's Well That Ends Well, Othello, Sorrows of Stephen, Girls Girls Girls, Zastrozzi, Painting Churches, Uncle Vanya, Romance Language, To Gillian on Her 37th Birthday, Man and Superman, Zero Positive, Bright Room Called Day, Lips Together Teeth Apart, Booth, Last Yankee, Three Tall Women*, Bdwy in *Lady from Dubuque* (1980), *Our Town, Secret Rapture* (also OB), *Some Americans Abroad* (also OB), *Two Shakespearian Actors, In the Summer House, Broken Glass.*

CONROY, JARLATH. Born Sept. 30, 1944 in Galway, Ire. Attended RADA. Bdwy debut 1976 in *Comedians*, followed by *The Elephant Man, Macbeth, Ghetto, The Visit, On the Waterfront*, OB in *Translations, The Wind that Shook the Barley, Gardenia, Friends, Playboy of the Western World, One-Act Festival, Abel & Bela/Architect, The Matchmaker.*

CONROY, MARYELLEN. Born Aug. 31, 1947 in White Plains, NY. Graduate Pace U. Bdwy debut 1994 in *Inspector Calls.*

CONWAY, KEVIN. Born May 29, 1941 in New York City. Debut 1968 in *Muzeeka* followed by *Saved, Plough and the Stars, One Flew Over the*

Cuckoo's Nest, When You Comin' Back Red Ryder, Long Day's Journey into Night, Other Places, King John, Other People's Money, Man Who Fell in Love with His Wife, Ten Below, Bdwy in *Indians* (1969), *Moonchildren, Of Mice and Men, Elephant Man, On the Waterfront.*

COOK, VICTOR T. Born Aug. 19, 1967 in New York City. Debut 1976 OB in *Joseph and the Amazing Technicolor Dreamcoat* followed by *Haggadah, Moby Dick, Romance in Hard Times*, Bdwy in *Don't Get God Started* (1988), *Starmites* (also OB), *Smokey Joe's Cafe.*

COOPER, MARILYN. Born Dec. 14, 1936 in New York City. Attended NYU. Bdwy in *Mr. Wonderful, West Side Story, Brigadoon, Gypsy, I Can Get It for You Wholesale, Hallelujah Baby, Golden Rainbow, Mame, A Teaspoon Every 4 Hours, Two by Two, On the Town, Ballroom, Woman of the Year, The Odd Couple, Cafe Crown, Fiorello in Concert*, OB in *The Mad Show, Look Me Up, The Perfect Party, Cafe Crown, Milk and Honey, Petrified Prince.*

COOPER, ROY. Born Jan. 22, 1930 in London, Eng. Bdwy debut 1968 in *Prime of Miss Jean Brodie* followed by *Canterbury Tales, St. Joan, Inspector Calls* (1994), OB in *Month in the Country, Mary Stuart, Henry IV Part I.*

CORBALIS, BRENDAN. Born Mar. 19, 1964 in Dublin, Ire. Graduate NYU. Debut 1988 OB in *April Snow* followed by *The Indians of Venezuela, Finding the Sun, Beekeeper's Daughter.*

CORBO, GEORGINA. Born Sept. 21, 1965 in Havana, Cuba. Attended SUNY/Purchase. Debut 1988 OB in *Ariano,* followed by *Born to Rumba, Mambo Louie and the Dancing Machine, Ghost Sonata, You Can't Win, Dog Lady.*

CORCORAN, JAY. Born Oct. 16, 1958 in Boston, MA. Graduate Catholic U., Harvard U. Debut 1985 OB in *Caligula* followed by *Why to Refuse, Jerker, Play* and wrote *The Fey and The Christening.*

CORMIER, TONY. Born Nov. 2, 1951 in Camp Roberts, CA. Attended Pierce Col., Wash. St. U. Debut 1984 in *Kennedy at Colonus*, followed by *Pericles, Something Cloudy Something Clear, Three Sisters, Love's Labour's Lost, Angel in the House, Measure for Measure, Titus Andronicus, Hamlet.*

CORPUS, WILLY. Born Apr. 18 in New York City. Graduate Bronx C.C., Stella Adler Consv. Debut 1980 OB in *Peking Man* followed by *F.O.B.*

CORREA, ANAMARIA. Born Mar. 26 in Brooklyn, NY. Graduate Hunter Col. Debut 1995 OB in *Simpson Street.*

CORSAIR, JANIS. Born June 18, 1948 in Providence, RI. Debut 1984 OB in *Coarse Acting Show* followed by *In the Boom Boom Room, Love and the Rebound.*

COSGRAVE, PEGGY. Born June 23, 1946 in San Mateo, CA. Graduate San Jose Col., Catholic U. Debut 1980 OB in *Come Back to the Five and Dime Jimmy Dean* followed by *Sandbox*, Bdwy in *The Nerd* followed by *Born Yesterday, Shadow Box.*

COSTA, RICHARD. Born Dec. 29, 1963 in Camden, NJ. Graduate Shenandoah U. Debut 1988 in Radio City Christmas Spectacular followed by Bdwy in *Gentlemen Prefer Blondes* (1995).

COSTALLOS, SUZANNE. Born Apr. 3, 1933 in New York City. Attended NYU, Boston Consv., Juilliard. Debut 1977 OB in *Play and Other Play by Beckett*, followed by *Elizabeth 1, The White Devil, Hunting Scenes from Lower Bavaria, Selma, In Miami as It is in Heaven, Peacetime, Most Massive Woman Wins*, Bdwy in *Zorba* (1983).

COSTER, NICHOLAS. Born Dec. 3, 1934 in London, Eng. Attended Neighborhood Playhouse. Bdwy debut 1960 in *Beckett* followed by *90 Day Mistress, But Seriously, Twigs, Otherwise Engaged*, OB in *Epitaph for George Dillon, Shadow and Substance, Thracian Horses, Oh Say Can You See, Happy Birthday Wanda June, Naomi Court, Old Glory, Jack's Holiday.*

COUNCIL, RICHARD E. Born Oct. 1, 1947 in Tampa, FL. Graduate U. Fl. Debut 1973 OB in *Merchant of Venice,* followed by *Ghost Dance, Look We've Come Through. Arms and the Man, Isadora Duncan Sleeps with the Russian Navy, Arthur, The Winter Dancer, The Prevalence of Mrs. Seal, Jane Avril, Young Playwrights Festival, Sleeping Dogs, The Good Coach, Subfertile*, Bdwy in *Royal Family* (1975), *Philadelphia Story, I'm Not Rappaport, Conversations with My Father, Pal Joey, Uncle Vanya.*

COURTNEY, TOM. Born Feb. 25, 1937 in Hull, Eng. Graduate RADA. Bdwy debut 1977 in *Otherwise Engaged* followed by *The Dresser, Uncle Vanya.*

COVER, BRADFORD. Born Jan. 26, 1967 in New York City. Graduate Denison U., U. Wis. Debut 1994 OB in *King Lear* followed by *Beaux Strategem, Venetian Twins, Oedipus at Colonus, Mrs. Warren's Profession.*

CRAVENS, MARY ELLEN. Born June 11, 1982 in Dallas, TX. Bdwy debut 1994 in *An Inspector Calls.*

CRAVENS, PIERCE. Born Jan. 8, 1986 in Dallas, TX. Debut 1993 OB in *All's Well that Ends Well*, Bdwy 1994 in *Beauty and the Beast.*

CRISTE, MIRLA. Born in Davao City, PI. Graduate Oberlin Col., U. Cal./Irvine. Bdwy debut 1991 in *Miss Saigon*, OB 1995 in *Rita's Resources.*

CRONIN, JANE. Born Apr. 4, 1936 in Boston, MA. Bdwy debut 1965 in

Postmark Zero, OB in *The Bald Soprano, One Flew over the Cuckoo's Nest, Hot l Baltimore, The Gathering, Catsplay, The Vialano Virtuoso, Afternoons in Vegas, The Frequency, A Month in the Country, The Trading Post, Booth, Love Diatribe, Evangeline and God.*

CROSBY, B.J. Born Nov. 23, 1952 in New Orleans, LA. Bdwy debut 1995 in *Smokey Joe's Cafe.*

CROSBY, KIM. Born July 11, 1960 in Fort Smith, AR. Attended SMU, Man. Schl. Music. Bdwy debut 1985 in *Jerry's Girls*, followed by *Into the Woods, Guys and Dolls*, OB in *Philemon.*

CRUDUP, BILLY. Born July 8, 1968 in Manhasset, NY. Graduate UNC, NYU. Debut 1994 OB in *America Dreaming*, Bdwy 1995 in *Arcadia* for which he received a Theatre World Award.

CUERVO, ALMA. Born Aug. 13, 1951 in Tampa, Fl. Graduate Tulane U. Debut 1977 in *Uncommon Women and Others* followed by *A Foot in the Door, Put Them All Together, Isn't It Romantic?, Miss Julie, Quilters, The Sneaker Factor, Songs on a Shipwrecked Sofa, Uncle Vanya, The Grandma Plays, The Nest, Secret Rapture, Christine Alberta's Father, Music from Down the Hall, Donahue Sisters*, Bdwy in *Once in a Lifetime, Bedroom Farce, Censored Scenes from King Kong, Is There Life After High School?, Ghetto, Secret Rapture.*

CULP, KAREN. Born July 31, 1964 in Charlotte, NC. Graduate UNC/Chapel Hill. Bdwy debut 1995 in *Crazy for You.*

CUMPSTY, MICHAEL. Born in England. Graudate UNC. Bdwy debut 1989 in *Artist Descending a Staircase* followed by *La Bete, Timon of Athens, Translations, Heiress*, OB in *The Art of Success, Man and Superman, Hamlet, Cymbeline, The Winter's Tale, King John, Romeo and Juliet, All's Well That Ends Well.*

CUNNINGHAM, JOHN. Born June 22, 1932 in Auburn, NY. Graduate Yale, Dartmouth U. OB in *Love Me a Little, Pimpernel, The Fantasticks, Love and Let Love, The Bone Room, Dancing in the Dark, Father's Day, Snapshot, Head Over Heels, Quartermaine's Terms, Wednesday, On Approval, Miami, Perfect Party, Birds of Paradise, Naked Truth, Cheever Evening, Camping with Henry and Tom, Sylvia*, Bdwy in *Hot Spot* (1963), *Zorba, Company, 1776, Rose, The Devil's Disciple, Six Degrees of Separation* (also OB), *Anna Karenina, The Sisters Rosensweig, Allegro in Concert.*

CUNNINGHAM, T. SCOTT. Born Dec. 15 in Los Angeles, CA. Graduate NC School of Arts. Debut 1992 OB in *Pterodactyls*, followed by *Takes on Women, Stand-In, Don Juan in Chicago*, Bdwy in 1995 in *Love! Valour! Compassion!*

CURRIER, TERENCE P. Born Nov. 5, 1934 in Cleveland, OH. Graduate Harvard U., Boston Consv. Bdwy debut 1994 in *Damn Yankees.*

CURTIS, KEENE. Born Feb. 15, 1925 in Salt Lake City UT. Graduate U. Utah. Bdwy debut 1949 in *Shop at Sly Corner*, with APA in *School for Scandal, The Tavern, Anatole, Scapin, Right You Are, Importance of Being Earnest, Twelfth Night, King Lear, Seagull, Lower Depths, Man and Superman, Judith, War and Peace, You Can't Take It with You, Pantaglieze, Cherry Orchard, Misanthrope, Cocktail Party, Cock-a-Doodle Dandy, and Hamlet, A Patriot for Me, The Rothschilds, Night Watch, Via Galactica, Annie, Division Street, La Cage aux Folles, White Liars/Black Comedy*, OB in *Colette, Ride Across Lake Constance, The Cocktail Hour.*

CURRY, MICHAEL. Born July 11, 1967 in St. Louis, MO. Graduate Fl. St. U./Asolo. Debut 1995 OB in *Two Boys in a Bed on a Cold Winter's Night.*

CWIKOWSKI, BILL. Born Aug. 4, 1945 in Newark, NJ. Graduate Smith and Monmouth Col. Debut 1972 OB in *Charlie the Chicken,* followed by *Summer Brave, The Desperate Hours, Mandrogola, Two by Noonan, Soft Touch, Innocent Pleasures, 3 from the Marathon, Two Part Harmony; Bathroom Plays, Little Victories, Dolphin Position, Cabal of Hypocrites, Split Second, Rose Cottages, The Good Coach, Marathon '88, Tunnel of Love, Dead Man's Apartment, De Donde?, Scarlett Letter.*

DABDOUB, JACK. Born Feb. 5 in New Orleans, LA. Graduate Tulane U. OB in *What's Up, Time for the Gentle People, The Peddler, The Dodo Bird, Annie Get Your Gun, Lola*, Bdwy in *Paint Your Wagon* (1951), *My Darlin' Aida, Happy Hunting, Hot Spot, Camelot, Baker Street, Anya, Her First Roman, Coco, Man of LaMancha, Brigadoon, Moose Murders, One Touch of Venus, Sally in Concert, The Most Happy Fella, Show Boat.*

DAILY, DANIEL. Born July 25, 1955 in Chicago, IL. Graduate Notre Dame, U. Wash. Debut 1988 OB in *Boy's Breath*, followed by *A Ronde, Iron Bars, Chekhov Very Funny, Macbeth, As You Like It, Free Zone, Scarlet Letter.*

DALE, JIM. Born Aug. 15, 1935 in Rothwell, Eng. Debut 1974 OB in *Taming of the Shrew (Young Vic)* followed by *Privates on Parade, Tavels with My Aunt*, Bdwy in *Scapino* (also OB), *Barnum, Joe Egg, Me and My Girl.*

DANE, SHELTON. Born Apr. 22, 1985 in San Antonio, TX. Debut 1992 OB in *Words Divine* followed by *Merry Wives of Windsor, Baby Anger, Cryptogram.*

D'ANGELO, BEVERLY. Born Nov. 15, 1954 in Columbus, OH. Debut 1994 OB in *Simpatico* for which she received a Theatre World Award.

DANIS, AMY. Born Jan. 20 in Dayton, OH. Member of Joffrey Ballet before Bdwy debut 1980 in *Brigadoon*, OB in *Fire in the Basement, The Rehearsal.*

DANNER, BLYTHE. Born Feb. 3, 1944 in Philadelphia, PA. Graduate Bard Col. Debut 1966 OB in *The Infantry* followed by *Collision Course, Summertree, Up Eden, Someone's Comin' Hungry, Cyrano, Miser* for which she received a 1969 Theatre World Award, *Twelfth Night, New York Idea, Much Ado about Nothing, Love Letters, Sylvia,* Bdwy in *Butterflies are Free, Betrayal, Philadelphia Story, Blithe Spirit, Streetcar Named Desire.*

DANSON, RANDY. Born Apr. 30, 1950 in Plainfield NJ. Graduate Carnegie-Mellon U. Debut 1978 OB in *Gimme Shelter,* followed by *Big and Little, The Winter Dancers, Time Steps, Casualties, Red and Blue, The Resurrection of Lady Lester, Jazz Poets at the Grotto, Plenty, Macbeth, Blue Window, Cave Life, Romeo and Juliet, One-Act Festival, Mad Forest, Triumph of Love, The Treatment, Phaedra.*

DANZINGER, MAIA. Born Apr. 12, 1950 in New York City. Attended NYU. Bdwy debut 1973 in *Waltz of the Toreadors,* OB in *Total Eclipse, Milk of Paradise, Rachel Plays, Kill, Madwomen of Chaillot.*

DARDEN, NORMA JEAN. Born Nov. 4 in Newark, NJ. Graduate Sarah Lawrence Col. Bdwy debut 1968 in *Weekend,* OB in *Underground, Les Femmes Noires, Uncle Tom's Cabin, Spoonbread and Strawberry Wine.*

DARLOW, CYNTHIA. Born June 13, 1949 in Detroit, MI. Attended NC Sch of Arts, Penn State U. Debut 1974 OB in *This Property Is Condemned* followed by *Portrait of a Madonna, Clytemnestra, Unexpurgated Memoirs of Bernard Morgandigler, Actor's Nightmare, Sister MaryIgnatius Explains..., Fables for Friends, That's It Folks!, Baby with the Bath Water, Dandy Dick, Naked Truth, Cover of Life,* Bdwy in *Grease* (1976), *Rumors, Prelude to a Kiss* (also OB).

DAVIDGE, DONNA. Born Jan. 15, 1955 in Stamford, CT. Graduate UNH, Loma Linda U., Neighborhood Playhouse. Debut 1989 OB in *Two Girls on a Porch* followed by *Postmarks, Hotline, Trash City and Death, Fools in the West, Down Dark Deceptive, Streets.*

DAVIDSON, RICHARD M. Born May 10, 1940 in Hamilton, Ont., Can. Graduate U. Toronto, LAMDA. Debut 1978 OB in *The Beasts* followed by *The Bacchae, The Broken Pitcher, Knights Errant, The Entertainer, Lunatics and Lovers, Let Us Now Praise Famous Men, Miami Stories, Have You Spoken to Any Jews Lately?,* Bdwy in *The Survivor* (1981), *The Ghetto.*

DAVIES, JOSEPH C. Born June 29, 1928 in Charlton, IA. Attended Mich. St.Col., Wayne U. Debut 1961 OB in *7 at Dawn* followed by *Jo, Long Voyage Home, Time of the Key, Good Soldier Schweik, Why Hanna's Skirt Won't Stay Down, Ghandi, Coney Island Kid, The Cause,* Bdwy in *Skin of Our Teeth* (1975).

DAVIS, BRUCE ANTHONY. Born Mar. 4, 1959 in Dayton, OH. Attended Juilliard. Bdwy debut 1979 in *Dancin',* followed by *Big Deal, A Chorus Line, High Rollers, Damn Yankees,* OB in *Carnival.*

DAVIS, CLIFTON. Born Oct. 4, 1945 in Chicago, IL. Attended Oakwood Col. Debut 1968 OB in *How to Steal an Election* followed by *Horseman Pass By, To Be Young Gifted and Black, No Place to Be Somebody, Do It Again* for which he received a 1971 Theatre World Award, *Hapgood,* Bdwy 1967 in *Hello Dolly!, Jimmy Shine, Look to the Lillies, Engagement Baby, Two Gentlemen of Verona.*

DAVIS, MICHAEL ALLEN/ALAN. Born Aug. 23, 1953 in San Francisco, CA. Attended Clown Col. Bdwy debut 1981 in *Broadway Follies* for which he received a Theatre World Award, *Sugar Babies, Comedy Tonight.*

DAVIS, SHEILA KAY. Born May 30, 1956 in Daytona, FL. Graduate Spelman Col. Debut 1982 OB in *Little Shop of Horrors* followed by *Rent.*

DEAK, TIM. Born Mar. 15, 1968 in Ravennam, OH. Graduate Otterbein Col. Debut 1974 OB in *Kentucky Cycle* followed by *Dark of the Moon, Childe Byron.*

DEAL, FRANK. Born Oct. 7, 1958 in Birmingham, AL. Attended Duke U. Debut 1982 OB in *The American Princess* followed by *Richard III, Ruffian on the Stair, A Midsummer Night's Dream, We Shall Not All Sleep, The Legend of Sleepy Hollow, Three Sisters, The Triangle Project, One Neck, Window Man, Othello, Junk Bonds.*

DeANDA, PETER. Born Mar. 10, 1940 in Pittsburgh, PA. Attended Pittsburgh Playhouse, Actors Workshop. Bdwy debut 1965 in *Zulu and the Zayda* followed by *The Guide,* OB in *The Blacks, Dutchman, Sound of Silence, Kitchen, Passing Through from Exotic Places, House of Leather, Ballad for Bimshire.*

DECAREAU, DICK. Born Jan. 19, 1950 in Lynn, MA. Graduate Salem St.Col. Bdwy debut 1986 in *Raggedy Ann* followed by *Gentlemen Prefer Blondes* (1995), OB in *Mlle. Colombe, Dragons, Music Man, Alias Jimmy Valentine.*

de HAAS, DARIUS. Born Sept. 29, 1968 in Chicago, IL. Graduate AMDA. Bdwy debut 1994 in *Kiss of the Spider Woman* followed by *Carousel.*

DeLAURENTIS, SEMINA. Born Jan. 21 in Waterbury, CT. Graduate Southern CT St.Col. Debut 1985 OB in *Nunsense,* followed by *Have I Got a Girl for You, Nunsense II.*

DE LA PENA, GEORGE. Born in New York City in 1956. Performed with Am. Bal. Th. before Bdwy debut 1981 in *Woman of the Year* followed by *On Your Toes, Red Shoes, Chronicle of a Death Foretold.*

DENMAN, JEFFREY. Born Oct. 7, 1970 in Buffalo, NY. Graduate U. Buffalo. Bdwy debut 1995 in *How to Succeed...*

DENNEHY, BRIAN. Born July 9, 1938 in Bridgeport, CT. Debut 1988 OB in *Cherry Orchard* followed by Bdwy 1995 in *Translations.*

DeSHIELDS, ANDRE. Born Jan. 12, 1946 in Baltimore, MD. Graduate U. Wis. Bdwy debut 1973 in *Warp,* followed by *Rachel Lily Rosenbloom, The Wiz, Ain't Misbehavin'* (1978/1988), *Haarlem Nocturne, Just So, Stardust,* OB in *2008-1/2 Jazzbo Brown, The Soldier's Tale, The Little Prince, Haarlem Nocturne, Sovereign State of Boogedy Boogedy, Kiss Me When It's Over, Saint Tous, Ascension Day, Casino Paradise, The Wiz, Angel Levine.*

DESMOND, DAN. Born July 4, 1944 in Racine, Wis. Graduate U. Wis., Yale U, Bdwy debut 1981 in *Morning's at 7* followed by *Othello, All My Sons, Rumors,* OB in *Perfect Diamond, The Bear, Vienna Notes, On Mt. Chimborazo, Table Settings, Moonchildren, Festival of 1-Acts, Marathon '88, Death Defying Acts.*

DeMATTHEWS, RALPH. Born Apr. 22, 1950 in Somerville, NJ. Debut 1984 OB in *Agamemnon* followed by *Bury the Dead, A Place Called Heartbreak, Any Corner, The Strike, On the Waterfront.*

DeSOTO, EDOUARD. Born June 13, 1941 in Santa Isabel, PR. Graduate Davis & Elkins Col. Debut 1977 in *I Took Panama* followed by *El Macho, Betances, Blackamoor, Spanish Eyes, Death and the Maiden,* Bdwy 1995 in *Chronicle of a Death Foretold.*

DeVRIES, JON. Born Mar. 26, 1947 in New York City. Graduate Bennington Col. Pasadena Playhouse. Debut 1977 OB in *The Cherry Orchard,* followed by *Agamemnon, The Ballad of Soapy Smith, Titus Andronicus, The Dreamer Examines his Pillow, Sight Unseen Patient A, Scarlet Letter,* Bdwy in *The Inspector General, Devour the Snow, Major Barbara, Execution of Justice.*

DIAZ, NATASCIA. Born Jan. 4, 1970 in Lugano, Swit. Graduate Carnegie-Mellon U. Debut 1993 OB in *Little Prince* followed by *I Won't Dance.*

DiBENEDETTO, JOHN. Born Oct. 9, 1955 in Brooklyn, NY. Attended Hunter Col., HB Studio. Debut 1979 OB in *Prisoners of Quai Dong* followed by *Greatest of All Time, Apple Crest, Tales of Another City, Out at Sea, Heartdrops, Good Woman of Setzuan, Squeeze, Drunken Boat, Venus Dances Nightly, Not a Single Blade of Grass, Flashpoint, Sea Gull, Bruno's Donuts, Happy Birthday America, Full Circle, Across Arkansas, Jurlyburly, Wedding, Candide, Unrecognizable Characters, Secret Sits in the Middle.*

DIXON, MacINTYRE. Born Dec. 22, 1931 in Everett, Ma. Graduate Emerson Col. Bdwy debut 1965 in *Xmas in Las Vegas,* followed by *Cop-Out, Story Theatre, Metamorphosis, Twigs, Over Here, Once in a Lifetime, Alice in Wonderland, 3 Penny Opera,* OB in *Quare Fellow, Plays for Bleecker Street, Stewed Prunes, The Cat's Pajamas, Three Sisters, 3 X 3, Second City, Mad Show, Meow!, Lotta, Rubbers, Conjuring an Event, His Majesty the Devil, Tomfollery, A Christmas Carol Times and Appetites of Toulouse-Lautrec, Room Service, Sills and Company, Little Murders Much Ado about Nothing, A Winter's Tale, Arms and the Man, Hamlet, Pericles, Luck Plauck Virtue.*

DONNELLY, DONAL. Born July 6, 1931 in Bradford, Eng. Bdwy debut 1966 in *Philadelphia, Here I Come!,* followed by *A Day in the Death of Joe Egg, Sleuth, The Faith Healer, The Elephant Man, Execution of Justice, Sherlock's Last Case, Ghetto, Dancing at Lughnasa, Translations,* OB in *My Astonishing Self* (solo), *The Chalk Garden, Big Maggie.*

DOWE, KATE. Born Dec. 5, 1968 in Salem, MA. Graduate Northwestern U. Bdwy debut 1994 in *Beauty and the Beast.*

DOUGLAS, GARY. Born Jan. 31, 1953 in Detroit, MI. Attended Am. Consv.Music. Bdwy debut 1994 in *Crazy for You.*

DOVEY, MARK. Born Jan. 13, 1954 in Vancouver, Can. Attended U. British Columbia. Bdwy debut 1980 in *Chorus Line* followed by *Little Prince and the Aviator, Cabaret* (1987), *Christmas Carol.*

DRAKE, DAVID. Born June 27, 1963 in Baltimore, Md. Attended Essex Col., Peabody Consv. Debut 1984 in *Street Theatre,* followed by *Pretty Boy, Vampire Lesbians of Sodom, The Life, The Night Larry Kramer Kissed Me, Pageant, The Normal Heart* (benefit), *Language of Their Own.*

DRAKE, DONNA. Born May 21, 1953 in Columbia, SC. Attended USC/Columbia. Bdwy debut 1975 in *Chorus Line* followed by *It's So Nice to Be Civilized, 1940s Radio Hour, Women of the Year, Sophisticated Ladies, Wind in the Willows,* OB in *Memories of Riding with Joe Cool, Body Shop.*

DUDLEY, CRAIG. Born Jan. 22, 1945 in Sheepshead Bay, NY. Graduate

AADA, Am. Th. Wing. Debut 1970 OB in *Macbeth*, followed by *Zou, I Have Always Believed in Ghosts, Othello, War and Peace, Dial "M" for Murder, Misalliance, Crown of Kings, Trelawny of The Wells, Ursula's Permanent.*

DUNDAS, JENNIFER. Born Jan. 14, 1971 in Boston, MA. Bdwy debut 1981 in *Grownups* followed by *Arcadia*, OB in *Before the Dawn, I Love You I Love You Not, The Autobiography of Aiken Fiction.*

DURAN, MICHAEL. Born Nov. 25, 1953 in Denver, CO. Graduate U.Col. Debut 1981 OB in *Godspell* followed *Anonymous, Dragons*, Bdwy 1986 in *Into the Light, Crazy for You.*

DuSOLD, ROBERT. Born June 7, 1959 in Waukesha, Wl. Attended U.Cinn.Consv. Bdwy debut in *Les Miserables* (1991) followed by *Kiss of the Spider Woman.*

DVORSKY, GEORGE. Born May 11, 1959 in Greensburg, PA. Attended Carnegie-Mellon. Bdwy debut 1981 in *The Best Little Whorehouse in Texas* followed by *Marilyn: An American Fable, Brigadoon. Cinderella, Passion, Gentlemen Prefer Blondes* (1995), OB in *Dames at Sea* (1985).

EDELMAN, GREGG. Born Sept. 12, 1958 in Chicago, IL. Graduate Northwestern U. Bdwy debut 1982 in *Evita*, followed by *Oliver!, Cats, Cabaret, City of Angels, Falsettos, Anna Karenina, Passion, Fiorello in Concert, Out of This World in concert*, OB in *Weekend, Shop on Main Street, Forbidden Broadway, She Loves Me, Babes in Arms, Make Someone Happy, Greetings.*

EDMEAD, WENDY. Born July 6, 1956 in New York City. Graduate NYU. Bdwy debut 1974 in *The Wiz*, followed *by Stop the World…, America, Dancin', Encore, Cats*, OB 1995 in *Petrified Prince.*

EIS, MARK. Born June 18, 1964 in Schenectady, NY. Graduate SUNY/Albany, U.N.Carolina. Debut 1994 OB in *Oh What a Lovely War* followed by *Botticelli, Romeo and Juliet, Measure for Measure, Titus Andronicus.*

EISENBERG, NED. Born Jan. 13, 1957 in New York City. Attended Acl. Inst.of Arts. Debut 1980 OB in *The Time of the Cuckoo* followed by *Our Lord of Lynchville, Dream of a Blacklisted Actor, Second Avenue, Moving Targets, Claus, Titus Adronicus, Saturday Morning Cartoons*, Bdwy 1995 in *Pal Joey* (Encores).

ELDARD, RON. Born in 1964 in New York City. Attended HS Performming Arts. Bdwy debut 1986 in *Biloxi Blues, On the Waterfront*, OB in *Tony 'n' Tina's Wedding*, followed by *Servy-n Bernice 4 Ever, The Years, Aven' U. Boys.*

ELDER, DAVID. Born July 7, 1966 in Houston, TX. Attended U.Houston. Bdwy debut 1992 in *Guys and Dolls* followed by *Beauty and the Beast.*

ELLIOTT, PATRICIA. Born July 21 in Gunnison, CO. Graduate U.Col., LAMDA. Debut 1968 with LC Rep in *King Lear* and *Cry of Players* followed OB by *Henry V, The Persians, Doll's House, Hedda Gabler, In Case of Accident, Water Hen, Polly, But Not for Me, By Bernstein, Prince of Homberg, Artichokes, Wine Untouched, Misalliance, Virginia, Sung and Unsung Sondheim, Voice of the Turtle, Lillian Wald, Bunker Reveries, Phaedra, Dance Durang*, Bdwy debut 1973 in *A Little Night Music* for which she received a Theatre World Award, followed by *Shadow Box, Tartuffe, 13 Rue de L'Amour, Elephant man, Month of Sundays.*

EMERY, LISA. Born Jan. 29 in Pittsburgh, PA. Graduate Hollins Col. Debut 1981 OB in *Connecticut*, followed by *Talley & Son, Dalton's Back, Growaups!, The Matchmaker, Marvin's Room*, Bdwy in *Passion* (1983), *Burn This, Rumors.*

EMICK, JARROD. Born July 2, 1969 in Ft. Eustas, VA. Attended S. Dakota State U. Bdwy debut 1990 in *Miss Saigon* followed by *Damn Yankees* for which he received a 1994 Theatre World Award.

EMMETT, ROBERT/BOB. Born Sept. 28, 1921 in Monterey, CA. Attended U.Cal., Neighborhood Playhouse. Bdwy credits include *Peter Gynt* (1951), *Two on the Aisle, Mid-Summer*, OB in *Knight of the Burning Pestle, Madam Will You Walk, Eye of the Beholder Doll's House.*

ENG, RICHARD. Born July 29, 1943 in Spokane, WA. Graduate Wa.St.U. Debut 1988 OB in *Loose Ends* followed by *School for Wives.*

ERBE, KATHRYN. Born in 1965 in New York City. Graduate NYU. Bdwy debut 1990 in *Grapes of Wrath*, followed by *Speed of Darkness, Month in the Country*, OB in *The My House Play, Down the Shore.*

ERIC, DAVID. Born Feb. 28, 1949 in Boston, MA. Graduate Neighborhood Playhouse. Debut 1971 OB in *Ballad of Johnny Pot* followed by *Love Me Love My Children, Oklahoma*, Bdwy in *Shenandoah* (1975), *Yentl, Naughty Marietta* (NYCO), *Sunset Blvd.*

ESPOSITO, GIANCARLO. Born Apr. 26, 1958 in Copenhagen, Den. Bdwy debut 1968 in *Maggie Flynn*, followed by *The Me Nobody Knows, Lost in the Stars, Seesaw, Merrily We Roll Along, Don't Get God Started, 3 Penny Opera*, OB in *Zooman and the Sign* for which he received a 1981 Theatre World Award, *Keyboard, Who Loves the Dancer, House of Ramon Iglesias, Do Lord Remember Me, Balm in Gilead, Anchorman, Distant Fires, The Root, Trafficking in Broken Hearts.*

ESTABROOK, CHRISTINE. Born Sept. 13 in Erie, PA. OB credits include *Pastorale, Win/Lose/Draw, Ladyhouse Blues, Baby with the Bathwater, Blue Windows, North Shore Fish, The Boys Next Door, For Dear Life, The Widow's Blind Date, What a Man Weighs*, Bdwy in *I'm Not Rappaport* (1978), *The Sisters Rosensweig.*

ESTEY, SUELLEN. Born Nov. 21 in Mason City, IA. Graduate Stephens Col., Northwestern U. Debut 1970 OB in *Some Other Time*, followed by *June Moon, Buy Bonds Buster, Smile Smile Smile, Carousel, Lullaby of Broadway, I Can't Keep Running, The Guys in the Truck, Stop the World…, Bittersuite—One More Time, Passionate Extremes, Sweeney Todd, Love in Two Countries, After the Ball*, Bdwy in *The Selling of the President* (1972), *Barnum, Sweethearts in Concert, Sweeney Todd* (1989).

EVANS, HARVEY. Born Jan. 7, 1941 in Cincinnati, OH. Bdwy debut 1957 in *New Girl in Town*, followed by *Annie Get Your Gun, Nash at 9, West Side Story, Redhead, Gypsy, Anyone Can Whistle, Oklahoma, Hello Dolly!, George M!, Our Town, The Boy Friend, Follies, Barnum, Damn Yankees, La Cage aux Folles, Damn Yankees, Sunset Blvd.*, OB in *The Rothschilds, Sextet, Annie Warbucks.*

EVANS, SCOTT ALAN. Born Oct. 18, 1955 in Irvington-on-Hudson, NY. Graduate Boston U. Bdwy debut 1983 in *Moose Murders* followed by OB 1995 in *Androcles and the Lion.*

EYRE, PETER. Born Mar. 11, 1942 in New York City. With London's Old Vic before Bdwy debut in *Hamlet* (1995).

FABER, RON. Born Feb. 16, 1933 in Milwaukee, WI. Graduate Marquette U. OB Debut 1959 in *An Enemy of the People*, followed by *The Exception and the Rule, America Hurrah, They Put Handcuffs on Flowers, Dr. Selavy's Magic Theatre, Troilus and Cressida, The Beauty Part, Woyzeck, St. Joan of the Stockyards, Jungle of Cities, Scenes from Everyday Life, Mary Stuart, 3 by Pirandello, Times and Appetites of Toulouse-Lautrec, Hamlet, Johnstown Vendicator, Don Juan of Seville, Between the Acts, Baba Goya, Moving Targets, Arturo Ui, Words Divine, Dracula, 3 By Beckett*, Bdwy in *Medea* (1973), *First Monday in October.*

FACTORA, MARSHALL. Born Aug. 19 in the Philippines. Graduate U.St. Thomas, NYU. Debut 1990 OB in *The Wash* followed by *Rita's Resources.*

FARER, RONNIE (aka Rhonda). Born Oct. 19, 1951 in Colonia, NJ. Graduate Rider Col. Debut 1973 on Bdwy in *Rachel Lily Rosenbloom*, followed by *They're Playing Our Song*, OB in *The Dog beneath the Skin, Sally and Marsha, The Deep End, Tamara, Festival of One-Acts, Catch Me If l Fall, Gift Horse.*

FARWICK, RICK. Born Sept. 13, 1954 in Vincinnati, OH. Graduate Northwestern U. Debut 1988 OB in *Leave It to Me* followed by *Boy Meets Boy.*

FAVRE, KENNETH. Born Mar. 15, 1956 in New York City. Graduate Hunter Col. Debut 1989 OB in *Working Her Way Down* followed by *Sundance, Morning Song, Tartuffe, Judgement Day, Macbeth, Rosencrantz and Guildenstern are Dead, Sea Plays, Anatomy of Sound, As You Like It, Twelfth Night.*

FAYE, PASCALE. Born Jan. 6, 1964 in Paris, France. Bdwy debut 1991 in *Grand Hotel*, followed by *Guys and Dolls.*

FEAGAN, LESLIE. Born Jan. 9, 1951 in Hinckley, OH. Graduate Ohio U. Debut 1978 OB in *Can-Can*, followed by *Merton of the Movies, Promises Promises, Mowgli*, Bdwy in *Anything Goes* (1978), *Guys and Dolls.*

FELDER, CLARENCE. Born Sept. 2, 1938 in St. Matthew, SC. Debut 1964 OB in *The Room* followed by *Are You Now or Have You Ever Been, Claw, Henry V, Winter Dancers, Goose and Tom, 2*, Bdwy in *Red White and Maddox* (1969), *Love for Love, Rules of the Game, Golden Boy, Memory of Two Mondays, They Knew What They Wanted.*

FELDON, BARBARA. Born Mar. 12, 1941 in Pittsburgh, PA. Attended Camegie Tech. Bdwy debut 1960 in *Caligula*, followed by *Past Tense*, OB. in *Faces of Love/Portrait of America, Cut the Ribbons, Love for Better and Verse.*

FELDSHUH, TOVAH. Born Dec. 28, 1953 in New York City. Graduate Sarah Lawrence Col., U.Minn. Bdwy debut 1973 in *Cyrano*, followed by *Dreyfus in Rehearsal, Rodgers and Hart, Yentl* for which she received a Theatre World Award, *Sarava, Lend Me a Tenor*, OB in *Yentl the Yeshiva Boy, Straws in the Wind, Three Sisters, She Stoops to Conquer, Springtime for Henry, The Time of Your Life, Children of the Sun, The Last of the Red Hot Lovers, Mistress of the Inn, A Fierce Attachment, Custody, Six Wives, Hello Muddah Hello Faddah, Best of the West, Awake and Sing.*

FERLAND, DANIELLE. Born Jan. 31, 1971 in Derby, CT. OB Debut 1983 in *Sunday in the Park with George*, followed by *Paradise, Young Playwrights Festival, Camp Paradox, Uncommon Women and Others*, Bdwy in *Sunday in the Park with George* (1984), *Into the Woods* for which she received a Theatre World Award, *A Little Night Music* (NYCO/LC), *Crucible, A Little Hotel on the Side.*

FIEDLER, JOHN. Born Feb. 3, 1925 in Plateville, WI. Attended Neighborhood Playhouse. OB in *The Sea Gull, Sing Me No Lullaby, The Terrible Swift Sword, The Rasberry Picker; The Frog Prince, Raisin in the Sun, Marathon '88, Human Nature,* Bdwy in *One Eye Closed* (1954), *Howie, Raisin in the Sun, Harold, The Odd Couple, Our Town, The Crucible, A Little Hotel on the Side.*

FIELD, CRYSTAL. Born Dec. 10, 1942 in New York City. Attended Juilliard, Hunter Col., Debut 1960 OB in *A Country Scandal,* followed by *A Matter of Life and Death, The Heart That Eats Itself, Ruzzante Returns from the Wars, An Evening of British Music Hall, Ride That Never Was, House Arrest, Us, Beverly's Yard Sale, Bruno's Donuts, Coney Island Kid, Till The Eagle Hollars, Rivalry of Dolls, Pineapple Face, It is It is Not, Little Book of Prof. Enigma.*

FIENNES, RALPH. Born Dec. 22, 1962 in Suffolk, England. Graduate RADA. Bdwy debut 1995 in *Hamlet* for which he received a Theatre World Award.

FINCH, SUSAN. Born Aug. 30, 1959 in Germantown, PA. Attended Juilliard. Debut 1986 OB in *Orchards* followed by *Fair Fight.*

FISHER, AMRY BETH. Born in Plainfield, NJ. Graduate Rutgers U., Debut 1978 OB in *Are You Now or Have You Ever Been?* followed by *Extremities, Radical Mystique.*

FITZGERALD, TARA. Born in 1967 in London, Eng. Graduate London Drama Centre. Bdwy debut 1995 in *Hamlet.*

FISHER, DAVID. Born Nov. 18, 1951 in Tel Aviv, Israel. Bdwy debut 1993 in *Les Miserables.*

FITZGIBBON, JOHN. Born Sept. 13, 1946 in New York City. Graduate Fordham U. LAMDA. Debut 1967 in *Macbeth,* followed by *Macbird!, Screens, False Confessions, Julius Caesar, Gaugin in Tahiti, Moon Mysteries, Twelfth Night, Zion!, Richard III,* Bdwy in *The Incomparable Max* (1981).

FITZPATRICK, ALLEN. Born Jan. 31, 1955 in Boston, MA. Graduate U. Va. Debut 1977 OB in *Come Back Little Sheba* followed by *Wonderful Town, Rothschilds, Group One Acts, Jack's Holiday,* Bdwy in *Gentlemen Prefer Blondes* (1995).

FLAGG, TOM. Born Mar. 30 in Canton, OH. Attended Kent State U., AADA. Debut 1975 OB in *The Fantasticks,* followed by *Give Me Liberty, The Subject Was Roses, Lola, Red Hot and Blue, Episode 26, Dazy, Dr. Dietrick's Process,* Bdwy in *Legend* (1976), *Shenandoah, Players, The Will Rogers Follies, Best Little Whorehouse Goes Public, How to Succeed.*

FLEISS, JANE. Born Jan. 28, in New York City. Graduate NYU. Debut 1979 OB in *Say Goodnight Gracie* followed by *Grace, The Beaver Coat, The Harvesting, D., Second Man, Of Mice and Men, Niedecker, The Undertakers,* Bdwy in *5th of July* (1981), *Crimes of the Heart, I'm Not Rappaport, Search and Destroy, My Thing of Love.*

FLETCHER, SUSANN. Born Sept. 7, 1955 in Wilmington, DE. Graduate Longwood Col., Bdwy debut 1980 in *The Best Little Whorehouse in Texas,* followed by *Raggedy Ann, Jerome Robbins' Broadway, Goodbye Girl, Guys and Dolls,* OB in *Homo Americanus, Stairway to Heaven.*

FLOCKHART, CALISTA. Born Nov. 11 in Stockton, IL. Graduate Rutgers U. Debut 1989 OB in *Beside Herself* followed by *Bovver Boys, Mad Forest, Wtong Turn at Lungfish, Sophistry, All for One, The Loop,* Bdwy in *Glass Menagerie* (1994) for which she received a Theatre World Award.

FLYNN, SUSAN (formerly Susan Elizabeth Scott). Born Aug. 9 in Detroit, MI. Graduate U.Denver. Debut 1971 OB in *The Drunkard* followed by *Mother, Company, Dames at Sea, Yiddle with a Fiddle, Broadway Jukebox, Dames at Sea, Body Shop,* Bdwy in *Music Is* (1976), *On the 20th Century, Fearless Frank The 1940's Radio Hour, Merry Widow* (NYCO).

FOOTE, HALLIE. Born 1955 in New York City. OB in *Night Seasons, Roads to Home, Widow Claire, Courtship, 1918, On Valentine's Day, Talking Pictures, Laura Dennis, Young Man from Atlanta*

FOREMAN, LORRAINE. Born May 25, 1929 in Vancouver, BC, Canada. Bdwy debut 1989 in *Oklahoma!,* followed by *Kiss of the Spider Woman, Show Boat.*

FORMAN, KEN. Born Sept. 22, 1961 in Boston, MA. Attended NYU. Debut 1985 OB in *Measure for Measure,* followed by *Rosencrantz and Guildenstern Are Dead, Macbeth, I Stand Before You Naked, Romeo and Juliet, 3 by Wilder, As You Like It, SS Glencairn, Goose and Tom Tom, Twelfth Night, Anatomy of Sound,* Bdwy in *Wilder Wilder Wilder* (1983).

FOSTER, FRANCES. Born June 11 in Yonkers, NY. Bdwy debut 1955 in *The Wisteria Trees,* followed by *Nobody Loves an Albatross, Raisin in the Sun, The River Niger, First Breeze of Summer, Tap Dance Kid, Fences, Mule Bone, Having Our Say,* OB in *Take a Giant Step, Edge of the City, Tarnmy and the Doctor, The Crucible, Happy Ending, Day of Absence, An Evening of One Acts, Man Better Man, Brotherhood, Akokawe, Rosalee Pritchett, Sty of the Blind Pig, Ballet Behind the Bridge, Good Woman of Seeuan* (LC), *Behold! Cometh the Vanderkellans, Origin, Boesman and Lena, Do Lord Remember Me, Henrietta, Welcome to Black River, House of Shadows, Miracle Worker, You Have Come Back, Ground People, Young Man from Atlanta.*

FOSTER, HERBERT. Born May 14, 1936 in Winnipeg, Can. Bdwy in *Ways and Means, A Touch of the Poet, The Imaginary Invalid, Tonight at 8:30, Henry V, Noises Off, Me and My Girl, Lettice and Lovage, Timon of Athens, Government Inspector,* OB in *Afternoon Tea, Papers, Mary Stuart, Playboy of the Western World, Good Woman of Setzuan, Scenes from American Life, Twelfth Night, All's Well That Ends Well, Richard II, Gifts of the Magi, Heliotrope Bouquet.*

FOWLER, CLEMENT. Born Dec. 27, 1924 in Detroit, MI. Graduate Wayne State U. Bdwy debut 1951 in *Legend of Lovers* followed by *The Cold Wind and the Warm, The Fragile Fox, The Sunshine Boys, Hamlet* (1964), *Richard II,* OB in *The Eagle Has Two Heads, House Music, The Transfiguration of Benno Blimpie, The Inheritors, Paradise Lost, The Time of Your Life, Children of the Sun, Highest Standard of Living, Cymbeline, The Chairs, Venetian Twins.*

FOX, JAMES. Born May 19, 1959 in London, Eng. Attended Central School of Speech and Drama. Bdwy debut 1995 in *Uncle Vanya.*

FOY, HARRIETT D. Born Aug. 24, 1962 in New Bern, NC. Graduate Howard U. Debut OB 1993 in *Fire's Daughters* followed by *Mr. Wonderful, Struttin', Trinity, Inside Out.*

FRANCIS-JAMES, PETER. Born Sept. 16, 1956 in Chicago, IL. Graduate RADA. Debut 1979 OB in *Julius Caesar,* followed by *Long Day's Journey into Night, Antigone, Richard II, Romeo and Juliet, Enrico IV, Cymbeline, Hamlet, Learned Ladies, 10th Young Playwrights Festival, Measure for Measure, Amphitryon, Troilus and Cressida.*

FRANZ, ELIZABETH. Born June 18, 1941 in Akron, OH. Attended AADA. Debut 1965 in *In White America,* followed by *One Night Stands of a Noisey Passenger, The Real Inspector Hound, Augusta, Yesterday Is Over, Actor's Nightmare, Sister Mary Ignatius Explains It All, The Time of Your Life, Children of the Sun,* Bdwy in *Rosencrantz and Guildenstern Are Dead, The Cherry Orchard, Brighton Beach Memoirs, The Octette Bridge Club, Broadway Bound, The Cemetery Club, Getting Married, Uncle Vanya.*

FRANZ, JOY. Born in 1944 in Modesto, CA. Graduate U.Mo. Debut 1969 OB in *Of Thee I Sing,* followed by *Jacques Brel Is Alive..., Out of This World Curtains, I Can't Keep Running in Place, Tomfoolery, Penelope, Bittersuite, Assassins, New Yorkers,* Bdwy in *Sweet Charity, Lysistrata, A Little Night Music, Pippin, Musical Chairs, Into the Woods.*

FRASER, ALISON. Born July 8, 1955 in Natick, MA. Attended Camegie-Mellon, Boston Consv. Debut 1979 OB in *In Trousers,* followed by *March of the Falsettos, Beehive, Four One-Act Musicals, Tales of Tinseltown, Next Please!, Up Against It, Dirtiest Show in Town, Quarrel of Sparrows, The Gig, Cock-a-Doodle Dandy, Swingtime Canteen,* Bdwy in *The Mystery of Edwin Drood* (1986), *Romance Romance, The Secret Garden.*

FRAZIER, RONALD C. Born Feb. 18, 1942. Graduate Carnegie Tech. Bdwy debut 1970 in *Wilson in the Promised Land* followed by *Enemy of the People, What Every Woman Knows, Death Story, Shadow Box,* OB in *Another Language.*

FRECHETTE, PETER. Born Oct. 3, 1956 in Warwick, RI. Debut 1979 OB in *Hornbeam Maze* followed by *Journey's End, In Cahoots, Harry Ruby's Songs My Mother Never Sang, Pontifications on Pigtails and Puberty, Scooter Thomas Makes It to the Top of the World, We're Home, Flora the Red Menace, Hyde in Hollywood, Absent Friends, And Baby Makes Seven, Destiny of Me, La Ronde, Raised in Captivity, Night and Her Stars,* Bdwy in *Eastern Standard* (1989-also OB) for which he won a Theatre World Award, *Our Country's Good, Any Given Day.*

FREEMAN, JONATHAN. Born Feb. 5, 1950 in Bay Village, OH. Graduate Ohio U. Debut 1974 OB in *The Miser* followed by *Bil Baird Marionette Theatre, Babes in Arms, Confessions of Conrad Gerhardt, Bertrano, Clap Trap, In a Pig's Valise,* Bdwy in *Sherlock Holmes* (1974), *Platinum, 13 Days to Broadway, She Loves Me, How to Succeed...*

FRENCH, ARTHUR. Born in New York City and attended Brooklyn Col. Debut 1962 OB in *Raisin' Hell in the Sun,* followed by *Ballad of Bimshire, Day of Absence, Happy Ending, Brotherhood, Perry's Mission, Rosalee Pritchell, Moonlight Arms, Dark Tower, Brownsville Raid, Nevis Mountain Dew, Julius Caesar, Friends, Court of Miracles, The Beautiful LaSalles, Blues for a Gospel Queen, Black Girl, Driving Miss Daisy, The Spring Thing, George Washington Slept Here, Ascension Day, Boxing Day Parade, A Tempest, Hills of Massabielle, Treatment, As You Like It, Swamp Dwellers, Tower of Burden, Henry VI,* Bdwy in *Ain't Supposed to Die a Natural Death, The Iceman Cometh, All God's Chillun Got Wings, The Resurrection of Lady Lester, You Can't Take It with You, Design for Living, Ma Rainey's Black Bottom, Mule Bone, Playboy of the West Indies.*

FROMMER, PAULINE. Born Mar. 25 in New York City. Graduate Wesleyan U. Debut 1995 OB in *Angel Levine.*

FRUGE, ROMAIN. Born Mar. 4, 1959 in Los Angeles, CA. Graduate Allentown Col. Bdwy debut 1986 in *Big River* followed by *Tommy*, OB in *Shabbatai* (1995).

FULLER, ELIZABETH. Born Sept. 22, 1946 in Cleveland, OH. Attended Oh. St. U. Debut 1994 OB in *Me and Jezebel*.

FULLER, PENNY. Born in 1940 in Durham, NC. Attended Northwestern U. Bdwy in *Barefoot in the Park* (1965) followed by *Cabaret, Richard II, As You Like It, Henry IV, Applause, Rex*, OB in *Cherry Orchard, Three Viewings*.

GALANTICH, TOM. Born in Brooklyn, NY. Debut 1985 OB in *On the 20th Century*, followed by *Mademoiselle Colombe, Doll's Life*, Bdwy in *Into the Woods* (1989), *City of Angels*.

GALLAGHER, MEGAN. Born Feb. 6, 1960 in Reading, PA. Graduate Juilliard. Debut 1983 OB in *Tartuffe*, followed by *Miss Julie, Come and Go, Play*, Bdwy in *A Few Good Men* (1989) for which she received a Theatre World Award, *Angels in America*.

GALLAGHER, PETER. Born Aug. 19, 1955 in Armonk, NY. Bdwy debut 1977 in *Hair*, followed by *Grease, A Doll's Life* for which he received a 1983 Theatre World Award, *The Corn is Green. The Real Thing, Long Day's Journey into Night* (1986), *Guys and Dolls* (1992), *Pal Joey* (Encores).

GAMMON, JAMES. Born Apr. 20, 1940 in Newman, IL. Debut 1978 OB in *Curse of the Starving Class* followed by *Lie of the Mind, Simpatico*.

GANUN, JOHN. Born Aug. 23, 1966 in Blissfield, MI. Graduate U. Mich. Bdwy debut 1991 in *The Will Rogers Follies* followed by *Damn Yankees*, OB in *Forever Plaid*.

GARBER, VICTOR. Born Mar. 15, 1949 in London, Can. Debut 1973 OB in *Ghosts* for which he received a Theatre World Award, followed by *Joe's Opera, Cracks, Wenceslas Square, Love Letters, Assassins, Christmas Memory*, Bdwy in *Tartuffe, Deathtrap, Sweeney Todd, They're Playing Our Song, Little Me, Noises Off, You Never Can Tell, Devil's Disciple, Lend Me a Tenor, Two Shakespearean Actors, Damn Yankees, Arcadia*.

GARITO, KEN. Born Dec. 27, 1968 in Brooklyn, NY. Graduate Brooklyn Col. Debut 1991 OB in *Tony 'n' Tina's Wedding*, followed by *Peacetime, A Map of the City, Watbanaland*.

GATTON, VINCE. Born Oct. 18, 1969 in Louisville, KY. Graduate U. Ill./Urbana. Debut 1995 OB in *Party*.

GAYSUNIS, CHERYL. Born Jan. 8, in Westminster, CA. Graduate Otterbein Col. Bdwy debut 1991 in *La Bete* followed by *Molière Comedies*, OB in *Finding the Sun* (1994), *An Enraged Reading, Fragments*.

GIAMATTI, MARCUS. Born Oct. 31, 1961 in New Haven, CT. Graduate Bowdoin Col. Debut 1989 OB in *Measure for Measure* followed by *Italian American Reconciliation, All This and Moonlight, Durang Durang*.

GIBBS, RON. Born June 15 in St. Louis, MO. Graduate So. We. Mo. St. U. Debut 1988 OB in *Give My Regards to Broadway*, Bdwy in *Show Boat* (1994).

GIBSON, TERI. Born Dec. 23, 1959 in Mahopac, NY. Graduate Adelphi U. Bdwy debut 1981 in *Marlowe*, OB in *Too Many Girls, Nunsense 2*.

GILES, NANCY. Born July 17, 1960 in Queens, New York City. Graduate Oberlin Col. Debut 1985 OB in *Mayor* for which she received a Theatre World Award, followed by *Mother, Circus of Death, Pinky, Oh You Hostage, Snicker Factor, Tiny Mommy Sparks in the Park, Czar of Rock and Roll, Johnny Business, Urban Blight, Police Boys*.

GILLETTE, ANITA. Born Aug. 16, 1938 in Baltimore, MD. Debut 1960 OB in *Russell Paterson's Sketchbook* for which she received a Theatre World Award, followed by *Rich and Famous, Dead Wrong, Road Show, Class 1-Acts, The Blessing, Moving Targets, Juno, Able-Bodied Seaman, Decline of the Middle West*, Bdwy in *Carnival, Gypsy, Gay Life, All American, Mr. President, Kelly, Don't Drink the Water, Cabaret, Jimmy, They're Playing Our Song, Brighton Beach Memoirs, Chapter Two*.

GILPIN, JACK. Born May 31, 1951 in Boyce, VA. Harvard graduate. Debut 1976 OB in *Goodbye and Keep Cold*, followed by *Stray, Soft Touch, Beyond Therapy, Lady or the Tiger, Middle Ages, Rise of Daniel Rocket, No Happy Ending, Strange Behavior, Foreigner, Marathon '86, Spring Thing, Human Nature, Cheever Evening*, Bdwy in *Lunch Hour* (1980), *A Christmas Carol* (1990).

GILPIN, MARTHA. Born June 23, 1960 in Santa Fe, NM. Graduate UNM, Rutgers U. Debut 1988 OB in *Angalak* followed by *Morning Coffee, Occupation*.

GIONSON, MEL (DUANE). Born Feb. 23, 1954 in Honolulu, HI. Graduate U. HI. Debut 1979 OB in *Richard II*, followed by *Sunrise, Monkey Music, Behind Enemy Lines, Station J, Teahouse, A Midsummer Night's Dream, Empress of China, Chip Shot, Manoa Valley, Ghashiram, Shogun, Macbeth, Life of the Land, Noiresque, Three Sisters, Lucky Come Hawaii, Henry IV Parts 1 & 2, Working 1-Acts '91, School for Wives*.

GIRARDEAU, FRANK. Born Oct. 19, 1942 in Beaumont, TX. Attended Rider Col. Debut 1972 OB in *22 Years*, followed by *The Soldier, Hughie,*

An American Story, El Hermano, Dumping Ground, Daddies, Accounts, Shadow Man, Marathon '84, Dennis, Marathon '89, Marathon '90, Talking Pictures, Night Seasons.

GLEASON, LAURENCE. Born Nov. 14, 1956 in Utica, NY. Graduate Utica Col. Debut 1984 OB in *Romance Language* follwed by *Agamemnon, A Country Doctor, The Misanthrope, The Sleepless City, Electra, Morning Sound, Like To Live, Macbeth, 3 by Wilder, As You Like It, S.S. Glencairn, Twelfth Night, Goose and Tom Tom, Anatomy of Sound*, Bdwy in *Wilder Wilder Wilder* (1993).

GLEZOS, IRENE. Born June 15, in Washington, DC. Graduate Catholic U. Debut OB in *Modigliani* followed by *The Last Good Moment of Lily Baker, Antigone, The Rose Tattoo, Top Girls, Lie of the Mind*.

GLOVER, JOHN. Born Aug. 7, 1944 in Kingston, NY. Attended Towson St. Col. Debut 1969 OB in *Scent of Flowers* followed by *Government Inspector, Rebel Women, Treats, Booth, Criminal Minds, Fairy Garden, Digby*, Bdwy in *Selling of the President, Great God Brown, Don Juan, Visit, Chemin de Fer, Holiday, Importance of Being Earnest, Frankenstein, Whodunit, Design for Living, Love! Valour! Compassion!* (also OB).

GLYNN, CARLIN. Born Feb. 19, 1940 in Cleveland, OH. Attended Sophie Newcomb Col., Actors Studio. Debut 1959 OB in *Waltz of the Toreadors* followed by *Cassatt, Winterplay, Outside Waco, Cover of Life, Young Man from Atlanta*, Bdwy in *Best Little Whorehouse...* (1978, also OB) for which she received a Theatre World Award.

GOLDBERG, RUSSELL. Born Mar. 28, 1964 in Flushing, NY. Graduate Syracuse U. Debut 1988 OB in *All's Fair* followed by *Sherlock Holmes and the Red-Headed League, The Emperor's New Clothes, Peg O'My Heart, The High Life in Concert, Hello Muddah Hello Faddah, Fairy Garden, Body Shop*.

GOLDEN, ANNIE. Born Oct. 19, 1951 in Brooklyn, NY. Bdwy debut 1977 in *Hair* followed by *Leader of the Pack*, OB in *Dementos, Dr. Selavy's Magic Theatre, A...My Name is Alice, Little Shop of Horrors, Class of '86, Assassins, Hit the Lights!, Sugar Bean Sisters*.

GOLDES, JOEL. Born Sept. 28, 1963 in Carmel, CA. Graduate U. Cal/Irvine. Debut 1993 OB in *News in Revue* followed by *3 By Wilder, Mourning Becomes Electra, Edward II*.

GOLDSMITH, MERWIN. Born Aug. 7, 1937 in Detroit, MI. Graduate UCLA, Old Vic. Bdwy debut 1970 in *Minnie's Boys* followed by *The Visit, Chemin de Fer, Rex, Leda Had a Little Swan, Trelawney of the Wells, Dirty Linen, 1940's Radio Hour, Slab Boys, Me and My Girl, Ain't Broadway Grand*, OB in *Naked Hamlet, Chickencoop Chinaman, Real Life Funnies, Wanted, Rubbers and Yanks, Chinchilla, Yours Anne, Big Apple Messengers, La Boheme, Learned Ladies, An Imaginary Life, Little Prince, Beau Jest, After-Play*.

GOLDSTEIN, STEVEN. Born Oct. 22, 1963 in New York City. Graduate NYU. Debut 1987 OB in *Boy's Life*, followed by *Oh Hell, Three Sisters, Marathon '91, Angel of Death, Five Very Live, Casino Paradise, Orpheus in Love, Nothing Sacred, Jolly, Marathon Dancing, Shaker Heights, The Lights, El Greco, Luck Pluck Virtue*, Bdwy in *Our Town* (1988).

GOODNESS, JOEL. Born Jan. 22, 1962 in Wisconsin Rapids, WI. Graduate U. Wisc. Debut 1991 OB in *Custody*, followed by *Georgy*, Bdwy in *Crazy for You* (1992).

GORDON, MARK ALAN. Born Aug. 22, 1960 in Columbus, OH. Graduate Niagara U., Ohio U. Debut 1991 OB in *Ambrosia* followed by *King James and the Indian, Giggle and Scream, Oscar Over There, Math and Aftermath*.

GORNEY, KAREN LYNN. Born Jan. 28, 1945 in Los Angeles, CA. Graduate Carnegie Tech, Bradeis U. Debut 1972 OB in *Dylan* followed by *Life on the Third Rail, Academy Street, Unconditional Communication, Something to Eat, Curved Ladder, Love Museum*.

GOULD, MURIEL. Born Oct. 12, 1928 in Brooklyn, NY. Graduate Brooklyn Col., Columbia U. Debut 1975 OB in *Little Night Music* followed by *Pelicans Please Mute, Tronzini Ristorante, Baby Luv*.

GRACE, GINGER. Born in Beaumont, TX. Graduate U. Tex., Penn. State U. Debut 1981 OB in *Peer Gynt* followed by *Wild Oats, The Ghost Sonata, The Cherry Orchard, Faust, Hamlet, The Oresteia, Mourning Becomes Electra, Craig's Wife*.

GRAHAM, RONNY. Born Aug. 26, 1919 in Philadelphia, PA. Bdwy debut in *New Faces of 1952* for which he received a Theatre World Award, followed by *Tender Trap, Something More*, OB in *Deja Revue*.

GRANITE, JUDITH. Born Apr. 22, 1936 in Rochester, NY. Graduate Syracuse U., NYU. Bdwy debut 1965 in *The Devils* followed by *Criss-Crossing, Cemetery Club*, OB in *Lovers in the Metro, So Who's Afraid of Edward Albee, Macbird, World of Gunter Grass, Survival of St. Joan, Equinox, Savings, Flatbush Faithful, Special Interest, Miami Stories, Have You Spoken to Any Jews Lately*.

GRANT, SCHUYLER. Born Apr. 29, 1970 in San Jose, CA. Attended

Yale U. Debut 1987 OB in *Hooded Eye* followed by *Mortal Friends, Banner.*

GRAY, CHARLES. Born July 15, 1960 in Annapolis, MD. Attended Towson St. U. Bdwy debut 1995 in *Grease.*

GREEN, AMANDA. Born Dec. 29, 1963 in New York City. Debut 1984 OB in *The New Yorkers* followed by *Sheik of Avenue B*, Bdwy in *Wonderful Town* (1994—NYCO).

GREENHILL, SUSAN. Born Mar. 19 in New York City. Graduate U.PA, Catholic U. Bdwy debut 1982 in *Crimes of the Heart*, OB in *Hooters, Our Lord of Lynchville, Sept. in the Rain, Seascape with Sharks and Dancer, Murder of Crows, Better Days, Marathan '89, Tounges of Stone, Festival of One Acts, Watbanaland.*

GREGORIO, ROSE. Born in Chicago, IL. Graduate Northwestern, Yale U. Debut 1962 OB in *The Days and Nights of Beebee Fenstermaker* followed by *Kiss Mama, The.Balcon!: Bivouac at Lucca, Journey to the Day, Diary of Anne Frank, Weekends Like Other People, Curse of the Starving Class, Dreams of a Blacklisted Actor, The Last Yankee, King Richard, Madwoman of Chaillot*, Bdwy in *The Investigation, Daphne in Cottage D, The Owl and the Pussycat, The Cuban Thing, Jimmy Shine, The Shadow Box, A View from the Bridge* (1983), *M. Butterfly.*

GRENE, GREGORY. Born Oct. 6, 1965 in Chicago, IL. Graduate Dublin's Trinity Col. Debut 1993 OB in *Importance of Being Earnest*, Bdwy in *Philadelphia Here I Come* (1994).

GREY, JOEL. Born Apr. 11, 1932 in Cleveland, OH. Attended Cleveland Playhouse. Bdwy debut 1951 in *Borscht Capades* followed by *Come Blow Your Horn, Stop the World I Want to Get Off, Half a Sixpence, Cabaret* (1966/1987), *George M!, Goodtime Charley, Grand Tour*, OB in *Littlest Revue, Harry Noon and Night, Marco Polo Sings a Solo, Normal Heart, Greenwich Village Follies.*

GROENER, HARRY. Born Sept. 10, 1951 in Augsburg, Germany, Graduate U. Washington. Bdwy debut 1979 in *Oklahoma!* for which he received a Theatre World Award, followed by *Oh, Brother!, Is There Life After High School, Cats, Harrigan 'n' Hart, Sunday in the Park with George, Sleight of Hand, Crazy for You*, OB in *Beside the Seaside, Twelve Dreams.*

GUTTMAN, RONALD. Born Aug. 12, 1952 in Brussels, Belg. Graduate Brussels U. Debut 1986 OB in *Coastal Disturbances*, followed by *Modigliano, Free Zone, Escurial, Liliom, Philanthropist, Funky Crazy Bugaloo Boy, No Exit, Sabina*, Bdwy in *Coastal Disturbances* (1987).

HADGE, MICHAEL. Born June 6, 1932 in Greensboro, NC. Bdwy debut 1958 in *Cold Wind and the Warm* followed by *Lady of the Camelias, Impossible Years*, OB in *Local Stigmata, Hunter, Night Seasons, Laura Dennis.*

HAGERTY, JULIE. Born June 15, 1955 in Cincinnati, OH, Attended Juilliard. Debut 1979 OB in *Mutual Benefit Life* followed by *Wild Life, The Years, Wifey, Valentine Fairy, Cheever Evening*, Bdwy in *House of Blue Leaves* (1986—also OB) for which she recieved a Theatre World Award, *Front Page, 3 Men on a Horse.*

HAINING, ALICE. Born Oct. 8, 1967 in Jackson, MS. Graduate Mississippi Col. Debut 1986 OB in *Fresh Horses* followed by *Emerald City, Rain, Some Fish No Elephants, Swim Visit, Learned Ladies, Cowboy in His Underwear, Cover of Life*, Bdwy in *On Borrowed Time* (1991).

HALSTON, JULIE. Born Dec. 7, 1954 in New York. Graduate Hofstra U. Debut OB 1985 in *Times Square Angel*, followed by *Vampire Lesbians of Sodom, Sleeping Beauty or Coma, The Dubliners, Lady in Question, Money Talks, Red Scare on Sunset, I'll Be the Judge of That, Lifetime of Comedy, Honeymoon Is Over, You Should Be So Lucky.*

HAMILTON, LAUREN. Born Nov. 10, 1959 in Boston, MA. Graduate Bard Col., Neighborhood Playhouse. Debut 1988 OB in *Famine Plays*, followed by *Tiny Dimes, Rodents and Radios, Hunger, Homo Sapien Shuffle, A Murder of Crows, A Vast Wreck, Gut Girls, Acts of Desire, Swoop.*

HAMMER, BEN. Born Dec. 8, 1925 in Brooklyn, NY. Graduate Brooklyn Col. Bdwy debut 1955 in *Create Sebastians*, followed by *Diary of Anne Frank, The Tenth Man, Mother Courage, The Deputy, Royal Hunt of the Sun, Colda, Broadway Bound*, OB in *The Crucible. Murderous Angels, Richard III, Slavs!*

HAMMER, MARK. Born Apr. 28, 1937 in San Jose, CA. Graduate Stanford U., Catholic U. Debut 1966 OB in *Jouney of the Fifth Horse* followed by *Witness for the Prosecution, Cymbeline, Richard III, The Taming of the Shrew, As You Like It, Henry VI, Twelve Dreams*, Bdwy in *Much Ado about Nothing* (1972).

HANKET, ARTHUR. Born June 23, 1934 in Virginia. Graduate UVA, Fla. State U. Debut 1979 OB in *Cuchculain Cycle*, followed by *The Boys Next Door, In Perpetuity Throughout the Universe, L'Illusion, White Collar, Heaven on Earth, One Act Festival, Kingitsh, Love and Anger, One-Act Festival, Amphitryon.*

HANNA, LISA. Born Feb. 26, 1965 in Biddeford, ME. Graduate Boston Consv. Bdwy debut 1995 in *Gentlemen Prefer Blondes.*

HA'O, WILLIAM. Born Aug. 10, 1953 in Honolulu, HI. Attended Chaminade Col., Leeward Col., Debut 1981 OB in *Shining House* followed by *Gaugin in Tahiti, Teahouse, Midsummer Night's Dream, Rain, Dream of Kitamura, Sleepless City, Heart of the Earth.*

HARADA, ANN. Born Feb. 3, 1964 in Honolulu, HI. Attended Brown U. Debut 1987 OB in *1-2-3-4-5* followed by *Hit the Lights!, America Dreaming*, Bdwy in *M. Butterfly* (1988).

HARDEN, MARCIA GAY. Born Aug. 14, 1959 in La Jolla, CA. Graduate U. MD, U. Tex., NYU. Debut 1989 OB in *The Man Who Shot Lincoln*, followed by *One of the Guys, The Years, Simpatico*, Bdwy in *Angels in America* for which she recieved a 1993 Theatre World Award.

HARDING, JAN LESLIE. Born in 1956 in Cambridge, MA. Graduate Boston U. Debut 1980 OB in *Album*, followed by *Sunday Picnic, Buddies, The Lunch Girls, Marathon '86, Traps, Father Was a Peculiar Man, A Murder of Crows, David's Red-Haired Death, Strange Feet, Impassioned Embraces, Storm Patterns, Bondage, My Head was a Sledgehammer, Bremen Freedom, Shades of Grey, I've Got the Shakes, Swoop.*

HARGREAVES, AMY. Born Jan. 27, 1970 in Rockville Center, NY. Graduate Fairfield U., NYU. Debut 1995 in *Living Proof* followed by *Trust, Tell Me I'm Beautiful.*

HARMAN, PAUL. Born July 29, 1952 in Mineola, NY. Graduate Tufts U. Bdwy debut 1980 in *It's So Nice to Be Civilized* followed by *Les Miserables, Chess*, OB in *City Suite, Sheik of Avenue B, Decline of the Middle West.*

HARRELSON, HELEN. Born in Missouri. Graduate Goodman Theatre. Bdwy debut 1950 in *The Cellar and the Well*, followed by *Death of a Salesman, Days in the Trees, Romeo and Juliet*, OB in *Our Town, His and Hers, House of Atreus, He and She, Missing Persons, Laughing Stock, Art of Self-Defense, Hour of the Lynx, Mother and Child.*

HARRINGTON, DELPHI. Born Aug. 26 in Chicago, IL. Graduate Northwestern U. Debut 1960 OB in *Country Scandal* followed by *Moon for the Misbegotten, Baker's Dozen, The Zykovs, Character Lines, Richie, American Garage, After the Fall, Rosencrantz and Guildenstern Are Dead, Good Grief, Hay Fever, Madwoman of Chaillot, Too Clever by Half*, Bdwy in *Thieves* (1974), *Everything in the Garden, Romeo and Juliet, Chapter Two, Sea Gull.*

HARRIS, BAXTER. Born Nov. 18, 1940 in Columbus, KS. Attended U. Kan. Debut 1967 OB in *America Hurrah*, followed by *The Serpent, Battle of Angels, Down by the River…, Ferocious Kisses, The Three Sisters, The Dolphin Position, Broken Eggs, Paradise Lost, Ghosts, The Time of Your Life, The Madwoman of Chaillot, The Reckoning, Wicked Women Revue, More Than You Deserve, him, Pericles, Selma, Gradual Clearing, Children of the Sun, Marathon '90, Go to Ground, Marathon '92 & '93, Long Ago and Far Away, Incommunicado*, Bdwy in *A Texas Trilogy* (1976), *Dracula, The Lady from Dubuque.*

HARRIS, CYNTHIA. Born in New York City. Graduate Smith Col. Bdwy debut 1963 in *Natural Affection* followed by *Any Wednesday, Best Laid Plans, Company, Greenwich Village Follies, Madwoman of Chaillot, Too Clever by Half.*

HARRIS, ED. Born Nov. 28, 1950 in Tenafly, NJ. Attended Columbia U, U. Ok., Debut 1983 OB in *Fool for Love* followed by *Simpatico*, Bdwy in *Precious Sons* for which he received a Theatre World Award.

HARRIS, JULIE. Born Dec. 2, 1925 in Grosse Pointe, MI. Yale graduate. Bdwy debut 1945 in *It's a Gift*, followed by *Henry V, Oedipus, Playboy of the Western World, Alice in Wonderland, Macbeth, Sundown Beach* for which she received a Theatre World Award, *The Young and the Fair, Magnolia Alley, Montserrat, Member of the Wedding, I Am a Camera, Mlle. Colombe, The Lark, Country Wife, Warm Peninsula, Little Moon of Alban, A Shot in the Dark, Marathon '33, Ready When You Are C. B., Hamlet* (CP), *Skyscraper, 40 Carats, And Miss Reardon Drinks a Little, Voices, The Last of Mrs. Lincoln, Au Pair Man, In Praise of Love, Belle of Amherst, Mixed Couples, Break a Leg, Lucifer's Child, A Christmas Carol, Glass Menagrie*, OB in *Fiery Furnace.*

HARRIS, NEIL PATRICK. Born June 15, 1973 in Albuquerque, NM. Debut 1995 OB in *Luck Pluck and Virtue.*

HARTLEY, MARIETTE. Born June 21, 1940 in New York City. Debut 1988 OB in *King John* followed by *Love and Shrimp, Sylvia.*

HAVOC, JUNE. Born Nov. 8, 1917 in Seattle, WA. Bdwy debut 1936 in *Forbidden Melody* followed by *The Women, Pal Joey, Mexican Hayride, Sadie Thompson, Ryan Girl, Dunnigan's Daughter, Dream Girl, Affairs of State, Infernal Machine, Beaux Stratagem, Warm Peninsula, Dinner at 8, Habeas Corpus, Annie*, playwright-director of *Marathon '33, Old Lady's Guide to Survival.*

HAWKE, ETHAN. Born Nov. 6, 1970 in Austin, TX. Debut 1991 OB in *Casanova* followed by *A Joke, Sophistry, Sons and Fathers, Hesh, Great Unwashed*, Bdwy in *The Sea Gull* (1992).

HAWKINS, TRISH. Born Oct. 30, 1945 in Hartford, CT. Attended Radcliffe, Neighborhood Playhouse. Debut 1970 OB in *Oh! Calcutta!* followed by *Iphigenia, Hot l Baltimore* for which she received a 1973 Theatre World Award, *him, Come Back Little Sheba, Battle of Angels, Mound Builders, The Farm, Ulysses in Traction, Lulu, Hogan's Folly, Twelfth Night, A Tale Told, Great Grandson of Jedediah Kohler, Time Framed, Levitations, Love's Labour's Lost, Talley & Son, Tomorrow's Monday, Caligula, Quiet in the Land, Road Show, Why We Have a Body,* Bdwy in *Some of My Best Friends (1977), Talley's Folly.*

HAWLEY, LYNN. Born Nov. 12, 1965 in Sharon, CT. Graduate Middlebury Col. Debut 1992 OB in *Woyzeck* followed by *Owners, The Illusion, Truth Teller.*

HAYDEN, MICHAEL. Born July 28 1963 in St. Paul, MN. Graduated Juilliard. Debut 1991 OB in *The Matchmaker* followed by *Hello Again, Off-Key, Nebraska,* Bdwy debut 1994 in *Carousel* for which he received a Theatre World Award.

HAYDEN, TAMRA. Born Aug. 18, 1962 in Littleton, CO. Graduate U. No. Co. Debut 1994 OB in *Doll's Life* followed by Bdwy in *Les Miserables* (1995).

HAYENGA, JEFFREY. Born Aug. 13, in Sibledy, IA. Graduate U. Mn. Bdwy in *The Elephant Man* (1980) followed by *Ah! Wilderness!, Long Day's Journey into Night,* OB in *King Lear, Mother Courage, The Actors' Nightmare, Burkie, Brand, Hamlet, Breaking Up, Two Rooms, Patient A, Jeffrey, Hapgood.*

HAYNES, BRYAN S. Born June 20, 1967 in Bronx, NY. Graduate Yale U. Bdwy debut 1995 in *Gentlemen Prefer Blondes.*

HAYNES, ROBIN. Born July 20, 1953 in Lincoln, NE. Graduate U. Wash. Debut 1976 OB in *A Touch of the Poet* followed by *She Loves Me, Romeo and Juliet, Twelfth Night, Billy Bishop Goes to War, Max and Maxie,* Bdwy in *The Best Little Whorehouse in Texas* (1978), *Blood Brothers.*

HAYS, REX (aka David). Born June 17, 1946 in Hollywood, CA. Graduate San Jose St. U., Brandeis U. Bdwy debut 1975 in *Dance with Me,* followed by *Angel, King of Hearts, Evita, Onward Victoria!, Woman of the Year, La Cage aux Folles, Grand Hotel,* OB in *Charley's Tale, Shabbotai.*

HEALD, ANTHONY. Born Aug. 25 1944 in New Rochelle, NY. Graduate Mich. St. U. Debut 1980 OB in *Glass Menagerie,* followed by *Misalliance* for which he received a Theatre World Award, *The Caretaker, The Fox, Quartermaine's Terms, Philanthropist, Henry V, Digby, Principia Scriptoriae, Lisbon Traviata, Elliot Loves, Pygmalion, Lips Together Teeth Apart,* Bdwy in *Wake of Jamey Foster* (1982), *Marriage of Figaro, Anything Goes, Small Family Business, Love! Valour! Compassion!*

HEARN, GEORGE. Born June 18, 1934 in St. Louis, MO. Graduate Southwestern Col. OB in *Macbeth, Antony and Cleopatra, As You Like It, Richard III, Merry Wives of Windsor, Midsummer Night's Dream, Hamlet, Horseman Pass By, The Chosen,* Bdwy in *A Time for Singing, Changing Room, An Almost Perfect Person, I Remember Mama, Watch on the Rhine, Sweeney Todd, A Doll's Life, Whodunit, Cage aux Folles, Ah! Wilderness!, Ghetto, Meet Me in St. Louis, Sunset Blvd.*

HEBERT, RICH. Born Dec. 14, 1956 in Quincy, MA. Graduate Boston U. Debut 1978 OB in *Rimers of Eldritch* followed by *110 in the Shade, Dazy, Easy Money, Ballad of Sam Grey,* Bdwy in *Rock 'n' Roll: First 5000 Years* (1982), *Cats, Les Miserables, Sunset Blvd.*

HECHT, PAUL. Born Aug. 16, 1941 in London, Eng. Attended McGill U. OB in *Sjt. Musgrave's Dance, Macbird, Phaedra, Enrico IV, Coriolanus, Cherry Orchard, Androcles and the Lion, Too Clever by Half, London Suite,* Bdwy in *Rosencrantz and Guildenstern Are Dead, 1776, Rothschilds, Ride Across Lake Constance, Great God Brown, Don Juan, Emperor Henry IV, Herzl, Caesar and Cleopatra, Night and Day, Noises Off.*

HEDWALL, DEBORAH. Born in 1952 in Washington State. OB includes *Blind Date, Intimacy, Amulets against the Dragon Forces, Savage in Limbo, Ertremities, Sight Unseen, Wreck on the 5:25, Iphigenia and Other Daughters, Why We Have a Body,* Bdwy in *Heidi Chronicles* (1989).

HEINZ, LEE. Born Apr. 29 in Warren, OH. Graduate Vassar Col. Wayne St. U., Oxford U. Debut 1985 OB in *Daddy and Sue at the Beach* followed by *Halloween, Here Everything Still Floats, Mamet Women, The Old Bachelor,* Bdwy 1980 in *Peter Pan.*

HENRITZE, BETTE. Born May 23 in Betsy Layne, KY. Graduate U. TN. OB in *Lion in Love, Abe Lincoln in Illinois, Othello, Baal, A Long Christmas Dinner, Queens of France, Rimers of Eldritch, Displaced Person, Acquisition, Crime of Passion, Happiness Cage, Henry VI, Richard III, Older People, Lotta, Catsplay. A Month in the Country, The Golem, Daughters, Steel Magnolias, All's Well That Ends Well,* Bdwy in *Jenny Kissed Me* (1948), *Pictures in the Hallway, Giants Sons of Giants, Ballad of the Sad Cafe, The White House, Dr. Cook's Garden, Here's Where I Belong, Much Ado about Nothing, Over Here, Angel Street, Man and Superman, Macbeth* (1981), *Present Laughter, The Octette Bridge Club, Orpheus Descending,*

Lettice and Lovage, On Borrowed Time, Hedda Gabler, Uncle Vanya.

HENRY, BUCK. Born Dec. 9, 1930 in New York City. Dartmouth Graduate. Bdwy debut 1952 in *Bernadine* followed by OB in *The Promise, Fortress of Glass, Kingfish, Three Viewings.*

HENSLEY, DALE. Born Apr. 9, 1954 in Nevada, MO. Graduate Southwest MO State U. Debut 1980 OB in *Annie Get Your Gun,* Bdwy in *Anything Goes* (1987), *Guys and Dolls* (1992), *Sunset Blvd.*

HERBST, JEFF. Born Jan. 8, 1963 in Sioux Falls, SD. Graduate U. Wv. Madison, Fla. State U. Debut 1988 OB in *On Tina Tuna Walk,* followed by *A Funny Thing Happened on the Way to the Forum, Doll's Life,* Bdwy in *A Change in the Heir* (1990).

HERINGES, FREDERIC. Born in Santa Maria, CA. Attended Pacific Consv. of Performing Arts. Bdwy debut in *Phantom of the Opera* (1991).

HERNANDEZ, PHILIP. Born Dec. 12, 1959 in Queens, NY. Graduate SUNY. Debut 1987 OB in *The Gingerbread Lady* followed by *Ad Hock, Troilus and Cressida,* Bdwy in *Kiss of the Spider Woman* (1993).

HESS, ELIZABETH. Born July 17, 1953 in Ontario, Can. Graduate York U. Debut 1982 OB in *Frances Farmer Story* followed by *Nothing But Bukowski, Modest Proposal.*

HEYMAN, BARTON. Born Jan. 24, 1937 in Washington, DC. Attended UCLA. Bdwy debut 1969 in *Indians* followed by *Trial of the Catonsville 9, Talent for Murder, Doll's House,* OB in *Midsummer Night's Dream, Sleep, Phantasmagoria Historia, Enclave, Henry V, Signs of Life, Crack, Private View, Night Hank Williams Died, Him.*

HICKOK, JOHN. Born Aug. 31, 1957. OB in *Eye of the Beholder* followed by *I Sent a Letter to My Love.*

HICKS, SHAUNA. Born Jan. 15, 1962 in Neenah WI. Graduate American U. Debut 1987 OB in *The Gingerbread Lady* followed by *Buzzsaw Berkeley,* Bdwy in *Meet Me in St. Louis* (1989), *Blood Brothers.*

HIKEN, GERALD. Born May 23, 1927 in Milwaukee, WI. Attended U. Wi. Bdwy in *Lovers* (1968) followed by *Cave Dwellers, Nervous Set, Fighting Cock, 49th Cousin, Gideon, Foxy, Three Sisters, Golda, Strider, Fools,* OB in *Cherry Orchard, Sea Gull, Good Woman of Setzuan, Misanthrope, Iceman Cometh, New Theatre, Strider, The Chosen, Slavs!*

HILL, ERIN. Born Feb. 13, 1968 in Louisville, Ky. Graduate Syracuse U. Debut 1991 OB in *Return to the Forbidden Planet* followed by *Rent.*

HILLNER, JOHN. Born Nov. 5, 1952 in Evanston, IL. Graduate Deniston U. Debut 1977 OB in *Essential Shepard,* followed by *To Whom It May Concern, At Home, Let 'Em Rot, The Proposition,* Bdwy in *They're Playing Our Song, Little Me, Woman of the Year, Crazy for You.*

HINES, MIMI. Born July 17, 1933 in Vancouver, Can. Bdwy debut 1965 in *Funny Girl* followed by *Grease* (1994), OB in *From Rodgers and Hart with Love, Little Me* (in previews).

HINGSTON, SEAN MARTIN. Born Dec. 16, 1965 in Melbourne, Australia. Bdwy debut 1994 in *Crazy for You.*

HIRSCH, VICKI. Born Feb. 22, 1951 in Wilmington, DE. Graduate U. Del., Villanova U. Debut 1985 OB in *Black County Crimes* followed by *Casualties, Mr. Universe, Working Magic, Tempest.*

HOCK, ROBERT. Born May 20, 1931 in Phoenixville, PA. Yale Graduate. Debut 1982 OB in *The Caucasian Chalk Circle* followed by *Adding Machine, Romeo and Juliet, Edward II, Creditors, Two Orphans, Macbeth, Kitty Hawk, Heathen Valley, Comedy of Errors, Phaedra, The Good Natur'd Man, Oedipus the King, Game of Love and Chance, Twelfth Night, Mrs. Warren's Profession, Oedipus at Colonus, King Lear, Beaux Stratagem,* Bdwy in *Some Americans Abroad* (1990).

HODGES, BEN. Born Sept. 17, 1969 in Morristown, TN. Graduate Otterbein Col. Debut OB 1992 in *Loose Ends* followed by *Hysteria, Beyond Therapy.*

HOFFMAN, AVI. Born Mar. 3, 1958 in Bronx, NY. Graduate U. Miami. Debut 1983 in *The Rise of David Levinsky,* followed by *It's Hard to Be a Jew, A Rendezvous with God, The Golden Land, Songs of Paradise, Finkel's Follies, Milk and Honey, Too Jewish?*

HOFFMAN, SUSANNAH. Born Mar. 20, 1963 in Montreal, Can. Attended Dawson Col. Bdwy debut 1994 in *An Inspector Calls.*

HOGAN, JONATHAN. Born June 13, 1951 in Chicago, IL. Graduate Goodman Th. Debut 1972 OB in *The Hot l Baltimore,* followed by *Mound Builders, Harry Outside, Cabin 12, 5th of July, Glorious Morning, Innocent Thoughts Harmless Intentions, Sunday Runners, Threads, Time Framed, Balcony Scene, The Professional,* Bdwy in *Comedians* (1976), *Otherwise Engaged, 5th of July* (also OB), *The Caine Mutiny Court Martial, As Is* (also OB), *Burn This!* (also OB), *Taking Steps, The Homecoming.*

HOLGATE, RONALD. Born May 26, 1937 in Aberdeen, SD. Attended Northwestern U., New Eng. Consv. Debut 1961 OB in *Hobo,* followed by *Hooray It's a Glorious Day, Blue Plate Special, Milk and Honey,* Bdwy in *A Funny Thing Happened..., Milk and Honey, 1776, Saturday Sunday*

 Bryan Batt

 Jane Connell

 Paul Castree

 B.J. Crosby

 Dylan Chalfy

 Donna Davidge

 Keene Curtis

 Jennifer Dundas

 Darius de Haas

 Patricia Elliott

 Mark Eis

 Barbara Feldon

 Jarrod Emick

 Jane Fleiss

 Jonathan Freeman

 Nancy Giles

 Charles Gray

 Schuyler Grant

 Gregory Grene

 Ann Harada

 Neil Patrick Harris

 Shauna Hicks

 Ethan Hawke

 Jennifer Holliday

 George Hearn

 Cherry Jones

 John Hoshko

 Ella Joyce

 Zeljko Ivanek

 Juliette Koka

211

Monday, The Grand Tour, Musical Chairs, 42nd Street, Lend Me a Tenor, Guys and Dolls (1993).

HOLLIDAY, JENNIFER. Born Oct. 19, 1960 in Houston, TX. Bdwy debut 1980 in *Your Arms Too Short to Box with God* followed by *Dreamgirls* for which she received a 1992 Theatre World Award, *Grease* (1995).

HOLMES, RICHARD. Born Mar. 16, 1963 in Philadelphia, PA. Graduate Gettysburg Col., NY. Debut 1990 OB in *Richard III*, followed by *Othello, Shadow of a Gunman, Mr. Parnell, Christina Alberta's Father, Dog Opera,* Bdwy in *Saint Joan* (1993), *Timon of Athens, Government Inspector.*

HOLTZMAN, MERRILL. Born Sept. 1, 1959. Bdwy debut 1989 in *Mastergate,* OB in *Chelsea Walls, Nebraska, A Darker Purpose, The Stand-In, La Ronde.*

HONDA, CAROL A. Born Nov. 20 in Kealakekus, HI. Graduate U. HI. Debut 1983 OB in *Yellow Fever,* followed by *Empress of China, Manoa Valley, Once Is Never Enough, Life of the Land, Rosie's Cafe, And the Soul Shall Dance, The Wash, Before It Hits Home, The Dressing Room.*

HOOPES, WENDY. Born Nov. 4, 1968 in Kuala Lampur, Malasia. Graduate American U., NYU. Debut 1994 OB in *Sub Urbia* followed by *Quick Bright Things.*

HOPE, STEPHEN. Born Jan. 23, 1957 in Savannah, GA. Attended U. Louisville, Cin. Consv. Bdwy debut 1982 in *Joseph and the...Dreamcoat* followed by OB in *Rabboni, Dames at Sea, Anyone Can Whistle, Manhattan Showboat.*

HORNE, CHERYL. Born Nov. 15 in Stamford, CT. Graduate SMU. Debut 1975 OB in *The Fantasticks,* followed by *Indomitable Huntresses, Andorra, Lady Windermere's Fan, Let's Get a Divorce, Mourning Becomes Electra, Uncle Vanya, Live Witness, Craig's Wife, Edward II.*

HORSFORD, ANNA. Born Mar. 6, 1947 in New York City. Attended Inter-American U. Debut 1969 OB in *Black Quartet* followed by *Perfect Party, Les Femmes Noires, Ladies in Waiting, Sweet Talk, In the Well of the House, Coriolanus, Peep, Dancing on Moonlight,* Bdwy 1976 in *For Colored Girls...*

HORTON, RUSSELL. Born Nov. 11, 1941 in Los Angeles, CA. Graduate UCLA. Debut 1966 OB in *Displaced Person* followed by *How's the World Treating You, Galileo and Antigone* (LC), *What Did We Do Wrong?, Last Resort, Scribes, City Sugar, Androcles and the Lion.*

HOSHKO, JOHN. Born July 28, 1959 in Bethesda, MD. Graduate U. So. Cal. Bdwy debut 1989 in *Prince of Central Park* followed by *Gentlemen Prefer Blondes,* OB in *Two by Two.*

HOWARD, KEN. Born Mar. 28, 1944 in El Centro, CA. Graduate Yale. Bdwy debut 1968 in *Promises Promises,* followed by *1776* for which he received a Theatre World Award, *Child's Play, Seesaw, Little Black Sheep* (LC), *The Norman Conquests, 1600 Pennsylvania Avenue, Rumors, Love Letters,* OB in *Camping with Henry and Tom* (1995).

HOWARD, LAUREN. Born May 20, 1957 in Bayonne, NJ. Graduate Franklin and Marshall Col. Debut 1993 in *Who Will Carry the Word?* followed by *Reproducing Georgia, Prosthetics and the $25000 Pyramid.*

HOWER, NANCY. Born May 11 in Wyckoff, NJ. Graduate Rollins Col., Juilliard. Debut 1991 OB in *Othello,* followed by *As You Like It, The Years, Why We Have a Body,* Bdwy in *Government Inspector* (1994).

HOXIE, RICHMOND. Born July 21, 1946 in New York City. Graduate Dartmouth Col., LAMDA. Debut 1975 OB in *Straw for an Evening* followed by *The Family, Landscape with Waitress, 3 from the Marathon, The Slab Boys, Vivien, Operation Midnight Climax, The Dining Room, Daddies, To Gillian on Her 37th Birthday, Dennis, Traps, Sleeping Dogs, Equal Wrights EST Marathon '93, Dolphin Project, Rain.*

HOYLEN, TONY. Born in Maracaibo, Venezuela. Attended Eastern New Mex. U.,TCU. Debut 1978 OB in *Thread of Scarlet* followed by *Middle of Nowhere, Sugar Hill, Noa Noa, Rent,* Bdwy in *Peter Pan* (1980), *The News.*

HUBER, KATHLEEN. Born Mar. 3, 1947 in New York City. Graduate U. Cal. Debut 1969 OB in *Scent of Flowers,* followed by *Virgin and the Unicorn, Constant Wife, Milestones, Tamara, Romeo and Juliet, Richard III.*

HUFF, NEAL. Born in New York City. NYU. Graduate. Debut 1992 OB in *Young Playwrights Festival* followed by *Joined at the Head, Day the Bronx Died, Macbeth, House of Yes, Class 1-Acts, Saturday Mourning Cartoons.*

HUFFMAN, FELICITY. Born Dec. 9, 1962 in Westchester, NY. Graduate NYU, AADA, RADA. Debut 1988 OB in *Boys' Life,* followed by *Been Taken, Grotesque Lovesongs, Three Sisters, Shaker Heights, Jolly, Cryptogram,* Bdwy in *Speed-the-Plow* (1988).

HYMAN, EARLE. Born Oct. 11, 1926 in Rocky Mount, NC. Attended New School, Am. Th. Wing. Bdwy debut 1943 in *Run Little Chillun,* followed by *Anna Lucasta, Climate of Eden, Merchant of Venice, Othello, Julius Caesar, The Tempest, No Time for Sergeants, Mr. Johnson* for which he received a Theatre World Award, *St. Joan, Hamlet, Waiting for Godot, The Duchess of Malfi, Les Blancs, The Lady from Dubuque, Execution of*

Justice, Death of the King's Horseman, The Master Builder, OB in *The White Rose and the Red, Worlds of Shakespeare, Jonah, Life and Times of J. Walter Smintheus, Orrin, The Cherry Orchard, House Party, Carnival Dreams, Agamemnon, Othello, Julius Caesar, Coriolanus, Pygmalion, Richard II, East Texas Hot Links, Merchant of Venice.*

IVANEK, ZELJKO. Born Aug. 15, 1957 in Lujubljana, Yugo. Graduate Yale U., LAMDA. Bdwy debut 1981 in *The Survivor* followed by *Brighton Beach Memoirs, Loot, Two Shakespearean Actors, Glass Menagerie* (1994), OB in *Cloud 9, A Map of the World, Cherry Orchard.*

IVES, JANE. Born Nov. 6, 1949 in New York City. Attended Conn. Col. Debut 1981 OB in *Murder in the Cathedral* followed by *Street Scene, Night Games, Frog in His Throat, Too Clever by Half.*

JACKSON, KIRK. Born Feb. 8, 1956 in Albany, NY. Graduate Binghamton U., Yale U. Debut 1990 OB in *Stirrings Still* followed by *Bremen Freedom, The Secret Lives of Ancient Egyptians, Underground Soap, Heartbreak House, Untitled Lindberg, Listen to Me, Inktomi, The Almond Seller, Necropolis, Private Property, Apocrypha, Storm Patterns,* Bdwy in *Love!Valour!Compassion!* (1995).

JACOBS, MAX. Born Apr. 28, 1937 in Buffalo, NY. Graduate U. Ariz. 8dwy debut 1965 in *The Zulu and the Zayda,* OB in *Full Circle, The Working Man, Hallowed Halls, The Man in the Glass Booth, Different People, Different Rooms, Second Avenue, Othello, Birth of a Poet, Shaking the Foundation, Madonna & Mike, Romeo and Juliet, Arms and the Man.*

JACOBY, MARK. Born May 21, 1947 in Johnson City, TN. Graduate GA State U., FL State U., St. John's U. Debut 1984 OB in *Bells Are Ringing,* Bdwy in *Sweet Charity* for which he received a 1986 Theatre World Award, *Grand Hotel, The Phantom of the Opera, Show Boat.*

JAKUBOWSKI, ZANIZ. Born in the UK. Graduate Am. Col./Switzerland. Debut 1995 OB in *Ecstacy.*

JAMES, ELMORE. Born May 3, 1954 in New York City. Graduate SUNY/Purchase. Debut 1970 OB in *Moon on a Rainbow Shawl* followed by *The Ups and Downs of Theopholus Maitland, Carnival, Until the Real Thing Comes Along, A Midsummer Night's Dream, The Tempest, Jacques Brel Is Alive...,* Bdwy in *But Never Jam Today* (1979), *Your Arms Too Short to Box with God, Big River, Beauty and the Beast.*

JAMES, KRICKER. Born May 17, 1939 in Cleveland, OH. Graduate Denison U. Debut 1966 OB in *Winterset,* followed by *Out of Control, Rainbows for Sale, The Firebugs, Darkness at Noon, The Hunting Man, Sacraments, Trifles, Batting Practice, Uncle Vanya, Mourning Becomes Electra, Shelter, Edward II.*

JANKO, IBI. Born Feb. 18, 1966 in Carmel, CA. Graduate Yale U. debut 1993 OB in *Somewhere I Have Travelled* followed by *Vinegar Tom, Waiting, Your Mom's a Man, Cinoman and Rebeck, Kidnapped.*

JARRETT, BELLA. Born Feb. 9, 1931 in Adairsville, GA. Graduate Wesleyan Col. Debut 1958 OB in *Waltz of the Toreadors* followed by *Hedda Gabler, The Browning Version, Cicero, Pequod, Welcome to Andromeda, The Trojan Women, Phaedra, The Good Natur'd Man, Twelfth Night, German Games,* Bdwy in *Once in a Lifetime* (1978), *Lolita.*

JBARA, GREGORY. Born Sept. 28, 1961 in Wayne, MI. Graduate U. MI, Juilliard. Debut 1986 OB in *Have I Got a Girl for you, Serious Money, Privates on Prarade, Forever Plaid,* Bdwy in *Serious Money* (1988), *Born Yesterday* (1989), *Damn Yankees* (1994).

JENKINS, DANIEL. Born Jan. 17, 1963 in New York City. Attended Columbia U. Bdwy debut 1985 in *Big River* followed by *Angels in America,* OB in *Feast Here Tonight, Young Playwrights Festival, The Triumph of Love, Johnny Pye and the Foolkiller.*

JENNINGS, KEN Born Oct. 10, 1947 in Jersey City, NJ. Graduate St. Peter's Col. Bdwy debut 1975 in *All God's Chillun Got Wings,* followed by *Sweeney Todd* for which he received a 1979 Theatre World Award, *Present Laughter, Grand Hotel, Christmas Carol,* OB in *Once on a Summer's Day, Mayor, Rabboni, Gifts of the Magi, Carmilla, Sharon, Mayor, Amphigory, Shabbatai.*

JEROME, TIMOTHY. Born Dec. 29, 1943 in Los Angeles, CA. Graduate Ithaca Col. Bdwy debut 1969 in *Man of La Mancha,* followed by *The Rothschilds. Creation of the World..., Moony Shapiro Songbook, Cats, Me and My Girl, Grand Hotel,* OB in *Beggars Opera, Pretzels, Civilization and Its Discontents, Little Prince, Colette Collage, Room Service, Romance in Hard Times, Petrified Prince.*

JOHANSON, DON. Born Oct. 19, 1952 in Rock Hill, SC. Graduate USC. Bdwy debut 1976 in *Rex* followed by *Cats, Jelly's Last Jam, Best Little Whorehouse in Texas Goes Public, Christmas Carol,* OB in *The American Dance Machine.*

JOHNSON, JEREMY. Born Oct. 2, 1933 in New Bedford, MA. Graduate CCNY, Columbia U. Debut 1975 OB in *Moby Dick,* followed by *Anna Christie, Harrison Texas, Romeo and Juliet, Much Ado about Nothing,*

212

Merchant of Venice, Winter's Tale.

JOHN, TAYLOR. Born Nov. 25, 1981 in New York City. Bdwy debut 1991 in *Les Miserables.*

JOHNSON, JULIE. Born Nov. 16 in Whitewright, TX. Graduate Austin Col. Debut 1994 OB in *Das Barbecu* for which she received a 1995 Theatre World Award, followed by *The Rink.*

JOHNSON, PAGE. Born Aug. 25, 1930 in Welch, WV. Graduate Ithaca Col. Bdwy 1951 in *Romeo and Juliet,* followed by *Electra, Oedipus, Camino Real, In Apr.* for which he received a Theatre World Award, *Red Roses for Me, The Lovers, Equus, You Can't Take It with You, Brush Arbor Revival,* OB in *The Enchanted Guitar, 4 in 1, Journey of the Fifth Horse, APA's School for Scandal, The Tavern,* and *The Seagull,* followed by *Odd Couple, Boys in the Band, Medea, Deathtrap, Best Little Whorehouse in Texas, Fool for Love, East Texas.*

JOINER, DORRIE. Born in Dublin, GA. Graduate U. So. Al. Debut 1989 OB in *Steel Magnolias* followed by *Fortune's Fools.*

JONES, CHERRY. Born Nov. 21, 1956 in Paris, TN. Graduate Carnegie-Mellon. Debut 1983 OB in *The Philanthropist,* followed by *He and She, The Ballad of Soapy Smith, The Importance of Being Earnest, I Am a Camera, Claptrap, Big Time, A Light Shining in Buckinghamshire, The Baltimore Waltz, Goodnight Desdemona, And Baby Makes 7,* Bdwy in *Stepping Out* (1986), *Our Country's Good, Angels in America, The Heiress.*

JONES, JAY AUBREY. Born Mar. 30, 1954 in Atlantic City, NJ. Graduate Syracuse U. Debut 1981 OB in *Sea Dream,* followed by *Divine Hysteria, Inacent Black and the Brothers, La Belle Helene,* Bdwy in *Cats* (1986), *How to Succeed...*

JONES, NEAL. Born Jan. 2, 1960 in Wichita, KS. Attended Weber Col. Debut 1981 OB in *The Dear Love of Comrades,* followed by *The Tavern, Spring's Awakening, Billy Liar, Groves of Academe, A Darker Purpose, Diminished Capacity, The Undertakers, Public Enemy,* Bdwy in *Macbeth* (1982), *The Corn Is Green* (1983).

JONES, TAD. Born May 5, 1955 in Stutgart, Germany. Graduate AADA. Debut 1983 OB in *The Inheritors* followed by *Paradise Lost, Rain, Hasty Heart, Time of Your Life, Children of the Sun, Craig's Wife.*

JONES, WALKER. Born Aug. 27, 1956 in Pensacola, Fl. Graduate Boston U., Yale U. Debut 1989 OB in *Wonderful Town* followed by *Scapin, Byzantium, Merry Wives of Windsor, Merchant of Venice.*

JOSLYN, BETSY. Born Apr. 19, 1954 in Staten Island, NY. Graduate Wagner Col. Debut 1976 OB in *The Fantasticks,* followed by *Light Up the Sky, Colette Collage, Decline of the Middle West,* Bdwy in *Sweeney Todd* (1979), *A Doll's Life, The Goodbye Girl, Lady in the Dark in Concert.*

JOY, ROBERT. Born Aug. 17, 1951 inMontreal,Can. Graduate Oxford U. Debut 1978 OB in *Diary of Anne Frank,* followed by *Fables for Friends, Lydie Breeze Sister Mary Ignatius Explains It All, Actor's Nightmare, What I Did Last Summer, The Death of von Ricthofen, Lenny and the Heartbreakers, Found a Peanut, Field Day, Life and Limb, Hyde in Hollywood, The Taming of the Shrew, Man in His Underwear, Goodnight Desdemona, No One will Be Immune,* Bdwy in *Hay Fever* (1985), *The Nerd, Shimada.*

JOYCE, ELLA. Born June 12, 1954 in Rural Township, IL. Attended E. Mich. U. Debut 1989 OB in *Don't Get God Started* followed by *Crumbs from the Table of Joy.*

KADEN, EILEEN. Born Feb. 25, 1968 in Rahway, NJ. Graduate Carnegie Mellon U. Debut 1991 OB in *Company* followed by *Anyone Can Whistle, Jesus Christ Superstar.*

KAGAN, DIANE. Born in Maplewood, NJ. Graduate Fla. State U. Debut 1963 OB in *Asylum,* followed by *Days and Nights of Beebec Fenstermaker, Death of a Well-Loved Boy, Mme. de Sade, Blue Boys, Alive and Well in Agentina, Little Black Sheep, The Family, Ladyhouse Blues, Scenes from Everyday Life, Marvelous Gray, Enrico IV, Five Women in a Chapel, Clothes for a Summer Hotel,* Bdwy in *Chinese Prime Minister* (1964), *Never Too Late, Any Wednesday, Venus Is, Tiger at the Gates, Vieux Carre.*

KANTOR, KENNETH. Born Apr. 6, 1949 in Bronx, NY. Graduate SUNY, Boston U. Debut 1974 OB in *Zorba,* followed by *Kiss Me Kate, A Little Night Music, Buried Treasure, Sounds of Rodgers and Hammerstein, Shop on Main Street, Kismet, The Fantasticks, Colette Collage, Snow White, Philemon,* Bdwy in *The Grand Tour* (1979), *Brigadoon* (1980), *Mame* (1983), *The New Moon* (NYCO/LC), *Me and My Girl, Guys and Dolls* (1992).

KAUFMAN, ERIC H. Born Sept. 11, 1961 in New York City. Attended U. Wis., NYU. Bdwy debut 1986 in *L'Chaim to Life,* followed by *Gypsy* (1989), *Christmas Carol.*

KEITH, LAWRENCE/LARRY. Born Mar. 4, 1931 in Brooklyn, NY. Graduate Brooklyn Col., Ind. U. Bdwy debut 1960 in *My Fair Lady* followed by *High Spirits, I Had a Ball, Best Laid Plans, Mother Lover,* OB in *The Homecoming, Conflict of Interest, The Brownsville Raid, M. Amilcar, The Rise of David Levinsky, Miami, Song for a Saturday, Rose Quar-*

tet, I Am a Man, Androcles and the Lion, Madwoman of Chaillot, Too Clever by Half, After-Play.

KELLER, JEFF. Born Sept. 8, 1947 in Brooklyn, NY. Graduate Monmouth Col. Bdwy 1974 in *Candide* followed by *Fiddler on the Roof, On the 20th Century, 1940's Radio Show, Roast, Dance a Little Closer, Sunday in the Park with George, Phantom of the Opera, Christmas Carol,* OB in *Bird of Paradise, Charlotte Sweet, Roberta in Concert, Personals.*

KELLY, JOHN-CHARLES. Born Apr. 28, 1946 in Salem, OR. Graduate U. Or., U. AZ. Debut 1984 OB in *Bells Are Ringing* followed by *The High Life in Concert, Christmas Carol.*

KELLY, TARI. Born Dec. 12, 1969 in Madison, WI. Attended U. Wis, DePaul U. Bdwy debut 1994 in *Show Boat.*

KENER, DAVID. Born May 21, 1959 in Brooklyn, NY. Graduate NYU. Debut 1987 OB in *The Rise of David Levinsky,* followed by *Songs of Paradise, Lady and the Clarinet, Coming Through.*

KENNEDY, COLLEEN. Born Feb. 5 in Warren, OH. Graduate Boston Consv. Bdwy debut 1994 in *An Inspector Calls.*

KENNEDY, LAURIE. Born Feb. 14, 1948 in Hollywood, CA. Graduate Sarah Lawrence Col. Debut 1974 OB in *End of Summer,* followed by *A Day in the Death of Joe Egg, Ladyhouse Blues, he and she, The Recruiting Officer, Isn't It Romantic, The Master Builder, Candida, 2,* Bdwy in *Man and Superman* (1978) for which she received a Theatre World Award, *Major Barbara, Angels in America.*

KERNER, NORBERTO. Born July 19, 1929 in Valparaiso, Chile. Attended Piscator Workshop, Goodman Theatre. Debut 1971 OB in *Yerma,* followed by *I Took Pananma, F.M. Safe, My Old Friends, Sharon Shashanovah, Blood Wedding, Crisp, The Great Confession, Cold Air, Don Juan of Seville, Human Voice, Ox Cart,* Bdwy 1995 in *Chronicle of a Death Foretold.*

KERSHEN, ED. Born Dec. 5, 1958 in Hempstead, NY. Graduate SUNY/Purchase. Debut 1994 OB in *Gift Horse.*

KERWIN, BRIAN. Born Oct. 25, 1949 in Chicago, IL. Graduate U. S. Cal. Debut 1988 OB in *Emily* for which he received a Theatre World Award, followed by *Lips Together Teeth Apart, One Shoe Off, Raised in Captivity.*

KHALAF, RAMZI. Born Jan. 17, 1982 in Lebanon. Debut 1993 OB in *The Little Prince* followed by *Christmas Carol.*

KIARA, DOROTHY. Born June 27, 1954 in Providence, Rl. Graduate Boston Consv, Bdwy debut 1980 in *They're Playing Our Song* followed by *Nine,* OB in *Forbidden Broadway* ('88/89/93), *Kokoro.*

KILNER, KEVIN. Born May 3, 1958 in Baltimore, MD. Graduate Johns Hopkins U. Debut 1988 OB in *Marriage of Betty and Boo* followed by *St. George, Night and Her Stars,* Bdwy 1994 in *Glass Menagerie* for which he received a Theatre World Award.

KIM, DANIEL DAE. Born Aug. 4, 1968 in Korea. Graduate Haverford Col. Debut 1991 OB in *Romeo and Juliet* followed by *Love Letters from a Student Revolutionary, A Doll House., School for Wives.*

KIMBROUGH, CHARLES. Born May 23, 1936 in St. Paul, MN. Graduate Ind. U, Yale U. Bdwy debut 1969 in *Cop-Out* followed by *Company, Love for Love, Rules of the Game, Candide, Mr. Happiness, Same Time Next Year, Sunday in the Park with George, Hay Fever,* OB in *All for Love, Struts and Frets, Troilus and Cressida, Secret Service, Boy Meets Girl, Drinks before Dinner, Dining Room, Later Life, Sylvia.*

KIRK, JUSTIN. Born May 28, 1969 in Salem, OR. Debut 1990 OB in *The Applicant,* followed by *Shardston, Loose Ends, Thanksgiving, Lovequest Live,* Bdwy in *Any Given Day* (1993), *Love! Valour! Compassion!* (also OB).

KIRSH, BOB. Born Sept. 26, 1962 in Bristol, PA. Graduate Temple U., NYU. Debut 1990 OB in *Beautiful Soup,* followed by *Time Piece, Hyacinth Macaw, Prince and the Pauper, Hundreds of Hats.*

KITTRELL, MICHELLE. Born Dec. 16, 1972 in Cocoa Beach, FL. Debut 1993 OB in *Girl of My Dreams* followed by *New Yorkers, Joseph and the... Dreamcoat.*

KLEIN, LAUREN. Born Jan. 4, 1946 in Brooklyn, NY. Graduate Santa Fe Col. Debut 1983 OB in *Becoming Memories,* followed by *Zastrozzi, After the Fall, Twice Shy, What's Wrong with This Picture?, Death Defying Acts,* Bdwy debut 1994 in *Broken Glass.*

KLEMPERER, WERNER. Born Mar. 20, 1920 in Cologne, Ger. Graduate Pasadena Playhouse. Bdwy debut 1947 in *Heads or Tails* followed by *Galileo, Insect Comedy, 20th Century, Dear Charles, Night of the Tribades, Cabaret, Sound of Music* (LC), *Uncle Vanya,* OB in *Master Class.*

KNELL, DANE. Born Sept. 27, 1932 in Winthrop, MA. Bdwy debut 1952 in *See the Jaguar,* followed by *Lettice and Lovage,* OB in *Ulster, Moon Dances, Court of Miracles, Gas Station, Zeks, She Stoops to Conquer, Modigliani, Just Another Lousy Musical.*

KNUDSON, KURT. Born Sept. 7, 1936 in Fargo, ND. Attended ND St. U, U. Miami. Debut 1976 OB in *Cherry Orchard* followed by *Geniuses, Room Service, Without Apologies,* Bdwy in *Curse of an Aching Heart* (1982),

Sunday in the Park with George, Take Me Along, Beauty and the Beast.

KOKA, JULIETTE. Born Apr. 4 in Finland. Attended Helsinki Dramatic Arts school. Debut 1977 OB in *Piaf...A Remembrance* for which she received a Theatre World Award, followed by *Ladies and Gentlemen Jerome Kern, Salon, Concert that Could Have Been,* Bdwy in *All Star Players Club Centennial Salute* (1989).

KOLINSKI, JOSEPH. Born June 26, 1953 in Detroit, MI. Attended U. Detroit. Bdwy debut 1980 in *Brigadoon,* followed by *Dance a Little Closer, The Human Comedy* (also OB), *The Three Musketeers, Les Miserables, Christmas Carol,* OB in *HiJinks!, Picking up the Pieces.*

KOREY, ALIX (formerly Alexandra). Born May 14 in Brooklyn, NY. Graduate Columbia U. Debut 1976 OB in *Fiorello!,* followed by *Annie Get Your Gun, Jerry's Girls, Rosalie in Concert, America Kicks Up Its Heels, Gallery, Feathertop, Bittersuite, Romance in Hard Times, Songs You Might Have Missed, Forbidden Broadway 10th Anniversary, Camp Paradox, Cinderella* (LC), *Best of the West, Jack's Holiday,* Bdwy in *Hello Dolly* (1978), *Show Boat* (1983), *Ain't Broadway Grand.*

KRSTANSKY, ADRIANNE. Born July 7, 1964 in Chicago, IL. Graduate Beloit Col., U. Cal./San Diego. Debut 1995 OB in *Luck Pluck and Virtue.*

KUBALA, MICHAEL. Born Feb. 4, 1958 in Reading, PA. Attended NYU. Bdwy debut 1978 in *A Broadway Musical* followed by *Dancin', Woman of the Year, Marilyn, Jerome Robbins' Broadway, Crazy for You,* OB in *Double Feature* (1981).

KUDISCH, MARC. Born Sept. 22, 1966 in Hackensack, NJ. Attended Fl. Atlantic U. Debut 1990 OB in *Quiet on the Set,* Bdwy in *Joseph and the...Dreamcoat* (1994), *Beauty and the Beast.*

KURTZ, MARCIA JEAN. Born in Bronx, NY. Juilliard graduate. Debut 1966 OB in *Jonah,* followed by *American Hurrah, Red Cross, Muzeeka, Effect of Gamma Rays..., Year Boston Won the Pennant, The Mirror, The Orphan, Action, The Dybbuk, Ivanov, What's Wrong with This Picture?, Today I Am a Fountain Pen, Chopin Playoffs, Loman Family Picnic, Human Nature, When She Danced, The Workroom, The Cowboy the Indian and the Fervent Feminist, Extensions, Credo,* Bdwy in *The Chinese and Dr. Fish* (1970), *Thieves, Execution of Justice.*

LaBRECQUE, DOUG. Born Jan. 5, 1966 in Battle Creek, MI. Graduate U. Mi. Bdwy debut 1994 in *Show Boat.*

LaCHANZE. Born Dec. 16, 1961 in St. Augustine, FL. Attended Morgan State U., Philadelphia Col. Bdwy debut 1986 in *Uptown It's Hot,* followed by *Dreamgirls* (1987), *Once on This Island* (also OB) for which she received a 1991 Theatre World Award, *Out Of This World* (Encores).

LaDUCA, PHIL. Born Dec. 10, 1954 in Chicago, IL. Attended DePaul U., Goodman Theatre. Bdwy debut 1980 in *Brigadoon,* followed by *Pirates of Penzance, Singing' in the Rain, Damn Yankees* (1994), OB in *Buskers, Pajama Game.*

LaFLECHE, MICHEL. Born May 2, 1962 in Winnipeg, Can. Bdwy debut 1994 in *Show Boat.*

LAGE, JORDAN. Born Feb. 17, 1963 in Palo Alto, CA. Graduate NYU. Debut 1988 OB in *Boy's Life,* followed by *Three Sisters, The Virgin Molly, Distant Fires, Macbeth, Yes But So What?, The Blue Hour, Been Taken, The Woods, Five Very Live, Hot Keys, As Sure as You Live, The Arrangement, The Lights, Shaker Heights, Missing Persons, Blaming Mom, Night and Her Stars,* Bdwy in *Our Town* (1989).

LAMB, MARY ANN. Born July 4, 1959 in Seattle, WA. Attended Neighborhood Playhouse. Bdwy debut 1985 in *Song and Dance,* followed by *Starlight Express, Jerome Robbins' Broadway, The Goodbye Girl, Fiorello!* (Encores), *Out of This World* (Encores), *Pal Joey* (Encores).

LAMISON, TAMIKA. Born May 26, 1961 in Richmond, VA. Graduate American U., Howard U. Debut 1984 OB in *Tower of Burden* followed by *For Colored Girls...*

LANDRIEU, NELSON ROBERTO. Born July 6, 1949 in Montevideo, Uruguay. Graduate AADA. Bdwy debut 1995 in *Chronicle of a Death Foretold,* OB in *Ceremony for a Black Man, Happy Birthday Mama, Yepeto.*

LANE, NATHAN. Born Feb. 3, 1956 in Jersey City, NJ. Debut 1978 OB in *A Midsummer Night's Dream,* followed by *Love, Measure for Measure, Claptrap, The Common Pursuit, In a Pig's Valise, Uncounted Blessings, The Film Society, The Lisbon Traviata, Bad Habits, Lips Together Teeth Apart,* Bdwy in *Present Laughter* (1982), *Merlin, Wind in the Willows, Some Americans Abroad, On Borrowed Time, Guys and Dolls, Laugher on the 23rd Floor, Love! Valour! Compassion!* (also OB).

LANG, STEPHEN. Born July 11, 1952 in New York City. Graduate Swarthmore Col. Debut 1975 OB in *Hamlet,* followed by *Henry V, Shadow of a Gunman, Winter's Tale, Johnny on a Spot, Barbarians, Ah Men, Clownmaker, Hannah, Rosencrantz and Guildenstern Are Dead, Awake and Sing,* Bdwy in *St. Joan* (1977), *A Few Good Men, Death of a Salesman* (1984), *Speed of Darkness, Hamlet* (1992).

LANGE, ANN. Born June 24, 1953 in Pipestone, MN. Attended Carnegie-Mellon U. Debut 1979 OB in *Rats Nest,* followed by *Hunting Scenes from Lower Bavaria, Crossfire, Linda Her and the Fairy Garden, Little Footsteps, 10th Young Playwrights Festival, Jeffrey, Family of Mann, 12 Dreams,* Bdwy in *The Survivor* (1981), *The Heidi Chronicles.*

LaPAGLIA, ANTHONY. Born Jan. 31, 1960 in Adelaide, Aust. College Grad/B. A. degree. Debut 1987 OB in *Bouncers* followed by *On the Open Road, Mere Mortals,* Bdwy 1995 in *Rose Tattoo* for which he received a Theatre World Award.

LARSEN, LIZ. Born Jan. 16, 1959 in Philadelphia, PA. Attended Hofstra U., SUNY/Purchase. Bdwy debut 1981 in *Fiddler on the Roof,* followed by *Starmites, A Little Night Music,* (NYCO/LC), *The Most Happy Fella, Damn Yankees,* OB in *Kuni Leml, Hamlin, Personals, Starmites, Company, After These Messages, One Act Festival, The Loman Family Picnic, Teibele and Her Demon.*

LAUREN, JULIE. Born in New York City. Graduate Dartmouth Col., Neighborhood Playhouse. Debut 1993 OB in *The Survivor, Ryan Interview.*

LAURENCE, JAMES HOWARD. Born Sept. 23, 1945 in Chicago, IL. Attended Ind. U. Bdwy debut 1969 in *Henry V,* OB in *The Moths, El Grande de Coca Cola, Madwoman of Chaillot.*

LAURENT, WENDELL. Born Dec. 1, 1961 in New Orleans, LA. Graduate Loyola U. Debut 1992 OB in *You're a Good Man Charlie Brown,* followed by *My Sister Eileen, Holy Ghosts.*

LAVIN, LINDA. Born Oct. 15, 1939 in Portland, ME. Graduate Wm. & Mary Col. Bdwy debut 1962 in *A Family Affair* followed by *Riot Act, The Game Is Up, Hotel Passionata, It's a Bird It's Superman!, On a Clear Day You Can See Forever, Something Different, Cop-Out, Last of the Red Hot Lovers, Story Theatre, The Enemy Is Dead, Broadway Bound, Gypsy* (1990), *The Sisters Rosensweig,* OB in *Wet Paint* (1965) for which she received a Theatre World Award, *Death Defying Acts.*

LAW, JUDE. Born Dec. 29, 1972 in Lesisham, Eng. Bdwy debut 1995 in *Indiscretions* for which he received a Theatre World Award.

LAWRENCE, TASHA. Born Jan. 31, 1967 in Alberta, Can. Graduate U. Guelph. 1992 OB in *Loose Ends,* followed by *Cowboy in His Underwear, Ten Blocks on the Camino Real, 3 by Wilder, Who Will Carry the Word?, Anatomy of Sound, Goose and Tom Tom,* Bdwy in *Wilder Wilder Wilder* (1993).

LAWRENCE, MAL Z. Born Sept. 2, 1937 in New York City. Attended CCNY. Bdwy debut 1991 in *Catskills on Broadway,* OB in *Petrified Prince.*

LEACH, NICOLE. Born May 10, 1979 in New Jersey. Debut 1994 OB in *Bring in the Morning* followed by *Crumbs from the Table of Joy.*

LEASK, KATHERINE. Born Sept. 2, 1957 in Munich, Ger. Graduate SMU. Debut 1988 OB in *Man Who Climbed the Pecan Trees* followed by *Cahoots, Melville Boys, Amphitryon.*

LEAVEL, BETH. Born Nov. 1, 1955 in Raleigh, NC. Graduate Meredith Col., UNC/Greensboro. Debut 1982 OB in *Applause,* followed by *Promises Promises, Broadway Juke Box, Unfinished Song,* Bdwy in *42nd Street* (1984), *Crazy for You.*

LECESNE, JAMES. Born Nov. 24, 1954 in NJ. Debut 1982 OB in *One-Man Band* followed by *Cloud 9, Word of Mouth, Extraordinary Measures.*

LEE, DARREN. Born June 8, 1972 in Long Beach, CA. Bdwy debut 1990 in *Shogun,* followed by *Miss Saigon,* OB in *Petrified Prince* (1994).

LEEDS, JORDAN. Born Nov. 29,1961 in Queens, NY. Graduate SUNY/Binghamton. Bdwy debut 1987 in *Les Miserables,* followed by OB in *Beau Jest, Angel Levine.*

LEFFERT, JOEL. Born Dec. 8, 1951 in New York City. Graduate Brown U. Debut 1976 OB in *Orphee* followed by *Heroes, Last Burning, Relatively Speaking, The Bachelor, Scaramouche, Macbeth, Don Juan in Hell, Village Wooing, Long Smoldering, Loveplay, The Straw, Richard III.*

LEHL, PHILIP. Born Apr. 29, 1964 in Terra Haute, IN. Graduate Drake U., Juilliard. Bdwy debut 1993 in *Blood Brothers,* followed by *Kentucky Cycle,* OB in *Hay Fever, Hundreds of Hats.*

LEIBMAN, RON. Born Oct. 11, 1937 in New York City. Attended Ohio Wesleyan Col., Actors Studio. Bdwy debut 1963 in *Dear Me the Sky is Falling,* followed by *Bicycle Ride to Nevada, The Deputy, We Bombed in New Haven* for which he received a Theatre World Award, *Cop-Out,* OB in *The Academy, John Brown's Body, Scapin, The Premise, Legend of Lovers, Dead End, Poker Session, Transfers, Room Service, Love Two, Rich and Famous, Children of Darkness, Non Pasquale, Give the Bishop My Faint Regards, Merchant of Venice.*

LENOX, ADRIANE. Born Sept. 11, 1956 in Memphis, TN. Graduate Lambuth Col. Bdwy debut 1979 in *Ain't Misbehavin,* followed by *Dreamgirls,* OB in *Beehive, Merrily We Roll Along, America Play, Identical Twins from Baltimore.*

LEONARD, ROBERT SEAN. Born Feb. 28, 1969 in Westwood, NJ. Debut 1985 OB in *Sally's Gone She Left Her Name,* followed by *Coming of Age in Soho, Beach House, Young Playwrights Festival, And the Air Didn't Answer, When She Danced, Romeo and Juliet, Pitching to the Star, Good Evening, Great Unwashed,* Bdwy in *Brighton Beach Memoirs* (1985), *Breaking the Code, Speed of Darkness, Candida, Philadelphia Here I Come, Arcadia.*

LeSTRANGE, PHILIP. Born May 9, 1942 in Bronx, NY. Graduate Catholic U., Fordham U. Debut 1970 OB in *Getting Married,* followed by *Erogenous Zones, The Quilling of Prue, The Front Page, Six Degrees of Separation,* Bdwy in *A Small Family Business* (1992), *Guys and Dolls, Rose Tattoo.*

LEUNG, KEN. Born Jan. 21, 1970 in New York City. Graduate NYU. Debut 1994 OB in *Ghost in the Machine.*

LEWIS, JERRY (Joseph Levitch). Born Mar. 16, 1926 in Newark, NJ. Bdwy debut 1995 in *Damn Yankees.*

LEWIS, MARK. Born Feb. 28, 1957 in Rosario, Argentina. Graduate SMU, Portland St. U. Debut 1988 OB in *Julius Caesar* followed by *Midsummer Night's Dream, Tamara, A Doll House, Othello.*

LEWIS, MATTHEW. Born Jan. 12, 1937 in Elizabeth, NJ. Graduate Harvard U. Debut 1970 OB in *Chicago '70,* followed by *Fathers and Sons, The Freak, Happy Days Are Here Again, Levitation, The Sea Cull, My Papa's Wine, Apocalyptic Butterflies, White Collar, Group, 2,* Bdwy in *Angels Fall* (1983).

LEWIS, TODD. Born May 26, 1952 in Chicago, IL. Graduate Lewis U. Debut 1989 OB in *Flying Blind* followed by *Willie and Sahara, Sawney Bean, Perfect Diamond, Soup du Soir, Blood, Field in Heat.*

LEWIS, VICKI. Born Mar. 17, 1969 in Cincinnati, OH. Graduate Cinn. Consv. Bdwy debut 1982 in *Do Black Patent Leather Shoes Really Reflect Up?,* followed by *Wind in the Willows, Damn Yankees, Pal Joey* (Encores), OB in *Snoopy, A Bundle of Nerves, Angry Housewives, 1-2-3-4-5, One Act Festival, The Love Talker, Buzzsaw Berkeley, Marathon '90, The Crucible, I Can Get It for You Wholesale, Don Juan and the Non Don Juan.*

LEYVA, SELENIS. Born May 26, 1972. Graduate Marymount Manhattan Col. Debut 1995 OB in *Simpson Street.*

LINARES, CARLOS. Born July 26, 1954 in El Salvador, CA. Attended Lehman Col. Debut 1988 OB in *Senora Carrar's Rifles,* followed by *Tafpoletigermosquitos at Mulligan's, The Cause.*

LINEHAN, ROSALEEN. Born Jan. 6, 1937 in Dublin, Ire. Graduate U. Dublin. Bdwy debut in *Dancing at Lughnasa* (1991), OB in *Mother of all the Behans* (1994).

LINVILLE, LARRY. Born Sept. 29, 1939 in Ojai, CA. Attended U. Co., RADA. Appeared with APA for 4 seasons before Bdwy 1967 in *More Stately Mansions* followed by *Rumors,* OB 1995 in *Travels with My Aunt.*

LOAR, ROSEMARY. Born in New York City. Attended U. Ohio, U. Ore. Bdwy debut 1984 in *You Can't Take It With You* followed by *Chess, Cats, Sunset Blvd.,* OB in *Encore, Sally in Concert, Chess.*

LOESSER, EMILY. Born June 2, 1965 in New York City. Graduate Northwestern U. Debut 1988 OB in *Secret Garden,* followed by *Together Again for the First Time, The Witch, Follies, Yiddle with a Fiddle, Music in the Air in Concert, Swingtime Canteen,* Bdwy in *The Sound of Music* (LC/90).

LOPEZ, CARLOS. Born May 14, 1963 in Sunnyvale, CA. Attended Cal. St. U./Hayward. Debut 1987 OB in *Wish You Were Here,* followed by Bdwy in *The Pajama Game* (NYCO–1989), *A Chorus Line, Grand Hotel, Guys and Dolls, Grease, Wonderful Town* (NYCO).

LOUDON, DOROTHY. Born Sept. 17, 1933 in Boston, MA. Attended Emerson Col., Syracuse U. Debut 1961 OB in *World of Jules Feiffer,* followed by *The Matchmaker,* Bdwy 1962 in *Nowhere to Go But Up* for which she received a Theatre World Award, followed by *Noel Coward's Sweet Potato, Fig Leaves Are Falling, Three Men on a Horse, The Women, Annie, Ballroom, West Side Waltz, Noises Off, Jerry's Girls, Comedy Tonight.*

LOUGANIS, GREGORY. Born Jan. 29, 1960 in San Diego, CA. Graduate U. Miami, U. Cal./Irvine. Debut 1993 OB in *Jeffrey,* followed by *Only Thing Worse You Could Have Told Me.*

LOVEMAN, LENORE (a.k.a. Lenore Koven). Born Feb. 23, 1934 in Brooklyn, NY. Attended Columbia U., SUNY. Debut 1954 OB in *Miss Julie,* followed by *Two by Linney, Cafe Crown, The Return, Subways Hallways Rooftops, Where Memories Are Magic and Dreams Invented, World of Sholem Aleichem, A Backward Glance of Edith Wharton, Academy Street, Greetings, Unorthodox Behaviour,* Bdwy in *Checking Out* (1976).

LOVETT, MARCUS. Born in 1965 in Glen-Ellen, IL. Graduate Carnegie-Mellon U. Bdwy 1987 in *Les Miserables,* followed by *Aspects of Love, Phantom of the Opera, Carousel,* OB in *And the World Goes Round.*

LOW, MAGGIE. Born Apr. 23, 1957 in Nyack, NY. Debut 1982 OB in *Catholic School Girls* followed by *Action, Thoughts Modern, Candle in the Window.*

LOWE, FRANK. Born June 28, 1927 in Appalachia, VA. Attended Sorbonne. Debut 1952 OB in *Macbeth,* followed by *Hotel De Breney, The Lady's Not for Burning, Fox Trot on Gardiner's Bay, As You Like it, A Sleep of Prisoners, Cymbeline, Did Elvis Cry!, Man with a Raincoat, Donkey's Years, Ring Round the Moon!, Moon for the Misbegotten, Twelfth Night, Titus Andronicus, Henry VI.*

LOY, PATRICK. Born Aug. 21, 1961 in Canton, OH. Graduate Cleveland State U. Bdwy debut 1994 in *Beauty and the Beast.*

LUCAS, ROXIE. Born Aug. 25, 1951 in Memphis, TN. Attended U. Houston. Bdwy debut 1981 in *Best Little Whorehouse in Texas* followed by *Harrigan 'n' Hart, My Favorite Year, Damn Yankees,* OB in *Forbidden Broadway, Best of Forbidden Broadway, 20 Fingers 20 Toes.*

LUDWIG, JAMES W. Born Nov. 16, 1967 in Subic Bay Naval Base, PI. Graduate U. MI, U. Wash. Debut 1995 OB in *jon & jen.*

LUDWIG, SALEM. Born July 31, 1915 in Brooklyn, NY. Attended Brooklyn Col. Bdwy debut 1946 in *Mirack in thc Mountains,* followed by *Camino Real, Enemy of the People, All You Need Is One Good Break, Inherit the Wind, Disenchanted, Rhinoceros, Three Sisters, Zulu and the Zahda, Moonchildren, American Clock, Month of Sundays,* OB in *Brothers Karamazov, Victim, Troublemaker, Man of Destiny, Night of the Dunce, Corner of the Bed, Awake and Sing, Prodigal Babylon, Burnt Flower Bed, Friends Too Numerous to Mention, After the Fall, What's Wrong with This Picture?, Spinoza.*

LUKER, REBECCA. Born 1961 in Birmingham, AL. Graduate U. Montevello. Bdwy debut in *Phantom of the Opera* followed by *Secret Garden, X* (NYCO), *Show Boat,* OB in *Jubilee, Music in the Air, No No Nanette, Trouble in Tahiti, Gay Divorce.*

LuPONE, PATTI. Born Apr. 21, 1949 in Northport, NY. Graduate Julliard. Debut 1972 OB in *School for Scandal* followed by *Women Beware Women, Next Time I'll Sing to You, Beggars Opera, Scapin, Robber Bridegroom, Edward II, The Woods, Edmond, America Kicks Up Its Heals, Cradle Will Rock,* Bdwy in *Water Engine* (1978), *Working, Evita, Oliver!, Accidental Death of an Anarchist, Anything Goes, Pal Joey* (Encores).

LuPONE, ROBERT. Born July 29, 1956 in Brooklyn, NY. Graduate Julliard. Bdwy debut 1970 in *Minnie's Boys,* followed by *Jesus Christ Superstar, The Rothschilds, Magic Show, A Chorus Line, Saint Joan, Late Night Comic, Zoya's Apartment,* OB in *Charlie Was Here, Twelfth Night, In Connecticut, Snow Orchid, Lemon, Black Angel, The Quilling of Prue, Time Framed, Class 1 Acts, Remembrance, Children of Darkness, Kill, Winter Lies, The Able-Bodied Seamon, Clothes for a Summer Hotel.*

LYNCH, MICHAEL. Born Nov. 14, 1964 in El Paso, TX. Graduate Manhattan School of Music. Bdwy debut 1989 in *Jerome Robbins' Broadway,* followed by *Fiddler on the Roof* (1990), *Starmites, Les Miserables* (1993), OB in *How to Write a Play, Silence Cunning Exile.*

LYNDECK, EDMUND. Born Oct. 4, 1925 in Baton Rouge, LA. Graduate Montclair St. Col., Fordham U. Bdwy debut 1969 in *1776* followed by *Sweeney Todd, Doll's Life, Merlin, Into the Woods, Artist Descending a Staircase,* OB in *King and I* (JB), *Mandragola, Safe Place, Amoureuse, Piaf: A Remembrance, Children of Darkness, Kill, The Interview.*

MA, JASON. Born in Palo Alto, CA. Graduate UCLA. Bdwy debut 1989 in *Chu Chem,* followed by *Prince of Central Park, Shogun, Miss Saigon,* OB in *Wilderness* (1994).

MacDONALD, DAVID ANDREW. Born June 1, 1961 in Washington, DC. Graduate Col. Col., Juilliard. Bdwy debut 1991 in *Two Shakespearean Actors,* OB in *Strike of '92, History of President JFK, Night and Her Stars.*

MACKAY, LIZBETH. Born Mar. 7 in Buffalo, NY. Graduate Adelphi U., Yale. Bdwy debut 1981 in *Crimes of the Heart,* for which she received a Theatre World Award, followed by *Death and the Maiden, Abe Lincoln in Illinois, Heiress,* OB in *Kate's Diary, Tales of the Lost Formicans, Price of Fame, Old Boy, Durang Durang.*

MACKLIN, ALBERT. Born Nov. 18, 1958 in Los Angeles, CA. Graduate Stanford U. Debut 1983 in *Doonesbury,* followed by *The Floating Light Bulb, I Hate Hamlet,* OB in *Ten Little Indians, Poor Little Lambs, Anteroom, Finding Donis Anne, The Library of Congress, Howling in the Night, Fortinbras, The Houseguests, Dog Opera, Jeffrey, Hide Your Love Away.*

MacLEAY, LACHLIN. Born Dec. 4, 1952 in St. Louis, MO. Graduate U. Tex. Debut 1984 OB in *Romantic Arrangements* followed by *The Albino, Moondance, Dead Wrong, The Professional.*

MacPHERSON, LORI. Born July 23 in Albany, NY. Attended Skidmore Col. Bdwy debut 1988 in *The Phantom of the Opera.*

MAIER, CHARLOTTE. Born Jan. 29, 1956 in Chicago, IL. Graduate Northwestern U. Debut 1984 OB in *Balm in Gilead* followed by *Gunplay, Last Girl Singer,* Bdwy in *Abe Lincoln in Illinois* (1993), *Picnic* (1984).

MAILER, STEPHEN. Born Mar. 10, 1966 in New York City. Attended

Middlebury Col., NYU. Debut OB 1989 in *For Dear Life,* followed by *What's Wrong with This Picture?, Peacetime, Innocents Crusade, Awake and Sing,* Bdwy 1993 in *Laughter on the 23rd Floor.*

MALCOLM, GRAEME. Born July 31, 1951 in Dunfermline, Scot. Graduate Central School. Debut 1985 OB in *Scapin* followed by *Pantaleone, Rough Crossing, The Return, Hapgood,* Bdwy in *Benefactors* (1986), *Death and the King's Horsemen.*

MALLON, BRIAN. Born May 12, 1952 in Detroit, MI. Attended U. Mich. Debut 1980 OB in *Guests of the Nation* followed by *Molière in Spite of Himself, Mr. Joyce Is Leaving Paris, Shadow of a Gunman, Derek, Doll House, Rasputin,* Bdwy 1995 in *Translations.*

MANDVIWALA, AASIF. Born May 5, 1966 in Bombay, India. Graduate U.S.Fl. Debut 1994 OB in *Sub Urbia* followed by *Death Defying Acts.*

MANHEIM, CAMRYN. Born Mar. 8, 1961 in Caldwell, NJ. Graduate U.Cal./Santa Cruz, NYU. Debut 1987 OB in *Stella* followed by *Alice in Wonderland, Henry IV Parts I & II, Woyzeck, St. Joan of the Stockyards, Two Gentlemen of Verona, Triumph of Love, Missing Persons.*

MANIS, DAVID. Born Nov. 24, 1959 in Ann Arbor, MI. Graduate U.Wash. Debut 1983 OB in *Pericles,* followed by *Pieces of Eight, A New Way to Pay Old Debts, As You Like It, Skin of Our Teeth, And They Dance Real Slow in Jackson, Rough Crossing Starting Monday, Henry IV Parts I & II,* Bdwy 1993 in *Abe Lincoln in Illinois* followed by *Arcadia.*

MARGOLIS, MARK. Born Nov. 26, 1939 in Malta. Attended Temple U. Bdwy debut 1962 in *Infidel Caesar,* followed by *The World of Sholom Aleichem,* OB in *Second Avenue Rag, My Uncle Sam, The Golem, The Big Knife, Days to Come, The Crimes of Vautrin, Balm in Gilead, Cross Dressing in the Depression, Three Americanisms, Moe's Lucky 7, Madwoman of Chaillot.*

MARIE, JEAN. Born Dec. 14, 1968 in Mountainside, NJ. Attended Fordham U. Bdwy debut 1992 for *Crazy for You.*

MARKELL, JODIE. Born Apr. 13, 1959 in Memphis, TN. Attended Northwestern U. Debut 1984 OB in *Balm in Gilead,* followed by *Carring School Children, UBU, Sleeping Dogs, Machinal, Italian American Reconciliation, Moe's Lucky 7, La Ronde, House of Yes, Saturday Mourning Cartoons.*

MARKS, JACK R. Born Feb. 28, 1935 in Brooklyn, NY. Debut 1975 OB in *Hamlet,* followed by *A Midsummer Night's Dream, Getting Out, Basic Training of Pavlo Hummel, We Bombed in New Haven, Angel Street, Birthday Party, Tarzan and Boy, Goose and Tom Tom, The Carpenters, Appear and Show Cause, Uncle Vanya, Acts of Faith,* Bdwy in *The Queen and the Rebels, Ma Rainey's Black Bottom.*

MARQUETTE, CHRISTOPHER. Born Oct. 3, 1984 in Stuart, FL. Bdwy debut 1994 in *An Inspector Calls.*

MARSDEN, LES. Born Feb. 26, 1957 in Fresno, CA. Graduate Cal.St.U./Fresno. Debut 1986 OB in *Groucho: A Life in Revue* followed by *New Yorkers.*

MARSHALL, DONNA LEE. Born Feb. 27, 1958 in Mt. Holly, NJ. Attended AADA. Debut 1987 OB in *By Strouse* followed by *Human Comedy, Sidewalkin', Charley's Tale,* Bdwy in *Pirates of Penzance, Christmas Carol.*

MARTELLA, DIANE. Born Dec. 10, 1943 in Pueblo, CO. Attended USCO. Debut 1979 OB in *Wine Untouched,* followed by *Time of the Cuckoo, Trial of Vaclav Havel, The Chain, Fayebird, Under Control,* Bdwy 1995 in *Rose Tattoo.*

MARTENS, RICA. Born Jan. 8, 1925 in Eliasville, TX. Graduate N.Tex.U. Bdwy debut 1947 in *Laura* followed by *The Shrike,* OB in *Assent of F6, Bird the Bear and the Actress, Edward My Son, Oedipus and Jocasta, Beckett, My Great Dead Sister, Tied by the Leg, Saved, Ah Wilderness!, Naomi Court, Gods in Summer, Manners, Waiting for the Parade, Rule of Three, The Blindfold, Saturday Mourning Cartoons.*

MARTIN, ANDREA. Born Jan. 15, 1947 in Portland, ME. Graduate Stephens Col., Emerson Col., Sorbonne/Paris. Debut 1980 OB in *Sorrows of Stephen,* followed by *Hardsell, She Loves Me, Merry Wives of Windsor,* Bdwy in *My Favorite Year* (1992) for which she received a Theatre World Award, *Out of This World* (Encores).

MARTIN, GEORGE N. Born Aug. 15, 1929 in New York City. Bdwy debut 1970 in *Wilson in the Promised Land,* followed by *The Hothouse, Plenty, Total Abandon, Pack of Lies, The Mystery of Edwin Drood, The Crucible, A Little Hotel on the Side, Broken Glass, On the Waterfront,* OB in *Painting Churches, Henry V, Springtime for Henry.*

MARTIN, LEILA. Born Aug. 22, 1932 in New York City. Bdwy debut 1944 in *Peepshow,* followed by *Two on the Aisle, Wish You Were Here, Guys and Dolls, Best House in Naples, Henry Sweet Henry, The Wall, Visit to a Small Planet, The Rothschilds, 42nd Street, The Phantom of the Opera,* OB in *Ernest in Love, Beggar's Opera, King of the U.S., Philemon, Jerry's Girls.*

MARVEL, ELIZABETH. Born 1970 in California. Graduate Juilliard. Debut 1995 OB in *Silence Cunning Exile.*

MASON, KAREN. Born Mar. 30 in New Orleans, LA. Attended U.Ill. De-

but 1980 OB in *Matinee Kid* followed by *Bundle of Nerves, Carnival, And the World Goes Round, Don Juan and the Non Don Juan,* Bdwy in *Play Me a Country Song, Torch Song Trilogy, Jerome Robbins' Bdwy, Sunset Blvd.*

MASTRO, MICHAEL (formerly Mastrototaro). Born May 17, 1962 in Albany, NY. Graduate NYU. Debut 1984 OB in *Victoria Station,* followed by *Submarines, Naked Truth/Name Those Names, Darker Purpose, Hot Keys, Crows in the Cornfield, City, Escape from Happiness, Naked Faith, Alone But Not Lonely,* Bdwy 1995 in *Love! Valour! Compassion!*

MATTER, JORDAN. Born Oct. 6, 1966 in New York City. Graduate U.Richmond. Debut 1993 OB in *Boys Next Door* followed by *Heart of a Dog, Loose Ends,* Bdwy in *Glass Menagerie* (1994).

MAYER, JERRY. Born May 12, 1941 in New York City. Debut 1968 OB in *Alice in Wonderland,* followed by *L'Ete, Marouf, Trelawny of the Wells, King of the Schnorrers, Mother Courage, You Know Al, Goose and Tom-Tom, The Rivals, For Sale, Two Gentlemen of Verona, Julius Caesar, A Couple with a Cat, Silence Cunning Exile,* Bdwy in *Much Ado about Nothing* (1972), *Play Memory.*

MAXWELL, JAN. Born Nov. 20, 1956 in Fargo, ND. Graduate Moorhead St.U. Bdwy debut 1990 in *City of Angels,* followed by *Dancing at Lughnasa,* OB in *Everybody Everybody, Hot Feet, Light Years to Chicago, Ladies of the Fortnight, Two Gentlemen of Verona, Marriage Fool, Oedipus Private Eye, Inside Out, The Professional.*

MAYES, SALLY. Born Aug. 3 in Livingston, TX. Attended U.Houston. Bdwy debut 1989 in *Welcome to the Club,* for which she received a Theatre World Award, followed by *She Loves Me,* OB in *Closer Than Ever, Das Barbecu.*

MAZZIE, MARIN. Born Oct. 9, 1960 in Rockford, IL. Graduate W.MI U. Debut 1983 OB in *Where's Charley?, And the World Goes Round,* Bdwy in *Big River* (1986), *Passion.*

McCARTHY, JEFF. Born Oct. 16, 1954 in Los Angeles, CA. Graduate Amer.Consv. Bdwy debut 1982 in *Pirates of Penzance,* followed by *Zorba* (1983), *Beauty and the Beast,* OB in *Gifts of the Maji, On the 20th Century.*

McCARTY, CONAN. Born Sept. 16, 1955 in Lubbock, 1-X. Attended U.S.Cal., AADA/West. Debut 1980 OB in *Star Treatment,* followed by *Beyond Therapy, Henry IV Part 1, Titus Andronicus, Man Who Shot Lincoln, Madwoman of Chaillot,* Bdwy in *Macbeth* (1988), *A Few Good Men.*

McCLANAHAN, MATT. Born July 1 in Kenmore, NY. Graduate SUNY/Purchase. Debut 1988 OB in *Psycho Beach Party,* followed by *Vampire Lesbians of Sodom, A Little Night Music, Balancing Act, Forever Plaid, Hearts and Voices,* Bdwy in *Les Miserables* (1992).

McCLANAHAN, RUE. Born Feb. 21, 1935 in Healdton, OK. Bdwy debut 1965 in *Best Laid Plains* followed by *Jimmy Shine, Father's Day, Sticks and Bone, California Suite,* OB in *Secret Life of Walter Mitty, Big Man, MacBird, Tonight in Living Color, Who's Happy Now?, Dark of the Moon, God Says There Is No Peter Ott, Dylan, Crystal and Fox, After Play.*

McCORMICK, CAROLYN. Born Sept. 19, 1959 in Texas. Graduate Williams Col. Debut 1988 OB in *In Perpetuity Throughout the Universe,* followed by *Lips Together Teeth Apart, Laureen's Whereabouts, Donahue Sisters.*

McCORMICK, MICHAEL. Born July 24, 1951 in Gary, IN. Graduate Northwestern U. Bdwy debut 1964 in *Oliver!,* followed by *Kiss of the Spider Woman,* OB in *Coming Attractions, Tomfoolery, The Regard of Flight, Charlotte's Secret, Half A World Away, In a Pig's Valise, Arturo Ui, Scapin.*

McCOURT, MALACHY. Born Sept. 20, 1931 in New York City. Debut 1958 OB in *Playboy of the Western World,* followed by *Plunkitt of Tammany Hall, Waiting for Godot, Shadow of a Gunman, Hostage, Couple of Blaguards, Da, Remembrance,* Bdwy in *MassAppeal* (1983), *Translations.*

McDERMOTT, SEAN. Born Oct. 23, 1961 in Denver, CO. Attended Loretto Heights. Debut 1986 on Bdwy in *Starlight Express,* followed by *Miss Saigon, Falsettos,* OB in *New Yorkers.*

McGILLIN, HOWARD. Born Nov. 5, 1953 in Los Angeles, CA. Graduate U.Cal./Santa Barbara. Debut 1984 OB in *La Boheme,* followed by Bdwy in *Mystery of Edwin Drood* for which he received a Theatre World Award, *Sunday in the Park with George, Anything Goes, 50 Million Frenchmen in Concert, The Secret Garden, She Loves Me, Kiss of the Spider Woman.*

McGINN, CHRIS. Born Dec. 13, 1955 in St. Louis, MO. Graduate NE Mo. St.U. Debut 1994 in *Butterfingers Angel.*

McGIVER, BORIS. Born Jan. 23, 1962 in Cobleskill, NY. Graduate Ithaca Col., SUNY/Cobleskill, NYU. Debut 1994 OB in *Richard II,* followed by *Hapgood.*

McGRATH, MATT. Born June 11, 1969 in New York City. Attended Fordham U. Bdwy debut 1978 in *Working,* followed by *Streetcar Named Desire,* OB in *Dalton's Back* (1989), *Amulets Against the Dragon Forces, Life During Wartime, The Old Boy, Nothing Sacred, The Dadshuttle, Fat Men in Skirts, A Fair Country.*

McGUIRE, MAEVE. Born in Cleveland, OH. Graduate Sarah Lawrence Col., Cleveland Playhouse. Debut 1968 with LC Rep in *Cyrano de Bergerac,* followed by *Miser, Charades,* OB in *Vera with Kate, Light Up the Sky, Steel Magnolias, Clothes for a Summer Hotel.*

McMARTIN, JOHN. Born in Warsaw, IN. Attended Columbia U. Debut 1959 OB in *Little Mary Sunshine* for which he received a Theatre World Award, followed by *Too Much Johnson, Misanthrope, Sung and Unsung Sondheim, Julius Caesar,* Bdwy in *Conquering Hero* (1961), *Blood Sweat and Stanley Poole, Children from Their Games, Rainy Day in Newark, Sweet Charity, Follies, Great God Brown, Don Juan, The Visit, Chemin de Fer, Love for Love, Rules of the Game, Happy New Year, Solomon's Child, A Little Family Business, Artist Descending the Stairs, Show Boat* (1994).

McMILLAN, LISA. Born May 28, 1955 in Oregon. Juilliard graduate. Debut 1980 OB in *City Junket,* followed by *Identical Twins from Baltimore,* Bdwy in *Moose Murders* (1983).

McNAMARA, DERMOT. Born Aug. 24, 1925 in Dublin, Ire. Bdwy debut 1959 in *A Touch of the Poet,* followed by *Philadelphia Here I Come!, Donnybrook, The Taming of the Shrew,* OB in *The Wise Have Spoken, 3 by Synge, Playboy of the Western World, Shadow and Substance, Happy as Larry, Sharon's Grave, A Whistle in the Dark, Red Roses for Me, The Plough and the Stars, Shadow of a Gunman, No Exit, Stephen D., Hothouse, Home Is the Hero, Sunday Morning Bright and Early, Birthday Party, All the Nice People, Roots, Grandchild of Kings, On the Waterfront, Evangeline and God.*

McNAMARA, ROSEMARY. Born Jan. 7, 1943 in Summit, NJ. Attended Newark Col. OB in *Master Builder,* followed by *Carricknabuana, Rocket to the Moon, The Details, Hooray It's a Glorious Day, Cut the Ribbons, Most Happy Fella, Matchmaker, Anyone Can Whistle, Facade, Marya, Good Year for the Roses, Countess Mitzi, Quilters, Lie of the Mind, Little White Lies,* Bdwy in *Student Gypsy* (1963), *Fig Leaves Are Falling, Dancing at Lughnasa.*

MEARA, ANNE. Born Sept. 20, 1929 in Brooklyn, New York City. Attended HB Studio. OB in *Silver Tassle,* followed by *Dandy Dick, Month in the Country, Spookhouse, After-Play* (which she wrote), Bdwy in *Eastern Standard* (1989—also OB).

MEISNER, VICKI. Born Aug. 2, 1935 in New York City. Graduate Adelphi Col. Debut 1958 OB in *Blood Wedding,* followed by *The Prodigal, Shakuntala, Nathan the Wise, Decathlon, Afternoon in Las Vegas, The Beauty Part, Trelawny of the Wells, Rimers of Eldritch, Mothers and Daughters.*

MELLOR, STEPHEN. Born Oct. 17, 1954 in New Haven, CT. Graduate Boston U. Debut 1980 OB in *Paris Lights,* followed by *Coming Attractions, Plenty, Tooth of the Crime, Shepard Sets, A Country Doctor, Harm's Way, Brightness Falling, Terminal Hip, Dead Mother, A Murder of Crows, Seven Blowjobs, Pericles, The Illusion, The Hyacinth Macaw, Careless Love, Teibele and Her Demon, Terminal Hip, Strange Feet, Dream Express,* Bdwy in *Big River* (1985).

MENDILLO, STEPHEN. Born Oct. 9, 1942 in New Haven, CT. Graduate Colo.Col., Yale U. Debut 1973 OB in *Nourish the Beast,* followed by *Gorky, Time Steps, The Marriage, Loot, Subject to Fits, Wedding Band, As You Like It, Fool for Love, Twelfth Night, Grotesque Lovesongs, Nowhere, Portrait of My Bikini, The Country Girl, The Last Yankee,* Bdwy in *National Health* (1974), *Ah! Wilderness, View from the Bridge, Wild Honey, Orpheus Descending, Guys and Dolls.*

MENNIER, LOUISE-MARIE. Born May 1 in St. John, New Brunswick, Can. Attended McGill U., Banff Ctr.for Arts. Bdwy debut in *Show Boat* (1994).

MERRITT, GEORGE. Born July 10, 1942 in Raleigh, NC. Graduate Catholic U. Bdwy debut in *Porgy and Bess* (1976), followed by *Ain't Misbehavin'* (1983), *Big River,* OB in *Step into My World, Midsummer Night's Dream, Petrified Prince.*

METCALF, ALLISON. Born Mar. 3, 1970 in Houston, TX. Graduate Carnegie-Mellon U. Bdwy debut 1994 in *Grease.*

METCALF, LAURIE. Born June 16, 1955 in Edwardsville, IL. Graduate Ill. St.U. Debut 1984 OB in *Balm in Gilead* for which she received a Theatre World Award, followed by *Bodies Rest and Motion, Educating Rita,* Bdwy in *My Thing of Love* (1995).

METTNER, JERRY. Born Aug. 21, 1958 in Detroit, MI. Bdwy debut 1982 in *Present Laughter,* OB in *Confessional* (1983), *Look Back in Anger, Jerusalem Mountain, 3 by Wilder, Somewhere I Have Never Traveled, The Eye of the Beholder, Cinoman and Rebeck, Live Witness, Edward II.*

METZO, WILLIAM. Born June 21, 1937 in Wilkes-Barre, PA. Graduate King's Col. Debut 1963 OB in *Bald Soprano,* followed by *Papers, Moon for the Misbegotten, Arsenic and Old Lace, Super Spy, Cradle Song, Bachelor's Wife, New Yorkers,* Bdwy in *Cyrano* (1973), *Arsenic and Old Lace, Cafe Crown.*

MEYERS, T.J. Born July 18, 1953 in Pittsburgh, PA. Graduate Phoenix

Col., Mesa Col. Bdwy debut 1984 in *Sunday in the Park with George,* followed by *Big River, Prince of Central Park, Metamorphosis, Passion,* OB in *Richard II* (1994), *Luck Pluck and Virtue.*

MICHAELS, KIMBERLEY. Born Dec. 30, 1961 in Rochester, NY. Graduate SUNY/Fredonia, SUNY/Brockport. Bdwy debut in *Show Boat* (1994).

MILLENBACH, GEORGE. Born Aug. 24, 1953 in Toronto, Can. Graduate U. Toronto. Debut 1982 OB in *Cinderella,* followed by *As You Like It, A Cricket on the Hearth, Ceremony in Bohemia, Lion in Winter, Little Lies, What the Butler Saw, The Rehearsal.*

MILLER, ALICIA. Born Nov. 17, 1963 in New York City. Graduate George Wash.U. Debut 1987 OB in *Wish You Were Here,* followed by *Budd, That Time of Year.*

MILLER, JONATHAN. Born Nov. 22, 1954 in Allison Park, PA. Graduate Duke U., Ohio U. Bdwy debut in *Amadeus* (1983), OB in *Comedy of Errors, Measure for Measure, Titus Andronicus.*

MILLER, JOSH. Born Dec. 1, 1973 in West Palm Beach, FL. Attended AMDA. Debut 1994 OB in *Fantasticks.*

MILLER, MARJORIE ANN. Born July 6, 1959 in Margaretville, NY. Graduate Syracuse U. Debut 1988 OB in *Peg O' My Heart,* followed by *Midsummer Night's Dream.*

MILLER, PENELOPE ANN. Born Jan. 13, 1964 in Santa Monica, CA. Attended Menlo Col. Bdwy debut in *Biloxi Blues* (1985), followed by *Our Town, On the Waterfront,* OB in *Moonchildren.*

MINOT, ANNA. Born in Boston, MA. Attended Vassar Col. Bdwy debut 1942 in *The Strings My Lord Are False,* followed by *The Russian People, The Visitor, The Iceman Cometh, An Enemy of the People, Love of Four Colonels, The Trip to Bountiful, Tunnel of Love, Ivanov,* OB in *Sands of the Niger, Gettin Out, Vieux Carre, State of the Union, Her Great Match, Rivals, Hedda Gabler, All's Well That Ends Well, Tarfuffe, The Good Natur'd Man, Little Eyolf, Beaux Stratagem.*

MIRREN, HELEN. Born 1945 in London. After distinguished career in England and US tv & film, Bdwy debut in *Month in the Country* (1995) for which she received a Theatre World Award.

MISTRETTA, SAL. Born Jan. 9, 1945 in Brooklyn, New York City. Graduate Ithaca Col. Bdwy debut in *Something's Afoot* (1976), followed by *On the 20th Century, Evita, King and I, Sunset Blvd.,* OB in *Charley's Tale, Education of Hyman Kaplan.*

MITCHELL, BRIAN. Born Oct. 31, 1957 in Seattle, WA. Bdwy debut 1988 in *Mail* for which he received a Theatre World Award, followed by *Oh Kay!, Jelly's Last Jam, Kiss of the Spider Woman.*

MITCHELL, GREGORY. Born Dec. 9, 1951 in Brooklyn, NY. Graduate Juilliard, Principle with Eliot Feld Ballet before Bdwy debut 1983 in *Merlin,* followed by *Song and Dance, Phantom of the Opera, Dangerous Games, Aspects of Love, Man of La Mancha* (1992), *Kiss of the Spider Woman, Chronicle of a Death Foretold,* OB in *Kicks* (1961), *One More Song One More Dance, Young Strangers, Tango Apasionado.*

MITCHELL, JOHN CAMERON. Born Apr. 21, 1963 in El Paso, TX. Attended Northwestern U. Bdwy debut 1985 in *Big River,* followed by *Six Degrees of Separation* (also OB), *Secret Garden,* OB in *Destiny of Me, No to Nine, It's Our Town Too, Hello Again, Little Monsters, Missing Persons, Hedwig and the Angry Inch.*

MOFFAT, DONALD. Born Dec. 26, 1930 in Plymouth, England. Attended RADA. Bdwy debut 1957 in *Under Milkwood,* followed by *Much Ado about Nothing, The Tumbler, Duel of Angels, Passage to India, The Affair, Father's Day, Play Memory, The Wild Duck, Right You Are, You Can't Take It with You, War and Peace, The Cherry Orchard, CockaDoodle Dandy, Hamlet, Iceman Cometh, The Heiress,* OB in *The Bald Soprano, Jack, The Caretaker, Misalliance, Painting Churches, Henry IV Part 1, Titus Andronicus, As You Like It.*

MOGENTALE, DAVID. Born Dec. 28, 1959 in Pittsburgh, PA. Graduate Auburn U. Debut 1987 OB in *Signal Season of Dummy Hoy,* followed by *Holy Note, Killers, Battery, Necktie Breakfast, Under Control, 1 Act Festival, Charmer, Killer Joe.*

MOHAT, BRUCE. Born Oct. 25, 1948 in Galion, OH. Graduate Miami U. Debut 1984 OB in *Flesh Flash and Frank Harris,* followed by *Good Woman of Setzuan, Portrait of a Woman.*

MONK, DEBRA. Born Feb. 27, 1949 in Middletown, OH. Graduate Frostburg State Col., SMU. Bdwy debut 1982 in *Pump Boys and Dinettes,* followed by *Prelude to a Kiss, Redwood Curtain, Picnic,* OB in *Young Playwrights Festival, A Narrow Bed, Oil City Symphony, Assassins, Man in His Underwear, Innocents Crusade, Three Hotels, Death Defying Acts.*

MONSON, LEX. Born Mar. 11, 1926 in Grindstone, PA. Attended DePaul U., U.Detroit. Debut 1961 OB in *The Blacks,* followed by *Pericles, Macbeth, See How They Run, Telemachus Clay, Keyboard, Oh My Mother Passed Away, Confession Stone, Linty Lucy, Burnscape, God's Trombones,*

Gift Horse, Bdwy in *Moby Dick, Trumpets of the Lord, Watch on the Rhine, Grapes of Wrath.*

MOORE, CRISTA. Born Sept. 17 in Washington, DC. Attended Am. Ballet Th.Schl. Debut 1987 OB in *Birds of Paradise*, followed by *Rags, Marathon '93, Long Ago and Far Away*, Bdwy in *Gypsy* (1989) for which she received a Theatre World Award, *110 in the Shade* (LC/NYCO), *Cinderella* (LC/NYCO), *Crazy For You, Wonderful Town* (NYCO).

MOORE, DANA. Born in Sewickley, PA. Bdwy debut 1982 in *Sugar Babies*, followed by *Dancin', Copperfield, On Your Toes, Singin' in the Rain, Sweet Charity, Dangerous Games, A Chorus Line, Will Rogers Follies, Pal Joey* (Encores), *Petrified Prince.*

MOORE, JUDITH. Born Feb. 12, 1944 in Princeton, WV. Graduate Ind.U. Debut 1971 OB in *The Drunkard*, followed by *Ten by Six, Boys from Syracuse, The Evangelist, Miracle of the Month, Midsummer Nights, Petrified Prince*, Bdwy in *Sunday im the Park with George* (1984—also OB), *Into the Woods.*

MOORE, KIM. Born Jan. 11, 1956 in Weaton, MN. Graduate Moorhead St.U. LAMDA. Debut 1985 OB in *Fantasticks*, followed by *Frankie, A Doll's House.*

MORALES, MARK. Born Nov. 9, 1954 in New York City. Attended Trenton St.U, SUNY/Purchase. Debut 1978 OB in *Coolest Cat in Town*, followed by *Transposed Heads*, Bdwy in *West Side Story* (1980), *Cats, Sunset Blvd.*

MORAN, DAN. Born July 31, 1953 in Corcoran, CA. Graduate NYU. Debut 1977 OB in *Homebodies*, followed by *True West, Pericles, The Merchant of Venice, The Vampires, Sincerely Forever, The Illusion, Class 1-Acts*, Bdwy in *Month in the Country* (1995).

MORAN, MARTIN. Born Dec. 29, 1959 in Denver, CO. Attended Stanford U., Am.Cons.Theatre. Debut 1983 OB in *Spring Awakening*, followed by *Once on a Summer's Day, 1-2~3~4~5, Jacques Brel Is Alive* (1992), Bdwy in *Oliver!* (1984), *Big River, How to Succeed...* (1995).

MORATH, KATHRYN/KATHY. Born Mar. 23, 1955 in Colorado Springs, CO. Graduate Brown U. Debut 1980 OB in *The Fantasticks*, followed by *Dulcy, Snapshot, Alice in Concert, A Little Night Music, The Little Prince, Professionally Speaking, The Apple Tree, Prom Queens Unchained, All in the Timing*, Bdwy in *Pirates of Penzance* (1982), *Nick & Nora.*

MORFOGEN, GEORGE. Born Mar. 30, 1933 in New York City. Graduate Brown U., Yale. Debut 1957 OB in *The Trial of D. Karamazov*, followed by *Christmas Oratorio, Othello, Good Soldier Schweik, Cave Dwellers, Once in a Lifetime, Total Eclipse, Ice Age, Prince of Homburg, Biography: A Game, Mrs. Warren's Profession, Principia Scriptoriae, Tamara, Maggie and Misha, The Country Girl, Othello, As You Like It* (CP), *Uncle Bob*, Bdwy in *The Fun Couple* (1962), *Kingdoms, Arms and the Man, An Inspector Calls.*

MORGAN, CASS. Born Apr. 15 in Rochester, NY. Attended Adelphi U. Debut 1984 OB in *La Boheme*, followed by *Another Paradise, The Knife, Catfish Loves Anna, Feast Here Tonight, Can Can, Merrily We Roll Along, Inside Out*, Bdwy in *Hair* (1969), *Pump Boys and Dinettes, Human Comedy, Beauty and the Beast.*

MORSE, ROBIN. Born July 8, 1963 in New York City. Bdwy debut 1981 in *Bring Back Birdie*, followed by *Brighton Beach Memoirs, Six Degrees of Separation*, OB in *Greenfields, Dec. 7th, Class 1 Acts, Eleemosynary, One Act Festival, Patient X, Uncommon Women and Others.*

MOSCOW, DAVID. Born 1975 in Bronx, NY. Attended Hampshire Col. Bdwy debut 1994 in *What's Wrong with This Picture?*, OB in *Bloodlines, The Tree, Steeel Town, On Ice.*

MOSES, BURKE. Born in New York City. Graduate Carnegie-Mellon U. Debut 1986 OB in *Wasted*, followed by *Way of the World*, Bdwy in *Most Happy Fella* (NYCO), *Guys and Dolls* (1993), *Beauty and the Beast* for which he received a 1994 Theatre World Award.

MUENZ, RICHARD. Born in 1948 in Hartford, CT. Attended Eastern Baptist Col. Bdwy debut 1976 in *1600 Pennsylvania Avenue*, followed by *The Most Happy Fella, Camelot, Rosalie in Concert, Chess, The Pajama Game, Nick and Nora, 110 in the Shade* (LC), *Wonderful Town* (LC).

MULLALLY, MEGAN. Born Nov. 12, 1958 in Los Angeles, CA. Attended Northwestern U. Bdwy debut in *Grease* (1994), followed by *How to Succeed...* (1995).

MURPHY, DONNA. Born Mar. 7, 1959 in Corona, NY. Attended NYU. Bdwy debut 1979 in *They're Playing Our Song*, followed by *Human Comedy* (also OB), *Mystery of Edwin Drood, Passion*, OB in *Francis, Portable Pioneer and Prairie Show, Little Shop of Horrors, A...My Name is Alice, Showing Off, Privates on Parade, Song of Singapore, Hey Love, Hello Again, Twelve Dreams.*

MURPHY, ROSEMARY. Born Jan. 13, 1927 in Munich, Ger. Attended Neighborhood Playhouse, Actors Studio. Bdwy debut in *Tower Beyond Tragedy* (1950), followed by *Look Homeward Angel, Death of Bessie Smith, Butterflies Are Free, Ladies at the Alamo, Cheaters, John Gabriel*

Borkman, Coastal Disturbances (also OB), *Devil's Disciple*, OB in *Are You Now or Have You Ever Been?, Learned Ladies, Uncommon Women and Others, The Arbor, Cold Sweat, Night of the Iguana.*

MURRAY, BRIAN. Born Oct. 9, 1939 in Johannesburg, SA. Debut 1964 OB in *The Knack*, followed by *King Lear, Ashes, The Jail Diary of Albie Sachs, A Winter's Tale, Barbarians, The Purging, A Midsummer Night's Dream, The Recruiting Officer, The Arcata Promise, Candide in Concert, Much Ado About Nothing, Hamlet, Merry Wives of Windsor, Travels with My Aunt*, Bdwy in *All in Good Time* (1965), *Rosencrantz and Guildenstern Are Dead, Sleuth, Da, Noises Off, A Small Family Business, Black Comedy.*

MURTAUGH, JAMES. Born Oct. 28, 1942 in Chicago, IL. Debut OB in *The Firebugs*, followed by *Highest Standard of Living, Marathon '87, Other People's Money, Marathon '88, I Am a Man, Wreck on the 5:25*, Bdwy in *Two Shakespearean Actors* (1991).

NAGY, KEN. Born Dec. 7, 1963 in Bucks County, PA. Bdwy debut 1992 in *The Most Happy Fella*, followed by *Sally Marr and Her Escorts, Gentlemen Prefer Blondes* (1995).

NAKAHARA, RON. Born July 20, 1947 in Honolulu, HI. Attended U.HI, U.Tenn. Debut 1981 OB in *Danton's Death*, followed by *Flowers and Household Gods, Rohwer, A Midsummer Night's Dream, Teahouse, Song for Nisei Fishermen, Eat a Bowl of Tea, Once Is Never Enough, Noiresque, Play Ball, Three Sisters, And the Soul Shall Dance. Earth and Sky, Cambodia Agonistes, A Doll House, School for Wives*, Bdwy in *A Few Good Men* (1989).

NAKAMURA, MIDORI. Born in Missoula, MT. Graduate Yale U. U.Chicago. Debut 1991 OB in *Piece of My Heart*, followed by *King Lear, Madame de Sade, Prometheus Bound, Kokoro.*

NAUFFTS, GEOFFREY. Born in Arlington, MA. Graduate NYU. Debut 1987 OB in *Moonchildren*, followed by *Stories from Home, Another Time Anothet Place, The Alarm, Jerusalem Oratorio, The Survivor, Spring Awakening, Summer Winds, Saturday Mourning Cartoons*, Bdwy in *A Few Good Men* (1989).

NAUGHTON, AMANDA. Born Nov. 23, 1965 in New York City. Attended HB Studio. Debut 1982 OB in *Life with Father*, followed by *Wonderful Town, Romance in Hard Times, Three Postcards, Hundreds of Hats.*

NELSON, MARI. Born July 27, 1963 in Tacoma, WA. Graduate U. Wash., Juilliard. Debut 1989 OB in *Up Against It*, followed by *Twelfth Night, Slain in the Spirit*, Bdwy in *Six Degrees of Separation* (1990), *Translations.*

NEUBERGER, JAN. Born Jan. 21 1953 in Amityville, NY. Attended NYU. Bdwy debut 1975 in *Gypsy*, followed by *A Change in the Heir*, OB in *Silk Stockings, Chase a Rainbow, Anything Goes, A Little Madness, Forbidden Broadway, After These Messages, Ad Hock, Rags, Christina Alberta's Father, All in the Timing.*

NEVARD, ANGELA. Born Mar. 19, 1963 in Montreal, Can. Graduate Skidmore Col. Debut 1988 OB in *Faith Hope and Charity*, followed by *3 by Wilder, Macbeth, The Balcony, Harm's Way, Judgment Day, Tartuffe, Morning Song, Who Will Carry the Word, Sea Plays, Twelfth Night, Camino Real, As You Like It, Goose and TomTom*, Bdwy in *Wilder Wilder Wilder* (1993).

NEWTON, JOHN. Born Nov. 2, 1925 in Grand Junction, CO. Graduate U.Wash. Debut 1951 OB in *Othello*, followed by *As You Like It, Candida, Candaules Commissioner, Sextet, LC Rep's, The Crucible, A Streetcar Named Desire, The Rivals, The Subject was Roses, The Brass Ring, Hadrian VII, The Best Little Whorehouse in Texas, A Midsummer Night's Dream, Night Games, A Frog in His Throat, Max and Maxie, The Lark, Measure for Measure, Down by the Ocean*, Bdwy in *Weekend, First Monday in October, Present Laughter, Hamlet* (1992), *Abe Lincoln in Illinois.*

NICHOLAW, CASEY. Born Oct. 6, 1992. Attended UCLA. Debut 1986 OB in *Pajama Game*, followed by *Petrified Prince*, Bdwy in *Crazy for You* (1992), *Best Little Whorehouse Goes Public.*

NIXON, CYNTHIA. Born Apr. 9, 1966 in New York City. Debut 1980 in *The Philadelphia Story* (LC) for which she received a Theatre World Award, followed by *The Real Thing, Hurlyburly, Heidi Chronicles, Angels in America, Indiscretions*, OB in *Lydie Breeze, Hurlyburly, Sally's Gone She Left Her Name, Lemon Sky, Cleveland and Half-Way Back, Alterations, Young Playwrights, Moonchildren, Romeo and Juliet, The Cherry Orchard, The Balcony Scene, Servy-n-Bernice 4Ever, On the Bum, The Illusion, Scarlet Letter.*

NOLTE, BILL. Born June 4, 1953 in Toledo, OH. Graduate Cin.Consv. Debut OB in *Wonderful Town* (1977), Bdwy in *Cats* (1985), *Me and My Girl, The Secret Garden, Joseph and the Amazing Technicolor Dreamcoat* (1993), *Christmas Carol.*

NOONAN, JIMMY. Born Jan. 31, 1958 in Massapequa Park, NY. Bdwy debut in *Inspector Calls* (1994).

O'CONNELL, PATRICIA. Born May 17 in New York City. Attended Am.Th.Wing. Debut 1958 OB in *Saintliness of Margery Kemp*, followed by *Time Limit, An Evening's Frost, Mrs. Snow, Electric Ice, Survival of St. Joan, Rain, Rapists, Who Killed Richard Corey?, Misalliance, Singular*

Life of Albert Nobbs, Come Back Little Sheba, Starting Monday, Uncommon Women and Others, Bdwy in *Criss-Crossing* (1970), *Summer Brave, Break a Leg, Man Who Came to Dinner, The Miser.*

ODO, CHRIS. Born Feb. 7, 1954 in Kansas City, MO. Attended Southwest Mo. State U. Debut 1984 OB in *Midsummer Night's Dream,* followed by *Oedipus, Sleepless City, Summer Face Woman, White Cotton Sheets, Chikamatsu's Forest,* Bdwy in *M. Butterfly* (1988).

O'GORMAN, HUGH. Born June 11, 1965 in New York City. Graduate Cornell U., U. Wash. Debut 1991 OB in *The Tempest,* followed by *Cloud 9, Taming of the Shrew, Time of Your Life,* Bdwy in *Translations.*

O'HARA, PAIGE. Born May 10, 1956 in Ft. Lauderdale, FL. Debut 1975 OB in *Gift of the Magi,* followed by *Company, Great Backstage American Musical, Oh Boy!, Rabonni, Sitting Pretty, Cat and the Fiddle,* Bdwy in *Show Boat* (1983), *Mystery of Edwin Drood, Les Miserables.*

OLIVER, ROCHELLE. Born Apr. 15, 1937 in New York City. Attended Brooklyn Col. Bdwy debut 1960 in *Toys in the Attic,* followed by *Harold, Who's Afraid of Virginia Woolf?, Happily Never After,* OB in *Brothers Karamazov, Jack Knife, Vincent, Stop You're Killing Me, Enclave, Bits and Pieces, Roads to Home, A Flower Palace, Fayebird, After-Play.*

O'MALLEY, KERRY. Born Sept. 5, 1969, in Nashua, NH. Graduate, Duke U., Harvard U. Bdwy debut 1993 in *Cyrano,* followed by *Translations.*

O'MARA, MOLLIE. Born Sept. 5, 1960 in Pittsburgh, PA. Attended Catholic U. Debut 1989 OB in *Rodents and Radios,* followed by *Crowbar, Famine Plays, Homo Sapien Shuffle, Vast Wreck, Gut Girls, Apocrypha, Budd.*

O'NEILL, MICHELLE. Born Apr. 26 in Bend, OR. Graduate U. Utah, Juilliard. Bdwy debut 1993 in *Abe Lincoln in Illinois,* followed by *Heiress.*

OPPENHEIMER, ALAN. Born Apr. 23, 1930 in New York City. Graduate Carnegie-Mellon U., Neighborhood Playhouse. Bdwy debut in *Sunset Blvd.* (1994).

ORBACH, RON. Born Mar. 23, 1952 in Newark, NJ. Graduate Rider Col. Debut 1985 OB in *Lies and Legends,* followed by *Philistines, Skin of Our Teeth, Mrs. Dally Has a Lover,* Bdwy in *Laughter on the 23rd Floor* (1993), *Pal Joey* (Encores).

O'ROURKE, KEVIN. Born Jan. 25, 1956 in Portland, OR. Graduate Williams Col. Debut 1981 OB in *Declassee,* followed by *Sister Mary Ignatius…, Submariners, A Midsummer Night's Dream, Visions of Kerouac, Self Defense, Spring Thing, Joined at the Head, Laureen's Whereabouts, Breaking Up, Radical Mystique,* Bdwy in *Alone Together* (1984), *Cat on a Hot Tin Roof, Spoils of War.*

O'SHEA, MILO. Born June 2, 1926 in Dublin, Ire. Bdwy debut 1968 in *Staircase,* followed by *Dear World, Mrs. Warren's Profession, Comedians, Touch of the Poet, Mass Appeal* (also OB), *Corpse, Meet Me in St. Louis, Philadelphia Here I Come* (1994), OB in *Waiting for Godot, Return of Herbert Bracewell, Educating Rita, Alive Alive Oh!, Remembrance.*

OSIAN, MATTE. Born June 21, 1960 in Boston, MA. Graduate Colgate U., Brandeis U., Debut 1989 OB in *Cheri,* followed by *Silence Cunning Exile.*

O'SULLIVAN, BRIAN. Born Dec. 11, 1958 in Jackson, MI. Graduate Mi. St. U. Debut 1987 OB in *Mud,* followed by *All's Well That Ends Well, Tempest, Elephant Man, Oh What a Lovely War!.*

OWENS, GEOFFREY. Born Mar. 18, 1961 in Brooklyn, NY. Graduate Yale U. Debut 1985 OB in *Man Who Killed the Buddah,* followed by *Midsummer Night's Dream, Richard II, Luck Pluck and Virtue, Macbeth, As You Like It, Othello.*

PAGE, KEN. Born Jan. 20, 1954 in St. Louis, MO. Attended Fontbonne Col. Bdwy debut in *Guys and Dolls* (1976) for which he received a Theatre World Award, followed by *Ain't Misbehavin'* (1978/1988), *Cats, Out of This World* (Encores), OB in *Louis, Can't Help Singing.*

PARKER, SARAH JESSICA. Born Mar. 25, 1965 in Nelsonville, OH. Bdwy debut 1978 in *Annie,* OB in *The Innocents, One-Act Festival, To Gillian on Her 37th Birthday, Broadway Scandals of 1928, Heidi Chronicles, Substance of Fire, Sylvia.*

PARLATO, DENNIS. Born Mar. 30, 1947 in Los Angeles, CA. Graduate Loyola U. Bdwy debut 1979 in *Chorus Line,* followed by *The First, Chess,* OB in *Becket, Elizabeth and Essex, The Fantasticks, Moby Dick, The Knife, Shylock, Have I Got a Girl for You, Romance! Romance!, The Earl, Violent Peace, Traveler in the Dark, Hello Again, Jack's Holiday, Down by the Ocean.*

PARRIS, STEVE. Born Nov. 25 in Athens, Greece. Graduate CCNY. Debut 1964 OB in *The Comforter,* followed by *Consider the Lillies, Christmas Carol, Man with the Flower in His Mouth, King David and His Wives, 3 by Pirandello, Nymph Errant, Tamer Tamed, The Blindfold.*

PARSONS, ESTELLE. Born Nov. 20, 1927 in Lynn, MA. Attended Boston U., Actors Studio. Bdwy debut 1956 in *Happy Hunting,* followed by *Whoop Up, Beg Borrow or Steal, Mother Courage, Ready When You Are C.B., Malcolm, Seven Descents of Myrtle, And Miss Reardon Drinks a Lit-*

tle, Norman Conquests, Ladies at the Alamo, Miss Marguerida's Way, Pirates of Penzance, Shadow Box (1994), OB in *DemiDozen, Pieces of Eight, The Threepenny Opera, Automobile Graveyard, Mrs. Dally Has a Lover* (1963) for which she received a Theatre World Award, *Next Time I'll Sing to You, Come to the Palace of Sin, In the Summer House, Monopoly, The East Wind, Galileo, Peer Gynt, Mahagonny, People Are Living There, Barbary Shore, Oh Glorious Tintinnabulation, Mert and Paul, Elizabeth and Essex, Dialogue for Lovers, New Moon* (in concert), *Orgasmo Adulto Escapes from the Zoo, Unguided Missile, Baba Goya, Extended Forecast, Deja Revue.*

PASSELTINER, BERNIE. Born Nov. 21, 1931 in New York City. Graduate Catholic U. OB in *Square in the Eye, Sourball, As Virtuously Given, Now Is the Time for All Good Men, Rain, Kaddish, Against the Sun, End of Summer, Yentl the Yeshiva Boy, Heartbreak House, Every Place Is Newark, Isn't It Romantic?, Buck, Pigeons on the Walk, Waving Goodbye, Sunshine Boys, Free Zone, God of Vengeance, Miami Stories,* Bdwy in *The Office, The Jar, Yentl.*

PATELLA, DENNIS. Born July 24, 1945 in Youngstown, OH. Graduate Wayne St. U. Debut 1974 OB in *Cherry Orchard* followed *Original Cast, Three Sisters, The Tiger, Warning Signals, Lovliest Afternoon of the Year, La Ronde, Androcles and the Lion, Madwoman of Chaillot,* Bdwy in *Romeo and Juliet.*

PATTERSON, JOSEPH. Born June 22, 1964 in London, Eng. Attended LAMDA. Bdwy debut in *Hamlet* (1995).

PATTON, LUCILLE. Born in New York City. Attended Neighborhood Playhouse. Bdwy debut 1946 in *Winter's Tale,* followed by *Topaz, Arms and the Man, Joy to the World, All You Need is One Good Break, Fifth Season, Heavenly Twins, Rhinoceros, Marathon '33, The Last Analysis, Dinner at 8, La Strada, Unlikely Heroes, Love Suicide at Schofield Barracks, The Crucible, A Little Hotel on the Side,* OB in *Ulysses in Nighttown, Failures, Three Sisters, Yes Yes No No, Tango, Mme. de Sade, Apple Pie, Follies, Yesterday is Over, My Prince My King, I Am Who I Am, Double Game, Love in a Village, 1984, A Little Night Music, Cheri, Till the Eagle Hollers, Money Talks, EST Marathon '92, German Games, Three Tall Women.*

PAWK, MICHELE. Born Nov. 16, 1961 in Pittsburgh, PA. Graduate Cin. Consv. Bdwy debut 1988 in *Mail,* followed by *Crazy for You,* OB in *Hello Again, Decline of the Middle West, john & jen.*

PEARLMAN, STEPHEN. Born Feb. 26, 1935 in New York City. Graduate Dartmouth Col. Bdwy debut 1964 in *Barefoot in the Park,* followed by *La Strada, Six Degrees of Separation* (also OB), *Any Given Day,* OB in *Threepenny Opera, Time of the Key, Pimpernel, In White America, Viet Rock, Chocolates, Bloomers, Richie, Isn't It Romantic, Bloodletters, Light Up the Sky, Perfect Party, Come Blow Your Horn, A Shayna Madel, Value of Names, Hyde in Hollywood, Wrong Turn at Lunfish, You Should Be So Lucky.*

PENNINGTON, GAIL. Born Oct. 2, 1957 in Kansas City, MO. Graduate SMU. Bdwy debut 1980 in *The Music Man,* followed by *Can-Can, America, Little Me* (1982), *42nd Street, Most Happy Fella, Christmas Carol,* OB in *The Baker's Wife.*

PEPE, NEIL. Born June 23, 1963 in Bloomington, IN. Graduate Kenyon Col. Debut 1988 OB in *Boys' Life,* followed by *Three Sisters, Virgin Molly, Return to Sender, Five Very Live, Down the Shore, The Lights, Trafficking in Broken Hearts.*

PEREZ, LAZARO. Born Dec. 12, 1945 in Havana, Cuba. Bdwy debut 1969 in *Does A Tiger Wear a Necktie?,* followed by *Animals, Streetcar Named Desire* (1992), *Chronicle of a Death Foretold,* OB in *Romeo and Juliet, 12 Angry Men, Wonderful Years, Alive, G.R. Point, Primary English Class, Man and the Fly, Last Latin Lover, Cabal of Hypocrites, Balm in Gilead, Enrico IV.*

PEREZ, LUIS. Born July 28, 1959 in Atlanta, GA. With Joffrey Ballet before 1986 Bdwy debut in *Brigadoon* (LC), followed by *Phantom of the Opera, Jerome Robbins' Broadway, Dangerous Games, Grand Hotel, Man of La Mancha* (1992), *Ain't Broadway Grand, Chronicle of a Death Foretold,* OB in *Wonderful Ice Cream Suit, Tango Apasionada.*

PERKINS, PATTI. Born July 9 in New Haven, CT. Attended AMDA. Debut 1972 OB in *The Contrast,* followed by *Fashion, Tuscaloosa's Calling Me, Patch, Shakespeare's Cabaret, Maybe I'm Doing It Wrong, Fabulous LaFontaine, Hannah 1939, Free Zone, New Yorkers,* Bdwy in *All Over Town* (1974), *Shakespeare's Cabaret.*

PERRY, ELIZABETH. Born Oct. 18, 1937 in Pawtucket, RI. Attended RI State U., Am. Th. Wing. Bdwy debut 1956 in *Inherit the Wind,* followed by *The Women,* with AP in *The Misanthrope, Hamlet, King Dies, Macbeth, and Chronicles of Hell, Deepest Laughter, 84 Charing Cross Road, Coastal Disturbances, Musical Comedy Murders,* OB in *Royal Gambit, Here Be Dragons, Lady from the Sea, Heartbreak House, him, All the Way Home, The Frequency, Fefu and Her Friends, Out of the Broom Closet, Ruby Ruby Sam Sam, Did You See the Elephant?, Last Stop Blue Jay Lane, Difficult*

| Page Johnson | Alix Korey | Jay Aubrey Jones | Dorothy Loudon | Marc Kudisch | Patti LuPone |

| Nathan Lane | Karen Mason | Jordan Leeds | Rosemary McNamara | Robert Sean Leonard | Anne Meara |

| Albert Macklin | Donna Murphy | Assif Mandviwala | Midori Nakamura | Matt McClanahan | Kerry O'Malley |

| Matt McGrath | Sarah Jessica Parker | Josh Miller | Michele Pawk | Mark Morales | Adina Porter |

| Martin Moran | Faith Prince | David Moscow | Patricia Randell | Geoffrey Nauffts | Leslie Rohland |

220

Borning, Bresque Isle, Isn't It Romantic?, The Chairs, Joined at the Head, Modest Proposal.

PERRY, LYNETTE. Born Sept. 29, 1963 in Bowling Green, OH. Graduate Cin.Consv. Debut 1987 OB in *The Chosen*, followed by *Lucy's Lapses, New York Rock, Oedipus Private Eye*, Bdwy in *Grand Hotel* (1989).

PETERS, MARK. Born Nov. 20, 1952 in Council Bluffs, IA. Yale graduate. Debut 1977 OB in *Crazy Locomotive*, followed by *Legend of Sleepy Hollow, Kismet, Awakening of Spring, Appelemando's Dreams, Most Men Are.*

PETLOCK, RAFAEL. Born Sept. 23, 1974 in Sarasota, FL. Debut 1994 OB in *Andrew My Dearest One.*

PEVSNER, DAVID. Born Dec. 31, 1958 in Skokie, IL. Graduate Carnegie-Mellon U. Debut 1985 OB in *A Flash of Lightning*, followed by *Rags, Rag on a Stick and a Star*, Bdwy in *Fiddler on the Roof* (1990).

PHILLIPS, AMY JO. Born Nov. 15, 1958 in Brooklyn, NY. Graduate Ithaca Col. Debut OB in *Little Shop of Horrors* (1986), followed by *Burnscape, Pretty Faces*, Bdwy in *Show Boat* (1994).

PHILLIPS, SIAN. Born May 14, 1934 in Carmarthenshire, Wales. Graduate U. Wales, RADA. Bdwy debut in *An Inspector Calls* (1995).

PHOENIX, REGGIE. Born Sept. 11, 1960 in New York City. Attended Brooklyn Col. Debut 1980 OB in *Lion and the Jewel*, followed by *Home Seekers, Angel Levine*, Bdwy in *Chorus Line* (1983).

PIERCE, LINDA. Born Oct. 18, 1946 in Sevierville, TN. Graduate UNC. Debut 1995 OB in *Night and Her Stars.*

PINE, LARRY. Born Mar. 3, 1945 in Tucson, AZ. Graduate NYU. Debut 1967 OB in *Cyrano*, followed by *Alice in Wonderland, Mandrake, Aunt Dan and Lemon, Taming of the Shrew, Better Days, Dolphin Project, Have You Spoken to Any Jew Lately?*, Bdwy in *End of the World* (1984), *Angels in America.*

PINHASIK, HOWARD. Born June 5, 1953 in Chicago, IL. Graduate Ohio U. Debut 1978 OB in *Allegro*, followed by *Marya, The Merchant, Street Scene, Collette Collage, Hopscotch, Doll's Life.*

PINKINS, TONYA. Born May 30, 1962 in Chicago Il. Attended Carnegie-Mellon U. Bdwy debut 1981 in *Merrily We Roll Along*, followed by *Jelly's Last Jam, Chronicle of a Death Foretold*, OB in *Five Points, A Winter's Tale, An Ounce of Prevention, Just Say No, Mexican Hayride, Young Playwrights '90, Approximating Mother, Merry Wives of Windsor.*

PIONTEK, MICHAEL (E). Born July 31, 1956 in Canoga Park, CA. Graduate FSU. Bdwy debut 1987 in *Into the Woods*, followed by *3 Penny Opera, Grand Hotel*, OB in *Reckless, Florida Crackers, Banner.*

PITTU, DAVID. Born Apr. 4, 1967 in Fairfield, CT. Graduate NYU. Debut 1987 OB in *Film is Evil: Radio is Good*, followed by *Five Very Live, White Cotton Sheets, Nothing Sacred, Stand-In, The Lights, Three Postcards*, Bdwy in *Tenth Man* (1989).

POCHOS, DEDE. Born Apr. 27, 1960 in Lake Forest, IL. Graduate U. Pa. Bdwy debut 1993 in *Wilder Wilder Wilder*, OB in *Midsummer's Night Dream, Macbeth, Tomorrow Was War, Judgment Day, Tartuffe, Who Will Carry the Word?, As You LIke It, Anatomy of Sound.*

PODELL, RICK. Born Nov. 16, 1946 in Los Angeles, CA. Attended San Fran St. U. Debut 1972 OB in *Two if By Sea*, followed by *Buy Bonds Buster*, Bdwy in *Mother Earth* (1972), *Sunset Blvd.*

PONTING, DAVID. Born Apr. 16, 1936 in Denizes, Eng. Graduate U. Bristol, U. London, Syracuse U. Debut 1972 OB in *Man and the Myth*, Bdwy in *Gentlemen Prefer Blondes* (1995).

PORTER, ADINA. Born Feb. 18, 1963 in New York City. Attended SUNY/Purchase. Debut 1988 OB in *Debutante Ball*, followed by *Inside Out, Tiny Mommie, Footsteps in the Rain, Jersey City, The Mysteries?, Aven U' Boys, Silence Cunning Exile, Girl Gone, Dancing on Moonlight, Saturday Mourning Cartoons.*

PORTER, BILLY. Born Sept. 21, 1969 in Pittsburgh, PA. Graduate Carnegie-Mellon U. Debut 1989 OB in *Romance in Hard Times*, followed by *Merchant of Venice*, Bdwy in *Miss Saigon, Five Guys Named Moe, Grease.*

POSER, TOBY. Born Apr. 16, 1969 in Huntingdon, PA. Graduate Tulane U. Debut 1993 OB in *Greetings!*, followed by *Killer Inside Me.*

POSEY, LEAH. Born Oct. 28, 1953 in Laurens, SC. Debut 1981 OB in *Little Murders*, followed by *Danny and the Deep Blue Sea, Belles, More Than Madness, Bible Burlesque, Nightwalking.*

PRESTON, WILLIAM. Born Aug. 26, 1921 in Columbia, PA. Graduate Penn. St. U. Debut 1972 OB in *We Bombed in New Haven*, followed by *Hedda Gabler, Whisper into My Good Ear, Nestless Bird, Friends of Mine, Iphigenia in Aulix, Midsummer, Fantasticks, Frozen Assets, The Golem, Taming of the Shrew, His Master's Voice, Much Ado About Nothing, Hamlet, Winter Dreams, Palpitations, Rumor of Glory, Killers, Not Partners, Rumor of Glory, Great Shakes, The Bacchae, Holy Ghosts*, Bdwy in *Our Town* (1988).

PRICE, PAIGE. Born July 6, 1964 in Middlesex, NJ. Attended NYU. Debut 1993 OB in *Gay Divorce*, Bdwy in *Beauty and the Beast* (1994).

PRINCE, FAITH. Born Aug. 5, 1957 in Augusta, GA. Graduate U. Cinn. Debut 1981 OB in *Scrambled Feet*, followed by *Olympus on My Mind, Groucho, Living Color, Bad Habits, Falsettoland*, Bdwy in *Jerome Robbins Broadway* (1989), *Nick & Nora, Guys and Dolls* (1992), *Fiorello* (Encores), *What's Wrong with This Picture.*

PRITCHETT, JAMES. Born Oct. 27 in Lenoir, NC. Graduate UNC, U. Chicago, AADA. Debut 1955 OB in *Ideal Husband*, followed by *Report to the Stockholders, Electra, Home of the Brave, New Girl in Town, Embers, The Killer, Death of Bessie Smith, Round with a Ring, An Evening's Frost, Phaedre, The Inheritors, Night Seasons, Young Man from Atlanta*, Bdwy in *Two for the Seesaw (1959), Sail Away, Lord Pengo.*

PRUITT, RICHARD. Born Jan. 20, 1950 in New Albany, IN. Graduate Ind. U. Debut 1987 OB in *Wicked Philanthropy*, Bdwy in *On the Waterfront* (1995).

PRUNZIK, KAREN. Born July 21, 1957 in Pittsburgh, PA. Attended Pittsburgh Playhouse. Bdwy debut in *42nd St.* (1980), followed by *Gentlemen Prefer Blondes* (1995).

PUGH, RICHARD WARREN. Born Oct. 20, 1950 in New York City. Graduate Tarkio Col. Bdwy debut 1979 in *Sweeney Todd*, followed by *Music Man, Five O'Clock Girl, Copperfield, Zorba* (1983), *Phantom of the Opera*, OB in *Chase a Rainbow.*

PULLIAM, DARCY. Born Nov. 15 1943 in Schenectady, NY. Graduate Tufts U., Wayne State U. Bdwy debut 1986 in *La Cage aux Folles*, followed by *Anna Karenina, Christmas Carol*, OB in *American Bagpipes, Royal Game, Werewolf.*

QUIGLEY, BERNADETTE. Born Nov. 10, 1960 in Coldspring, NY Debut 1983 OB in *Ah Wilderness*, followed by *Relative Values, God of Vengeance, Public Enemy.*

QUINN, PATRICK. Born Feb. 12, 1950 in Philadelphia, PA. Graduate Temple U. Bdwy debut 1976 in *Fiddler on the Roof*, followed by *Day in Hollywood/Night in the Ukraine, Oh, Coward!, Lend Me a Tenor, Damn Yankees*, OB in *It's Better with a Bank, By Strouse, Forbidden Broadway, Best of Forbidden Broadway, Raft of Medusa, Forbidden Broadway's 10th Anniversary, A Helluva Town, After the Ball.*

QUINN, TARYN. Born July 29, 1959 in Hamilton, OH. Attended Wittenberg U., Actors Studio. Debut 1979 OB in *Pudding Lake, Holy Junkie, Savage in Limbo, Danger of Strangers, Place Where Love Is, Half and Half, Fish in a Chimney, Environmental, Down Dark Deceptive Streets.*

RAIKEN, LAWRENCE/LARRY. Born Feb. 5, 1949 on Long Island, NY. Graduate Wm. & Mary Col., UNC. Debut 1979 OB in *Wake Up It's Time to Go to Bed*, followed by *Rise of David Levinsky, Bells Are Ringing, Pageant, Talley's Folly*, Bdwy in *Woman of the Year* (1981), *Sheik of Avenue B.*

RAINEY, DAVID. Born Jan. 30, 1964 in Tucson, AZ. Graduate E. N. Mex. U., Juilliard. Debut 1987 OB in *Richard II*, followed by *Henry IV Part 1, Julius Caesar, Love's Labour's Lost, Boy Meets Girl, Phantom Tolihooth, Black Eagles, Cash Cow.*

RAITER, FRANK. Born Jan. 17, 1932 in Cloquet, MN. Yale graduate. Bdwy debut 1958 in *Cranks*, followed by *Dark at the Top of the Stairs, J. B., Camelot, Salome*, OB in *Soft Core Pornographer, The Winter's Tale, Twelfth Night, Tower of Evil, Endangered Species, A Bright Room Called Day, Learned Ladies, 'Tis Pity She's A Whore, Othello, Comedy of Errors, Orestes, Marathon Dancing, Sudden Devotion.*

RAMOS, RICHARD RUSSELL. Born Aug. 23, 1941 in Seattle, WA. Graduate U. Minn. Bdwy debut 1968 in *House of Atreus*, followed by *Arturo Ui*, OB in *Adaptation, Screens, Lotta, Tempest, Midsummer Night's Dream, Gorky, The Seagull, Entertaining Mr. Sloane, Largo Desolato, Henry I V Parts I and 2, Dog Opera.*

RAMSAY, REMAK. Born Feb. 2, 1937 in Baltimore, MD. Graduate Princeton U. Debut 1964 OB in *Hang Down Your Head and Die*, followed by *Real Inspector Hound, Landscape of the Body, All's Well That Ends Well* (CP), *Rear Column, Winslow Boy, Dining Room, Save Grand Central, Quartermaine's Terms*, Bdwy in *Half a Sixpence, Sheep on the Runway, Lovely Ladies Kind Gentlemen, On the Town, Jumpers, Private Lives, Dirty Linen, Every Good Boy Deserves Favor, The Devil's Disciple, Woman in Mind, Nick and Nora, St. Joan, Moliere Comedies, Heiress.*

RANDALL, MARTHA. Born in Searcy, AK. Graduate Martha Wash. Col., U. Va. Bdwy debut in *Be Your Age* (1953), followed by *Glass Menagerie* (1994).

RANDLE, PATRICIA. Born Mar. 18 in Worcester, MA. Graduate Boston U. Debut 1995 OB in *Durang Durang.*

RASCHE, DAVID. Born Aug. 7, 1944 in St. Louis, MO. Graduate Elmhurst Col., U. Chicago. Debut 1976 OB in *John*, followed by *Snow White, Isadora Duncan Sleeps with the Russian Navy, End of the War, A Sermon, Routed, Geniuses, Dolphin Position, To Gillian on Her 37th Birthday, Custom of the Country, Country Girl, Marathon '91, No One Will Be Immune*, Bdwy in

Shadow Box (1977), *Loose Ends, Lunch Hour, Speed-the-Plow, Mastergate, Christmas Carol.*

RAYNER, MARTIN. Born Aug. 1, 1949 in Ryde, Eng. Attended London Drama Studio. Debut 1995 OB in *Travels with My Aunt.*

REAMS, LEE ROY. Born Aug. 23 in Covington, KY. Graduate U.Cinn. Consv. Bdwy debut in *Sweet Charity (1966)*, followed by *Oklahoma* (LC), *Applause, Lorelei, Show Boat* (JB), *Hello Dolly* (1978), *42nd St., La Cage aux Folles, Beauty and the Beast*, OB in *Sterling Silver, Potholes, The Firefly in Concert.*

REDDY, HELEN. Born Oct. 25, 1941 in Melbourne, Aust. Bdwy debut in *Blood Brothers* (1995).

REDGRAVE, VANESSA. Born Jan. 30, 1937 in London, Eng. Attended Central School of Speech and Drama. Bdwy debut in *Lady from the Sea* (1976), followed by *Orpheus Descending* (1989), OB in *Vita and Virginia.*

REED, MAGGI-MEG. Born in Columbus, OH. Graduate Harvard U. Debut 1984 OB in *She Stoops to Conquer*, followed by *Playboy of the Western World, Triangles, Beyond the Window, El Greco, Shabbatai.*

REES, ROGER. Born May 5, 1944 in Wales. Graduate Glade School of Fine Art. Bdwy debut 1975 in *London Assurance*, followed by *Nicholas Nickleby* (1981), *Red Shoes (previews only), Indiscretions*, OB in *End of the Day* (1992).

REINER, ALYSIA. Born July 21, 1970 in Gainesville, FL. Graduate Vassar Col. Debut 1993 OB in *Bye Bye Blackbird*, followed by *Mirage, And the Sky Opened Up, Recklessness, Single and Proud, A Play of One's Own.*

REISSA, ELEANOR. Born May 11 in Brooklyn, NY. Graduate Brooklyn Col. Debut 1979 OB in *Rebecca and the Rabbi's Daughter*, followed by *That's Not Funny That's Sick, Rise of David Levinsky, Match Made in Heaven, Song for a Saturday. No No Nanette, Songs of Paradise, Those Were the Days, Funky Crazy Boogaloo Boy.*

RENDERER, SCOTT. Born in Palo Alto, CA. Graduate Whitman Col. Bdwy debut 1983 in *Teaneck Tanzi*, OB in *And Things That Go Bump in the Night, Crossfire, Just Like the Lions, Dreamer Examines His Pillow, Nasty Little Secrets, Unidentified Human Remains, Hairy Ape.*

RICHARDS, JEAN. Born in New York City. Attended Yale U. Debut 1969 OB in *Man with the Flower in His Mouth*, followed by *Madwoman of Chaillot, Poor Old Simon, Whining and Dining, Hamlet.*

RICKABY, BRETT. Born Dec. 15, 1964 in Minneapolis, MN. Graduate U.Mn./Duluth, NYU. Debut 1990 OB in *Richard III*, followed by *Two Gentlemen of Verona, Dracula, All's Well That Ends Well, Carnal Knowledge*, Bdwy in *Glass Menagerie* (1994).

RIEBLING, TIA. Born July 21, 1954 in Pittsburgh, PA: Attended NYU, Carnegie-Mellon. Debut 1983 OB in *American Passion*, followed by *Preppies, Hamlin, Wish You Were Here*, Bdwy in *Smile* (1986), *Fiddler on the Roof, Les Miserables, Grease.*

RIFKIN, RON. Born Oct. 31, 1939 in New York City. Graduate NYU. Bdwy debut 1960 in *Come Blow Your Horn*, followed by *The Goodbye People, The Tenth Man, Broken Glass, Month in the Country*, OB in *Rosebloom, Art of Dining, Temple, Substance of Fire, Three Hotels, Fair Country, Greenwich Village Follies.*

RIGG, DIANA. Born July 20, 1938 in Doncaster, England. Attended RADA. Bdwy debut 1964 in *Comedy of Errors*, followed by *King Lear, Abelard and Heloise, The Misanthrope, Medea.*

RIGBY, TERENCE. Born Jan. 2, 1937 in Birmingham, Eng. Attended RADA. Bdwy debut in *The Homecoming* (1967), followed by *No Man's Land* (1976), *Hamlet* (1995), OB in *Richard III* (BAM).

RILEY, ERIC. Born Mar. 22, 1955 in Albion, MI. Graduate U.Mich. Bdwy debut 1979 in *Ain't Misbehavin'*, followed by *Dreamgirls, Ain't Misbehavin'* (1988), *Once on This Island* (also OB), *Christmas Carol*, OB in *Weird Romance.*

RIPLEY, ALICE. Born Dec. 14, 1963 in San Leandro, CA. Graduate Kent State U. Bdwy debut 1993 in *Tommy*, followed by *Sunset Blvd.*

ROBBINS, REX. Born in Pierre, SD. Bdwy debut 1964 in *One Flew over the Cuckoo's Nest*, followed by *Scratch, The Changing Room, Gypsy, Comedians, An Almost Perfect Person, Richard III, You Can't Take It with You, Play Memory, Six Degrees of Separation, Sisters Rosensweig*, OB in *Servant of Two Masters, The Alchemist, Arms and the Man, Boys in the Band, Memory of Two Mondays, They Knew What They Wanted, Secret Service, Boy Meets Girl, Three Sisters, The Play's The Thing, Julius Caesar, Henry IV Part 1, Dining Room, Urban Blight, Deja Revue.*

ROBERTSON, SCOTT. Born Jan. 4, 1954 in Stanford, CT. Bdwy debut 1976 in *Grease*, followed by *The Pajama Game* (LC), *Damn Yankees* (1994), OB in *Scrambled Feet, Applause, A Lady Needs a Change, A Baker's Audition, She Loves Me, Secrets of a Lava Lamp, Love in Two Countries.*

ROBINS, LAILA. Born Mar. 14, 1959 in St. Paul, MN. Graduate U.Wis., Yale. Bdwy debut 1984 in *The Real Thing*, OB in *Bloody Poetry, The Film*

Society, For Dear Life, Maids of Honor, The Extra Man, Merchant of Venice.

ROBINSON, LARRY. Born Oct. 15, 1929 in New York City. Bdwy in *On Borrowed Time, Life with Father, Richard III, The Victors, Grass Harp, Time Out for Ginger*, OB in *Love and the Rebound.*

ROCHA, KALI. Born Dec. 5, 1971 in Memphis, TN. Graduate Carnegie-Mellon U. Bdwy debut in *In the Summer House* (1993), followed by *Inspector Calls.*

RODRIGUEZ, AL D. Born Mar. 5, 1963 in New York City. Graduate LIU. Debut 1981 OB in *Who Collects the Pain?*, followed by *Charge It Please, Born to Rumba, English Only Restaurant, Caucasian Chalk Circle.*

RODRIGUEZ, RAYMOND. Born Dec. 6, 1961 in Puerto Rico. Attended Cerritos Col., Orange County Col. Bdwy debut in *Kiss of the Spider Woman* (1993).

RODRIGUEZ, TRESHA. Born Sept. 2, 1969 in El Paso, TX. Graduate U.Tex., Am.Rep.Th./Harvard. Debut 1995 OB in *Circus Life.*

ROGERS, DIANA. Born Feb. 5, 1952 in Cincinnati, OH. Graduate Cin. Consv., N.Ky,U. Bdwy debut 1994 in *Les Miserables.*

ROHLAND, LESLIE. Born Feb. 7, 1965 in Okinawa, Japan. Graduate U.Ut., Fl.St.U. Debut 1995 OB in *The Choice.*

ROSAGER, LARS. Born Mar. 21, 1956 in San Francisco, CA. Attended U.Cal./Santa Cruz. Bdwy debut 1980 in *42nd St.*, followed by *Cabaret* (1987), *American Ballroom Theatre.*

ROSE, BRIAN. Born Nov. 26, 1951 in New York City. Graduate Hofstra U., CUNY, Oh.St.U. Debut 1970 OB in *Chronicles of Hell*, followed by *Gift Horse.*

ROSE, NORMAN. Born June 23, 1917 in Philadelphia, PA. Graduate George Washington U. Bdwy in *Cafe Crown, St. Joan, Land of Fame, Richard III, The Fifth Season*, OB in *Career, Hemingway Hero, Wicked Cooks, Empire Builders, The Old Ones, The Wait, Edith Rose, Gift Horse.*

ROSENBAUM, DAVID. Born in New York City. Debut 1968 OB in *America Hurrah!*, followed by *The Cave Dwellers, Evenings with Chekhov, Out of the Death Cart, After Miriam, The Indian Wants the Bronx, Allergy, Family Business, Beagleman and Brackett, The Last Sortie, Awake and Sing*, Bdwy in *Oh! Calcutta!, Ghetto.*

ROSENBLATT, MARCELLE. Born July 1 in Baltimore, MD. Graduate UNC, Yale U. Debut 1979 OB in *Vienna Notes*, followed by *The Sorrows of Stephen, The Dybbuk, Twelfth Night, Second Avenue Rag, La Boheme, Word of Mouth, Twelve Dreams, Don Juan, A Midsummer Night's Dream, Mud, The Return of Pinocchio, Ladies of Fisher Cove*, Bdwy in *Stepping Out* (1986), *Our Town, What's Wrong with This Picture.*

ROSENTHAL, MARK. Born July 24, 1966 in Kettering, OH. Attended DePaul U./Goodman School. Debut 1991 OB in *Marvin's Room* for which he received a Theatre World Award, followed by *Basement at the Bottom of the End of the World, Balm in Gilead, Carne Vale, Phaedra.*

ROSS, JAMIE. Born May 4, 1939 in Markinch, Scot. Attended RADA. Bdwy debut 1962 in *Little Moon of Alban*, followed by *Moon Beseiged, Ari, Different Times, Woman of the Year, La Cage aux Folles, 42nd Street, Gypsy* (1990), *Gentlemen Prefer Blondes* (1995), OB in *Penny Friend, Oh Coward!, Approaching Zanzibar.*

ROSS, NATALIE. Born Jan. 24, 1932 in Minneapolis, MN. Graduate U.Wash., RADA. Bdwy debut 1961 in *Come Blow Your Horn*, followed by OB in *Butterfly Dream* (1966), *Dietrich Process, Tales from Hollywood, Madwoman of Chaillot.*

ROTH, STEPHANIE. Born in 1963 in Boston, MA. Juilliard graduate. Bdwy debut 1987 in *Les Liaisons Dangereuses*, followed by *Artist Descending a Staircase*, OB in *The Cherry Orchard, Measure for Measure, A Body of Water, Uncommon Women and Others, Crumbs from the Table of Joy.*

ROZNOWSKI, ROBERT. Born July 16, 1963 in Baltimore, MD. Graduate Point Park Col., Ohio St.U. Debut 1992 OB in *Lightin' Out*, followed by *Young Abe Lincoln, Identical Twins from Baltimore.*

RUBES, JAN. Born June 6, 1920 in Volyne, Czeh. Graduate Charles U. Prague, Guelph U. Debut 1995 OB in *Twelve Dreams.*

RUEHL, MERCEDES. Born Feb. 28, 1948 in Jackson Heights, New York City. Attended New Rochelle Col. Debut 1985 OB in *Coming of Age in Soho*, followed by *Marriage of Betty and Boo, Other People's Money*, Bdwy in *I'm Not Rapaport* (1985), *Lost in Yonkers, Shadow Box* (1994), *Rose Tattoo* (1995).

RUIZ, ANTHONY. Born Oct. 17, 1956 in New York City. Attended NYCC. Debut 1987 OB in *Wonderful Ice Cream Suit*, followed by *Danny and the Deep Blue Sea. Born to Rumba!.*

RUNOLFSSON, ANNE. Born in Long Beach, CA. Attended UCLA. Bdwy debut 1989 in *Les Miserables*, followed by *Aspects of Love, Cyrano.*

RUSH, JO ANNA (formerly Lehmann). Born Nov. 13, 1947 in Montclair. NJ. Bdwy debut 1986 in *Pousse Cafe*, followed by *Shirley MacLaine at the Palace*, OB in *Love Me Love My Children, Broadway Scandals of*

1928, Options, Inside Out, O Sappho O Wilde, Grandma Sylvia's Funeral.

RUSH, SUSAN. Born Nov. 17, 1943 in Mansfield, PA. Graduate Mansfield St.Col., U.Az. Debut 1970 OB in *The Drunkard,* followed by Bdwy in *Knickerbocker Holiday* (1977), *Guys and Dolls, Gentlemen Prefer Blondes* (1995).

RYALL, WILLIAM. Born Sept. 18, 1954 in Binghamton, NY. Graduate AADA. Debut 1979 OB in *Canterbury Tales,* followed by *Elizabeth and Essex, He Who Gets Slapped, Sea Gull, Tartuffe,* Bdwy in *Me and My Girl* (1986), *Grand Hotel, Best Little Whorehouse Goes Public, How to Succeed...* (1995).

RYAN, STEVEN. Born June 19, 1947 in New York City. Graduate Boston U., U.Minn. Debut 1978 OB in *Winning Isn't Everything,* followed by *The Beethoven, September in the Rain, Romance Language, Love's Labour's Last, Love and Anger, Approximating Mother, Merry Wives of Windsor, Unexpected Tenderness,* Bdwy in *I'm Not Rappaport* (1986), *Guys and Dolls* (1992), *On the Waterfront.*

RYDER, AMY. Born Jan. 8, 1958 in San Diego, CA. Attended San Francisco State U. Debut 1984 OB in *Options,* followed by *Falsies, Taboo in Revue, On Again, Songs in Blume, Friends and Music, Toulouse, Pretty Faces, Merrily We Roll Along, Most Massive Woman Wins,* Bdwy in *Damn Yankees* (1994).

SAGE, ALEXANDRIA. Born June 25, 1968 in San Francisco, CA. Graduate Yale U. Debut 1993 OB in *Ceremony of Innocence,* followed by *Fragments, The Co-Op, Jacob's Blanket.*

SALATA, GREGORY. Born July 21, 1949 in New York City. Graduate Queens Col. Bdwy debut 1975 in *Dance with Me,* followed by *Equus, Bent,* OB in *Piaf: A Remembrance, Sacraments, Measure for Measure, Subject of Childhood, Jacques and His Master, Androcles and the Lion, Madwoman of Chaillot.*

SALINGER, ROSS. Born Oct. 14, 1960 in Norwalk, Ct. Graduate Northwestern U. Debut 1992 OB in *On the Bum,* followed by *War of the Worlds, Bertolt Brecht: In Dark Times, Somewhere in the Pacific.*

SANDERS, JACKIE. Born July 17, 1967 in Thornston, GA. Graduate Brenau U., AMDA. Debut 1994 OB in *Judy at the Stonewall Inn,* followed by *Swingtime Canteen.*

SANTIAGO, DOUGLAS. Born July 4, 1972 in Rio Piedras, PR. Attended Fashion Inst. Debut 1995 OB in *Simpson St.*

SANTIAGO, SAUNDRA. Born Apr. 14, 1957 in New York City. Graduate U.Miami, SMU. Bdwy debut 1983 in *View from the Bridge,* followed by *Chronicle of a Death Foretold,* OB in *Road to Nirvana, Spike Heels, Hello Again.*

SANTIAGO, SOCORRO. Born July 12, 1957 in New York City. Attended Juilliard. Debut 1977 OB in *Crack,* followed by *Poets from the Inside, Unfinished Women, Family Portrait, Domino, The Promise, Death and the Maiden, Phaedra,* Bdwy in *The Bacchae* (1980).

SANTORIELLO, ALEX. Born Dec. 30, 1956 in Newark, NJ. Attended Ks.St.U., Kean St. Debut 1986 OB in *Belle Helene,* followed by *Romantic Detachment, Passionate Extremes, Winterman,* Bdwy in *Les Miserables* (1987), *3 Penny Opera.*

SANTORO, MARK. Born Jan. 28, 1963 in New Haven, CT. Bdwy debut 1974 in *Gypsy,* followed by *Carrie, Pajama Game* (NYCO/LC), *Damn Yankees* (1994).

SARSGAARD, PETER. Born Mar. 7, 1971 in Scott A.F.B., IL. Graduate Washington U. Debut 1995 OB in *Laura Dennis.*

SAVAGE, JACK. Born Dec. 5, 1953 in Paterson, NJ. Graduate Manhattan Sch.Music, Fl.St.U. Debut 1984 OB in *Kuni-Lemi,* followed by *New Yorkers.*

SBARGE, RAPHAEL. Born Feb. 12, 1964 in New York City. Attended HB Studio. Debut 1981 OB in *Henry IV Part I,* followed by *The Red Snake, Hamlet, Short Change, Ghosts,* Bdwy in *The Curse of an Aching Heart, Ah Wilderness!, Twilight of the Golds, Shadow Box* (1994).

SCALAMONI, SAM. Born Oct. 21, 1962 in Bloomfield, NJ. Bdwy debut 1989 in *Les Miserables,* followed by *Cyrano,* OB in *Shabbatai.*

SCHNEIDER, JAY. Born May 8, 1951 in Brooklyn, New York City. Graduate Brandeis U. Debut 1979 OB in *On a Clear Day...,* followed by *Pal Joey, Very Warm for May,* Bdwy 1994 in *Philadelphia Here I Come.*

SCHOEFFLER, PAUL. Born Nov. 21, 1958 in Montreal, Can. Graduate U.CA/Berkley, Carnegie-Mellon U. Brussels. Debut 1988 OB in *Much Ado about Nothing,* followed by *Cherry Orchard, Carnival, Doll's Life,* Bdwy in *Cyrano the Musical* (1993).

SCHREIBER, AVERY. Born Apr. 9, 1935 in Chicago, IL. Graduate Goodman Th. Debut 1965 OB in *Second City at Square East,* followed by *Conerico Was Here to Stay, Awake and Sing,* Bdwy in *Metamorphosis, Dreyfus in Rehearsal, Can-Can* (1981), *Welcome to the Club.*

SCOTT, MICHAEL. Born Jan. 24, 1954 in Santa Monica, CA. Attended Cal.St.U. Bdwy debut 1978 in *Best Little Whorehouse in Texas* (also OB),

followed by *Happy New Year, Show Boat* (1994), OB in *Leave It to Me.*

SEALE, DOUGLAS. Born Oct. 28, 1913 in London, Eng. Graduate Washington Col., RADA. Bdwy debut 1974 in *Emperor Henry IV,* followed by *Frankenstein, The Dresser, Noises Off, Madwoman of Chaillot.*

SEARS, JOE. Born July 23, 1949 in Bartlesville, OK. Graduate Northeastern St.U. Debut 1982 OB in *Greater Tuna,* Bdwy 1994 in *Tuna Christmas.*

SECADA, JON. Born 1962 in Cuba. Graduate U.Miami. Bdwy debut 1995 in *Grease.*

SEFF, RICHARD. Born Sept. 23, 1927 in New York City. Attended NYU. Bdwy debut 1951 in *Darkness at Noon,* followed by *Herzl, Musical Comedy Murders,* OB in *Big Fish Little Fish, Modigliani, Childe Byron, Richard II, Time Framed, The Sea Gull, Only You, Countess Mitzi, Two Schnitzler One Acts, Truth Teller.*

SERABIAN, LORRAINE. Born June 12, 1945 in New York City. Graduate Hofstra U. Debut OB in *Sign of Jonah* (1960), followed by *Electra, Othello, Secret Life of Walter Mitty, Bugs and Veronica, The Trojan Women, American Gothic, Gallows Humor, Company, Dorian, Deathtrap, Tonight at 8:30, The Rink,* Bdwy in *Cabaret, Zorba, The Flowering Peach.*

SERBAGI, ROGER. Born July 26, 1937 in Waltham, MA. Attended Am. Th.Wing. Bdwy debut 1969 in *Henry V,* followed by *Gemini,* OB in *Certain Young Man, Awake and Sing, The Partnership, Monsters, Transfiguration of Benno Blimpie, Family Snapshots, Till Jason Comes, 1984, Hanry Lampur, Dog Opera.*

SETLOCK, MARK. Born June 26, 1968 in Cleveland, OH. Graduate Kent St.U., Am.Rep.Th./Harvard. Debut 1995 OB in *Don Juan in Chicago.*

SETRAKIAN, ED. Born Oct. 1, 1928 in Jenkinstown, WVA. Graduate Concord Col., NYU. Debut 1966 OB in *Dreams in the Night,* followed by *Othello, Coriolanus, Macbeth, Hamlet, Baal, Old Glory, Futz, Hey Rube, Seduced, Shout Across the River, American Days, Sheepskin, Inserts, Crossing the Bar, The Boys Next Door, The Mensch, Adoring the Madonna, Tack Room, Water and Wine,* Bdwy in *Days in the Trees* (1976) *St. Joan, The Best Little Whorehouse in Texas.*

SEWELL, RUFUS. Born 1968 in London, Eng. Attended London Central School of Speech and Drama. Bdwy debut 1995 in *Translations* for which he received a Theatre World Award.

SHANICE. Born 1963 in Pittsburgh, PA. Bdwy debut 1995 in *Les Miserables.*

SHANNON, SARAH. Born May 23, 1966 in LaCrosse, WI. Graduate U.Wis. Bdwy debut 1992 in *Cats,* followed by *Beauty and the Beast.*

SHEA, JERE. Born June 14, 1965 in Boston, MA. Graduate Boston College, NYU. Debut 1992 OB in *As You Like It,* Bdwy 1992 in *Guys and Dolls,* followed by *Passion,* for which he received a 1994 Theatre World Award.

SHEIN, KATE. Born Oct. 13 in Tarrytown, NY. Graduate San Fran.St.U. Debut 1985 OB in *Alvrone,* followed by *Secret Sits in the Middle.*

SHELLEY, CAROLE. Born Aug. 16, 1939 in London, Eng. Bdwy debut 1965 in *The Odd Couple,* followed by *The Astrakhan Coat, Loot, Noel Coward's Sweet Potato, Hay Fever, Absurd Person Singular, The Norman Conquests, The Elephant Man, The Misanthrope, Noises Off, Stepping Out, The Miser,* OB in *Little Murder, The Devil's Disciple, The Play's the Thing, Souble Feature, Twelve Dreams, Pygmalion, Christmas Carol, Jubilee in Concert, Waltz of the Toreadors, What the Butler Saw, Maggie and Isha, Later Life, Destiny of Me, Lady in the Dark in Concert, Richard II, London Suite.*

SHELTON, SLOANE. Born Mar. 17, 1934 in Asheville, NC. Attended Bates Col., RADA. Bdwy Debut 1967 in *The Imaginary Invalid,* followed by *Touch of the Poet, Tonight at 8:30, 1 Never Sang for My Father, Sticks and Bones, Runner Stumbles, Shadow Box, Passione, Open Admission,* Orpheus Descending, OB in *Androcles and the Lion, The Maids, Basic Training of Pavlo Hummel, Play and Other Plays, Julius Caesar, Chieftans, Passione, Chinese Viewing Pavilion, Blood Relations, Great Divide, Highest Standard of Living, Flower Palace, April Snow, Nightingale, Dearly Departed, Other People's Money, Dog Opera.*

SHEPARD, JOAN. Born Jan. 7 in New York City. Graduate RADA. Bdwy debut 1940 in *Romeo and Juliet,* followed by *Sunny River, Strings My Lors Are False, This Rock, Foolish Notion, A Young Man's Fancy, My Romance, Member of the Wedding,* OB in *Othello, Plot Against the Chase Manhattan Bank, Philosophy in the Boudoir, Knitters on the Sun, School for Wives, Importance of Being Earnest, Enter Laughing, World War Won, Richard III.*

SHEPHERD, LEE. Born July 20 in Kansas City, MO. Graduate U.Mo. Debut 1983 OB in *Waiting for Lefty,* followed by *Till the Day I Die, Sympathy, Tracers, Isadora Duncan Sleeps with the Russian Navy, Living Proof.*

SHEPHERD, SUZANNE. Born Oct. 31, 1934 in Elizabeth, NJ. Graduate Bennington Col. Debut 1977 OB in *World of Sholem Aleichem,* followed by *End Game, House Arrest, Appointment with a High Wire Lady, Life Flashes before His Eyes, Lie of the Mind,* Bdwy in *Awake and Sing* (1984).

SHERMAN, JONATHAN MARC. Born Oct. 10, 1968 in Morristown,

NJ. Attended Carnegie-Mellon U., AADA. Debut 1986 OB in *The Chopin Playoffs*, followed by *Sophistry, Wild Dogs, Great Unwashed, Unexpected Tenderness.*

SHENKEL, LES. Born May 20, 1944 in Brooklyn, New York City. Attended Rider Col. Attended AADA. Debut 1969 OB in *The Fantasticks*, followed by *Time of Harry Harass, Moon and Mongols, Coiled Spring, The Occupation.*

SHEW, TIMOTHY. Born Feb. 7, 1959 in Grand Forks, ND. Graduate Millikin U., U. Mich. Debut 1987 OB in *The Knife*, Bdwy in *Les Miserables, Guys and Dolls.*

SHIELDS, BROOKE. Born May 31, 1965 in New York City. Graduate Princeton U. Debut 1985 OB in *Eden Cinema*, followed by Bdwy 1994 in *Grease* for which she received a Theatre World Award.

SNIMIZU, KEENAN. Born Oct. 22, 1956 in New York City. Bdwy debut 1965 in *South Pacific*, followed by *King and I*, OB in *Rashomon, Year of the Dragon, The Catch, Peking Man, Flowers and Household Cods, Behind Enemy Lines, Station J, Rosie's Cafe, Boutique Living, Gonza the Lancer, Letters to a Student Revolutionary, Fairy Bones, Fall Guy.*

SHIPLEY, SANDRA. Born Feb. 1 in Rainham, Kent, Eng. Attended New Col. of Speech and Drama, London U. Debut 1988 OB in *Six Characters in Search of an Author*, followed by *Big Time, Kindertransport*, Bdwy 1995 in *Indiscretions.*

SIMMONS, J.K. (formerly Jonathan). Born Jan. 9, 1955 in Detroit, MI. Graduate U. Minn. Debut 1987 OB in *Birds of Paradise*, followed by *Dirty Dick, Das Barbecu*, Bdwy in *A Change in the Heir* (1990), *A Few Good Men, Peter Pan* (1990/1991), *Guys and Dolls, Laughter on the 23rd Floor.*

SIMS, BARBARA CAREN. Born June 17 in Ft. Worth, TX. Graduate U. Houston. Debut OB in *Trip to Bountiful*, followed by *Night Seasons, Laura Dennis.*

SISTO, ROCCO. Born Feb. 8, 1953 in Bari, Italy. Graduate U. Ill., NYU. Debut 1982 OB in *Hamlet*, followed by *The Country Doctor, The Times and Appetites of Toulouse-Lautrec, The Merchant of Venice, What Did He See, A Winter's Tale, The Tempest, Dream of a Common Language, 'Tis Pity She's a Whore, Mad Forest, Careless Love, All's Well That Ends Well, The Illusion, Merry Wives of Windsor*, Bdwy 1995 in *Month in the Country.*

SITLER, DAVID. Born Apr. 7, 1957 in Harrisburg, PA. Graduate Franklin-Marshall College, Catholic U. Debut 1991 OB in *Necktie Breakfast*, followed by *Blues for Mr. Charlie*, Bdwy in *An Inspector Calls* (1994).

SKELTON, PATRICK. Born Jan. 24, 1956 in Idaho Falls, ID. Graduate U. S. Cal. Debut 1982 OB in *Isolde of White Hands*, followed by *Mirandolina, Soul of an Intruder.*

SKINNER, EMILY. Born June 29, 1970 in Richmond, VA. Gradaute Carnegie-Mellon U. Bdwy debut 1994 in *Christmas Carol*, OB in *Watbanaland.*

SKINNER, KATE. Born Aug. 10, 1953 in Chicago, IL. Graduate Cal. St. U, UCLA. Debut 1995 OB in *Putside Waco*, followed by *Common Pursuit, Marvin's Room*, Bdwy in *Uncle Vanya* (1995).

SKINNER, MARGO. Born Jan. 3, 1950 in Middletown, OH. Graduate Boston U. Debut 1980 OB in *Missing Persons*, followed by *The Dining Room, Mary Barnes, The Perfect Party, Spare Parts, Oedipus the King, Game of Love and Chance, Durang Durang, Mrs. Warren's Profession.*

SLYTER, JILL. Born Dec. 29, 1964 in San Jose, CA. Attended UC/San Diego. Debut 1987 OB in *Satchmo:America's Musical Legend*, Bdwy 1994 in *Show Boat.*

SMILEY, BRENDA. Born 1947 in Indiana. Attended Ind. U., NYU. Debut 1966 OB in *America Hurrah*, followed by *Scuba Duba* for which she received a 1968 Theatre World Award, *Enactment, Jimmy Paradise, You're as Old as Your Arteries, Wedding Portrait, Sea Gull, Shanghai Gambit, Andrew My Dearest One.*

SMITH, DANA. Born Nov. 30, 1953 in New York City. Graduate Syracuse U., Yale U. Debut 1983 OB in *Richard III*, followed by *Nora, Miami Stories.*

SMITH, DEREK. Born Dec. 4, 1959 in Seattle, WA. Juilliard Graduate. Debut 1986 OB in *Cruise Control*, followed by *Ten by Tennessee, Traps, Hyde in Hollywood, Sylvia*, Bdwy in *Timon of Athens* (1993), *Government Inspector.*

SMITH, SHEILA. Born Apr. 3, 1933 in Coneaut, OH. Attended Kent St. U., Cleveland Play House, Bdwy debut 1963 in *Hot Spot*, followed by *Mame* for which she received a Theatre World Award, *Follies, Company, Sugar, Five O'Clock Girl, 42nd Street, Show Boat* (1994), OB in *Taboo Revue, Anything Goes, Best Foot Forward, Sweet Miami, Fiorelio!, Taking My Turn, Jack and Jill, M. Amilcar, The Sunset Gang, Backers Audition.*

SMITH-CAMERON, J. Born Sept. 7 in Louisville, KY. Attended Florida State U. Bdwy debut 1982 in *Crimes of the Heart*, followed by *Wild Honey, Lend Me a Tenor, Our Country's Good, The Real Inspector Hound, 15 Minute Hamlet*, OB in *Asian Shade, The Knack, Second Prize: Two Weeks in Leningrad, The Great Divide, The Voice of the Turtle, Women of Man-*

hattan, *Alice and Fred, Mi Vida Loca, Little Egypt, On the Bum, Traps/ Owners, Desdemona, Naked Truth, Don Juan in Chicago.*

SOMMER, JOSEF. Born June 26, 1934 in Griefswald, Ger. Graduate Carnegie Tech. U. Bdwy debut 1970 in *Othello*, followed by *Children Children, Trial of the Catonsville 9, Full Circle, Who's Who in Hell, Shadow Box, Whose Life Is It Anyway?*, OB in *Enemies, Merchant of Venice, The Dog Ran Away, Drinks before Dinner, Lydie Breeze, Black Angel, The Lady and the Clarinet, Love Letters on Blue Paper, Largo Desolato, Hamlet, Later Life, Hapgood.*

SOPHIEA, CYNTHIA. Born Oct. 26, 1954 in Flint, MI. Bdwy debut 1981 in *My Fair Lady*, followed by *She Loves Me*, OB in *Lysistrata, Sufragette, Golden Apple, Winter's Tale, Petrified Prince.*

SPAISMAN, ZYPORA. Born Jan. 2, 1920 in Lublin, Poland. Debut 1955 OB in *Lonesome Ship*, followed by *My Father's Court, A Thousand and One Nights, Eleventh Inheritor, Enchanting Melody, Fifth Commandment, Bronx Express, The Melody Lingers On, Yoshke Musikant, Stempenya, Generation of Green Fields, Ship, A Play for the Devil, Broome Street America, The Flowering Peach, Riverside Drive, Big Winner, The Land of Dreams, Father's Inheritance, At the Crossroads, Stempenyu, Mirele Efros.*

SPEROS, TIA. Born May 3, 1959 in San Francisco, CA. Graduate San Jose St. U. Debut 1985 OB in *Tenderloin*, followed by *Tatterdemalion, The Taffetas, Little by Little.*

SPIEGEL, BARBARA. Born Mar. 12 in New York City. Debut 1969 in LC Rep's *Camino Real, Operation Sidewinder*, and *Beggar on Horseback*, OB in *The Disintegration of James Cherry, Feast for Fleas, Museum, Powder, The Bleachers, Nightshift, Cassatt, Rope Dancers, Friends Too Numerous to Mention, Bronx Dreams, Green Fields, Festival of l-Acts, What's Wrong with This Picture?, Jewish Wife, Where Do We Go from Here?, Those Summer Nights, Circus, SWAK, World Without Men, The Bleachers, Miami Stories, Beau Jest.*

SPINDELL, AHVI. Born June 26, 1954 in Boston, MA. Attended Ithaca Col., U.NH, Juilliard. Bdwy debut 1977 in *Something Old Something New*, followed by *Ghetto*, OB in *Antony and Cleopatra, Forty Deuce, Alexandria, Emma, Art of Finesse, Broken English.*

SPINELLA, STEPHEN. Born Oct. 11, 1956 in Naples, Italy. Graduate NYU. Debut 1982 OB in *The Age of Assassins*, followed by *Dance for Me Rosetta, Bremen Coffee, Taming of the Shrew, L'Illusion, Burrhead, Love! Valour! Compassion!* Bdwy 1993 in *Angles in America*, for which he received a Theatre World Award.

SPOLAN, JEFFREY. Born July 14, 1947 in New York City. Graduate Adelphi U. Debut 1982 OB in *Yellow Fever*, followed by *Savage in Limbo, Three Sisters, East of Evil, Saved, Romersholm, Dead End, The Boor, Running Home, Tombstone, Dining Out Alone, Montpelier Pa-Zazz, Soul of an Intruder, Living Proof.*

SPELLMAN, KERRIANNE. Born Jan. 7, 1966 in NJ. Graduate AADA, AMDA. Bdwy debut 1993 in *Les Miserables*, followed by OB in *Cover of Life.*

SPYBEY, DINA. Born Aug. 29, 1965 in Columbus, OH. Graduate Oh. State U., Rutgers. Debut 1993 OB in *Five Women Wearing the Same Dress* for which she received a Theatre World Award, followed by *Girl Gone, Dates and Nuts, Don Juan in Chicago.*

STAHL, MARY LEIGH. Born Aug. 29, 1946 in Madison, WI. Graduate Jacksonville State U. Debut 1974 OB in *Circus*, followed by *Dragons, Sullivan and Gilbert, World of Sholem Aleichem*, Bdwy in *The Phantom of the Opera* (1988).

STANLEY, DOROTHY. Born Nov. 18 in Hartford, CT. Graduate Ithaca Col., Carnegie-Mellon U. Debut 1978 OB in *Gay Divorce*, followed by *Dames at Sea*, Bdwy in *Sugar Babies* (1980), *Annie, 42nd Street, Broadway, Jerome Robbins' Broadway, Kiss of the Spider Woman, Show Boat* (1984).

STANLEY, FLORENCE. Born July 1 in Chicago. Graduate Northwestern U. Debut 1960 OB in *Machinal*, followed by *It's Only a Play, Mexican Hayride*, Bdwy in *Glass Menagerie* (1965), *Fiddler on the Roof, Safe Place, Prisoner of Second Ave., Secret Affairs of Mildred Wild, What's Wrong with This Picture?* (also OB).

STANTON, ROBERT. Born Mar. 8, 1963 in San Antonio, TX. Graduate George Mason U., NYU. Debut 1985 OB in *Measure for Measure*, followed by *Rum and Coke, Cheapside, Highest Standard of Living, One Act Festival, Best Half-Foot Forward, Sure Thing, Emily, Ubu, Casanova, Owners/Traps, Visits from Mr. Whitcomb, All in the Timing, Cheever Evening*, Bdwy in *A Small Family Business* (1992).

STAPLETON, JEAN. Born Jan. 19 1923 in New York City. Attended Hunter Col., Am. Th. Wing. Bdwy debut 1953 in *In the Summer House*, followed by *Damn Yankees, Bells Are Ringing, Juno, Rhinoceros, Funny Girl, Arsenic and Old Lace*, OB in *Mountain Language/The Birthday Party, Learned Ladies, Roads to Home, Night Seasons.*

224

STATTEL, ROBERT. Born Nov. 20, 1937 in Floral Park, NY. Graduate Manhattan College. Debut 1958 in *Heloise,* followed by *When I Was a Child, Man and Superman, The Storm, Don Carlos, The Taming of the Shrew, Titus Andronicus, Henry IV, Peer Gynt, Hamlet, Danton's Death, The Country Wife, The Caucasian Chalk Circle, King Lear, Iphigenia in Aulis, Ergo, The Persians, Blue Boys, The Minister's Black Veil, Four Friends, Two Character Play, The Merchant of Venice, Cuchulain, Oedipus Cycle, Guilles de Rais, Woyzeck, The Fuehrer Bunker, Learned Ladies, Domestic Issues, Great Days, The Tempest, Brand, A Man for All Seasons, Bunker Reveries, Enrico IV, Selling Off, Titus Andronicus,* Bdwy in *Zoya's Apartment* (1990), *Black Comedy, Philadelphia Here I Come.*

STEHLIN, JACK. Born June 21, 1936 in Allentown, PA. Graduate Julliard. Debut 1984 OB in *Henry V,* followed by *Gravity Shoes, Julius Caesar, Romeo and Juliet, Phaedra Britannica, Don Juan of Seville, Uncle Vanya, Henry IV Part I, Life on Earth, Danton's Death, Casanova, Washington Square Moves, Richard II, Macbeth.*

STEIN-GRAINGER, STEVEN. Born Oct. 17, 1958 in Chicago, IL. Graduate N. Ill. U., Am. Consv. Music. Bdwy debut 1994 in *Show Boat.*

STEINHARDT, LEE. Born Sept. 4, 1959 in Philadelphia, PA. Graduate Brooklyn Col., NYU, ACT. Debut 1986 OB in *Beautiful Truth,* followed by *Twelfth Night, Stranger on the Road to Jericho, M Club, Tell Veronica.*

STENBORG, HELEN. Born Jan. 24, 1925 in Minneapolis, MN. Attended Hunter College. OB in *A Doll's House, A Month in the Country, Say Nothing, Rosmersholm, Rimers of Eldritch, Trial of the Catonsville 9, The Hot l Baltimore, Pericles, Elephant in the House, A Tribute to Lili Lamont, Museum, 5th of July, In the Recovery Lounge, The Chisholm Trail, Time Framed, Levitation, Enter a Free Man, Talley and Son, Tomorrow's Monday, Niedecker, Heaven on Earth, Daytrips, A Perfect Ganesh,* Bdwy in *Sheep on the Runway* (1970), *Da, A Life, Month in the Country.*

STENDER, DOUG. Born Sept. 14, 1942 in Nanticoke, PA. Graduate Princeton U., RADA. Bdwy debut 1973 in *Changing Room,* followed by *Run for Your Wife, The Visit,* OB in *New England Elective, Hamlet, Second Man, How He Lied to Her Husband, Bhutan, Clothes for a Summer Hotel.*

STEPHENSON, DON. Born Sept. 10, 1964 in Chattanooga, TN. Graduate U. Tenn. Debut 1986 OB in *Southern Lights,* followed by *Hypothetic, The Tavern, Young Rube, A Charles Dickens Christmas, Follies, Wonderful Town* (LC/NYCO).

STERN, ARLENE. Born Mar. 23 in Boston, MA. Graduate Northwestern U. Debut 1986 OB in *First Night of Pygmalion,* followed by *Final Curtain, Papa's Violin, Pericles, Ceremony of Innocence.*

STERNHAGEN, FRANCES. Born Jan. 13, 1932 in Washington, DC. Graduate Vassar Col. OB in *The Admirable Bashful, Thieves Carnival, Country Wife, Ulysses in Nighttown, Saintliness of Margery Kemp, The Room, A Slight Ache, Displaced Person Playboy of the Western World, The Prevalence of Mrs. Seal, Summer, Laughing Stock The Return of Herbert Bracewell, Little Murders, Driving Miss Daisy, Remembrance, Perfect Ganesh,* Bdwy in *Great Day in the Morning, The Right Honourable Gentleman,* with APA in *The Cocktail Party* and *CockaDoodle Dandy, The Sign in Sidney Brustein's Window, Enemies The Good Doctor, Equus, Angel, On Golden Pond, The Father, Growaups, Home Front, You Can't Take It With You, The Heiress.*

STEWART, GWEN. Born Sept. 5 in Newark, NJ. Debut 1986 OB in *Mama I Want to Sing,* followed by *God's Creation, Suds, Oedipus Private Eye,* Bdwy 1989 in *Starmites, Truly Blessed.*

STILLER, JERRY. Born June 8, 1931 in New York City. Graduate U. Syracuse. Debut 1953 OB in *Coriolanus,* followed by *Power and the Glory, Golden Apple, Measure for Measure, The Taming of the Shrew, The Carefree Tree, Diary of a Scoundrel, Romeo and Juliet, As You Like It, Two Gentlemen of Verona, Passione, Hurlyburly, Prairie/Shawl, Much Ado about Nothing,* Bdwy in *The Ritz* (1975), *Unexpected Guests, Passione, Hurlyburly, 3 Men on a Horse, What's Wrong with This Picture?.*

STONE, DANTON. Born in Queens, New York City. Debut 1976 OB in *Mrs. Murray's Farm,* followed by *In This Fallen City, Say Goodnight Gracie, Angels Fall, Balm in Gilead, Fortune's Fools,* Bdwy 1980 in *5th of July.*

STONEBURNER, SAM. Born Feb. 24, 1934 in Fairfax, VA. Graduate Georgetown U., AADA. Debut 1960 OB in *Ernest in Love,* followed by *Foreplay, Anyone Can Whistle, Twilight Cantata, Flaubert's Latest, Little White Lies,* Bdwy in *Different Times* (1972), *Bent, Macbeth* (1981), *The First, Six Degrees of Separation* (also OB).

STOUT, MARY. Born Apr. 8, 1952 in Huntington, WV. Graduate Marshall U. Debut 1980 OB in *Plain and Fancy,* followed by *The Sound of Music, Crisp, A Christmas Carol, Song for a Saturday, Prizes, Golden Apple, Identical Twins from Baltimore,* Bdwy in *Copperfield* (1981), *A Change in the Heir, My Favorite Year.*

STRAM, HENRY. Born Sept. 10, 1954 in Lafayette, IN. Attended Juilliard. Debut 1978 OB in *King Lear,* followed by *Shout and Twist, The Cradle Will Rock, Prison-made Tuxedos, Cinderella/Cendrillon, The Making of Americans, Black Sea Follies, Eddie Goes to Poetry City, A Bright Room Called Day, The Mind King, On the Open Road, My Head was a Sledge Hammer, Christina Alberta's Father, All's Well that Ends Well, Jack's Holiday.*

STRANSKY, CHARLES / CHUCK. Born Jan. 31, 1946 in Boston, MA. Graduate S. Ill. U., Brandeis U. Bdwy debut 1984 in *Glengarry Glen Ross,* followed by *Front Page,* OB in *Pantomime, Death Defying Acts.*

STRITCH, ELAINE. Born Feb. 2, 1925 in Detroit, MI. Bdwy debut 1946 in *Loco,* followed by *Made in Heaven, Angel in the Wings, Call Me Madam, Pal Joey, On Your Toes, Bus Stop, Sin of Pat Muldoon, Goldilocks, Sail Away, Who's Afraid of Virginia Woolf?, Wonderful Town* (CC), *Company, Love Letters, Show Boat* (1994), OB in *Private Lives, Rogers and Hart Revue.*

STUART, TOM. Born Mar. 19, 1970 in Berkeley, CA. Graduate AADA. Debut 1994 OB in *Fantasticks,* followed by *Dames at Sea, Party.*

SULLIVAN, BRAD. Born Nov. 18, 1931 in Chicago, IL. Graduate U. Me., Am. Th. Wing. Debut 1961 OB in *Red Roses for Me,* followed by *South Pacific, Hot House, Leavin' Cheyenne, Ballad of Soapy Smith, Cold Sweat, As You Like It, Somewhere I Have Never Travelled,* Bdwy in *Basic Training of Pavlo Hummel* (1977), *Working, Wake of Jamie Foster, Caine Mutiny Court Martial, Orpheus Descending, On the Waterfront.*

SULLIVAN, K. T. Born Oct. 31, 1953 in Coalgate, OK. Graduate Okla. U. Bdwy debut 1989 in *3 Penny Opera,* followed by *Gentlemen Prefer Blondes* (1995), OB 1992 in *A ... My Name Is Still Alice.*

SWARBRICK, CAROL. Born Mar. 20, 1948 in Inglewood, CA. Graduate UCLA, NYU. Debut 1971 OB in *Drat!,* followed by *Glorious Age,* Bdwy in *42nd St., Whoopee!, Side by Side By Sondheim, Gentlemen Prefer Blondes* (1995).

TALBERTH, KENNETH. Born June 22, 1956 in Boston, MA. Graduate NYU. Debut 1981 OB in *Total Eclipse,* followed by *Henry IV Part I, The Misanthrope, Stray Dog Story, A Winter's Tale, After the Rain, King Lear, Emperor of the Moon, Lucky Man.*

TALBOT, SHARON. Born Mar. 12, 1949 in Denver, CO. Graduate Denver U. Bdwy debut 1975 in *Musical Jubilee,* OB in *Man with a Load of Mischief, Curtain Call, Royal Gambit, Edsel was a Mistake, Angel and Dragon, Alph, JB, Goering, Holy Ghosts, Housewives Cantata, Legend of Sharon Shashanobah.*

TALCOTT, LINDA. Born July 5, 1960 in Edwards AFB, CA. Attended San Diego State U. Bdwy debut 1989 in *Jerome Robbins' Broadway,* followed by *Goodbye Girl, Beauty and the Beast.*

TALMAN, ANN. Born Sept. 13, 1957 in Welch, WV. Graduate Penn. St. U. Debut 1980 OB in *What's So Beautiful about a Sunset over Prairie Avenue?,* followed by *Louisiana Summer, Winterplay, Prairie Avenue, Broken Eggs, Octoberfest, We're Home, Yours Anne, Songs on a Shipwrecked Sofa, House Arrest, One Act Festival, Freud's House,* Bdwy in *Little Foxes* (1981), *House of Blue Leaves, Some Americans Abroad* (also OB), *Better Days.*

TARANTINA, BRIAN. Born Mar. 27, 1959 in New York City. Debut 1980 OB in *Innocent Thoughts and Harmless Intentions,* followed by *Time Framed, Fables for Friends, Balm in Gilead, V & V Only, Portrait of My Bikini, Shades of Grey,* Bdwy in *Angels Fall,* for which he received a 1983 Theatre World Award, *Biloxi Blues, Boys of Winter.*

TATUM, BILL. Born May 6, 1947 in Philadelphia, PA. Graduate Catawba Col. Bdwy debut 1971 in *Man of La Mancha,* OB in *Missouri Legend, Time of the Cuckoo, Winner Take All, Last Girl Singer.*

TAYLOR, MYRA. Born July 9, 1960 in Ft. Motte, SC. Graduate Yale U. Debut 1985 OB in *Dennis,* followed by *The Tempest, Black Girl, Marathon '86, Phantasie, Walking the Dead, I Am a Man, Marathon Dancing, Come Down Burning,* Bdwy in *A Streetcar Named Desire, Mule Bone, Chronicle of a Death Foretold.*

TAYLOR, SCOTT. Born June 29, 1962 in Milan, TN. Attended Mis. St. U. Bdwy in *Wind in the Willows* (1985), followed by *Cats, Crazy for You.*

TAYLOR-MORRIS, MAXINE. Born June 26 in New York City. Graduate NYU. Debut 1977 OB in *Counsellor-at-Law,* followed by *Manny, Devil's Disciple, Fallen Angels, Billy Liar, Uncle Vanya, What the Butler Saw, Subject Was Roses, Goodnight Grandpa, Thirteenth Chair, Comedy of Errors, Second Avenue, One Act Festival, Midsummer, Broken English.*

TEMPERLEY, STEPHEN. Born July 29, 1949 in London, England. Attended AADA. Debut 1968 OB in *Invitation to a Beheading,* followed by *Henry IV Parts I & II, Up Against It,* Bdwy in *Crazy for You* (1992).

TESTA, MARY. Born June 4, 1955 in Philadelphia, PA. Attended URI. Debut 1979 OB in *In Trousers,* followed by *Company, Life Is Not a Doris Day Movie, Not-So-New Faces of 1982, American Princess, Mandrake, 4 One-Act Musicals, Next, Please!, Daughters, One-Act Festival, The Knife, Young Playwrights Festival, Tiny Mommy, Finnegan's Funeral and Ice Cream Shop, Peter Breaks Through, Lucky Stiff, 1-2-3-4-5, Scapin, Hello Muddah Hello Faddah, Broken English,* Bdwy in *Barnum* (1980), *Marilyn,*

The Rink.

THOLE, CYNTHIA. Born Sept. 21, 1957 in Silver Springs, MD. Graduate Butler U. Debut 1982 OB in *Nymph Errant,* followed by *Christmas Carol,* Bdwy 1985 in *42nd St., Me and My Girl, Meet Me in St. Louis, Nick & Nora.*

THOMAS, MARLO. Born Nov. 21, 1938 in Detroit, MI. Graduate US Cal. Bdwy debut 1974 in *Thieves,* followed by *Social Security, Shadow Box* (1994).

THOMAS, RAY ANTHONY. Born Dec. 19, 1956 in Kentwood, LA. Graduate U. Tex./El Paso. Debut 1981 OB in *Escape to Freedom,* followed by *The Sun Gets Blue, Blues for Mr. Charlie, Hunchback of Notre Dame, Ground People, The Weather Outside, One Act Festival, Caucasian Chalk Circle, Virgin Molly, Black Eagles, Distant Fires, Shaker Heights, The Lights, Dancing on Moonlight.*

THOMPSON, JENN. Born Dec. 13, 1967 in New York City. Debut 1975 OB in *Wooing of Lady Sunday,* followed by *Cowboy Jack Street, The Wobblies, Looie, One Time One Place, You're a Good Man Charlie Brown, I Ought to Be in Pictures, Frankenstein, Wedding of the Siamese Twins,* Bdwy in *Annie* (1978), *The Heiress* (1995).

THOMPSON, JENNIFER LAURA. Born Dec. 5, 1969 in Southfield, MI. Graduate U. Mi., AADA. Debut 1994 OB in *A Doll's Life.*

THOMPSON, RICHARD. Born Sept. 25, 1963 in Kinsha, Zaire. Graduate Georgetown U., Catholic U. Debut 1992 OB in *Baltimore Waltz,* followed by Bdwy 1995 in *The Heiress.*

THORNE, RAYMOND. Born Nov. 27, 1934 in Lackawanna, NY. Graduate U. Ct. Debut 1966 OB in *Man with a Load of Mischief,* followed by *Rose, Dames at Sea, Love Course, Blue Boys, Jack and Jill, Annie Warbucks, New Yorkers,* Bdwy in *Annie* (1977), *Teddy and Alice.*

TICOTIN, NANCY. Born Sept. 4, 1957 in New York City. Bdwy debut 1980 in *West Side Story,* followed by *Jerome Robbins' Broadway, Damn Yankees,* OB in *The King and I,* (CC), *A... My Name is Still Alice.*

TIRELLI, JAIME. Born Mar. 4, 1945 in New York City. Attended U. Mundial, AADA. Debut 1975 OB in *Rubbers, Yanks 3 Detroit 0,* followed by *Sun Always Shines on the Cool, Body Bags, Bodega, Blade to the Heat,* Bdwy in *In the Summer House* (1993), *Chronicle of a Death Foretold.*

TOBIE, ELLEN. Born Mar. 26 in Chambersburg, PA. Graduate Ohio Wesleyan U., Wayne St. U. Debut 1981 OB in *Chisholm Trail Went Through Here,* followed by *Welded, Talking With, The Entertainer, Equal Wrights, Remembrance,* Bdwy 1995 in *Rose Tattoo.*

TOMEI, MARISA. Born Dec. 4, 1964 in Brooklyn, NY. Attended Boston U., NYU. Debut 1986 OB in *Daughters* for which she received a Theatre World Award, followed by *Class 1 Acts, Evening Star, What the Butler Saw, Marathon '88, Sharon and Billy, Chelsea Walls, Summer Winds, Comedy of Errors, Fat Men in Skirts, Slavs!*

TONER, THOMAS. Born May 25, 1928 in Homestead, PA. Graduate UCLA. Bdwy debut 1973 in *Tricks,* followed by *The Good Doctor, All Over Town, The Elephant Man, California Suite, A Texas Trilogy, The Inspector General, Me and My Girl, The Secret Garden,* OB in *Pericles, The Merry Wives of Windsor, A Midsummer Night's Dream, Richard III, My Early Years, Life and Limb, Measure for Measure, Little Footsteps, Saturday Mourning Cartoons.*

TRACEY, OLIVIA. Born July 11, 1960 in Dublin, Ire. Graduate U. College/Dublin, Actors Centre/London. Debut 1995 OB in *Donahue Sisters.*

TRUCCO, ED. Born June 3, 1963 in New York City. Attended HB Studio. Debut 1988 OB in *Ariano,* followed by *Boiler Room, Royal Affair.*

TSOUTSOUVAS, SAM. Born Aug. 20, 1948 in Santa Barbara, CA. Attended U. Cal., Juilliard. Debut 1969 OB in *Peer Gynt,* followed by *Twelfth Night, Timon of Athens, Cymbeline, School for Scandal, The Hostage, Women Beware Women, Lower Depths, Emigre, Hello Dali, The Merchant of Venice, The Leader, The Bald Soprano, The Taming of the Shrew, Gus & Al, Tamara, The Man Who Shot Lincoln, Puppetmaster of Lodz, Richard III, Snowing at Delphi, Richard II, Phaedra,* Bdwy in *Three Sisters, Measure for Measure, Beggar's Opera, Scapin, Dracula, Our Country's Good, The Misanthrope.*

TUCCI, MARIA. Born June 19, 1941 in Florence, Italy. Attended Actors Studio. Bdwy debut 1963 in *Milk Train Doesn't Stop Here Anymore,* followed by *The Rose Tattoo, The Little Foxes, Cuban Thing, Great White Hope, School for Wives, Lesson from Aloes, Kingdoms, Requiem for a Heavyweight, Night of the Iguana,* OB in *Corruption in the Palace of Justice, Five Evenings, Trojan Women, White Devil, Horseman Pass By, Yerma, Shepherd of Avenue B., The Gathering, Man for All Seasons, Love Letters, Substance of Fire, A Fair Country.*

TUCKER, SHONA. Born in Louisville, KY. Graduate Northwestern U., NYU. Debut 1989 OB in *Investigation of the Murder of El Salvador,* followed by *A Light from the East, Diary of an African American, Light Shining in Buckinghamshire, Caucasian Chalk Circle, Greeks, Marvin's Room, From*

the Mississippi Delta, Come Down Burning, Othello, A Doll House.

TUMEO, VINCENT. Born Aug. 17 in Columbus, OH. Graduate Columbus Col. Bdwy debut 1994 in *Sunset Blvd.*

TURNER, KATHLEEN. Born June 19, 1954 in Springfield, MO. Graduate So. West Mo. St. U. Bdwy debut 1978 in *Gemini,* followed by *Cat on a Hot Tin Roof* (1990) for which she received a Theatre World Award, *Indiscretions.*

TURQUE, MIMI (aka Strongpin). Born Sept. 30, 1939 in Brooklyn, New York City. Graduate Brooklyn Col. Bdwy debut 1945 in *Carousel,* followed by *Seeds in the Wind, The Enchanted, Cry of the Peacock, Anniversary Waltz, Carnival, Man of LaMancha, Threepenny Opera, Kiss of the Spider Woman,* OB in *Johnny Summit, The Dybbuk, Romeo and Juliet, Happy Journey, God Bless You Mr. Rosewater, 13, Tale of Two Toms, The Misanthrope, The Haggadah, A Bintel Brief, The Chosen.*

TUTHILL, CHARLES. Born Nov. 11, 1961 in Cleveland, OH. Graduate NYU. Debut 1992 OB in *Ten Blocks on the Camino Real,* followed by *Night and Her Stars.*

TWAINE, MICHAEL. Born Nov. 1, 1936 in Lawrence, NY. Graduate Oh. St. U. Bdwy debut 1956 in *Mr. Roberts,* OB in *Kill the One-Eyed Man, Duchess of Malfi, Recess, Empire Builders, Pictures at an Exhibition, Holy Heist, The Seagull: The Hamptons, As You Like It, Last Sortie, Yellow Fever.*

VAN ARK, JOAN. Born June 16, 1943 in New York City. Attended Yale U., Actors Studio. Bdwy debut 1965 in *Barefoot in the Park,* followed by *School for Wives,* for which she received a 1971 Theatre World Award, *Rules of the Game,* OB in *3 Tall Women* (1995).

VAN DYCK, JENNIFER. Born Dec. 23, 1962 in St. Andrews, Scotland. Graduate Brown U. Debut OB 1977 in *Gus and Al,* followed by *Marathon '88, Secret Rapture, Earth and Sky, Man in His Underwear, Cheever Evening,* Bdwy in *Secret Rapture, Two Shakespearean Acrors, Dancing at Lughnasa.*

VAN TREUREN, MARTIN. Born Dec. 6, 1952 in Hawthorne, NJ. Graduate Montclair St. Col. Debut 1978 OB in *Oklahoma!,* followed by *The Miser, Allegro in Concert, Christmas Carol.*

VARON, CHARLIE. Born in New York City. on Nov. 1, 1958. Debut 1995 OB in *Rush Limbaugh in Night School.*

VENNEMA, JOHN C. Born Aug. 24, 1948 in Houston, TX. Graduate Princeton U., LAMA, Bdwy debut 1976 in *The Royal Family,* followed by *The Elephant Man, Otherwise Engaged,* OB in *Loot, Statements after an Arrest, The Biko Inquest, No End of Blame, In Celebration, Custom of the Country, The Basement, A Slight Ache, Young Playwrights Festival, Danday Dick, Nasty Little Secrets, Mountain, Light Up the Sky, Joined at the Head, Quarrel of Sparrows, The Illusion, After-Play.*

VENTRISS, JENNIE. Born Aug. 7, 1935 in Chicago, IL. Graduate DePaul U. Debut 1954 OB in *Ludlow Fair,* followed by *I Can't Keep Running in Place, Lautrec, The Contest, Warren G, Mirage, Look after Lulu, Between Daylight and Boonville, Bodies Rest and Motion, Flags Unfurled,* Bdwy 1966 in *Luv, Prisoner of Second Ave., Gemini, Sherlock's Last Case, Some Americans Abroad, On Borrowed Time.*

VICKERS, LARRY. Born June 8, 1947 in Harrisonburg, VA. Attended Howard U. Bdwy debut 1970 in *Purlie,* followed by *Shirley MacLaine at the Palace, Shirley MacLaine on Broadway, Jesus Christ Superstar* (1995).

VIDNOVIC, MARTIN. Born Jan. 4, 1948 in Falls Church, VA. Graduate Cinn. Consv. Of Music. Debut 1972 OB in *The Fantasticks,* followed by *Lies and Legends,* Bdwy in *Home Sweet Homer* (1976), *The King and I, Oklahoma!* (1979), *Brigadoon* (1980), *Baby, Some Enchanted Evening* (also OB), *Guys and Dolls* (1994).

VIRTA, RAY. Born June 18, 1958 in L'Anse, MI. Debut 1982 OB in *Twelfth Night,* followed by *The Country Wife, The Dublilners, Pericles, Tartuffe, The Taming of the Shrew, No One Dances, Jacques and His Master, Progress, Snowing at Delphi, The Eye of the Beholder, King Lear.*

VIVONA, JEROME. Born Mar. 7, 1967 in Bayville, NY. Attended Quinnipac Col., Ind. U., Nassau CC. Bdwy debut 1994 in *Guys and Dolls,* followed by *How to Succeed...* (1995).

WAGER, MICHAEL. Born Apr. 29, 1925 in New York City. Graduate Harvard U. Bdwy debut 1949 in *Streetcar Named Desire,* followed by *Small Hours, Bernadine, Merchant of Venice, Misalliance, Remarkable Mr. Pennypacker, Othello, Henry IV, St. Joan, Firstborn, Cradle Will Rock, Three Sisters, Cuban Thing,* OB in *Noontide, Brecht on Brecht, Sunset, Penny Friend, Trelawny of the Wells, Taming of the Shrew, Inn at Lydda, Richard III, Rhinestone, Madwoman of Chaillot.*

WALBYE, KAY. Born in Ft. Collins, CO. Attended Kan. St. U. Debut 1984 OB in *Once on a Summer Day,* followed by *Majestic Kid, Gin and Bitters,* Bdwy 1989 in *Run for Your Wife, Rose Tattoo* (1995).

WALKEN, CHRISTOPHER. Born Mar. 31, 1943 in Astoria NY. Attended Hofstra U. Bdwy debut 1958 in *J.B.,* followed by *High Spirits, Baker Street, Lion in Winter, Measure for Measure, Rose Tattoo* (CC) for which he received

Jimmy Noonan

Marcell Rosenblatt

Milo O'Shea

Mercedes Ruehl

Ken Page

Jackie Sanders

Rafael Petlock

Margo Skinner

Lee Roy Reams

Tia Speros

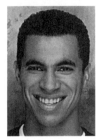

Raymond Rodriguez

Florence Stanley

Douglas Santiago

Elaine Stritch

Mark Setlock

Sharon Talbot

Tom Stuart

Jennifer Van Dyck

Vincent Tumeo

Jennie Ventriss

Ray Walker

Lauren Ward

James Waterston

Leigh-Anne Wencker

Frank Whaley

Lynne Wintersteller

Walter Willison

Jo Anne Worley

Michael Winther

Karen Ziemba

a 1967 Theatre World Award, *Unknown Soldier and His Wife, Rosencrantz and Guildenstern Are Dead, Scenes from American Life, Cymbeline, Enemies, Plough and the Stars, Merchant of Venice, The Tempest, Troilus and Cressida, Macbeth, Sweet Bird of Youth,* OB in *Best Foot Forward* (1962), *Iphigenia in Aulis, Lemon Sky, Kid Champion, Sea Gull, Cinders, Hurlyburly, House of Blue Leaves, Love Letters, Coriolanus, Othello, Him* (which he wrote).

WALKER, RAY. Born Aug. 13, 1963 in St. Johnsbury, VT. Graduate NYU. Debut 1985 OB in *Christmas Spectacular,* followed by *Merrily We Roll Along, Chess,* Bdwy 1987 in *Les Miserables, Grease.*

WALLER, KENNETH. Born Apr. 12, 1945 in Atlanta, GA. Graduate Piedmont Col. Debut OB 1976 in *Boys from Syracuse,* Bdwy in *Sarava* (1979), *Onward Victoria, Me and My Girl, Phantom of the Opera.*

WALLNAU, COLLEEN SMITH. Born June 28, 1948 in Trenton, NJ. Graduate Trenton St.Col., Rutgers U. Debut 1993 OB in *Through Darkest Ohio,* Bdwy in *Crazy for You* (1994).

WALSH, JUANITA. Born May 3, 1951 in Milwaukee, WI. Graduate Stephens Col. Debut 1980 OB in *Mo' Tea Miss Ann,* followed by *This Land Is Bright, Modern Sanctuary, All on Her Own, The Bookworm, Another Part of the Forest, Little Foxes, Doves on a Lark.*

WALTER, WENDY. Born Nov. 13, 1961 in Dallas, TX. Attended U. Kan. Bdwy debut 1994 in *Sunset Blvd.*

WANDS, SUSAN. Born Oct. 20 in Denver, CO. Graduate U. Wash. Debut 1985 OB in *Whining and Dining,* followed by *And They Dance Real Slow in Jackson, Henry IV Parts I & 2, Talking Pictures.*

WANN, JIM. Born Aug. 30, 1948 in Chattanooga, TN. Graduate UNC. Debut 1975 OB in *Diamond Studs,* followed by *King Mackerel and the Blues Are Running,* Bdwy 1982 in *Pump Boys and Dinettes.*

WARD, FRED. Born in 1943 in San Diego, CA. Debut 1994 OB in *Simpatico.*

WARD, JANET. Born Feb. 19 in New York City. Attended Actors Studio. Bdwy debut 1945 in *Dream Girl,* followed by *Anne of a Thousand Days, Detective Story, King of Friday's Men, Middle of the Night, Miss Lonelyhearts, J.B., Cheri, The Egg, Impossible Years, Of Love Remembered,* OB in *Chapparal, The Typist, The Tiger, Summertree, Dreams of a Blacklisted Actor, Crusing Speed 600 MPH, One Flew over the Cuckoo's Nest, Love Gotta Come by Saturday Night, Home Is the Hero, Love Death Plays, Olympic Park, Hillibilly Wives, Q.E.D., Yello Dog Contract, Laura Dennis.*

WARD, LAUREN. Born June 19, 1970 in Lincoln, NE. Graduate NC School of Arts. Bdwy debut 1994 in *Carousel,* OB in *Jack's Holiday.*

WARING, WENDY. Born Dec. 7, 1960 in Melrose, MA. Attended Emerson Col., Debut 1987 OB in *Wish You Were Here,* Bdwy in *Legs Diamond* (1988), *Will Rogers Follies, Crazy for You.*

WASHINGTON, SHARON. Born Sept. 12, 1959 in New York City. Graduate Dartmouth Col., Yale U. Debut 1988 OB in *Coriolanus,* followed by *Cymbeline, Richard III, The Balcony, Caucasian Chalk Circle, Before It Hit Home, Radical Mystique.*

WATT, GREGORY. Born Mar. 28, 1963 in Framingham, MA. Graduate U. Mich., Am. Consv. Th. Bdwy debut 1994 in *Blood Brothers.*

WATERSTON, JAMES. Born in New York City. Debut 1993 OB in *Another Time,* followed by *Good Evening* (dir).

WEAVER, FRITZ. Born Jan. 19, 1926 in Pittsburgh, PA. Graduate U. Chicago, Bdwy debut 1955 in *Chalk Garden* for which he received a Theatre World Award, followed by *Protective Custody, Miss Lonelyhearts, All American, Lorenzo, The White House, Baker Street, Child's Play, Absurd Person Singular, Angels Fall, The Crucible* (1991), *A Christmas Carol,* OB in *The Way of the World, White Devil, Doctor's Dilemma, Family Reunion, Power and the Glory, Great God Brown, Peer Gynt, Henry IV, My Fair Lady* (CC), *Lincoln, Biko Inquest, The Price, Dialogue for Lovers, A Tale Told, Time Framed, Wrong Turn at Lungfish, The Professional.*

WEBER, JAKE. Born Mar. 12, 1963 in London, Eng. Graduate Middlebury Col. Juilliard Debut 1988 OB in *Road,* followed by *Twelfth Night, Maids of Honor, Richard III, Big Funk, Othello, Mad Forest, As You Like It* (CP) *Othello, Radical Mystique,* Bdwy in *A Small Family Business* (1992).

WEIL, SEAN. Born May 28, 1961 in Bronx, NY. Attended Sienna College. Debut 1991 in *Nebraska,* followed by *Heart of Earth, Dalton's Back, Superman is Dead, Performance.*

WEISS, JEFF. Born in 1940 in Allentown, PA. Debut 1986 OB in *Hamlet,* followed by *Front Page, Casanova, Hot Keys,* Bdwy in *Macbeth,* (1988), *Our Town, Mastergate, Face Value, Real Inspector Hound/15 Minute Hamlet, Carousel* (1994).

WELLS, CHRISTOPHER. Born June 18, 1955 in Norwalk, CT. Graduate Amherst Col. Debut 1981 OB in *Big Apple Country,* followed by *Broadway Juxebox, Savage Amusement, Overrules, Heart of Darkness, Ancient History, One Act Festival,* Bdwy 1985 in *Harrigan 'n'Hart, Broadway, Teddy and Alice, Crazy for You.*

WENCKER, LEIGH-ANNE. Born June 16 in St. Louis, MO. Graduate Webster U. Bdwy debut 1993 in *Crazy for You.*

WESTENBERG, ROBERT. Born Oct. 26, 1953 in Miami Beach, FL. Graduate U. Cal./Fresco. Debut 1981 OB in *Henry IV Part I,* followed by *Hamlet, Death of von Richthofen, 3 Birds Alighting on a Field,* Bdwy in *Zorba* (1983) for which he received a Theatre World Award, *Sunday in the Park with George, Into the Woods, Les Miserables, Secret Garden, Abe Lincoln in Illinois, Christmas Carol.*

WESTON, CELIA. Born in South Carolina. Attended Salem Col., NC School of Arts. Bdwy debut 1979 in *Loose Ends,* OB in *Bargains, Laura Dennis.*

WETHERALL, JACK. Born Aug. 5, 1950 in Sault Ste. Marie, Can. Graduate Glendon Col., York U. Bdwy debut 1979 in *Elephant Man,* followed by OB in *Tamara, Henry VI.*

WHALEY, FRANK. Born July 20, 1963 in Syracuse, NY. Graduate SUNY/Albany. Debut 1986 OB in *Tigers Wild,* followed by *The Years, Good Evening, Veins and Thumbtacks, Hesh, Great Unwashed.*

WHEELER, TIMOTHY. Born July 21, 1957 in Waterville, ME. Debut 1993 OB in *Oedipus the King,* followed by *Game of Love and Chance, Silence Cunning Exile.*

WHITE, AMELIA. Born Sept. 14, 1954 in Nottingham, England. Attended London Central School. Debut 1984 OB in *The Accrington Pals* for which she received a Theatre World Award, followed by *American Bagpipes,* Bdwy in *Crazy for You* (1992), *The Heiress* (1995).

WHITE, JANE. Born Oct. 30, 1922 in New York City. Attended Smith Col. Bdwy debut 1942 in *Strange Fruit,* followed by *Climate of Eden, Take a Giant Step, Jane Eyre, Once Upon a Mattress* (also OB), *Cuban Thing,* OB in *Razzle Dazzle, Insect Comedy, Power and Glory, Hop Signor, Trojan Women, Iphigenia in Aulis, Cymbeline, Burnt Flowerbed, Rosmersholm, Jane White Who?, Ah Men, Lola, Madwoman of Chaillot, Vivat! Vivat! Regina!, King John, Tropical Breeze Hotel, Petrified Prince.*

WHITE, LILLIAS D. Born July 21, 1951 in Brooklyn, New York City. Graduate NYCC. Debut 1975 OB in *Solidad Tetrad,* followed by *The Life, Romance in Hard Times, Back to Bacharach,* Bdwy in *Barnum* (1981), *Dreamgirls, Rock n' Roll: The First 5000 Years, Once on This Island, Carrie, How to Succeed…* (1995).

WHITE, TERRI. Born Jan. 24, 1953 in Palo Alto, CA. Attended USIU. Debut 1976 OB in *The Club,* followed by *Juba, Nunsense 2,* Bdwy in *Barnum* (1980), *Ain't Misbehavin', Welcome to the Club.*

WHITEHURST, SCOTT. Born Dec. 24, 1962 in Indianapolis, IN. Graduate Columbia U., Rutgers U. Debut 1991 OB in *Black Eagles,* followed by *Gunplay, Incommunicado.*

WHITTON, MARGARET (formerly Peggy). Born Nov. 30 in Philadelphia, PA. Debut 1973 OB in *Baba Goya,* followed by *Arthur, Nourish the Beast, Another Language, Chinchilla, Othello, The Art of Dining, One Tiger to a Hill, Henry IV Parts 1 and 2, Don Juan, My Uncle Sam, Aunt Dan and Lemon, Ice Cream and Hot Fudge, The Merry Wives of Windsor, Silence Cunning Exile, Three Viewings,* Bdwy in *Steaming* (1982).

WIDDOES, KATHLEEN. Born Mar. 21, 1939 in Wilmington, DE. Attended Paris Theatre de Natoons. Bdwy debut 1958 in *The Firstborn,* followed by *World of Suzy Wong, Much Ado about Nothing, Importance of Being Earnest, Brighton Beach Memoirs, Hamlet,* OB in *Three Sisters, The Maids, You Can't Take It with You, To Clothe the Naked, World War 2, Beggars Opera, As You Like It, Midsummer Night's Dream, Hamlet, Tower of Evil, Truth Teller.*

WILKS, ELAYNE. Born Sept. 25, 1933 in Bronx, NY. Graduate Adelphi U., NYU. Debut 1995 OB in *Baby Luv.*

WILLEY, CHARLES. Born Sept. 18, 1956 in Abington, PA. Graduate Syracuse U. Debut 1991 OB in *Necktie Breakfast,* followed by *Battery, Holy Note, Blue Window, Single and Proud, The Firebugs.*

WILLIAMS, CARLA RENATA. Born Sept. 16, 1961 in Cherry Point, NC. Graduate Howard U. Debut 1992 OB in *The Balmyard,* followed by *Back to Bacharach,* Bdwy 1995 in *How to Succeed…*

WILLIAMS, DATHAN B. Born Oct. 30, 1960 in Wash., DC. Graduate Wheeling Jesuit Col., W.Va. U. Bdwy debut 1994 in *Show Boat* (1994).

WILLIAMSON, RUTII. Born Jan. 25, 1954 in Baltimore, MD. Graduate U. Md. Bdwy debut 1981 in *Annie,* followed by *Smile, Guys and Dolls,* OB in *Preppies, Bodo, A Helluva Town.*

WILLISON, WALTER. Born June 24, 1947 in Monterey Park, CA. Bdwy debut 1970 in *Norman Is That You?,* followed by *Two by Two* for which he received a Theatre World Award, *Wild and Wonderful, Celebration of Richard Rodgers, Pippin, Tribute to Joshua Logan, Tribute to George Abbott, Grand Hotel, Christmas Carol,* OB in *South Pacific in Concert, They Say It's Wonderful, Broadway Scandals of 1928* and *Options,* both of which he wrote, *Aldersgate '88.*

WILLS, RAY. Born Sept. 14, 1960 in Santa Monica, CA. Graduate Wichita St. U., Brandeis U. Debut 1988 OB in *Side by Side by Sondheim*, followed by *Kiss me Quick, Grand Tour, The Cardigans, The Rothschilds, Little Me, A Backers Audition, All in the Timing*, Bdwy in *Anna Karenina* (1993).

WINDE, BEATRICE. Born Jan. 6 in Chicago, IL. Debut 1966 OB in *In White America*, followed by *June Bug Graduates Tonight, Strike Heaven on the Face, Divine Comedy, Crazy Horse, My Mother My Father and Me, Steal Away, The Actress, Richard II, 1-2-3-4-5, Le Bourgeois Gentilhomme, American Plan, Night Seasons, Young Man from Atlanta*, Bdwy 1971 in *Ain't Supposed to Die a Natural Death* for which she received a Theatre World Award.

WING, VIRGINIA. Born Nov. 9 in Marks, MS. Graduate Miss. Col. Debut 1989 OB in *Two by Two*, followed by *Food and Shelter, Cambodia Agonistes, America Dreaming*.

WINTERSTELLER, LYNNE. Born Sept. 18, 1955 in Sandusky, OH. Graduate U. Md. Bdwy debut 1982 in *Annie*, followed by *Grand Night for Singing*, OB in *Gifts of the Magi* (1984), *Rise of David Levinsky, Nunsense, Closer Than Ever, Music in the Air in Concert, I Sent a Letter to My Love*.

WINTHER, MICHAEL. Born Feb. 1, 1962 in San Francisco, CA. Graduate Williams Col. Debut 1988 OB in *Tony 'n' Tina's Wedding*, followed by *Forever Plaid, Hapgood*, Bdwy 1989 in *Artist Descending the Staircase*.

WISEMAN, JOSEPH. Born May 15, 1919 in Montreal, Canada. Attended CCNY. Bdwy in *Journey to Jerusalem, Abe Lincoln in Illinois, Candle in the Wind, The Three Sisters, Storm Operation, Joan of Lorraine, Anthony and Cleopatra, Detective Story, That Lady, King Lear, Golden Boy, The Lark, Zalmen or the Madness God, The Tenth Man*, OB in *Marco Cillions, Incident at Vichy, In the Matter of Robert Oppenheimer, Enemies, Duchess of Malfi, Last Analysis, The Lesson, The Golem, Unfinished Stories, Slavs!*

WOJDA, JOHN. Born Feb. 19, 1957 in Detroit, MI. Attended U. Mich. Bdwy debut 1982 in *Macbeth*, followed by *Merchant of Venice, Two Shakespearean Actors*, OB in *Natural Disasters, Merchant of Venice, Coming of Mr. Pine, Henry IV Parts 1 & 2, Crackdancing, Black, Hnery VI, Ecstacy*.

WOLF, CATHERINE. Born May 25 in Abington, PA. Attended Carnegie-Tech U., Neighborhood Playhouse. Bdwy debut 1976 in *The Innocents*, followed by *Otherwise Engaged, An Inspector Calls*, OB in *A Difficult Burning, I Can't Keep Running in Place, Cloud 9, The Importance of Being Earnest, Miami*.

WONG, B.D. Born Oct. 24, 1962 in San Francisco, CA. Debut 1981 OB in *Androcles and the Lion*, followed by *Applause, The Tempest, Language of Their Own*, Bdwy in *M. Butterfly* for which he received a Theatre World Award, *Face Value*.

WOODESON, NICHOLAS. Born in England. Graduate RADA. Debut 1978 OB in *Strawberry Fields*, followed by *Taming of the Shrew, Backers Audition, Art of Success*, Bdwy 1978 in *Man and Superman, Piaf, Good, Inspector Calls*.

WOODMAN, BRANCH. Born Aug. 31, 1962 in Upland, CA. Attended Chaffee Col., Cal. St. U./Fullerton. Debut 1989 OB in *Out of This World*, Bdwy 1994 in *Crazy for You*.

WORKMAN, JASON. Born Oct. 9, 1962 in Omaha, Neb. Attended U. Ky., Goodman School. Bdwy debut 1989 in *Meet Me in St. Louis* for which he received a Theatre World Award, followed by *Damn Yankees* (1994), OB in *Haunted Host, Safe Sex, Music in the Air in Concert*.

WORLEY, JO ANN. Born Sept. 6, 1937 in Lowell, IN. Attended CCLA, Pasadena Playhouse. Bdwy debut 1961 in *Billy Barnes Revue*, followed by *Prince of Central Park, Grease* (1994), OB in *That Thing at the Cherry Lane, Hotel Passionata, Mad Show, Second City Revue*.

WROE, CRAIG. Born Apr. 8, 1958 in Los Angeles, CA. Graduate Loyola U., Catholic U. Debut 1989 OB in *The Tempest*, followed by *Othello, Measure for Measure, Winter's Tale, 2*.

WYLIE, JOHN. Born Dec. 14, 1925 in Peacock, TX. Graduate No. Tex. St. U. Debut 1987 OB in *Lucky Spot*, followed by *Venetian Twins*, Bdwy 1989 in *Born Yesterday, Crand Hotel*.

XIFO, RAYMOND. Born Sept. 3, 1942 in Newark, NJ. Graduate Don Bosco College. Debut 1974 OB in *The Tempest*, followed by *Frogs, My Uncle Sam, Shlemiel the First, Murder of Crows, Dracula, Threepenny Opera, Phaedra*, Bdwy in *City of Angels* (1989), *3 Penny Opera, Black Comedy*.

YANCEY, KIM. Born Sept. 25, 1959 in New York City. Graduate CCNY. Debut 1978 OB in *Why Lillie Won't Spin*, followed by *Escape to Freedom, Dacha, Blues for Mr. Charlie, American Dreams, Ties That Bind, Walking Through, Raisin in the Sun, Don Juan of Seville, Heliotrope Bouquet, Come Down Burning, Dancing on Moonlight*.

YANO, YOSHI. Born Nov. 10, 1959 in Gifu, Japan. Attended Kyoto Indus U. OB includes *In My Father's House, Twilight Crane, Story of Three Women, Exchange Cafe Mimosa, American Ballroom Theatre*.

ZADORA, PIA. Born in 1954 in Hoboken, NJ. Bdwy debut 1961 in *Midgie Purvis*, followed by *Fiddler on the Roof, Applause, Crazy for You*.

ZERKLE, GREG. Born Aug. 19, 1957 in Wisconsin. Graduate U. Wis., U. Washington. Debut 1986 OB in *Sherlock Holmes and the Redheaded League*, followed by *Bittersuite, Juba, Richard II*, Bdwy in *Into the Woods* (1988), *Grand Hotel, Secret Garden, Kiss of the Spider Woman*.

ZIEMBA, KAREN. Born Nov. 12 in St. Joseph, MO. Graduate U. Akron. Debut 1981 OB in *Seesaw*, followed by *I Married an Angel, Sing for Your Supper, 50 Million Frenchmen, And the World Goes Round, 110 in the Shade* (NYCO/LC), *A Grand Night for Singing*, Bdwy in *Crazy for You* (1994), *Allegro in Concert, Crazy for You*.

ZINN, RANDOLYN. Born Aug. 23, 1952 in Hamilton, OH. Graduate Sawyer Col. Bdwy debut 1971 in *The Rothschilds*, OB in *1951, Frank Frank*.

ZISKIE, DANIEL. Born in Detroit MI. Debut 1970 OB in *Second City*, followed by *Sea Gull, Ballymurohy, The Rivals, Listen to the Lions, Halloween, Bandit, Mamet Plays, At Home, The Castaways, Marathon '93, Bed and Breakfast, Flyboy*, Bdwy in *Mornings at 7, Breakfast with Les and Bess, I'm Not Rappaport*.

ZISKIE, KURT. Born Apr. 16, 1956 in Oakland, CA. Graduate Stanford U., Neighborhood Playhouse. Debut 1985 OB in *A Flash of Lightning*, followed by *Ulysses in Nighttown, Three Sisters, Marathon '92, Cincinnati Saint, Beaux Stratagem, King Lear*, Bdwy in *Broadway* (1987).

ZUSY, JEANNIE. Born in Washington, DC. Graduate SMU. Debut 1993 OB in *Top Girls*, followed by *Lie of the Mind*.

George Abbott

Lindsay Anderson

Danny Apolinar

Robert Bolt

OBITUARIES

(June 1, 1994-May 31, 1995)

GEORGE ABBOTT, 107, New York-born director, producer, author, and actor, died Jan. 31, 1995 in Miami Beach, FL. In tribute to this theatre giant, all the lights on Broadway were dimmed for one minute on Feb. 1, 1995. He made his first acting appearance in 1913's *The Misleading Lady.* Broadway productions he produced, directed, co-authored, or acted in include *Three Wise Fools, Yeoman of the Guard, Dulcy, White Desert, Processional, Fall Guy, A Holy Terror, Love 'Em and Leave 'Em, Broadway, Chicago, Four Walls, Coquette, Great Magoo, Gentlemen of the Press, Ringside, Those We Love, Sweet River, Lily Turner, Twentieth Century, Ladies Money, Small Miracle, John Brown, Three Men on a Horse, Jumbo, Boy Meets Girl, On Your Toes, Brother Rat, Room Service, All That Glitters, Boys from Syracuse, Too Many Girls, Pal Joey, Best Foot Forward, Kiss and Tell, Snafu, Beat the Band, Sweet Charity, Get Away Old Man, On the Town, Billion Dollar Baby, Beggar's Holiday, Barefoot Boy with Cheek, The Dancer, High Button Shoes, Look Ma I'm Dancin', Where's Charley, Call Me Madam, A Tree Grows in Brooklyn, Wonderful Town, Me and Juliet, Pajama Game, On Your Toes* (1954), *Damn Yankees, Skin of Our Teeth, New Girl in Town, Once Upon a Mattress, Fiorello!, Tenderloin, Call on Kuprin, Take Her She's Mine, A Funny Thing Happened on the Way to the Forum, Never Too Late, Fade Out–Fade In, Flora the Red Menace, How Now Dow Jones, The Education of H*Y*M*A*N K*A*P*L*A*N, Three Men on a Horse* (1969), *Norman Is That You, Not Now Darling, Twentieth Century* (1971), *Pajama Game* (1973), *Music Is* (1975), *On Your Toes* (1983). In 1989, at age 102, he wrote and co-directed Off Broadway's *Frankie* and he was a consultant on the 1994 revival of *Damn Yankees.* He won four Tony awards and a Pulitzer Prize (for *Fiorello!*). Survived by his third wife, a sister, and grandchildren.

REZA ABDOH, 32, Tehran-born director, died May 11, 1995 in Manhattan, NY, of AIDS. For his theatre ensemble, Da a Luz, he devised *Hip-Hop Waltz of Eurydice, Bogeyman, Law of Remains,* and *Quotations from a Ruined City,* between 1990 and 1993. Survived by his companion, three brothers, his mother, and sister.

RONALD ALEXANDER, 78, playwright, died April 24, 1995 in the Bronx, NY. Broadway plays included *Nobody Loves an Albatross, Time Out for Ginger,* and *Holiday for Lovers.* Survived by three daughters.

RANDY ALLEN, 38, Indiana-born performance artist, died May 11, 1995 in Philadelphia of AIDS. His last illness forced him to withdraw from the Actors' Playhouse's *Me and Jezebel.* Off-Broadway included *P.S. Bette Davis, Marilyn: Something's Got to Give,* and *Dressing Up.* Survived by his longtime companion, his parents, a sister, and two brothers.

FRANZ ALLERS, 89, Czechoslovakian-born conductor, died Jan. 26, 1995 in Las Vegas, NV of pneumonia. His Broadway shows included *Day Before Spring, Brigadoon, Paint Your Wagon, My Fair Lady,* and *Camelot.* He conducted for Richard Rodgers Music Theatre of Lincoln Center in the 1960s. Survived by a daughter and brother-in-law.

HERBERT ANDERSON, 77, California-born actor, died June 11, 1994 in Palm Springs, CA. He appeared on Broadway in *Caine Mutiny Court Martial* (1953). Survived by his wife, a son, a daughter, and grandchildren.

LINDSAY ANDERSON, 71, British director, died Aug. 30, 1994 in France of a heart attack. A director of British theatre and film, his New York credits included *Home, The Kingfisher,* and Off-Bdwy's *Holly and the Ivy* and *In Celebration.* Survived by a brother and nephew.

DANNY APOLINAR, 61, Brooklyn-born composer and performer, died Mar. 23, 1995 in Manhattan of kidney failure. Best known as co-writer of the successful 1968 Off-Bdwy musical *Your Own Thing,* he also wrote lyrics for *Changes* and several cabaret revues. Survived by his longtime companion, John Britton, and a brother.

BENNY BAKER, 87, St. Louis-born comedian, died Sept. 20, 1994 in Woodland Hills, CA. 1931 Bdwy debut in *You Said It* followed by *DuBarry Was a Lady, Let's Face It, The Tempest* and, during the 1973–74 season, *No No Nanette.* Survived by his wife, a daughter, and two grandchildren.

RANDY BARCELO, 48, costume/set designer and playwright, died Dec. 6, 1994 in Manhattan, NY. Bdwy included *Jesus Christ Superstar, Lenny, Magic Show,* and *Ain't Misbehavin'* (Tony nom.). Off-Bdwy included *Midsummer Night's Dream* and *Mass.* He wrote the off-Off-Bdwy play *Songs From the Jukebox.* Survived by his mother and a sister.

COURTENAY E. BENSON, 80, actor, died Feb. 5, 1995 in Mt. Kisco, NY, of heart failure. He appeared in *Ross* during the 1961–62 season. Survived by his wife, son, daughter, and granddaughter.

BARRY K. BERNAL, 31, San Diego-born born actor/dancer died Oct. 31, 1994 in San Diego of AIDS. Bdwy debut in *Cats* followed by *Starlight Express, Miss Saigon,* and *Goodbye Girl.* Survived by his parents, two brothers, and three sisters.

DAVID BISHOP, 66, stage manager/actor died Aug. 19, 1994 in Myrtle Beach, SC, of cancer. NYC credits included *Desperate Hours, Tiger Rag, How to Succeed...* and the NY Shakespeare Festival. As an actor he starred in Bdwy and touring companies of *Happiest Millionaire* from 1956–58. Survived by his mother.

ROBERT BOLT, 70, English playwright, died Feb. 20, 1995 in Petersfield, Hampshire, England. Best known for his 1960 play *A Man for All Seasons,* he was also an Oscar-winning screenwriter. Other plays include *The Critic and the Heart, Flowering Cherry, Thwarting of Baron Bollingrew, Vivat! Vivat! Regina,* and *State of Revolution.* Married four times to three different women, he is survived by wife, actress Sarah Miles, and four children.

PHILIP BOSAKOWSKI, 47, playwright, died Sept. 11, 1994 in Middletown, CT, of cancer. His plays include *Chopin in Space* (1985), *Crossin' the Line,* and *Nixon Apologizes to the Nation.* Survived by his wife, father, sister, and two brothers.

Christopher Chadman **Alex Colon** **Peter Cook** **Jake Dengel**

PHILIP BURTON, 90, Wales-born actor/director, died Feb. 4, 1995 in Davenport, FL, of a stroke. His NYC directorial debut was *Purple Dust* (1958) followed by *Cock-a-Doodle Dandy*. He was director of the American Musical and Dramatic Academy. Burton discovered Richard Jenkins (Richard Burton) whom he informally adopted in 1943.

CAB CALLOWAY, 86, New York-born performer, died Nov. 18, 1994 in Hosckessin, DE, following a stroke. Well known as a radio/film/nightclub performer from the 1930s through the present, his most notable theatre credit was the 1952 production of *Porgy and Bess*, playing Sportin' Life, a role he inspired. He starred opposite Pearl Bailey in the all-black *Hello Dolly!* (1967) on Broadway. Survived by his wife and four daughters.

DONNA CAMERON, 71, Vancouver-born actress/performer, died Feb. 25, 1995 in Los Angeles, CA, of cancer. She appeared Off-Bdwy in 1958's *Garden District* and she toured worldwide. Survived by two sons.

DORIS CARSON, 83, actress, died Feb. 20, 1995 in Rancho Mirage, CA. Bdwy included 1929's *Show Girl* (substituting for Ruby Keeler) followed by *Strike Up the Band, Cat and the Fiddle,* and *On Your Toes*. She also appeared in the West End. Survived by her husband and a sister.

JANIS CARTER, 80, Cleveland-born actress, died July 30, 1994 in Durham, NC. In addition to films and television, she appeared in Bdwy's *DuBarry Was a Lady* (1939) and *Panama Hattie*. Survived by her husband.

CHRISTOPHER CHADMAN, 47, dancer/choreographer, died Apr. 30, 1995 in New York City of AIDS. He choreographed the smash 1992 revival of *Guys and Dolls* and won a Tony for his work. He also choreographed *Merlin* (1983), *Peter Allen and the Rockettes,* and worked with Bob Fosse on *Pippin, Chicago,* and *Big Deal*. As a performer he debuted in 1968's *Darling of the Day* and starred in the 1976 Bdwy *Pal Joey*.

ALICE CHILDRESS, 77, South Carolina-born playwright/novelist/actress, died Aug. 14, 1994 in Queens, NY, of cancer. Plays included *Wedding Band, Florence, Gold Through Trees,* and, co-written with husband Nathan Woodard, *Moms, Gullah, Young Martin Luther King,* and *Sea Island Song*. As a member of the American Negro Theatre she acted in *Strivers Row, Natural Man, Three's a Family,* and *Anna Lucasta*. Survived by her husband and granddaughter.

DOROTHY COLLINS, 67, Ontario-born singer/actress, died July 21, 1994 in Watervliet, NY, of a heart attack. After radio and TV popularity, she came to Bdwy in the notable 1971 musical *Follies*. Survived by ex-husband Ron Holgate, three daughters, and grandchildren.

ALEX COLON, 53, Puerto Rican-born actor, died Jan. 6, 1995 in Los Angeles, CA, after an extended illness. Bdwy debut 1970 in *Gingerbread Lady* followed by *6 Rms Riv Vu* and Off-Bdwy's *Macbeth, Winterset, Crossroads, Golden Streets, Hatful of Rain,* and *Each Day Dies with Sleep*. Survived by a sister and daughter.

ELISHA COOK JR., 91, San Francisco-born actor, died May 18, 1995 in Big Pine, CA. Cook was chosen by Eugene O'Neill for the lead in Bdwys's *Ah Wilderness* (1933). Theatre includes *Crooked Friday* (1925), *Hello Lola!, Henry–Behave, Gertie, Her Unborn Child, Kingdom of God, Many a Slip, Privilege Car, Lost Boy, Merry-Go-Round, Chrysalis, Three-Cornered Moon, Crime Marches On, Come Angel Band,* and *Arturo Ui* (1963). Cook acted in over 100 films. No known survivors.

PETER COOK, 57, English comedian/actor/writer, died Jan. 9, 1995 in London, England, of a gastrointestinal hemorrhage. First on Bdwy in 1962 with *Beyond the Fringe* (which he co-created with Dudley Moore, Alan Bennett, and Jonathan Miller) followed by *Good Evening* with Moore in 1973–74. Survived by his third wife and two daughters.

VALERIE COSSART, 87, London-born actress, died Dec. 31, 1994 in Manhattan, NY, of pneumonia. Bdwy debut 1930 in *Lost Sheep* followed by *Call It a Day, Shadow and Substance, The Haven,* and *Blithe Spirit*. Survived by a stepdaughter, stepson, and grandchildren.

SEVERN DARDEN, 65, actor, died May 26, 1995 in Santa Fe, NM, of heart failure. A founding member of the Second City Troupe, he appeared on and off-Bdwy with Improvisational troupes and in *Leda Had a Little Swan*. Survived by his wife and son.

JAKE DENGEL, 61, Wisconsin-born actor died Nov. 14, 1994 in Sherman Oaks, CA, of cancer. Debut Off-Bdwy in *Fantasticks* followed by *Red Eye of Love, Fortuna, Abe Lincoln in Illinois, Dr. Faustus, Evening with Garcia Lorca, Shrinking Bride, Where Do We Go from Here?, Woyzeck, Endgame, Measure for Measure, Ulysses in Traction, Twelfth Night, Beaver Coat, Great Grandson of Jedediah Kohler, Caligula, Mound Builders,* and *Quiet in the Land*. He also appeared on Bdwy in *Royal Hunt of the Sun, Cock-a-Doodle Dandy, Hamlet,* and *Changing Room*. In addition to regional theatre, he also worked in films and TV. Survived by four daughters.

JOHN DI CARLO, 36, performer/playwright, died June 27, 1994 in Manhattan, NY, of AIDS. His work as a playwright includes Off-Bdwy's *22 Cigarettes Past 3:00* (1987) and *Waves*. As a performer he was active in Manhattan cabarets. Survived by his companion, actor Paul Maisano, and his father, sister, and brother.

JACK DODSON, 63, Pittsburgh-born actor, died Sept. 16, 1994 at Encino-Tarzana (CA) Medical Center. Spotted by Andy Griffith in the 1964 Bdwy *Hughie*, he worked with Griffith in his popular TV show. Other New York credits included Off-Bdwy debut in 1957's *Country Wife, Our Town, The Balcony, Under Milk Wood, Infancy, Six Characters in Search of an Author,* and *You Can't Take It with You*. Survived by his wife and two daughters.

NORMA DONALDSON, 68, Harlem-born singer/actress, died Nov. 22, 1994 in Los Angeles of cancer. Best known for the 1976 revival of *Guys and Dolls*, she also appeared on Bdwy in *Purlie, No Place to Be Somebody,* and *Great White Hope*. Survived by her godmother, cousin, and two nieces.

JOHNNY DOWNS, 80, Brooklyn-born actor, died June 6, 1994 in Coronado, CA, of cancer. Best known as a star of the Our Gang silent film comedies he also appeared on Bdwy in *Strike Me Pink, Growing Pains, Are You With It?,* and *Hold It*. Survived by his wife, four daughters, and a son.

MARY DRAYTON, 89, Arkansas-born playwright, died June 24, 1994 in Sarasota, FL, of a blood clot. Two of her plays, *Debut* (1956) and *The Playroom* (1965) were performed on Bdwy. Survived by her daughter and husband.

WILLIAM DUFF-GRIFFIN (William Joseph Duffy), 54, actor, died Nov. 13, 1994 in Manhattan, NY, of prostate cancer. New York credits included *Greek Trilogy, Good Woman of Szechuan, Cherry Orchard,* and much NY Shakespeare Festival work including *Measure for Measure, Twelfth Night,* and *Taming of the Shrew*. He is survived by his companion, actor Robert Joy.

| John DiCarlo | Robert Emhardt | Tom Ewell | Ed Flanders |

NORA DUNFEE, 78, Ohio-born actress/teacher, died Dec. 23, 1994 in Manhattan. Stage work included *Madam Will You Walk?* (1953), *Midnight Caller, The Visit, Last Days of Lincoln,* and *Crowbar* (1990). She taught acting at NYU for many years. Survived by her husband, two daughters and grandchildren.

ROBERT EMHARDT, 78, Indianapolis-born actor, died Dec. 29, 1994 in Ojai, CA. New York credits included *The Pirate, Harriet, Deep Are the Roots, Life with Mother, Ghosts, Hedda Gabler, The Man, Curious Savage, Seven Year Itch, Janus, Nature's Way,* and *Girls in 509.*

TOM EWELL, 85, Kentucky-born actor, died Sept. 12, 1994 in Woodland Hills, CA. New York debut in 1934's *They Shall Not Die* followed by *Sunny River, Ethan Frome, Family Portrait, Merchant of Yonkers, Liberty Jones, Tobacco Road, Brother Rat, Apple of His Eye, John Loves Mary, Small Wonder, The Seven Year Itch* (Tony Award), *Tunnel of Love, Thurber Carnival, Xmas in Las Vegas.* He acted in films, including repeating *Seven Year Itch* opposite Marilyn Monroe, and TV. In 1946 he married Ann Abbott, daughter of George Abbott, but the marriage ended in divorce. Survived by his second wife and a son.

JOHN FEARNLEY, 80, Connecticut-born director, died Nov. 29, 1994. He directed more than 20 musical revivals at City Center and also directed musicals for the Jones Beach summer theatre. Survived by his sister, a niece, and two nephews.

NELLE FISHER, 79, California-born dancer/choreographer, died Oct. 19, 1994 in Edmonds, WA, of Parkinson's disease. Part of the Martha Graham dance troupe, she also danced in Bdwy musicals including *One Touch of Venus, On the Town, Make Mine Manhattan, Can–Can,* and *Golden Apple.* Survived by her sister.

ED FLANDERS, 60, Minnesota-born actor, died Feb. 22, 1995 in Denny, CA. He commited suicide by a gunshot to the head. Well known as a TV actor, he made his Bdwy debut in *The Birthday Party* (1967) followed by *Man for All Seasons, Crucible, Trial of the Catonsville 9, Moon for the Misbegotten,* and *Last Licks.*

BERT FREED, 74, NYC-born actor, died Aug. 2, 1994 in West Sechelt, British Columbia of a heart attack. Bdwy debut 1942 in *Johnny Two by Four* was followed by *Strip for Action, Counterattack, One Touch of Venus, Firebrand of Florence, Kiss Them for Me, Day Before Spring,* and *Joy to the World.* He acted in over 200 TV shows and over 75 films. Survived by his wife, son, daughter, stepson, and grandchildren.

MICHAEL V. GAZZO, 71, actor/playwright, died Feb. 14, 1995 in Los Angeles of a stroke. His 1955 drama *A Hatful of Rain* was praised and turned into a 1957 film. He also wrote *Night Circus* (1958). He acted Off-Bdwy and in films. Survived by his wife, a daughter, and two sons.

ZELMA GEORGE, 90, Texas-born singer/musicologist, died July 3, 1994 in Cleveland. She was the first black woman to play a white role in 1950's *The Medium.* Survived by two sisters and a brother.

WILLIAM GIBBERSON, 74, St. Louis-born actor/announcer, died Sept. 25, 1994 in Manhattan of a stroke. Bdwy debut in 1947's *It Takes Two* followed by *For Love or Money, Two Blind Mice, Mr. Barry's Etchings, The Heiress,* and *Mame.* Survived by his longtime companion.

PHILLIP GILMORE, 38, actor/singer, died Aug. 29, 1994 in NYC. Credits included *Dreamgirls, House of Flowers, Betsey Brown, Bubbling Brown Sugar,* and *Apollo It Was Just Like Magic.* His last work was the national tour of *Five Guys Named Moe.* Survived by his companion, parents, brother, and sister.

MURRAY GITLIN, 67, Connecticut-born dancer/stage manager, died June 22, 1994 in Manhattan of AIDS. He danced in *The King and I, Golden Apple, Can–Can,* and *Irma La Douce.* He stage managed many Bdwy and Off-Bdwy shows. Survived by his mother and a brother.

PETER D. GOULD, 50, production designer, died Oct. 17, 1994 in Boston, MA, following surgery. Bdwy credits included *Starlight Express, Sophisticated Ladies, Little Me* (1984), *The Real Thing, I'm Not Rappaport, Cats, Miss Saigon,* and *Sunset Blvd.,* which he was working on at the time of his death. He worked extensively in regional theatre. Survived by his wife, a daughter, two sons, his mother, and a brother.

DOLLY HAAS, 84, German-born actress and wife of theatre artist Al Hirschfeld, died Sept. 16, 1994 in Manhattan, NY, of ovarian cancer. New York debut in *Circle of Chalk* (1941) followed by *War and Peace, Lute Song* (replacing Mary Martin), *Crime and Punishment, Threepenny Opera* and *Brecht on Brecht.* Survived by her husband, her daughter Nina, and grandchildren.

ALBERT HACKETT, 95, NYC-born playwright, died Mar. 16, 1995 of pneumonia. With his first wife and collaborator, Frances Goodrich, he won a Pulitzer Prize for *The Diary of Anne Frank* (1955). Starting in 1930 with *Up Pops the Devil* (in which he also performed), the Hackett-Goodrich team wrote *Bridal Wise, Great Big Doorstep* and many screenplays. Hackett began as a child actor at six in *Lottie the Poor Saleslady* (playing a girl) and *Peter Pan.* Survived by his second wife.

JAMES LEE HANSEN, JR., 36, playwright, died Dec. 1, 1994 in NY after a long illness. His play *What's a Girl to Do* was produced Off-Bdwy.

LARRY HANSEN, 42, West Virginia-born actor/singer, died Mar. 4, 1995 in New York City of AIDS. Bdwy credits included *Show Boat, Me and My Girl,* and *Anna Karenina.* New York debut 1978 in Off-Bdwy's *Can–Can* was followed by *Box Office of the Damned, Pageant,* and *Allegro in Concert.* He wrote the lyrics for the theme song for Broadway Cares. Survived by his sister and her family.

ROBERT HARRIS, British actor, died May 18, 1995 near London. After London work, he made his New York debut in *The Will* (1923) and was Marchbanks opposite Katharine Cornell in *Candida* (1937). Later plays included *Edwina Black* and a 1963–64 US tour of *Man for All Seasons.* Survived by a brother.

LLEWELLYN HARRISON, 47, designer/production manager, died Nov. 11, 1994 in Richmond, VA, of cardiac arrest. He was set designer for Off-Bdwy's *Mama I Want to Sing* and numerous productions at New Federal Theatre and Negro Ensemble Company. Survived by his parents and a sister.

JACK HARROLD, 74, New Jersey-born singer/actor, died July 22, 1994 in Manhattan, NY, of lung cancer. In addition to almost 50 seasons at New York City Opera, his Bdwy credits include *Merry Widow* (1943), *Carousel, Mr. Strauss Goes to Boston, Chocolate Soldier, Lady from Paris, The Vamp, Unsinkable Molly Brown, Rugantino, Cradle Will Rock,* and *Good Woman of Setzuan.* Survived by his brother.

Bert Freed

Dolly Haas

Larry Hansen

Jack Harrold

JULIE HAYDON, 84, Illinois-born actress, died Dec. 24, 1994 in La Crosse, WI, of abdominal cancer. She created the role of Laura in the original production of *The Glass Menagerie* which opened on Bdwy in 1945. In 1980 she played the mother in an Off-Bdwy revival. Other Bdwy roles included 1935's *Bright Star, Shadow and Substance, Time of Your Life, Sweeney in the Trees, Magic, Hello Out There, The Patriots, Miracle in the Mountains,* and *Our Lan.* Married to drama critic George Jean Nathan from 1955 until his 1958 death, she is survived by her sister.

LILLIAN HAYMAN, 72, Maryland-born actress/singer, died Oct. 25, 1994 in Hollis, NY, of a heart attack. A Tony winner for her role in the 1967 musical *Hallelujah Baby!,* her distinctive style also enlivened Bdwy in *Kiss Me Kate, Show Boat, Kwamina, 70 Girls 70, No No Nanette* and Off-Bdwy in *Dream About Tomorrow* and *Along Came a Spider.* She toured internationally with *Porgy and Bess* for more than three years. Survived by a sister.

JOSEPH HOLLAND, 84, Virginia-born actor, died Dec. 28, 1994 in Santa Fe, NM, of heart failure. He made his debut with Katharine Cornell in *Romeo and Juliet* (1934) and worked with her again in *Saint Joan* and *Anthony and Cleopatra.* A founding member of the Mercury Theatre, he played *Julius Caesar* in the first Mercury production (1937). Later work included *The Show-Off* (1950) and *Bad Seed* (1954). Survived by his longtime companion.

CHARLES HORNE, 48, playwright, died Sept. 2, 1994 in Syracuse, NY, of AIDS. His play *The Smoking Room* was set in a hospital AIDS ward. Survived by his companion, his parents, and three brothers.

HARRY HORNER, 84, Czechoslovakian-born set designer, died Dec. 5, 1994 in Pacific Palisades, CA, of pneumonia. As a member of the Max Reinhardt Theatre company, he visited NYC in 1935 and stayed to design *All the Living* (1937), *The World We Make, Family Portrait, Banjo Eyes, Let's Face It, Lady in the Dark, Star and Garter, Winged Victory, Christopher Blake, Me and Molly, Joy to the World* and other plays, operas, and films. Survived by his wife, three sons, and grandchildren.

RICHARD V. IRIZARRY, 38, playwright/political aide, died Sept. 19, 1994 in Manhattan, NY, of AIDS. His Off-Bdwy play *Ariano* won the Nat'l Drama Award of Puerto Rico. His musical *Newyorico!* was being developed at the Public Theatre at the time of his death. Survived by his companion, his parents, a brother, and sister.

BURL IVES, 85, Illinois-born singer/actor, died April 14, 1995 in Anacortes, WA. He suffered from mouth cancer and a degenerative bone disease. Prized in the theatre for his memorable "Big Daddy" in *Cat on a Hot Tin Roof,* he reprised the role in the film version. Other Bdwy roles include his debut in 1938's *Boys from Syracuse, This Is the Army, Sing Out Sweet Land, She Stoops to Conquer, Show Boat* (1954) and *Dr. Cook's Garden.* As recently as 1988 he played Walt Whitman in a Santa Barbara, CA, production, *The Mystic Trumpeter.* During a seven decade career as a folk singer he recorded more than 70 albums. Survived by his second wife, his son, three stepchildren, and grandchildren.

RAUL JULIA (Raul Rafael Carlos Julia y Arcelay), 54, Puerto Rican-born actor, died Oct. 24, 1994 in Manhasset, Long Island (NY) of complications from a stroke. Popular both on Bdwy and off (especially with the NY Shakespeare Festival), his worked spanned a wide range: classics and new work, plays, and musicals. Starting in 1964 with *Life Is a Dream,* a Spanish language production, his credits included *Macbeth* (1966), *Ox Cart, Titus Andronicus, No Exit, The Memorandum, Your Own Thing, The Cuban Thing* (Bdwy debut 1968), *Frank Gagliano's City Scene, Christmas Carol, Indians, The Persians, Castro Complex, Pinkville, Two Gentlemen of Verona, Hamlet* (1972), *Via Galactica, As You Like It, King Lear, Emperor of Late Night Radio, Robber Bridegroom, Where's Charley?, Threepenny Opera* (1976), *Cherry Orchard, Taming of the Shrew, Dracula* (succeeding Frank Langella), *Betrayal, Nine, Design for Living, Arms and the Man, Macbeth* (1990) and *Othello* (1991). His last NYC appearance was the 1992 Bdwy revival of *Man of La Mancha.* He was also active in film and TV. Survived by his second wife, two sons, his mother, and two sisters.

Julie Haydon

Lillian Hayman

Burl Ives

Raul Julia

Nancy Kelly

Michael Kermoyan

Burt Lancaster

Henry Mancini

MICHAEL KASDAN, 66, NYC-born producer/stage manager, died Oct. 22, 1994 in Mahpoac, NY, of lymphoma. He managed *Whose Afraid of Virginia Woolf?, Tiny Alice, Boys in the Band, Everything in the Garden, Grass Harp,* and many dance companies. No reported survivors.

BRIAN KAUFMAN, 40, Oregon-born stage manager, died Aug. 22, 1994 of AIDS. Bdwy credits included *Heidi Chronicles, Oh Kay!, Mandy Patinkin: Dress Casual,* and *Any Given Day.* Off-Bdwy included *Marvin's Room, Closer Than Ever, Kathy and Mo Show,* and *Three Guys Naked from the Waist Down.* Survived by his parents and two brothers.

SALLY MOFFET KELLIN, 63, actress, died May 8, 1995 in Nyack, NY of lung cancer. Her NY credits started in the 1940s and included *Young and Fair, Member of the Wedding, Desk Set, Under Milkwood,* and *Perfect Analysis Given by a Parrot.* She worked in regional theatre and on TV. Survived by her actress mother Sylvia Field, three sons, and a daughter.

NANCY KELLY, 73, Massachusetts-born actress, died Jan. 2, 1995 in Bel Air, CA, of diabetes. Bdwy debut 1931 as a child actress in *Give Me Yesterday* followed by *One Good Year, Susan and God, Flare Path, Big Knife, Season in the Sun, Twilight Walk, The Bad Seed* (1954) for which she won a Tony, *Genius and the Goddess, The Rivalry, A Mighty Man Is He, Giants Sons of Giants, Who's Afraid of Virginia Woolf?, Quotations from Chairman Mao Tse-Tung,* and the national tour of *Gingerbread Lady.* She worked in film where she reprised her *Bad Seed* role. Survived by a daughter and grandchildren.

MICHAEL KERMOYAN, 73, California-born actor/singer, died Sept. 21, 1994 in Manhattan of cancer. Bdwy debut 1954 in *Girl in the Pink Tights* followed by *Whoop-Up, Happy Town, Camelot, Happiest Girl in the World, Fly Blackbird, Ross, Tovarich, Anya, The Guide, Desert Song,* and the 1977 *King and I.* Off-Bdwy included *Carousel, Sandhog,* and *Angels of Andarko.* Survived by his wife, a brother, a stepson, and grandchildren.

SIDNEY KINGSLEY (Kirshner), 88, NYC-born playwright, died March 20, 1995 in Oakland, NJ, of a stroke. Winner of a Pulitzer Prize for his first play *Men in White* (1933), his well-known *Dead End* (1935) and *Detective Story* (1949) won praise for their gritty realism. Other plays included *The Patriots, Darkness at Noon, 10 Million Ghosts, World We Make, Lunatics and Lovers,* and *Night Life.* His actress wife Madge Evans predeceased him. No survivors.

IRWIN KOSTAL, 83, Chicago-born orchestrator/conductor, died Nov. 30, 1994 in Studio City, CA, of a heart attack. Theatre work included *West Side Story* (co-orchestrator) and *A Funny Thing Happened on the Way to the Forum.* He orchestrated musical films including adaptations of Bdwy's *Sound of Music* and *West Side Story.* Survived by three children.

BURT LANCASTER (Burton Stephen Lancaster), 80, East Harlem-born actor, died Oct. 20, 1994 in Century City, CA, of a heart attack. A screen legend for more than 40 years, he won a Theatre World Award for his Bdwy debut in 1945's *A Sound of Hunting.* Prior to Bdwy he worked in vaudeville and circus acts as an acrobat. Survived by his third wife and five children.

JERRY LESTER, 85, Chicago-born comedian, died March 23, 1995 in Miami, FL, of Alzheimers disease. Bdwy work included 1940s' productions including *Beat the Band* and *Jackpot.* Later work included 1965 tour of *A Funny Thing Happened on the Way to the Forum,* and 1969 *South Pacific* at Jones Beach. Survived by his wife, a son, two daughters, and grandchildren.

ROBERT LANSING, 66, California-born actor, died Oct. 23, 1994 in the Bronx, NY, of cancer. Bdwy debut 1951 in *Stalag 17* followed by *Cyrano de Bergerac, Richard III, Charley's Aunt, The Lovers, Cue for Passion, Great God Brown, Cut of the Axe, Little Foxes, Finishing Touches,* and Off-Bdwy's *The Father, Cost of Living, Sea Plays, The Line, Phaedra, Mi Vida Loca , Sum of Us, Disciple of Discontent,* and *Damian.* Survived by his wife and two children.

ROBERT E. LEE, 75, Ohio-born playwright, died July 18, 1994 in Los Angeles, CA, of cancer. His collaboration with Jerome Lawrence spanned 1942 to the present and produced *Inherit the Wind* (1955), *Call on Kuprin, First Monday in October* (1978), *Night Thoreau Spent in Jail, Look Ma I'm Dancin', Auntie Mame* (1956) and the book for the musical version *Mame* (1966). Their last play *Whisper in the Mind* has been produced regionally. Survived by actress wife Janet Waldo, a son, daughter, and grandchildren.

WILLIAM LIEBERSON, 79, Brooklyn-born director/playwright, died Jan. 14, 1995 in Manhattan, NY, of a heart ailment. He founded the Quaigh Theatre where he directed many plays and was artistic director. His plays include *Private Stock* and the 1951 Bdwy comedy *Springtime Folly.* Survived by his wife, two sons, and a daughter.

VALERIE COSSART LIVINGSTON, 87, London-born actress, died Dec. 31, 1994 in Manhattan, NY, of pneumonia. After moving to NYC in the 1930s she appeared in *Lost Sheep, Blithe Spirit, Call It a Day, Shadow and Substance,* and *The Haven.* Survived by two stepchildren and grandchildren.

KARL LUKAS, 75, actor, died Jan. 16, 1995 in Agoura Hills, CA. After starting at the Barter Theatre in Virginia, he worked on Bdwy in *Mister Roberts* (1948) and *Remains to Be Seen.* He also worked in film and TV.

BRUCE MAILMAN, 55, producer/theatre owner, died June 9, 1994 in Manhattan, NY, of AIDS. In 1965 he bought buildings he developed into the Astor Place Theatre and Truck and Warehouse Theatre (currently New York Theatre Workshop). In the 1970s he produced *Dirtiest Show in Town, Neon Woman,* and *The Faggot.* Survived by his longtime companion.

HENRY MANCINI, 70, Cleveland-born composer, died June 14, 1994 in Los Angeles of pancreatic cancer. One of the best-known film composers, he was working on expanding his score for the stage musical *Victor Victoria* when he died. The show opened on Bdwy in Oct. 1995. His film musicals included *Darling Lili* and *Victor Victoria* (1982). Survived by his wife, twin daughters, son, and grandchildren.

ERNEST H. MARTIN (Markowitz), 75, Pittsburgh-born producer, died May 7, 1995 in Los Angeles, CA, of liver cancer. With Cy Feuer, he co-produced some of the most successful musicals ever. Starting in 1948 they presented *Where's Charley?, Guys and Dolls, Can-Can, Boy Friend, Silk Stockings, Whoop-Up, How to Succeed in Business…, Little Me, Sky-scraper, Walking Happy,* the drama *Goodbye People* and *The Act* (1977). They also produced the film versions of *Cabaret* and *Chorus Line.* Survived by his third wife and three daughters.

DAN McCOY, 37, actor/singer/dancer, died Feb. 7, 1995 in Manhattan, NY, of AIDS. He performed "Munkustrap" in Bdwy's *Cats* during 1992–93 after playing in two national touring companies of the show. Other major tours included *Woman of the Year, La Cage aux Folles,* and *Jesus Christ Superstar.* Mr. McCoy was the live action model for "Gaston" in Disney's animated *Beauty and the Beast.* Survived by his parents and a sister.

Dan McCoy

Keith McDaniel

Gunter Meisner

Mildred Natwick

KEITH McDANIEL, 38, Chicago-born dancer, died Jan. 2, 1995 in Los Angeles, CA, of AIDS. A principal dancer with the Alvin Ailey company, he performed on Bdwy in *Leader of the Pack* (1985) and was a lead dancer in *Kiss of the Spider Woman* (1993). Survived by his companion, father, and brother.

KENNETH J. McLAUGHLIN, 41, actor, died Sept. 23, 1994 in Manhattan, NY, of AIDS. In addition to films and TV, he often performed at the 78th St. Theatre Lab in New York. Survived by his companion, mother, and brother.

GUNTER MEISNER, 66, German-born actor, died Dec. 5, 1994 in Berlin, Germany. Debut 1983 OB in *Report to an Academy* followed by *Fairwell.* Survived by his wife.

CRAIG MILLER, 43, lighting designer, died June 7, 1994 in Manhattan, NY, of cancer. Nominated for a Tony for 1980's *Barnum,* other Bdwy included *Most Happy Fella, Oh Kay!, Romance Romance, Safe Sex, On Golden Pond, Wind in the Willows,* and *Take Me Along.* He also worked with many Off-Bdwy companies. Survived by his mother, brother, sister-in-law, and niece.

JEROME MINSKOFF, 78, Bronx-born theatre owner/producer, died Aug. 13, 1994 in London, England, of a heart attack. The Minskoff Theatre opened on Bdwy in 1973 on the site of the old Astor hotel. Mr. Minskoff produced *Irene* (1973), *Can-Can, Sweet Charity, Noises Off, Big Deal,* and London productions *Sweet Bird of Youth* (Lauren Bacall) and *Apple Cart* (Peter O'Toole). Survived by his wife, two brothers, a son, two daughters, and a grandson.

CAMERON MITCHELL, 75, Pennsylvania-born actor, died July 6, 1994 in Pacific Palisades, CA, of lung cancer. Winner of a Theatre World Award for his role in the original 1949 *Death of a Salesman* his New York credits include *At a Certain Hour* (1938 Off-Bdwy), *Peace and Plenty,* and Bdwy's *Jeremiah* (1939), *Taming of the Shrew, Trojan Woman* (1941), *Southern Exposure, Les Blancs,* and *November People* (1978). He made more than 90 films and worked steadily on TV. Survived by his wife, six children, and grandchildren.

NOMI MITTY, 54, actress, died Aug. 24, 1994 in Los Angeles, CA, of cancer. As a child she appeared on Bdwy in *A Tree Grows in Brooklyn* (1951) and later toured in *Who's Afraid of Virginia Woolf?.* Survived by her husband, son, two step-daughters, three brothers, and a sister.

SALLY MOFFET, 63, NYC-born actress, died May 8, 1995 in Upper Nyack, NY, of lung cancer. Bdwy debut 1948 in *Young and Fair* followed by *Member of the Wedding, Desk Set,* and Off-Bdwy's *Under Milk Wood, Perfect Analysis,* and *Rasputin.* Survived by her companion, mother, three sons, a daughter, step-brothers, and grandchildren.

JAMES MONKS, 81, a NYC-born actor/model, died Oct. 9, 1994 in Manhattan, NY, of cancer. Bdwy included *Brother Rat* (1936), *Yesterday's Magic, Eve of St. Mark, Othello, Story of Mary Surratt, Town House,* and *Auntie Mame.* In the mid 1950s he shifted focus to modeling. Survived by his brother.

ELIZABETH MONTGOMERY, 62, Los Angeles-born actress, died May 18, 1995 in Los Angeles, CA, of cancer. Winner of a Theatre World Award for her Bdwy debut in 1953's *Late Love,* other NY theatre included *Loud Red Patrick* and *Romanoff and Juliet.* Later she appeared in *Love Letters* in NY and L.A. with husband Robert Foxworth. Best known for her lead role in TV's "Bewitched," she is survived by her husband and three children.

PRISCILLA MORRILL, 67, Massachusetts-born actress, died Nov. 9, 1994 in Los Angeles of a kidney infection. Bdwy debut 1950 in *The Relapse* followed by *Buy Me Blue Ribbons, Way of the World* (OB), *Duchess of Malfi* (OB), *Love's Labour's Lost* (OB), *Night of the Iguana, Touch of the Poet, Still Life,* and *Tonight at 8:30.* Survived by her husband.

GILBERT MOSES, 52, Cleveland-born director, died April 14, 1995 in Manhattan, NY, of multiple myeloma. He directed Bdwy shows including *Ain't Supposed to Die a Natural Death, The Wiz, 1600 Pennsylvania Avenue,* and Off-Bdwy's *Slaveship* (1969 Obie Award). Moses co-founded the Free Southern Theatre which toured the South during the 1960s. Survived by his companion, two daughters, his mother, two brothers, and four sisters.

FRED NATHAN, 38, Brooklyn-born press agent, died June 28, 1994 in New York City of AIDS. One of Bdwy's most prominent publicists, his shows included *Oklahoma* (1979), *42nd St., Brigadoon, Sophisticated Ladies, Little Foxes* (Elizabeth Taylor), *Entertaining Mr. Sloan, Oh Brother!, The First, Curse of an Aching Heart, Joseph and the…Dreamcoat, Little Johnny Jones, Cats, View from the Bridge, Marcel Marceau, Private Lives* (Taylor & Burton), *Cradle Will Rock, Corn is Green, Zorba, Noises Off, Oliver, Sunday in the Park with George, Heidi Chronicles, Jerome Robbins' Broadway, Largely New York, Miss Margarida's Way, Grapes of Wrath, Lettice and Lovage, Aspects of Love, Big Love, Miss Saigon,* and *Ain't Broadway Grand* (1993). Survived by his mother, sister, and brother.

MILDRED NATWICK, 89, Baltimore-born actress, died Oct. 25, 1994 in Manhattan, NY. The versatile actress had a long career on the NY stage. 1932 debut in *Carry Nation* followed by *Amourette, Spring in Autumn, Wind and the Rain, Distaff Side, Night in the House, End of Summer, Love from a Stranger, Candida* (1937, 1942, & 1946), *Star Wagon, Missouri Legend, Stars in Your Eyes, Christmas Eve, Lady Who Came to Stay, Blithe Spirit, Playboy of the Western World, Grass Harp, Coriolanus, Waltz of the Toreadors* (Tony nom.), *Day the Money Stopped, The Firstborn, Good Soup, Critic's Choice, Barefoot in the Park, Our Town* (1969), *Landscape, 70 Girls 70* (Tony nom.) and *Bedroom Farce* (1979). She also worked in film including reprising *Barefoot in the Park.* No reported survivors.

GERALD NOBLES, 58, actor/stage manager, died Aug. 23, 1994 of AIDS. He stage managed at the Allenberry (PA) Playhouse and was production manager at Philadelphia's Walnut St. Theatre for nine seasons. He toured with *Oliver* and worked in summer stock. Survived by his mother, brother, and two nieces.

BRAD O'HARE (Steven Bradford O'Hare), 43, actor/psychotherapist, died Oct. 1, 1994 in Manhattan, NY, of AIDS. A founding member of Off-Bdwy's Production Co., he appeared in *Three Postcards, Blue Window,* and Bdwy's *Amadeus.* He worked at major regional theatres, film, and TV. Survived by his longtime companion, mother, and brother.

| Patrick O'Neal | Nicholas Pennell | Donald Pleasence | Martha Raye |

PATRICK O'NEAL, 66, Florida-born actor, died Sept. 9, 1994 in Manhattan, NY, of respiratory failure. Bdwy debut 1961 in *A Far Country* followed by *Night of the Iguana* and Off-Bdwy's *Ginger Man and Children of Darkness*. He owned many Manhattan restaurants with his wife and brother including the "Ginger Man" named after his stage role, "O'Neals Baloon," and "Landmark Tavern". Survived by his wife and two sons.

JOHN OSBORNE, 65, British playwright, died Dec. 24, 1994 in Shropshire, England, of diabetes and other health problems. Often called the first angry young man, he ushered in a new generation of rebellious and disillusioned dramatists with his 1956 drama *Look Back in Anger*. The play reached Bdwy in 1957 and his work in London and NYC included *Epitaph for George Dillon, The Entertainer, World of Paul Slickey, Luther* (Tony Award), *Blood of the Bambergs, Under Plain Cover, Inadmissible Evidence, Patriot for Me, Time Present, Hotel in Amsterdam,* and *Dejavu* (1992). Survived by his fifth wife and daughter.

TESSIE O'SHEA, 82, Wales-born actress/singer, died April 21, 1995 in East Lake Weir, FL, of heart failure. A stage and radio star in England, she made Bdwy debut 1963 in *Girl Who Came to Supper* and won a Tony Award. Other Bdwy included *Time for Singing* and *Something's Afoot* (1976). No reported survivors.

LOUIS PADILLA JR., 38, singer/actor, died April 19, 1995 in New York City after a long illness. He appeared in the Bdwy and Off-Bdwy versions of *The Human Comedy* (1983–84) and in national tours including *Joseph and the…Dreamcoat* and *Evita*. Survived by his companion, his mother and four sisters.

DOUGLAS A. PAGLIOTTI, 36, Santa Barbara-born stage manager, died Sept. 27, 1994 in San Diego, CA, of AIDS. Production stage manager of the 1994 *Damn Yankees* and Off-Bdwy's *Cocktail Hour,* he managed more than 150 productions at San Diego's Old Globe Theatre. He worked at many major regional theatres. Survived by his companion, director Will Roberson, until his AIDS death in Dec. '94, his parents, three sisters, and a brother.

NICHOLAS PENNELL, 56, British-born actor, died Feb. 22, 1995 in Ontario, Canada. A member of the Stratford Festival acting company for 23 consecutive seasons, he appeared in more than 75 plays. Survived by a brother and three nephews.

MICHAEL PETERS, 46, Brooklyn-born choreographer/director, died Aug. 29, 1994 in Los Angeles, CA, of AIDS. Mr. Peters shared a Tony with Michael Bennett for their choreography for 1981's *Dreamgirls*. Other Bdwy included *Comin' Uptown* (1979) and directing *Leader of the Pack* (1985). He worked on major music videos, films, and TV shows. Survived by his mother, two aunts, and an uncle.

LYDIA PETERKOCH, 29, actress, died Oct. 30, 1994 in Los Angles, CA, in a car accident. She had a lead in Westside Arts Theatre's *Time of Your Life* and worked in films. Survived by a brother.

DONALD PLEASENCE, 75, British-born actor, died Feb. 2, 1995 in France after a recent heart sugery. Best known for his many films, he acted onstage in England before Bdwy in *Antony and Cleopatra, Caesar and Cleopatra, The Caretaker* (Tony nom.), *Poor Bitos* (Tony nom.), *Man in the Glass Booth* (Tony nom.) and *Wise Child* (1972) where he played a transvestite. He worked on the London stage last in a 1991 revival of *The Caretaker*. Survived by his fourth wife and five daughters.

BOB RANDALL (Stanley B. Goldstein), 57, Bronx-born playwright, died Feb. 13, 1995 in New Milford, CT, of AIDS. His plays included the 1972 Bdwy comedy *6 Rms Riv Vu,* the book for the musical *Magic Show* (1974), and the 1991 drama *David's Mother*. He also wrote for films and TV. Survived by his longtime companion, son, daughter, and sister.

SAMUEL D. RATCLIFFE, 50, Florida-born actor/writer, died Dec. 14, 1995 in Manhattan, NY, of AIDS. In 1969 he played Matt in *The Fantasticks* and appeared in Bdwy's *Fiddler on the Roof* and *Hurry Harry* before focusing on televison writing which won him an Emmy. Survived by his companion, actor Jeffrey Hayenga, his parents, and three sisters.

MARTHA RAYE (Margaret Teresa Yvonne Reed), 78, Montana-born comedian/singer, died Oct. 19, 1994 in Los Angeles, CA, after a series of ailments. A popular film performer, she made her Bdwy debut 1934 in *Calling All Stars* followed by *Earl Carroll's Sketchbook, Hold on to Your Hats, Hello Dolly!* (1967, replacing Ginger Rogers), and *No No Nanette*. Survived by her seventh husband and a daughter.

OLIVER REA, 71, Manhattan-born producer/theatre founder, died Mar. 31, 1995 in Manhattan, NY, of cardiac arrest. He produced the landmark 1947 Judith Anderson *Medea, Crime and Punishment, Member of the Wedding,* and *Slave Ship*. In 1963 he co-founded the Guthrie Theatre in Minneapolis. Survived by his wife, a son, three daughters, a brother, and grandchildren.

MURIEL RESNIK, 78, New Haven-born playwright, died Mar. 6, 1995 in Manhattan, NY, of heart failure. In addition to many novels she wrote the Bdwy play *Any Wednesday* (1964). Survived by her husband, two sons, two sisters, and grandchildren.

JESS RICHARDS (Richard Sederholm), 51, Seattle-born actor, died Nov. 6, 1994 in Indianapolis, IN, of AIDS. A versatile actor whose career spanned Bdwy, Off-Bdwy and regional theatre, he won a Theatre World Award for his role in the 1971 Bdwy *On the Town*. Other Bdwy included his debut in 1966's *Walking Happy, South Pacific* (LC), *Blood Red Roses, Two by Two, Mack and Mabel, Nash at Nine, Musical Chairs,* and *Barnum*. Off-Bdwy included *One for the Money, Lovesong, Josh Logan's Musical Scrapbook, Lullaby of Broadway, All Night Strut, Dames at Sea,* and the Lyrics and Lyricists series. His nat'l tours included *Hello Dolly!, Irene, Mack and Mabel,* and *Phantom of the Opera*. Survived by his mother and a brother.

RON RICHARDSON, 43, Pennsylvania-born actor/singer, died April 5, 1995 in Bronxville, NY, of AIDS. Winner of a Tony Award for the 1985 musical *Big River,* he re-created his role of Jim in the musical "Huck Finn" adaptation in Japan. Other Bdwy included *Timbuktu, Oh Kay!,* and *Boys Choir of Harlem and Friends*. He was in *Ground People* off-Bdwy and tours included *Dreamgirls, I Do! I Do!,* and many Philadelphia area productions. Recently he appeared in *Carmen Jones* in London. Survived by his parents, two brothers, and a sister.

Jess Richards

Paul Roebling

Lilia Skala

Lionel Standler

WILL ROBERSON, 36, Indiana-born director/playwright, died Dec. 13, 1994 in San Diego, CA, of AIDS. Assistant Director for Bdwy's 1994 *Damn Yankees,* he was best known for his direction of many shows at San Diego's Old Globe Theatre. His Old Globe credits included directing *Suds* (1989) which played across the country. He was predeceased by his longtime companion, Old Globe stage manager Douglas Pagliotti, who died in Sept. of AIDS. Survived by his parents, a sister, and brother.

PAUL ROEBLING, 60, Philadelphia-born actor, commited suicide July 27, 1994 on a Navajo Indian reservation in Arizona. Winner of a Theatre World Award for *A Desert Incident* (1959), he was a great-great-grandson of John A. Roebling, who designed the Brooklyn Bridge. Bdwy debut 1953 in *A Girl Can Tell* followed by *Dark is Light Engough, The Lark, Romeo and Juliet, This Side of Paradise* (1962 OB–Obie Award), *Milk Train Doesn't Stop Here Anymorek,* and *Four Seasons* (OB). He also directed Off-Bdwy's *Zelda* and worked in films and TV. During the 1980s he was chairman of "Save the Theatres," campaigning to landmark NYC's historic theatres. He was predeceased by actress wife Olga Bellin in 1987 and is survived by his son.

GINGER ROGERS (Virginia Katherine McMath), 83, Missouri-born actress/dancer, died April 25, 1995 in Rancho Mirage, CA. One of the biggest screen stars of the 1930s and 1940s, she made movie musical history in her pairings with Fred Astaire. Bdwy debut in 1929's *Top Speed* was followed by the original 1930 *Girl Crazy, Love and Let Love* (1951), and *Hello Dolly!* (1965-67). She played Mame in London and toured in *Bell Book and Candle, Annie Get Your Gun, Unsinkable Molly Brown,* and played a pre-Bdwy run of *The Pink Jungle.* She even directed a 1985 production of *Babes in Arms* in Tarrytown, NY. Married five times, she never had children.

WILLIAM ROSS, 78, producer/stage manager, died Aug. 23, 1994 in Manhattan, NY, of heart failure. He managed *Born Yesterday, Two's Company, Marriage Go Round,* and the 1966 *Annie Get Your Gun.* His "Century Productions" produced many tours of big musicals and he was active in Actors Equity. Survived by two daughters and a brother.

NORMAN ROSTEN, 81, NYC-born playwright/novelist, died Mar. 7, 1995 in Brooklyn, NY, of heart failure. Although his first play, *First Stop to Heaven* (1941), ran only eight performances, his 1956 *Mister Johnson* (adapted from the Joyce Cary novel) was a notable success. Other plays included *Mardi Gras, Golden Door,* and *Come Slowly Eden.* Survived by his companion, daughter, and sister.

SARAH RUBINSTEIN, 94, Yiddish theatre actress, died July 19, 1994 in New York of a stroke. Under the stage name Sarah Silverberg, she was a popular member of the Artef, a NYC company, from 1920–40. Survived by her daughter.

JOHN SCANLAN, 73, Milwaukee-born actor, died June 26, 1994 in Closter, NJ, of heart failure. In a career spanning more than forty years, his Bdwy roles included *Mastergate, Best Man,* and *Capt. Brassbound's Conversion.* Off Bdwy included *Plough and the Stars, Master Builder, No Exit,* and lastly 1992's Central Park *As You Like It.* Survived by his wife, three sons, a daughter, and two sisters.

THOMAS B. SHOVESTULL, 45, company manager, died June 25, 1994 of AIDS. Credits included *Gemini, Fifth of July, Foxfire, A Nightingale Sang,* and *Oedipus Rex.* He worked with Baltimore's Center Stage and other regional theatres. Survived by his longtime companion, mother, sister, niece, and nephew.

DAVID J. SILBER, 41, New Haven-born actor, died Dec. 29, 1994 in Brookline, MA, of AIDS. Credits included Bdwy's *Aren't We All?, Pygmalion, Breaking the Code, Zoya's Apartment* (1990), and Off-Bdwy's *The Changeling* (1978), *Doctor's Dilemma,* and *Story of the Gadsbys.* Survived by his companion, parents, and seven siblings.

LILIA SKALA, 90s, Vienna-born actress, died Dec. 18, 1994 in Bay Shore, NY. In 1939, fleeing Hitler, she came to America. Bdwy debut 1941 in *Letters to Lucerne* followed by *With a Silk Thread, Call Me Madam, Diary of Anne Frank, Threepenny Opera* (1965), *Zelda, 40 Carats, The Survivor,* and Off-Bdwy's *Medea and Jason, Gorky,* and *Shop on Main Street* (1981). Survived by two sons and grandchildren.

THOMAS SKELTON, 66, Maine-born lighting designer, died Aug. 9, 1994 in Akron, OH, of lung cancer. He won three Tony nominations for *The Iceman Cometh, Indians,* and *All God's Chillun Got Wings.* Other Bdwy included *Mame, Coco, Oklahoma, King and I, Brigadoon, Lena Horne: Lady and Her Music, A Few Good Men, Carousel, Shakespeare for My Father,* and many others. Survived by his companion of 30 years, choreographer Heinz Poll.

MARTIN SMITH, 37, Scotish-born actor/singer, died Nov. 12, 1994 in London, England, of AIDS. One of the Phantoms in London's *Phantom of the Opera,* other London leads included *Evita, Les Miserables, A Swell Party,* and lastly, *City of Angels.*

VIOLA SPOLIN, 88, teacher/author, died Nov. 22, 1994 in Los Angeles, CA. Her improvisational games, collected in her book "Improvisations for the Theatre" trained generations of actors. Her son, actor Paul Sills, continued the tradition with theatre companies like Chicago's "Second City" and "Compass" along with Story Theatre which was performed all over the country. Survived by two sons, her third husband, sister, and grandchildren.

KATHERINE SQUIRE, 92, Ohio-born actress, died Mar. 29, 1995 in Lake Hill, NY. Bdwy debut 1932 in *Black Tower* followed by *Goodbye Again, High Tor, Hipper's Holiday, What a Life, Liberty Jones, The Family, Shadow of a Gunman, Traveling Lady* and Off-Bdwy's *Roots, This Here Nice Place, Boy on a Straight-Back Chair, Catsplay, Hillbilly Women, Memory of Whiteness,* and *Hedda Gabler.* She acted in regional theatre and films. Survived by three stepdaughters.

LIONEL STANDLER, 86, Bronx-born actor, died Nov. 30, 1994 in Brentwood, CA, of lung cancer. A familiar character actor in films and TV, he appeared in more than two dozen Bdwy plays before turning 30. Debut in *Him* followed by O'Neill's Glencairn Cycle and many classics, often at the Provincetown Playhouse in Greenwich Village. Survived by his sixth wife and five daughters.

Barry Sullivan

Ted Thurston

Willard Waterman

David Wayne

K. T. STEVENS (Gloria Wood), 74, Hollywood-born actress, died June 13, 1994 in Brentwood, CA, of lung cancer. A child actress under the name Katherine Stevens, she made her Bdwy debut 1941 in *Land is Bright*. Other Bdwy included *Nine Girls* and *Laura*. Survived by two sons.

JULE STYNE (Julius Kerwin Stein), 88, London-born composer/producer, died Sept. 20, 1988 in Manhattan, NY, of heart failure. One of Bdwy's greatest composers, his shows produced dozens of classic standards. Stars who introduced his work include Carol Channing, Ethel Merman, and Barbra Streisand. After composing many film musicals, his theatre work started with 1944's *Glad to See You* (closed in Philadelphia but produced "I Guess I'll Hang My Tears Out to Dry") followed by *High Button Shoes* ("Poppa Won't You Dance With Me"), *Gentlemen Prefer Blondes* ("Diamonds are a Girl's Best Friend," "Bye Bye Baby"), *Two On the Aisle* ("If"), *Hazel Flagg* ("Every Streets a Boulevard"), *Peter Pan* ("Neverland"), *Bells are Ringing* ("Just in Time," "The Party's Over"), *Say Darling*, *Gypsy* ("Some People," "Everythings Coming Up Roses," "Small World," "Together"), *Do Re Mi* ("Make Someone Happy"), *Subways are for Sleeping* ("Comes Once in a Lifetime"), *Arturo Ui, Funny Girl* ("People," "Don't Rain on My Parade"), *Fade Out Fade In, Hallelujah Baby!* (Tony Award), *Darling of the Day, Look to the Lillies, Prettybelle, Sugar, Lorelei, One Night Stand,* and his final show *The Red Shoes* (1993). His work as a producer included 1952's *Pal Joey* and *Will Success Spoil Rock Hunter?* Survived by his wife, two sons, a daughter, a sister, and grandchildren.

ELAINE SULKA, 61, NYC-born actress/director, died Dec. 24, 1994 in Manhattan, NY, of a heart attack. Off-Bdwy debut 1962 in *Hop Signor!* followed by *Brotherhood, Brothers, Last Prostitute, The Courting,* and Bdwy's *Passion of Josef D* and *Medea* (1972). She was co-founder of the National Shakespeare Company in 1963 and NYC's Cubiculo Theatre with husband Philip Meister who died in 1982. . Survived by her daughter, mother, and two sisters.

BARRY SULLIVAN, 81, NYC-born actor, died June 6, 1994 in Sherman Oaks, CA, of a respitory ailment. Bdwy debut 1936 in *I Want a Policeman* followed by *Caine Mutiny Court Martial* (1954 succeeding Henry Fonda) and *Too Late the Phalarope* (1956). He acted in films and TV and is survived by two daughters and a son.

E. W. SWACKHAMER, 67, New Jersey-born actor/stage manager/director, died Dec. 5, 1994 in Berlin, Germany, of a ruptured aortic aneurysm. He appeared in *Time Remembered* (1957) with Helen Hayes and Richard Burton. He stage managed the original *Cat on a Hot Tin Roof*. He directed Off-Bdwy's *Exiles, Rules of the Game,* and *Ascent of F-6*. He had success as a television director working on many series and miniseries. Survived by his second wife, actress Bridget Haney, three daughters, and a son, Ten Eyck Swackhamer, who is general manager of the Cleveland Playhouse. Also survived by a brother and grandchildren.

JESSICA TANDY, 85, London-born actress, died Sept. 11, 1994 in Connecticut of ovarian cancer. A leading theatre star best known for creating "Blanche DuBois" in the original 1949 *Streetcar Named Desire,* she had a rich and varied life in the theatre. She started acting as a teenager in her native England and appeared in *Manderson Girls, The Rumour* (1929), *Children in Uniform, Twelfth Night,* and *Henry V* with Olivier, as Ophelia to John Gielgud's Hamlet and *King Lear* and *Tempest* also with Gielgud. After her 1940 divorce from actor Jack Hawkins, she moved to the US where she met and married actor Hume Cronyn. Bdwy debut in 1930's *The Matriarch* followed by *Last Enemey, Time and the Conways, White Steed, Geneva, Jupiter Laughs, Anne of England, Yesterday's Magic, Streetcar Named Desire* (Tony Award), *Hilda Crane, The Fourposter, The Honeys, Day by the Sae, Man in the Dog Suit, Triple Play, Five Finger Exercise, The Physicists, Delicate Balance, Home, All Over, Camino Real, Not I, Happy Days, Noel Coward in Two Keys, Rose* (Tony nom.), *The Gin Game* (Pulitzer Prize, 1978 Tony Award for Tandy), *Foxfire* (1983 Tony Award), *Glass Menagerie, Salonika,* and lastly *The Petition* (1986). In 1994 , Tandy and Cronyn received the first Tony Lifetime Achievement Award. Her many films included the 1989 screen version of *Driving Miss Daisy* which won her an Oscar. Survived by Cronyn, daughters Susan and Tandy, and son Christopher.

ROBIN TATE, 40, actor, died Aug. 19, 1994 in Manhattan, NY, of lung cancer. Off-Bdwy included *Umbrellas of Cherbourg* and *Jacques and His Master*. For three years he was in McCarter Theatre's acting company and appeared at many regional theatres. At his death, he was performing in *Comedy of Errors* in Garrison, NY. Survived by his longtime companion, parents and siblings.

TED THURSTON, 77, Minnesota-born actor, died July 23, 1994 in East Hampton, NY, of stomach cancer. Bdwy included 1951 debut in *Paint Your Wagon, Girl in Pink Tights, Kismet, Buttrio Square, Seventh Heaven, Most Happy Fella, Li'l Abner, 13 Daughters, Happiest Girl in Town, Luther, Celebration* (also OB), *Gantry, Wild and Wonderful,* and *Onward Victoria*. Off-Bdwy included *Bible Salesman Smith, Fiddler on the Roof, Turns,* and *Taking My Turn*. Involved in Actors Equity, he was instrumental in the creation of Manhattan Plaza, a federally subsidized apartment complex for performing artists. Survived by his wife Danya Krupska Thurston, two daughters, a sister, stepson, and grandchildren.

DANITRA VANCE, 35, Chicago-born actress, died Aug. 21, 1994 in Markham, IL, of breast cancer. Off-Bdwy included *Danitra Vance and the Mel-O-White Boys, Colored Museum, Spunk* (1990 Obie Award), and *Marisol* (1993). After her breast cancer diagnosis, she created a performance piece, *The Radical Girl's Guide to Radical Mastectomy*. Survived by her companion, mother, sister, grandfather, and niece.

Jessica Tandy

SYDNEY WALKER, 73, Philadelphia-born actor, died Sept. 30, 1994 in San Francisco. He made his Bdwy debut 1960 in *Becket* and was nominated for a Tony for *Wild Duck*. Other NYC credits included *Volpone, Julius Caesar, King Lear, The Collection, Scent of Flowers, The Nuns, You Can't Take It With You, War and Peace, Right You Are, School for Scandal, We Comrades Three, Pantagleize, Cherry Orchard, Misanthrope, Cocktail Party, Cock-a-Doodle Dandy, Blood Red Roses, Playboy of the Western World, Good Woman of Setzuan, Enemy of the People, Antigone, Mary Stuart, Narrow Road to the Deep North, Twelfth Night, Crucible, Enemies, Plough and the Stars, Merchant of Venice, Streetcar Named Desire,* and *Minister's Black Veil.* He worked with American Conservatory Theatre and appeared in films including the screen *Prelude to a Kiss.* Survived by two sisters.

FREDI WASHINGTON, 90, Georgia-born actress, died June 28, 1994 in Stamford, CT, of pneumonia and a stroke. One of the first black actresses to gain wide recognition, she worked for equal rights for blacks in the arts by founding the Negro Actors Guild. Credits included 1921's *Shuffle Along, Black Boy* (opposite Paul Robeson–used her stage name Edith Warren), *Run Little Chillun, Great Day, Singing the Blues, Mamba's Daughters, Lysistrata,* and *Long Way from Home,* based on Gorky's *Lower Depths.* Survived by three sisters and a brother.

WILLARD WATERMAN, 80, Wisconsin-born actor, died Feb. 2, 1995 in Burlingame, CA, of bone marrow disease. Bdwy included *Mame* (1966 & 1983) and *Pajama Game* (1973). National tours included *How to Succeed...* and *A Funny Thing Happened on the Way to the Forum.* He often worked in radio drama and series. Survived by his wife, two daughters, and grandchildren.

DAVID WAYNE (Wayne James McKeekan), 81, Michigan-born actor, died Feb. 9, 1995 in Santa Monica, CA, of lung cancer. He won a Theatre World Award and a Tony Award for his memorable leprechaun in the musical *Finian's Rainbow* (1947). He won another Tony for the his portrayal of a Japanese man in *Teahouse of the August Moon* (1954). Bdwy included *Escape This Night* (1938 debut), *Dance Night, American Way, Scene of the Crime, Merry Widow, Peepshow, Park Avenue, Mister Roberts, Ponder Heart, Loud Red Patrick, Say Darling, Send Me No Flowers, Venus at Large, Too True to Be Good, Marco Millions, But for Whom Charle, Incident at Vichy, The Yearling, Show Boat* (LC) and *Happy Time* (1968 Tony nom.). He worked often in film and TV and is survived by twin daughters and grandchildren.

CALDER WILLINGHAM, 72, Atlanta-born playwright/novelist, died Feb. 19, 1995 in Laconia, NH. Best known for his novels and screenplays, he had great success adapting his 1947 novel *End as a Man* to the NY stage in 1953. Survived by his wife, four sons, and two daughters.

BILLY WILSON, 59, Philadelphia-born choreographer/director, died Aug. 14, 1994 in Manhattan of AIDS. He directed and choreographed 1976's *Bubbling Brown Sugar* and the 1976 *Guys and Dolls.* Other Bdwy included *Eubie, Merlin, Odyssey/Home Sweet Homer, Stop the World...* (1978), and *Dance a Little Closer.* As a performer his debut was a City Center *Carmen Jones* followed by *Bells are Ringing, Jamaica,* and London's *West Side Story.* He worked with many dance companies and taught dance. Survived by his ex-wife dancer Sonja van Beers, a daughter, son, brother, sister, and grandchildren.

INDEX

242

264

Salinger, Marilyn, 108
Salinger, Ross, 141, 223
Salla, Jerry Della, 100
Sally Marr And Her Escorts, 76
Salome, Lou, 89
Salonga, Lea, 68, 193
Saloutos, Connie, 97, 154, 169
Salovey, Todd, 180
Salt, Jennifer, 193
Saltarelli, Kim, 150
Salucci, Gianennio, 181
Salvador, Luis A., 83
Salvador, Michelle V., 83
Salvato, Laura Jane, 120
Salvio, Robert, 193
Salzman, Thomas, 154
Sama, Lenys, 85, 99
Sameth, Marten, 85
Sametz, Laura, 162
Sams, Jeremy, 47, 52
Samuel Beckett Theatre, 93, 95-96,
    100, 115
Samuels, Gayle, 160
Samuels, Peggy R., 79
Samuelsohn, Bethany, 61
Samuelsohn, Howard, 175
Samuelson, Sam, 60
San Diego Repertory Theatre, 180
Sanchez, Adam, 158
Sanchez, Alex, 177
Sanchez, Edwin, 123, 166
Sanchez, Jaime, 158, 193
Sanchez, Karenjune, 115, 148-149
Sanchez, Monica, 180
Sanchez, Rene, 115
Sanchez-Scott, Milcha, 153
Sanctifying Grace, 80
Sanders, Erin, 143
Sanders, Jackie, 78, 105, 223, 227
Sanders, Nathan, 146
Sanders, Pete, 26, 58, 64, 90, 112
Sanders, Ty, 139
Sanderson, Austin, 117, 175
Sanderson, Kirsten, 117
Sandhu, Rommy, 23
Sandoval, Vincent, 177
Sandow, Nick, 106
Sandri, Remi, 151
Sandri, Thomas, 69
Sands, Ben, 160
Sands, Diana, 192
Sanes, Camilia, 80, 90, 149
Sanford Meisner Theatre, 90, 93, 101,
    112, 115
Sanford, Tim, 141
Sanni, Nick, 182
Santangelo, Luly, 98, 117
Santeiro, Luis, 110
Santiago, Douglas, 121, 142, 223, 227
Santiago, Jualkyris, 96
Santiago, Socorro, 111, 223
Santiago-Hudson, Ruben, 163
Santoro, Mark, 61, 97, 223
Santos, Lorinda, 50, 164
Santos, Mylene, 83
Santos, Ray, 68
Sanz, Carlos, 163
Saposnick, Michael, 182
Sarbinska, Tatiana, 151
Sargeant, Greig, 108
Sargent, Peter E., 160, 179
Sarnataro, Patricia, 107
Saroyan, William, 78
Sarsgaard, Peter, 144, 223
Sasfai, Conny, 177
Sastre, Elizabeth, 166
Saturday Mourning Cartoons, 118
Saturday Sunday Monday, 171
Sauer, John E., 140
Sauli, James, 92, 100
Saunders, Alonzo, 177

Sauter, Luisa, 99
Sauve, Gloria, 79
Savage, Ashley, 148
Savage, Busairi, 162
Savage, Sheila, 163
Saverine, Nicholas F., 67
Savino, Frank, 171
Sawyer, Forrest, 143
Sawyer-Dailey, Mark, 148-149
Sbarge, Raphael, 19, 223
Scala, C. George, 86
Scalamoni, Sam, 122, 223
Scanlon, Patricia, 78, 89, 102
Scarborough, Adrian, 156
Scardino, Don, 141
Scardino, Frank P., 12
Scarlet Letter, The, 126
Scatuorchio, Tee, 125
Schaechter, Ben, 99, 127
Schaefer, Richard, 139
Schaeffer, Berton, 175
Schaffer, Kareth M., 163
Schaffner, Catherine, 150
Schak, John, 79
Schall, Thomas, 57, 140
Schaller, Mark, 91, 107
Schany, Bryan, 121
Schanzer, Jude, 100
Scharolais, B., 82
Schaufer, Lucy, 90
Schechter, David, 155, 179
Schecter, Amy, 64
Scheerer, Bob, 192
Schelble, Bill, 52, 65, 89, 138, 143
Schelter, Jennifer, 176
Schenker, Diane, 78
Schenkkan, Robert, 81
Schenkweiler, John, 50
Scher, Jerry, 99
Scher, Judith, 89
Scherer, John, 48
Schertler, Nancy, 138, 152
Scherzer, Wayne, 67
Schiappa, John, 60
Schiavo, Janna, 80
Schiavone, Carmen, 64
Schiff, Charlie, 141
Schiliro, David, 89
Schilke, Raymond, 75, 84, 88, 112,
    113, 130
Schiller, Friedrich, 90
Schilling, Thom, 24
Schiro, Frank, 95
Schiro, Gary, 101
Schisgal, Murray, 104
Schlee, Nicholas, 81
Schlesinger, Toni, 102
Schlossberg, Julian, 95, 105, 113
Schmidt, Douglas W., 63, 101
Schmidt, Ed, 162
Schmidt, Harvey, 72, 169
Schmidt, Marlene, 117
Schmidt, Mary Ethel, 98, 107
Schmidt, Paul, 181, 184
Schmidtke, Ned, 163
Schneider, Claudia, 154
Schneider, Gary, 75
Schneider, Gerard J., 85
Schnier, Stan, 64
Schoeffler, Paul, 147, 223
Schofield, Elizabeth M., 115
Scholl, Jessica, 67
Schommer, David, 85
Schonberg, Claude-Michel, 67-68
School For Husbands, The, 30
School For Wives, 165
Schottland, Alixx, 115
Schreiber, Avery, 127, 169, 223
Schreier, Dan Moses, 9, 56, 129, 136-
    137, 141
Schrot, Richard A., 174

Schuck, John, 182
Schuette, James, 80, 138, 148
Schulberg, Budd, 56
Schulfer, Roche, 163
Schulman, Craig, 67
Schulman, Susan H., 117, 141
Schulman, Susan L., 62, 84, 97, 115
Schulte, Mark, 84
Schultz, Carol, 179
Schulz, Paul, 81
Schumacher, Joanie, 82, 93
Schumacher, Michelle, 156
Schurr, Carl, 148
Schuster, Alan J., 56, 63, 95
Schwab, Kaipo, 112
Schwartz, Clifford, 23, 34
Schwartz, Craig, 16, 197
Schwartz, Erica, 83
Schwartz, Gary, 66
Schwartz, Glenn, 80
Schwartz, Robert Joel, 140
Schwartzman, Amy, 84
Schwarz, Kristen, 160
Schwarz, William, 163
Schweizer, David, 183
Schweppe, Jeanna, 64
Schworer, Angie L., 62
Sciaino, Ryan Loftus, 177
Sciarra, Anthony Brian, 95
Scofield, Paula, 86
Scolari, Peter, 48
Scott, Adjowah, 80
Scott, Brian, 148
Scott, Christopher, 72, 96
Scott, Eric Dean, 78
Scott, George C., 192
Scott, H. Hylan, 64
Scott, James, 119, 165, 179
Scott, Michael, 12, 223
Scott, Mimi, 35, 121-122, 148
Scott, Pippa, 192
Scott, Seret, 143, 162, 176
Scott, Sherie, 64, 70
Scrofano, Paula, 163
Scruggs, Sharon, 80, 155
Scurria, Anne, 183
SDD Productions, 102
Seacat, James, 148
Search And Destroy, 80
Sears, Joe, 26, 223
Sebastian, Gabriel, 151
Secada, Jon, 64, 223
Second Stage, 73, 143
Secret Garden, The, 150, 169
Secret Of Life, The, 108
Secret Sits In The Middle, The, 114
Secretaries, The, 138
Sedgwick, Kyra, 193
Seduced, 106
Seelbach, Jeff, 177
Seer, Richard, 193
Seff, Richard, 125, 223
Segal, David F., 63, 166, 174, 176
Segal, Jeff, 84, 108
Segal, Laura, 115
Segal, Martin E. ., 193
Segal, S., 162
Segal, Yaniv, 128
Seidel, Virginia, 193
Seier, Teri, 98
Seitz, John, 125, 184
Sekeres, Caleb, 166
Sekora, Elizabeth, 169
Selby, Jamison, 173
Seldes, Marian, 74
Seleznev, Vladimir, 124
Sell, Janie, 193
Sellars, Lee, 152
Sellars, Peter, 163
Sellon, Kim, 59
Selner, Jenny, 180

Seltzer, Daniel, 193
Selznick, Daniel Mayer, 101
Seminar For Responsible Living, A,
    149
Semonin, David, 93
Sempliner, Woody, 140
Separate Flights, 91
Sephers, James III, 174
Serabian, Lorraine, 118, 150, 223
Seraphim Theater Company, 98
Serdiuk, Tanya, 121
Sergel, Christopher, 158, 174
Serino, Renee, 153
Sermol, Luisa, 97
Serra, Jack, 98
Servitto, Matt, 97
Setlock, Mark, 106, 138, 223, 227
Setrakian, Ed, 117, 223
Setrakian, Mary, 186
Setterfield, Valda, 138
Settling Accounts, 82, 110
Seven Guitars, 163
Sewell, Rufus, 40, 191, 194, 223
Sexton, Brent, 169
Sexton, Coleen Ann, 177
Seyd, Richard, 151
Seymour, Caroline, 88, 113
Seymour, Christina, 160
Shabbatai, 122
Shade, Clarencia, 82
Shades Of Grey, 97
Shadow Box, The, 19
Shae, Ed De, 48
Shafer, Margaret, 48, 164
Shaffer, Malinda, 50, 63
Shaffer, Pamela Jean, 80
Shaffer, Peter, 7, 168
Shafransky, Renee, 6
Shakespeare For My Father, 165
Shakespeare, William, 57, 81, 84-85,
    88, 91, 97, 101, 104, 108, 116,
    119, 124, 136-137, 140, 151, 160,
    163, 165-167, 175-176, 178, 180,
    183-184
Shamas, Laura, 120
Shamos, Jeremy, 95
Shanaphy, Meghan, 150
Shane, Lester, 108
Shane, Lorna, 50, 64
Shaner, Tom, 108
Shangraw, Howard, 181
Shanice, 67, 223
Shanks, Priscilla, 171
Shannon Falank,, 29
Shannon, Kyle, 79
Shannon, Marguerite, 90
Shannon, Sarah Solie, 59, 61
Shapanus, Laura, 123
Shapiro, Anna D., 123
Shapiro, Max, 123
Shapiro, Ron, 96
Shapiro, Steve, 127
Sharogradsky, Arkadii, 124
Sharon, Michael, 164
Sharp, Alex, 164
Sharp, Jon Marshall, 93, 111
Sharp, Randy, 106
Shatner, William, 192
Shattuck, Bart, 81
Shaver, Helen, 193
Shaw, Bernard, 88, 95, 140, 152, 179
Shawhan, April, 108, 193
Shawn, Allen, 123, 129
Shay, Michele, 163
Shayna Maidel, A, 182
Shayne, Tracy, 69
She Loves Me, 76-77, 174
Shea, Ed, 160, 179, 183
Shea, Jere, 193, 223
Shea, John V., 193
Shearer, Andy, 21, 48, 91-92, 105, 123

269

Walter, John, 75, 162
Walter, Rik, 116
Walter, Wendy, 16, 228
Walters, Lara, 175
Walton, Bob, 12
Walton, Jim, 163, 186
Walton, Judith Marie, 113
Walton, Laurie, 12
Walton, Scott, 36
Walton, Tony, 23, 156
Walz, Christopher, 163
Wampler, Calude, 115
Wanda Visit, 132
Wands, Susan, 144, 228
Wang, Ben, 114
Wang, Luo Yong, 156
Wann, Jim, 103, 228
Wanselius, Bengt, 124
Wanstreet, David, 150
Warbeck, Stephen, 65
Ward, Anthony, 119
Ward, Buzz, 160
Ward, Elsa, 136
Ward, Emilie, 94
Ward, Fred, 136, 228
Ward, George, 151
Ward, Jamie C., 101
Ward, Janet, 144, 228
Ward, Lauren, 141, 227-228
Ward, Michael, 101
Ward, Nancy, 86
Ward, Theara J., 23
Warfel, Andy, 114
Warfield, Anjua, 112
Warfield, Cheryl, 12
Warfield, Marlene, 193
Warik, Joe, 154
Waring, Wendy, 62, 228
Warmen, Timothy, 14, 70
Warner, Amy, 150
Warner, David Strong, 57, 70
Warnette, Noelia, 80
Warren, Casey, 64, 114, 118, 140
Warren, David, 117, 132, 145, 164
Warren, Jennifer, 193
Warren, Leslie Ann, 193
Warren, Will, 80
Warrender, Scott, 91
Warshofsky, David, 56
Warwick, Pam, 94
Washington Square Church, 75
Washington, Sharon, 132-133, 171, 228
Wasser, Alan, 67, 69
Wasserstein, Wendy, 143
Wasson, Susanne, 107
Wasswemann, Molly, 50
Watanabe, Gedde, 170
Watbanaland, 146
Water And Wine, 117
Watermark Theater, 78, 102, 117
Waterston, James, 130, 227
Watkins, Dana, 91
Watkins, Jeffrey, 29
Watkins, Tuc, 118
Watson, Becky, 177, 182
Watson, David, 166
Watson, Douglass, 192
Watson, Judy, 180
Watson, Lincoln, 114
Watson, Lloyd, 177
Watt, Gregory, 60, 228
Wattenmaker, Adrian, 106
Watts, Andrew, 79
Watts, Steve, 124
Waxman, Jessica, 177
Waxman, Rebecca, 127
Way Of The World, The, 176
Wayne, Carys, 80
Wayne, David, 192, 238-239
We Take The Town, 94
Weaver, Fritz, 125, 192, 228

Weaver, Rose, 183
Webb, Alexander, 174
Webb, Elmon, 148
Webb, Helena, 80
Webb, Jeremy, 165
Webber, Julian, 92, 100
Weber, Brent, 34
Weber, Fredricka, 193-195
Weber, Jake, 132, 228
Weber, Jeffrey, 14
Weber, Robert, 68, 84, 115
Weber, Steven, 78
Webster, Bryan, 78
Webster, Doug, 175
Webster, Leigh, 61
Webster, Trey, 86, 108
Webster, Whitney, 23, 111
Wedemeyer, Kristi, 136
Weeden, Janet, 82
Weeks, Jimmie Ray, 181
Weeks, Todd, 123, 166
Weems, Andrew, 148, 152
Wehrle, Thomas, 87
Weidler, Bethlyn, 81
Weil, Tim, 138
Weill, Kurt, 155
Wein, Glenn, 87
Wein-Reis, Dina, 56
Weinberg, Helene, 165
Weinberg, Vanessa, 85
Weinberger, Barry, 87
Weiner, Arn, 182
Weinstein, Arnold, 82, 117
Weinstein, Irv, 182
Weinstock, Jack, 43, 170
Weiss, Christine, 85
Weiss, Daniel, 91
Weiss, Gordon Joseph, 148
Weiss, Jeff, 170, 228
Weiss, Marc B., 9, 48, 89
Weiss, Marthe, 130
Weiss, Mitchell, 56
Weissberg, Iona, 90
Weissberger Theater Group, 119
Weitzman, Ken, 81
Welch, Christopher Evan, 170
Welch, Dan, 183
Welch, David, 121
Welch, Karen Ann, 110
Welch, Lucinda Dohanian, 183
Welcome To The Club, 94
Weldon, Ann, 181
Well, Sam, 181
Weller, Allison, 175
Welles, Orson, 175
Wellington, Roxanne, 174
Wellman, John, 175
Wellman, Mac, 92
Wellmann, John, 140
Wells, Billy K., 95
Wells, Kimberly, 169
Wemitt, Monica M., 186
Wen, A, 122
Wcndc O'Rcilly, 93
Wendland, Mark, 126, 160, 170, 179, 181, 183
Wendt, Angela, 138
Werner, Howard, 86, 123, 179
Wernick, Nancy, 118
Wertenbaker, Timberlake, 151
Wesp, Richard, 182
West Bank, 103, 108
West, Brandon, 160
West, Charles, 164
West, Cheryl L., 132, 160, 176, 181
West, Darron L., 83, 91, 118, 138
West, Irv, 169
West, Jennifer, 193
West, Matt, 59
West, Nathaniel, 123
West, Peter, 175

Westbeth Music Hall, 91
Westbeth Theatre Center, 96
Westenberg, Robert, 23, 100, 193, 228
Wester, Bradley, 113, 115
Westfeldt, Jennifer, 150
Westgate-Moore, Meredith, 87, 95
Weston, Douglas, 60, 173
Westside Theatre, 84, 90, 104, 109
Wetherall, Jack, 101, 228
Whaley, Frank, 130, 227-228
Whalley-Kilmer, Joanne, 193
What The Butler Saw, 152
What's Wrong With This Picture?, 24-25
Wheeler, David, 178
Wheeler, Ed, 143
Wheeler, Hugh, 163
Wheeler, Julie, 115
Wheeler, Timothy, 137, 228
Whelehan, Brian, 121
Whenry, Christopher, 176
Where Or When, 98
Whigham, Shea, 112
Whishman, Court, 154
Whitcomb, Cornelia, 88
White St. Theater, 114
White, Al, 193
White, Alton, 50, 70
White, Amelia, 39, 193, 228
White, Andrew, 172
White, Bradley, 118
White, Brian D., 86, 99, 106
White, Chip, 138
White, J. Steven, 137
White, Jane, 104, 136, 228
White, Jason Tyler, 99
White, Jason, 160
White, Jo Ann Hawkins, 12
White, Julie, 143
White, Kevin, 180
White, Lillias, 42-43, 79, 170, 228
White, Spence, 57
White, Susan R., 119, 138
White, Terri, 90, 228
White, Welker, 136
Whitefield, Bill, 164
Whitehead, Paxton, 110
Whitehead, Robert, 50
Whitehead-Winn, Torri, 159
Whitehill, B.T., 81, 90, 105
Whitehurst, Scott, 94, 107, 160, 228
Whitescarver, Randall, 188
Whitfield, Dondre T., 171
Whitlock, Isiah Jr., 162, 170
Whitmore, James, 192
Whitner, Daniel, 107, 112
Whitney, Ann Stevenson, 163
Whitney, Sewell, 173
Whitton, Kathy, 193
Whitton, Margaret, 132, 136-137, 228
Who's Tommy, The, 70, 188
Why We Have A Body, 92
Wiater, David, 170
Wickcns, Lauric, 91
Wickham, Saskia, 156
Wickler, Cate Van, 150
Wicklow Plays, The, 84
Widdoes, James, 193
Widdoes, Kathleen, 125, 228
Widmann, Thom, 19, 137
Widmer, Philip, 83, 100, 140
Wiener, Matthew, 153
Wierzbicki, Ed, 166
Wierzel, Robert, 141, 155, 160, 178, 184
Wieselman, Doug, 20, 170
Wiest, Dianne, 193
Wiggins, James H. III, 164
Wiggins, Pamela, 160, 179
Wigle, Christopher, 39
Wilber, Susan, 108

Wilborn, Carlton, 136
Wilbur, Richard, 30, 181
Wilcox, Charlotte W., 56, 63-64
Wilcox, Kim, 117
Wilcox, Patricia, 102
Wilde, Oscar, 108, 134
Wilder, Andrew, 50, 164
Wilder, Billy, 16
Wilder, Thornton, 83, 117, 173
Wildman, James, 132
Wildman, Robert, 171
Wilhelm, Le, 82, 86, 108, 115
Wilkes, Fiona, 73
Wilkins, W. David, 175
Wilkinson, Colm, 193
Wilkinson, Wade, 78
Wilkner, Pierre, 124
Wilkof, Lee, 94, 155
Wilks, Elayne, 115, 228
Will Rogers Follies, The, 169, 196
Will, Joseph, 108
Willems, Stephen, 106
William Redfield Theatre, 106, 110, 121
Williams, Carla Renata, 43, 170, 188, 228
Williams, Clarence III, 193
Williams, Dathan B., 12, 228
Williams, Elizabeth, 62
Williams, Eric, 144
Williams, Erin, 181
Williams, Garry, 117
Williams, Geoffrey D., 167
Williams, Jacqueline, 163
Williams, Janice, 86
Williams, Jaston, 26
Williams, Jeff, 94
Williams, Jeffrey Eugene, 84
Williams, Jerry, 134
Williams, Laurie, 170, 180
Williams, Matthew J., 87
Williams, Penny Koleos, 154
Williams, Ralph, 12
Williams, Robert, 110
Williams, Sam, 20
Williams, Tennessee, 7, 15, 55, 147, 166, 174, 178, 181
Williams, Tim, 26, 115
Williams, Todd, 101
Williams, Vanessa, 21, 66, 191, 195
Williams-Sellers, Alton, 180
Williamson, Chad Lee, 180
Williamson, Laird, 176
Williamson, Nance, 135-136, 183
Williford, Lou, 141, 177
Willinger, David, 121
Willis, Gay, 12
Willis, Jack, 160
Willis, Richard, 134
Willis, Susan, 169
Willison, Walter, 22-23, 111, 193, 227-228
Willow Cabin Theatre Co., 94, 104, 111
Wills, Michael MacKenzic, 101
Wills, Ray, 71, 229
Willson, Andrea, 169
Willson, Michael, 78
Wilner, Lori, 155
Wilshusen, Carrie, 99
Wilson, August, 155, 163, 182
Wilson, C.J., 136
Wilson, Chandra, 193
Wilson, Cintra, 112
Wilson, Collette, 136
Wilson, Darlene, 16, 61
Wilson, Glenn, 87
Wilson, Gregory A., 174
Wilson, Jessica-Snow, 67
Wilson, Kathryn Gay, 84
Wilson, Mary Louise, 176